EMPEROR AND AUTHOR:
THE WRITINGS OF JULIAN THE APOSTATE

EMPEROR AND AUTHOR:
THE WRITINGS OF JULIAN THE APOSTATE

Editors

Nicholas Baker-Brian

and

Shaun Tougher

Contributors

Nicholas Baker-Brian, Hal Drake, Susanna Elm,
Jill Harries, Mark Humphries, David Hunt, Liz James,
J. H. W. G. Liebeschuetz, Jacqueline Long, Josef Lössl,
Arnaldo Marcone, Benet Salway, Fernando López Sánchez,
Andrew Smith, Rowland Smith, Shaun Tougher,
Michael Trapp, Eric R. Varner, John W. Watt

The Classical Press of Wales

First published in 2012 by
The Classical Press of Wales
15 Rosehill Terrace, Swansea SA1 6JN
Tel: +44 (0)1792 458397
www.classicalpressofwales.co.uk

Distributor
Oxbow Books,
10 Hythe Bridge Street,
Oxford OX1 2EW
Tel: +44 (0)1865 241249
Fax: +44 (0)1865 794449

Distributor in the United States of America
The David Brown Book Co.
PO Box 511, Oakville, CT 06779
Tel: +1 (860) 945–9329
Fax: +1 (860) 945–9468

ISBN 978-1-905125-50-0

A catalogue record for this book is available from the British Library.

Typeset, printed and bound in the UK by Gomer Press, Llandysul, Ceredigion, Wales

————————————

The Classical Press of Wales, an independent venture, was founded in 1993, initially to support the work of classicists and ancient historians in Wales and their collaborators from further afield. More recently it has published work initiated by scholars internationally. While retaining a special loyalty to Wales and the Celtic countries, the Press welcomes scholarly contributions from all parts of the world.

The symbol of the Press is the Red Kite. This bird, once widespread in Britain, was reduced by 1905 to some five individuals confined to a small area known as 'The Desert of Wales' – the upper Tywi valley. Geneticists report that the stock was saved from terminal inbreeding by the arrival of one stray female bird from Germany. After much careful protection, the Red Kite now thrives – in Wales and beyond.

CONTENTS

Contents

ACKNOWLEDGEMENTS

This volume of papers is the proceedings of an international conference, 'Emperor and Author: The Writings of Julian the Apostate', held in the Main Building Council Chamber at Cardiff University between 16th–18th July 2009.

It is a pleasure to record here various debts of gratitude. In the first instance, we would like to express our warmest thanks to all the authors whose papers appear in this volume. Their contributions during the conference made the event an enjoyable and rewarding experience, and their co-operation afterwards during the preparation of the proceedings smoothed considerably the editorial passage of their work. We are immeasurably indebted to Anton Powell of the Classical Press of Wales. His enthusiasm for a conference and volume on Julian as author chimed with his own projects on the writings of both Julius Caesar and Augustus. His keen editorial eye has been invaluable.

It is a pleasure also to acknowledge the cheerful assistance of Adam Anders and Michal Zytka in running the event during those balmy days in mid-July. The administrative support supplied by Claire Rees from the Cardiff School of History, Archaeology, and Religion (then the Cardiff School of History and Archaeology) was valued. We would also like to thank all the delegates who attended and participated at the conference, especially David Buck, Ken Donovan, Pilar García Ruiz, Roger Green, Angie Jimenez, Alberto Quiroga, Bella Sandwell, and Hans Teitler. The attention to detail of Lis Fouldai and her catering team at Aberdare Hall made the conference dinners all the more enjoyable.

Especial thanks are owed to the Loeb Classical Library Foundation for awarding a generous grant which made the conference possible. We are appreciative of the contribution to the opening event of the conference made by The Society for the Promotion of Byzantine Studies. Crucial support for the project in its early stages was provided by Glen Bowersock, Gillian Clark and Mary Harlow, and we remain very grateful to all of them. This volume is dedicated to John Drinkwater, for his long-standing enthusiasm and support for all matters Julian, and to Amy Rosemary who arrived too late for the conference, but in time for the book.

Nicholas Baker-Brian and Shaun Tougher
Cardiff, Wales, April 2012

LIST OF CONTRIBUTORS

NICHOLAS BAKER-BRIAN is Lecturer in New Testament and Early Christian Studies in the Cardiff School of History, Archaeology and Religion at Cardiff University.

HAL DRAKE is Research Professor of History at the University of California, Santa Barbara.

SUSANNA ELM is Professor of History and Classics at the University of California, Berkeley.

JILL HARRIES is Professor of Ancient History in the School of Classics at the University of St. Andrews.

MARK HUMPHRIES is Professor of Ancient History in the Department of History and Classics at Swansea University.

DAVID HUNT is a retired Senior Lecturer in the Department of Classics and Ancient History at Durham University.

LIZ JAMES is Professor of Art History in the Department of Art History at the University of Sussex.

WOLFGANG LIEBESCHUETZ is Professor Emeritus in Classics at the University of Nottingham.

JACQUELINE LONG is Associate Professor in the Department of Classical Studies at Loyola University Chicago.

FERNANDO LÓPEZ SÁNCHEZ is Investigador Rámon y Cajal at Universidad Jaume I, Castellón.

JOSEF LÖSSL is Professor of Historical Theology and Intellectual History in the Cardiff School of History, Archaeology and Religion at Cardiff University.

ARNALDO MARCONE is Professor of Roman History at Università Roma Tre.

BENET SALWAY is Senior Lecturer in the Department of History at University College London.

ANDREW SMITH is Associate Director of the Centre for the Study of the Platonic Tradition at Trinity College Dublin.

ROWLAND SMITH is Lecturer in Ancient History in the School of Historical Studies at Newcastle University.

SHAUN TOUGHER is Senior Lecturer in Ancient History in the Cardiff School of History, Archaeology and Religion at Cardiff University.

MICHAEL TRAPP is Professor of Greek Literature and Thought in the Department of Classics at King's College London.

ERIC R. VARNER is Associate Professor in the Departments of Art History and Classics at Emory University.

JOHN WATT is Honorary Research Fellow in the Cardiff School of History, Archaeology and Religion at Cardiff University.

ABBREVIATIONS

AJA	*American Journal of Archaeology*
AncW	*Ancient World*
AntTard	*Antiquité tardive*
Blockley	R. C. Blockley, *The Fragmentary Classicising Historians of the Later Roman Empire: Eunapius, Olympiodorus, Priscus and Malchus*, vol. 2, *Text, Translation and Historiographical Notes* (Liverpool, 1983)
Byz	*Byzantion*
BZ	*Byzantinische Zeitschrift*
CIL	*Corpus Inscriptionum Latinarum*
CQ	*Classical Quarterly*
DNB	*Dictionary of National Biography*
DOP	*Dumbarton Oaks Papers*
GRBS	*Greek, Roman and Byzantine Studies*
ILS	*Inscriptiones Latinae Selectae*
JECS	*Journal of Early Christian Studies*
JHS	*Journal of Hellenic Studies*
JLA	*Journal of Late Antiquity*
JRA	*Journal of Roman Archaeology*
JRS	*Journal of Roman Studies*
LIMC	*Lexicon Iconographicum Mythologiae Classicae*
Num. Chron.	*Numismatic Chronicle*
PG	*Patrologia Graeca*, ed. J.-P. Migne
PLRE	*Prosopography of the Later Roman Empire, vol. 1,* AD *260–305*, ed. A. H. M. Jones, J. R. Martindale and J. Morris (Cambridge, 1971)
RIC	*Roman Imperial Coinage*

INTRODUCTION

Nicholas Baker-Brian and *Shaun Tougher*

The Roman emperor Julian (r. AD 361–363) is famous for being the last pagan ruler of the Roman empire, who attempted to bring a halt to the religious revolution initiated by his uncle the emperor Constantine I (r. 306–337), the first Christian Roman emperor, better known as Constantine the Great.[1] The emperor Julian is often known simply as Julian the Apostate, because he was brought up a Christian but converted to paganism as a young man, in his twentieth year he says.[2] However, Julian should not just be remembered as the last pagan Roman emperor, but as an emperor who was an author, and a prolific one at that. He turned his hand to a wide variety of literary forms: letters, hymns, satires, panegyrics, invectives, and even history (e.g. his lost account of the battle of Strasbourg).[3] The tenth-century Byzantine encyclopaedia known as the *Suda* reflects well this dichotomous aspect of Julian, despite certain confusions of fact. Its entry for the emperor begins:

> Julian the Transgressor and the Apostate, emperor of the Romans, [nephew (ἀνεψιὸς)] of the emperor Constantine the Great, born of his brother Dalmatus and a mother named Galla. He wrote the so-called *Caesars*, which dealt with the emperors of the Romans starting with Augustus, and another book *On the Three Figures* and the so-called *Kronia* and the *Beard-hater* or *Antiochic*, *Whence the Evils*, *To the Uneducated*, *To Heraclitus the Cynic How to be a Cynic*, various letters, and other things.[4]

Julian was an inveterate communicator; he confessed to the people of Antioch that his 'fingers are nearly always black from using a pen'.[5] Glen Bowersock has memorably observed that Julian's writings 'provide an insight into character and disposition such as can be had for no other classical figure apart from Cicero'.[6]

Julian's emergence as an author can be explained to a large extent by the degree of education he experienced (ranging from having a personal tutor when a boy to attendance at university when a young man) as a member of the imperial family, an education which was exacerbated by the political circumstances of his youth. Julian was born 331 or 332 in Constantinople into the imperial family, his father Julius Constantius being the half-brother of the Augustus Constantine I, since they had the same father, the emperor Constantius I (Caesar from 293–305, and Augustus from 305–306).

The rich sources for Julian's life provide us with glimpses (not always as clear as one would like) of his education.[7] An important early tutor was the eunuch Mardonius, who taught Julian from seven years old, and who had also taught Julian's mother Basilina (who died shortly after Julian's birth). Mardonius is credited by Julian himself as being a formative influence upon him, endowing him in particular with his great love of Homer. The bishop of Nicomedia, Eusebius (who became patriarch of Constantinople in the late 330s, after the death of Constantine), also seems to have had a part to play in Julian's upbringing, being a relative of the boy.[8] In 337 Julian's life was dramatically fractured, for in this year the emperor Constantine died; in the political fallout nine of Julian's male relatives were killed, including his father. The main figure in these deaths was Constantine's son Constantius II (337–361), and from this point on Julian felt the controlling hand of his cousin upon his life, a situation which had profound ramifications for his education. Soon after 337 Julian (together with his half-brother Gallus) was to spend a six year stint (probably from 342 – soon after Eusebius died – to 348) at the imperial estate of Macellum in Cappadocia. It is often assumed that a key figure in their intellectual formation at this time was the bishop of Cappadocian Caesarea, George, for later on, when George was murdered in 361 in Alexandria (having becoming patriarch of that city), Julian requisitioned his library, commenting to the Prefect of Egypt that George had previously lent him some of his books when he was in Cappadocia, and that they comprised many on rhetoric and philosophy as well as on Christianity.[9]

After Macellum, Julian appears to have spent time studying in both Constantinople and Nicomedia. He was taught grammar by the Spartan Nicocles, and rhetoric by the sophist Hecebolius, a Christian who converted to paganism during Julian's reign. There is some question about whether Julian was taught philosophy by Themistius, an expert in Aristotle, though he was dogged throughout his long career by accusations of being a sophist rather than a philosopher. Famously, it was at Nicomedia that Julian encountered the great Antiochene sophist Libanius. Forbidden to attend Libanius' lectures, Julian accessed them though written versions. Libanius was later to assert that, given the similarity of Julian's style to his own, it was assumed that Julian had been his pupil. It is of note that one of the most important manuscripts for the works of Julian, the *Vossianus gr.* (V) dating to the late twelfth or early thirteenth century, predominantly consisted of a collection of Libanius' letters, to which Julian's works were appended (as a third volume of three).[10]

It was also at Nicomedia that Julian's interest in philosophy developed further, for he moved on from there to seek out Neoplatonic philosophers at Pergamum. These were headed by Aedesius, a pupil of Iamblichus (whose thought was a key influence upon Julian), but also included his own pupils Eusebius of Myndus and Chrysanthius of Sardis (and perhaps it was in Pergamum that Julian met the doctor and author Oribasius, for the city was his home town).[11] Discussions with these men brought the figure of Maximus of Ephesus to Julian's attention, another Neoplatonist, one celebrated for his adeptness at theurgy. Thus Julian left Pergamum for Ephesus, where Maximus seems to have been instrumental in Julian's final abandonment of Christianity and embracing of paganism, about 351.

Julian's formal education developed further a few years later. Having been summoned to Milan under a cloud in the wake of Gallus' execution for treason in 354 (Gallus having been appointed Caesar by Constantius in 351), he was eventually despatched to Athens in the summer of 355 to attend the university, Julian's enthusiasm for the intellectual life being well known at the imperial court. Spending a few months at the university, Julian came into contact with a range of celebrated intellectuals. Fellow pupils included the future Church Fathers, Basil of Caesarea and Gregory of Nazianzus. It is possible that he was taught by the sophists Prohaeresius (a Christian) and Himerius (the son-in-law of the Platonist Nicagoras). He may also have met the Neoplatonist Priscus, another pupil of Aedesius. Julian's study in Athens was short-lived; he was soon recalled to Milan, where he was appointed Caesar himself, on 6th November 355. Julian's elevation to an imperial role, however, was to provide the platform for his literary career. Almost at once he utilised the pen as well as the sword, his first major work being a panegyric of the emperor, the nature of the imperial office and imperial power being subjects that were to preoccupy him greatly in his writings.[12]

In general, Julian's religious identity has been the primary interest of the emperor for historians and writers, witness for instance Henrik Ibsen's *Emperor and Galilean* (1873), which in 2011 was staged for the first time in England, at the National Theatre in London (9th June to 10th August). Its preoccupation with religious fanaticism – as well as its culmination in a doomed invasion – gave it a certain currency.[13] This is not to say that Julian's writings have been neglected. A key figure in making Julian's texts widely available and accessible (they are accompanied by English translations) was Wilmer Cave Wright, the Professor of Greek at Bryn Mawr College from 1897–1933,[14] whose editions and translations of Julian's works appeared in three volumes in the Loeb Classical Library series (volumes 1 and 2 in 1913, and volume 3 in 1923).[15] Volume 1 contained Julian's two panegyrics on Constantius, his speech of thanks to Constantius' wife the empress Eusebia, and his hymns to the Mother of the

Gods and Helios. Volume 2 comprised his two speeches against the Cynics, his consolation to himself on the departure of Salutius, his letters to the Athenians and Themistius (as well as a fragment of a letter to a priest), and his satires the *Caesars* and the *Misopogon*. Volume 3 was devoted primarily to his letters, but also contained the fragments of his anti-Christian tract *Against the Galileans*. For the text of Julian's works Wright utilised with some revisions the edition of F. C. Hertlein (published in 1875–76 in the Teubner series; the editio princeps by Dionysius Petavius – Denis Pétau – had appeared in 1630). However, a new edition (with French translation, for the *Belles Lettres* series) was soon initiated by Joseph Bidez,[16] the first volume (1.2, confusingly) appearing in 1924 (letters and fragments) and the second (1.1) in 1932 (containing the discourses Julian wrote as Caesar: the two panegyrics to Constantius, the speech of thanks to Eusebia, the consolation to himself on the departure of Salutius, and his letter to the Athenians).[17] The final two volumes appeared in the 1960s, produced by other scholars. The third volume (2.1) (containing the letter to Themistius, the speeches against the Cynics, and the hymn to the Mother of the Gods) by Gabriel Rochefort appeared in 1963, and the final volume (2.2) (containing the *Caesars*, the hymn to Helios, and the *Misopogon*) by Christian Lacombrade in 1964.[18] Notably, the *Belles Lettres* edition amended the numbering of Julian's works, to place them in chronological sequence, but the numbering deployed by Wright also remains in use as her volumes are the most accessible and familiar (her numbering is indeed followed in this volume unless otherwise indicated).

A string of further editions of individual or linked texts of Julian have been published since 1964, usually with translations and commentaries (thus adding significantly to the brief remarks of Wright on the texts, and the fundamental but concise introductions of Bidez and his fellow *Belles Lettres* editors). For instance, an edition of Julian's letter to Themistius was published in 1984 by Carlo Prato and Alfonsina Fornaro.[19] Prato, in conjunction with Jacques Fontaine (who provided the introduction) and Arnaldo Marcone (who provided commentaries and Italian translations), published in 1987 editions of Julian's *Letter to Themistius* (again), *Misopogon*, and hymns to the Mother of the Gods and Helios.[20] The hymn to the Mother of the Gods was edited once more in 1992 by Valerio Ugenti.[21] Prato had already published an edition of the *Misopogon* in 1979 with Dina Micalella, with whom he also produced an edition of Julian's speech against the Cynics in 1988.[22] Julian's attack on the Cynic Heraclius was the subject of an edition by Rosanna Guido, published in 2000.[23] Julian's attack on the Christians has not been neglected either, Emanuela Masaracchia producing an edition in 1990.[24] In 1973 Bertold Weis published the letters of Julian with Greek text (mostly following Bidez) and German translation.[25] The satires have also attracted further attention. In 1998 Friedhelm Müller published editions of the *Caesars* (or *Symposion*) and the *Misopogon* (or *Antiochikos*), with German translation and commentary, and the *Caesars* was reedited by Rosanna Sardiello in 2000.[26] Julian's panegyrics have also received some notice. In 1997 Ignazio Tantillo published a text of Julian's first panegyric of Constantius II (with Italian translation and commentary), but this simply reproduced almost entirely unchallenged Bidez's edition, as Tantillo acknowledges.[27] Despite all this piecemeal work, however, one eagerly awaits the new edition of the works of Julian by Heinz-Günther Nesselrath, which is scheduled to be published by De Gruyter in September 2012.

Thus Julian's works have continued to receive study and attention since the still vital editions published by the Loeb Classical Library and *Les Belles Lettres*, though it is noticeable that most of the further editing, translating and commenting has not been done by English-speaking scholars (it is a surprising, and telling fact, as Rowland Smith notes in this volume, that one of Julian's most fêted works, the *Caesars* – his satire on the emperors of Rome – has not yet been published in English translation with a commentary). While historians have drawn upon Julian's works to illuminate his life and thought – and in the case of Jean Bouffartigue's magisterial study *L'Empereur Julien et la culture de son temps* (1992) to reveal Julian as an avid reader of classical and philosophical writings – there is the sense that still not enough attention has been devoted to the emperor's writings in their own right. More fundamentally, the topic of Julian as author needs to be placed centre stage. Recent publications reveal the potential for such work, as well as the limitations of current study. For instance, Julian's writings have been the subject of detailed discussion in a volume of papers entitled *Kaiser Julian 'Apostata' und die philosophische Reaktion gegen das Christentum*, edited by Christian Schäfer (2008). The chapters in this volume consider his writings primarily from a philosophical and cultural point of view, thereby shedding light on Julian's own role in mediating certain philosophical ideas and ideals current in the late empire. Within this narrow remit, notable contributions include Theo Kobush's examination of *Against the Galileans*, Matthias Perkams' consideration of the second oration on Constantius, *Against Heraclius the Cynic*, and the *Letter to Themistius*, Martin Hose on the hymns to Helios and the Mother of the Gods, Markus Janka's literary dissection of the *Misopogon*, and the analysis of Julian's letters by Katharina Luchner. In addition, in 2009 volume seventeen of the journal *Antiquité Tardive* was devoted to 'L'empereur Julien et son temps' (edited by Jean-Michel Carrié). This begins with an intriguing posthumous chapter by Jean Martin on Julian's autobiographical writings,[28] though the rest of the volume is divided into sections on 'Biography', 'Julian as Legislator', 'Julian and Religions', 'The Antioch of Julian', and articles on various late antique topics. Some of the other articles on Julian do deal with him as author, such as Alberto Quiroga's study of the *Misopogon*'s subversion of rhetoric, and Carrié's consideration of the style of Julian's laws,[29] but the majority dealt with more traditional historical aspects of the reign.

Hence it was the objective of our conference (held in Cardiff in July 2009) to consider Julian primarily as an author, to explore his writings as literary texts, and to place him and his work in the broader context of the cultural milieu of the Roman empire in the fourth century. The conference also sought to examine the relationship between Julian's imperial identity and his literary output. A further goal was to consider all forms of communication of the emperor, thus letters, laws, epigraphy, coinage and art were examined too, not just his major literary works. The current volume maintains these objectives and contains all the papers given at the conference. It is topped and tailed by chapters by Susanna Elm and Jacqueline Long, designed to introduce and conclude the other contributions, just as they had done at the conference. Susanna Elm places Julian in his cultural and historical context. She considers in particular how Julian came to be characterised as 'The Apostate' by his Christian opponents, but also demonstrates that the impact of Julian was vital in forming Christian identity, to such an extent that he is in his own right a Church Father (a conclusion to which one can well imagine his own reaction). Jacqueline Long provides a review of the chapters in the volume, drawing together the threads of the discussions and establishing ways ahead for further study. The main contributions follow a broadly chronological structure, though there is also thematic grouping at play. Shaun Tougher, Hal Drake and Liz James discuss Julian's three imperial panegyrics, all questioning the Caesar's purposes in these texts. The two panegyrics on Constantius II are taken in sequence, in order to keep the focus on this emperor, even though the speech of thanks to Eusebia probably predates the second panegyric on Constantius and is often closely associated with the first panegyric on Julian's cousin. All three panegyrics speak of Julian's relationship with the imperial court during his Caesarship in Gaul, as do the next two texts considered, discussed by Josef Lössl and Mark Humphries respectively: Julian's consolation to himself on the departure of Salutius (who was a key support for Julian in Gaul but was recalled by Constantius) and his letter to the Athenians, Julian's famous justification of his 'usurpation' and opposition to Constantius. Letters are kept in focus by the following duo of papers, John Watt's consideration of Julian's letter to Themistius and Michael Trapp's reflections on Julian's letter collection and his art as a letter writer in general. The letter to Themistius is a fascinating text as it deals with Julian's perception of the nature of the imperial office, and seemingly sets him at odds with the views of Themistius, a leading pagan philosopher cum sophist who was strongly associated with the court and ideology of Constantius (and to add further to the interest of the letter, it may date to 355, at the time of Julian's elevation to the Caesarship, rather than to his eventual emergence as sole Augustus on the sudden death of his cousin in late 361). Moreover, as Watt discusses, it is possible that Themistius' reply to Julian's rejoinder exists in an Arabic translation.

Trapp's paper also forms part of a subset of chapters all dealing with various other forms of communication deployed by Julian beyond his major works: Jill Harries considers Julian's laws, Benet Salway the inscriptions issuing from him, Fernando López Sánchez the coinage of Julian, and Eric Varner not just the coinage but all the art associated with the emperor. It was decided to place these contributions at this point in the volume as they emphasise the emergence of Julian as sole ruler, taking on the administration of the whole empire, making his mark upon his subjects. Also, it was deemed that these other forms of communication were as integral to Julian's oeuvre as his major texts, and to group them at the end of the volume might have conveyed an erroneous impression that they were considered less important or an afterthought: they were an integral part of the conference plan from the start. One of the issues that emerges from these other sources is religion, which is picked up by the subsequent chapters of J. H. W. G. Liebeschuetz, Andrew Smith, Arnaldo Marcone and David Hunt, who all discuss Julian's religious project. Liebeschuetz considers Julian's hymn to the Mother of the Gods in the general context of the emperor's attempt to revive paganism, Smith focuses on Julian's use of Neoplatonic concepts in his hymn to Helios, Marcone explores Julian's hostility to the Cynics in his attacks against Heraclius individually and then the Cynics as a group, while Hunt also considers invective, this time against the Christians (or the 'Galileans', as Julian called them), showing how the emperor's own Christian upbringing had given him a strong grasp of the Christian disputes of his time.

The final two main contributions consider Julian's famous satires, the *Caesars* and the *Misopogon*, but the chronological sequence of the texts is inverted because Rowland Smith's discussion of the *Caesars* is greatly concerned with its reception. Nicholas Baker-Brian's treatment of the *Misopogon* returns us to the preoccupations of imperial ideology and

Constantius II, highlighting the centrality of the virtue of self-control in the text, and revealing Julian to be competing with his cousin even after his death. Smith considers the reception of Julian's *Caesars* (and effectively of Julian himself) from the sixteenth down to the eighteenth century, revealing how fascinating – and important – an aspect of the study of Julian this approach is.[30] It also reveals how deep an interest there has been in Julian, one in fact that shows no signs of abating. For such a short-lived emperor, Julian has had a major impact on historians and thinkers, writers and artists. This is not just because of his attempt to restore paganism and undermine Christianity, but also because he was an emperor who was an author.

Notes

[1] For recent accounts of Julian's life and reign, see for instance Rosen 2006 and Tougher 2007. For a recent treatment of Constantine I, see Barnes 2011.

[2] *Ep.* 47 434d, Wright 1923, 148–9.

[3] Julian's memoir of the battle of Strasbourg is mentioned by Eunapius (Blockley, fragment 17). See also Matthews 1989, 378.

[4] 'Julian.' Suda On Line. Tr. Abram Ring. 24 August 2004. 1 April 2012 <http://www.stoa.org/sol-entries/iota/437>. Ring translates 'ἀνεψιὸς' as 'cousin', but it can mean 'nephew', which we give here. For the correct identities of Julian's father and mother see the subsequent discussion. Flavius Dalmatius was a paternal uncle of Julian. Galla was the first wife of Julian's father, and the mother of Julian's half-brother Gallus.

[5] *Misop.* 339b, trans. Wright 1913, vol. 2, 425.

[6] Bowersock 1978, 4.

[7] For an overview of Julian's education, and a discussion of the sources for its reconstruction, see Bouffartigue 1992, 13–49. It should be noted that the chronological problems and details of Julian's early life will be discussed at length in John Vanderspoel's forthcoming monograph on the emperor, and we would like to thank him for sending us copies of unpublished papers which reveal his train of thought.

[8] For Eusebius see for instance Gwynn 1999.

[9] *Ep.* 24, Wright 1923, 74–7. *Ep.* 38, Wright 1923, 122–5, also mentions George's library, and notes that it was extensive and comprehensive, and that it contained diverse philosophical works and histories as well as books by Christians.

[10] For the manuscript tradition of Julian's works see especially Bidez 1929, but also Bidez 1932, xv–xxx.

[11] For Oribasius see for instance Baldwin 1975. Oribasius is first mentioned in connection with Julian when it is reported that Julian took him to Gaul when he was appointed Caesar, but Julian indicates that he was already his friend by then: Eunap. *VS* 498, Jul. *Ep. ad Ath.* 277c. Julian remarks that when appointed Caesar he entrusted Oribasius with the care of his books. Julian later commissioned Oribasius to write two epitomes of medical texts, one of the works of Galen and the other of diverse medical authors.

[12] It is possible that Julian's *Letter to Themistius* also dates to the beginning of his Caesarship. This letter was a response to one of Themistius', congratulating him on his elevation to the Caesarship (or to sole power in 361). In it Julian questions Themistius' conception of the nature of the imperial office: see the chapter by John Watt in this volume.

[13] The part of Julian was played by Andrew Scott, familiar to TV audiences for playing the role of Moriarty in the BBC TV series *Sherlock*. In addition to inspiring plays, poems and paintings, Julian has been the subject of numerous historical novels, the most recent of which is Paul Waters' *The Philosopher Prince*, published in 2010. This focuses on Julian's time in Gaul, and a sequel seems inevitable (it is itself already a sequel to his *Cast Not the Day*, which begins the story of his protagonists, the lovers Drusus and Marcellus). However, probably the most famous – and best – of the novels about Julian is Gore Vidal's *Julian*, a best seller when it was published in 1964. Notably Vidal writes primarily in the voice of Julian (as well as voicing Libanius and Priscus), and shows interest in the subject of Julian as a writer as well as a pagan and politician. Shaun Tougher aims to discuss Vidal's novel more fully elsewhere.

[14] For a fascinating account of the career of Wright see Emerson 1954.

[15] Wright 1913–23.

[16] Bidez and Franz Cumont had already published a collection and edition of Julian's letters, laws and fragments in 1922: Bidez and Cumont 1922. Bidez also wrote an important history of Julian's life and reign: Bidez 1930.

[17] Bidez 1924 and 1932.

[18] Rochefort 1963 and Lacombrade 1964.

[19] Prato and Fornaro 1984.

[20] Fontaine, Prato and Marcone 1987.

[21] Ugenti 1992.

[22] Prato and Micalella 1979 and 1988.

[23] Guido 2000.

[24] Masaracchia 1990.

[25] Weis 1973. For Julian's letter writing see Caltabiano 1991.

[26] Müller 1998, Prato and Micalella 1979, and Sardiello 2000.

[27] Tantillo 1997, 52. In 2008 Stefano Angiolani published an Italian translation of Julian's speech of thanks to Eusebia, but did not provide an edition: Angiolani 2008.

[28] Martin 2009.

[29] Quiroga 2009, Carrié 2009.

[30] For treatment of the reception of Julian see especially Braun 1978 and Richer 1981, but also Browning 1975, esp. 226–35, and Rosen 2006, esp. 399–462.

JULIAN THE WRITER AND HIS AUDIENCE

Susanna Elm

Julian arrived in Constantinople on 11th December 361 as sole Augustus of the Roman empire and legitimate successor of his recently deceased cousin Constantius II. Julian's peaceful *adventus* into the city of his birth was not, however, the predictable result of dynastic regularity. As Caesar, Julian had challenged Constantius' supremacy; he had, in fact, been a usurper. Julian himself acknowledged this, albeit somewhat obliquely. His march against Constantius, resolved by the latter's death, had been accompanied by another campaign, one of letters. Acclaimed as Augustus by his troops, Julian while *en route* against his cousin the reigning Augustus devoted significant time and effort to composing letters to cities in the west – Rome, Corinth, Sparta, Athens, in sum, cities with a great degree of cultural cachet – to persuade his implied audience of the legitimacy, indeed the divinely-preordained inevitability of his actions. In fact, writing about the divine in relation to his imperial mandate was to be one of Julian's central occupations. No sooner had he arrived in Constantinople as emperor than he invited a wide circle of persons to court with the intention of engaging them (and through them all his subjects) in philosophical debates, in which he proclaimed his own perspectives and positions regarding the correct way to rule the *oikoumenē*.[1]

Indeed, no Roman emperor wrote more and no Roman emperor is therefore better known to modern historians than Julian. But this prolific productivity has not elicited a corresponding response from these same modern historians. Despite innumerable scholarly works on the emperor Julian (indeed, if we consider all works on the emperor they extend in near uninterrupted sequence from the time of his death in 363 to today), his writings have received far less scrutiny than one would assume.[2] Similarly investigations of Julian's audience, in particular the response of his Christian audience, have been few. Though every scholar of Julian is more than aware of the emperor's famous edict regarding teachers and its impact on his Christian contemporaries, the extent and the contours of that impact have usually been presupposed rather than studied in detail.

Such investigations as there are tend to be limited to the few Christian works attacking the emperor directly (after his demise).[3] And yet a few months after Julian's *adventus* into Constantinople, at the same time as he proclaimed his *Hymn to the Mother of the Gods* in March 362,[4] one of Julian's immediate contemporaries apologized to his family and friends in a small city in Cappadocia for choosing to lead henceforth 'the true philosophical life'. About a year later, the young man presented a formal, written form of that apology which was to exert an enormous impact over the subsequent centuries. Julian's writings had been a catalyst both for his choice of the philosophical life and its subsequent written formulation: Gregory of Nazianzus' entire literary oeuvre, in fact, responded to Julian's writings, and it stands paradigmatic for much of the response of Julian's Christian subjects, after all a significant part of the imperial audience. And yet, students of Julian have paid comparatively scant attention to that response as formulated in Gregory's ample writings or in those of other Christian contemporaries of the emperor such as Basil of Caesarea or Gregory of Nyssa, and in the subsequent generation as represented by John Chrysostom, Theodore of Mopsuestia, Theodoret of Cyrrhus and many others.

The reasons for such comparative lack of interest are not difficult to see. After all, Julian the emperor and 'Apostate', and Gregory of Nazianzus, 'the Theologian', are also emblematic of the relationship between Christianity and the later Roman empire and its scholarly conceptualization. Both belonged to the first generation of Romans born after Constantine had made Christianity legal, and hence made it a real career option for elite men. These elite men were, without exception, deeply imprinted by their formation in *paideia*. Every Christian writer who mattered had undergone training on the basis of the writings of Homer, Hesiod, Thucydides, Herodotus, Plato, Aristotle (or in the case of the Latins Cicero, Varro, Livy, Sallust, Vergil, Ovid, Seneca, and so forth). These Christian writers were forensic rhetoricians, physicians, and teachers (of the imperial family too, regardless of its religious affiliation); they were also high imperial administrators of the emperor and his court, and were leaders, advisors and administrators of their fellow Christians in the empire. For them, in sum, as for all other members of the elites, classical learning was *the* status marker as well as the *conditio sine qua non* for any leadership position: Christian members of the elites were thus very similar to their non-Christian elite contemporaries.[5]

And yet, the relationship between Rome and Christianity continues in modern times to be cast in the grand narrative according to which the Roman empire declined and fell soon after Christianity had triumphed.

According to this narrative, the origin of which can be found in the Christian histories of Late Antiquity, non-Christian 'Romans' became labeled as pagans: the empire and its pagan 'Romans' were thus regarded as being destined to fade away, at the very latest when christianized barbarians arrived at Rome's gates. We are all familiar with the many variations of this theme. Such a narrative assumes, of course, that the Roman empire and Christianity acted as distinct entities, oil and water, preserving their essential nature even when thrown together. On the one side, the Roman empire of the pagan gods; on the other, Christianity, which was catapulted into the Graeco-Roman world fully formed. Recent scholarship has modified and nuanced this binary model to a considerable degree. Yet, old dichotomies are hard to shake, and the division of the late Roman world into pagans and Christians has proven particularly resilient. This has direct consequences for Julian the writer and his audience, especially his Christian audience.

Julian's Christian contemporaries, men such as Gregory, emphasize the deep gulf separating themselves from those 'on the outside', their 'pagan' relatives, friends, and neighbors. Julian's hostility to his Christian cousin Constantius and all those similarly deluded fairly leaps off the pages of his writings. Modern scholarly disciplines are not conducive to bridging that gulf constructed (*nota bene*) by our sources.[6] Scholars of ancient history commonly end their studies with Constantine's precursor Diocletian (often appending a short last chapter gesturing toward a Roman empire ruled by a Christian and hence no longer part of their intellectual domain). Those who venture further into that Christian Roman realm tend to remain on the safe side of individual emperors and their rule, that is, by studying questions of imperial legislation, administration, and the army, with occasional forays into Christian councils, especially those where imperial involvement is palatable. Here, the emperor Julian provides welcome relief as a 'pagan' emperor and thus 'normal' material for 'real' ancient historians. The strangeness of his paganism (potentially tainted by his Christian up-bringing) can be tempered by leaving his philosophical writings, such as his *Hymn to the Mother of the Gods* or his *Hymn to King Helios*,[7] to philosophers, better equipped to deal with such obscure musings than ancient historians concerned with the *realia* of governance. Alas, most philosophers interested in classical philosophy are just that, so that for many of them Julian's philosophical writings have little to offer, since Julian (as emperor) was no 'professional' philosopher and his writings thus lack originality or system; he was undoubtedly no Iamblichus or Proclus.

With Julian's impact on the writings of his most prominent Christian contemporaries we enter the realm of social historians (who are very interested in the writings of these men, but not so much in their theology, that is, in the 'philosophical' dimension of these men's literary output where Julian's impact might, after all, be located), and that of theologians and Church historians.[8] The latter two in particular have their own concerns and scholarly traditions, which do not necessarily privilege dedicated searches for the 'pagan' roots of the fundamentals of Christian thought and action. Julian, therefore, makes cameo appearances in more historical studies of Gregory, while most strictly-theological studies devoted to Gregory of Nazianzus, Basil of Caesarea and other contemporaries directly affected by Julian's rule pay no attention to the emperor's writings and thus do not investigate their potential impact.[9]

Of course, all those involved in the study of Late Antiquity, whether from a secular or theological vantage point, labor hard to cross disciplinary boundaries, to disrupt and complicate narratives of triumph and decline, and to soften the divide between non-Christian and Christian, both orthodox and heretical. To speak of 'transformation' has therefore been one of the hallmarks of recent scholarship, and despite welcome and necessary caveats that admittedly somewhat vague term continues to be of heuristic value.[10] To speak of transformation implies a small but significant point: the Roman empire became a Christian Roman empire over time and through numerous incremental steps, in a dynamic process of challenge and response, trial, error, dialogue and fierce debate. Very little was set in stone. Many of the developments we now take for granted need not have turned out the way they did, were it not, for example, for the short reign of Julian and for the long and stable reigns of Theodosius I (379–395) and especially Theodosius II (408–450). But to posit transformation (in our context the transformation of the late Roman elites from pagan to Christian) is one thing, to prove and demonstrate such a process of small but significant adjustments in detail is quite another. The *adventus* of Julian into Constantinople as sole Augustus, his actions, laws and especially his writings and the response they elicited from his audience, as captured by the young man who purposely embraced the 'true philosophical life' only a few months later, was just such an incremental step.

Julian and Gregory

Emperor Julian's reign lasted a mere 20 months. He died during the night of 26th June 363, fatally wounded on the battlefield while in retreat from Ctesiphon – the ignominious end of his glorious Persian campaign.[11] Yet these 20 months reverberate until today. Ostensibly repulsed by his cousin Constantius, whom Julian accused of having murdered several members of their family in order to secure his rule when Julian was seven years old,

Julian also rejected the Christianity into which he had been born and which he associated with his cousin's criminal deeds. Inspired instead by Plato's definition of the ideal ruler as philosopher king, Julian understood and presented himself as philosopher, priest, and emperor,[12] divinely inspired and called to rule by the gods who had created Greece's greatness, Zeus, Helios the Sun, Athena, Hermes. Therefore, immediately upon his accession, Julian began to publish imperial letters and edicts aimed at strengthening and invigorating the triad he considered the basis of the greatness of Greek culture: *logoi*, *hiera* and the *polis* – Greek language and culture, its gods and all things sacred, and the city as the physical locus of Greek culture, government and religion. These three he also considered the wellspring of Rome's supremacy and hence guarantor of its *imperium*, without which the *oikoumenē* of the Romans could not be safeguarded, far less prosper. For Julian, Rome and its empire was the divinely appointed heir to Greece. In his words:

> the Greek colonies civilized the greater part of the *oikoumenē* thus preparing it to more easily submit to the Romans. For the Romans are not only Greek by origin (οὐ γένος μόνον Ἑλληνικόν), but also the sacred laws and the pious belief in the gods, which they have instituted and preserve, are from beginning to end Greek.[13]

Greek language, culture and learning, worship of the gods that had inspired them all, and the invigoration of the municipalities were therefore Julian's political program. That and the war against Persia; victory where his cousin had failed was to be the ultimate sign that his imperial power had indeed been bestowed *nutu caelesti*, by divine grace (Amm. Marc. 22.2.3).

Part and parcel of that political program was an attempt at re-education. The Christians, so Julian thought, had foolishly deserted – apostate is the Greek term for deserter – the community of educated, civilized men, namely the community of the Greeks and Romans, and the universality they represented because they had succumbed to childish myths about a so-called god. That 'god' was at best responsible for a tiny corner of the vast *oikoumenē*, Galilee, and by adopting him his followers had in fact deserted their Greek and Roman roots to become 'Galilean'. How this myth had fogged their minds Julian could not fathom. It was as if they not only suddenly declared the governor of an insignificant region more powerful than the emperor of the entire known world (following the mistake of the followers of Moses), but then had deserted even that minor lord too 'to worship the corpse of the Jews'.[14] But Julian considered it an important part of his imperial philanthropy 'to teach, but not to punish, the insane',[15] that is, to reintegrate the demented Christians into the universal community of the civilized. One way to achieve that aim was to point out – by imperial letter with the force of law – that those who did not believe in the gods who had laid the foundation of Greek and Roman civilization, especially its philosophy, could not then use that philosophy to elucidate the simplistic assumption of their myth (for example, how *one* God could be Father, a Son born of a human woman, and a Divine Spirit, elucidations which forced them 'to gnaw at the learning of the Greeks').[16] Such persons could, further, not publicly engage in teaching and living the true philosophical life though they were welcome to expound Matthew and Luke in the churches of the Galileans.[17]

Julian's entire program, but especially the imperial letter concerning Christian teachers of late June or early July 362 (*Ep.* 36), sent shockwaves through the Christian elites. Among those directly affected was Gregory of Nazianzus. He was Christian, he had just returned from advanced study of philosophy at Athens, he had been teaching as a public (though unpaid) rhetorician, and he had decided to embark precisely on the kind of philosophical life now declared unfit for Christians by the new emperor. Julian had grown up not far from Nazianzus (at Macellum, an imperial estate near Caesarea), Gregory had met him at Athens, where both had studied philosophy, and Gregory's younger brother Caesarius was one of Julian's personal physicians.[18] In sum, Gregory had a fair idea what Julian proposed, he had means to gain access to the emperor's writings and pronouncements beyond imperial letters, and he was personally affected by them. The affront Julian's actions, thoughts, and writings represented for Gregory galvanized him into a response with far-reaching consequences. Spurred by Julian's laws, edicts, writings and above all by his self-presentation as Platonic emperor and philosopher-priest, devoted to lead his *oikoumenē*, the empire, to salvation as a servant (really slave) of the true gods of the Greeks and the Romans, Gregory developed his own concept of the Christian leader as philosopher and priest, now in the form of the bishop as servant (really slave) of the God *Logos*. Both followed Plato in considering the philosophical life *the* condition for leadership. Since Julian had proclaimed that those who did not believe in the Gods who had founded Greek philosophy could not use its techniques, for example to define the nature of the Trinity as three in one, Gregory set out to do just that in a manner that took into account Julian's writings on the relationship between the Supreme Divine Father and his Sons (Helios, Apollo, Asclepius etc.). Where Julian had denied that Christianity could be the foundation of Rome's world rule as proven by Constantius' amorality and his corresponding losses in Persia, Gregory sought to show the opposite, especially after the emperor's disastrous death on the Persian battlefields. As I will briefly address below, it is Gregory who created the image of Julian as 'the Apostate', an image which is still predominant today.

Because Julian sought to force Christians to do without 'pagan' learning, Gregory and other Christians had to acknowledge and grapple with the 'pagan' elements in their ways of thinking as never before. One result was Gregory's entire oeuvre of 45 orations in all classical genres and 19,000 verses in all meters, in which he 'rewrote' the key-concepts of the 'pagans' – Plato's notions of leadership as laid down in the *Republic* and the *Laws*; Aristotle's use of logic; Homeric themes; how Christians should be honored through funeral orations; how to praise emperors, compose letters; write poetry as Christian – to lay the foundations of Byzantine and much western thought.[19] He did so by incorporating Christian elements into the classical matrix. As a result, Gregory became one of the leading intellectuals of his day and one of the most widely read authors of Byzantium – only the Scriptures had a wider manuscript distribution – with a significant impact on such westerners as Jerome, Ambrose, Augustine and pope Gregory the Great. He became none other than Saint Gregory of Nazianzus, the 'Theologian', whose signal contributions to the formulation of the Trinity – 'the God who is one must be preserved and three *hypostaseis* professed, each with its own specific properties (τὸν ἕνα Θεὸν τηρεῖν καὶ τὰς τρεῖς ὑποστάσεις ὁμολογεῖν, καὶ ἑκάστην μετὰ τῆς ἰδιότητος)' (Greg. Naz. *Or.* 2.38) – dominated Christian doctrine for generations and made him one of the three Hierarchs of the Orthodox Church (and a favorite of Pope Benedict XVI). And the emperor was henceforth Julian 'the Apostate'.[20]

Historiography once more – Pagan vs. Christian

Paradoxically, however, Gregory's very success as 'the Theologian' and one of the leading Fathers of the Christian Church as a whole turned him – historiographically speaking – into a somewhat marginal figure. Scholars consider him so Christian, so passionately devoted to philosophical retreat and pure thought, as to be constitutionally incapable of functioning in the real world of Church and other politics. In fact, if (influenced, for example, by Max Weber or Hans von Campenhausen) one considers normative the bishop as an institutional figurehead wedded to one see and characterized by his sacramental functions, then Gregory was indeed an abject ecclesiastical failure.[21] He was a reluctant priest and a lack-luster adjunct bishop. After his ordination as bishop of Sasima he refused to assume his duties – he never even went there, though the place was close by. Instead he disappeared for three years of retreat, from where he emerged – somewhat inexplicably for modern scholars – as the leader of the 'orthodox' Christian congregation in Constantinople in 379. Less than a year later, the new emperor Theodosius I made him bishop of the capital, but a mere nine months after that, while presiding at the first ecumenical council of 381, Gregory resigned, left Constantinople, and retired to his estate near Nazianzus.[22] Fits and starts, which have garnered him scholarly characterizations as sensitive soul and a *romantique avant la lettre* or as an indecisive, pusillanimous, and labile man, who simply could not make up his mind and stick with it.[23] These near-canonical scholarly characterizations of Gregory as gifted theologian but 'weltfremder' man and disastrous bishop were also what piqued my own curiosity. Could a man, made bishop of Constantinople at a very tense time by the mandate of the very emperor Theodosius who made catholic Christianity the *religio* of the entire realm – could such a man really have been such a clueless loser?

My answer is 'No', but to arrive at that conclusion required first an opening of the Christian bubble in which scholars have sealed Gregory so hermetically. What if, say, Gregory had not just contemplated the Christian Scriptures in solitary splendor, but had actually read Julian's writings and responded to them? Which would mean that he had shaped his concept of the bishop as philosopher, alternating periods of active political involvement with those of retreat and writing, in direct response to Julian's claim to embody just such a philosopher as leader. A possibility, I should point out, categorically excluded by nearly all scholars who have ever published on Gregory, with the exception of Leonardo Lugaresi and Ugo Criscuolo.[24] And yet, that was the case. This was the model of the orthodox Christian bishop Gregory had first delineated in the apology I mentioned above, his famous *Oration* 2, entitled by the manuscript editors 'Apology for his Flight' or 'On the Priesthood'. This was the model he propagated time and again in his subsequent orations, a model that became normative for Ambrose, Augustine, and Gregory the Great – and Julian had been the catalyst for this model.

To puncture Gregory's Christian bubble required a similar operation on the part of Julian, for his part encased in the historiographical bubble of the pagan 'Apostate' intent on persecuting Christians, albeit in a somewhat more subtle manner than by throwing them to the lions.[25] Julian had been brought up Christian: George of Cappadocia, later bishop of Alexandria, had been among his teachers. But, to cite Klaus Rosen, 'there is no trace of his Christianity to be found in his rather obtuse philosophical speculations'.[26] As a consequence of this view, which Rosen shares with other scholars engaged with Julian, there is little reason to mention a single work of Gregory in connection with the emperor – with the exception of Gregory's two invectives against Julian which I will address shortly. Thus,

Julian's precise knowledge of the Christian debates of his time, and his engagement in these debates through his ('pagan') philosophical and other writings have not been elucidated, nor as a consequence has the Christian response to that 'pagan' challenge, which was as significant as the challenge had been. Therefore, despite the enormous scholarly attention lavished on Julian, scholarship has not truly investigated *all* of his writings – including his philosophical works. It has only scratched the surface of the actual impact of Julian's writings on his contemporaries, that is, on the thoughts and writings of the emperor's Christian contemporaries, also known as the Fathers of the Church, who were then formulating the tenets of orthodoxy.[27] Julian's works have not been fully appreciated, for instance, by historians with 'an active interest in secular aspects of the end of the Roman world, such as its political, economic and military history', and who are thus understandably reluctant to probe Julian's philosophy for Christian influences.[28] Nor have they been appreciated by theologians and most church historians, who are reluctant for equally understandable reasons to concede that Gregory may have read a single piece of writing by the emperor, even when he cites its title, had a brother at court, and claims that the emperor targeted him and Basil of Caesarea especially because he had known them since their days in Athens (*Or.* 5.39), and despite the fact that Gregory's entire oeuvre does in fact respond to Julian's writings point by point.[29]

Creating the Apostate
To add substance to my remarks, I would like to discuss briefly some aspects of the two orations by Gregory discussed both by all historians concerned with Julian and all church historians concerned with Gregory, namely Gregory's *Orations* 4 and 5. These are the famous 'invectives' in which Gregory 'created' Julian as *the Apostate*. For many, they stand symptomatic for Gregory and his value as a historical source. 'Simultaneously hysterical and pedantic, fiercely caustic and pompously ponderous' (according to Raymond Van Dam), these literary products exhibit above all their author's lack of historical sensibility.[30] Church historians also dislike these orations since 'this kind of joyful scalp dance on the body of a dead enemy of yesterday is somewhat embarrassing'.[31] Indeed, it is a challenge to integrate the picture of a happily dancing Gregory, swinging Julian's bloody scalp, with that of the 'sweet and gentle man', paragon of a 'spirit of high culture, brilliant and gracious, a sweet and tender soul through a lack of practical sense, perhaps, badly armed to sustain the battles into which the hazards of life will throw him' – the historiographical Gregory in a nutshell.[32]

In fact, the metaphor of the dance with the scalp is apt. Gregory's orations against Julian were a performance piece. First, Gregory explicitly and emphatically did not wish to write history (*Or.* 4.20). Second, he claimed to perform a sacred ritual. His orations were a *panegyric,* a celebratory hymn (*Or.* 4.7, 4.8; *Or.* 5.35) and a 'bloodless sacrifice of words to the Word', Christ, the *Logos* (*Or.* 4.3). As such his performance stood in sharp contrast to that of the emperor. While Gregory' oration performed a sacred ritual, Julian's entire reign had been nothing but theater, a 'fiction without any roots in reality' (*Or.* 4.113 and 114), 'making one laugh rather than cry' (*Or.* 4.78). Gregory's aim was to make Julian lose face and so he presented the man and his rule as histrionics. And through his performance of Julian's past as theater Gregory, as it turned out, formed his future. His picture of Julian's reign shaped historiography more than anything the emperor had ever done or written in the short twenty months of his reign.

Though usually treated as one piece, Gregory wrote the two orations against Julian over one year apart and for different, albeit overlapping, audiences. *Oration* 4, prepared while Julian was still alive but completed after the emperor's death, probably in 364 during the first months of Valentinian I's and Valens' rule, addressed an (intended) audience more concerned with the theological controversies that so dominated the early 360s. *Oration* 5, in contrast, was written during the interlude of Procopius' usurpation (365–366), and uses the specter of Julian and the glorification of his memory by men such as Libanius – after all Julian was a duly divinized legitimate Roman ruler – to argue against Procopius and in favor of Valens. It thus enters a debate regarding the legitimacy of Julian's successors. Both orations, despite their differences, address an audience consisting, so far as we can tell, of members of the new service elite then in the process of becoming an empire-wide aristocracy. These men, many of whom sat in the new Constantinopolitan senate, were scions of the native municipal elites, such as Gregory's brother Caesarius.[33] Most of these men were Christian, and it was for their benefit that Gregory formulated in these two orations the correct ways in which, as Christian public men, they ought to conduct themselves and the affairs of the *politeia.*

As his two orations against Julian reveal, Gregory shared Julian's assessment regarding the centrality of *logoi, hiera* and the *polis,* Greek culture, the sacred and the city. He also saw them as intrinsically linked with each other as well as foundational for the well-being of the Roman empire, the *oikoumenē* of the Romans – both Julian and Gregory use the same terms. Gregory differed sharply, of course, with regard to the divinity that had originated all three, four if we count the empire. Those whom Julian had considered gods, Gregory considered demons, and the figure Julian had declared to be the pseudo-divinity of a marginal people was Gregory's universal *pantokratōr*: a small but significant difference. As a result, Julian had, according to Gregory, misconstrued the sacred, with the consequence that his understanding of *logoi* and the *polis* was equally faulty. In a private person such a mistake might be merely reprehensible, but in an emperor, 'such comportment alone suffices to pillory (*stēliteusai*) the moral character of a ruler', because a ruler's comportment affects the fundamentals of the state (*Or.* 4.81). And that is one of the central issues at stake in Gregory's allegedly a-historic orations: the Roman empire (*archē*), the roots of its power, and the manner in which the community of the Romans ought to be governed – according to Gregory (*Or.* 4.74). To clarify his views regarding these matters, Gregory focused on the most central places in which the emperor performed imperial rule and where his impact on the triad *logoi*, *hiera* and *polis* was most directly visible: the theater and the market place.

The theater – as is well known and was abundantly clear to Gregory – was of crucial importance for the self-representation and self-constitution of any city. Here the city's elites were seated in hierarchical order and proportional overabundance, viewing the results of their own financial munificence as they were observed in so doing by the non-elites (*Or.* 4.113). In addition, the theater was 'the primary vehicle for the inculcation of classical culture' because here mimes and pantomimes performed the tragedies and comedies as well as all the essential myths regarding the gods of the Greeks and Romans: the essence of *logoi* and the *hiera*.[34] These very same *logoi* and the *hiera* at their center were what Julian had sought to reinvigorate, albeit not their theatrical performance. That interpretation was Gregory's obvious defamation. Like many intellectuals, Julian and Gregory shared the ambivalence the theater evoked.[35] It was powerful and attractive, it transmitted Greek culture, but it did so in a popular, mocking, and often rather licentious fashion. To be a mime and pantomime was considered shameful, *infamus*.[36] Theater was by its very nature dissimulation, fiction, lie. To call Julian's entire reign nothing but theater (*Or.* 4.113) said it all.[37] Julian had erected 'a polis constructed of words' that could not be sustained by deeds, because it lacked 'the force of a system that is derived from divine inspiration' (*Or.* 4.44, 4.113; Pl. *Resp.* 369c). All of Julian's imperial acts were simulations of reality destined to be fleeting – recall that the men whom Gregory here addressed, all Christian, were also the ones who continued to fund just such theatrical games for public enjoyment and at immense costs to themselves.[38]

Gregory's argument works on several levels. First, if Julian's acts and deeds, including his legislative acts and deeds, were 'theater', demonically inspired dissimulations destined to be transitory, then Gregory's words were 'reality' rooted in deeds and lasting because they expressed a divinely inspired system. Thus, his words overwrote Julian's (legislative) acts and deeds. Second, in a long treatment of the nature of the myths portrayed in the theater, myths so dear to Julian, Gregory dismantled the religious and thus ethical foundations upon which Julian's transient '*polis*' – that is, his rule – rested. Like their theater performances, the myths of Julian's gods were devoid of all the ethical prerequisites of appropriate rule, such as restraint, justice, prudence, philanthropy, and, above all, piety; no wonder, therefore, that Julian's disastrous performance as ruler showed such deficiencies (*Or.* 4.113–123). For, third, Gregory's attack aimed not only at Julian's deeds and works but also at his person. Gregory knew that Julian personally disdained the theater almost as much as he did, and for similar reasons. Julian considered the mockery of the Gods and the licentious displays of their myths shameful. And he had made his feelings known, for example in the *Antiochikos* or *Misopogon*, which Gregory cited by title in his *Oration* 5.41.[39] Of course, Julian's actual attitude towards the theater was of no consequence. At every stage Gregory sought to portray the emperor as a bad actor who did not comport himself as a real emperor should. When Gregory had first laid eyes on Julian in Athens and observed him twittering and twitching, he could already divine what the future would bring:

> What more can I say? I looked at the man prior to his deeds and recognized him by them...and I said to [my companions]: 'what disaster is the Roman state nurturing here!'[40]

The theater was a place where the emperor interacted directly with his subjects, where he performed imperial rule and was seen doing so. It was also one of the places where imperial letters and decrees were received and read aloud in a highly ritualized manner as if the emperor were present.[41] A second site where the same interaction occurred was the *agora*, the market place, and it is here too, of course, that Gregory engaged Julian.

Even though they are usually characterized as invectives, and even though he followed the structural demands of that genre, Gregory himself emphatically declared that his *Orations* 4 and 5 against Julian were not invectives, because he considered himself incapable of writing a *psogos* that could do justice to Julian's misdeeds (*Or.* 4.79). The distinction is relevant. By explicitly foregoing the genre *psogos* (as well as that of history) Gregory also chose to forego the role of the prosecutor arguing his case to elicit a conviction (the generic conceit characteristic of the *psogos*).[42] Instead, he called his orations a '*stēlographia*', a 'writing-on-a-stēlē' or pillar (*Or.* 4.20). As Alois Kurmann has pointed out, the term is a neologism deriving from the verb *stēliteuein*, to inscribe the name of convicted criminals after their execution onto a pillar in the market place. Persons thus inscribed or pilloried were marked and shamed forever and for all to see.[43] In Gregory's eyes, thus, Julian had already received his sentence. By divine decree he had been convicted and executed in the theater of war. God had been prosecutor, judge and executioner. Gregory merely proclaimed the sentence and explicated it to all present and to those in the future. Anticipating Augustine in the *City of God* (5.21), that God grants earthly rule both to the pious and to the impious, but that he does so advisedly, Gregory's oration provided a providential explanation for Julian's rule and the calamity it entailed for the entire community of the empire. God had permitted Julian's rise to chastise the Christians, who had not used their new power wisely. But, he had also decreed his demise by ensuring that his rule was as transient as a theater performance.

That Gregory called this sentence a 'writing-on-a-stēlē', furthermore, draws attention to the act of *stēliteuein* as a public proclamation of legal acts. Such public proclamations were the domain of those who ruled. On just such pillars in the public places Julian's edict and imperial letters had been posted, including the *Misopogon*, in which Julian had presented himself as the embodiment of the just Platonic philosopher-king outlined in the *Laws*, or his famous letter excluding Christians from *logoi*. Gregory's *Oration* 4, consequently, labors hard to showcase Julian as the embodiment of the unjust ruler, whose legislation cannot be allowed to stand since it is driven by mistaken assumptions of justice, lack of ethical fiber and above all bad craftsmanship as shown in the incorrect use of grammar and rhetoric that led Julian to exclude Christians from 'speaking Greek' (*Or.* 4.100–107). In his metaphorical counter-stēlē Gregory – in a performative act of his own – overwrote all of Julian's acts and most of his concepts, one by one. And while Julian's words, written on stone, would pass like dried grass, Gregory's words though written on flimsy linen or wax tablets would last:

> Here our *stēlē* for you, higher and more visible than those of Hercules, because those are merely planted in one place and are visible only to those who go there. This *stēlē* instead cannot but move about and make itself known to all. It will even be received in the future, of that I am certain, to pillory you and your works and to teach everyone not to attempt such a rebellion 'apostasy' against God, so that they may not be punished in like manner for having committed similar crimes.[44]

Emperor and priest

Julian was a deserter (*apostate*) whom God had judged and condemned to execution in war. In so doing God had issued a stern warning regarding the conduct of imperial rule and of the governance of the *oikoumenē* of the Romans. What was at stake for Gregory was in fact the relationship between Christian God, emperor, and priest. By calling his discourse a 'writing on a stēlē', Gregory signaled that he was posting a divine decree that overwrote imperial ones. And by attacking Julian as lacking imperial *gravitas* and the crucial capability of acting as a just Roman imperial legislator, he at the same time defined what being a true and just Christian emperor entailed. To further highlight his point, Gregory juxtaposed Julian's negative image with a positive portrayal of his cousin Constantius as the paragon of an ideal Christian ruler. Constantius' sole fault had been too much philanthropy out of which he had permitted Julian to survive (*Or.* 4.3).[45] Other than that, Constantius 'knew very well, because he reflected upon such things in a manner more elevated and imperial than most, that the Roman power had grown together with Christianity and that the *imperium* arrived together with Christ' (*Or.* 4.37). To assure the greatness of the empire thus required the appropriate nurturing of all things Christian, the unity of Christian teaching (or *orthodoxa*); the appropriate protection of Christian *hiera*, and, of course, the creation through tax exemptions, removal of 'pagan' symbols, and so on, of the Christian *polis*. Julian, this 'best of all governors of the commonwealth' (*Or.* 4.74), had failed to realize that to eradicate Christianity, 'now that it ruled sovereign', was 'to rip out the roots of Roman rule and to place the entire commonwealth into grave danger' all because of his newfangled philosophy on the throne, which brought nothing but disorder and war.

Gregory, to recall, wrote these two orations during the reign of Julian's successors who were all Christian. But much remained uncertain: how would these new emperors comport themselves as Christian emperors? Julian's edicts needed to be rescinded, but would the new emperors do that given that he had been a legitimate and duly divinized emperor? How would *they* treat Christian *logoi*? After all, Julian had been raised as a Christian from childhood, but he had deserted. Instead of adhering to what his priests and bishops had taught him, he had gone off to invent his own *logoi* – a stern warning to Christian emperors not to deviate from the words of their bishops such as Gregory. And what about the theater and the marketplace? How was a Christian emperor to comport himself there? For example, as Neil McLynn has so persuasively pointed out, the manner in which a Christian emperor should perform imperially in the new theater – the church – was at that point entirely unclear: how was one to integrate the emperor into the liturgy?[46] And by the time of *Oration* 5 the issue had become even more pressing: Procopius, after all, had justified his usurpation against Valens because of his shared dynastic lineage with Julian and Constantine the Great. A call to support Valens instead (as which *Oration* 5 in fact functions) had therefore to be very convincing indeed.[47]

To conclude, characterizing Julian as a bad actor performing badly the part of a ruler allowed Gregory to achieve a number of aims. It permitted him to define what he considered appropriate Christian rule by opposing Julian and Constantius, tyrannical and just legislation, disastrous and justified conduct of war, appropriate behavior in the *agora* and its opposite. And it allowed him to do far more. Gregory also used the theater to attack Julian's understanding of myth as the emperor had defined it in his writings against Heraclius[48] and in his two hymns to the Mother of the Gods and to King Helios. In so doing, Gregory addressed at the same time emerging debates regarding the correct exegesis of the Bible, literally or allegorically, which also erupted as a consequence of Julian's views on myth and its allegorical interpretations.[49] Further, Gregory used arguments he had sharpened in *Oration* 4 against Julian's use of 'being Greek' (*hellēnizein*) against Eunomius and other Christians he considered heretical or 'Arian' in his famous so-called *Theological Orations*. Perhaps most importantly, by associating a number of ways of acting and arguing as a Greek person with the emperor Julian, Gregory created '*hellēnizein*' as a way of being Greek henceforth clearly delineated as Julianic and thus not acceptable for his audience. At the same time he also clarified that what remained of being and speaking Greek, including its philosophy (the true *logoi*), and the shape of the *polis* as configured by Gregory, was 'ours', i.e. Christian, and had been so since the beginning. After all, the *imperium* of the Romans had begun with Christ. Hellene, as we know, became the equivalent of pagan.[50]

Point by point, argument by argument, Gregory's orations counter Julian and his notions. What is true for *Orations* 4 and 5 also applies to the rest of Gregory's phenomenally influential oeuvre. Julian's rule, then, may have been a transient theater performance, but the effect of his writings on his Christian audience proved to be of a magnitude that has yet to be fully appreciated. Bringing Julian's and Gregory's writings into dialogue shows that both men had far more in common than divided them: merely the definition of the divinity that had created Greek and Roman supremacy. Integral for all and to everything these men thought and wrote was the 'pagan learning' they all shared. Phrased differently, without paganism no Christianity, without Julian's writings no Gregory the Theologian. And what is true for Gregory's writings also applies to a number of his important contemporaries and successors. Thus, paradoxical though it may sound, through the Christian (and especially Gregory's) response to the pagan Apostate's writings, Julian became in effect yet another Father of the Church.

15

Acknowledgements

I would like to thank Nicholas Baker-Brian and Shaun Tougher for the wonderful conference in Cardiff dedicated to Julian the writer, at which this paper was presented. I benefited enormously.

Notes

[1] For Julian's rise see now Tougher 2007, 16–21, 31–43. The view of Szidat 1997 that Julian was technically not a usurper has not found widespread scholarly acceptance. For Julian's *Letter to the Athenians* see the chapter by Mark Humphries in this volume. For a comprehensive account of Julian's reign see Rosen 2006.

[2] See now the important contributions in Schäfer 2008.

[3] For a summary of the scholarly debates regarding this edict see Germino 2004.

[4] For Julian's *Hymn to the Mother of the Gods* see the chapter by J. H. W. G. Liebeschuetz in this volume.

[5] The essential discussion of *paideia* in Late Antiquity continues to be Brown 1992. See also the contributions in Borg 2004.

[6] See Elm 2003 for additional bibliography, as well as Elm 2012. For approaches to Julian the philosopher see the remarks in Bouffartigue 1992; O'Meara 2003; and now Schäfer 2008 and Cürsgen 2008.

[7] For the *Hymn to King Helios* see the chapter by Andrew Smith in this volume.

[8] For a social historical approach see especially Van Dam 2002a, 2002b and 2003; and the important papers now collected in McLynn 2009. See also McGuckin 2001 and Gautier 2002.

[9] The best and most recent work devoted to Gregory's theology is Beeley 2008.

[10] See in particular Ward-Perkins 2005; Kelly 2009.

[11] Matthews 1989, 181; Tougher 2007, 63–71.

[12] E.g. *Ep. ad Them.* 267a. For Julian's *Letter to Themistius* see the chapter by John Watt in this volume.

[13] *Or.* 4 152d–153a.

[14] *C. Gal.* fr. 36 171e; fr. 43 194d. For Julian's *Against the Galileans* see the chapter by David Hunt in this volume.

[15] *Ep.* 36 (for the numbering of Julian's letters I follow the Loeb Classical Library edition of Julian's writings by W. C. Wright).

[16] *C. Gal.* fr. 55 229c–d.

[17] *Ep.* 36.

[18] For Gregory's engagement as rhetorician after returning from Athens see McLynn 2006, 220–4; for biographic details see Beeley 2008, 7–14.

[19] Daley 2006, 1–61.

[20] For Gregory's reception of the honorific 'the Theologian', and for his later impact, see McGuckin 2001, xxii–vii, 399–402.

[21] For an overview of scholarly constructions of the bishop see now the seminal work by Rapp 2005, esp. 3–22 and 24–33; also Sterk 2004, esp. 119–40. Still foundational is Campenhausen 1953.

[22] Beeley 2008, 3–16, 34–62.

[23] For bibliographic details see Elm 2009, 281–2.

24 Lugaresi 1993, 15, and 1997; Criscuolo 1987, 205.

25 Tougher 2007, 55–62, for a discussion of scholarly views.

26 Rosen 2006, 287, translation mine.

27 What has been studied is the tip of the iceberg: decidedly anti-Julianic texts such as Gregory's orations *Against Julian* (Orr. 4 and 5) and other direct responses to Julian's writings, especially to his *Against the Galileans*, most notably by Cyril of Alexandria.

28 Ward-Perkins 2005, 180.

29 Elm 2012. There are notable exceptions, especially Thome 2004, and García Garrido 2000.

30 Quasten 1974, 242; Bowersock 1978, 5, considers Gregory's work a useful collection of gossip; Van Dam 2002b, 194–5.

31 'cette espèce de danse allègre du scalp sur le corps d'un ennemi mort de la veille a quelque chose de gênant': Bernardi 1978a, 91, trans. mine.

32 '...esprit de haute culture, brillant et grâcieux, âme douce et tendre, mal armée, faute peut-être de sens pratique, pour soutenir les luttes dans lesquelles le hazard de la vie le jettera': P. Godet as cited by Lugaresi 1993, 13–14, trans. mine.

33 For the dating see Elm 2012, Bernardi 1983, 11–37, and Lugaresi 1993, 39–48, whose suggestions concerning a later date for Or. 5 I am following. Sarris 2004, esp. 62; Banaji 2001, 49–51.

34 Leyerle 2001, 13–20, quote 18.

35 Compare denunciations of the Roman senators' lust for the theater in Lugaresi 2003, 299.

36 Lim 2003, 87–91.

37 As Gregory elaborates in *Or.* 4.113–19, Julian's claim to Greek culture and the sacred was nothing but a recourse to the 'fictions and vain words of the poets' (*Or.* 4.118), particularly those of 'Homer...the great comediograph, or better tragediograph of your gods' (*Or.* 4.116).

38 Lim 2003, 84–6; also Sarris 2004, 63.

39 For Julian's *Misopogon* see the chapter by Nicholas Baker-Brian in this volume.

40 *Or.* 5.32. This is the famous and widely quoted characterization of Julian's physique; Bowersock 1978, 12; Rosen 2006, 18.

41 Matthews 2000, 195–9.

42 Koster 1980, 7–17, 38–9, focuses on Latin authors but is nonetheless fundamental (he does not treat Christian writers).

43 Kurmann 1988, 19–20.

44 *Or.* 5.42.

45 Note that in Julian's *Misopogon* (357b) he asserts that Constantius did the Antiochenes harm in one thing, not executing Julian when he had appointed him Caesar.

46 McLynn 2004, 235–6.

47 A few years later Gregory reversed the call to support Valens, of course, as evident in his famous description of the somewhat hostile encounter between an emperor and a bishop in a church. Again, Gregory used the term stēlē. Now the bishop, Basil, was the solid pillar and the public display of power took place in the church. Lo and behold, the emperor, now Valens, twitched again. The winner was, of course, the bishop Basil (*Or.* 43.52).

[48] For Julian's attack on the Cynic Heraclius (*Or.* 7) see the chapter by Arnaldo Marcone in this volume.

[49] As shown in Thome 2004, an excellent monograph.

[50] Elm 2010a.

READING BETWEEN THE LINES: JULIAN'S *FIRST PANEGYRIC* ON CONSTANTIUS II

Shaun Tougher

Introduction

Of all Julian's writings it is probably safe to say that his panegyrics have excited least interest.[1] This may have been because of the dim view traditionally taken of this type of literature (witness Syme's verdict on Pliny the Younger's speech of thanks to Trajan, that it 'has done no good to the reputation of the author or the taste of the age'),[2] but also because of the unseemly scenario of Julian flattering his cousin the emperor Constantius II (337–361), the man held responsible for the deaths of so many of Julian's relatives (not least his half-brother the Caesar Gallus, executed in 354). However, in the course of the twentieth century there was a sea-change in the attitude to panegyric, from one of instinctive distaste to one of greater understanding and appreciation, a development which shows no signs of abating in the twenty-first century.[3] Further, it has been realised that Julian's panegyrics (and his writings in general) should not necessarily be taken at face value. This is true in particular of the *Second Panegyric on Constantius II* (*Or.* 2): Polymnia Athanassiadi detected in the speech an 'auto-panegyrical flavour', while Florin Curta developed this notion further and interpreted it as 'a veritable political program of the future emperor'.[4] The character of Julian's *Speech of Thanks to the Empress Eusebia* (*Or.* 3) (Constantius' wife) as supposedly sincere and spontaneous has been questioned, and it has been argued that beneath its surface are found deeper, more personal concerns, as well as criticism of the regime of Julian's cousin.[5] These conclusions about the other two panegyrics suggest that the *First Panegyric on Constantius II* (*Or.* 1) deserves to be considered with a sharper eye.[6] This is the objective of the present chapter. I will begin by establishing and scrutinising accepted truths about the date and context of the panegyric before concentrating especially on the question of the models Julian used for his speech. These issues all bring into focus my key question: how should we read Julian's *First Panegyric on Constantius*?

Accepted truths

To start with, let us establish key accepted truths about the text, all found in Joseph Bidez's classic assessment of it. It has been dated to the early years of Julian's Caesarship. In the speech Julian himself alludes to his appointment to the Caesarship (6th November 355) in the aftermath of Constantius II successfully crushing usurpers in the west in the 350s; Julian focuses mainly on the cases of Vetranio and Magnentius, but also refers to the suppression of Silvanus. Thus some have tied the speech closely to Julian's elevation to the Caesarship in Milan, and have asserted that it was written before his departure for Gaul in December.[7] However, in the speech Julian also asserts that he has not as yet conducted a military campaign of his own, but has only shared in one of Constantius, which has led to AD 356, prior to the capture of Cologne in that year, being proposed as the date of the speech.[8] Yet the panegyric has also been placed in the context of specific military and political events in 356–357: the failure of the Master of Cavalry Marcellus to relieve Julian at Sens (where he was wintering) and the subsequent allegations of Marcellus against Julian at Constantius' court in Milan (accusing the Caesar of arrogance and 'strengthening his wings so as to rise up higher')[9] as well as the concomitant mission of Julian's chamberlain the eunuch Eutherius to the court, to defend the Caesar. It has been suggested that the panegyric came with Eutherius to Milan, and was designed to convince Constantius of Julian's trustworthiness and loyalty: in effect, the panegyric has been read as diplomatic in character, a deliberate attempt to secure the favour of the emperor.[10]

Regarding the literary nature of the speech, it has been declared that Julian has followed closely the model laid down for composing *basilikoi logoi* in the rhetorical handbook attributed to Menander Rhetor (see below and the Appendix).[11] Wilmer Cave Wright asserts that Julian 'follows with hardly a deviation the rules for the arrangement and treatment of a speech in praise of an emperor...as we find them in Menander's handbook', while Bidez observes that the speech was composed 'suivant toutes les règles de l'art; on dirait même que Julien...avait sous les yeux un traité analogue aux conseils de Ménandre'.[12] Indeed Athanassiadi pronounced that the

> panegyric follows so faithfully the model...that it arouses the suspicion that its author saw in slavish imitation the only way of absolving himself from the charge of lying. By refusing to make intelligent use of the ready-made model before his eyes he proclaimed unambiguously that his true self...was not participating in the composition of this disgraceful panegyric.[13]

She also described it as a work of 'studied unoriginality'.[14] In addition, it is often remarked that Julian had certain other models in mind when he wrote his speech, in particular speeches written by the oratorical giants of his day, Themistius and Libanius.[15] Themistius especially was associated with praising Constantius II. He addressed his oration *On Love of Mankind* (*Or.* 1) to the emperor in person at Ancyra, probably in 347 (though possibly in 350), a speech which also goes by the title *Constantius*.[16] He took the emperor as his subject again in 355, in his *Speech of Thanks to Constantius* (*Or.* 2), written in response to his adlection to the Senate of Constantinople by the emperor.[17] This speech was not delivered in person, for in 355 Constantius was in the west. Interestingly the speech touches on Julian directly as by that date he had been chosen as Caesar,[18] and of course Themistius also wrote a letter (*protrepticus*) to Julian on his appointment as Caesar.[19] As for Libanius, probably in 348/9 he had delivered a panegyric on Constantius and his brother Constans (*Or.* 59) at Nicomedia, though neither emperor was present.[20] These three orations are considered to have been literary models for Julian's first speech on Constantius II, and it is notable that Julian sent a copy of his panegyric to Libanius; Bidez assumed that Themistius also received a copy.[21]

Deconstruction time

Let us begin by scrutinising the issues of dating and context more closely, before concentrating especially on the question of Julian's models. Regarding the date of the speech, it is clear that Julian is already Caesar, but the question of which joint campaign with Constantius he is referring to is a live one since the details of his early career have been problematised by Vanderspoel. Vanderspoel has suggested that, prior to becoming Caesar, Julian had already been involved with his cousin in a campaign against the Alamanni, in 354.[22] Thus the *First Panegyric* could indeed date to late 355, rather than 356. However, if that was the case, it seems rather odd that the speech does not emphasise more Julian's elevation to the Caesarship and make of it a *Speech of Thanks*, akin to his *Speech of Thanks to Eusebia*, written after a visit of the empress to Rome in 356.[23] Regarding the dating of the panegyric to 357 Tantillo has also associated it with this year, but in a rather different context to the one usually imagined.[24] He connects it with Constantius' triumphal visit to Rome in April and May 357, celebrating his victory over Magnentius, and suggests that Julian's wife Helena brought the speech (as well as the one for Eusebia) with her to Rome. This is certainly an intriguing hypothesis, but I would still lean towards favouring 356 because of the reference to the lack of an independent military campaign.[25] However, what deserves to be emphasised more than issues of dating is that the panegyric is Julian's first major extant literary work, unless one dates his *Letter to Themistius* to 355/6 rather than 361/2.[26] Even if the

Letter was written prior to the *Panegyric*, more thought needs to be devoted to why at all Julian turned to writing panegyric (and three times!). As we have seen, diplomacy has been assumed to be the answer, but is this the only answer, or even correct at all? I will return to these questions below when considering further the models for Julian's speech. Certainly the theory that the speech was sent with Eutherius to Constantius should be questioned, as indeed Tantillo has done.[27] There is no evidence to support this; it has simply been chosen as a suitable context for a speech assumed to be diplomatic in purpose. Indeed one could argue that it was in Julian's interests to be generally diplomatic with Constantius, so the speech could have been sent or delivered at other times. One should also ponder further whether Constantius ever heard the speech or received a copy of it. The only person we know who apparently read it was Libanius, since he wrote to Julian about it.[28] A host of questions deserve to be asked. Did Julian intend the speech for Constantius at all? Did he write it for an audience in Gaul? Did he write it primarily for himself? We cannot know for sure, of course, but further reflections below will attempt to illuminate the question of the audience for the speech. It also deserves to be emphasised that the panegyric was written by a Caesar, not by just a philosopher (Themistius) or a sophist (Libanius). It should be asked, how has this fact affected the nature of the work, if at all?

Julian's models

In this section I will explore in particular the question of the Menandrian nature of the panegyric, but first the question of the influence of the other models will be considered further.

Both Themistius and Libanius had strong associations with Julian. Themistius had dealings with Julian prior to his elevation to the Caesarship (whether he actually taught him or not),[29] and Libanius was a stylistic inspiration for Julian even though, famously, Julian was not taught by him.[30] In the case of the *First Panegyric*, Themistius has usually been seen as the more influential model.[31] Themistius' panegyric on Constantius (*Or.* 1) is noted for several distinct features: Themistius took the pose of the philosopher who could only tell the truth,[32] and thus, he asserted, his speech was better than others which had praised the emperor; he took as his theme virtue, especially philanthropy (the supreme royal virtue, he says); and he conjured up a picture of the ideal ruler, which he implied (rather than demonstrated) was Constantius II.[33] Themistius, thus, did not embrace the Menandrian model (which was heavily biographical)[34] but avowed that he was pursuing his own path.[35] Libanius, on the other hand, appears to have taken an entirely more traditional sophistic approach in his panegyric on Constantius and Constans (*Or.* 59).[36] It has been described as being 'very carefully modelled on Menander's rules' (just like Julian's),[37] Malosse going so far as to observe that one has the impression that Libanius had the treatise in front of his eyes.[38] So how is it that Themistius has tended to be seen as the more influential model?[39] It is clear, in fact, that Julian was attempting a hybrid panegyric, embracing elements of Themistius' approach (the pose of the philosopher, the concern for truth and the rejection of flattery, the emphasis on virtue, the identification of the ideals of kingship) as well as of Libanius' (the detailed factual content, the greater use of the Menandrian model). Like Themistius, Julian asserts that he was attempting something new, and I would suggest that his claim should be taken more seriously.

Whether Julian had copies of the speeches of Themistius and Libanius before his eyes is a moot point,[40] but it also raises another question that deserves further thought: were there other models in play? It is often noted that Themistius himself was influenced in particular by Dio Chrysostom's four *Kingship Orations*.[41] For instance, Dio also adopts the role of the truth-telling philosopher, concerned with ideals rather then factual details. The question arises as to whether Julian was directly influenced by the writings of Dio, or whether the influence was mediated through the orations of Themistius.[42] It is interesting to note that Dio's championing of truth and rejection of flattery (in *Or.* 3) finds particular echo in Julian's *Or.* 1 where he says that panegyric has come into disrepute as a form of flattery (4b–c). Dio in his oration indicates that truth was the currency of the day under the present emperor (supposedly Trajan); it was under a previous regime (supposedly that of Domitian) that the taint had occurred (*Or.* 3.12–13). The possibility that other models were at play too has not been ignored (and that Dio and Julian were both influenced by a third, unknown, author has been hypothesised).[43] What has not been explored, and surely should have been, is that other contemporary figures, whose works have not survived intact, may have influenced Julian. To limit the discussion of influence to surviving texts seems short-sighted, if understandable. Someone who should have been named and discussed more fully, I suggest, is Himerius, the sophist from Bithynian Prusias who carved out a teaching career in Athens.[44] Like Themistius and Libanius, he had a personal association with Julian, the future Caesar, having met him (apparently) when he was studying in Athens in the summer of 355 (though it is possible that they could have met earlier, in Nicomedia or in Constantinople). Further, it seems that Himerius also wrote a speech lauding Constantius (in which he praised Gallus and Julian too), for it has been suggested that one of Himerius' fragments (1.6) was part of a speech addressed to the emperor, given when Gallus was made Caesar in March 351.[45] Himerius, famed for his poetic eloquent style, his love of Homer, and his Atticism, should not be ignored as a possible influence on Julian.[46]

One further thought should be stressed too: the consideration of specific models and their influence should not be allowed to obscure Julian's own significance as a panegyrist. For instance Themistius is often seen as the great innovator, the unusual voice, but when Julian wrote *Or.* 1 as far as is known Themistius had only written two speeches on Constantius (and the second of these was only written after Julian's elevation to the Caesarship). Julian's *Letter to Themistius* (which may date to 355/6 rather than 361/2) challenges the views of the philosopher and indicates the more radical nature of Julian's thinking about the nature of the imperial office,[47] and the possibility of Julian's influencing Themistius' subsequent thought needs to be further recognised and appreciated.[48] Bouffartigue himself has emphasised that not only was Themistius a model for Julian, he was also a rival whom the Caesar endeavoured to surpass.[49] The same could also be said of the relationship of Julian and Libanius.

These questions of originality, or lack of it,[50] bring us to the central topic of the Menandrian model.

Julian and Menander

It should be said at once that some, including Bidez himself,[51] have already noted that Julian, although he knows the Menandrian rules by heart, is not a slave to the Menandrian model. However, this fact has tended to be obscured, and deserves to be highlighted.

Let us begin by summarising the Menandrian handbook's advice on how to write a *basilikos logos*.[52] First there is expounded the essential fact that 'the imperial oration is an encomium of the emperor' and 'will thus embrace a generally agreed amplification of the good things attaching to the emperor', allowing 'no ambivalent or disputed features'. Eleven key sections in a panegyric are identified. First comes the prooemium (1), where the orator introduces the speech. After this follow the remaining elements, which form the topics under which one praises the life, character and deeds of the emperor. One begins with the native country of the emperor, which also comprises reflection on his ancestors (2). There follows the subject of the emperor's birth (3), then his nature (*phusis*) (4) and nurture (*anatrophē*) (5) as a youth. Next come accomplishments (*epitēdeumata*) (6), which 'are qualities of character not involved with real competitive actions' and which 'display character'. Then there is the heart of the imperial panegyric: the emperor's actions (*praxeis*) (7). These are divided into two types: war-time and peace-time actions. War-time actions are to be discussed first and under the virtues of courage and wisdom, allowing for an allusion to the emperor's humanity (*philanthrōpia*) also, while peace-time actions are to be analysed under the virtues of justice, temperance and wisdom. Thus the deeds of the emperor were to be categorised by the four cardinal virtues of justice, courage, temperance and wisdom (*dikaiosunē, andreia, sōphrosynē, phronēsis*). The advice asserts that the virtue of wisdom was especially important as it 'enables lawgiving and temperance and all other virtues to come to successful fruition'.[53] After actions there is to follow a discussion of the emperor's fortune (*tychē*) (8), and subsequently a comparison (*sunkrisis*) of the whole reign with previous reigns (9), 'not disparaging' these 'but admiring them while granting perfection to the present'. The epilogue (10) came next (providing an assessment of the state of the empire), and then finally the prayer (11), 'beseeching God that the emperor's reign may endure long, and the throne be handed down to his children and his descendants'.

Turning now to Julian's panegyric, the Caesar usefully supplies a summary of its structure which indicates that he will diverge from the 'norm'. He states that he will begin with a consideration of the virtues of Constantius' ancestors. Next he will describe the emperor's 'upbringing and education', moving on to his achievements, then 'set forth all those personal qualities from which evolved all that was noble in your projects and their execution'.[54] Here Julian declares

> It is in this respect that I think my speech will surpass those of all the others. For some limit themselves to your exploits, with the idea that a description of these suffices for a perfect panegyric, but for my part I think one ought to devote the greater part of one's speech to the virtues that were the stepping-stones by which you reached the height of your achievements.

So, from the outset of his speech Julian indicates that he intends it to be unusual, ascribing his alternative approach to his training in philosophy rather than rhetoric.[55] Yet let us not take Julian's word for it, but analyse the structure ourselves. He begins with the prooemium (1), progresses to native land and ancestors (2), then moves on to birth (3). Next he skims over nature (4) and nurture (5), concentrating instead on education (*paideia*), which the handbook had recommended only if the subject lacked a 'distinguished nurture'. This section on education focuses heavily on Constantius' physical training and practical military experience. Education is followed up with a discussion of the emperor's accomplishments (6), illustrating his personal qualities. From this point on, Julian's panegyric indeed diverges sharply from the Menandrian model (as he indicated it would). He devotes almost half of the panegyric to the narration of Constantius' actions, then finishes off the speech by analysing how these actions illustrated Constantius' virtues (though virtues are also considered in the course of the narrative). So, war-deeds are not treated as a distinct topic, and not analysed under the virtues of courage and wisdom. Fortune is not treated as a separate subject, but appears briefly in the narrative. Peace-time deeds are not treated as a separate subject either, and the virtues of temperance and wisdom are briefly discussed in the final section, while courage and justice are not.[56] Humanity also surfaces in the final section. There is no final comparison, no defined epilogue, and no prayer (which some assume has been lost, but which others doubt was ever there).[57] The speech thus ends rather abruptly, albeit on a note of finality, with the assertion that 'To such a degree does every act of yours incline towards clemency and is stamped with the mint-mark of perfect virtue'.[58]

While some have realised that Julian does not follow the Menandrian model slavishly, the significance of the changes Julian made to the model has not been considered, beyond asserting that Julian was following a philosopher's path rather than a rhetor's (though in actual fact trying to combine the two). Given that it is well understood that in panegyric alterations of scheme, decisions about what to include and what to exclude, can be highly revealing,[59] surely one would have expected further comment on this aspect of the speech? Is Julian implying that Constantius has no courage and no justice, that he has not much to say about the virtues of the emperor? Or is he just making the best of the material that he can, emphasising certain prominent aspects of Constantius II over others? Is the absence of the prayer (if it has not simply been lost) a sign that he had no wish to pray for the prolonged reign of his cousin, or a recognition of the sensitive truth that Constantius had no son and Julian himself was next in line to the throne? In either case, his innovative structure could justify its absence. It is striking that Libanius' panegyric lacks a final prayer too, but the Antiochene at least discusses this omission, and justifies it on the grounds that there is nothing left to pray for![60]

Thus a closer consideration of the structure of Julian's panegyric raises intriguing questions. These are compounded when one also analyses Julian's treatment of his subject matter, for here too he diverges from the handbook. Concerning the topic of birth it is recommend that 'if any divine sign occurred at the time of [the emperor's] birth...work it up', and 'if it is possible to invent...do not hesitate'. When Julian comes to discuss the birth of Constantius he deliberately excludes any attempt to make it portentous, commenting 'it is foolish even to state that at the hour of your birth all the circumstances were brilliant and suited to a prince' (characterising such ideas as belonging to the realm of poetry) (10b).[61] It is notable that Libanius also decries such stories, but he still manages to praise the emperors, asserting that there were very real tangible signs that coincided with the births of the brothers, these being the successes and victories during the reign of their father Constantine I; he comments 'Are not these things better than a vine flourishing in dreams, are they not surer signs than the flight of birds? Are they not more credible than a phenomenon of snakes?'[62]

Even more striking is Julian's flouting of the cardinal rule that only good things should be discussed and nothing ambivalent or disputed should appear. At various points he tempers his praise of Constantius.[63] He declares to the emperor that 'In your dealings with your brothers, your subjects, your father's friends, and your armies you displayed justice and moderation', but then adds 'except that, in some cases, forced as you were by the critical state of affairs, you could not, in spite of your own wishes, prevent others from going astray' (*Or.* 1 16d–17a) (which, to compound the oddity, seems to be an allusion to the massacre of 337, or even the execution of Gallus in 354). Again, on the topic of taxation, Julian states 'you were content, I understand, with the original revenues, except in cases where, for a short time, and to meet an emergency, it was necessary that the people should find their services to the state more expensive' (*Or.* 1 21d). On the topic of Constantius' friends, whom he has promoted and enriched (a running theme, and perhaps potentially negative; he says Constantius 'gave others the means of luxury in abundance': *Or.* 1 16b), Julian observes 'there is no man who having once been held worthy of the honour of your friendship, ever suffered any punishment great or small, even though later he proved to be vicious (*mochthēros*)' (*Or.* 1 46c). In relation to Constantius' triumph in subduing the usurper Vetranio (by power of words rather than force of arms), Julian has been so dismissive of the character of Vetranio as a feeble old man that he apparently has to back-pedal and assert that Vetranio was an opponent worthy of Constantius, and not just an easy pushover, 'a man not by any means to be despised, as many people think' (*Or.* 1 32d–33a).[64] In relation to military matters Julian's treatment of the battle of Singara seems peculiar too (23a–25b). When Libanius had dealt with Singara he treated it simply as a success, but Julian raises doubts by indicating that there was debate about the assessment of the battle (though he does ultimately declare it a success).[65] Regarding the battle he also observes that Constantius' soldiers were not easily controlled as they were used to victory under his father Constantine. It also seems odd that Julian is willing to touch on presumably sensitive family matters. In his panegyric on Constantius and Constans, Libanius avoided any mention of their dead brother Constantine II or even their mother Fausta, but Julian explicitly mentions these figures and praises them, lauding Fausta for the purity of her family relations (in contrast to Parysatis who was married to her brother) (9b–d).[66] He even includes Crispus, whom he describes as a son of Fausta.[67] Julian also implies that Constantius was weak in the face of his brothers, for they made things more difficult for him (18c) and he had to cede the greater share of the empire to them (19b). He does, however, stress the closeness of Constantius with his father, though this could have a sinister edge.[68]

One also wonders if Julian's comments on the genre of panegyric itself might have been disconcerting. He makes it quite clear that panegyric is a type of literature that calls for inflation and grants 'unlimited license to invent' (2b). He states that such speeches of praise can be about people who deserve no praise. He exposes the formulae and rules of panegyric and comments that 'panegyric has come to incur a grave suspicion due to its misuse, and is now held to be base flattery rather than trustworthy testimony to heroic deeds' (4c). But then, of course, he attested his devotion, as a philosopher, to truth, the same device Themistius had used.

In addition to issues of structure and treatment of subject matter, the nature of the imperial ideal that Julian presents in the speech should be considered further. It has been observed that, in the second panegyric on Constantius, the ideal ruler that Julian presents bears little relation to the emperor, and in the first panegyric too Julian despatches supposed sacred cows of the regime of his cousin. In Themistian panegyric the emperor is defined as law incarnate, and as above the law,[69] but in Julian (and in Libanius too) Constantius is praised for acting 'like a citizen who obeys the laws, not like a king who is above the laws' (45d; and see also 14a).[70] The dynastic basis for the claim to power is often thought to be fundamental to Constantius and not to Julian, and although in the first panegyric Julian concerns himself with the rich imperial ancestry of his cousin (and himself, of course), he also makes it clear that virtue is key and that the emperor is someone who has had a special education fitting him for the role of emperor.[71] Further, in the speech Julian asserts that the emperor is not just God-favoured, but emulates the divine himself (48a).[72] Perhaps, however, one should rather question the extent to which the classic Themistian image was Constantius' preferred one. The speech of Libanius seems also to have been pleasing to Constantius for the sophist appears to have been rewarded for his efforts by being recalled to Constantinople.[73] Perhaps Constantius was open to variations of imperial ideology, or the difference between the two has been overstated.[74]

Conclusion
Thus I would argue that Julian's *First Panegyric on Constantius*, like his *Second Panegyric on Constantius* and his *Speech of Thanks to Eusebia*, rewards much

closer reading, for it is not as straightforward as it seems to be and contains elements that might be considered disconcerting in a speech of praise. The question is, how are we to understand these disconcerting elements, or more essentially, how are we to read the panegyric? One response might be that Julian was simply not very adept as a writer. Alternatively, one could suggest that Julian's declared devotion to the truth, despite being a commonplace, is entirely sincere, causing him not to dodge difficult subjects or awkward facts. Certainly panegyric could be a vehicle for advice, if not criticism. Even Themistius' panegyrics on Constantius, which most are content to declare that the emperor was happy with, can seem rather pointed and more in the vein of creating an ideal the emperor should aspire to. Nevertheless, some of Julian's remarks can seem rather near the knuckle. This raises a further possibility, that Julian is being deliberately subversive, directing a speech of praise to a rather different end. This might be thought a rather risky strategy, as Bidez recognised, but he also recognised that there was indeed a limit to Julian's flattery. Further, Julian was not averse to taking risks in others of his writings, such as the subsequent two panegyrics, but also in his *Letter to Themistius*, itself also a text associated with the period of Julian's Caesarship, whatever precise date is ascribed to it. Alternatively, perhaps Julian was in fact having it both ways, creating a speech for more than one audience which could be understood in different ways by the different audiences. It is not without interest that Malosse has argued that Libanius' own panegyric on Constantius and Constans could have different meanings for different audiences. In Julian's case, one can appreciate for instance that Constantius would have been pleased by Julian's assertion that Constantine's greatest achievement 'was that he begat, reared and educated' Constantius (9a), but one can imagine that Libanius (who we know read the panegyric) would probably have reacted to this remark in a different manner. Further, one could posit that Julian was writing for himself too. His attention to Constantine's relationship with Athens could reflect more about his own concern with, and experience of, that ancient Greek city (8c–d).[75] In contrast to the panegyrics of Themistius and Libanius on Constantius it is often remarked that Julian's features a significant narrative of the deeds of the emperor.[76] Could it be that Julian was utilising the panegyric to take the opportunity to assess the political condition of the empire by the mid-350s and to reflect on the nature of imperial power and the role of the emperor? Indeed, such is the amount of detailed information Julian provides on the family, life and reign of Constantius II that it has been observed that the panegyric constitutes a major historical source for his cousin's career.[77] It is worth observing too that when considering Julian as a writer we should not forget Julian the historian. His own narrative of the Battle of Strasbourg may be lost but we can catch glimpses of historiographical writing in other works of his.

Ultimately, how we read Julian's first panegyric on Constantius II depends on how we understand Julian himself. I would see him as an ambitious and subversive risk-taker, but others see him as cautious and concerned not to offend Constantius. However we read it, though, I would argue that it is a text that deserves (and rewards) much closer scrutiny.

Appendix

Structures of Panegyrics

A. Advice of 'Menander Rhetor'
1. Prooemium
2. Native Country (including ancestors)
3. Birth of the Emperor
4. Nature (as a youth)
5. Nurture (as a youth)
6. Accomplishments
7. Actions (actions in war-time – virtues of courage and wisdom, and including discussion of humanity of the emperor; actions in peace-time – virtues of justice, temperance and wisdom)
8. Fortune
9. Complete Comparison
10. Epilogue
11. Prayer

B. Julian, *First Panegyric on Constantius II*
1. Prooemium (Loeb pp. 4–12)
2. Native Country (including ancestors) (Loeb pp. 12–24)
3. Birth of the Emperor (Loeb pp. 24–26)
4. Nature and 5. Nurture (but Julian emphasises education) (Loeb pp. 26–40)
6. Accomplishments (Loeb pp. 40–44)
7. Actions (Loeb pp. 44–104)
8. Virtues demonstrated by actions narrated (Loeb pp. 106–126)

Notes

[1] Julian wrote three panegyrics, two for his cousin the emperor Constantius II and one for the empress Eusebia, Constantius' wife.

[2] Syme 1958, 114, cited also in Radice 1968, 169.

[3] On distaste see for example Vanderspoel 1995, 5. For understanding and appreciation see for example Russell and Wilson 1981, Nixon and Rodgers 1994, and Whitby (ed.) 1998. For the twenty-first century see for example Rees 2002 and Malosse 2003.

[4] Athanassiadi 1992, 64, and also 66: 'a panegyric of his own deeds...an extraordinary piece of propaganda for his own cause'. Curta 1995, 182, and also 209: 'a genuine political manifesto veiled in rhetoric'. For earlier recognition of this aspect of the speech see for instance Bowersock 1978, 43–5, and ultimately Bidez 1932, 113. On the speech see the contribution of Hal Drake in this volume.

[5] Tougher 1998a. On the speech see also Vatsend 2000, and the contribution of Liz James in this volume.

[6] For previous analysis of the speech see especially Bidez 1932, 3–9, and Tantillo 1997. Tantillo provides a very full commentary on the panegyric, but his introduction (pp. 11–50) is rather limited in scope.

[7] E.g. Wright 1913, 2, Boulenger 1927, 22, and Browning 1975, 74. Boulenger asserts that Constantius asked Julian to write the panegyric.

[8] Bowersock 1978, 37.

[9] Amm. Marc. 16.7.2.

[10] Bidez 1932, 3, an hypothesis repeated by Athanassiadi 1992, 61. For the diplomatic character of the speech see also Bowersock 1978, 37, and Cameron 1993, 89.

[11] For the handbook see Russell and Wilson 1981.

[12] Wright 1913, 2, and Bidez 1932, 4. See also Boulenger 1927, 22–3, Lieu and Montserrat 1996, 162, and Tantillo 1997, 17.

[13] Athanassiadi 1992, 61.

[14] Athanassiadi 1992, 62.

[15] On these models see for instance Bidez 1932, 5, Curta 1995, esp. 190 and n. 48, and Tantillo 1997, 33–6. On Julian and Themistius see also Bouffartigue 1992, 296–300, and Vanderspoel 1995, 115–34.

[16] See Heather and Moncur 2001, 69–96.

[17] See Heather and Moncur 2001, 97–114.

[18] See Vanderspoel 1995, 94. Interestingly, in the oration Themistius describes Constantius as a philosopher and observes that he has appointed another philosopher to share power with him, on the grounds of virtue rather than dynastic right: see for instance Vanderspoel 1995, 92.

[19] See for instance Heather and Moncur 2001, 139–40, and Vanderspoel 1995, 118–19.

[20] For the oration see Malosse 2003, and Lieu and Montserrat 1996, 147–209. Perhaps Julian was in Nicomedia when the oration was performed.

[21] Bidez 1932, 3 n. 2. This providing of copies of speeches was a common practice. Themistius sent copies of his speeches to Libanius: Heather and Moncur 2001, 11 n. 36.

[22] Vanderspoel 1995, 86 and n. 63, and also 116 (Julian at Sirmium in 351 and at Arles in 353). Vanderspoel plans to expand on his hypotheses on Julian's early life in

a forthcoming monograph on the emperor, and I would like to thank him for providing me with unpublished papers on the subject.

[23] Bidez 1932, 104 n. 2. Eusebia visited Rome again in 357, though on that occasion with her husband.

[24] Tantillo 1997, 36–40.

[25] For the dating of the first panegyric see also the chapter by López Sánchez in this volume, in which he suggests that it may date to as early as 353. This seems to me extremely hypothetical.

[26] On the question of the dating of the *Letter to Themistius* see for instance Bradbury 1987, and the contribution of John Watt in this volume. I will return to the letter below.

[27] Tantillo 1997, 37–8.

[28] Lib. *Ep.* 30, Norman 1992, 444–51. See also Bidez 1924, 2–5.

[29] On the possibility of Themistius teaching Plato to Julian see for instance Smith 1995, 27, though Themistius' interest in Aristotle needs to be recognised too.

[30] See for example Tougher 2007, 25–6. The famous story is that Julian was in Nicomedia when Libanius was teaching there but was forbidden to attend his lectures so accessed them through written copies. Libanius himself remarked that people assumed that Julian was his pupil.

[31] See for example Bouffartigue 1992, 298.

[32] Though notably Themistius' career was dogged by assertions that he was a sophist and not a philosopher.

[33] Heather and Moncur 2001, 68, note that the speech contains 'little informed comment on the policies and issues of its day'. Vanderspoel 1995, 73 and 79, comments that the speech 'rarely alludes to historical events', and observes that a 'theoretical exposition of desirable characteristics has become a treatment of Constantius' virtues'.

[34] Vanderspoel 1995, 6, notes that the biographical 'structure can be observed in most panegyrics of the fourth century'. See also Heather and Moncur 2001, 7.

[35] Heather and Moncur 2001, 7, consider that Themistius was innovating, '[a]s far as we can tell'. Vanderspoel 1995, 6, declares that 'Themistius differs from contemporary panegyrists in the content and structure of his speeches'.

[36] See also the comment of Vanderspoel 1995, 131 n. 72.

[37] Lieu and Montserrat 1996, 160.

[38] Malosse 2003, 73.

[39] Note, however, that Tantillo 1997, 35, does emphasise the debt to Libanius.

[40] Bouffartigue 1992, 297, maintains that Julian definitely consulted Themistius' two orations, but finds no textual borrowings. Lieu and Montserrat 1996, 162, remark that 'it is clear that Julian did not have access to a copy of Libanius' work' due to the lack of 'verbal agreement'; see also Bouffartigue 1992, 182.

[41] For these orations see especially Moles 1990, and also Whitmarsh 2001, esp. 200–16. They are usually understood to have been written for the emperor Trajan (AD 98–117). Other influences on Themistius identified are Aelius Aristides, Demosthenes, and Isocrates, and the latter two in particular had an impact on Julian also.

[42] On the question of Dio's influence see for instance Bouffartigue 1992, 293–4. He is of the view that Julian had read Dio's kingship orations but not copied them.

[43] Curta 1995, 182. Bouffartigue 1992, 294, favours the view that Dio and Julian were simply expressing common humanist views.

[44] For Himerius see especially Penella 2007.

[45] See Barnes 1987, and now Penella 2007, 2 and 273–4.

[46] Indeed Boulenger 1927, 25, comments on Julian's *Or.* 2 being akin to Himerius' work in its poetic reminiscences.

[47] Curta 1995, 192, describes Julian's second panegyric on Constantius as his 'first political program', but it is possible that this honour should be held by the letter to Themistius. On the letter to Themistius see for instance Bouffartigue 2006 and Schofield 2000, both of whom favour the earlier date.

[48] It has been identified as an issue by Curta 1995, 209. See also n. 70 below.

[49] Bouffartigue 1992, 299–300.

[50] Bouffartigue 1992, 516.

[51] Bidez 1932, 4. Bouffartigue 1992, 516, notes that Julian himself indicates the difference of his speech from the Menandrian model. Bouffartigue 1992, 538, says it is clear that Julian knew the Menandrian model by heart.

[52] See Russell and Wilson 1981, 76–95. All quotations from 'Menander' are from Russell and Wilson's translation.

[53] It is also observed that 'when you are about to pass from one heading to another, there ought to be a prooemium about the subject you are now going to treat, so as to make the hearer attentive and not allow the intended scheme of the main headings to pass unobserved or concealed'. The importance of making comparisons under each heading is emphasised too.

[54] All translations from Julian's panegyric are from the Loeb Classical Library edition by Wright 1913.

[55] A stance taken by Themistius also, as has been seen.

[56] Menander advised that 'If the empress [was] of great worth and honour' she should be mentioned under the virtue of temperance, however Julian does not mention Eusebia (though there is a general reference to Constantius respecting marriage ties: *Or.* 1 47a, Wright 1913, 120, Bidez 1932, 66). It has been assumed that Julian was saving the subject of Eusebia for his *Speech of Thanks*, which was written after her visit to Rome in 356. Perhaps the different structure of Julian's speech could account for the omission too.

[57] For example, Boulenger 1927, 23, notes the brusque end of the panegyric and suggests that the text has been mutilated.

[58] Tantillo 1997, 38, notes that all of Julian's panegyrics end by returning to virtue.

[59] On the significance of the absence of expected subjects see for instance Malosse 2003, 37. See also Curta 1995, 190, who notes that in his speech of thanks to Julian for his appointment to the consulship for 362 Claudius Mamertinus avoids dealing with the topic of *genos*.

[60] Lieu and Montserrat 1996, 161, suggest that Libanius did not include a prayer because of his pagan sympathies, but this seems unlikely to me; presumably he could have written something suitably vague and monotheistic.

[61] Isoc. *Evag.* 21, refuses to discuss portents relating to the birth of Evagoras, though not because he doubts them but because knowledge of them is only possessed by a few. Tantillo 1997, 200–1, places Julian's comments in the context of his writing a panegyric as a philosopher.

[62] *Or.* 59.29, trans. Lieu and Montserrat 1996, 171. Malosse 2003, 188, comments that Libanius follows the rationalist stance adopted by Aelius Aristides (*To Zeus* 43.8).

[63] As he also does in his *Speech of Thanks* to Eusebia: see Tougher 1998a, 119–20.

[64] In Julian's *Caesars* (329a) Constantine's success against Licinius is degraded by characterising Licinius as a feeble old man.

[65] Lieu and Montserrat 1996, 163, also note that Libanius avoided dealing with Nisibis but Julian includes it.

[66] See also Tantillo 1997, 194–5. It seems that Fausta was rehabilitated after the death of Constantine I, but it is still noteworthy that Libanius does not mention her yet Julian does.

[67] Barnes and Vanderspoel 1984 argued against the identification of Crispus, but Malosse 1997, 522, argues for it, and I agree with him. Malosse hypothesises that possibly Constantius restored Crispus' memory between Libanius' oration and Julian's, but perhaps Julian is simply being bold for his own purposes. On the mention of Crispus see also Tantillo 1997, 196–7.

[68] For the presence of Constantine in the panegyric see Tantillo 1997, 47.

[69] See for example Heather and Moncur 2001, 93–4.

[70] On this see also Tantillo 1997, 398–404. He notes that Themistius only mentions the emperor being above the law in *Or.* 1 (not in his other orations on Constantius) and that he returned to the concept in his panegyric on Jovian.

[71] Though see n. 18 above for such ideas in Themistius too.

[72] See also Tantillo 1997, 421. These ideas are expressed by Julian in his *Letter to Themistius* too. In the panegyric Julian also declares that Constantius was more like a priest then an emperor in his peaceful defeat of Vetranio (33b) and that his war against Magnentius had a sacred quality (33c).

[73] Malosse 2003, 10.

[74] See the comments of Malosse 2003, 59 and n. 1, and also Schofield 2000, 664.

[75] In addition to Julian's own experiences of Athens it is interesting to note that Himerius in a speech of praise to Julian asserted that Athens was the mother city of Constantinople: Penella 2007, 37. Ammianus Marcellinus also knows this 'fact': 22.8.8.

[76] Libanius confesses his lack of knowledge: *Or.* 59.8–9. It is notable that when Themistius wrote *Or.* 3 he did provide hard detail on Constantius' campaigns which he had not provided in *Or.* 1: see Heather and Moncur 2001, 119. Perhaps Themistius was influenced by the example of Julian?

[77] Bidez 1932, 7, characterises it as 'une de nos meilleures sources d'information pour le règne de son cousin'. On the historical value of the panegyric see also for instance Tantillo 1997, 31–3.

'BUT I DIGRESS…':
RHETORIC AND PROPAGANDA IN JULIAN'S
SECOND ORATION TO CONSTANTIUS

Hal Drake

I intend to speak today about Julian's second speech to Constantius. This reminds me of a speech that Dio Chrysostom gave to Trajan, a speech that would probably please you more, because you love sophists. But I digress. I was actually talking about Julian. He spoke Greek. In fact, he spoke a lot of Greek. This reminds me of the time when I discovered, through personal experience, that the Greek alphabet (a word derived from the first two letters, which in Hebrew are 'aleph' and 'beth') – as I was saying, the Greek alphabet, as I learned, has no character for the sound 'aitch'. But you are small-minded people who cannot be expected to understand the profundity of this discovery. Therefore, though many of you might not consider it appropriate, because I make no claim to expertise on the subject, I will speak about Julian. The facts, be that as it may, are what they are. I would be the first to tell you, but I am just too busy.

Such is a one-paragraph version of what this chapter would have sounded like if I had taken the same approach to Julian as he took in his Second Oration to Constantius, had it ever been delivered. One paragraph can hardly give the full sense of this work's strangeness. Using Robin Lane Fox's estimate of two hours for Constantine's *Oration to the Saints*,[1] Julian's speech would have taken at least three hours, and probably closer to four, to deliver – similar in length to his first panegyric to Constantius, both of which are three to four times the length of any offering in the *Panegyrici Latini* (excepting Pliny's, which was heavily reworked). Length, of course is a relative matter: by the reckoning of modern American politics, this is a great, swollen beast of an oration, but by the standards of the old Supreme Soviet a speech of such a length would not have been unusual, and for Fidel Castro on a good day it is downright terse.

Still, to my untutored ear Julian's second oration to Constantius sounds like nothing so much as a schoolboy stalling on an assignment, constantly picking up and dropping a topic that he never quite gets to. But in this conclusion I am decidedly in the minority. In fact, the majority of scholars consider this oration to be a masterly work, if not a masterpiece. A case for such a conclusion can indeed be made. Assuming that Julian wrote this piece only a year or so after the equally lengthy first oration to Constantius,[2] what was left to be said? Julian must indeed have been haunted by what William Stuart Maguinness long ago identified as the 'two great fears' of the imperial panegyrist – 'that of saying something which has not been said before, and that of saying it in the same way as it has before been said'.[3] Under the circumstances, an elaborate, long-winded comparison to personages in the *Iliad* might have seemed an inspired option.

Table 1 (the tables are appended at the end of this chapter) gives the outline of a rather stylish oration in which Julian seizes on what he describes as Constantius' diligent study of the *Iliad* to call attention to the famous conflict between Agamemnon and Achilles that ignites the misfortunes of the Greeks in Homer's tale. In contrast to Agamemnon, Julian claims, Constantius constantly shows mercy and forgiveness, a theme to which he returns throughout this oration. As he proceeds to compare Constantius' battles and sieges with events in the *Iliad*, Julian demonstrates that Constantius is not only more merciful than Agamemnon but also braver than Achilles, stronger than Ajax, wiser than either Nestor or Odysseus and more pious than Hector. In the course of these comparisons, Julian discusses at length the revolt and death of Magnentius (50c–51a), the Persian siege of Nisibis (62b–67b), and Constantius' own siege of Aquileia (71c), concluding that the emperor's achievements are simply too many to enumerate. During the course of this display – as Heinz Janssen demonstrated in an exhaustive dissertation – Julian covers all of the standard panegyrical virtues, albeit not in the standard panegyrical way.[4]

But it is only possible to construct such a rational discourse by hopscotching all over the speech and ignoring its most distinctive trait, which in addition to its length is the extensive amount of space devoted to digressions. The estimate of these digressions will vary, necessarily given a speech that is so discursive there are digressions within digressions. Some of these topics are listed in Table 2, but this summary does not give a real sense of how scatterminded this oration really is. At points, Julian is scarcely able to finish a sentence without haring off after some diversion or another.

Scholars have wrestled with the nature of the speech. When Joseph Bidez analyzed this oration in 1924, he saw it as composed of two parts – one rhetorical, the other philosophical – working together in what he saw as a single, harmonious whole.[5] But more recent authors have been more inclined to see the two parts as contradictory, one praising Constantius, the other directly or indirectly attacking him. To give just one example, early in the oration Julian uses the greater size of Constantius' army and empire to demonstrate his superiority to Agamemnon (73d), whereas later he specifically says that such hallmarks of power have nothing to do with identifying a real king (84a). Accordingly, when scholars call this work a masterpiece they usually are not referring to its superficial intent, but rather to what they see as the cleverness with which Julian undermines his own efforts. In her intellectual biography of Julian, for instance, Polymnia Athanassiadi attributed the two voices of this oration to a conflict going on within Julian himself – an urge to revolt tempered by the knowledge that such disloyalty 'would have been an act of desertion and even stupidity'.[6] Athanassiadi's judgment relied on insights into Julian's psyche. Florin Curta took a different approach, but reached a similar conclusion. Focusing on the digressions, Curta used techniques of literary analysis to argue that these were not incidental, but played an important role in the oration, serving as a counterpoint to the effusive flattery of the ostensible comparisons being made and thereby constituting a sort of 'anti-oration'.[7]

Julian's comparisons with barbarians, especially Persians, are one place to find examples of this subversive message. After describing Shapur's efforts to take Nisibis and the way he executed subordinates for the failure, Julian remarks, 'This is in fact the regular custom among the barbarians in Asia, to shift the blame of their ill-success on to their subjects' (66d).[8] At another point, he calls attention to Darius' greed, which was so insatiable that it even led him to raid 'the tombs of the dead' (85c). Since greed and jealousy are two failings with which Julian and Ammianus repeatedly fault Constantius, such passages easily qualify as representative of that genre of implicit criticism through the use of 'letters from abroad' that Montesquieu, for one, would use to such devastating effect in his *Letters from Persia*.[9]

Julian's prominent use of Homer, whom he cites by name thirteen times, makes the scenes and imagery drawn from this poet the most popular place to hunt for counter-messages,[10] and so many of Julian's heroic similes fall flat that it is hard not to assume this must have been the intent. In one particularly tortured, albeit heartfelt, comparison, Julian likens Constantius' refusal to listen to slanderers to the taking of Troy (97a), and in another he calls the emperor superior to Nestor and Odysseus as a speaker because his speeches, although admittedly unpolished, get the job done.[11] Other Homeric scenes are far less subtle. These include the opening lines, which call attention to the famous confrontation between Agamemnon and Achilles that Julian used to compare with Constantius' mercifulness and generosity.

Constantius' mercifulness comes up again towards the end of the oration, in a famous passage where Julian abandons all restraint to rail against calumniators and slanderers. The exercise consumes an entire chapter, and in the course of it he strikes some of his most eloquent poses: 'what a terrible thing is slander (λοιδορία)! How truly does it devour the heart and wound the soul as iron cannot wound the body!' (96a). Or again:

> If anyone does not believe me, and thinks it no great achievement [to repel such attacks], let him observe himself when a misfortune of this sort happens to him...and I am convinced that he will not think that I am talking with exceeding folly.[12]

Yet even here, the outburst turns into an occasion for Julian to praise his cousin. He personally, Julian tells us, has witnessed the emperor reject such slurs 'with great restraint' (ἐγκρατῶς), an achievement he finds no less laudable than the taking of Troy (97a), and he devotes the remaining chapters of the oration to a celebration of Constantius' mercifulness.

Granted, there is something backhanded about all this: given the picture we have of him, praising Constantius' mercy is a bit like celebrating Bill Clinton's chastity or Gordon Brown's charismatic oratory, and after Julian's great victory at Strasbourg it is not unreasonable to postulate some risk-taking on the Caesar's part. But it is virtually impossible now to read this oration without looking for indicators of the drama that we know will unfold, when Julian first revolts against his cousin then institutes a radical shift in imperial religious policy, only to be cut short by his ill-fated Persian campaign. Knowing what the future portends, for instance, the opening dispute between Agamemnon and Achilles inevitably makes us think of Julian's own complaint that Constantius had stolen credit for his victory at Strasbourg. Yet as Curta has pointed out, the dispute between Agamemnon and Achilles seems to have been a popular theme in the fourth century,[13] and in any case Julian quickly backs away from a fight, concluding that Homer's point was to warn hot-blooded generals as much as arrogant kings. The scene becomes an opportunity to compare Constantius favorably to Agamemnon, contrasting his generosity with the Homeric king's arrogant stinginess. This approach sets a pattern for the whole oration, in which Julian seems to be constantly skating to the brink, only to pull back at the last moment.

There is no need to preclude the possibility of taunts, but at best they are a cat-and-mouse game, and at some point we have to ask, for what purpose? Scholarly answers have not been particularly persuasive. Bidez recognized some 'impertinences et...maladresses' in what he took to be a 'political manifesto'.[14] But a manifesto for what? Curta's distinction of an oration and anti-oration gives us one answer, because the implicit comparison between the two parts of the oration would be between Julian and Constantius himself. Presumably, something of the sort was what Athanassiadi also saw when she called this oration 'a panegyric of his [Julian's] own deeds', sent as a warning to Constantius.[15]

Still, the amount of hindsight required by these explanations is unsettling. The premise of an 'anti-oration' cannot fully explain this behavior, because these contradictions can occur in the same chapter, even the same sentence. And reading these passages as signs of Julian's desire to confront Constantius while at the same time professing his loyalty[16] serves rather to remind us of how much we do not know.

We do not know, for instance, exactly when this oration was written. Obviously, it was after the first, which Athanassiadi dates to winter 356/7,[17] and a reference to his personal experience with Gallic tribes suggests Julian would not have written it before late 357 or early 358.[18] But Curta has argued for a significantly later date – 359, and possibly even 360.[19] Since Ammianus tells us Julian was still minding his p's and q's right up to the moment when Constantius demanded he send Gallic troops to use against the Persians (Amm. Marc. 21.2), it seems we are caught in a genuine Catch-22: the more subversive and confrontational we take the speech to be, the less likely it is to have been written before Julian had made up his mind to risk a break with Constantius. So the more rebellious the oration sounds, the later a date it requires.

Another thing we do not know is when, if ever, the oration was delivered at Constantius' court. Scholars are divided on this issue – older authorities, products of a more genteel age, presumed it was never delivered, while the hardened intellects of our own day assume that it was.[20] Let us suppose for a minute that it was delivered. What would the response have been? Fury and outrage is assumed, but this is because we have grown up with the picture of a court filled with fawning, incompetent backstabbers and presided over by a craven, suspicious, murdering coward. But this picture of Constantius and his court comes from unswervingly hostile sources, of which Julian himself and his admirer Ammianus form the greater part (the remainder is comprised mostly of Church historians who depend heavily on Athanasius for their accounts, and Athanasius had little reason to admire Constantius). The result is a caricature; a picture that is so one-sided that at one point Ammianus even tells us of a suspicion that the only reason Constantius sent Julian to Gaul was to have him fail (Amm. Marc. 16.11.13), a suggestion which on the slightest reflection makes no sense at all, but one that is nevertheless often accepted at face value.

If Julian did send in his oration, there is a good chance that it was simply 'received and placed on file' (or whatever the fourth-century equivalent of that bureaucratic notation was). Even if it was delivered, we should hesitate before assuming an outraged court. The supposed taunts in this oration are clear to us because we know Julian's feelings, as well as his future actions. But they need not have been all that obvious at the time. Why should Constantius not have taken Julian's protestations of loyalty and his excessive, though not by any means unusual, praise at face value? Two can play the stereotype game, and if we try to look at Julian through the eyes of an experienced and capable court, what we would see would be an over-educated, archaizing fop who had also shown some unexpected capacity as a commander and an equally unexpected ability to be a distinct pain in the posterior. Those confrontations with imaginary critics that strike us now as such subversive passages in the oration were part of the persona cultivated by philosophers, and Julian had obviously adopted that persona in this speech. A court used to indulging such *parrhēsia* might well have taken this outspokenness as nothing more than harmless role-playing, along the lines of Dio Chrysostom's famous series of orations on kingship to Trajan, with which Julian evidently was familiar.[21] His references to the gods, and temples, his excursuses on Homer and Plato, so provocative sounding to us, easily might have been dismissed as simply more examples of Julian showing off.

If the oration was ever received and if it provoked anger at court, there were far better grounds for such a reaction than these harmless exclamations, for the true subversion in this oration lies in what it does not say. We are not particularly well-informed about Constantius' activities in Sirmium in 357–8, save for his alleged chagrin over Julian's own brilliance. If all he had been doing was pushing around bishops, Julian's failure to discuss Constantius' actions might be understandable.[22] But we do know that Constantius was also engaged in operations against the Sarmatians and the Quadi, the latter in particular apparently as part of a two-pronged offensive against the Alamanni that, if we knew more about it, might shed additional light on Julian's own successes as the other prong of this strategy. Julian surely knew about these events. But perhaps the oration was written before these actions were completed; even so, they certainly had been planned and were at least underway, so we would still have to suppose that for some reason Julian did not wish even to forecast a successful outcome, perhaps for security reasons, although that seems far-fetched.

Even if there were some reason to keep Julian from celebrating Constantius' recent military achievements, he still would have had the emperor's activities as a builder to celebrate.[23] These were always fodder for panegyric, as Themistius showed in 357 (*Orr.* 3, 4) and Procopius would again under Justinian I (527–565), to name but two obvious examples.[24] Yet from Julian only silence, and a rehashing of events at least five and maybe more years earlier. We are entitled to ask whether this choice was deliberate.

Perhaps this is too speculative. If we are to assume that this oration was meant for Constantius' ears, then about the only safe conclusion to draw from its contents is that Julian still felt the need to compose something in recognition of a traditional event, and this in turn suggests that he did not at this moment feel confident enough to risk an open breach with late imperial etiquette. But we have another option. Instead of postulating an elaborate cat-and-mouse game that would only have been grasped in any case by *cognoscenti*,[25] why not just take this speech for what it appears to be: a parody? We are, after all, talking about the author of the *Caesars*, and the supposedly satirical *Misopogon*.[26] A *divertissement* along the lines of Seneca's equally tasteless *Apocolocyntosis* – a work entitled *The Deeds of Constantius* that had little or nothing to say about such deeds – would have been a delightful way for Julian and his coterie to while away one or more winter nights in a Paris that at this time had little else to offer. Moreover, if the oration was a parody, then the bantering that Curta identified as one of its novel aspects[27] would be entirely appropriate, as would all of the inside jokes. And if we decide that it was never sent to Constantius and never meant to be sent, we also can enjoy the jokes without worrying about what the political consequences might have been, or whether or not Julian was deliberately trying to provoke them.

Even as a parody, the oration still has much to teach us. As Jean Bouffartigue once observed, Julian is one of the most self-referential – one might even say self-absorbed – of all ancient authors.[28] Even in jest, he cannot help telling us about himself. This is especially true for the longest of his digressions, an extended discussion of the ideal ruler that has given the oration its subtitle of *basilikos logos*. Table 3 summarizes the traits of this ruler. The title is slightly misleading, on two counts. First, in much of this section Julian's point is not praise of kingship but praise of virtue, arguing that the virtuous individual always prevails over fortune.[29] This had been a philosophical platitude since Plato's day. Thus, when Julian claims that the virtuous individual has more nobility than the one who receives nobility from birthright, he is not necessarily undermining either the dynastic basis for kingship or poking fun at Constantius but simply repeating a claim that, as he himself observes, had long been commonplace (80a). Second, certain of the characteristics of Julian's ideal prince – he values discourse, is a workaholic (φιλόπονος), allows himself little time for sleep – sounds very much like he has a specific individual in mind. The only thing he left out is 'wins a major battle against the Alamanni'; maybe we should take that omission as a *terminus ante quem*.

Thus, just as with the rest of the oration, too much can be read into this section on the ideal ruler by assuming it was meant for Constantius. On these grounds, Bidez took it to be the basis of Julian's 'political manifesto', for instance, and it presumably helped Athanassiadi decide that the work was meant to be a thinly disguised panegyric to himself.[30] Instead, we could do worse than think of it as Julian's homage to one of his heroes, Marcus Aurelius: it is a soliloquy, reflecting his thoughts about what kind of leader he wanted to be.[31] The result is something virtually unique in ancient panegyric: a *speculum principis* written not for but by the prince.

Julian's religious program comes through loud and clear. Not only does he lament despoliation of the temples and abandonment of the old ways (80c), but he envisions a ruler who would be something of a priest-king (70c–d), a ruler he describes at one point as 'a priest or prophet' (καθάπερ ἱερέα καὶ προφήτην, 68b) and at another as 'prophet and vice-regent' (προφήτην καὶ ὑπηρέτην, 90a) of the highest god. The ruler is, repeatedly, 'beloved of God' (θεοφιλῆς).[32] Julian occasionally identifies this god as Zeus, but for the most part what is striking about his language is how compatible it is with major currents of religious thought in the fourth century. Curta and others have explained his use of such terms as 'higher power' (τοῦ κρείττονος, 70d) and 'greatest god' (ὁ μέγιστος θεός, 89a) as well as the supreme importance he gives to the Sun god, Helios, as reflecting Neoplatonic influence.[33] This is undoubtedly correct, but wider connections can be made – to Constantine's language, for instance, and to Sol mosaics in fourth-century synagogues in Palestine.[34] What they all point to is a lingua franca of religious thought in the fourth century, centered on vaguely monotheistic thought and framed around solar imagery.

Julian's adoption of this language testifies to the viability of such a religious program, but other parts foreshadow why the program he eventually introduced failed. In the passage just cited, for instance, he attaches great importance to observing 'the traditional form of worship' (τῆς ἐννόμου θεραπείας), which as emperor he would honor through a costly and flamboyant revival of blood sacrifice. Elsewhere, he calls for careful scrutiny of appointments (89d, 91c) so that offices only go to individuals who are suited to them – precisely the reason he will give for his controversial ban on Christians from teaching positions.[35] Unlike the more universalizing parts of his religious program, these policies served only to polarize and disrupt.

42

Although our attention naturally goes to these religious markers, Julian actually spends far more time discussing the ruler's military duties. The space Julian devotes to the importance of the commander living simply and sharing hardship with his men we may put down to more of what Michel Rambaud long ago characterized as 'indirect self-praise',[36] and I forbear to mention his ridiculous excursus on Aquileia and the geography of Italy (71d–72d) – another page out of Caesar's book. More revealing is the contempt Julian consistently shows for what might be called 'defensive strategies'. This comes out most clearly in what he has to say about the wall the Achaeans build in the *Iliad*. Julian is unusually preoccupied with this wall, making it clear that he considers it a major blunder. It is the occasion for one of his most scathing comments, when he dismisses Nestor's advice to build it as 'a cowardly notion and worthy indeed of an old man' (75d). Julian's reason for this judgment is extremely revealing:

> For before that [building the wall], they [the Achaeans] thought that they were themselves protecting the ships like a noble bulwark. But when they realised that a wall lay in front of them, built with a deep moat and set at intervals with sharp stakes, they grew careless and slackened their valour, because they trusted to the fortification.[37]

To Julian, such defensive measures were bad for morale; the best defense, to coin a phrase, is a good offense.

It is clear from Ammianus that Julian scorned Constantius' defensive posture, as did Ammianus himself. So this passage might be a sly dig at his senior commander. But if these passages also reflect Julian's own musings, then what we have here is a foreshadowing of the policy that would prove his undoing in Persia, especially his disastrous decision to burn his fleet, only to realize when it was too late that his army's morale was hurt, rather than strengthened, by this maneuver.[38]

Ultimately, the greatest value in thinking of this oration as a parody might be that it reminds us of the limited and one-sided picture we have of Constantius and his court, for which Julian and Ammianus are ultimately responsible. As already noted, this picture is in many ways a caricature. There has been ample discussion of animosity towards Julian in Constantius' court, but too little attention paid to the animosity against Constantius in Julian's court. This is not the place to conduct a defense of Constantius, but it would be a useful exercise to try to tell the story of Julian and Constantius from the opposite perspective. It would undoubtedly be the story of a pretentious schoolboy sent to Gaul merely to show the imperial colors, a schoolboy who turned out to be much more than that, to the surprise and chagrin of the court officials who expected to run things themselves. This story would also remind us how Constantius backed Julian in every one of his monumental clashes with these officials, at least until reports of Julian's hostility and ambitions became too numerous to ignore. It might even point out how Julian's reckless and unilateral reduction of taxes in Gaul boosted his own popularity but crippled imperial resources. But most of all, it would remind us that, despite everything Julian and Ammianus throw at Constantius II, the fact remains that this suspicious and scandal-ridden ruler held the empire together for a quarter of a century, husbanding enough resources for Julian to squander on his dream of emulating Alexander.

But then, I digress...

Table 1: The Oration

I. Constantius surpasses the heroes of the *Iliad*
A comparison of Homeric war with Constantius' wars
    1. He surpasses Agamemnon in genealogy and generosity: 50c, 51a
    2. He surpasses Achilles, Ajax and Sarpedon in bravery, Hector in piety: 49c–51d, 54a–55c, 67b–68c,71a–b
    3. He has larger armies, rules greater territory: 73c–75a

II. Constantius' exploits are greater
    1. In defense: Nisibis withstood a siege: 62b–63d, 64b–67b compared with *Iliad*: 67a
    2. In offense: he took Aquileia: 71c compared with Alexander: 72d–73c

III. In wisdom and wise counsel he surpasses Nestor and Odysseus: 73c–74d
    1. His speaking and deliberation: 75a

IV. Constantius' virtues make him emperor
    1. He behaved justly to his family: 94b–c
    2. He cares for his subjects, who love him in return: 98b
    3. He scorns pleasure
    4. He is merciful to all

Table 2: Digressions in Julian's Second Oration

panegyric vs. true praise: 63d–64a, 74d, 78b–d, 79c–d, 92d–93c
    rules for panegyric say digression irrelevant to his speech: 63d–64a
armies, habits of barbarians:
    Persians do not use infantry: 63c
    they blame others for failure: 66d
    they rob graves and steal from temples: 80b, 85c–d
priestly role of king: 68c–70d
origins and geography of Aquileia: 71d–72d
Homer: e.g. 60d–62b, 78d

Plato: 68c–69d
birth vs. virtue: 81a (stories of Argives, Celts, Cretans)
beasts and tyrants: 84a–85d (virtue protects from 80b)
calumniators: 96a–b, 101a
demons: 90a–b
interpretation of myth: 82d
the good king: 78c–92d

Table 3: The Good King (78c–92d)

power, territory do not make a king: 84a–b
pious, god-beloved (θεοφιλῆς): 80b, 84a, 90c
    does not neglect worship of the gods; pious to family, reveres gods who protect family: 86a
military qualities: enforces discipline (87a–b); shares life style of troops (87d); defensive walls destroy morale (76a); Nestor's building of wall 'a cowardly notion worthy of an old man': 75d
religion: should not say gods lie (82c); Helios=virtue (80c–d), cannot be hurt by despoiling temples; 'higher power' (τοῦ κρείττονος, 70d); 'greatest god' (ὁ μεγίστος θεός, 89a)
ruler: aware of own affinity to god (70c); interpreter and vice-regent (προφήτην καὶ ὑπηρέτην) (90a); follows traditional forms of worship (70d); fond of work (φιλόπονος, 86c); allows little time for sleep (87c); scrutinizes appointments (89d, 91c)

Notes

[1] Lane Fox 1986, 628.
[2] For the first panegyric see the chapter by Shaun Tougher in this volume.
[3] Maguinness 1932, 45.
[4] Janssen 1953.
[5] Bidez 1924, 109–10.
[6] Athanassiadi-Fowden 1981, 60.
[7] Curta 1995, 196–7: 'The key notions here make up a subsidiary, asyntactical oration based on isolated concepts rather than on their relationships or developments, forming the "anti-oration"…which permanently undermines the "explicit oration"'.
[8] Unless otherwise indicated, all translations of Julian come from the Loeb Classical Library edition by Wright 1913–23.
[9] For a recent analysis, see Runyon 2005. The *Persian Letters* are newly translated by Mauldon 2008.
[10] For Homer, see Athanassiadi-Fowden 1981, 70. Curta 1995, 185 observes that in all his works Julian cites Homer directly and indirectly more than any of his contemporaries, and most of all in this oration.
[11] *Or.* 2 75a–77b, esp. 77a.
[12] *Or.* 2 97a.
[13] Curta 1995, 177.

[14] Bidez 1924, 113, 115.

[15] Athanassiadi-Fowden 1981, 66.

[16] As Athanassiadi-Fowden 1981, 63: 'This elephantine hint is followed by a stern warning, but a warning combined with an implicit statement of Julian's ultimate loyalty to Constantius, that we need not doubt'.

[17] Athanassiadi-Fowden 1981, 61. On the dating of the first panegyric see also the chapter by Shaun Tougher in this volume, as well as the observations by Fernando López Sánchez in his chapter in this volume.

[18] Bidez 1924, 108.

[19] Curta 1995, 196.

[20] Curta 1995, 210.

[21] Wright 1896, 101–2, dismissed the suggestion that Julian was imitating Dio, but Bidez still found parallels between the two noteworthy: Bidez 1924, 111. Cf. Curta 1995, 182.

[22] Constantius' autocratic manner in seeking doctrinal unity drew the ire of the Church historians, and Ammianus characteristically derided the frequency with which the emperor summoned bishops to councils at 21.16.18, where he says that the imperial post was crippled by Constantius' efforts to make the Church 'conform to his own will' (*ad suum trahere conatur arbitrium*). On Constantius and the clergy, see Klein 1977; Michaels-Mudd 1979, 99–103. On Constantius' military objectives, see Thompson 1956.

[23] On these, see Henck 2001a.

[24] For Procopius' panegyric on Justinian's buildings, see Haury and Wirth 1964. Themistius praised Constantius' buildings in *Orr.* 3 and 4, as did Julian himself in his first oration to Constantius (*Or.* 1 41a). See Henck 2001a, 284–6.

[25] As observed by Curta 1995, 185.

[26] For the *Caesars* and the *Misopogon* see the chapters of Rowland Smith and Nicholas Baker-Brian in this volume.

[27] Curta 1995, 190.

[28] Bouffartigue 1978, 15.

[29] Brauch 1980, 146.

[30] Athanassiadi-Fowden 1981, 66. Bidez 1924, 113, is echoed by Curta 1995, 190.

[31] Julian lavished praise on Marcus in his *Caesars* for his commitment to philosophy and desire to imitate the gods. See esp. *Caes.* 317c–d, 328b–d, 333b–335a, and Hunt 1995.

[32] Curta 1995, 193, translated θεοφιλής as 'a favorite of the gods' and described the term as 'a recurring epithet'.

[33] Curta 1995, 193.

[34] Baynes 1929, 102, attributed the 'solar apologetic of the period' to Constantinian influence; see also Drake 2009. For the Sol mosaics, see Noga-Banai 2008, Levine 2000, 570–3.

[35] For Julian's ban on Christian teachers, see Amm. Marc. 22.10.7 and 25.4.20; Hardy 1986; Banchich 1993; Watts 2006, 68–78. It is worth noting that Ammianus praises Constantius' standards for appointments at 21.16.1–3.

[36] Rambaud 1966.

[37] *Or.* 2 76a.

[38] The record of Julian's Persian campaign is in Amm. Marc. 24.

4

IS THERE AN EMPRESS IN THE TEXT? JULIAN'S *SPEECH OF THANKS* TO EUSEBIA

Liz James

The *Speech of Thanks* to Eusebia is an intriguing piece of writing: its subject is unusual, its context mysterious and its audience unknown. How far is it a speech about Eusebia, how far about Constantius, and how far about Julian himself? The text is usually dated to 355/356, to Julian's early years as Caesar in Gaul, and is often taken as Julian's own commentary on his relationship with the empress. Read with Ammianus Marcellinus' account of Julian's dealings with Eusebia, the *Speech* has been employed to create a picture of Eusebia as a kind, merciful woman, well-disposed towards Julian.[1] Bidez described it as 'sincere and spontaneous'.[2] It was she, so Ammianus and Julian suggested, who reconciled Julian and Constantius; it was she who persuaded Constantius to send Julian to Athens and then to make him Caesar and send him to Gaul.[3] The *Speech* has also been used to look at Julian's life at this critical moment of his appointment to the position of Caesar, and thus as a commentary by Julian on his own political position.[4] It has also been employed in the assessment of Julian as author and in the context of his intellectual concerns.[5] In it, Julian is said to have expressed his admiration of Eusebia.[6] In this chapter, Julian will, of course, play a part, as one of the issues developed here is that of how the text works as rhetoric, and the consideration of authorial intention. However, Eusebia will be given a more central role, as what I am primarily concerned with is how far Julian's *Speech* was about Eusebia and what it did, and did not, say about her as both person and empress. I will argue that the *Speech*, especially when backed by Ammianus, created a false impression on both counts.

The *Speech* is the only surviving panegyric about a woman. Whether it was addressed to Eusebia is another matter, for she is never directly addressed within it. Where, in his first oration to Constantius, Julian frequently addressed the subject of his speech as 'you', in the *Speech*, Eusebia is only ever referred to in the third person. Whether this reflected a convention of politeness is unclear; it seems improbable that empresses were only addressed in the third person. Instead, this may be an early

47

indication that this was perhaps neither a speech to Eusebia nor for her, but, rather, about her for a different audience.

It has been proposed that, in writing it, Julian was forced to adapt the rules laid out in the rhetorical handbooks, because they gave no rules or examples for speeches on women.[7] While it is true that Hermogenes, Menander and Aphthonius, authors of the major rhetorical handbooks, did not discuss what to do if the subject of a speech was female, it is implausible that Julian's was the first, or the last, speech of praise ever addressed to an empress, any more than the surviving encomia for emperors represent every encomium ever delivered. In fact, the *Speech* is not the only surviving address to an empress from Late Antiquity. Other pieces include Gregory of Nyssa's funeral orations for Flacilla (wife of Theodosius I) and for Pulcheria (Flacilla's and Theodosius' daughter); and four poems celebrating empresses: Claudian's poem, the *Laus Serenae*, in praise of Serena, niece of Theodosius I and wife of Stilicho; a short anonymous poem praising Eudocia, wife of Theodosius II; Proclus' praise of Pulcheria, sister of Theodosius II; and Corippus on Justin II and Sophia.[8] What these texts imply is that praise of an empress was not unknown and that Julian's *Speech* should be seen as part of a broader tradition of speeches made to imperial women. Considering that 'wife of the emperor' was a position of considerable power, this is hardly a surprise.[9]

In discussing the *Speech*, it is vital to understand the rhetorical conventions under which it operated. The *Speech* was a piece of panegyrical writing. Although it is often called an *encomium*, a speech of praise, actually, strictly speaking, it was a speech of thanks, a *gratiarum actio*. However, the two forms were closely related in the rhetorical handbooks, for both deal in praise.[10] It is apparent from the surviving handbooks, notably the one ascribed to Menander Rhetor, that encomia had very definite progressions.[11] The audience expected an *introduction*, amplifying and justifying the subject; the orator would then move on to hail the *native land* (if it was famous for anything) and the *family* of the subject (in imperial cases, if this last was undistinguished, the emperor's divine nature could be stressed). After this, the speech should praise the *physical appearance* of the *laudandus*, encompassing good looks, upbringing and habits, and making comparisons with gods and heroes, before dealing with his *deeds* in peace and war (if the subject was a successful general, then war came first; deeds in peace included success in government and the happiness of the ruled), and his command of the *virtues* of courage, righteousness, justice and mercy, foresight and prudence or moderation and good sense, wisdom, philanthropy and good fortune. Under the heading of virtues, education might be emphasised, for a proper education in philosophy enabled the subject to deal with his tasks wisely. Finally, in the *conclusion*, the prosperity of his reign (if the subject were an emperor) should be praised and prayers were to be offered for his well-being and dynastic security. After the conversion of Constantine, the requisite virtues and appropriate heroic role models took on a Christian slant. Constantine's own panegyricist, Eusebius, stressed that the four cardinal virtues of a ruler, clemency, justice, piety, and love for mankind, or *philanthrōpia*, were taught to the ruler by God, his own divine ruler, and chastity was increasingly emphasised as a praiseworthy characteristic.[12]

In speaking of Eusebia, most of this model was used by Julian. He began with an *introduction* justifying why it was acceptable to make a speech of this nature on this subject: praise is a good thing; ingratitude is base; women no less than men can be excellent.[13] He claimed that he would borrow Homer's model from the *Odyssey* of Athena's speech on queen Arete (which, of course, means 'excellence' or 'virtue', thus allowing him to draw out a series of word-plays throughout the speech) and he listed Eusebia's virtues: temperance, justice, mildness, goodness, love for her husband, generosity with money, honouring of her own kin.[14] These virtues echo the standard virtues of an encomium, with the significant addition of love for one's husband and honour for one's own kin, and with the notable exception of courage. As the speech unfolded, Julian amplified and elaborated on these virtues, and explained his omission of the martial virtues.

The *Speech* then progressed through the stages of the encomium as laid down by Menander and in Julian's Homeric example: the concept of *native land* led to a passage on Macedonia, with special mention of kings Philip and Alexander; under *family*, Julian spoke of Eusebia's father, emphasising that he was the first of the family to be a consul, and then later of her mother, who remained chaste in her widowhood.[15] Under *physical appearance*, Eusebia was described as beautiful and chosen as wife by a brave, wise, temperate and just emperor who recognised her qualities of wit, wisdom and beauty and saw her as fit to bear sons for empire.[16] In this context, marriage was hailed as the first (and last) of a woman's deeds: Julian commended Constantius for his choice of Eusebia and compared her to prudent Penelope who persuaded her husband Odysseus to stay faithful to her and to return to her, and who was a partner in her husband's counsels.[17] Not only was Eusebia merciful, she also encouraged Constantius to be even more merciful. She pleaded for people before him and he, according to Julian, gave in unwillingly; there were no cases where she had been the cause of punishment and she had never bade the emperor to inflict injury or harm.[18] She was philanthropic, for she influenced the emperor in awarding offices, especially to her own family and friends, a perfectly acceptable virtue in Late Antiquity.[19] The final proof of her virtue was her treatment of Julian himself: she intervened for him with the emperor, warding off suspicion from him and encouraging him to take the post of Caesar.[20] Her deeds were her virtues: she was devoted to her husband.

Still on the theme of *deeds and virtues*, Julian clarified the exclusion of courage: would one prefer a wife like Semiramis and others who 'played men's parts in no very seemly fashion' or one like Penelope, discrete, loving her husband and family, speaking mildly, providing many blessings to those around her?[21] He then compared Eusebia, slightly obliquely, with Pericles as someone who never caused the death of anyone or took money or sent people into exile. As Pericles was praised for those qualities, so too was Eusebia.[22] Finally, *in conclusion*, Julian said that he would not describe her visit to Rome but would rather praise her goodness, temperance and wisdom.[23] And then the *Speech* ended, abruptly.

This brief summary underlines that Julian did not have to do very much to Menander's model in order to make his encomium fit a woman: with a few judicious changes to the appropriate virtues and role models, it was relatively straightforward. Courage disappeared, to be replaced by wifely devotion; gods and heroes were exchanged for two Homeric characters, Arete, and prudent, chaste, wifely Penelope, and, at a remove, Pericles. Julian offered a picture of Eusebia as virtuous, devoted, well-educated, kind, generous, philanthropic, merciful and just. Whether this was a 'true' picture of Eusebia, however, is beside the point. The fact is that the picture of Eusebia created in the *Speech*, and the range of virtues ascribed to her by Julian, and, indeed, in his *History* of Ammianus Marcellinus, and even the comparison with Penelope, were the very basic and very familiar set of imperial female virtues apparent in a range of texts from Late Antiquity, through to Procopius in the sixth century and via almost every historian of the period.[24] The *Laus Serenae*, for example, shares them. This poem stressed Serena's humility before God and her pious works and emphasised her chastity and loyalty to her family and husband through a series of classical comparisons, above all with Penelope. It praised her ancestry, both male and female, and celebrated her birth. The same virtues of wifely devotion, piety and philanthropy appeared again in Gregory of Nyssa's funeral oration for Flacilla. This, a piece written for a specific ceremonial and public event, emphasised the piety, philanthropy, zeal for faith, wifely love and humility of the empress, underlining these as key virtues of a good empress. Flacilla was generous to widows, orphans and virgins, chaste and clement, dignified but approachable, modest but ready to speak boldly. These virtues recurred in a visual form in the sixth century. In the frontispiece to her manuscript of the *Herbal of Dioscurides*, Anicia Juliana was shown flanked by personifications of generosity (*megalopsychia*) and prudence (*sōphrosynē*), while gratitude of the arts, which is surely another version of education, kneels at her feet.[25] That marital devotion was the most important single virtue for women was underlined by Dio Chrysostom's statement in his *Kingship Orations*: 'His wife, moreover, he (the ruler) regards not merely as the partner of his bed and affections, but also as his helpmate in his counsel and action, and indeed in his whole life'.[26] Dio's comment also made it clear that behind every empress, indeed every woman, no matter how important, was always a man, be it her husband, brother or father. Her role was to make his life better.

What these parallels expose is that Julian's *Speech* is one that deals in 'types' as much as it does with individuals. Julian's Eusebia was a recognisable type. She was the model of a fit and proper empress worthy of praise because she possessed the correct imperial female virtues, just as Constantius in Julian's *First Panegyric* was praised for possessing the correct set of male virtues.[27] Even Julian's perceived emphasis on Eusebia's education can be seen as part of the same rhetorical tradition, for he merely employed one of the standard tropes of panegyric, that the subject should be well-educated. This does not indicate that Eusebia was an intellectual, as has been suggested.[28] Indeed, the proof that Julian adduced of Eusebia's educational standards was that she sent him off to Athens with a parcel of books; this does not indicate that she had ever read them. The Eusebia of the *Speech* was the model of a 'good' empress; how far this should be recognised as 'personal' was irrelevant since that was not how panegyrics worked.

Rhetoric was the art of persuasion. Its primary purpose was not to convey unambiguous pieces of information in a neutral or unbiased way, but to articulate a particular point of view in a persuasive manner: famously, it can make the worse the better.[29] Ruth Webb has made the point that epideictic, or panegyrical, oratory was concerned with persuasion as much as judicial or deliberative oratory was, and that it too dealt in argumentation and proof.[30] For an epideictic speech to be successful, the orator was compelled to use reasoned arguments to show that the subject was worthy of praise. This is apparent in the *Speech of Thanks* in which Julian stated explicitly that he would have to bring proof of what he said, that he would need evidence 'as in a law court'.[31] The rules of epideictic meant that he could not merely state that Eusebia was wise or kind; he needed to provide demonstrations of this. Here, the choice of proof adduced by Julian is interesting: Eusebia was a worthy subject of praise because of her lineage and homeland; she performed good deeds because she was kind and supportive of Julian in various ways. Employing argumentation in this way underlined the orator's role of persuading the audience to appreciate the qualities of his subject. In this context, epideictic oratory needs also to be understood as a dynamic medium: its aim was to influence or even to change the audience's understanding of the subject; and the audience was there not to be dazzled by virtuoso displays of oratorical brilliance, but to be convinced of the appropriateness of the speech, to be won over if necessary.[32] Julian's *Speech*, as it must, both proved a point ('Eusebia is a good empress worthy of thanks because she helped me...') and highlighted correct social values ('Eusebia is a good empress because she is virtuous...'). It also gave the one praised a standard to live up to; as Julian put it, 'it makes them zealous to aim at a still higher level of conduct'.[33] By praising Eusebia, was Julian encouraging her to raise her game? These aspects gave epideictic oratory a public role, for praise has a social function. It reminds the audience of their shared values and, by intensifying these it makes them all the more significant.[34] The *Speech* thus drew attention to proper (female) imperial conduct. Again, it was less about Eusebia per se, and more about the correct way to behave. 'Realism' was not the issue at stake; recognisability was. Eusebia was instantly recognisable from the *Speech*, not as an individual woman but as a good empress; to argue her case as anything else was perhaps failure on the orator's part.

However, while the *Speech* persuaded its audience that Eusebia possessed all the right values and none of the wrong ones (whether or not that was true), was it also possible that it used those same arguments to comment on Constantius? Shaun Tougher has argued that this is a speech as much about Constantius as about Eusebia, that the emperor is paramount.[35] Is it possible then, to see the *Speech* as critical of Constantius? Julian's comparison of Eusebia with Pericles as someone who never caused the death of anyone or took money or sent people into exile could be interpreted as a comment on Constantius as someone who did. His praise of Eusebia's mildness, justice and temperance could be set against an unspoken background of Constantius' own reputation (according to Ammianus Marcellinus and Julian) for punishment and killing. Was Constantius meant to be crafty Odysseus to Eusebia's patient Penelope?[36] If this double-edged meaning is present in the *Speech*, then Julian can also be seen as criticising Constantius for being manipulated by his wife in his treatment of others – for uxoriousness, in fact, which was perceived as a shameful blot on any man's character – and for not matching up to a woman's standards of behaviour: he was merciful and just, but Eusebia was more so.[37] Such a trope did exist, 'figured speech' or *eschēmatismenos logos*, that says one thing on the surface but means something different, though it is not a technique that seems to have been explicitly applied to epideictic in the theoretical texts.[38] We might push this reading a stage further, for it is conceivable that the *Speech* was also implicitly critical of Eusebia. Julian claimed that her father was the first of the family to be consul, perhaps suggesting a lack of nobility, that Constantius saw her as fit to bear sons for empire, which might be construed as a reminder of Eusebia's lack of progeny, that she was the perfect devoted wife – to the hated Constantius. What sort of woman did that make her?

In answer to this last, both Ruth Webb and Laurent Pernot have made the point that it is inappropriate to look for veiled dissent about the subject in epideictic rhetoric.[39] Rather, they suggest that both orator and audience shared a background of knowledge against which the speech operated and in which they shared a complicit silence. In other words, the orator may have persuaded or sought to persuade his audience of something different from what they knew against the background of their shared knowledge: in Julian's case, for example, that Constantius could be called merciful, just and kind when everyone was aware that he had killed Julian's father and much of his family. If Julian were able to persuade his audience to share a complicit silence on this issue, it would make both this 'Speech' and the two orations on Constantius remarkable feats of oratory, and it is a matter for debate as to whether he did achieve this.

In contrast, therefore, to Webb's and Pernot's position, the issue of veiled criticism needs more consideration. In setting the *Speech* against a background of implicit shared knowledge, however, in which the ostensible subject was Eusebia, rather than Constantius, it is perhaps possible that in persuading his audience of Eusebia's virtues, the complicit silence around Constantius was perhaps heightened. Consequently, reading the *Speech* as hostile to both Constantius and Eusebia relies on reading it through an understanding of Julian as a man who hated and loathed Constantius and was prepared to express that. This is a reading, however, that raises a fundamental question in our understanding of the text: when and where was it delivered? Could Julian have got away with a public speech critical of Constantius?

Panegyrics were public speeches embedded in specific contexts.[40] They were then expanded for publication in a written form. The *Speech*, as we have it, if it was ever delivered, has therefore been worked over for public consumption. It is often dated to 355 or 356 on the basis of its references to Julian's career in Gaul and his rebellion against Constantius, though the closing section refers to a visit made to Rome by Eusebia without

Constantius in 356, but we have no knowledge about whether it was ever delivered before being written down.[41] Scholars have made a variety of suggestions. It may have been written down and sent to Constantius to be read (if so, was that privately or performed at court?).[42] It may have been given to a small and select audience in Gaul of Julian's friends (for what reason?).[43] It is unknown whether Eusebia ever received it. Is it significant in this context that in comparison to other encomia, she was never directly addressed but was only present in the third person? What these questions of audience also highlight is the issue of the intended purpose of the *Speech*. Was it as straightforward as saying 'thank you very much' to Eusebia?[44]

In part, considering these questions returns us to the problem of people and personalities. It is generally accepted that criticism of any emperor was not usually well received. Could Julian really have criticised Constantius to the extent to which this *Speech* might suggest and have survived?[45] The response to that depends in part on our reading of Constantius' character.[46] Our chief source for this is the pagan author Ammianus Marcellinus, who took Julian as the hero of his history and the Arian Christian Constantius as the villain. Equally, Julian, in his own writings, as one would expect, offered a negative and hostile picture of Constantius.[47] Without a clearer picture of Constantius, it is impossible to resolve the issues around the *Speech*. However, it is conceivable that this *Speech* was written retrospectively by Julian. If so, it might have served as propaganda in which Julian justified his actions against Constantius. By both appearing to credit Eusebia (and thus Constantius) and to criticise them, he could gain his audience's approval of his manners towards Constantius, coupled with its awareness of his relationship with his predecessor.[48]

In the context of this paper, Julian's Eusebia in the *Speech*, the personification of all the female imperial values and help-mate of the monstrous Constantius, bears comparison with Ammianus' Eusebia, the apparently split personality: the kind, good woman who protected Julian and spoke up for him to Constantius, and the malevolent one who poisoned Julian's wife, Helena.[49] Ammianus mentioned Eusebia four times: in 354, 'through the favour of divine power', Eusebia befriended Julian, ensuring his safety (15.2.8) and he was then allowed to travel to Greece; in 355, she opposed those who thought the title Caesar should not be awarded to Julian, either because she had no wish to travel to Gaul with Constantius or because she felt that favouring a kinsman was always a better option than favouring anyone else; (15.8.3); in 357, she brought Julian's wife, Helena, to Rome, and coaxed her to drink a 'rare potion' to ensure that she would miscarry every time she conceived (16.10.18). Ammianus then went on to say, without naming names, that Helena had previously borne Julian a child but the midwife had been bribed to make sure it did not survive. The proximity of the two stories has seemed to scholars to implicate Eusebia. Finally, in a retrospective comment, Ammianus noted Constantius' third marriage, characterising the dead Eusebia as 'a woman distinguished before many others for beauty of person and character and kindly in spite of her lofty station' (21.6.4).

Ammianus was hardly enthusiastic in his treatment of Eusebia. Her support of Julian was portrayed as the result of divine intervention and of either self-interest or self-preservation; in both cases, a dig at Constantius is apparent. Constantius was depicted in turn as uxorious, weak and even manipulated by a woman to his own later downfall, something that several later pagan sources also noted. Zosimus, for example, suggested that Constantius was influenced by Eusebia, whom he represented as devious, a standard trope for any woman who might influence a man, and Eutropius claimed that Constantius was 'excessively influenced' by his wives.[50] Criticism of an empress was always a good means of attacking, directly or indirectly, an emperor, as indeed Procopius' attack on Theodora showed. An emperor led by a woman appeared weak, unmanly and lacking in proper virtues; a woman leading a man was devious and lacking in proper virtue; by both, the natural order was disrupted. In this context, Ammianus' retrospective character study is seen as credible because it matches Julian's account in the *Speech*, but in its terms of praise, it is actually nothing more than a conventional encomium. Tougher has suggested that this passage is, in fact, Ammianus praising Eusebia's brothers. Again, however, the 'good' and the 'bad' are equally constructions, which may reflect nothing of the 'true' Eusebia, whoever and whatever she may have been, but instead serve the purposes of the texts in which they appear.

Eusebia's poisoning of Helena fits the type of the evil scheming woman described in the line of malevolent empresses from Suetonius' Livia to Julia Domna and onwards into Byzantium. Such a woman would have been an appropriate mate for Constantius. A very clear picture of how an empress could be turned into a domineering, rapacious, murderous, lustful whore is presented in Procopius' *Secret History*, written of the sixth-century empress Theodora.[51] Compared to that characterisation, Eusebia escaped lightly. Both Elizabeth Fisher and Averil Cameron have shown that the *Secret History* is a construction utilising types rather than an 'accurate' character study of Theodora, that the murderous whore need not have been any closer to the 'real' Theodora than the pious spouse of Justinian described elsewhere by Procopius.[52]

Ammianus' miscarriage story is also just that: a good story. As Roger Scott has argued, Late Antique readers loved a good story, and their category of 'good' needed little relationship to 'true'.[53] What they enjoyed were stories that made recognisable points, often originally points of propaganda, but that illustrated something about the characters concerned, stories that conveyed messages. The *Secret History* perhaps took this to extremes in its treatment of Justinian and Theodora. The miscarriage story is only one of many that might be seen as good stories and which recur in different forms with different names throughout Late Antique and Byzantine history, sexual morality being a central theme in such tales. That such stories need not ever be true is irrelevant: Socrates, unhappy with the idea that Theodosius I was ever married to an Arian, claimed instead that the Arian Galla was his first wife and only after her death did Theodosius marry the unimpeachably orthodox Flacilla, hailed as a paragon of all the virtues; whether Pulcheria and Marcian ever had a marriage in more than name depended on the historian in question; Theodora's attempt to save prostitutes from sin was a successful measure in Malalas, a dismal failure in Procopius.[54] These stories, which challenge our credulity, doubtless survived as true history because they were good stories which audiences continued to demand. What is interesting here is that the stories told about Constantius and Eusebia by Christian historians were very different to those of Ammianus, Julian and other pagan writers. As Scott points out, for stories to continue in circulation, they needed to remain within the limits of what was accepted as a true representation of the past, a story that made sense to later audiences.

It is therefore significant that the miscarriage story dropped out of the Christian sources. These presented a very different empress. One of the Christian stories about Eusebia described how, perceiving herself as insulted by bishop Leontius, she attempted to persuade Constantius to punish him. Constantius, however, was impressed by the bishop's forthrightness and refused to intervene.[55] Similar stories of bishops putting empresses down recur in other sources making two points: one is the putting of over-mighty women in their place; the other is demonstrating the courage of various bishops, underlining their claims to holiness.[56] Another story claimed that Eusebia was afflicted with a disease of the womb, to the distress of Constantius. He recalled the monk Theophilus from exile; begged pardon for the injuries caused to him and entreated him to heal Eusebia. As soon as the monk laid hands on her, she was healed: the moral of the story being that faith solves everything.[57] Fifth- and sixth-century historians were all very concerned with Eusebia's piety, her primary virtue, or vice, as far as they were concerned. Indeed, her faith was almost the only thing mentioned about her by writers such as Sozomen, Socrates, and Philostorgius. Like Constantius, Eusebia was renowned as an Arian

Christian and the historians reacted to this along religious lines. Sozomen, who wished to stress Constantius' orthodoxy, explained that it was Eusebius the Arian who converted the empress and who influenced the court. The empress in turn, influenced her husband.[58] Here we see that the theme of empresses being influenced by wicked men is a recurrent one that reflects women's fallibility. It was also one that served to clear the emperor of heresy, convicting him instead of weakness and being led astray by his wife, itself a parody of the virtue of wifely devotion. Socrates had a similar but different version of this: a priest in the household of Constantius' sister, Constantia, converted the court eunuchs, often dubious characters, then the empress and then finally the emperor.[59]

The Christian Eusebia was in no way closer to the 'real' Eusebia than Ammianus' or Julian's creations were. Instead, by putting Christian and pagan sources together, we can see what interested different authors. It is unsurprising that Ammianus made no mention of Eusebia's faith. Julian's omission of piety, one of the key virtues that an encomium was supposed to extol, is equally expected. Nor is it surprising that Julian used no Christian role models in his praise of Eusebia. But what that does again is emphasise that the *Speech* is a construction and that what it tells us, just as was the case with the accounts of historians and chroniclers, was the choice of the author for his own purposes. It has been noted that the *Speech* was perhaps more about Julian than Eusebia. This is true; Eusebia as a 'person' was not present, though the *Speech* tells us a great deal about how to portray a good empress. Both Julian's picture of Eusebia in the *Speech* and Ammianus' apparently conflicting images of her underline that the Flavian empresses play a relatively small part in the histories of this period. Their appearances are linked to themes of family, dynasty and childbearing, to religion, and also to support of the emperor or putative emperor. To this end, they appeared time and again in the written sources as resisting or supporting usurpers, manipulating events for their own children, and, in the case of Eusebia and Helena, as competing for the eventual succession. Their presence in texts, of whatever sort, engages us, but serves to underline the role of those texts as sites to play out different dramas often unconnected to their 'real' lives.

Acknowledgments
My thanks to Shaun Tougher, Jill Harries, Suzanna Elm and Pilar Garcia for discussion of the subject matter of this paper, and to Michelle O'Malley for commenting on the written version. Thank you also to David Hunt, who taught me about Julian.

Notes

[1] Bowersock 1978, 33; Aujoulat 1983a and 1983b.

[2] Bidez 1932, 72.

[3] Amm. Marc. 15.2.8; 15.8.3.

[4] Tougher 1998a.

[5] Tougher 1998b.

[6] Radošević 1995.

[7] Tougher 1998a.

[8] Gregory of Nyssa, *Oratio funebris in Flacillam Imperatricem*; *Oratio consolatoria in funere Pulcheriae*; Claudian, *Laus Serena*, ed. and trans. Consolino 1986; anonymous poem, *Greek Anthology* 1, 105; Proclus, *On the Resurrection*; Corippus, *In laudem Iustini Augusti minoris*, ed. and trans. Averil Cameron 1976. See also Vatsend 2000, 46–7; 81–5.

[9] James 2001.

[10] On *gratiarum actio*, see Pernot 1993, 108–9.

[11] Men. Rhet. *On epideictic*, ed. and trans. Russell and Wilson 1981. Also Russell 1998; Webb 2003; Mary Whitby 2003.

[12] Euseb. *Vit. Const.* e.g. 3.1–3; Kennedy 1983; Averil Cameron 1991; Rapp 1998.

[13] Julian, Eusebia (=*Or.* 3), 104b.

[14] *Or.* 3 106b.

[15] Vatsend 2000, 51–8.

[16] *Or.* 3 109b.

[17] *Or.* 3 110c, 112d.

[18] *Or.* 3 114b–c.

[19] *Or.* 3 116.

[20] *Or.* 3 118b, 121a–c.

[21] *Or.* 3 127. On the comparisons with Arete and Penelope, see also Vatsend 2000, 93–5, 97–9 and 104–6.

[22] *Or.* 3 128c.

[23] *Or.* 3 129c.

[24] James 2001, chap. 2.

[25] Vienna, Nationalbibliothek, cod. Med. Gr. 1, fol. 6v; Weitzmann 1977, 60 and 61.

[26] Dio Chrys. *Or.* 3.122. My thanks to Shaun Tougher for this reference.

[27] Julian, *Or.* 1, e.g. 32b.

[28] *Or.* 3 118c and d, 123d. Eusebia as educated: e.g. Aujoulat 1983a, 93–4, 102–3.

[29] Jeffreys 2003, Vinson 2003.

[30] Webb 2003, 130–1.

[31] *Or.* 3 116d.

[32] Webb 2003, 135.

[33] *Or.* 3 103c; trans. Wright, vol. 1, 277.

[34] Webb 2003, 133.

[35] Tougher 1998a, 116.

[36] On Constantius II as Odysseus, see Vatsend 2000, 108–10. Vatsend 2000, 99–100, also suggests that parallels were drawn between the emperor and empress and Zeus and Hera at 114a–b. These would not necessarily flatter either party.

[37] This may be the case in Julian's *Ep. ad Ath.*

[38] My thanks to Ruth Webb on this point.

[39] Webb 2003, 134; Pernot 1993.

[40] Russell 1998, 49; Braund 1998, 59.

[41] For the visit to Rome, *Or.* 3 129b–c. For discussions of the date, see Bidez 1932, 71–2, suggesting it was written at the same time as the *Oration* on Constantius; Tantillo 1997, 36–40, making a case for its delivery in Rome in 357; Vatsend 2000, 11–12, suggesting 356–7.

[42] Tantillo 1997, 36–40, suggests that Helena took the two speeches to Rome.

[43] Athanassiadi 1992, 61 (sent to court); Aujoulat 1983a, 97 (read by Constantius); Tougher 1998a, 110 (read in Gaul).

[44] This might be suggested by the portrayal of Eusebia in Julian's *Ep. ad Ath.*

[45] Heather 1998, 140, on the life-expectancy of those who savaged an emperor in public.

[46] DiMaio and Arnold 1992, esp. 168, on Constantius' character.

[47] See for example, *Ep. ad Ath.* 277d, 278a–b.

[48] This may also be the case in the *Ep. ad Ath.*, where Julian justifies his right to replace Constantius. Mark Humphries (1998) saw a savage humour in Hilary of Poitiers' treatment of Constantius; there may be scope for the same in Julian's *Speech.*

[49] Amm. Marc. 16.10.18–19. On the two Eusebias, see Tougher 2000. For Ammianus and women, see Sabbah 1992, which suggests Ammianus treated women as stereotypes. I am grateful to Pilar Garcia for this reference. The Eusebia of the *Ep. ad Ath.* is another treatment of the empress and I regret that space does not allow me to discuss her here.

[50] Zos. 3.1; Eutr. *Brev.* 10.15. Amm. Marc. 21.16.16 has him as 'easily influenced'.

[51] Procop. *SH* 15.

[52] Fisher 1984; Averil Cameron 1985, chap. 5.

[53] Scott 2010.

[54] Theodosius and Galla: Socrates, *Hist. eccl.* 4.31; Mal. 13.37 also has Galla as the first wife. Marcian and Pulcheria: discussed by Scott 2010; Theodora: Mal. 18.24; Procop. *SH* 17.3. Also see Urbainczyk 1998, 313–15 on Socrates' and Sozomen's different treatments of Julian.

[55] The story is preserved in the tenth-century *Souda* lexicon, sv Leontius, ed. Adler 1928–38, 525.

[56] A similar story is also told of Justina (second wife of Valentinian I) and bishop Ambrose: Paulinus, *Life of Ambrose* 6.20.

[57] Philostorgius, *Hist. eccl.* 4.7.

[58] Sozom. *Hist. eccl.* 3.1.

[59] Socrates, *Hist. eccl.* 2.2. At 1.25 this same priest is responsible for converting Constantine to Arianism. Michael the Syrian, *Chronicle* 7.3 and 4 repeats the story.

5

JULIAN'S *CONSOLATION TO HIMSELF ON THE DEPARTURE OF THE EXCELLENT SALUTIUS*: RHETORIC AND PHILOSOPHY IN THE FOURTH CENTURY

Josef Lössl

In his monumental study on Julian and the culture of his time, Jean Bouffartigue included a brief note on Julian's *Consolation to Himself on the Departure of the Excellent Salutius*.[1] I shall take this helpful note as a point of departure and discuss briefly some of the issues raised in it. My aim is to make a small contribution to the exegesis of a work which, despite its relative brevity, is quite remarkable in its own right as well as in the context of Julian's intellectual and political life.

Referring to the work as Julian's 'Letter to Saloustios', Bouffartigue begins by saying that the manuscript tradition clearly establishes it as a *consolatio*, παραμυθητικὸς λόγος. This genre, he continues, is claimed in equal measure by philosophers and rhetors. Menander Rhetor's manual, known to Julian, contains a model of consolatory speech. However, this is restricted to cases of bereavement. Julian must therefore have drawn on other models dealing with separation. At any rate, Julian follows Menander's suggested structure. He divides his speech into three parts: present grief (240b–244c), past examples (244c–246b), future hope (246b–252d). The same structure applies to προσωποποιία, which Julian puts to use in his *Consolatio* in a remarkable way. His speech of Pericles (246b–248b) generates a whole new layer of meaning and allows Julian to switch narrative levels at will. Thus at one point he lets Pericles muse how quickly a man's thoughts can 'dart' from Thrace and Illyria to Gaul and back (247b), an allusion to his and Salutius' situation. Bidez attributed this sudden switching of levels to Julian's possible loss of concentration: 'Julian seems to forget that it is Pericles who is speaking here'.[2] In Bouffartigue's opinion it is a deliberate rhetorical technique to cut through the different narrative layers and pack the past into the present and vice versa. Yet Julian's motivation for doing so is ultimately not a desire to generate rhetorical effect but, on the contrary, a concern for philosophy. His aim is to break up the rigid and opaque surface of conventional rhetoric and infuse philosophical meaning. Julian says as much himself, when he questions the use of too many *topoi*. He compares them to oversized machinery in a small theatre. What he wants to do, he says, is to spice up the ancient tales with philosophical teachings, like over-sweet wine with some bitter resin.[3] Thus Julian uses rhetoric, but would like to use less. He also wants to give philosophy her due. Overall, his technique is not original. He does not get everything from Menander, and it is apparent that he had access to other sources. Still, it is remarkable how he makes προσωποποιία, a marginal technique, the cornerstone of his little masterpiece.

Thus Bouffartigue. Now my discussion. Bouffartigue labels the *Consolatio* as Julian's 'Letter to Saloustios'. My questions are: Is it a letter? If so, is it addressed to Saloustios? And who is 'Saloustios'? Obviously, the text is addressed to someone, and this someone is named as Σαλούστιος in the superscription attested by the manuscript tradition, though nowhere in the body of the work. Though there is no reason to be over-critical, we may note that the manuscript tradition is not unanimous. At least one important manuscript does not have a superscription.[4] The remaining two groups have two variants. The older and more authentic one, which Bidez chose for his critical edition, reads: 'Julian Caesar's Consolation to Himself on the Departure of the Excellent Sallustius', Ἰουλιανοῦ Καίσαρος ἐπὶ τῇ ἐξόδῳ τοῦ ἀγαθωτάτου Σαλουστίου παραμυθητικὸς εἰς ἑαυτόν.[5] The other occurs in a more recently discovered 15th-century manuscript and omits the honorific address. It reads: 'By the same [Julian] a Consolation to Himself on the Departure of Sallustius', τοῦ αὐτοῦ [scil. Ἰουλιανοῦ] παραμυθητικὸς εἰς ἑαυτὸν ἐπὶ τῇ ἐξόδῳ Σαλουστίου.[6] A further version contained in the same codex is even shorter.[7]

Who is the Σαλούστιος of the manuscripts? He is generally assumed to be Secundus Saturninus Salutius,[8] who from 355 to 359, when the *Consolatio* was written, was most probably Julian's *quaestor sacri palatii*, his 'minister of justice'. He had held a series of offices previously in Gaul and Africa and went on to become Praetorian Prefect of the East from 361 to 365. He was offered the purple at least once, after Julian's death in 363, perhaps also after Jovian's death a year later, before he retired in 367.[9] Although a pagan, he enjoyed an excellent reputation across the whole religious spectrum. Gregory of Nazianzus, in an invective against Julian of all places, counted him as one of the ἄριστοι, a phrase that is reminiscent of the epithet ἀγαθώτατος in the superscription of the *Consolatio*.[10] He had been assigned to Julian as an adviser by Constantius II on Julian's appointment as Caesar in 355 and by 358 he seems to have been Julian's closest friend and ally in Gaul. It was this close relationship that was at least to contribute to the events that led to his being removed from his post and called to Constantinople.

Salutius is also believed to be the author of the Neoplatonic discourse *On the Gods and the Universe* and the dedicatee of Julian's *Hymn to King Helios*, but both these works date from the early 360s and will not be considered here.[11] Salutius is not identical with Flavius Sallustius,[12] who in 359 was probably Julian's *comes consistorii* or 'privy councillor' and went on to become Praetorian Prefect of Gaul in 361.

Thus I will from now on refer to the addressee of the *Consolatio* as 'Salutius'. But now, wait a moment: although the superscription refers to Salutius by name, it does not refer to him as addressee. According to the superscription the addressee is Julian himself. Of course, when we start reading the body of the work, it becomes immediately obvious that the addressee is the author's 'dear friend and comrade', φιλὸς ἑταῖρος,[13] who I assume is the Σαλούστιος of the superscription, our Salutius. But at the same time the author too is an addressee, for the thoughts he intends to share with his friend are thoughts which he addresses to himself to find some consolation in his grief. In fact, the opening paragraph presents us with a rather complex account of what the main purpose of the work actually is. Julian, according to his own account, wants to console himself, but he thinks that he can only do so by sharing his consolation with his friend, whom he assumes to be equally in need of a consolation. 'We must', he writes, 'find together (κοινόν) an effective remedy for whatever afflicts us in the present situation'.[14]

Julian's implication of himself in his work makes me inclined to think that his *Consolatio* is not, strictly speaking, a letter. By implicating himself Julian somehow universalizes the scope of the work; for he, as an addressee, now stands for anyone in a similar situation who might benefit from reading it, working it through as a philosophical exercise. This makes the *Consolatio* on the whole a speech, or discourse, although it retains in many places the characteristics of a letter, especially where it directly addresses Salutius (e.g. 251d–252d).

To illustrate my point, let me for a moment refer to a 'real' letter Julian wrote slightly more than half a year before the *Consolatio*, his letter to Oribasius. In it he describes the situation that probably contributed to Salutius' recall. Salutius had not been the only adviser, or minder, whom Constantius had assigned to Julian. There were others, and with most of them Julian was not on good terms. One of these was the Praetorian Prefect of Gaul, Flavius Florentius.[15] Julian writes to Oribasius how he rejected Florentius' tax plans for the province as extortionate and fraudulent[16] and justifies his stance on philosophical grounds: as a pupil of

Plato and Aristotle he had to follow his conscience (τὸ σύνειδος) and protect the poor provincials against 'those thieves'.[17] Like a soldier he had to stay at his post. God himself had put him there.[18] The rhetoric here may be slightly over the top, but it is at this point that Julian comes up with the idea of *consolatio*. He writes:

> But if by any chance I should come to harm in the process, to have acted with a clear conscience would be a great consolation (παραμυθία); if only the gods allowed me to keep my brave Salutius... But even if because of all this a successor were appointed, it would, I hope, not grieve me in the least; for it is far better to fulfill one's duty for a short time honestly than for a long time dishonestly.[19]

Whether or not, from hindsight, the idea of writing a *consolatio* originated from here, the letter to Oribasius may illustrate the difference between, on the one hand, writing to someone a letter about such events, and even about one's opinions and emotions in connection with them, and on the other, of 'working' or 'talking through', 'holding a discourse' (διαλέγειν) together with oneself, or with someone else, in order to address philosophical and emotional issues arising from such events, and then making this discourse available for others as a text. As we shall see further in a moment, this distinction is far from a clear cut one. A letter can indeed also be a discourse, but in the case of Julian's *Consolatio* the problem is that despite its obvious epistolary characteristics it does not strike one as a straightforward letter. One would feel uncomfortable classifying it as one without further comment.

'To work things through by myself', 'to talk to myself' (διαλέγειν πρὸς ἐμαυτόν), these are phrases which we do not only find in the superscription of the *Consolatio*, εἰς ἑαυτόν, but also in the body of the work, for example in the opening sentence. Where, to put it in Bouffartigue's terms, are Julian's models for this kind of writing? What follows are some wider reflections, not definite answers.

The phrase εἰς ἑαυτόν as a title, or part of a title, is reminiscent of Marcus Aurelius' work of the same title, a far more uncompromisingly philosophical, i.e. un-rhetorical, text than Julian's *Consolatio*. Themistius is purported to have referred to it as 'precepts', παραγγέλματα,[20] which recalls the 'philosophical applications', the ἐκ φιλοσοφίας προστιθέμενα, which Julian wants to infuse into his text to give it more philosophical force. However, there is no evidence that these associations are deliberate on Julian's part. We do not know whether Julian was aware of Marcus' philosophical work.[21]

If we think more specifically in terms of self-consolation, Cicero comes to mind. For the moment we leave aside the problem that he wrote in

Latin. Cicero, to begin with, is also one who defined *consolatio* as something much wider than *consolatio mortis*. In his *Tusculans* he writes that there exists a range of consolatory discourses for predicaments other than death including sudden fall into poverty, failure in public life, exile, ruin of one's country, slavery, illness, blindness, anything that can be labelled in some way or other a disaster.[22] From this tradition, which of course goes further back than Cicero, arises a host of letters and speeches that can be labelled consolatory including, in particular, works dealing with the predicament of exile, for example by Plutarch,[23] or by Dio Chrysostom, whose *Or.* 13 on his exile, ἐν Ἀθήναις περὶ φυγῆς, has in fact been suggested as a potential source for Julian's *Consolatio*,[24] though there is no more evidence of such an influence than there is, for example, in the case of the *Consolatio ad Apollonium*, an otherwise extremely influential consolatory work traditionally ascribed to Plutarch. On the other hand, Dio Chrysostom, in his work on grief, περὶ λύπης, provides a similar list to Cicero in the *Tusculans* (death, illness, loss of reputation, financial failure, stress, danger),[25] but adds that one should not try to deal with each of these separately through specially targeted forms of consolatory speech (καθ᾽ ἕκαστον…παραμυθίαν), because that way one would never come to an end, but one should take a radical approach, remove all emotional pain (τὸ πάθος) from the soul entirely (ὅλως) and get a grip on reality by using one's judgement (κρίνειν βεβαίως) and realising that someone guided by the intellect (τῷ νοῦν ἔχοντι)[26] must not be subject to any form of grief.[27] But although Dio's attitude comes close to Julian's in his *Consolatio*, Dio is not an advocate of self-consolation.

The classic self-consolation, of course, is Cicero's consolation to himself on the death of his daughter Tullia, a work of which now only fragments remain. Writing to his friend Atticus, Cicero says that he had done something which no one else before him had done, namely to write a *consolatio* as 'a letter to himself'.[28] A sentence later, and from then on consistently, he calls that 'letter' a 'book', *liber*.[29] It is clear that although the occasion of the work was quite specific, and without any doubt deeply authentic, the work was from the very beginning also intended for publication. Cicero wrote his *consolatio* for himself to alleviate his own grief, but he also sent it to his friends 'to share' it. And this sharing was not a sharing of his particular grief caused by losing his daughter, but of his general, universal, philosophical, way of dealing with it. It is more in this philosophical tradition rather than in the more rhetorical tradition of topical speeches that we have to situate Julian's *Consolatio*. But, of course, although the similarities with Julian's *Consolatio* are quite striking, they cannot count as evidence for any direct influence. On the other hand, there does not seem to be any such evidence in the Greek tradition either, although I am happy to take advice. Generally, I would not categorically rule out the possibility that Julian was influenced by Latin literature, although as a self-respecting Greek he would never have admitted to it or made it explicit.[30]

And there exist yet further possible parallels with Cicero, and also with possible Greek models of a particular tradition, namely discourses on friendship. Julian's *Consolatio* is packed with friendship *topoi*. Classic couples of friends referred to, both mythical and historical, include Theseus and Peirithous (242d), Scipio and Laelius (244c–245d), Pericles and Anaxagoras (245d, 246c), Achilles and Patroclus, the two Ajaxes and Antilochus (250d). Friendship-*topoi* used include sharing of pleasures and pains, words and deeds, private and public life, life at home and in the army (240b), open conversations, collaboration in all that is good, τῆς ἐν ἅπασι τοῖς καλοῖς κοινοπραγίας, unanimity, ἴσον θυμόν (241d).[31] Incidentally, it is here that Julian also remembers Mardonius,[32] his childhood tutor. A few paragraphs further on he cites the proverb attributed to Pythagoras, 'friends have all things in common' (245b), and insists that this does not only include material possessions, but intellect and wisdom (νοῦς καὶ φρόνησις) as well.

Julian thinks of his friendship with Salutius as some sort of natural bond, without the need of negotiated agreements, or oaths or things of that sort, but identity of thoughts and actions, ταῦτα νοοῦντες καὶ προαιρούμενοι (242d). It is based purely on virtue (243a). There is no need to follow one another's advice, because there is already unanimity. This is why Zeno is mistaken to say that to act on advice is more virtuous than to act on one's own decision, and Hesiod is right to say that the best man decides all things for himself (245a). The implication here is that those who try to slander Julian by saying that the real author of his achievements in Gaul is Salutius do not understand what it means to work in a team of friends. In the same way it was said of Laelius that he was the real author of Africanus' successes, whereas the truth is that both loved each other in an equal yoke of friendship and they both acted in unison (244c–d).

Perhaps, to return for a moment to one of Bouffartigue's concerns, Pericles' speech is better situated in the context of the friendship tradition rather than the consolatory one. The dangers associated with the separation of friends, especially the danger that a friendship might end, or a wedge might be driven between two friends because of long absence and physical distance, is an important *topos*, and the passage in the Pericles speech about the darting of thoughts between Thrace and Gaul, using a quote from the *Iliad* (15.80), ὡς δ' ὅτ' ἂν ἀΐξῃ νόος ἀνέρος, 'as when the mind of a man darts swiftly', clearly alludes to this danger. This is why the philosophical references to virtue and the intellect as the foundation of the friendship between him and Salutius are particularly important for Julian.

Although there are Greek sources for these *topoi*, it is again striking how most of them are actually concentrated in a philosophically systematic way in Cicero's dialogue *Laelius, On Friendship*: the idea that natural inclination is a better bond of friendship than need (27: *a natura mihi videtur potius quam ab indigentia orta amicitia*), and that *utilitas* is not the closest bond of friendship (51), that only good men, *boni*, can be friends (18), an idea that goes back to Aristotle,[33] and that virtue is the basis of friendship (20.27 ff.), not wisdom, as the Stoics say.[34] According to Cicero, Laelius wanted to be remembered for his friendship with Scipio rather than for his wisdom. As already with the consolatory motifs it is again difficult to find more contemporary Greek parallels. There are a number of works which Julian may have known, including Iamblichus' *Life of Pythagoras*,[35] which contains some substantial chapters on friendship, and Themistius' *Oration 22* (*On Friendship*), the date of which is uncertain, but which may have been published in 355.[36] But both works are not congenial with Julian's, mainly because they are written from a general perspective and focus on the basic principles of friendship, on how to acquire and maintain friendships, and how to deal with crises. For example, Iamblichus relates in detail how Pythagorean friendships are strictly regulated,[37] which is a far cry from Julian's romantic notion of friendship and his somewhat superficial interpretation of Pythagoras' principle that friends have all things in common (245b).

For a similar reason Libanius' *Oration* 8 (*On Friendship*) does not exactly fit the bill,[38] since it is mostly about the usefulness of many friends, whereas Julian's reflections are focused on the relationship between two, very intimate, friends. However, there seems to be an interesting similarity between parts of the opening sections of Julian's *Consolatio* and Themistius' *Oration* 22. Both highlight the contrast between listening to stories about the Trojan war (and other wars) and more uplifting discourses such as they themselves are offering. Thus Julian writes that he is not offering 'a tale of all the sufferings that the Greeks and Trojans inflicted on one another, but rather tales that dispel the grief from the souls of human beings and have power to restore cheerfulness and calm',[39] whereas Themistius asks his addressees:

> Why is it...that, if someone tells you how the Trojans and Achaeans fought one another..., you enjoy these tales and are spellbound by them...? How can you be so interested in conflict without ever having given thought to stories of friendship and how much friendship benefits human beings?[40]

But we may be dealing here merely with a frequent commonplace used to open a speech, similar to motifs like 'Orpheus' lyre', 'the Sirens' songs' and the 'drug nepenthe' from *Odyssey* 4.221ff.,[41] which can also be found in Themistius' *Oration* 32,[42] or in a work like Clement of Alexandria's *Protrepticus*, where it is used to adorn the idea that it is sweet to hear the new song of Moses, Clement's 'word of God'.[43] However, in this latter case it is, of course, highly significant that Julian should open his *consolatio* with an allusion to Helen's famous 'soothing drug', as he himself is embarking on a soothing, i.e. consolatory, discourse, which comes along, in some of its parts, in the guise of a discourse on friendship and is spiked with philosophical teachings.

Here the circle begins to draw to a close. The consolatory discourse is at the same time a discourse on friendship and vice versa. But as a whole this discourse is also intended to be something more. To return for a moment to Cicero: Cicero, in his *Laelius*, had defined friendship as 'unanimous agreement, combined with good will and charity, in all things divine and human'.[44] Now where are we here, between Julian and Salutius, with 'divine things'? They are not obvious from the outset. Religion does not feature in the opening address and what we are to make of the references to Orpheus, the Sirens and to Helen's lore in the next section is still open to question. These are not obviously allusions to theurgic hymn-singing but rather elements of a rhetorical opening gambit. What comes next is perhaps more revealing: 'It seems to me that pleasure and pain are connected at their apex and take their turns reciprocally'.[45] In other words, one cannot have both at the same time, and yet, one follows the other with necessity. This is almost mimicking the Socrates of the *Phaedo*, the Bible of philosophical consolatory writing. And it continues:

> Of all that befalls one who is guided by the intellect (τῷ νοῦν ἔχοντι) so the wise men say, the most severe trials cause him no more discomfort than comfort...and the bees extract sweet dew from the bitterest herb that grows on Hymettus and work it into honey.[46]

That is the ideal, Julian concludes, or at least the reality of those who have a sufficiently robust intellectual constitution and plenty of philosophical training. Julian does not necessarily count himself among them, as we saw earlier. He, upon examining himself, does feel distressed and in need of some rhetorical consolation. But his aim is also set: philosophy. This is not yet itself the divine sphere, but it sets the scene for the way in which divine matters will be discussed later on.

The first instances when God is mentioned are still literary allusions, or proverbs. The very first comes immediately after Julian's description of his and Salutius' friendship as 'one in heart' (*Il.* 17.720). Julian exclaims to his addressee, in the context of a series of further *Iliad* citations, 'a god (θεός) has removed you, as he did with Hector, beyond the reach of the arrow-shafts, which were so often aimed at you by sycophants, or rather at me, for they intended to wound me through you'.[47] The second is even less conspicuous, although at a closer look highly interesting. 'God grant', δοίη δὲ ὁ δαίμων, Julian prays, that the separation from Salutius may only last a short time.[48] The third instance is no less interesting: we ordinary mortals are more inferior to Plato than Plato was to God.[49] After that we slowly enter theological territory. After listing all the advantages and joys of friendship which Julian had enjoyed while being together with Salutius, he asks:

> But now that I am suddenly deprived of these, on which resource of arguments or words of encouragement (λόγοι) can I draw...so that they can persuade me to remain calm and stable in my mind and 'to bear nobly whatever God has sent my way'?[50]

The last phrase is a slightly altered citation from Demosthenes' *De Corona*,[51] which can also be found in one of the apocryphal letters to Iamblichus.[52] But what is really interesting about this passage is what immediately follows it: 'For surely', Julian adds, 'it is with this in mind that our great emperor has decreed this now in this way'.[53] This sentence strikes me as highly ambivalent, not only against the political background, but also in religious terms. Julian uses the monotheistic ὁ θεός and links it to the emperor, but in a rather awkward, allusive, way. And, of course, his source is a classical one. It is quite clear that he is not speaking of the Christian God.

This becomes far more obvious in the third part, where Julian outlines his thought on how philosophy links him with God (248d–249b). He puts it already in Pericles' mouth, in his speech (248b: νῷ γὰρ δὴ καὶ τῷ κρείττονι σύνεσμεν). But then he distances himself from the great Athenian hero of the past (μεγαλόφρων, τραφεὶς ἐλευθέρως ἐν ἐλευθέρᾳ τῇ πόλει) and laments that as a mortal of the present age[54] he is in need of a more human encouragement. How can he gain consolation? Not just by mere philosophy. Of course, at the outset is his ability to think for himself. No one can steal our thoughts. We can always communicate with ourselves, ἑαυτοῖς. But this does not happen in a naturalistic way, but 'perhaps God too will throw in a useful suggestion', ἴσως δὲ καὶ ὁ δαίμων ὑποθήσεταί τι χρηστόν (249a). For someone who entrusts himself to the superior being (τῷ κρείττονι) is not likely to be abandoned. But over him God (ὁ θεός) holds his hand,[55] strengthens and encourages him and puts into his mind ethical (πράκτεα) thoughts that make him do the good and avoid the bad, like

Socrates' 'divine voice' (δαιμονία φωνή). Homer, too, says of Achilles that [God] 'put a thought into his mind'.[56] This means that when our mind turns inward, to itself, εἰς ἑαυτόν, it communicates with itself through God and through itself with God, without mediation, and without limitation, through the world of the senses.[57]

This is Neoplatonist, not specifically recognisable as either Porphyrian or Iamblichan at this more popular level, but definitely not Christian, nor an attempt to accommodate Christianity, or to appear to do so. Obviously, it is not militantly anti-Christian, but then it is of course a *Consolatio* for a pagan, or rather, for two pagans. I would therefore not interpret Julian's habit of occasionally changing a Homeric Ζεύς or Ἥρη into a ὁ θεός as a christianising, or pretending to be christianising, *correctio* or ἐπανόρθωσις, as has been suggested. In fact I would even question whether we can speak here at all, even in terms of Lausbergian literary rhetoric, of ἐπανόρθωσις. Rather, the technique I see at work here is μετάφρασις, a form of παράφρασις, which deliberately adjusts terminology intending to create more consistency in its own presentation. Thus Julian is not embarrassed to use an Aristotelian κρείττων, a Socratic δαίμων, and a monotheistic ὁ θεός side by side, but he is trying to avoid the mythological, 'un-philosophical', Ζεύς and Ἥρη. Thus Julian's point is to outline some kind of philosophical monotheism, but not a kind of religion that could in any way be mistaken as Christian. Perhaps the conclusion to this section contains even a veiled anti-Christian reference. Julian says at the end of the section that he cannot now go into any details on how the mind participates in God, but there are witnesses to this phenomenon, and they are first-rate philosophers, not 'men not even fit to be classed with the Megarians', i.e. people beyond the pale.[58]

Clearly, it is important for Julian to believe in God in addition to human ingenuity. The gods loved Odysseus because he was so clever.[59] Generally, the Homeric heroes are models in that they achieve a lot through their own power and virtue, and on top of that they are supported by the gods.

Julian projects these thoughts on to Salutius, and because his text is 'to himself' they are reflected back on him. In the final section of the work he identifies himself with his friend: I heard you are going to Thrace, he writes. I was born and brought up there. Not that I want you to go. But it is a consoling thought to imagine you going there rather than somewhere else. In the meantime I stay here in 'our' country. I say 'our' because I now rank myself among the Celts, your tribe, which does not mean that you are not now an accomplished Greek philosopher, i.e. not a barbarian. Barbarians are those others who believe in incredible myths and paradoxical marvels, i.e. again perhaps the Christians.[60]

Thus by focusing on Salutius' main characteristics as being a Celt, a philosopher and a pagan, Julian, in his *Consolation to Himself*, also tells us something about himself, who within a few months of writing this text embarked on a campaign that led to him being proclaimed emperor in Gaul, in defiance of Constantius. Where does this leave us with the questions raised by Bouffartigue's note? I would conclude very briefly that from reading the work I can only confirm that as a *Consolatio* it can lay equal claim to being a work of rhetoric and of philosophy, a key text for understanding Julian's early career, and, more generally, an important text for understanding the intellectual culture of his time.

Notes

[1] Cf. Bouffartigue 1992, 539–40.

[2] Bidez 1932, 198 n. 3: 'Julien semble oublier qu'il fait parler Périclès. C'est Salluste qui est en Illyrie et va se rendre en Thrace, tandis que le César son ami demeure chez les Celtes'.

[3] Julian, *Or.* 4 244c (I am following Bidez's numbering and edition of Julian's works): ...τοῖς διηγήμασιν ἐκ φιλοσοφίας ἄττα προστιθέμενα τὸ δοκεῖν ἐξ ἱστορίας ἀρχαίας ὄχλον ἐπεισάγειν... Cf. Bidez 1932, 194 n. 3; Them. *Or.* 5 63b; Plat. *Leg.* 659e *et al.* Note that the imagery corresponds with that of the opening passage 240b–c, where the *Consolatio* is compared to nepenthe (*Od.* 4.219).

[4] Venice, Marcianus Graecus 366 (15th cent.) fol. 259v; cf. Bidez 1932, xxii–xxiii.

[5] Leiden, Vossianus Graecus Folio 77 (12th cent.).

[6] Χαλκή, Μονὴ τῆς Θεοτόκου 157 (15th cent.) fol. 265r; Cf. Bidez 1932, 189, xvi, xxvii.

[7] Χαλκή, Μονὴ τῆς Θεοτόκου 157 (15th cent.) fol. 277v: ἐπὶ τῇ ἐξόδῳ Σαλουστίου.

[8] *PLRE* 1, 814–17.

[9] For the details see *PLRE* 1.815 and 817. Amm. Marc. 25.5.3 reports that he was offered the purple after Julian's death in 363. Zos. 3.36.1–2 reports that he was offered it after Jovian's death a year later. It is possible that Zosimus incorrectly refers to the same event as Ammianus.

[10] Greg. Naz. *Or.* 4.91 (*PG* 35, 621): κατὰ τοὺς ἀρίστους τῶν πάλαι καὶ νῦν ἐπαινουμένων.

[11] For the *Hymn to King Helios* see the chapters by Andrew Smith and J. H. W. G. Liebeschuetz in this volume.

[12] *PLRE* 1, 797–8.

[13] For the implied meanings of ἑταῖρος in this context, both a 'political friend' and someone who shares in the intellectual life, cf. Cribiore 2007, 108–9.

[14] Julian, *Or.* 4 240b: κοινὸν εὑρίσκεσθαι χρὴ τῶν παρόντων, ὁποῖα ποτ' ἂν ᾖ, παιωνικὸν ἄκος.

[15] *PLRE* 1, 365.

[16] Julian, *Ep.* 14 (Bidez-Cumont = Wright 4) 385a–c. Julian refers to Florentius' reports as 'shameful and wholly abominable' (μιαρὰ καὶ πάσης αἰσχύνης ἄξια), 'outrageously disgraceful' (δεινῶς ἀσχημονεῖ) and as a means of handing the poor to the thieves (ἀνθρώπους ἀθλίους τοῖς κλέπταις ἐκδιδομένους); for his refusal of Florentius' plans cf. also Amm. Marc. 17.3.5.

[17] *Ep.* 14 385c: τὴν δὲ ὑπὲρ τῶν ἀθλίων ἀνθρώπων ἀπολείπειν τάξιν, ὅταν δέῃ πρὸς κλέπτας ἀγωνίζεσθαι τοιούτους.

[18] *Ep.* 14 385c–d: καὶ ταῦτα τοῦ θεοῦ συμμαχοῦντος ἡμῖν, ὥσπερ οὖν ἔταξεν; for the comparison between the call of conscience and the soldier's duty to stay at his post cf. both Christian and pagan sources, e. g. Pl. *Ap.* 28d, 1 Cor. 15.23, 1 Clem. 41.1.

[19] *Ep.* 14 385d: εἰ δὲ καὶ παθεῖν τι συμβαίη, μετὰ καλοῦ τοῦ συνειδότος οὐ μικρὰ παραμυθία πορευθῆναι. τὸν δὲ χρηστὸν Σαλούστιον θεοὶ μέν μοι χαρίσαιντο. κἂν συμβαίνῃ δὲ διὰ τοῦτο τυγχάνειν διαδόχου, λυπήσει τυχὸν οὐδέν· ἄμεινον γὰρ ὀλίγον ὀρθῶς ἢ πολὺν κακῶς πρᾶξαι χρόνον.

[20] Haines 1916, xv.

[21] Cf. Brunt 1974, 1 n. 4. Also, Hunt 1995.

[22] Cic. *Tusc.* 3.81: *sunt enim certa [scil. genera {orandi} aegritudinis], quae de paupertate, certa, quae de vita inhonorata et ingloria dici soleant; separatim certae scholae sunt de exilio, de interitu patriae, de servitute, de debilitate, de caecitate, de omni casu, in quo nomen poni solet calamitatis. haec Graeci in singulas scholas et in singulos libros dispertiunt.*

[23] Cf. Plut. *Mor.* 599a–607d (*De exilio*, περὶ φυγῆς); Gaertner 2007, 74. Plutarch wrote this as a *consolatio* for a friend in exile, not for himself. Cf. also Claassen 1999.

[24] Cf. Asmus 1895, 16–17. Compare, for example, Julian, *Or.* 4 249d and Dio Chrys. *Or.* 13.4 on Odysseus' lament.

[25] Dio Chrys. *Or.* 16.3: ἢ γὰρ προσήκοντος θάνατος ἢ νόσος ἐκείνων τινὸς ἢ καὶ αὐτοῦ· πρὸς δὲ τούτοις ἀδοξία, χρημάτων ἀποβολή, τὸ μὴ περᾶναί τι τῶν προκειμένων ἢ παρὰ τὸ δέον, ἀσχολία, κίνδυνος, μυρία ἄλλα ὅσα συμβαίνει κατὰ τὸν βίον.

[26] Cf. *Or.* 4 241a: τῶν προσπιπτόντων δὲ καὶ τὰ λίαν ἐργώδη φασὶν οἱ σοφοὶ τῷ νοῦν ἔχοντι φέρειν οὐκ ἐλάττονα τῆς δυσκολίας τὴν εὐπάθειαν.

[27] Dio Chrys. *Or.* 16.4: οὔκουν καθ᾽ ἕκαστον αὐτῶν δεῖ ποιεῖσθαι τὴν παραμυθίαν – ἀνήνυτον γὰρ τὸ πρᾶγμα καὶ λυπηρός ἐστιν ὁ βίος - ἀλλὰ ὅλως ἐξελόντα τῆς ψυχῆς τὸ πάθος καὶ τοῦτο κρίναντα βεβαίως, ὅτι μὴ λυπητέον ἐστὶ περὶ μηδενὸς τῷ νοῦν ἔχοντι, τὸ λοιπὸν ἐλευθεριάζειν...

[28] Cic. *Ep. ad Att.* 12.14.3: *quin etiam feci quod profecto ante me nemo ut ipse me per litteras consolarer. quem librum ad te mittam, si descripserint librarii;* cf. also 12.20.2.

[29] Cf. Cic. *Ep. ad Att.* 12.20.2; *Tusc.* 1.76 and 4.63.

[30] Generally on Julian's Latin cf. Bouffartigue 1992, 108–10, 408–12, and 500–1; Cribiore 2007, 208. There are testimonia, but they remain vague and cannot replace solid textual evidence. Libanius (*Or.* 12.92–94) writes that Julian knew Latin. Ammianus (16.5.7) refers to it as 'sufficient'. Julian himself complains in *Ep.* 8 (= W 3) that his long stay in Gaul had made a barbarian of him, out of touch with Greek education.

[31] *Or.* 4 241d: ἴσον θυμὸν ἔχοντες, is citing *Iliad* 17.720, which refers to the friendship of the two Ajaxes who are standing by each other fighting side by side against the Trojans, 'one in heart as they are in name', ἴσον θυμὸν ἔχοντες ὁμώνυμοι...

[32] *Or.* 4 241c–d: ἐγώ τοι καὶ αὐτὸς πεῖραν ἐμαυτοῦ λαμβάνων ὅπως πρὸς τὴν σὴν πορείαν ἔχω τὸ καὶ ἔξω, τοσοῦτον μὲν ὠδυνήθην, ὅσον ὅτε πρῶτον τὸν ἐμαυτοῦ καθηγεμόνα κατέλιπον οἴκοι· πάντων γὰρ ἀθρόως εἰσῄει με μνήμη, τῆς τῶν πόνων κοινωνίας, ὧν ἀλλήλοις συνδιηνέγκαμεν, τῆς ἀπλάστου καὶ καθαρᾶς ἐντεύξεως, τῆς ἀδόλου καὶ δικαίας ὁμιλίας, τῆς ἐν ἅπασι τοῖς καλοῖς κοινοπραγίας, τῆς πρὸς τοὺς πονηροὺς ἰσορρόπου τε καὶ ἀμεταμελήτου προθυμίας τε καὶ ῥώμης, ὡς μετ᾽ ἀλλήλων ἔστημεν πολλάκις ἴσον θυμὸν ἔχοντες, ὁμότροποι καὶ ποθεινοὶ φίλοι.

[33] Cf. Arist. *Eth. Eud.* 7.1235a; *Eth. Nic.* 8.1157a 16; cf. Pl. *Lys.* 214c–d; Xen. *Mem.* 2.6.16–20.

[34] Cf. Diog. Laert. 7.124; Sen. *Ep.* 81.12: *solus sapiens amicus.*

[35] Cf. Iambl. *VP* 69–70, 101–2, and 229–40; for the importance of the concept of παιδεία as developed in *VP* for Julian cf. Athanassiadi-Fowden 1981, 121–60.

[36] Thus Vanderspoel 1995, 228 n. 23; rejected by Penella 2000, 18 n. 67.

[37] Iambl. *VP* 233: ἐν τῇ μελλούσῃ ἀληθινῇ ἔσεσθαι φιλίᾳ ὡς πλεῖστα δεῖν ἔφασαν εἶναι τὰ ὡρισμένα καὶ νενομισμένα…

[38] Cf. Lib. *Or.* 8.

[39] *Or.* 4 240d: οὐχ ὅσα Ἕλληνες καὶ Τρῶες ἀλλήλους ἔδρασαν, ἀλλὰ ποταποὺς εἶναι χρὴ τοὺς λόγους, οἳ τὰς μὲν ἀλγηδόνας ἀφαιρήσουσι τῶν ψυχῶν, εὐφροσύνης δὲ καὶ γαλήνης αἴτιοι καταστήσονται.

[40] Them. *Or.* 22 264c–d: τί δή ποτε, ὦ μακάριοι, ἂν μέν τις ὑμῖν διηγῆται περὶ τῶν Τρώων καὶ Ἀχαιῶν, ὡς ἐπολέμησαν πρὸς ἀλλήλους … ἐκ τούτων μὲν ἥδεσθε τῶν λόγων καὶ κατέχεσθε κηλούμενοι … τῶν δὲ ὑπὲρ φιλίας λόγων καὶ ὁπόσα ἀνθρώπους ὀνίνησιν οὐδὲν πώποτε ἐφροντίσατε…

[41] *Or.* 4 240b–c: ἀλλὰ τίς ἂν ἡμῖν ἢ τὴν Ὀρφέως μιμήσαιτο λύραν ἢ τοῖς Σειρήνων ἀντηχήσειε μέλεσιν ἢ τὸ νηπενθὲς ἐξεύροι φάρμακον; εἴτε λόγος ἦν ἐκεῖνο πλήρης Αἰγυπτίων διηγημάτων, εἴθ' ὅπερ αὐτὸς ἐποίησεν, ἐν τοῖς ἑπομένοις ἐνυφήνας τὰ Τρωικὰ πάθη, τοῦτο τῆς Ἑλένης παρ' Αἰγυπτίων μαθούσης, οὐχ ὅσα Ἕλληνες καὶ Τρῶες ἀλλήλους ἔδρασαν, ἀλλὰ ποταποὺς εἶναι χρὴ τοὺς λόγους, οἳ τὰς μὲν ἀλγηδόνας ἀφαιρήσουσι τῶν ψυχῶν, εὐφροσύνης δὲ καὶ γαλήνης αἴτιοι καταστήσονται ('But who will be our Orpheus to play the lyre, or our Sirens to sing sweet melodies, or who will administer to us the magic soothing drug nepenthe (*Od.* 4.219), whether as a discourse saturated with Egyptian recipes, or as a story which the poet himself invented, when he wove the account of the suffering of Troy into the verses that follow (i.e. *Od.* 4.242 ff.)? Yet what Helen learned from the Egyptians was not a tale of how much suffering the Greeks and Trojans inflicted on one another but how a discourse has to look that will soothe grief-stricken human souls and have the power to restore cheerfulness and calm'). For the importance of Orpheus and the Sirens in this context cf. Lamberton and Keaney 1992, 23, 34, 65–6, 123, 164 and 169.

[42] Them. *Or.* 32 357a: φύεται ἐν τοῖς φιλοσοφίας λειμῶσιν φάρμακον πολύ τε καὶ ἰσχυρόν, ὁποῖον Ὅμηρος λέγει τὴν τοῦ Διὸς θυγατέρα Ἑλένην παρὰ Πολυδάμνης πορίσασθαι τῆς Αἰγυπτίας ('There grows in the meadows of philosophy a highly effective drug, with which, Homer tells us, Helen the daughter of Zeus was furnished by the Egyptian woman Polydamne' (cf. *Odyssey* 219 ff.)).

[43] Clem. Alex. *Protr.* 2.4 (4.25–29 ed. Marcovich 1995): τὸ ᾆσμα τὸ καινόν, τὸ Λευιτικόν, 'νηπενθές τ' ἄχολόν τε, κακῶν ἐπίληθες ἁπάντων' [*Od.* 4.221]. Γλυκὺ γάρ τι καὶ ἀληθινὸν φάρμακον πειθοῦς ἐγκέκραται τῷ ᾄσματι ('This is the new song, the song of Moses, 'it soothes grief and anger and makes us forget all the bad things'. There is a sweet and truthful medicine of persuasion mixed in with this song'). For Clement's use of the verse cf. Van der Poll 2001.

[44] Cic. *Lael.* 20: *est enim amicitia nihil aliud nisi omnium divinarum humanarumque rerum cum benevolentia et caritate consensio.*

[45] *Or.* 4 241a: καὶ γάρ πως ἔοικεν ἡδονὴ καὶ λύπη τῆς αὐτῆς κορυφῆς ἐξῆφθαι καὶ παρὰ μέρος ἀλλήλαις ἀντιμεθίστασθαι. Cf. Pl. *Phd.* 60b–c: [Socrates, scratching his leg:] ὡς ἄτοπον … ἔοικε … ἡδύ· ὡς θαυμασίως … τὸ λυπηρόν, τὸ ἅμα μὲν αὐτὸ μὴ θέλειν παραγίνεσθαι τῷ ἀνθρώπῳ, ἐὰν δέ τις διώκῃ τὸ ἕτερον καὶ λαμβάνῃ, σχεδόν τι ἀναγκάζεσθαι ἀεὶ λαμβάνειν καὶ τὸ ἕτερον, ὥσπερ ἐκ μιᾶς κορυφῆς ἡμμένω δύ' ὄντε.

[46] *Or.* 4 241a–b: τῶν προσπιπτόντων δὲ καὶ τὰ λίαν ἐργώδη φασὶν οἱ σοφοὶ τῷ νοῦν ἔχοντι φέρειν οὐκ ἐλάττονα τῆς δυσκολίας τὴν εὐπάθειαν, ἐπεὶ καὶ τὴν μέλιτταν ἐκ τῆς δριμυτάτης πόας τῆς περὶ τὸν Ὑμηττὸν φυομένης γλυκεῖαν ἀνιμᾶσθαι δρόσον καὶ τοῦ μέλιτος εἶναι δημιουργόν. For the last part of the sentence compare Julian, *Or.* 3 101a.

[47] *Or.* 4 241d–242a: ...σὲ μὲν κατὰ τὸν Ἕκτορα θεὸς ἐξήγαγεν ἔξω βελῶν, ὧν οἱ συκοφάνται πολλάκις ἀφῆκαν ἐπὶ σέ, μᾶλλον δὲ εἰς ἐμέ, διὰ σοῦ τρῶσαι βουλόμενοι...

[48] *Or.* 4 243a.

[49] *Or.* 4 243b.

[50] *Or.* 4 243d: τοσούτων δὲ ὁμοῦ ἐστερημένος, τίνων ἂν εὐπορήσαιμι λόγων, οἵ με...πείσουσιν ἀτρεμεῖν καὶ φέρειν ὅσα δέδωκεν ὁ θεὸς γενναίως;

[51] Dem. *De Cor.* 97: δεῖ δὲ τοὺς ἀγαθοὺς ἄνδρας ἐγχειρεῖν μὲν ἅπασιν ἀεὶ τοῖς καλοῖς, τὴν ἀγαθὴν προβαλλομένους ἐλπίδα, φέρειν δ᾽ ὅ τι ἂν ὁ θεὸς διδῷ γενναίως.

[52] Ps.-Julian, *Ep.* 75 439d (following Wright; the letter is summarized in Bidez as *Ep.* 185): The author discusses the limited options of either him or the addressee visiting one another and concludes: ἡμεῖς δέ, ὅ τι ἂν θεὸς διδῷ γενναίως οἴσομεν. Note that this author writes θεός without the definite article. On Julian's apocryphal correspondence cf. Barnes 1978 and Van Nuffelen 2002.

[53] *Or.* 4 243d: εἰς ταὐτὸ γὰρ ἔοικεν αὐτῷ νοῶν ὁ μέγας αὐτοκράτωρ ταῦθ᾽ οὕτω νυνὶ βουλεύσασθαι.

[54] *Or.* 4 248c: ἐγὼ δὲ γεγονὼς ἐκ τῶν οἷοι νῦν βροτοί εἰσιν citing Il. 5.304: οἷοι νῦν βροτοὶ εἰσ᾽.

[55] *Or.* 4 249a–b: ἀλλ᾽ αὐτοῦ καὶ ὁ θεὸς χεῖρα ἑὴν ὑπερέσχε 'metaphrasing' *Il.* 9.420: Ζεὺς χεῖρα ἑὴν ὑπερέσχε by replacing Ζεύς with ὁ θεός.

[56] *Or.* 4 249b: καὶ Ὅμηρος ὑπὲρ Ἀχιλλέως· τῷ γὰρ ἐπὶ φρεσὶ θῆκεν 'metaphrasing' *Il.* 1.55: τῷ γὰρ ἐπὶ φρεσὶ θῆκε θεὰ λευκώλενος Ἥρη. Julian actually hides the fact that according to the *Iliad* it is Hera who puts the thought into Achilles' mind and pretends that he refers only to 'the one God', ὁ θεός.

[57] *Or.* 4 248d–249b: εἵπετό τοι καὶ Σωκράτει δαιμονία φωνὴ κωλύουσα πράττειν ὅσα μὴ χρεὼν ἦν· φησὶ δὲ καὶ Ὅμηρος ὑπὲρ Ἀχιλλέως· τῷ γὰρ ἐπὶ φρεσὶ θῆκεν, ὡς τοῦ θεοῦ καὶ τὰς ἐννοίας ἡμῶν ἐγείροντος, ὅταν ἐπιστρέψας ὁ νοῦς εἰς ἑαυτὸν αὐτῷ τε πρότερον ξυγγένηται καὶ τῷ θεῷ δι᾽ ἑαυτοῦ μόνου, κωλυόμενος ὑπ᾽ οὐδενός.

[58] *Or.* 4 249d: οὐ γὰρ ἀκοῆς ὁ νοῦς δεῖται πρὸς τὸ μαθεῖν οὐδὲ μὴν ὁ θεὸς φωνῆς πρὸς τὸ διδάξαι τὰ δέοντα, ἀλλ᾽ αἰσθήσεως ἔξω πάσης ἀπὸ τοῦ κρείττονος ἡ μετουσία γίνεται τῷ νῷ· τίνα μὲν τρόπον καὶ ὅπως, οὐ σχολὴ νῦν ἐπεξιέναι· τὸ δ᾽ ὅτι γίνεται, δῆλοι καὶ σαφεῖς οἱ μάρτυρες, οὐκ ἄδοξοί τινες οὐδ᾽ ἐν τῇ Μεγαρέων ἄξιοι τάττεσθαι μερίδι, ἀλλὰ τῶν ἀπενεγκαμένων ἐπὶ σοφίᾳ τὰ πρωτεῖα. For an explanation of the proverbial phrase 'to rank among the Megarians' cf. Wright 1913, 189 n. 3.

[59] *Or.* 4 250c: οὕνεκ᾽ ἐπητής ἐσσι καὶ ἀγχίνοος καὶ ἐχέφρων. Cf. *Od.* 13.332.

[60] *Or.* 4 251d–252b: ...καὶ εἰς Θρᾷκας ἀφίξῃ καὶ τοὺς περὶ τὴν θάλατταν ἐκείνην οἰκοῦντας Ἕλληνας, ἐν οἷς γενομένῳ μοι καὶ τραφέντι πολὺς ἐντέτηκεν ἔρως ἀνδρῶν τε καὶ χωρίων καὶ πόλεων...καὶ τοῦτο μὲν οὐχ ὡς εὐχόμενος...ἀλλ᾽ ὡς, εἰ γένοιτο, καὶ πρὸς τοῦθ᾽ ἕξων οὐκ ἀπαραμυθήτως οὐδὲ ἀψυχαγωγήτος ἐννοῶ...Κέλτοις γὰρ ἐμαυτὸν ἤδη διὰ σὲ συντάττω, ἄνδρα εἰς τοὺς πρώτους τῶν Ἑλλήνων τελοῦντα καὶ κατ᾽ εὐνομίαν καὶ κατὰ ἀρετὴν τὴν ἄλλην, καὶ ῥητορείαν ἄκρον καὶ φιλοσοφίας οὐκ ἄπειρον, ἧς Ἕλληνες μόνοι τὰ κράτιστα μεληλύθασι, λόγῳ τἀληθές, ὥσπερ οὖν πέφυκε, θηρεύσαντες, οὐκ ἀπίστοις μύθοις οὐδὲ παραδόξῳ τερατείᾳ προσέχειν ἡμᾶς, ὥσπερ οἱ πολλοὶ τῶν βαρβάρων, ἐάσαντες.

6

THE TYRANT'S MASK?
IMAGES OF GOOD AND BAD RULE IN JULIAN'S
LETTER TO THE ATHENIANS

Mark Humphries

Introduction

Julian's *Letter to the Athenians* is a remarkable document. It presents a
vigorously-worded analysis of the duties of an emperor, written from the
perspective of one who was himself emperor. That it is expressed in such
trenchant terms, rather than as a set of quiet meditations, reflects, as the
bulk of this chapter will argue, the extraordinary political circumstances of
its composition: for it offers a personal justification of why in 361 Julian
decided to defend, by force if necessary, his impromptu elevation a year
earlier by the Gallic armies to the rank of Augustus and thus effectively to
declare civil war on his cousin Constantius II.[1] The *Letter* is, therefore, in
many ways unique, since no other text survives in which a challenger for
the imperial throne sets out his case so systematically. To be sure, there
survive other texts from similar circumstances, such as Magnus Maximus'
letter to pope Siricius, composed at a time when Rome lay within the
jurisdiction of Maximus' rival Valentinian II; but that deals with an
extremely specific set of circumstances connected to the role played by the
emperor in ecclesiastical affairs.[2] There are also texts that surely reflect the
claims made by individuals making a bid for power, such as the Latin
panegyrics that mirror the shifting claims to legitimacy made by
Constantine I before and after his conflict with Maxentius.[3] Yet none of
these examples comes close to Julian's *Letter to the Athenians* in offering a
personal defence of the claims of an individual whose bid for power was
effectively a challenge to civil war. As the frequent incidence of civil war
throughout the fourth century suggests, this was a period in which claims
to imperial legitimacy were repeatedly contested.[4] In this context, Julian's
Letter is a document of unparalleled importance.

   Such considerations make it remarkable that the text has generally
received only scant attention from scholars.[5] This is not to say that it has
been completely ignored, but rather that on the whole its contents have

been read in the light of other narratives of Julian's bid for power, such as those contained in Claudius Mamertinus' *Speech of Thanks* (*gratiarum actio*) of 1st January 362, Libanius' Julianic orations, and Ammianus Marcellinus' history.[6] There are perhaps other reasons for this lack of specific attention. On the one hand, the *Letter to the Athenians* deals with a rather embarrassing episode in Julian's otherwise illustrious career, in that it effectively justifies his willingness to plunge the empire into civil war: this sits uncomfortably with the tendency of some scholars to concentrate on the more heroic aspects of Julian's career, such as his vigorous defence of the Rhine frontier as Caesar between 355 and 360 or his valiant attempt as Augustus to restore the cultural and religious traditions of Hellenism.[7] On the other hand, while the *Letter* is by no means silent on the question of religion (see below), it does not offer a programmatic exposition of his religious, philosophical and cultural views in the same manner as, for instance, his *Hymn to King Helios* or his *Hymn to the Mother of the Gods*.[8]

It is the purpose of this chapter, then, to offer a detailed analysis of the *Letter to the Athenians*, concentrating precisely on its polemical nature by examining what it reveals about competing ideals of the imperial office in the context of the breach between Julian and Constantius. It will proceed along a number of lines. First, it will consider the date of the text and the form it takes, addressing amongst other issues its treatment of Athens and of the gods. From this it is possible to deduce something of what the text was intended to achieve. The next section of the chapter seeks to explain this further by sketching the political context in which the letter was written, since this is fundamental to any consideration of its contents. Following on from this, the largest part of the chapter will be devoted to examining how, in this charged atmosphere, Julian sought to offer a justification of a course of action that might possibly be regarded as an indefensible usurpation. The discussion will highlight Julian's deployment of two interrelated arguments: first, his insistence that he had not deliberately sought imperial power, either now or in the past, and that he was instead a victim of circumstances; and, secondly, his calculated subversion of Constantius II's qualities as emperor. As will be shown, these aspects of Julian's argument serve to depict Constantius, not Julian, as the chief cause of the impending civil war, and to present Julian as a worthy recipient of political support from the *Letter*'s addressees. After examining these various dimensions of the political import of the *Letter*, a final section will stress the historical specificity of the text by comparing it briefly with Mamertinus' panegyric, delivered only a few months after Julian's *Letter*. In this way it is hoped to demonstrate that the *Letter to the Athenians* is – as Roger Blockley noted about Mamertinus' panegyric – a text which presents a picture specifically calibrated to a particular time and place, and which sheds significant light on how Julian's propaganda was evolving amid a rapidly developing political situation.

Date, audience and form

There seems little doubt that the extant *Letter to the Athenians* – or, to give it the full title it is accorded in the manuscripts, the *Letter to the Assembly [Boulē] and People [Dēmos] of the Athenians* – is identical with that which the historical sources mention Julian wrote, along with letters to the Corinthians, Spartans, and the Senate at Rome.[9] They were written as Julian entered the Balkan and Danubian provinces in the middle of summer 361, and were dispatched most probably from the city of Naissus.[10] Of these letters, that to the Athenians is the only one that survives in its entirety. A scrap survives from the *Letter to the Corinthians*, quoted by Libanius in an oration delivered to Julian at Antioch in 362/3.[11] The contents of the letter to the Senate at Rome may be gauged from Ammianus' summary of it and the reaction it provoked. It was, claimed the historian, written once Julian had given up hope of reaching any agreement with Constantius, and contained a bitter invective that charged Constantius with opprobrious actions and misdeeds (*orationem acrem et invectivam, probra quaedam in eum explanantem et vitia*); and when it was read out to the senators, they smarted at its contents and unanimously shouted out, as if Julian were himself there: 'We demand that you revere your creator' (*auctori tuo reverentiam rogamus*).[12]

The description of the contents of the letter to Rome sounds akin to the contents of the *Letter to the Athenians*. As will be seen below, there too Julian is critical of Constantius and accuses him of various acts that might be described as *probra* and *vitia*. Such similarity between letters written at the same time might be expected, but it prompts questions about the *Letter to the Athenians*, such as the extent to which it was written specifically for an Athenian audience. After all, Athens was a city with which Julian had close associations: prior to his elevation as Caesar, he had been a student there.[13] Later accounts of Julian's reign associate him with a religious revival, both in the city's temples and at the nearby sanctuary of Demeter at Eleusis.[14] Some dubious surmises have been built on this, such as that Julian was responsible for a renovation of the Parthenon.[15] It needs to be borne in mind, however, that those who report Julian's active interventions in Athenian religious life, Libanius and Eunapius of Sardis, were enthusiastic supporters of the emperor's religious programme and perhaps likely to exaggerate his impact, especially in a centre such as Athens that was pregnant with cultural capital. In fact, a measured analysis of the *Letter to the Athenians* suggests that its references to both religious matters and to Athens were, for the most part, conventional.

What, then, does the *Letter* reveal about Julian's religion? Much has been made of Julian's initial reluctance to espouse openly his disavowal of Christianity and his adherence to the old gods: only months before gathering his forces and marching against Constantius, for example, he had attended the Epiphany celebrations at Vienne (6th January 361).[16] Not the least of the significant features of the *Letter to the Athenians*, it would seem, is that here, for the first time in a public document, Julian makes his religious allegiances plain through constant invocation of the role played by the gods in his bid for power.[17] He does this in various ways. At the various crisis points in his narrative – his elevation to the rank of Caesar, and his proclamation as Augustus – Julian asserts that he had submitted himself to the will of the gods.[18] He remarks too that when he was about to take up arms against Constantius he consulted the gods and offered them sacrifice.[19] Such comments might suggest that the *Letter to the Athenians* displays unmistakably the pagan hue of Julian's regime for the first time. Yet there is a danger here of reading too much into what may in fact be conventional statements, the sort of remarks that could be made by Christian and pagan alike.[20] There is certainly nothing in the letter that amounts to a revelation of the new religious programme on which Julian was shortly to embark. It should be remembered too that while some pagans like Eunapius and Libanius could look back on Julian's reign with nostalgia, at the time of his breach with Constantius, others, like the Roman senator L. Aurelius Avianus Symmachus who participated in the embassy to Constantius following the reading of Julian's letter to Rome, were just as keen to distance themselves from him.[21] Rather than act as a clarion call to pagan supporters, then, the references to the gods serve a different purpose. Throughout the letter, he repeatedly calls on the gods as witnesses to the justice of his cause.[22] This, and not any first blush of a pagan revival, is the function of the references to the gods in the *Letter*.

The same can be said of the appearance of Athens itself in the exhortations to support Julian's cause with which the *Letter* begins and ends. Julian's opening address extols the virtues shown by the Athenians in the past,[23] but does so in a way to highlight themes relevant to Julian's predicament in 361. Great emphasis is placed on the Athenians' wisdom, justice, and adherence to the law, by which they excel other Greek states; he stresses, for instance, that the Athenians triumphed over the tyranny imposed by Sparta not through violence, but through justice.[24] There is, here, a potent implication that Julian's relationship with Constantius directly parallels that of Athens with Sparta, and that the regime of

Constantius should be regarded similarly as tyrannical. Likewise, by referring to the episode in which Aristides the Just prevailed over Themistocles through his virtuous adherence to the cause of justice,[25] Julian was likely seeking to argue that his Athenian audience would similarly adhere to the cause of justice and support him against Constantius.

The references in the *Letter* to the gods and to Athens hardly amount to a programme of religious or cultural renewal of the sort that figures such as Libanius or Eunapius were later to extol. But if they are entirely conventional, they nevertheless conform to the wider purpose of the *Letter* in that, both by appealing to the gods to bear witness to the justice of his cause and in calling on the Athenians to be mindful of their reputation for justice, Julian is staking a claim for the justice of his position in marching against Constantius. As will be seen below, the major thrust of the majority of the *Letter* is precisely to underline Julian's legitimacy, and to remove from him any of the opprobrium usually associated with usurpation. The appeals to the gods and to the Athenian past are subordinate to this theme. And yet, in one sense the insights of Eunapius and Libanius are absolutely right: both speak of Julian as combating the tyranny of Constantius,[26] and in that respect their versions chime in harmony with the respective positions of Julian and Constantius as presented in the *Letter*. In 361, however, and as the members of the Senate at Rome recognised, the emperor with the best claim to be legitimate was Constantius. Presenting him effectively as a tyrant was, therefore, a drastic move; but as will now be shown, the political atmosphere in the summer and autumn of that year was precisely one that would require drastic measures.

The political background

By the time the *Letter to the Athenians* was written in the second half of 361, Julian and his army had already advanced to the middle Danubian frontier in preparation for confrontation with Constantius II, and had secured control of strategic vantage points such as the cities of Sirmium and Naissus and the Succi Pass.[27] The letters to Athens, Corinth, Sparta, and Rome aimed to undermine Constantius' grip on Illyricum and the west so that Julian could concentrate on the looming war. Yet Julian's success was uneven. As has been seen, the letter to Rome was angrily rejected and the Senate sent an embassy to Constantius, then residing at Antioch, to pledge its devotion to the man they considered legitimate Augustus.[28] Loyalty to Constantius was demonstrated in other parts of Italy, such as Aquileia, which was seized by troops opposed to Julian.[29] On occasion, Julian's success in gaining support might have been quite accidental. Zosimus reports that when Julian first approached Sirmium, the appearance of such a large army led the locals to assume that it was Constantius who had arrived; only too late did they realise that the forces bearing down on them were being led by Julian.[30] Such episodes are indicative of the highly-charged political atmosphere in late-summer and autumn 361.

Yet even by this stage, the likelihood of civil war had been looming for some time. According to Ammianus, Julian had already been offered the title of Augustus by his victorious troops after the battle of Strasbourg in 357, although on that occasion had refused it.[31] The second offer came in 360 at Paris in response to demands from Constantius II that Julian send hefty detachments of his Gallic army to serve in the east against Persia.[32] In the event, Julian did not actively seek to defend his elevation and thus to initiate hostilities for another year, a circumstance that could be read as marking reluctance on Julian's part to embark on a civil war. This was certainly how Julian himself would present the development of events (see below). But there is every reason to suppose that his protest was disingenuous. It has been argued persuasively that Julian, far from being the unwitting pawn of a disgruntled Gallic army, was in actuality instrumental in engineering his proclamation at Paris: analysis of the strategic disposition of the Rhine armies suggests that already in 359 Julian was adopting a more defensive strategy in preparation for a coming breach with Constantius.[33]

If Julian's bid for power shows every sign of having been carefully calculated, it remained nevertheless a risky undertaking. It was likely to provoke an apprehensive reaction, particularly in the west, which had witnessed a number of usurpations in the last decade. The year 350 had seen the usurpations of Magnentius in Gaul, Nepotianus at Rome, and Vetranio on the Danube. The elevation of Vetranio as would-be emperor had been neutralised swiftly and relatively peaceably, when Constantius himself, as part of his preliminary manoeuvres against Magnentius, negotiated Vetranio's surrender and retirement into private life; but the other two instances were remembered vividly for the violence with which they had been resolved. Nepotianus had been ousted swiftly amid bloody slaughter by forces sent to Rome by Magnentius. In turn, Constantius' campaign against Magnentius was a protracted and brutal affair, with battles fought at Mursa in Pannonia in 351 and Mons Seleucus in Gaul in 353.[34] A year later, while Constantius was in northern Italy, rumours emerged of another attempted usurpation by the *magister peditum* Silvanus, although it seems clear from Ammianus' account that Silvanus was pushed to revolt by the machinations of his enemies at Constantius' court.[35] Any bid for power would likely conjure up memories of these events. It would likely also evoke, and in the east too, the more recent memory of

Constantius' condemnation of his earlier Caesar, Julian's half-brother Gallus, who had been suspected of plotting against Constantius.[36]

To embark on a course of civil war was a project fraught with peril at any time, but in 360–361 it must have seemed particularly unwise, not least because Constantius recently had shown himself ruthlessly efficient in suppressing any opposition. Consideration of such circumstances makes it easy to understand why Julian's overtures to the Roman Senate were summarily rejected, why Aquileia was seized by partisans of Constantius, and why the inhabitants of Sirmium apparently expected the imperial army arriving at their gates to be led by Constantius. In such circumstances, it would be necessary for Julian to articulate his cause persuasively if he were to garner *any* support. The *Letter to the Athenians* permits insights into the tactics Julian adopted in order to buttress his cause.

Unmasking the tyrant

The reluctant aggressor

Any argument that Julian had justice on his side required that he present a picture of his elevation to the rank of Augustus that removed from him any stain of vaulting ambition and thus accusations of usurpation. He achieves this most famously in his tendentious presentation of his acclamation at Paris, with which the main narrative of the letter ends. Here Julian argues that he never sought the position of Augustus, that he actively sought to remove himself from the clutches of the troops who wanted to elevate him, and that he only succumbed to their acclamation when he had little option but to bow to their will.[37] Their motivation is ascribed not to Julian's ambition, but to conveniently anonymous pamphlets circulating among the troops.[38] Even after their acclamation of him, Julian remarks how he sought to negotiate with Constantius in respectful terms (for example, by not using the title of Augustus that the troops had just conferred on him) in the hope of obviating an open breach with his cousin.[39] Julian stresses that he would have been content to have remained in Gaul as Constantius' imperial colleague.[40] That this did not happen, he argues, was through no fault of his own, a claim that deftly rebuts suspicions that all blame for the impending civil war should be laid at Julian's feet. On the contrary, Julian argues that it was Constantius who was pushing the empire towards civil war by refusing to negotiate with Julian at all, by making strategic preparations for conflict (for example by stockpiling supplies in the Alpine provinces), and by encouraging, and even bribing, the Rhine barbarians to attack Julian in Gaul.[41]

The account thus offered by Julian was influential: significant aspects of it can be found, for instance, in Libanius' *Oration* 18 and in the narrative of Ammianus. Equally appreciated by modern scholars is the account's essential tendentiousness. It serves to underline how Julian's presentation of events serves a serious purpose in that it makes Julian not the aggressor in this looming civil war, but rather the innocent victim of political circumstances. More importantly, within the context of the *Letter*, it marks the culmination of a particular presentation of the respective positions of Julian and Constantius throughout the narrative, which stresses time and again how Julian was an unwilling recipient of imperial honours while Constantius was relentlessly suspicious and power-hungry. These aspects warrant detailed analysis.

Julian's unwillingness to accept elevation to the rank of Augustus neatly echoes the account earlier in the letter of his proclamation as Caesar by Constantius. Here too Julian makes a show of his reluctance to accept this position, even to the extent of stating that he would have preferred death to the rank of Caesar.[42] Yet however reluctant he had been to accept the position, Julian stresses that once he was Caesar he was keen only to act as Constantius' servant, displaying in the Gallic regions Constantius' imperial robe and icon.[43] Other details of Julian's account of his early time as Caesar reinforce this image of devotion to Constantius. When, for instance, Constantius does not give Julian any active command of the Gallic troops, Julian acquiesces in the emperor's wishes;[44] later, when he does assume command of the Rhine legions, it is only at the behest of Constantius himself.[45] Julian's dutiful subservience to Constantius even after this is stressed repeatedly, for instance in his selfless bearing following his victory over the Alamanni at Strasbourg, which Julian asserts was Constantius' triumph, not his own.[46]

There is one key moment in the narrative that demands special attention: Julian's response to Constantius' demand that he send troops from Gaul to serve in the war with Persia. This is an episode of momentous significance, for it is precisely that demand which Julian asserts antagonised the Gallic soldiers to the extent that they proclaimed him Augustus. Yet in Julian's presentation, the episode is constructed in such a way as to exonerate Julian from any suspicion that he fomented the troops' anger; in other words, the account firmly blames Constantius for the breach that resulted, and for the impending civil war. First, when the demand from Constantius arrives, Julian stresses that he sought to honour it.[47] He underlines the fact that so difficult was the predicament in which this demand placed him that he even offered to resign his position as Caesar.[48] Secondly, his apparent delay in acting upon Constantius' request was itself motivated by Julian's subservience to the Augustus: he protests that he wished to await the arrival of Florentius and Lupicinus, Constantius' appointees to the positions of Praetorian Prefect and *magister equitum* in Gaul, before taking action.[49] From other sources it is apparent that there is deliberate dissimulation here: Julian omits to mention, for instance, that Florentius' and Lupicinus' delayed return to Paris was something that had been contrived by himself.[50] But that is not the image of himself that Julian aims at in his account. Rather, through actions such as his strenuous efforts to find troops to dispatch to the east, Julian displays himself as treating Constantius with greater honour than any Caesar had ever shown an Augustus.[51] If civil war threatens the empire, then it is not Julian's doing.

Other incidental details reinforce the image of Julian's subservience to Constantius, and his reluctance to take actions on his own initiative. Such initiative as Julian had shown would, he argues, surely be consonant with the wishes of the Augustus. Thus when, before being granted command of the Gallic legions, Julian did occasionally take initiative in local military affairs, he stresses that he had done so only when he noticed that something had been overlooked by Constantius' generals.[52] Similarly, when he campaigns against the Salian Franks and the Chamavi, he stresses that he does so only because Constantius ought to have known that making payments to these tribes to keep the peace was a dishonourable course of action.[53]

What we have throughout these passages is a consistent and (as the disingenuous account concerning Florentius and Lupicinus makes clear) calculated articulation of Julian's position that amounts to an elaboration on the theme of *recusatio imperii*.[54] Julian stresses that the positions first of Caesar and then of Augustus have been forced upon him. His activities in Gaul have been undertaken only at Constantius' behest. If such actions have brought him glory, then that is not a glory he has actively pursued. On the contrary, Julian stresses that his position in Gaul brought him only anxiety and danger.[55] By stressing his reluctance to accept the various positions imposed upon him, culminating with his unwillingness to accept his elevation at Paris, Julian is aiming at something quite deliberate in the context in which he was writing. For if in 361 Julian could be presented by Constantius' toadies (much as they had presented Silvanus and Gallus) as a usurper ruthlessly pursuing his ambitions for power, the central message of the *Letter to the Athenians* was to deny any such accusation.

The butcher in purple

But when the letter was written, it would have been reckless indeed if Julian had merely protested his innocence and that he was no usurper. By now civil war was inevitable and sides needed to be taken. Thus the *Letter to the Athenians* seeks to help its readers to make a momentous decision. It does so by stressing, in counterpoint to Julian as a reluctant Caesar and unwilling Augustus, an image of Constantius that impugns his qualities as emperor, casts him as bloodily power-hungry, and all but accuses him of tyranny. This is done in various ways throughout the *Letter*'s narrative, but is achieved primarily by means of drawing a deliberate contrast between the respective attitudes to power of Julian and Constantius. If Julian presented himself as someone who took on power unwillingly, no such image could be entertained about Constantius. In a number of ways, Constantius' actions are portrayed in stark contrast to those of Julian; cumulatively, they imply that it is Constantius, not Julian, who bears the hallmarks of a tyrant greedy for power. To be sure, the *Letter* holds back from articulating such an accusation in *explicit* terms; but the association of Constantius with modes of behaviour usually attributed to tyrants is *implicit* throughout.

In the first place, while Julian had power forced upon him and went to considerable lengths to stress his efforts to refuse it, Constantius is presented as someone who had actively sought power. The narrative section of the letter opens with a notice of Julian's family connections with Constantius, which is swiftly followed by an account of the murder of many of Julian's family, in which blame for the massacre is apportioned openly to Constantius.[56] Similarly, the career of Gallus is recounted in ways that represent his death as murder rather than legal execution, since Gallus, whatever his faults (and Julian makes little effort to obscure them), was never offered an opportunity to defend himself.[57] Such actions reflect the suspicious nature of Constantius and his determination to hold onto power in the face of challenges that are presented largely as the products of his paranoid imagination. Similar dangers also awaited Julian, who at numerous points alludes to the precariousness of his position because Constantius was so jealously suspicious.[58] Constantius' murders of members of Julian's family, whether in 337 or with the execution of Gallus, are re-elaborated at various points throughout the letter. They serve to emphasise that while Julian himself had never sought power, Constantius had come to the throne and had sought to hold on to power by drenching himself in the blood of his relatives.

This depiction serves to contrast Constantius and Julian in other ways too. While the murders of Julian's kin in 337 and the subsequent execution without trial of Gallus showed Constantius trampling underfoot the ties of blood and familial piety, Julian himself had only ever been dutiful and pious towards his cousin, like a father to a son. He prayed that Constantius' wife Eusebia might be delivered of a child – this in spite of the obvious fact that Constantius' acquisition of a son would have made Julian's survival even more precarious.[59]

Furthermore, the death of Gallus served to highlight another contrast. As has been noted above, Julian complains that Gallus had not received any sort of trial, but was summarily executed and so in effect murdered. Not even bandits are treated so capriciously, he remarks; he also observes that rights of defence against accusations are a feature of natural law, observed by Greeks and barbarians alike.[60] More significantly, he points out time and again how his own actions in legal matters contrast markedly with those of Constantius, who is excoriated more than once for his general lawlessness.[61] After the battle of Strasbourg, Julian does not kill the Alamannic king Chnodomar, since to have done so would have been to benefit from Chnodomar's misfortunes.[62] When Julian is compelled to take action against those agents of Constantius who were plotting against him in Gaul, he acts with due deference to the laws; indeed, Julian notes that he did not even confiscate their property, something that Constantius had done to him.[63] The implicit contrast becomes explicit at one point: Julian stresses his devotion even to the man who destroyed his family.[64] When he later remarks that 'such is the character of the laws in Constantius' empire',[65] he makes clear which one of them is exercising power in a just fashion.

Finally, in addition to his greed for power and his capricious application of the laws, Constantius emerges as a poor emperor in one other significant way: he does not act with the interests of the empire at heart. Thus he prepares to negotiate with or bribe barbarians rather than defeat them in battle.[66] Indeed, his only triumph is a vicarious one over the Rhine barbarians: it had been achieved by Julian at Strasbourg in 357, but the honour of the victory went to Constantius alone.[67] Julian professes no complaint at this, but the description serves to establish yet another tension between him and his cousin. Julian's enumeration of his military achievements as Caesar – four campaigns, three crossings of the Rhine, a thousand captives redeemed, two battles, one siege, some forty towns recovered[68] – contrasts starkly with the actions of Constantius, who prefers negotiation and bribery to war. Finally, after the proclamation at Paris, and as Julian does his best to prevent civil war, Constantius shows his true colours in dealing with the barbarians: he bribes them to attack Julian in Gaul, a misdemeanour for which, Julian claims, he has proofs.[69] Such tactics are unbecoming of an emperor. In the end, this example of Constantius' duplicity serves to explain why Julian, in spite of his best intentions, can no longer trust Constantius' fork-tongued professions of amity. Now Julian, having stated that he will not give further examples of Constantius' cruelty across the rest of the earth,[70] announces his intention to defend his position, but not for his own sake: rather he does so for all men, and especially for those in Gaul who have been so signally betrayed by Constantius.[71]

In short, if there is a tyrannical ruler in the *Letter*, it is clearly Constantius, and emphatically not Julian. It is Constantius, not Julian, who lusts for power, and does so through bloody purges of any perceived opponents. His actions fly in the face of natural law and familial piety, and he fails signally to secure the defence of the empire. In stark contrast, it is Julian who is the energetic defender of the empire and who rules according to the precepts of law and the interests of the empire's subjects; and he does all this in spite of never having wished for an imperial role and when the emperor to whom he shows nothing but devotion seeks to undermine him at every turn. In sum, the *Letter to the Athenians* leaves its readers in no doubt as to who is acting in a fashion more befitting the imperial office. It is Julian who behaves more as an emperor should; in opposition to him stands Constantius, an emperor who might be characterised, as the Gallic panegyrist Pacatus later described the usurper Magnus Maximus (383–388), as a 'butcher clad in purple' (*carnifex purpuratus*).[72] As the Roman world stood on the brink of civil war in 361, a reader persuaded by the contents of the *Letter to the Athenians* should have been left in no doubt as to which contender was more deserving of support.

The vicissitudes of propaganda

It is well known that the essential outlines of the conflict between Julian and Constantius presented in the *Letter to the Athenians* find significant reverberations in other pro-Julianic sources, notably in Libanius' orations, and above all in Ammianus' account. Other echoes may be found in a work composed and delivered within months of Julian's *Letter*, namely Claudius Mamertinus' *gratiarum actio* delivered at Constantinople on 1st January 362.[73] Some of the points made by Julian himself were made by the panegyrist also. For instance, the duplicitous dealings of Constantius with the barbarians as driving Julian to war are hinted at, as indeed is Julian's energetic defence of Gaul and the execrable character of Constantius' court, where eunuchs and sycophants hold sway and place Julian in danger.[74] It has equally been noted that Mamertinus presents certain aspects of Julian's bid for power in a different light from that offered by Julian himself. For example, the discussion of the war in Gaul is less caught up in details, depicting Julian's success there as if it had been secured through a single, mighty battle. Similarly, Mamertinus' observations on Constantius are of more studied neutrality than those offered by Julian himself. These differences, it has rightly been observed, arise from the particular circumstances in which Mamertinus was delivering his speech. On the shores of the Propontis, a specific emphasis on Gaul would not have served Julian particularly well: indeed, the geographical space evoked by Mamertinus, while it includes Gaul, is altogether broader, extending to Italy, Illyricum, Greece, and beyond.[75] Most importantly, in this context, Mamertinus makes no mention at all of that fateful night in Paris when the troops raised Julian as Augustus. The explicit contrast between the two claimants on the throne no longer served a purpose at the time Mamertinus delivered his speech. By New Year's Day 362, civil war had been forestalled by Constantius' sudden death at Mopsucrenae in Cilicia on 3rd November 361, before his and Julian's forces even met. Moreover, it was said that on his death-bed, Constantius had finally nominated Julian as his successor.[76] Hence the sharp distinction between Julian and Constantius that had been so important to the argument of the *Letter to the Athenians* was no longer useful. Now it was more politic for Julian to stress his *pietas* towards his predecessor and to seek continuities with Constantius' regime.[77] Indeed, as the gruesome show trials at Chalcedon soon demonstrated, Julian was forced to succumb to the demands of Constantius' partisans, even to the extent of acquiescing in the condemnation of individuals who had previously been supportive of him: it did Julian no credit whatsoever to allow the judges at Chalcedon to destroy Constantius' erstwhile *comes sacrarum largitionum* Ursulus, who had once ordered the *praepositus thesaurorum* in Gaul to meet all Julian's demands for money.[78] In time Julian would lament this decision, and allow Ursulus' daughter to inherit her father's fortune.[79]

Julian's agreement to the condemnation of his one-time ally is an indication of how quickly the political landscape was changing between late 361 and early 362, and how quickly Julian had to change with it. Mamertinus' panegyric similarly reflects how propaganda needed to be modulated – and moderated – to fit the new situation. In that respect, the panegyric of Mamertinus sheds interesting light on the *Letter to the Athenians* and emphasises how its message was tailored to circumstances in which civil war seemed about to envelop the empire. In those circumstances, Julian was compelled to offer an extreme justification of his views. His very life was at stake, and if he could not cultivate allies he risked the post mortem ignominy of being condemned as a nameless tyrant. That surely explains the most remarkable feature of the letter, in which Julian sought to divest himself of the accusation of tyranny and usurpation, and instead to place the mask of tyranny on the face of Constantius.

Acknowledgements
I am grateful first and foremost to Shaun Tougher and Nicholas Baker-Brian for their kind invitation to participate in the excellent Cardiff

conference, and for their editorial guidance (and exemplary patience) subsequently. Revision of the paper owes much to the comments of several participants at the conference, especially Jill Harries (who reined in my more eccentric ideas) and Hans Teitler. I am indebted too to Pilar García Ruiz, Nic Baker-Brian, and my colleague Maria Pretzler for locating works that I might otherwise have found difficult to access. None of those mentioned above bears any responsibility for the manifold shortcomings of the finished product.

Notes

[1] Julian, *Ep. ad Ath.* 287b–c, clearly anticipates war.

[2] *Coll. Avell.* 40.

[3] Rodgers 1989 is the most succinct treatment of this theme. For Constantine's shifting claims to legitimacy, see Humphries 2008.

[4] See Wardman 1984; Humphries (forthcoming b) will offer a detailed treatment of the theme.

[5] Rare examples include Labriola 1975 and 1991–1992; sadly incomplete at the time of his death was an edition and commentary (in its present condition quite rudimentary) on the *Ep. ad Ath.* by Jean Martin: Martin 2009, esp. 27–49.

[6] See Blockley 1972 on Claudius Mamertinus, and Matthews 1989, 84–100 *passim*, on Ammianus; cf. Bowersock 1978, 46–54, seeking to read the *Letter* alongside other sources, including Libanius' *Or.* 18, to produce a cogent account of events at Paris in 360. See also García Ruiz 2008a, 142–3, on links between the *Letter* and Lib. *Or.* 12.

[7] Renucci 2000 is the most explicit example, but Athanassiadi 1992 shows not entirely dissimilar tendencies.

[8] For these aspects of Julian's writings, see above all R. Smith 1995. For the *Hymn to King Helios* and the *Hymn to the Mother of the Gods* see the chapters by Andrew Smith and J. H. W. G. Liebeschuetz in this volume.

[9] Amm. Marc. 21.10.5–8 (letter to Rome); Zos. 3.10.4 (letters to Athens, Sparta, and Corinth). Mamert. 9.4, implies letters dispatched more widely across the Balkans (*cunctas Macedoniae Illyrici Peloponnessi civitates unis an binis epistulis*).

[10] Naissus is mentioned specifically in connection with the letter to Rome by Amm. Marc. 21.10.5–7; the narrative of Julian's movements in Zos. 3.10.4–11.1 implies that the letters were sent from Sirmium, but Kaegi 1975, 168, argues that Zosimus is confused here. Lib. *Or.* 18.113–115 identifies the letter as one sent during Julian's progress along the Danube, but gives no further precise detail. Julian's exact whereabouts in 361 between 6th January (when he attended Epiphany celebrations at Vienne) and 11th December (when he entered Constantinople) are uncertain: for an authoritative reconstruction, see Nixon 1991, 113–18, endorsed by Barnes 1993, 228; cf. Lieu 1989, xiii, for a slightly different chronology.

[11] Lib. *Or.* 14.29–30 = Julian, *Ep.* 20 Bidez = fr. 3 Wright.

[12] Amm. Marc. 21.10.7–8.

[13] Drinkwater 1983, 368–9.

[14] For Eleusis, see Lib. *Or.* 18.115; Eunap. *VS* 476; modern discussion in Kaldellis 2005.

[15] For discussion and rejection of this theory, see Frantz 1979.

[16] Amm. Marc. 21.2.4–5.

[17] Noted (but not discussed) by Drinkwater 1983, 355 n. 26.

[18] *Ep. ad Ath.* 275d–277a (elevation to the rank of Caesar their will), 282d, 284b–285a, and 285d (acclamation as Augustus their will); cf. 275a–b (including an appeal to the Athenian acropolis).

[19] *Ep. ad Ath.* 286d–287a.

[20] On this matter, see Humphries and Gwynn 2010.

[21] *PLRE* 1, 863–5, Symmachus 3; that he was pagan is clear from *CIL* 6.1698. His embassy to Constantius is mentioned at Amm. Marc. 21.12.24, plainly on the return leg of its journey.

[22] E.g. *Ep. ad Ath.* 280d, 284b, 285d.

[23] For Julian's attitudes to the Athenian past in the *Ep. ad Ath.*, see Bregman 1997, 355–7; and Labriola 1991–1992.

[24] *Ep. ad Ath.* 268a–269c, 270a–b.

[25] *Ep. ad Ath.* 269c–d.

[26] Eunap. *VS* 476, explicitly noting that the aim was to end Constantius' tyranny; cf. Lib. *Or.* 18.101 (distancing Julian from accusations of tyranny) and 113 (presenting Constantius, by contrast, as treacherous).

[27] Bowersock 1978, 46–65, Kaegi 1975, and esp. Drinkwater 1983, 370–83, describe the risks facing Julian in 360–361 particularly well.

[28] See n. 21 above.

[29] Amm. Marc. 21.11–12.

[30] Zos. 3.10.3.

[31] Amm. Marc. 16.12.64.

[32] See discussions at n. 27 above, together with the detailed analysis in Matthews 1989, 93–100.

[33] Drinkwater 1983, 370–1.

[34] For Constantius' campaigns against the western usurpers, see esp. Barnes 1993, 101–9. For the case of Nepotianus at Rome, see Humphries (forthcoming a).

[35] Amm. Marc. 15.5, with Hunt 1999.

[36] This much is suggested by the emphasis of Julian on Gallus' maltreatment: see n. 57 below.

[37] *Ep. ad Ath.* 284b ff.

[38] *Ep. ad Ath.* 283b.

[39] *Ep. ad Ath.* 285d–286a.

[40] *Ep. ad Ath.* 287a.

[41] *Ep. ad Ath.* 286b; cf. Lib. *Or.* 18.107, and Amm. Marc. 21.4; Heather 1999, 239, regards the story with scepticism.

[42] *Ep. ad Ath.* 275c–277a.

[43] *Ep. ad Ath.* 278a and d.

[44] *Ep. ad Ath.* 277d ff.

[45] *Ep. ad Ath.* 278d–279a.

[46] *Ep. ad Ath.* 279c–d.

[47] *Ep. ad Ath.* 280d (sends troops to Constantius); 282d–284a (Julian seeking ways to agree to Constantius' demand for troops in 360).

[48] *Ep. ad Ath.* 283a.

[49] *Ep. ad Ath.* 282d–283a.

[50] Drinkwater 1983, 378–9.

[51] *Ep. ad Ath.* 281a.

[52] *Ep. ad Ath.* 278c.

[53] *Ep. ad Ath.* 280a–b.

[54] The best treatment remains Béranger 1948.

[55] E.g. at *Ep. ad Ath.* 273c, 274d–275a, 277c, 278b.

[56] *Ep. ad Ath.* 270c–d, 271b, 274d.

[57] *Ep. ad Ath.* 271a–b, 272d.

[58] See the instances cited at n. 55 above.

[59] Julian's piety towards Constantius: *Ep. ad Ath.* 280d (like a son to a father); 275c–d (praying for Eusebia's child); cf. Drinkwater 1983, 357–8, for the likely implications for Julian of Constantius and Eusebia producing an heir.

[60] *Ep. ad Ath.* 272b (even for bandits); 272c (even among barbarians).

[61] *Ep. ad Ath.* 281b (general lawlessness of Constantius' regime); 286d (Constantius' worldwide cruelty).

[62] *Ep. ad Ath.* 279c–d.

[63] *Ep. ad Ath.* 281a–b (Julian's law-abiding defence of Constantius' partisans; cf. 273b, confiscation of Julian's property by Constantius).

[64] *Ep. ad Ath.* 281b.

[65] *Ep. ad Ath.* 281b–c.

[66] *Ep. ad Ath.* 279d, 280a–b.

[67] *Ep. ad Ath.* 279d.

[68] *Ep. ad Ath.* 280c–d.

[69] *Ep. ad Ath.* 286a.

[70] *Ep. ad Ath.* 286d.

[71] *Ep. ad Ath.* 287a.

[72] Mamert. 24.1. For the stereotypical depiction of tyrants, see esp. Barnes 1996.

[73] The most perceptive analysis remains Blockley 1972. Important analyses and commentaries also in Lieu 1989, 3–38; Nixon and Rodgers 1994, 386–436.

[74] Mamert. 6.1 (Constantius and the barbarians), 4.3 (Julian's defence of Gaul), 4.4–7 (Constantius' court). On the association of Constantius' court with eunuchs see also Tougher 1999, esp. 68–71.

[75] Discussion of these aspects in Blockley 1972, 446–9.

[76] Amm. Marc. 21.15.3 and 5, and 22.2.1, 3 and 5. On matters of political legitimacy after Constantius' death and its representation by Mamertinus and Libanius, see García Ruiz 2008, 142–50, esp. 142–4.

[77] The historical contingency is neatly elucidated in García Ruiz 2008a, *passim.*

[78] Amm. Marc. 22.3.7–9.

[79] Lib. *Or.* 18.152.

7

JULIAN'S *LETTER TO THEMISTIUS* – AND THEMISTIUS' RESPONSE?

John W. Watt

In seeking to understand Julian as both emperor and author, his letter to Themistius[1] is of particular interest, precisely since its principal concern is the relationship between political activity and philosophy. It is clearly a response to a previous letter, now lost, from Themistius to Julian, in which Themistius apparently acknowledged Julian's new position and expressed hopes for his success in it. Opinions are divided as to whether the occasion was Julian's appointment as Caesar in 355 or sole Augustus in 361,[2] but what is not in doubt is that Julian's letter touches on a fundamental issue in late antique philosophy and represents a sharp response to Themistius' exhortations in that preceding letter. It is not merely, as he says at the outset, that he fears falling short of the high hopes Themistius has expressed to him on his accession to power, but that the very nature of the exhortation has discouraged rather than encouraged him to live the active political life commended by Themistius. Later on he emphasises the point of his nervousness, expresses his desire to clarify the assertions in Themistius' letter which puzzle him, and proclaims his wish to be more precisely informed by Themistius about these questions. This can certainly be interpreted as an attempt on Julian's part to reach a working compromise with Themistius over the issues which divided them, a compromise based on their common allegiance to a Hellenism founded on the thought of Plato and Aristotle.[3]

Given the rather confident manner in which Julian expresses some views which are clearly at odds with Themistius' grand conception of kingship, the letter has also been interpreted as a sharp rebuttal of Themistius' views, a rebuttal which effectively ended their relations and left Themistius with no grounds to continue the debate.[4] If in fact Themistius did respond to this letter, such a radical reading of Julian's letter becomes rather questionable; at any rate it would not have been the way Themistius read it. Whether such a response was ever made is disputed, but on the basis of an extant Arabic text it cannot be ruled out, and has in fact been supported by a number of scholars.[5] Given these diametrically opposed readings of the letter, it may be of value to consider it as a challenge to Themistius,[6] a sharp challenge but not a terminal rebuttal, in which Julian calls on him to justify (if he can) his expectations for Julian's rule on the basis of what they might be able to agree, rather than on the basis of Themistius' theocratic conceptions of kingship which Julian finds himself unable to share.[7] The central point of agreement would be that the writings of Plato and Aristotle furnish the basis for discussion,[8] but what Julian contests is that these sages recommended philosophers to enter the public sphere, and that, in the public sphere as it now is, events are or can be governed by semi-divine philosopher-kings. Contemporary interpretations of the letter diverge over whether indeed Julian intended to close off the argument and in requesting assistance from the philosophers by all means in their power[9] was merely acting with courtesy,[10] or whether he was open to a response from Themistius, and may indeed have received one.

Julian's preference for the contemplative life of a philosopher over the active one of a ruler is a dominant thread running through the whole letter. Shivering at the thought of comparison with Alexander the Great or Marcus Aurelius, his pleasurable recollection of the Attic way of living and his love of this life of leisure is shattered by Themistius' exhortation to put away all thought of leisure[11] and exchange the philosophy of the portico for the open air.[12] This fearsome requirement from a friend is comparable to a navigator struggling to make his way safely through the Bosphorus now being required to set out on the Aegaean and Ionian seas and the Ocean,[13] or a man accustomed to take moderate exercise in his gymnasium at home now being catapulted into a competition in the Olympic stadium.[14] This, of course, was the *idée fixe* of Themistius, the obligation of philosophers to come out of their secluded study rooms and bring their influence to bear on the life of the state. For Themistius the true philosopher was the one who put his theoretical knowledge at the service of the state, and the supreme philosopher was the philosopher-king. But Julian has a different understanding of the role of the philosopher and the way he can benefit humanity. For him, Socrates ranks above Alexander in the benefit he brought to humanity, but Socrates was no ruler, and neither was Aristotle, who brought inestimable benefit to mankind especially by his 'theological treatise' (presumably *Metaphysics Lambda*). Military success is due to courage and fortune, but the greater glory of knowledge of God can only be obtained (on the principle of like knowing like) by him who becomes divine.[15] Neither were the other philosophers, to whom Themistius refers in support of his ideas, statesmen – Areius, Nicolaus, Thrasyllus, and Musonius – while Themistius himself is no general or public orator. But as a teacher of philosophy he is, according to Julian, more effective in making men act virtuously than the statesmen who urge them to do so by commands.[16]

Themistius was therefore mistaken, so Julian contends, in railing against Epicurus whose advice, praising leisure and discussions during walks, was to live in obscurity. No doubt Epicurus pressed the case too far, but it is nevertheless questionable whether someone lacking the appropriate natural aptitude should be forced into taking part in public life, as both Socrates and Glaucon realised. Furthermore, success in public life is determined not by virtue or wisdom, but by Fortune.[17] Therefore, as Plato in the *Laws* made clear, no ordinary man can provide perfect rule, but only one whose conduct is divine, as in the days of Kronos the God who, being philanthropic, set over men the higher race of daemons. Since so much is expected of a king, are not the advice of Epicurus, the gardens of Athens, and the little house of Socrates preferable to the splendour now around him as a gift of Fortune?[18]

In turning the theocratic passages of Plato against Themistius' beloved concept of the philosopher-king, Julian seems to be throwing down a gauntlet, having already declared that by nature there is nothing special about himself, who has merely fallen in love with philosophy.[19] But the challenge to Themistius, the great Aristotle-interpreter of his day, becomes even bolder when Julian cites Aristotle against him – asserting that far from 'bringing owls to the Athenians' he is merely showing the Aristotelian master that he does not entirely neglect Aristotle.[20] Themistius in his letter had cited Aristotle for his case, referring to his definition of happiness as acting well.[21] But if every living thing desires happiness, in the opinion of Julian only according to the Stoic definition of happiness could statesmen such as Cato or Dion of Sicily be considered to have been fortunate and happy.[22] And when, in the *Politics*, Aristotle speaks of 'correctly using the word "act" of the architects of public actions by virtue of their intelligence', he is speaking of lawgivers and political philosophers. They give counsel and instruction to those who do the work, but do not do it themselves. It is not Aristotle but Themistius who says that they are kings.[23]

The other thread running through the letter is Julian's rejection of the Hellenistic notion so enthusiastically espoused by Themistius (and many of his Christian contemporaries) that the king, being divinely appointed, was not only a perfect philosopher, but also participated in the divine virtues, especially the divine love of mankind, *philanthrōpia*, and far from being under law was himself the animate law (*nomos empsychos*).[24] Themistius' voice can be clearly heard in the statement reported by Julian that he has been placed, according to Themistius, in the place occupied of old by Heracles and Dionysus, who were at once both philosophers and kings.[25] Julian, however, was aware that by nature there was nothing special about himself, who had merely fallen in love with philosophy and, much as he loved it, had never attained to it.[26] Plato had shown that a ruler, although human by nature, had in his conduct to be divine and totally expel from his soul what is mortal and brutish, except what is necessary for the survival of his body.[27] In line with this, Aristotle criticised hereditary monarchy, as it required of a good king a virtue greater than that belonging to human nature, obliging him to reject his children as successors if they are no better than anyone else. One who rules as guardian of the laws is not called a king by Aristotle, and absolute monarchy, governance by the king's own will, is thought by some to be contrary to nature. The rule of reason is therefore that of God and the laws, not that of man, whose nature includes an element of the wild animal. Appetite (*epithumia*) is such, and anger (*thumos*), which perverts even the best men, but law is reason exempt from desire (*orexis*), and political affairs should be entrusted to it alone.[28] These views of Aristotle are in perfect harmony with Plato, who likewise asserted the need for the moral superiority of the governor to the governed – a thing not easy to find among men – and the need for the lawgiver to purify his mind and soul before framing the laws.[29]

One has to feel some sympathy for Themistius on receiving all this. Despite any previous contacts and any letters that had passed between them,[30] it would appear that Themistius had assumed that Julian would naturally accept the main tenets of his teaching. Julian, however, had not only disputed the lessons Themistius drew from Plato, but even had the effrontery to quote Aristotle against him. 'I want to make clear in your letter the points of difficulty for me', he wrote, 'for I desire to learn more clearly about them'.[31] It is reasonable to suspect that following this broadside against him, Themistius did not think it useful to make a frontal counter attack against Julian and present once again a full account of his views. To judge by all his later, post-Julianic orations, Themistius did not change his mind at all. In an oration defending his acceptance of the Prefecture of Constantinople, for example, he effectively gave an answer to Julian's 'presumptuous' effort to trip him up with Aristotle on the matter of human happiness. This, said Themistius, involves the virtuous action of the soul in the prevailing circumstances; we philosophise not to know, but as far as possible to achieve.[32] And the grand themes of Themistius – the public duty of philosophy, the philanthropic philosopher-king, the king as the animate law – all appear again in the orations after Julian's death, just as they did during the reign of his predecessor. But if Themistius did not want to let on to Julian what he really thought of his views, that does not necessarily mean that he did not want to respond to a challenge thrown down to him. No response at all might have implied an admission of defeat, and whatever their differences, they both shared a love of philosophy and Hellenism. What he needed to do, therefore, was to make the argument from a position 'further back in the rear' that would be acceptable to Julian. Granted that Julian could not be persuaded of certain things, Themistius might still be able to offer him, as he had requested, a philosopher's encouragement to take up public life by falling back on those concepts which they both shared.

There is no response of Themistius preserved in Greek, but two Arabic manuscripts are extant containing a 'Letter (*risāla*) of Themistius the philosopher to the emperor Julian, on government and the administration of the empire', or (in the other manuscript) a 'Letter of Themistius, minister of the emperor Julian, on government, translated by Ibn Zurʿa from Syriac'.[33] The text is very similar in the two manuscripts, and the first of those mentioned above records in the subscription that it was translated by Abū ʿUthmān Saʿīd Ibn Yaʿqūb al-Dimashqī, without specifying the language of the text from which it was derived. Al-Dimashqī belongs to the early tenth century, Ibn Zurʿa to the later part of it. Given the similarity of the two texts it is likely that al-Dimashqī translated it from an earlier Syriac version, and Ibn Zurʿa subsequently revised his translation making use of the same, but now lost, Syriac. Since the fundamental study of Jeanne Croissant in 1930,[34] a good case has existed for seeing in this text the response of Themistius to Julian's letter, or more likely, an epitome or modified (or deformed) version of that response, possibly shorn of its epistolary form and also perhaps of some of the classical and literary allusions which one might have expected Themistius to include. Although Croissant's defence of the authenticity of the *risāla* has been accepted by some scholars, the identity of both author and addressee has been challenged. Dagron has supposed it reasonable to believe that Syriac and Arabic traditions, knowing Themistius above all for his commentaries on Aristotle and aware that he was a contemporary of Julian, have associated the two with this text.[35] Such a hypothesis cannot be disproved, but is rather improbable. This is no paraphrase of Aristotle, and although Themistius was indeed quite well known in the Near East, his reputation was hardly so great that his name is likely to have been casually associated with a work such as this. There is in fact a clear example of the reverse process, the dissociation of his name from a work undeniably his. An Arabic paraphrase of a passage from his oration *On Friendship* (*Or.* 22), but clearly derived from the extant Syriac version rather than the Greek, appears in the chapter on friendship in Miskawayh's treatise on ethics,

Tahdhīb al-akhlāq, but in Miskawayh it is attributed not to Themistius but to Socrates.[36] Shahid, in the introduction to his edition of the *risāla*, believes that it was written by Themistius, but during the reign of Theodosius I. His grounds, however, are rather weak, and it is only if addressed to Julian, whose 'reactionary ideas of kingship'[37] were in contrast to those of all other emperors of Themistius' time and to those of Themistius himself, that the *risāla*, if addressed to an emperor at all, can be credibly attributed to Themistius. Daly's objections presuppose that Themistius would have given a full account of his own views, rather than, as Brauch suggests, signalling in this response 'his willingness to reach an accommodation with the emperor'.[38] Along the lines of Brauch, the *risāla* might well be interpreted as Themistius' response to Julian's letter, endeavouring to stake out a position he has reason to believe Julian will accept and thus provide some of the assistance which he had requested 'from you philosophers by all means in your power'.[39] Unlike Themistius' previous letter, however, this one, to judge from the Arabic, while intended to encourage Julian in his public life, is not in the form of a *protrepticus*, but in that of a short treatise of political philosophy.[40] As for the reliability of the Arabic text, while it is true that Syriac and Arabic translators frequently modified – whether by intention or incomprehension – Greek texts which they rendered, these modifications are rarely so severe as to obscure completely the import of the original.

In his letter Julian had effectively closed off Themistius' natural lines of response. There was no point turning to Plato's injunction that philosophers should become kings[41] when Julian had already averred that as regards philosophy he had only fallen in love with it, and the fates had rendered that love ineffectual by removing him from the contemplative life proper to it;[42] or in extolling the divine character of kingship when Julian had already asserted that by nature there was nothing remarkable about himself and doubted, following the example of Socrates and Glaucon, the rightness of forcing into the life of statesmanship any who were reluctant and conscious of their deficiencies.[43] Themistius had to find in Julian's letter some common ground from which to launch his response. He found it in the Platonic and Aristotelian psychology or anthropology cited by Julian with its linkage to government.[44] Since Julian did not wish 'to bring owls to the Athenians', Themistius could put him right on the proper interpretation of this point – without, of course, explicitly saying so. Julian had noted Aristotle's view that the rule of reason is that of God and the laws, not man, for appetite and anger pervert even the best men, and law is reason exempt from desire. But according to Themistius, if he is indeed the author of the *risāla*, that does not in practice exclude the rule of an individual man in whom the rational faculty is in full control and who therefore 'becomes divine'. Most significantly, Julian had referred to the myth of Kronos in Plato's *Laws*, at first accepting the allegorical interpretation as referring to a mortal, human by nature but divine by conduct, but later using the myth while abandoning or forgetting the interpretation and arguing that ruling is 'beyond a man' and requires 'a more divine nature'.[45] Themistius saw the inconsistency and exploited the opening. The 'natural' divinity of rulers was ancient myth, not truth; it merely resembled (259a *empherōs*) it. As Julian had at first in effect indicated, it was Plato himself who used the myth to assert that a human ruler could be divine in his conduct and totally expel from his soul what is mortal and brutish, except what is necessary for the survival of his body. But that is exactly the core of the *risāla*'s argument.

The *risāla* thus falls into two parts: an exposition of human psychology and society, followed by an account of the virtues of the most excellent king.[46] In the background, of course, is the close parallel in Plato's thought between the state (composed of elite philosopher-rulers and the ruled multitude) and the soul (composed of ruling reason and the ruled multitude of irrational passions and desires).[47] It begins with the announcement that God created man the most perfect of animals and placed in him three faculties: that of speech, reason or discernment; the animal faculty; and the nutritional, appetitive or vegetable faculty. The first is unique to man, the second shared with animals, and the third shared also with plants. This is in conformity with the psychology of the authentic orations of Themistius, where the human soul is partitioned into *logos*, *thumos* (life, passion, anger), and *epithumia* (appetition). The rational faculty or *logos* enables man to be virtuous and pious and excel all other animals on earth. If he is not governed by the rational faculty and he abandons himself to bodily appetites and pleasures, his life is that of the animals, but if the rational faculty does rule and he abandons bodily pleasures, he becomes divine (*muta'allih, theios*) and lives a life proper to man and pleasing to God.[48] Since man is composed of soul and body, God gave him appetites to fulfil the necessities of nourishment and reproduction, but the rational is designed to be the governing faculty in man, and the man in a praiseworthy condition is the man who by the rule of reason in his soul is not driven by pleasures and is angered only when anger (*ghaḍab, thumos*) is desirable or necessary.[49] The doctrine here is that of *metriopatheia*, moderation of the emotions, to which Themistius devoted an oration in which he claimed that all philosophers 'ascribe to [the doctrine] in practice, even though it is only the adherents of the Lyceum who assent to it in theory';[50] but what the *risāla* does not mention, unlike the orations, is that such a man is a philosopher.

Since man is composed of body and soul, he has various material and intellectual needs,[51] and since a single man cannot provide all of them by himself, men congregate in societies and build cities, for God created man disposed to community life and established for him laws and judges.[52] Thus man is exposed to evil from himself, from his fellow citizens, or from another city.[53] Against the evil which comes from himself, that is from the rule of the appetitive faculty associated with his body, man has the defence of his rational soul;[54] against the evil from his fellow citizens the defence of the laws;[55] against the evil from another city the defence works of his own city and the resort to war.[56] This shows what constitutes the excellence of rulers, why men are necessarily led to govern, and why it is the best of them who must rule: he who orders or defends something must demonstrate that he can do it in himself (in his soul) before he can perform it on others.[57] Because a plurality of heads corrupts government and produces division, it is necessary for a single man to rule, whether over a city, great cities, a country, great countries, or most of the world.[58] Only he who can govern his family and himself can govern the citizenry. He must be the best of the people (*afḍal ahl*) and a benevolent father (*wālid shafīq*) to them, combining all the virtues in himself, something which not every man is able to do.[59]

The following account, made 'in obedience to the command of the king', of the virtues necessary for the ruler if the people are to live in concord, picks up on the 'internal' (psychological) and 'external' (administrative) features of this philosophical justification of kingship.[60] The 'internal' include temperance, justice, generosity, and indifference to luxury[61] as well as insight into the judicious employment of men.[62] The 'external' include correct administration and selection of the army, preservation of frontiers, and care of the built environment.[63] Importantly, as they certainly would be for Themistius, they also include his support of the theoretical, manual, and mixed arts. For the first of these he mentions philosophy, rhetoric, grammar, and eloquence, and for the third medicine and music.[64] The ruler must leave to his successor a realm more prosperous than that he received,[65] but his son is not designated as his successor.

The author thus eschewed all explicit mention of the philosopher-king and the divine origin of kingship. In the *risāla* the virtues of the king do not include *philanthrōpia*, the divine virtue par excellence, and the king is not above the law or portrayed as the animate law. It is this absence of these characteristic themes of Themistius, interpreted by defenders of the *risāla*'s authenticity as an accommodation to Julian's ideas, which gives most weight to the sceptics' counter-argument that such an interpretation is almost entirely negative.[66] But aside from the questionable dismissal of the

Arabic manuscript evidence, the *risāla* can well be read as an astute response to Julian by Themistius, in contrast to his earlier *protrepticus* a more subtle exhortation to fulfil his kingly role in the form of a short philosophical treatise. By basing the treatise on the Platonic and Aristotelian psychology quoted at him by Julian, Themistius not only endeavoured to convince him of the necessity of kingship, but also that, contrary to Julian's view, the desirability of the kingship of the best man who becomes divine through rational governance of the passions is indeed the proper interpretation of both philosophers' writings. The superiority of the king over his subjects is not presented, therefore, as due to his divine origin, but to his moral excellence in virtue of the rule of reason in his soul. No doubt Themistius would have furthermore loved to say that he in whom reason reigns supreme is a philosopher, and that a philosopher thus not only can but also should exchange the philosophy of the portico for the open air. Having already said it once, however, in his previous letter and been rebuffed, he was wise enough not to chance his luck again. But having told Julian that only the rule of reason in his soul qualifies a man to rule over others, the implication is surely that only the philosopher, the philosopher according to Themistius' conception, is fit to rule, and that as a lover of philosophy Julian fulfils that requirement, even if his misconception concerning the public duty of a philosopher obliges Themistius not to make that misconception explicit. We do not know, if the *risāla* is indeed from Themistius, whether or not it did in fact 'encourage' Julian in his political life, but if his later behaviour was influenced by regarding himself as in some way divinised, as an adopted son of Helios and Athena,[67] then maybe it was Themistius who after all got the better of this verbal joust.

Whether or not the two of them reached a compromise which enabled Themistius to hold public office during Julian's reign continues to be disputed, and we cannot know whether this *risāla* played any part in encouraging Julian, despite his professed attachment to 'the philosophy of the portico', to assume the role of a ruler. However, after Julian's death the theocratic conception of kingship became firmly re-established, and Themistius' real views were given full expression again in the orations delivered during the reigns of subsequent emperors. Julian's re-assertion of a more classical Hellenic-Roman royal ideology would therefore appear to be, like his re-assertion of pagan religion, a fleeting episode of little or no significance in the longer march of events. Nearly two hundred years later, however, quite against the grain of prevailing contemporary thought, a rejection of the theocratic royal ideology reminiscent of Julian's more sceptical opinions found expression in a place which he himself would hardly have found congenial, namely, the theological-philosophical commentary on the creation story in the book of *Genesis* by John Philoponus, *De Opificio Mundi*.[68] Against the view he attributed to Theodore of Mopsuestia, that those who bear the image of God are judges and kings and on this account may even be called gods, Philoponus maintained that the 'image of God' is present in all men, and that mankind was given kingship by virtue of *logos* and *epinoiai* over the animal realm, within which also kingship such as the king bee exists by nature, but that human government exists only by convention (*thesis*) and the will of men. Most men are not kings, and kingship is not a natural form of government, and frequently, indeed, neither right nor rational.[69] If the views of Julian and Libanius are the clearest antecedents we know for these ideas,[70] neither of them seems a likely source for Philoponus' thinking.[71] As an Alexandrian philosopher of the school of Ammonius, he was, however, very familiar with the Aristotelian commentaries of Themistius, and made extensive use of them.[72] He would not have been in sympathy with the Themistius of the orations, but he might have had more time for the Themistius (or pseudo-Themistius) of this little treatise of 'political philosophy'. In claiming that kingship is frequently neither right nor rational, Philoponus' criticism goes well beyond the *risāla*, which maintained that monarchy was necessary to avoid dissension, and kingship and *logos* were inextricably linked. But what is clear in the *risāla* is something Philoponus believed also, namely, that the nature of the emperor is not divine in a way that is impossible for any other man.[73] It is of course no more than a speculation that Philoponus might have read Themistius' *risāla* as well as his Aristotelian paraphrases. But it would be a nice irony if, through the mediation of Themistius, the tolerant pagan philosopher whose memory remained in good repute among generations of later Christians (but not pagans),[74] the criticism of theocratic kingship by the imperial lover of 'portico philosophy' who attempted to obliterate Christianity as a cultural force found an appreciative response with the Christian 'portico philosopher' who mounted the most serious attack on paganism in the last great 'portico' of philosophy in antiquity.

Notes

[1] For text, translation and commentary, cf. Rochefort 1963; Prato and Fornaro 1984; Fontaine, Prato and Marcone 1987.

[2] For the former, cf., e.g., Bradbury 1987; Bouffartigue 2006, 120–7. For the latter, cf., e.g., Criscuolo 1983, 91. A compromise position in Barnes and Vanderspoel 1981, 187–9, cautiously commended by Brauch 1993, 83–5 and n. 18.

[3] Brauch 1993, 85–8.

[4] Bouffartigue 2006, 127–8, 136–7.

[5] In addition to Brauch 1993, 88–97, see Croissant 1930; Dvornik 1955 and 1966, 666–9.

[6] A 'challenge' is how Bradbury 1987, 242, characterises Julian's stance.

[7] Whether or not this was a challenge to a teacher from a former student is disputed; against is Bouffartigue 1992, 22, in favour Smith 1995, 27–9, who nevertheless 'suspect(s) that Themistius' importance as an intellectual influence on Julian was marginal from an early stage'.

[8] On the importance of Plato and Aristotle to Julian, cf. Bouffartigue 1992, 170–214, especially 192 (on the citing of Plato's *Laws*) and 198–200 (on the citing of Aristotle's *Politics*).

[9] *Ep. ad Them.* 266d.

[10] Bouffartigue 2006, 137.

[11] *Ep. ad Them.* 253b–254a.

[12] *Ep. ad Them.* 262d.

[13] *Ep. ad Them.* 254c–255b.

[14] *Ep. ad Them.* 263a.

[15] *Ep. ad Them.* 264b–265b.

[16] *Ep. ad Them.* 265b–266c. This assertion of Julian would have been all the more pointed if, following his reference to Aristotle's 'theological treatise', Julian had intended an allusion to the fact that Themistius wrote a paraphrase of *Metaphysics Lambda* (preserved fully only in Hebrew and partially in Arabic); cf. Brague 1999.

[17] *Ep. ad Them.* 255b–256a.

[18] *Ep. ad Them.* 257d–259b. Cf. Bouffartigue 1992, 192.

[19] *Ep. ad Them.* 254b.

[20] *Ep. ad Them.* 260c–261d.

[21] *Ep. ad Them.* 263c, citing Arist. *Pol.* 7.3.1325b. Elsewhere in Aristotle, happiness is only to be found in the contemplative life: *Eth. Nic.* 10.7.7–8, as also in the complete text of *Politics* 1325b. Cf. Bouffartigue 1992, 198–202, who draws the conclusion that at the time of writing Julian did not have available the text of (this chapter of) the *Politics*, but only what stood in Themistius' letter to him.

[22] *Ep. ad Them.* 256a–c.

[23] *Ep. ad Them.* 263c–264a.

[24] Cf. in general Leppin and Portmann 1998, 23–6, Renucci 2000, 420–34. According to Tantillo 1997, 398–404 (who adopts the 'compromise' position on dating, see above n. 2), Themistius' concept of the animate law existed only *in nuce* at the time of his letter to Julian.

[25] *Ep. ad Them.* 253c–254a.

[26] *Ep. ad Them.* 254b, and 266c–d. Cf. Bouffartigue 1992, 494–5.

[27] *Ep. ad Them.* 258d–259b.

[28] *Ep. ad Them.* 260c–261d. Cf. Arist. *Pol.* 3.15.1286b 22–27; 3.16.1287a 8–13 and 28–32.

[29] *Ep. ad Them.* 261d–262d.

[30] Cf. Bradbury 1987, 247–50.

[31] *Ep. ad Them.* 263b–c.

[32] Them. *Or.* 34.448, 22–6 (ed. and trans. Schneider 1966, 62–3, and commentary 106).

[33] Editions: Shahid 1974 (with Latin version), and Salim 1970 (text only). There is

a summary in French of the contents of the work by Bouyges 1924. Cf. Schamp, Todd and Watt forthcoming. In what follows, citations from the *risāla* are according to the paragraph number of Bouyges, followed by the page and line numbers of the edition of Shahid.

[34] Croissant 1930.

[35] Dagron 1968, 222–4.

[36] Cf. Rosenthal 1940, 402–5.

[37] The phrase is that of Dvornik 1955 and 1966.

[38] Daly 1980, 9; Brauch 1993, 92.

[39] *Ep. ad Them.* 266d.

[40] Vanderspoel 1995, 115, 127–34, 244–9, held that the emperor envisioned in the *risāla* was indeed Julian, and that its Greek original was the panegyric of Themistius in honour of Julian admired by Libanius (*Epp.* 818 and 1430), or an epitome of that panegyric. There is a panegyrical section in the *risāla*, 16, 102.6–104.9, but the work as a whole is more like a treatise than a panegyric.

[41] Pl. *Resp.* 5, 473c–d.

[42] *Ep. ad Them.* 254b.

[43] *Ep. ad Them.* 255c–d.

[44] *Ep. ad Them.* 260c–262d.

[45] *Ep. ad Them.* 259a–b, and 260c–d; Pl. *Leg.* 4, 713a–714b. Cf. Bouffartigue 2006, 130.

[46] Cf. Watt 2004, 135–8.

[47] Pl. *Resp.* 4, 435a–436a; Pl. *Leg.* 3, 689a–c.

[48] *Risāla* 1, 82.2 – 2, 84.15.

[49] *Risāla* 8, 92.2–94.3.

[50] Them. *Or.* 32, esp. 358a, 359b–360c. Cf. Them. *Or.* 34, 445.10–446.8. Cf. Croissant 1930, 9, 11–12.

[51] *Risāla* 4, 88.3–90.2

[52] *Risāla* 5, 90.2 – 6, 90.13.

[53] *Risāla* 7, 90.14–92.2.

[54] *Risāla* 9, 94.4–96.6.

[55] *Risāla* 10, 96.7–10.

[56] *Risāla* 11, 96.10–13.

[57] *Risāla* 12, 96.13–98.2.

[58] *Risāla* 13, 98.3–11.

[59] *Risāla* 14, 100.1 – 15, 100.10.

[60] *Risāla* 17, 104.10 – 18, 106.8.

[61] *Risāla* 19, 106.8 – 20, 108.7. Cf. Pl. *Resp.* 6, 485a–487a.

[62] *Risāla* 21, 108.8 – 22, 110.10.

[63] *Risāla* 23, 110.11 – 24, 114.3; 26, 116.11–118.2.

[64] *Risāla* 25, 114.4–116.11.

[65] *Risāla* 27, 118.3–6.

[66] Cf. Dagron 1968, 223: 'hypothèse ingénieuse...mais une interprétation presque entièrement négative...est très insuffisante pour prouver que Julien fut bien le destinataire de l'œuvre.'

[67] *Against Heraclius the Cynic* (*Or.* 7) 229c–234c. Cf. Schofield 2005, 665, who notes that 'Julian's assumption that a real king is not human (or not just human) but a divine

spirit seems to have remained an element in his thinking'. Themistius might well have felt that subsequently seeing Julian acting as a 'real king' (or as Schofield puts it, 'a fanatical autocrat') he had won the argument – albeit without seeing in Julian the religious tolerance and *philanthrōpia* supposed to characterise the philosopher-king and which Themistius praised in his successor (cf. *Or.* 5 67b–70a).

[68] We owe this observation to Dvornik 1966, 711–12.

[69] *De Opificio Mundi* 6, 16. The anonymous dialogue *On Political Science* from the reign of Justinian also runs against the grain of most thought of the time in subjecting the monarch to various limitations, not least law. Cf. Dvornik 1966, 707–11; O'Meara 2003, 178–82; Angelov 2004, 508–11.

[70] Dvornik 1966, 711.

[71] Admittedly Julian is remembered appreciatively by Ammonius; cf. Smith 1995, 218 and n. 7. But it is unlikely that the Christian Philoponus would have had the same appreciation of Julian as the pagan Ammonius.

[72] He may have silently drawn on Themistius many times, for example in commenting on the *Physics*; cf. Vitelli 1888, 992 s.v. Themistius; Sorabji 1990, 17.

[73] The *risāla* recognises three categories of men: those, the best, who do the good by themselves; those who do it under pressure from another; and those who refuse to do it and must be restrained by punishment. Men may be happy under the rule of a man whose nature is accepting of all the virtues necessary for governance (15, 100.10 – 16, 102.8). There is nothing in the *risāla* to suggest that all men of the first category could not meet that criterion.

[74] Cf. Leppin and Portmann 1998, 26.

8

THE EMPEROR'S SHADOW: JULIAN IN HIS CORRESPONDENCE

Michael Trapp

Letters by emperors, whether preserved in a regular manuscript tradition, or recovered from papyrus or stone, are not thick on the ground. Along with Julian's, the most substantial collections are the fifty-one letters of Trajan included in the last book of Pliny's collected correspondence, and the more numerous but also more dilapidated remains of Marcus Aurelius' correspondence with Fronto.[1] From inscriptions and papyri, we have such items as Octavian's letter to Ephesus about a purloined statue of Aphrodite,[2] and Claudius' message to the much-harangued people of Alexandria.[3] A notable quantity of material, albeit of excerpts not full letters, is quoted by Suetonius in his biographies of the Caesars and of Horace.[4] But Julian's collection at least at first sight seems to head the field by some way both in its size and in the diversity of its contents.[5]

Just how many items we are dealing with is, however, a tricky question. The manuscripts contain varying numbers in varying combinations, the largest being the 43 in Laurentianus 58.16.[6] Nineteenth-century editors, putting together all the manuscript evidence then available, seemed to have stabilized the number at 78 (Hercher in his *Epistolographi Graeci* of 1873) or 79 (Hertlein's Teubner of 1876); but six further items then turned up in 1885 in two fragmentary manuscripts on Halki;[7] and in any case the count even before this addition already included a number of manifestly spurious letters. Bidez and Cumont in 1922 got up to a total of 284 items, 157 genuine and 127 *spuriae vel dubiae*, by counting in and numbering separately letters or sets of letters now known only by report, and laws and edicts assembled from other sources. Wright in her Loeb of 1923, based on Hertlein and on Bidez-Cumont's earlier work on the manuscript tradition,[8] got to 73 genuine items and 10 *apocrypha*. But when you then compare Bidez-Cumont to Wright, you find that they regard as spurious or dubious no fewer than sixteen of the letters that she is prepared to accept as certainly or possibly genuine, and they have doubts about at least one more (73 W = 19 B–C).

The number of uncontroversial items thus seems to drop to somewhere in the fifties. But we must then add one further twist. What has been described so far is the material preserved in the collection of Julian's letters that circulated in manuscript tradition both in editions of his complete works, like Vossianus 77, and in epistolographic collections like Laurentianus 58.16, in which Julian's efforts rub shoulders with those of Phalaris, Brutus, Libanius, Basil and Gregory. But – as is well known – there are three further items that have been handed down not as part of the letter-collection, but among Julian's other works: the *Letter to Themistius*, the *Letter to the Athenians*, and the now truncated *Letter to a Priest* that was excavated by a seventeenth-century editor (Petavius)[9] from the *Letter to Themistius* with which it had become entangled.[10]

The total haul thus reduces to something between fifty-five and sixty items. This is still substantial, whether compared with the remainder of Julian's own surviving work, or with other sets of emperors' letters; though it is of course dwarfed on the other hand by the one thousand five hundred and forty four surviving letters of Libanius, or St. Basil's three hundred and sixty eight.

It is also a notably varied collection, bearing out the *Suda*'s attribution to Julian of ἐπιστολαὶ παντοδαπαί; compare the more uniform show put on by Fronto's Aurelius or Pliny's Trajan. Just how varied Julian looks does, though, depend to some extent on how much is to be rejected as spurious. The most sensitive items from this point of view are the so-called 'sophistic' letters: the elegant, sometimes very short messages, chiefly to close acquaintances, which stand apart from the remainder of the correspondence both in being undatable to any specific point in Julian's career, and in being concerned with the process of letter-writing as much as with its practical usefulness. We shall return to these later. But even if the 'sophistic' items are subtracted, what remains still shows us an intriguing range of epistolographic forms and styles: from news and requests to personal friends at one end of the scale, to the formal communications of emperor to civic communities at the other, with business and administrative messages to individuals in between; and this 'business and administrative' category in its turn divides in well-known fashion between run-of-the-mill imperial business on the one hand, and on the other hand, the more distinctive business brought on by Julian's religious revivalism (the so-called 'pastoral letters').[11] There is admittedly not much variety of mood and tone in evidence: Julian's range is essentially from seriousness to vehemence and back. But in terms of forms or kinds, this is a distinctive combination, making Julian as letter-writer comparable by turns not only with fellow Roman statesmen and rulers – Cicero,

Aurelius or Trajan – but also, thanks to the blend of managerial instruction with moral exhortation in the 'pastoral' letters, with Christian managers and leaders like Basil or Augustine.

Exactly how Julian's letters came to be collected in the first place, and what intermediate stages we should imagine intervening between first collection and the extant medieval manuscripts, is impossible to establish with certainty. Our difficulty in this regard is highlighted by the more circumstantial stories we can tell in connection with some of Julian's contemporaries and near contemporaries. In the case of Gregory of Nazianzus, we know that he himself in old age, at the request of his nephew Nicobulus, put together a selection that centred on his correspondence with Basil, but included also messages to other recipients, and was prefaced by a quartet of epistles on epistolography; and we can be sure that it was this authorial selection that formed the nucleus of the larger collections that come down to us in the manuscript tradition.[12] In the case of Libanius, though there is some room for argument over the precise circumstances of publication, the grounding of the collection in the writer's own duplicate correspondence files is comparably clear.[13] With Julian, in contrast, we are thrown back much more rapidly onto general plausibility and inferences from the pattern of later citation.

Zosimus in his *New History*, composed in the opening decades of the sixth century, can refer to Julian's discourses and letters as a rich source of information, open 'to anyone who wants', and 'from which it is eminently possible to comprehend his deeds across the whole world'.[14] But already more than a century earlier Eunapius, in his now fragmentary *Histories,* is to be found referring his readers to the correspondence as first-hand testimony to one of Julian's campaigns.[15] Given the general dependence of Zosimus on Eunapius, first alleged by Photius and substantiated by modern scholarly work,[16] it is likely that Zosimus' more generalizing comment on the letters also follows Eunapius' lead, not only in the thought but also in the wording. In between Eunapius and Zosimus in time, and apparently independently of the former, Sozomen in Book 5 of his *Ecclesiastical History* cites excerpts from three letters, to the people of Bostra and to the Alexandrians, and a fourth, the letter to Arsacius, in its entirety.[17] Closest in time to Julian himself, his correspondence is praised by both Libanius and Ammianus as much for its style and its excellence as epistolographic art as for its information content: Libanius, admiring the beauty that derives from the letters' unmatched combination of clarity and force (σαφήνεια and ἰσχύς), declares them the pinnacle of Julian's literary achievement; Ammianus speaks of the *cum gravitate comitas incorrupta* – blend of weight with unspoiled elegance – that characterises both them and the orations.[18]

Bidez and Cumont plausibly suggest that this combination of testimonies points to the existence by the late fourth century of two separate collections: one of Julian's private correspondence with friends and literary figures, and one of his edicts and official correspondence that centred on material dealing with Christians.[19] These two initially separate elements, put together for differing motives, literary and historico-polemical, would then have been combined and augmented in the fifth century, so as to produce a more comprehensive edition that was subsequently selected from in various ways by the ancestors of the surviving medieval manuscript tradition. On the further question of who put the proposed original collections together in the first place, and drawing on what material, Bidez and Cumont are properly tentative, suggesting Libanius as a possible candidate for the more literary of the two.[20] Another possibility might be the Nymphidianus, brother of Maximus of Ephesus, whom Eunapius recorded was Julian's Greek secretary (*ab epistulis graecis*).[21]

While of course it cannot be guaranteed that the real story was quite as neat and simple as this,[22] what it does seem to get right is the combination of motives and interests that was responsible for the correspondence being published in the first place. Julian's notorious entanglement with Christianity, and his consequently scandalous role in the evolving history of the Church, made the contents of much of his official correspondence hugely interesting to sacred and secular historians alike. The equally passionate attachment to Hellenic *paideia* and its contemporary champions, even if inextricably bound up with his religious *démarches*, gave an extra literary dimension to his letter-writing, and made of it also a cherishable heirloom for connoisseurs of the right kind of writing.

It is clear, furthermore, that the fuss made of the letters by immediate posterity is a fair reflection of the importance that letters and letter-writing had in Julian's own career and experience. As emperor, he was naturally bound *ex officio* to a punishing routine of formal correspondence, issuing edicts and rescripts, and instructions and responses to prefects, governors and agents.[23] The majority was done by dictation – Libanius in one place speaks admiringly of him 'showing up the slowness of his secretaries' hands with the speed of his tongue', and in another fantasises in Homeric vein that it would only have been if he had been able to speak with ten tongues that he would have had no need of any secretaries at all.[24] Not all of the physical labour thus fell on Julian alone, even if most of the tedium inevitably did. We need also to reckon with a substantial number of cases in which the body of the letter-text is not Julian's own unaided composition, but either a collaborative effort in consultation with the imperial consistory, or even drafted out whole by an individual secretary. The imperial hand itself generally then just signed, sometimes added a few concluding sentences, only very rarely physically wrote out a whole epistle by itself.[25] All this was simply the lot of any emperor, and following hallowed tradition Julian duly complains of it, poignantly, in the closing words of his very last datable letter.[26] But in addition to the inevitable routine that would have fallen to any emperor, Julian's own particular religio-cultural agenda gave him extra, and more individual reasons to multiply his correspondence, as he sought to instruct his burgeoning network of new-style pagan priests, and to beat back the disobliging rebelliousness of Christian leaders and communities.

Yet this supercharged epistolarity was not a feature of Julian's life that began only when he was firmly settled into the imperial throne. The circumstances of his accession too – moving in from the fringes, with the commanding heights of an empire to be talked round – gave extra importance to the letter as tool. And even before that, geography and cultural ambitions had already conspired to the same effect. Julian's enforced movements around the eastern half of the empire in childhood and adolescence, followed by the removal to Gaul, would in any case have given him enhanced reasons to correspond. But this was mightily compounded by two further factors: the circumstance of his finding his identity in a *paideia* that so valued letters as means to and proof of membership of the charmed circle; and his adherence to a paganism that, until his accession, had something of the feel of a secret society or underground movement, and so needed such tokens of solidarity with an extra urgency. The particular circumstances of Julian's career and projects thus made him not only correspond more, but also correspond with an extra self-consciousness about the way doing it right – in proper form – would project cultivation and Hellenism.

This point about *paideia*, and displaying it by getting your correspondence right, deserves to be pursued further, because it is so clearly central: central to getting the feel of the letters themselves, and to understanding a kind of verbalization that took up so much of Julian's time; and central also to understanding why the letters were so prized and praised by his admirers and by posterity.

The variety of the collection, in particular the range across both personal communication with individuals and messages to collectives and communities, means that there is no one single thing that counts as getting it right, but rather a range of kinds of cultivated performance, appropriate to the different forms of communication going on. There is not the space to attempt a complete survey, so I propose to concentrate on the personal communications, the centrally epistolary part of the picture. But by way of preface, a few words are necessary about Julian's performance in his public communications, the edicts and rescripts.[27] As already observed, much in these is likely not to be his own unaided composition. The release of each item was, however, sanctioned by him and went out over his signature, which means that they represent the public style that he wished to be known as his; and their acceptance into the corpus of his works means that they played their part in creating his persona and reputation as letter-writer.

In these public communications, though the sense that something epistolary is going on is not always entirely absent, the main element of correct and cultivated performance seems to lie in the adoption of a good oratorical style. A missive to a group has, from one point of view, as much in common with a speech as with a letter, which in its central form is standardly compared to the one-to-one medium of dialogue.[28] The sender-speaker's credentials as man of culture are therefore appropriately established by his ability to work with a vocabulary and a sentence-structure of the kind sanctioned by the Attic classics as right for mass communication. Displays of historical erudition or literary taste, though not ruled out categorically, are less to the point. A couple of characteristic examples of what results can be seen in the short rescript to the Thracians (*Ep.* 27 W = 73 B–C), and the second half of the proclamation to the Alexandrians about the murder of Bishop George (*Ep.* 21 W = 60 B–C), of which the second is relatively more likely and the first relatively less likely to be substantially Julian's own work.

The rescript to the Thracians consists of just five sentences, plus the concluding salutation:

Θραξίν. Βασιλεῖ μὲν πρὸς κέρδος ὁρῶντι χαλεπὸν ἂν ὑμῶν ἐφάνη τὸ αἴτημα, καὶ οὐκ ἂν ᾠήθη τὴν δημοσίαν εὐπορίαν καταβλάπτειν τῇ πρός τινας ἰδίᾳ χάριτι· ἐπεὶ δὲ ἡμεῖς οὐχ ὅτι πλεῖστα παρὰ τῶν ὑπηκόων ἀθροίζειν πεποιήμεθα σκόπον, ἀλλ ὅτι πλείστων ἀγαθῶν αὐτοῖς αἴτιοι γίγνεσθαι, τοῦτο καὶ ὑμῖν ἀπολύσει τὰ ὀφλήματα. ἀπολύσει δὲ οὐχ ἁπλῶς ἅπαντα, ἀλλὰ μερισθήσεται τὸ πρᾶγμα, τὸ μὲν εἰς ὑμᾶς, τὸ δὲ εἰς τὴν τῶν στρατιωτῶν χρείαν, ἐξ ἧς οὐκ ἐλάχιστα καὶ αὐτοὶ δήπου φέρεσθε τὴν εἰρήνην καὶ τὴν ἀσφάλειαν. τοιγαροῦν μέχρι μὲν τῆς τρίτης ἐπινεμήσεως ἀφίεμεν ὑμῖν πάντα, ὅσα ἐκ τοῦ φθάνοντος ἐλλείπει χρόνον· μετὰ ταῦτα δὲ εἰσοίσετε κατὰ τὸ ἔθος. ὑμῖν τε γὰρ τὰ ἀφιέμενα χάρις ἱκανή, καὶ ἡμῖν τῶν κοινῶν οὐκ ἀμελητέον. περὶ τούτων καὶ τοῖς ἐπάρχοις ἐπέσταλκα, ἵν᾿ ἡ χάρις ὑμῖν εἰς ἔργον προχωρήσῃ. ἐρρωμένους ὑμᾶς οἱ θεοὶ σώζοιεν τὸν ἅπαντα χρόνον.

To the people of Thrace. An emperor looking only to his revenues would have found your request a hard one to grant; he would not have thought it was right to damage public resources by granting a special favour to any individual group. But since we have made it our aim not to amass the largest possible sums from our subjects, but to be ourselves the authors of the largest possible number of blessings for them, this policy will extend to the cancellation of your debt. The cancellation will not however be absolute. The amount will be divided, some of it going to you, and some of it to meet the needs of the army, from which you too will not be least among the beneficiaries in terms of peace and security. We therefore remit the whole sum that is in arrears from the preceding period, up to the third assessment; thereafter you will pay your contribution in the usual way. For you, this remission is favour enough; I for my part must not neglect the common good. I have also sent orders to the Prefects on this matter, to ensure that the favour granted you takes effect. May the gods keep you in good health for all time!

Each sentence is carefully patterned, with sought balances and antitheses: τὴν δημοσίαν εὐπορίαν...τῇ πρός τινας ἰδίᾳ χάριτι; ὅτι πλεῖστα...ὅτι πλείστων; the epanorthosis ἀπολύσει...ἀπολύσει δὲ οὐχ; ὑμῖν τε γάρ...καὶ ἡμῖν with the switch from negative to positive statement, and so on. The patterning is both aesthetically significant – here is someone who can do good oratorical plain-style – and functional: here is an eminently judicious and reasonable response (even though in fact the emperor is not giving his plaintive subjects anything like what they were asking for). But although the style is oratorical, the length of the message is restricted, and a version of a standard epistolary formula is used to round it off (cf. e.g. *Ep.* 7 W = 10 B–C, to Alypius).

The message to the Alexandrians about the murdered George is rather longer and the markers of rhetorical style are correspondingly the more obtrusive, even though here too we do not get entirely away from epistolary reference. The opening sentences of the second half, from 379e onwards (Παραβάλλετε τοίνυν ταύτην μου τὴν ἐπιστολὴν κτλ.), identify the communication as a letter and challenge the recipients to compare it to another, written to them not long previously. But this then gives way to a string of exclamations, rhetorical questions, anticipated objections, and parenthetic comment. The recipients are apostrophised as ἄνδρες Ἀλεξανδρεῖς, like the audience of a formal oration; and the communication ends not with epistolary wishes for good health, but a command for its display which emphasises that this is a message for a plurality of recipients. The sentences are once again formally constructed, even if not with the symmetry and antitheses of the rescript to the Thracians, and the diction is carefully literate: register for instance the classicizing (Thucydidean) use of the neuter plus article in the phrase τὸ γὰρ τῆς ἐξουσίας ἀκαταφρόνητον καὶ τὸ ἀπηνέστερον καὶ καθαρὸν τῆς ἀρχῆς, (lit. 'the not-to-be-floutedness of authority and the austererness and purity of power'), and the delaying of the noun χαρακτήρ in the final sentence. The *paideia* is then once more in the diction, rather than in any overt display of learned references, though one might feel that the concluding hortatory reference to the Hellenism of the Alexandrians is meant in implication to go beyond the good moral character it officially refers to: if they are indeed good Hellenes, they will toe the imperial line because they appreciate the civilisation of Julian's style as well.

Epistolary markers, then, jostle with canons of oratorical diction in these public written pronouncements of Julian's. For the domain in which standards of appropriate performance are more solidly bound up with knowing what counts as right for a *letter*, and showing elegantly that you know it, we have to look elsewhere in the collection, at the messages to individuals.

To first appearances, the place where we find what we are now looking for in its most concentrated and manifest form is the so-called 'sophistic' letters, numbers 60 to 67 in Wright's numeration, the epistles to Eugenius, Sopater, Euclides, Hecebolius, Lucian, Elpidius and George (= 182, 188–9, 192–5, 197, 200–1 B–C). These letters show us epistolography at its most insistently and self-consciously epistolographic, and cultivated reference at its most ostentatiously cultivated. They are as much phatic as functional, seeming to aim at reinforcing the sender's and the recipient's shared sense of their own and each other's *paideia* as much as to convey any specific message. And they extend the letter's inbuilt propensity for reflexivity into a kind of elegantly playful meta-epistolary commentary.

Take for instance *Letter* 60 W to Eugenius (193 B–C):

Δαίδαλον μὲν Ἰκάρῳ φασὶν ἐκ κήρου πτερὰ συμπλάσαντα τολμῆσαι τὴν φύσιν βιάσασθαι τῇ τέχνῃ. ἐγὼ δὲ ἐκεῖνον μὲν εἰ καὶ τῆς τέχνης ἐπαινῶ, τῆς γνώμης οὐκ ἄγαμαι· μόνος γὰρ κηρῷ λυσίμῳ τοῦ παιδὸς ὑπέμεινε τὴν σωτηρίαν πιστεῦσαι. εἰ δέ μοι θέμις ἦν κατὰ τὸν Τήιον ἐκεῖνον μελοποιὸν εὐχῇ τὴν τῶν ὀρνίθων ἀλλάξασθαι φύσιν, οὐκ ἂν δήπου πρὸς Ὄλυμπον οὐδὲ ὑπὲρ μέμψεως ἐρωτικῆς, ἀλλ' εἰς αὐτοὺς ἂν τῶν ὑμετέρων ὀρῶν τοὺς πρόποδας ἔπτην, ἵνα σε τὸ μέλημα τῶμον, ὥς φησιν ἡ Σαπφώ, περιπτύξωμαι. ἐπεὶ δέ με ἀνθρωπίνου σώματος δεσμῷ κατακλείσασα ἡ φύσις οὐκ ἐθέλει πρὸς τὸ μετέωρον ἁπλῶσαι, τῶν λόγων οἷς ἔχω σε πτεροῖς μετέρχομαι, καὶ γράφω, καὶ σύνειμι τὸν δυνατὸν τρόπον. πάντως που καὶ Ὅμηρος αὐτοὺς οὐκ ἄλλου του χάριν ἢ τούτου πτερόεντας ὀνομάζει, διότι δύνανται πανταχοῦ φοιτᾶν, ὥσπερ οἱ ταχύτατοι τῶν ὀρνίθων ᾗ ἂν ἐθέλωσιν ἄττοντες. γράφε δὲ καὶ αὐτός, ὦ φίλος· ἴση γὰρ δήπου σοι τῶν λόγων, εἰ μὴ καὶ μείζων, ὑπάρχει πτέρωσις, ᾗ τοὺς ἑταίρους μεταβῆναι δύνασαι καὶ πανταχόθεν ὡς παρὼν εὐφραίνειν.

They say that Daedalus made wings for Icarus out of wax, thus daring to do violence to nature with his art. Though I may indeed praise him for his art, I do not admire his judgement: no-one else, after all, has ever brought himself to entrust his son's safety to soluble wax. If I were allowed, in the words of the famous lyricist of Teos, to change my form into a bird's in answer to a wish, I wouldn't fly to Olympus in pursuit of a lover's complaint, but to the very foothills of your mountains, so that, to quote Sappho, I could embrace you, my dear. But since Nature has bound me with the shackles of a human frame and refuses to unburden me for flight through the air, I will pursue you with such wings as I have, my words, and will write to you, and keep you company as far as I may. Surely it was for no other reason than this that Homer called them winged, that they can travel anywhere, speeding wherever they may wish like the swiftest of birds. Write to me too, my friend. You have as rich a plumage of words as I do, if not richer, with which to visit your friends, and to cheer them wherever they may be as if you were with them in person.

The message here is just 'write to me', but this is wrapped in mannered reflection on the standard epistolary *locus* about absence and presence,[29] which in turn is explored through and decorated with references to Daedalus and Icarus, Anacreon, Sappho, and Homer.[30] Or again, take *Letter* 67 W to the revenue official George (*Ep.* 188 B–C). The message is again exceedingly tenuous, something like 'thank you for your marvellous letters, here is one in return'; but it is built up into a meditation on the notions – again, standard epistolary *loci* – of letters as images and representatives of the sender's character, of letters as essentially brief, and letters as both markers and remedies for separation.[31] And this meditation is conducted through urbanely knowledgeable reference to the details of the art of Phidias and the poetry of Homer (with special reference to themes of exile, return, and identity, as embodied in the return of Telemachus, Odysseus revealing his identity to the Phaeacians, and Odysseus' desire to see even so much as the smoke rising from the hearths of his native land).[32]

If we could be sure that these epistles were genuine, we would have the far end of Julian's epistolary span nailed down at a satisfyingly distant point from his edicts and rescripts, in something much more self-consciously and showily cultivated. But editorial disagreements suggest that we cannot in fact be entirely sure of Julianic authorship. It may not be a specially good argument to urge that this kind of 'sophistic' preciousness is not consistent with the seriousness and intensity of Julian's public and religious communications; why should he not have commanded both registers? Nor is it necessarily suspicious that these letters are not firmly anchored, as others are, to specific places and dates in Julian's known career. But it is more worrying that in Greek epistolography overall, the kind of urbane meta-epistolarity one finds in these items is much more regularly characteristic of pseudepigrapha like the *Epistles of Phalaris* than of genuine correspondence. Playing for safe ground, then, we should bracket the sophistic letters and search on. If we have to deny Julian *this* style of engagement with the personal letter, and *this* degree of epistolary *paideia*, however provisionally, then what kinds of engagement can we more safely credit him with?

A proper answer would need a full survey of the 55 or so generally accepted letters that remain once both the rescripts and edicts, and the suspected items, have been removed. What this would reveal, and document, is that here too, within this apparently more homogeneous subset of the corpus, there is a variety of practice. Even to his individual correspondents, Julian has more than one way of being epistolary and of displaying his cultivation in letter-friendly form. He is more and less disposed by turns to make use of standard formula and conventions; he may or may not trick out a particular kind of message – for example, the invitation or summons – with a literary or philosophical reference. A good few of his personal letters make do with *neither* overt epistolary markers *nor* overtly learned reference. There is a good deal to be chased up and studied more closely along these lines. I suspect that it might be particularly interesting to focus on the pastoral letters. In their content and purpose, these can fairly easily be seen as instances of some well-represented general trends in ancient epistolography, a kind of blend of the letter of administrative instructions with the letter of moral advice or exhortation, in which Julian plays both the political superior and the moral *praeceptor*. Can then these exercises in a special kind of epistolary didacticism be felt as a distinct subset also in style and tone, somewhere between the more fully private among the personal letters, and the fully public mode of the edicts and decrees? And would we find ourselves wanting to argue that Julian was consciously and deliberately manipulating what he knew to be existing models and patterns, or that he had simply fallen co-incidentally into them in the course of pursuing his cultural political aims?

I hope those are at least good questions; but they are also questions that I am sketching without being able to give any confident answers. I propose to end more modestly, not with the comprehensive map of the whole territory of Julian's personal letters that following them through would eventually lead towards, but with another triangulation point. We have looked at some examples of the not-excessively-epistolary messages Julian dispatched in his public persona as emperor, responding to petitions and intervening in the communal life of cities; and we have looked at the cultivated phatic epistolography of the 'sophistic' letters, which may or may not belong to him. And I have given the briefest of sketches of the variegated terrain between these two extremes. Here to end is at least one marker that can be set down to give that intermediate terrain some shape.

Julian's interest in manifesting epistolary *paideia* may be uneven across the surviving works, but uneven distributions have their outer edges, their limiting cases. For Julian, if the sophistic epistles are bracketed, I think that the limiting edge comes with two items, *Ep.* 16 W = 30 B–C and *Ep.* 30 W = 40 B–C, the letters to Theodorus and Philip, both of which, though lacking the preciousness of the disputed sophistic epistles, nevertheless show a combination of a high, and surely conscious, density of epistolary reference with a well-marked erudition. So it is with these that I propose to end.

Letter 16, to the same Theodorus as is appointed to the high-priesthood of Asia in *Letter* 20 W = 89a B–C, is too long to be comfortably quotable. In summary, it combines instances of the epistolographic *loci* of receiving and opening letters, letters and friendship, letters as images of their senders' souls, letters and brevity, mutual support and reciprocity, and the anticipation of a physical meeting, with elaborate reference to Socrates and Musonius, the nature of the true philosopher, and the Theban hero Amphion's invention of music.

Letter 30, to the paganizing poet Philip, is shorter and shows more compendiously the same combination of conscious epistolarity with erudite allusion.

Ἰουλιανὸς Φιλίππῳ. ἐγὼ νὴ τοὺς θεοὺς ἔτι Καῖσαρ ἐπέστειλά σοι, καὶ νομίζω πλέον ἢ ἅπαξ. ὥρμησα μέντοι πολλάκις, ἀλλ᾽ ἐκώλυσαν ἄλλοτε ἄλλαι προφάσεις, εἶτα ἡ γενομένη διὰ τὴν ἀνάρρησιν ἐμοί τε καὶ τῷ μακαρίτῃ Κωνσταντίῳ λυκοφιλία. παντάπασι γὰρ ἐφυλλαττόμην ὑπὲρ τὰς Ἄλπεις ἐπιστεῖλαί τινι, μὴ πραγμάτων αὐτῷ χαλεπῶν αἴτιος γένωμαι. τεκμήριον δὲ μὴ ποιοῦ τῆς εὐνοίας τὸ γράφειν. οὐ γὰρ ἐθέλει πολλάκις ὁμολογεῖν ἡ γλῶττα τῇ διανοίᾳ. καὶ ἴσως ἔχει μέν τι πρὸς τὸ γαυριᾶν καὶ ἀλαζονεύεσθαι τοῖς ἰδιώταις ἡ τῶν βασιλικῶν ἐπιστολῶν ἐπίδειξις, ὅταν πρὸς τοὺς ἀσυνήθεις ὥσπερ δακτύλιοί τινες ὑπὸ τῶν ἀπειροκάλων φερόμενοι κομίζωνται. φιλία δὲ ἀληθινὴ γίνεται μάλιστα μὲν δι᾽ ὁμοιότητος, ἡ δευτέρα δέ, ὅταν τις ἀληθῶς, ἀλλὰ μὴ πλαστῶς θαυμάζῃ, καὶ παρὰ τοῦ τύχῃ καὶ συνέσει κρείττονος ὁ πρᾷος καὶ μέτριος καὶ σώφρων ἀγαπηθῇ. τὰ γραμματεῖα δὲ ταῦτα πολλοῦ τύφου καὶ πολλῆς φλυαρίας ἐστὶ μεστά, καὶ ἔγωγε πολλάκις ἐμαυτῷ μέμφομαι μακρότερα ποιούμενος αὐτὰ καὶ λαλίστερος ὤν, ἐξὸν Πυθαγόρειον διδάσκειν τὴν γλῶτταν.

ὑπεδεξάμην μέντοι τὰ σύμβολα, φιάλην ἀργυρᾶν, ἕλκουσαν μίαν μνᾶν, καὶ χρυσοῦ νόμισμα. καλέσαι δέ σε πρὸς ἐμαυτόν, ὥσπερ ἐπέστειλας, ἐβουλόμην. ἤδη δὲ ἔαρ ὑποφαίνει καὶ τὰ δένδρα βλαστάνει, χελιδόνες δὲ ὅσον οὔπω προσδοκώμεναι τοὺς συστρατευομένους ἡμᾶς, ὅταν ἐπεισέλθωσιν, ἐξελαύνουσι τῶν οἰκιῶν, καί φασι δεῖν ὑπερορίους εἶναι. πορευσόμεθα δὲ δι᾽ ὑμῶν, ὥστε μοι βέλτιον ἂν ἐντύχοις, ἐθελόντων θεῶν, ἐν τοῖς σαυτοῦ. τοῦτο δὲ οἶμαι ταχέως ἔσεσθαι (πλὴν εἰ μή τι δαιμόνιον γένοιτο κώλυμα), καὶ τοῦτο δὲ αὐτὸ τοῖς θεοῖς εὐχόμεθα.

115

Julian to Philip. As the gods are my witnesses, I wrote to you when I was still Caesar, and I think it was more than once. I set out to do so many times, but was prevented by different reasons on different occasions, and then on top of everything by the friendship of wolf and wolf that the proclamation conjured up between me and the late lamented Constantius. I was meticulously careful not to write to anyone on the other side of the Alps, for fear of getting him into serious trouble. Do not take writing as proof of goodwill: what the tongue says is often at odds with what the mind thinks. For private citizens, showing off letters from the emperor is a means of boasting and bragging, when they are carried about by tasteless individuals like some sort of seal-ring, and get into the hands of people who aren't used to them. Real friendship comes about above all from similar character, with a next-best version when someone is genuinely and without pretence admired, and an equable, moderate and chaste individual is cherished by one who is his superior in rank and intelligence. Letters of this kind are crammed with a mass of pretentiousness and nonsense, and I often reproach myself for making them longer than they should be, and for babbling on when I could perfectly well train my tongue into Pythagoreanism.

Yes, the tokens arrived safely: a silver bowl weighing one mina, and a gold piece. I should be happy to invite you to visit me, as you suggest in your letter, but the first signs of spring are now here – the trees are coming into bud, and when the swallows arrive, as we expect them to do at any moment, they drive us fellow campaigners out of our quarters and remind us that we ought to be across the border. Our route will take us through your part of the world, so you will have a better chance, gods willing, of meeting me in your own home territory. I expect this to be soon (unless the heavens interpose some obstacle), and pray the gods for it likewise.

Here, the erudite touch – just the one – is the use of the phrase 'school my tongue into Pythagoreanism' to mean simply 'shut up'.[33] This is employed to acknowledge and articulate the epistolary commonplace that letters ought properly to be short rather than long. But by the time we have reached this point in the letter, we have already had a wealth of other epistolary reference. Julian has started by apologizing for not having written more frequently, and continued by floating the paradox that, even though normally it is sending letters that manifests true friendship, in this case, given the circumstances, the friendly thing was not to send any. He has then meditated on the use and misuse that recipients of letters, in particular letters from emperors to private citizens, are liable to make, and the temptation for senders to compose them in an inappropriately and unhelpfully bombastic style – because, again as a matter of epistolographic commonplace, letters are best given in the simple style. All this before we get to the Pythagorean silence and epistolary brevity. The remainder of the letter acknowledges receipt of a set of gifts, and discusses the best way of arranging a physical meeting that Philip has asked for and that Julian too declares that he desires, thus both doing practical business and invoking the further epistolographic commonplaces of letters and reciprocal exchange, and letters and absence and presence. It all adds up to a very 'lettery' letter, both doing epistolary business and talking about it – making letters both medium and topic. In the course of it, the word ἐπιστέλλω and its cognates occur four times, and γράφω and cognates twice, though as it happens no absolutely straightforward epistolary markers – opening or closing wishes for health, for instance – are used.

Even without the 'sophistic' letters to his name, Julian does therefore – sometimes – indulge in self-conscious and reflexive epistolography, in which the almost automatic tendency of letters to self-reference is built on and pointed up. And this in turn reassures both Julian's correspondents, and any reader of a collected edition, that he (or she) is dealing with an insider to the circle of the cultivated. And we have with this at least some of the background and the justification for the enthusiasm for Julian's epistles shown by such a master epistolographer as Libanius.

But these stand-out items have in turn to be put back into the broader picture of Julian's whole epistolographic range. The overt erudition and obtrusive epistolarity of some items sits together with other letters that show their cultural credentials in their classicizing verbal style and diction rather than in overt subject-matter or declarations of generic allegiance, and with yet others that demonstrate competence and cultural allegiance in their contents; and others again that found their claims to respectful attention on the simple efficient and economical transaction of their primary business. And the whole assemblage of letters thus compounded needs to be set back into place in the larger story of Julian's career, over the closing years of his all-too-brief life. For another remarkable feature of the transmitted collection is how effectively it traces that career's key stages, in part, but only in part, because of Julian's own impulse to account for himself and his doings to his correspondents. In a manner already touched on, the correspondence shows us: Julian maintaining his literary and pagan-revivalist contacts during his spell in distant Gaul; drumming up support as he plays for and wins the imperial throne, both from cities and from key personal allies; pursuing both his plans for the revival of ancestral cult, and the management of Christian recalcitrance; and in the final stages moving eastwards on his last, fatal campaign.

To end, therefore, we may return to that last letter to Libanius, written from Hierapolis in Syria in early March 363 (*Ep.* 58 W = 98 B–C): a lengthy narrative letter, properly and self-consciously worried about not going on at unepistolary length (401d), tracing Julian's route from Litarbae in Chalcis to Hierapolis via Aleppo (Beroea) and Antioch. With superb dramatic irony this last dispatch leaves Julian on the edge of the unknown – we know, as he does not, that he is for the dark; and as the picture fades, in the last lines of the last letter, what is its writer doing?

Ἐκεῖθεν ἐδίκασα δίκην στρατιωτικήν, ὡς ἐμαυτὸν πείθω, πραότατα καὶ δικαιότατα. ἵππους περιττοὺς καὶ ἡμιόνους παρεσκεύασα, τὸ στρατόπεδον εἰς ταὐτὸ συναγαγών. ναῦς πληροῦνται ποτάμιαι πυροῦ, μᾶλλον δὲ ἄρτων ξηρῶν καὶ ὄξους. καὶ τούτων ἕκαστον ὅπως ἐπράχθη καὶ τίνες ἐφ' ἑκάστῳ γεγόνασι λόγοι, πόσου μήκους ἐστὶ συγγράφειν ἐννοεῖς. ἐπιστολαῖς δὲ ὅσαις ὑπέγραψα καὶ βίβλοις (ἑπόμενα ὥσπερ σκιά μοι καὶ ταῦτα συμπερινοστεῖ πανταχοῦ) τί δεῖ νῦν πράγματα ἔχειν ἀπαριθμούμενον;

I then presided over a court-martial, and am confident that I delivered an unimpeachably humane and just verdict. I have organized a reserve of horses and mules, and consolidated my forces into one unit. There are river-boats full of corn, or rather of baked bread and cheap wine. You can imagine how long I would have to go on in order to record how each of these pieces of business was done and what discussions each of them provoked. As for the number of letters and petitions I have put my signature to – these too follow me like my own shadow and keep me company in all my travels – why should I put myself to the trouble of counting them up now?

Complaining that however far he travels, he cannot get away from his cursed correspondence!

Notes

[1] Trajan's letters account for 51 of the 121 items in Book 10; there are between eighty and ninety letters by Aurelius (some very fragmentary) in Fronto's collection.

[2] Reynolds 1982, doc. 12; Trapp 2003, no. 64.

[3] P. Lond. 1912; ed. Hunt and Edgar 1934, vol. 2, 78–89.

[4] Suetonius quotes some 25 passages, plus a scatter of isolated phrases, from Augustus' correspondence in the *Lives* of Augustus, Tiberius, Claudius, Virgil and Horace (*Aug.* 51.3, 64.2, 71.2–4, 76.1–2, 86.3, 87.1; *Tib.* 21.4–7; *Claud.* 4.1–6; *Virg.* 31; *Hor.* [5 extracts and two phrases]); he quotes once each from the correspondence of Tiberius (*Tib.* 67.1) and Domitian (*Dom.* 13.2).

[5] Most recent writing on Julian's *Letters* concentrates on historical problems. Caltabiano 1991 provides an overview, Mazza 1998 discusses the context and purpose of the 'pastoral' letters, Luchner 2008 examines some philosophical aspects; older bibliography is given by Wright 1923, lxiv–lxvii. Questions concerning the authenticity of individual letters also continue to attract attention, as witness Spawforth 1994 and Van Nuffelen 2002. On the characteristics of ancient epistolography more generally, see Rosenmeyer 2001, Trapp 2003, and Morello and Morrison 2007.

[6] To which must be added two answering letters (one by Basil, one by Libanius), and a further letter of Libanius misattributed to Julian.

[7] Wright 1923, lxiv–lxv. The letters are numbers 2, 16, 29, 32, 34 and 73 W.

[8] Wright was able to take only a first look at their edition: it is acknowledged in her Introduction and its numeration included in her concordance.

[9] Pétau 1630.

[10] For the *Letter to Themistius* and the *Letter to the Athenians* see the chapters of John Watt and Mark Humphries in this volume.

[11] The name first given them by Edward Gibbon, in Chapter 23 of *The History of the Decline and Fall of the Roman Empire*: 'his pastoral letters, if we may use that name' (Womersley 1994, vol. 1, 879).

[12] Nicobulus: Bradbury 2004, 21; Gallay 1964–7, 2. xxi–xxiii; Greg. Naz. *Epp.* 52–3.

[13] Bradbury 2004, 19–23; Norman 1992, 2.28–43.

[14] Zos. 3.2.4. On this passage, and its probable relation to Eunapius, see Paschoud 1979, 65–6; 1994; and 2000, lxi.

[15] Eunap. *fr.* 14.7 Müller = 9 Blockley = Julian 25 Bidez-Cumont.

[16] See Paschoud 2000, x–xvi.

[17] Soz. *Hist. eccl.* 5.7.8–9 and 5.15.1–2 (Alexandria); 5.15.12 (Bostra); 5.164–15 (Arsacius).

[18] Lib. *Ep.* 716 (to Celsus) and *Or.* 18.302; Amm. Marc. 16.5.7; cf. Bidez-Cumont, *Testimonia*, 1–3. For some of the theoretical background to these verdicts, see Trapp 2003, 43–5.

[19] Bidez-Cumont, v.

[20] Bidez-Cumont, v.

[21] Eunap. *VS* 497.28 – a passage cited by Bidez and Cumont in their *testimonia*, but not used in their discussion of the origins of the collection. I own the suggestion that Nymphidianus might be relevant in this connection to the volume's editors.

[22] For instance, their suggestion that the hypothetical combined edition will have been known to Zosimus, but not already available in Eunapius' day, is weakened if, as suggested above, Zosimus is simply echoing Eunapius and not showing any independent knowledge of a different configuration of Julian's writings.

[23] Millar 1977, 213–28.

[24] Lib. *Orr.* 18.174 and 12.93.

[25] 'Own hand' additions: Wright 5 (Priscus), 6 (Alypius), 9 (Julian), 46 (Ecdicius); dictation: 52 (Libanius); full letter in own hand (by lamplight), 25 (Evagrius).

[26] *Ep.* 58 Wright = 98 B–C, for which see below. Compare the rueful remark of Seleucus, recorded by Plutarch in *An seni* 11.790a: 'If people only knew how laborious the mere writing and reading of so many letters was, they wouldn't pick up a discarded crown.'

[27] Eleven items: 21 W (Alexandrians), 24 (Alexandrians), 27 (Thracians), 31 (Decree on physicians), 36 (Rescript on Christian teachers), 39 (Byzantines), 41 (Bostra), 47 (Alexandrians), 48 (Alexandrians), 51 (Jews, perhaps inauthentic), 56 (Edict on funerals). On Julian's edicts and rescripts see also the chapter of Jill Harries in this volume.

[28] E.g. Demetr. *Eloc.* 223.

[29] Trapp 2003, 38–9.

[30] Anac. *fr.* 378 PMG; Sappho *fr.* 163 L–P. A comparison between the wax of Icarus' wings and the wax of the traditional writing tablet, thanks to which the 'winged' words of a letter 'fly', floats in the background, but is not explicitly articulated.

[31] Trapp 2003, 38–42.

[32] *Od.* 16.23, 9.19 and 1.57–9 (for the last of which, cf. Maximus of Tyre, *Or.* 21.8).

[33] Compare the joke in Lucian, *Demon.* 14, in which a tediously self-promoting philosopher-sophist is told 'Pythagoras is calling you'.

9

JULIAN THE LAWGIVER

Jill Harries

Imperial laws were the words of the emperor himself – or so the Roman world was led to believe.[1] In reality, an imperial law, or 'constitution', could boast a number of authors: the originator of a proposal (*suggestio*), who could have been an administrator, provincial official, army commander, or even a bishop, whose idea was adopted with little or no change to his text;[2] the quaestor or member of the palace secretariat, who drafted the law; the consistory, which discussed and perhaps amended it; the emperor, who signed it. Many legal extracts preserved in the law-codes of Theodosius II (438) and Justinian I (529, second edition 534) represent the emperors in responsive mode; the 'laws' as we have them, in truncated form, represent only one part of a complex process of negotiation between emperor, administrators and subjects, the details of which are now largely irrecoverable. The emperors of the Codes are, to some extent, the creations of a later bureaucratic machine and Julian, as we shall see, was no exception.

The extent to which Julian, or any other emperor, was directly the author of a constitution, in the sense that he, rather than the quaestor, wrote it himself, is perhaps impossible to determine. However, Julian, unlike most other emperors, also speaks as a lawgiver through his letters on legal matters, which survive mixed with more personal correspondence (see Michael Trapp's chapter in this volume). These letters he sent to cities, public bodies, and administrators in his capacity as emperor. Although often issued in response to a petition or report, they also contain new legal rulings or reaffirm existing policy, which are accompanied by often highly moralistic explanations and justifications of the emperor's actions. Moreover, Julian's distinctive character as legislator is further analysed by his (qualified) admirer, the Greek soldier-historian, Ammianus Marcellinus. Julian therefore, has three distinct legislative personae: he wrote in person some laws, perhaps, and letters with legal content (the two were not formally distinct in Late Antiquity); his legislation was selectively summarised and analysed by observers, such as Ammianus; and the laws issued in his name would be extracted (and expurgated) in the *Theodosian Code*, and later recycled by Justinian. Each authorial persona is worth a closer look.

In his own words?

Late Roman imperial constitutions intended to have general application in some sense were issued in the form of either letters or edicts, which explained and justified imperial policy. Imperial laws were, therefore, both legal enactments and rhetorical exercises in persuasion and propaganda, enjoining obedience on the basis, preferably, of consensus, rather than coercion. How far the reality constructed by the emperor's eloquence reflected the experience of the recipients was another matter. Julian's letter to the people of Bostra, written in response to a report on local religious disturbances,[3] laid blame exclusively on the unruly Christian clergy, alleging ingratitude on their part for his generous restoration of exiles and advising the Christian community to expel their turbulent bishop. Although ostensibly advocating religious toleration, the rhetoric is consistently anti-Christian; this is not the letter of a religious neutral. Partisan in a different sense is a letter sent to the Jewish community, which would have had a more favourable reception: while remitting past levies, Julian also lays blame for past excessive taxation on the greedy courtiers of Constantius II, 'barbarous in mind, godless in spirit', and assures them that he has rooted out the past tax records and destroyed them.[4]

But can it be established that Julian's *Letters* on matters legal were written (or dictated) by him personally, and not by the secretariats in charge of imperial correspondence? Julian's personal authorship of some must be in doubt. For example, a letter to the Thracians[5] is a formal response to a petition requesting the cancellation of several years' arrears of taxation. The reply reflects a compromise probably brokered by or with the finance offices: thanks to the emperor's generosity, the Thracians will receive a partial cancellation but must pay up the rest, which will go to support the army, which defends them. While Julian may have agreed its contents, there is nothing in the style to suggest his authorship. By contrast, Julian's discursive style is evident in a long disquisition on the ancient history and current public entertainments budgets of Corinth and Argos, addressed to an anonymous governor of Achaea, perhaps the great senator Vettius Agorius Praetextatus.[6] The letter was prompted by a report on a financial dispute between the two cities; Julian's final decision, to leave it to the governor, did not in itself require the justification of the Argives that precedes it.

Inevitably, the Julian of the *Theodosian Code* intersects with the Julian of the *Letters*, with curious consequences for our perception of imperial behaviour. Julian's dealings with the Prefect of Egypt, one Ecdicius, in the latter part of 362 reveal failures of communication on several fronts. The *Theodosian Code* preserved two extracts from a longer letter about rights of ownership in public spaces.[7] The emperor expressed his regret that his order to vindicate the status of the official residences of governors as public property had not been implemented and gave orders that it should be; he also reassured the builders of flats over public workshops that their rights as owners would be upheld. Julian's letters show that Ecdicius was slow off the mark in other respects as well. *Letter* 45 'informs' Ecdicius that the Nile flood has been very successful, rising on 20th September by 15 cubits: however, Julian had not learned this from Ecdicius (as he should have done) but from the *relatio* of one Theophilus. The casual attitude to legal rights mentioned by Ammianus is also in evidence in the emperor's sequestration, through Ecdicius, of the lynched George of Cappadocia's library for his personal use, regardless of the rights of George's hypothetical heirs.[8] And he pursues his personal cultural agenda in the creation of a boys' choir from suitably gifted Alexandrians, to be subsidised by the state and with hopes of further rewards at court.[9]

More serious was Ecdicius' failure to deal promptly with the unwelcome presence of the turbulent Athanasius in Alexandria. In an earlier 'edict' to the Alexandrians, Julian had explained that his edict permitting Christians exiled by Constantius to return to their 'native places' did not mean that they were to be reinstated as bishops; now he was ordering Athanasius to leave the city immediately on receipt of the order of exile.[10] Several months later, Ecdicius had failed to contact Julian about Athanasius and the emperor had lost patience: if Athanasius was not out of Egypt altogether by 1st December, the office staff would incur a fine of 100 pounds of gold, a huge sum by late Roman standards for penalising official misdemeanours.[11] In his own hand, Julian added a postscript, bitterly complaining that, in his reign, Athanasius had dared to baptize Greek aristocratic women into the faith. No doubt the sight of the emperor's own handwriting was to be a further stimulus to action. But the disproportionate size of the fine is evidence of the real dangers posed to officials, and subjects in general, by 'impulsive' emperors. We may find Julian's spontaneity endearing; the experience of his subjects could be far otherwise.

Julian and Ammianus

For Ammianus, the nature of Julian's legislation was bound up with his character. Julian, Ammianus observed, made a point of deferring to legal experts, when hearing cases, because he was aware of his own impulsiveness.[12] Yet Ammianus also conceded that Julian, when acting as judge, stepped out of line by questioning litigants on their religious convictions[13] and that his legal decisions were on occasion arbitrary and contrary to law.[14] But Ammianus was also eager to celebrate Julian's wisdom in refusing to be drawn on spurious treason charges[15] and his clemency towards his 'enemy' Thalassius, Constantius' former deputy head of the petitions department.[16] In a society founded on patronage, imperial use of discretion was bound to result in inconsistency.

Ammianus' choice of laws for discussion is designed to reinforce his picture of the emperor's character as a whole. He notes a law safeguarding the fees (or bribes) of patrons and advocates,[17] the emperor's excessive determination to recall decurions to the service of their city councils,[18] the recalling from exile of Christians banished by Constantius, and a general attack on corruption and over-subsidized officials.[19] Especially striking is Ammianus' disapproval of the edict banning Christians from the official teaching of the 'pagan' classics, a law which he trusted would be buried in perpetual silence.[20] It was natural for observers like Ammianus to pick out those elements of Julian's legislation which were distinctive or controversial, and to omit the more routine or duller elements preserved by the Codes. But Ammianus was also aware of an underlying sustained programme of reform: in line with what was expected of the 'good' legislator, Julian was praised for the lucidity of his many reforms, which 'removed ambiguities' (as the *Theodosian Code* would later claim to do) and explained clearly 'what was to be done and what was forbidden'.[21]

Julian in the *Theodosian Code*

Ammianus' Julian is more individual, more fallible and more radical than his encoded counterpart. For the Julian of the Codes is the emperor at work, dealing with the minutiae of routine queries, which, despite their relative triviality, required imperial answers. Thus, for example, on 23rd March, 362, the imperial consistory debated trial procedure.[22] The meeting, as the minutes recorded, was attended by the emperor Julian, his quaestor, Iovius, the Master of Offices, Anatolius, and Felix, the head of taxation and finance. Among the questions raised was the use of written evidence in legal trials. Speaking in Greek, the emperor declared that, in general, written 'instruments' had great force, provided that there was no ambiguity in the documents themselves, which required reference to other materials to clarify their meaning. The observation, along with others now lost, was duly minuted. 76 years later, in 438, the extract re-emerged as 'general law' in the *Theodosian Code*.

In this text, the emperor speaks directly; the words are his alone, not those of a secretary or other intermediary. But Julian is not known for his expertise in *instrumenta*; it is likely that he took advice on specialised matters, and that, in this case, the advice came from the man standing at his side, his legal consultant, the quaestor, Iovius. Moreover, the ruling may well have been a response to a referral (*relatio*) or report conveyed from a judge or other official. So, as the decision of the consistory, in response to an external prompt, the content is the creation of a group, even though the words are Julian's.

Julian in the *Theodosian Code* is uncharacteristically concise. In line with their instructions, to delete 'unnecessary words', while preserving the legal content (*ius*), the compilers of the *Theodosian Code* preserved the core of Julian's decision, not its possibly more lengthy justification. The much-edited and abbreviated Julian of the *Theodosian Code* is, with two possible exceptions,[23] Julian Augustus, not Julian the Apostate. Although Christians themselves, the compilers of Theodosius' *Code* accepted without question that Julian was a legitimate emperor and they respected the wording of his constitutions to a (to us) surprising extent. As we shall see, they did have access to his more contentious enactments on religion, and their treatment of, in particular, the edict on funerals and the constitution which, *inter alia*, banned Christians from acting as official teachers of the pagan classics is revealing of their method. I shall argue below that, in a reversal of the usual view taken of legal documents, that intention mattered more than wording, the Theodosian compilers exploited the fiction of Theodosius' authorship to extract appropriately worded regulations from earlier constitutions, and felt free to ignore the intention of the original legislator.

Julian's laws

The compilers of the *Theodosian Code* did not consciously set out to curtail Julian's individuality as legislator. Nevertheless, the focus on legal content, to the exclusion of superfluous rhetoric, resulted, inevitably, in a Julian who was more conformist, more dull – and more like a fifth-century emperor, the creature of legal bureaucrats.[24] As with all imperial administrators, Julian spent much of his time reiterating regulations to officials worried that he might differ from his predecessors (a reasonable concern, in his case) or hoping for a reinforcement of their authority. Thus, for example, Julian imitated Constantius' insistence on the place of the *vicarii* in the chain of referrals of reports and court records upwards to the higher courts; he also confirmed that governors could delegate cases of lesser importance to subordinate judges (although the meaning of 'lesser importance' is not defined in the existing text).[25] He also reiterated a principle derived from 'ancient law' that a procurator charged with the conduct of a lawsuit could continue to act, even after the death of the person who had given him the mandate.[26]

In other areas of the civil law, he was equally conformist. Early in 363, Julian took time off from his preparations against Persia to think about dowries, insisting to the Praetorian Prefect Mamertinus that the existing law on rights of retention of dowries under binding agreements was to be upheld, and, to Hypatius, the *vicarius* of Rome, that betrothal gifts in the form of land to under-age girls were to be valid, provided they were attested in the public records. Julian may well have been the author of these laws in name only. They respect existing conventions and, in the case of the constitution to Hypatius, contain some legalistic Latin on different categories of land, now obsolete for all practical purposes, which is unlikely to have emanated from Julian directly.[27] Julian also followed general conventions on appeals, reinforcing the duties of governors to accept and forward the appropriate documentation on penalty of a fine. The level of fine imposed, however, was inconsistent. In September 362,[28] the governor's office staff were threatened with a fine of 10 pounds of gold, if they missed the limit of 30 days after the lodging of the appeal but by the following March, the fine for the office staff for the same offence had doubled, while the governor himself was liable to a further 10 pounds of gold.[29] Julian's threat to levy one hundred pounds of gold from the dilatory Ecdicius, already noted, suggests that his use of fines, or the threat thereof, may have been somewhat erratic.

However, despite the best efforts of Theodosius' lawyers, Julian's anti-Christian bias emerges, for example in the constitution, which is a doublet, stating that decurions who seek exemption from curial duties on the grounds that they are 'Christians' (not 'clergy'), were to be recalled.[30] Still more individualistic were Julian's reactions to some Constantinian decisions. Significantly, these were unrelated to religion, suggesting that Julian's antipathy to Constantine went beyond his most high profile divergence from that emperor. For example, on a technical issue, concerning the right of a plaintiff to sue (or not) his own choice of coparties to a suit, provided no detriment could be shown to those excluded, Julian accused Constantine of assisting the chicaneries of defendant *possessores* (who had subsequently exploited the provision to delay matters) and abolished his constitution on the matter.[31] This attitude to a predecessor, more often found when reversing the enactments of *tyranni*, a point to which we shall return, contrasts with the restrained respect accorded by, say, Gratian to the grant of equestrian status to *navicularii* by 'the late (*divi*) emperors Constantine and Julian'.[32] Similarly, on the rights of under-age wives to sell property without a decree from a magistrate, Constantine, in line with his general urge to cut back on formalities, had allowed such transactions, subject to agreement by the husband; overturning Constantine's reform Julian reinstated the requirement that a decree be obtained, in line with the 'ancient law'.[33] In similar vein, he reinstated legal protection for free women who cohabited with slaves: where Constantine had ruled that such a woman automatically forfeited her free status, Julian reinstated the qualification stipulated under the SC Claudianum, that her status was unaffected, unless she received three formal warnings.[34] Constantine's wrong-headed innovations were not confined, it seemed, to his patronage of Christianity.

Julian's constitutions as preserved in the Codes also permit testing of Ammianus' broader assessment of Julian's legislation and policies. The impression that Julian the legislator was more conventional than Ammianus implies is confirmed by measures, even in areas where he was known to hope for change. The emperor reaffirmed that decurions were not liable to the *collatio lustralis*, the trade tax – unless the decurion was himself a trader – and that nominated doctors and men with large families (in the case cited, thirteen children) were exempt from curial duties.[35] Both confirmed existing policy. Where Julian differed from other emperors was in his generosity.[36] Public lands were to be restored to the *municipia* and leased at fair rates[37] and the *aurum coronarium* was to be treated, both by senators (perhaps the subject of a query raised by the Prefect) and by everybody else, as a voluntary tax (a concession revoked by Valentinian and Valens as regarded decurions).[38] City life was to be reinvigorated by the appointment of new officials, both religious and secular: the *zygostatēs*, for example, was a new creation, to be responsible for assessing the worth of clipped or damaged *solidi* and each city was to have one.[39]

On Julian's attempts to restore and maintain the membership of city councils, Ammianus' complaints are specific: the emperor ignored rights of exemption gained by years of service elsewhere and was over-strict on matters of domicile. The latter charge is supported by a law to Julianus, the *comes* of Phoenicia, that forbade exemptions to nominated decurions who claimed to be domiciled in another city.[40] On exemption from curial service on grounds of service elsewhere, however, Julian did agree that ten years of military service and fifteen of service in the imperial administration enabled exemption from curial duties[41] and, when nominations for the *boulē* at Antioch were challenged, he ordered a rerun, insisting that nominations were lawful from only two categories of people, namely sons of decurions and 'plebeian' citizens who met the property qualification.[42]

Ammianus also accused Julian of inconsistency in handling specific cases of curial exemptions. Like emperors themselves, who constantly and unsuccessfully advocated strict adherence to the rules on the one hand but the right to use discretion on the other, Ammianus ignored the omnipresence of patronage in Roman culture. Julian hoped to cut back on officialdom, but he still required administrators and some reforms, such as the creation of the *zygostatēs*, would require an increase in personnel. The bureaucracy at Constantinople was recruited largely from the ruling classes of the eastern cities and it was not in emperors' long-term interests to shut off the flow of talent to the capital. Moreover, it was sometimes in cities' own interests that their more prominent citizens had access to the heart of power through service at court. Julian was not alone in his attempts to revive the cities: like other emperors, however, when confronted by the various vested interests involved, he was forced to compromise.

But Julian had some limited success in reducing government expenditure. Ammianus' anecdote about the excessive perks enjoyed by the imperial barber is confirmed by various cost-cutting measures. A maximum of 50 *praesentales* stationed in barracks were to receive animal rations; those in excess of the quota were to return home.[43] Municipal accounting practices were to be tightened up, by the simple expedient of making accountants liable to torture; to this end, only accountants of low social status were to be employed.[44] Long-standing worries about the cost of the *cursus publicus* and the resultant burdens on provincials generated a flurry of regulations to prevent abuse of the system.[45] The right to issue post warrants was confined to the Praetorian Prefect, but Julian would donate a limited number of extra warrants in his own hand to *vicarii* and – after representations from the chief tax officer – governors could also issue warrants for the transport of taxes in kind, if no *vicarius* was available.[46] In Sardinia, the *cursus publicus* was abolished altogether, although exceptions would be made, again, for the transport of the *annona* to the ports.[47]

This clutch of regulations is characteristic of Julian's concern for cost-cutting, his willingness to take advice on unintended consequences of his ideas, such as the impact of cut-backs on tax-collection, and his generally hands-on approach to government – as illustrated in his promise to write out personally ten to twelve post warrants for every *vicarius* in the empire. No detail was too small for his attention. What Ammianus perceived as his concern for clarity may be illustrated in the decision to define a supernumerary horse (*parhippus*).[48] Although it should be obvious, wrote the lawgiver, in order to avoid chicanery he would explain that a *parhippus* was one over and above the number stipulated on the warrant: if the warrant stated one horse, the second was the *parhippus*, and if the warrant gave permission for two, then the third was the supernumerary. Obvious indeed, perhaps, yet not only Julian but also the compilers of both the Theodosian and Justinianic codes thought the point worth making.

Julian and the Christians

Thus far, we have seen that Julian the legislator, as represented in the *Theodosian Code*, is a more conventional and conformist figure than the one we meet in Ammianus, or indeed in his own writings. Although his dislike of Christians and of Constantine survived the editorial cuts of the compilers, the Julian of the *Code* is a pale version of Julian as seen by himself, by Ammianus and even by his detractors. Nonetheless, the Julian of the *Code* matters. His routine responses to day-to-day matters, however mundane, are a reminder of what even Julian as emperor had to do. Moreover, although the specific impact of advisers on individual constitutions cannot be identified, the knowledge, experience and advice of the unnamed backroom officials who acted as guardians of the legal tradition influenced and must often have dictated the emperor's public statements of what the law was. The voice of the 'dull' Julian of the Codes may be in truth that of his officials, the anonymous 'authors' of imperial pronouncements, but the voice of the officials was officially, still, the voice of the emperor himself.

So what are we to make of the two legislative initiatives where Julian's voice should be most distinctively heard, the so-called 'Edict on Funerals', and the law banning Christians from acting as official teachers of the pagan classics, both of which measures were explained and justified by imperial letters?[49] Both can be related to extracts in the *Theodosian Code*, but the nature of the relationship differs in each case. The former illustrates the ability of the Theodosian compilers to divorce wording from context, the latter the importance of selection in determining what law and legal history looked like in the early fifth century.

In banning the holding of funeral processions in daylight, because of the pollution risked by innocent citizens who came into contact with the dead, Julian was almost certainly not thinking only of traditional commemorations of the dead, but of Christian celebrations of martyrs, also held in daylight. The Edict could be used to ban both. Given the explicitly pagan framework of Julian's justification of the measure, as preserved in Greek, the decision of the Theodosian compilers to include extracts from the Latin version required careful management. Julian's argument in the 'letter' (which is described as confirmation of 'ancient law') began with a philosophical disquisition on the absolute separation of death from life, as mirrored in the separate spheres of the gods of the living and the dead. For this reason, the emperor argued, burials of the dead should take place only at night, to avoid troubling the crowds who go about their business by day and attend the temples and festivals of the gods. To ignore the absolute difference between life and death was to disrespect the divine order: those previously 'in error' will either obey willingly or expect 'the most serious retribution'. The content of the Edict is inseparable from Julian's Olympian theology: men are subject to the gods of Olympus in life and rejoin them in death; citizens intending to worship at the temples of the gods are unable to do so because of the pollution incurred by contact with a dead body; and the rites in the temples themselves are disrupted by the ill-omened laments of the funeral cortege. For Julian, the inappropriate conduct of funerals not only violated the cosmic order; it also disrupted civic rituals in honour of the divine.

The Latin version preserved in the *Theodosian Code* differs in emphasis but is still recognizably Julianic.[50] The Edict was a response to a report: the emperor 'has learned' that corpses were being transported through crowds. Julian is now covered: he is responding to a complaint. Funerals, the emperor states, are ill-omened events, which create pollution and no-one can pass to the gods (*sic*) and the temples from a funeral. Moreover, the measure benefits the bereaved as well: grief prefers privacy and funerals should not be exercises in ostentation. In the Theodosian version, this is preceded by a clause on the plundering of tombs, prohibiting the reuse of tomb-building materials for the ornamentation of dining rooms and porticoes. This last is a standard prohibition, which could stand on its own and was uncontentious; the compilers could have included it, while quietly deleting the more controversial measure on daytime funerals, complete with its reference to the gods (plural) and the temples. So why did it survive? First, the constitution's apparently unedited presence in the *Code* exemplifies the respect accorded by the compilers to the wording of past imperial laws. Secondly, as far as is known, the edict was never explicitly revoked. Thirdly, the law, taken literally, was unexceptionable. Nothing in the wording singles out martyr cults as the intended targets of the legislation. Indeed, for Christians, the martyrs were not dead in the conventional sense, therefore the edict, as phrased, was irrelevant to them. Thus the Theodosian compilers could respect and preserve the wording, while ignoring the intention of the legislator.

The law banning Christians from being appointed by city councils to official positions as teachers of the pagan classics on the grounds that it was inappropriate for them to teach what they did not believe to be 'sound' (although no child was excluded from receiving instruction) was controversial at the time and is not included in the *Theodosian Code*, despite its explicit designation by Julian as a *koinos nomos* (424a) or *lex generalis*. Instead the compilers included a related enactment, which was probably part of the same constitution, ordaining that city councils should scrutinise closely the moral qualifications of the teachers they appointed. Once the list was agreed, they were to refer it to the emperor personally, so that his endorsement could provide further honour for them. Taken with Julian's exclusion of 'Galileans' from official teaching posts, the implications are sinister: submission of the lists would provide the emperor with the means of enforcing his ban on Christians, and would probably scare the councillors into excluding Christians from the list altogether.[51] Out of context, however, the measure is innocuous and characteristic of the hands-on approach adopted by Julian in other areas, such as the issue of post warrants noted above. Again, the words, as distinct from the intention of the reform of teaching taken as a whole, were acceptable in the early fifth century, as a regulation issued by a legitimate emperor.[52] But by selecting only what was acceptable, and removing the controversial context, the Theodosian lawyers in effect retrospectively changed the law. The Theodosian Julian is, once again, tamed and relatively conventional; the ill-fated initiative of the original Julian the legislator was indeed buried 'perenni silentio'.

Rhetoric and legitimacy

Two features of Julian's original authorial voice as a legislator stand out. One is the rhetoric employed in his public pronouncements. Like the edicts of Constantine on religion – or, further back, Maximinus' rescript to Tyre and other cities on the rewards of right religion[53] – the rhetoric justifying a legal measure was an intrinsic part of the law itself. It is not an accident that Julian's constitutions are imbued with his personal philosophy and that he so often begins an edict or letter with a set of maxims and comments on his thinking; the rhetoric not only conveys the imperial persona, it also indicates to subjects how the law or the decision is to be read. Julian did not have to incite persecution of 'the Galileans' directly.[54] It was enough to indicate disapproval of their 'errors' and then allow events to take their course – as they did at Alexandria, Gaza[55] and Bostra.[56] Rufinus of Aquileia and the fifth-century church historians would testify that, on the ground, there was active persecution; their accounts are certainly exaggerated but some spin-off from Julian's hostile tone and toleration of anti-Christian behaviour could be expected.

The second notable feature of Julian as author of his laws is his explicit distancing of himself as legislator from aspects of the laws of Constantine. This was not idiosyncrasy or some stylistic quirk but deliberate policy, the aim of which was to subvert the legitimacy of Constantine and his Christian sons as emperors. Constantine and his sons had benefited from the patronage of a wrong god; Julian's accession, following the convenient and natural death of Constantius II, was a demonstration of divine support from the 'true' gods. If Constantine and his sons had claimed their right to rule on the basis of wrong religion, it could follow that their right to rule was itself undermined.

For this reason, Julian's accession was marked by many of the features of imperial regime change, presented by victorious emperors and their propagandists as the replacement of *tyranni*, usurpers, by legitimate emperors. Just as the acts and laws of *tyranni* were routinely repealed by their conquerors and their regimes systematically discredited, so the records of Constantine and Constantius II were openly or more covertly criticised. Constantine and Constantius II are never labelled as *tyranni*, in Julian's propaganda; an open challenge was impracticable, as Julian's own claim depended of course on his membership of the Flavian house and his descent from Constantius I. But for contemporaries, who could decipher the codes of imperial language, as we cannot, such labels may have been unnecessary.

This argument is reinforced by Julian's general behaviour in the early months of his reign. His unchallenged accession was attended by far more disruption in the governing class than was usual during a period of transition. The trials at Chalcedon saw a comprehensive clear-out of the top echelons of Constantius II's civil administration, with the execution or exile of both finance officers and the Master of Offices, as well as several former holders of the posts.[57] These deaths were explained as stemming from the hostility of the eastern armies, whom Julian was obliged to conciliate, combined with Julian's own urge to punish those who had engineered the destruction of his half-brother Gallus. However, this purge contrasted starkly with previous emperors' continuation of some appointments made under previous regimes, to ensure continuity and conciliate vested interests. In addition, Julian's government was openly distanced from that of his predecessor in Claudius Mamertinus' public speech of thanks for his consulship in January 362. Julian himself dismissed Constantine in his *Caesars* as the protegé of Luxury, Extravagance – and an all-forgiving Jesus – allowing him a respite from the attention of the Furies only because of his descent from Constantius I and Claudius Gothicus.[58] Julian's predecessors could never openly be labelled *tyranni*, but their legitimacy could be undermined because, as Christians, they lacked what mattered most, the endorsement of the true gods.

Conclusion

As lawgiver, Julian's authorial persona is complex. Although many measures were shaped by the conventional pattern of report or petition and response, his laws also bear his individual imprint, both by contrast with other emperors and in the light of his own writings. Like his hero Marcus Aurelius,[59] Julian aimed to function as both an emperor and a philosopher.[60] Nor were those two identities easily separated; laws had a moral purpose and Julian's, more than most, were advertised as implementing his view of empire in accordance with the will of the gods who had enabled his rise to power. It remained the case, certainly with strong and assertive emperors, that although responsive they were not passive, but after Julian, they would become less abrasively individualistic, as the bureaucracy at Constantinople tightened its collective grip on the levers of administration. The comparatively muted and boring Julian, who is more in evidence in the *Theodosian Code*, is the creation of the system as it evolved after his death. No emperor after 363 – perhaps fortunately – would so impose his personality on his legislation and, by extension, the whole public culture of his government.

Notes

[1] Millar 1977, 203–6, on imperial authorship of laws and speeches.

[2] On *suggestio*, Honoré 1986, 137–44, and 1998, 133–4; Harries 1999, 47–55; Millar 2006, 207-14.

3 Julian, *Ep.* 41 (following Wright's numeration, which I use throughout), cited by Sozom. *Hist. eccl.* 5.15.

[4] *Ep.* 51.

[5] *Ep.* 27, also discussed by Michael Trapp in this volume.

[6] *Ep.* 28.

[7] *Cod. Theod.* 15.1.8–9 (2nd December 362).

[8] Julian, *Ep.* 23. Whether or not George was involved with the disruptive activities of Artemius and others, he died as a result of lynching, not condemnation for a crime by due process. His goods, therefore, should have passed to his heirs, not to the *fiscus*. The letter also suggests separate treatment for the 'Galilean' texts.

[9] Julian, *Ep.* 49.

[10] Julian, *Ep.* 24. See also *Ep.* 15, to Aetius, which also refers to the recall of exiles under Constantius II.

[11] Julian, *Ep.* 46. On fines, see Honoré 1998, 26-9; Harries 2007, 69-70. Generally levels of fine, where specified, ranged between ten and thirty pounds of gold.

[12] Amm. Marc. 22.10.3. Cf. Julian's pre-empting of the consuls' role in the manumission of slaves at 'their' games (22.7.2, *ipse lege agi ocius dixerat*), for which he fined himself 10 lb. of gold; and his welcome to Maximus the philosopher in the senate in Constantinople (22.7.3). Also Amm. Marc. 25.4.16, that Julian accepted correction, when shown to be wrong.

¹³ Amm. Marc. 22.10.2

¹⁴ Amm. Marc. 22.10.6, *ni quaedam suo ageret, non legum arbitrio*. Perversely, Ammianus also celebrated the return of Justice to the earth as a feature of Julian's reign.

¹⁵ Amm. Marc. 22.9.8, on a rich man accused on the grounds that he had made himself a silk purple robe; Julian sent him a pair of shoes to match.

¹⁶ Amm. Marc. 22.9.16-17.

¹⁷ Amm. Marc. 22.6.5. *Cod. Theod.* 2.29.1 (To the People, 1st February 362) denies to those who bought favours by bribes the right to retrieve them by litigation or forced seizure, as the original contracts were not valid in law. The law was prompted by Egyptian litigants, with whom Julian in the end refused to deal in person.

¹⁸ Amm. Marc. 22.9.12. Decurions were not allowed to use exemptions already granted, length of army service or attachment by birth to a different city from the one claiming his services.

¹⁹ Amm. Marc. 22.4. Note the subsistence allowance paid to the emperor's barber (22.4.9), who received 20 daily bread rations and the equivalent amount of animal fodder, a huge annual salary (*annuum stipendium grave*), and many other lucrative perks

²⁰ Amm. Marc. 22.10.7, *obruendum perenni silentio*.

²¹ Amm. Marc. 22.10.7 (immediately preceding the verdict on the Christian teachers law): *Post multa enim etiam iura quaedam correxit in melius, ambagibus circumcisis, indicante liquide quid iuberet fieri vel vetari*. Cf. also 25.4.20, on Julian's laws, *absolute quaedam iubentia fieri vel arcentia praeter pauca*.

²² *Cod. Theod.* 11.39.5.

²³ *Cod. Theod.* 12.1.50 = 13.1.4 (13th March 362), the withdrawal of curial exemptions from 'Christians'; *Cod. Theod.* 9.17.5 = *Cod. Iust.* 9.19.5, part of the 'edict on funerals' which retains mention of 'the temples' and 'the gods'. The extract from the law banning Christians from teaching the pagan classics (*Cod. Theod.* 13.3.5) refers to a different aspect of Julian's reform of official teaching in cities.

²⁴ Cf. Honoré 1998, 159 (of Theodosius II), that (with one exception, at *Nov. Theod.* 23) 'it is difficult to point to any personal imprint of the emperor on the laws, apart from an emphasis on modesty and restraint'.

²⁵ *Cod. Theod.* 1.15.4 (6th June 362); for Constantius, see *Cod. Theod.* 1.15.2 and 3.

²⁶ *Cod. Theod.* 2.12.1 (6th February 363, to Salutius Secundus).

²⁷ *Cod. Theod.* 3.5.8 (21st February 363), *in praediis Italicis vel stipendiariis seu tributariis*, referring to distinctions from the Roman Republic between lands belonging to Italy and those of states subjected to the Roman empire. It is possible that the phrase is Hypatius' own and that his question sparked a debate in the consistory on dowries, generating the law to Mamertinus, dated five days later (*Cod. Theod.* 3.13.2) on dowries and pacts.

²⁸ *Cod. Theod.* 11.30.29 (22nd September 362), also to Hypatius, Vicar of Rome, illustrating how, even in Antioch, Julian was in regular contact with western officials.

²⁹ *Cod. Theod.* 11.30. 31 (23rd March 363), to Mamertinus, Praetorian Prefect.

³⁰ *Cod. Theod.* 12.1.50 = 13.1.4 (13th March 362). The law (as preserved) refrains, however, from labelling the Christians as 'Galileans'.

³¹ *Cod. Theod.* 2.4.2 (3rd September 362); *Cod. Theod.* 2.4.1 may be the relevant, or possibly a related, ruling concerning coparties of Constantine rescinded by Julian. If the same, the problem was abuse of the rule, not the rule itself.

³² *Cod. Theod.* 13.5.16.

[33] *Cod. Theod.* 3.1.3 (6th December 362), to Julianus, *comes orientis*.

[34] *Cod. Theod.* 4.5.6 (6th December 362), to Salutius Secundus, Praetorian Prefect. This could be a copy of another regulation in the same enactment as that addressed to Julianus (*Cod. Theod.* 3.1.3).

[35] *Cod. Theod.* 12.1.50.1 (*collatio lustralis*); *Cod. Theod.* 12.1.55 (13 children).

[36] As noted also by Amm. Marc. 25.4.15.

[37] *Cod. Theod.* 10.3.1 (15th March 362), to Salutius Secundus, Praetorian Prefect.

[38] *Cod. Theod.* 12.13.1, on the voluntary nature of the application of the crown gold levy to senators – or anyone else. This seems to have been a response to complaints from senators, not decurions. For the re-imposition of *aurum coronarium* on decurions, see *Cod. Theod.* 12.13.2 (28th August 364).

[39] *Cod. Theod.* 12.7.2 (23rd April 363) = *Cod. Iust.* 10.73.2, to Mamertinus, Praetorian Prefect. On the *zygostatēs*, a reform which lasted, see Banaji 2001, 62–3. 70.

[40] *Cod. Theod.* 12.1.52 (15th October 362).

[41] *Cod. Theod.* 12.11.56 (military service); *Cod. Theod.* 6.26.1 (court secretariats).

[42] *Cod. Theod.* 12.1.53.1 (18th September 362) to Sallustius, Praetorian Prefect.

[43] *Cod. Theod.* 6.24.1.

[44] *Cod. Theod.* 8.1.6 (17th January 362), to Auxonius, Corrector of Tuscany. After five years' service, accountants remained on the list for a further year, but, if not prosecuted, could retire with the rank of *perfectissimus*. In *Cod. Theod.* 8.1.7, to Salutius Secundus (1st March 362), the principle of degrading to low status to make liable for torture is extended to keepers of the public records, and in 8.1.8 (27th November 363) by Jovian to heads of accounting departments.

[45] Greg. Naz. *Or.* 4.75, praises Julian's administration of the public post, along with his tax reductions and appointments of magistrates. On the public post and Julian as reformer, or not, see Kolb 1998.

[46] *Cod. Theod.* 8.5.12 (22nd February 362) to Mamertinus; *Cod. Theod.* 8.5.13 (20th June 362), again to Mamertinus but in response to representations from the *comes sacrarum largitionum*. Cf. also *Cod. Theod.* 8.5.15, to Avitianus, *vicarius* of Africa, perhaps providing support for a clamp-down suggested by Avitianus on abuse of the system by influential provincials for the transport of marble.

[47] *Cod. Theod.* 8.5.16 (25th November 362) to Mamertinus. Local officials were expected to travel at their own expense.

[48] *Cod. Theod.* 8.5.14 (9th September 362) and Cod. Iust. 12.50.4. See also *Ep.* 15, to Aetius, allowing him one *parhippos*.

[49] *Cod. Theod.* 9.17.5 = *Cod. Ius.* 9.19.5; Julian, *Ep.* 56. For the *koinos nomos* (general law) banning the teaching of pagan classics, see Julian, *Ep.* 38; Amm. Marc. 22.10.7; Socrates, *Hist. eccl.* 3.16.1; Sozom. *Hist. eccl.* 5.18; Theodoret, *Hist. eccl.* 3.8. For the related constitution, a different extract from the lost Latin original, see *Cod. Theod.* 13.3.5. See also Banchich 1993.

[50] *Cod. Theod.* 9.17.5. pr. and 1.

[51] One prominent victim was the Christian Prohaeresius at Athens, Eunap. *VS* 493.

[52] But note the doubts expressed by Christopher Kelly in his review of J. Harries and I. Wood (eds) *The Theodosian Code* (1993) in *JRS* 86 (1996), 236, on the problem of exclusion of obsolete legislation from the *Code*, that the inclusion of 'a passage (albeit carefully edited) from Julian's notorious "Edict on Education"' was

problematic. My view is that the clause probably comes from the Latin version, and was not edited, but included because, unlike the ban on Christians, it was valid law.

[53] Copied and reproduced by Euseb. *Hist. eccl.* 9.7.

[54] Some violence against Christians did result, although later sources may exaggerate the atrocities for dramatic effect, e.g. Theodoret, *Hist. eccl.* 3.3 (virgins fed to pigs). See Penella 1990.

[55] Sozom. *Hist. eccl.* 5.9.12, Julian fails to show anger against the killers of three Christians.

[56] Julian, *Ep.* 41. At Edessa (*Ep.* 40), Julian exploited conflict between the rival Christian leaderships at Edessa to confiscate all their funds.

[57] *PLRE* 1, 988, Ursulus 1, *CSL*, 355-61, condemned to death due to hatred of soldiers at Chalcedon (Amm. Marc. 22.3.7–9; 20.11.15); *PLRE* 1, 285, Evagrius 5, *CRP* 360–1, exiled (Amm. Marc. 22.3.7); *PLRE* 1, 363, Florentius 3, *Mag. Off.* 359–61, exiled (Amm. Marc. 22.3.6).

[58] *Caes.* 336b.

[59] See Hunt 1995.

[60] Cf. Julian's thoughts on philosophy and the life of action in his *Letter to Themistius* (after 355), which cites Plato's *Laws* and Aristotle's *Politics*. See John Watt's chapter in this volume.

10

WORDS AND DEEDS:
JULIAN IN THE EPIGRAPHIC RECORD

Benet Salway

As part of a volume devoted to the writings of Julian, the assignment to discuss the inscriptions seems at first sight one of the easier ones. Of what may be conceived of as the documentary materials (legislation, epigraphy, numismatics), the inscriptions, being less plentiful than the coins and comprising a shorter extent of text than the legal pronouncements, arguably form the smallest body of evidence. Very many aspects of the emperor's life and short reign have been picked over in minute detail by scholars and the inscriptions relating to Julian are no exception. *Epigráfia* was one of the categories of material analysed in Javier Arce's *Estudios sobre el Emperador Fl. Cl. Iuliano*, arising from his 1975 doctoral dissertation on the sources for the history of Julian's reign, and, more recently, Stefano Conti produced a corpus of the inscriptions mentioning the emperor as Caesar or Augustus: *Die Inschriften Kaiser Julians* (2004).[1] Such inscriptions represent a relatively controllable, if slowly growing group. In 1975 Arce collected 125 inscriptions, by 1984 this number had risen to 131, while Conti's corpus, which still excludes banal mentions of Julian as consul in dating formulae,[2] includes 192 certain examples and sixteen *incertae*. Of these, twenty-six (plus three *incertae*) are Greek, the rest in Latin.

A reasonably diligent, if by no means exhaustive, trawl of epigraphic publications that have appeared in the decade since Conti's text was finalised (in about 2000) reveals an additional five examples of texts in which Julian certainly features. These comprise a Greek dedication to him from Samos,[3] the marginal case of a Greek statue base dedication to a Praetorian Prefect of Constantius Augustus and Julian Caesar from Batanaea in Arabia,[4] and three Latin milestones (all re-used): one from Tipasa in Mauretania Caesariensis;[5] the second from the Hierapolis (Pamukkale)-Laodicea (Denizli) road in Phrygia Prima;[6] and the third from the Antioch-Ptolemais road in Syria.[7] Neither in terms of distribution by genre or by location do these new finds alter the overall pattern discernable in Conti's collection, of which Shaun Tougher reproduced a brief but representative sample in his volume in the *Debates and Documents in Ancient History* series.[8] It is legitimate, therefore, to ask whether anything more of significance can be said on the subject. After all, there is a danger that a discussion of Julian's inscriptions might comprise little more than an extended review of Conti's monograph.[9] However, the present context – that is the analysis of Julian's *writings* – demands a different focus to that found in the studies by Arce and Conti. It is necessary to sift the corpus of Julianic inscriptions to sort those inscriptions that might reflect or represent writings *by* Julian from the far larger number comprising texts dedicated *to* Julian, be they milestones, dedicatory plaques, statue bases, altars, or building inscriptions.

The corpus of inscriptions relating to Julian

Before analysing the corpus in detail, a few general observations are worth making. First, the inscriptions need to be considered within the context of the various phases of Julian's life and reign. The absence of any epigraphic trace of Julian in the first two decades of his life is not surprising, given that much of the period was spent in enforced seclusion (AD 337–351). Still, it is not impossible that he received or commissioned inscribed monuments during the period that he lived in honourable *otium* as a student in Pergamum, Ephesus, and Athens (351–355);[10] but, if so, no examples have survived. As it is, Julian's epigraphic footprint relates entirely to his time in office as Caesar (6th November 355 to November 360 by his reckoning,[11] or to 3rd November 361 by that of his cousin Constantius) and Augustus (360/1 to 26th June 363).[12] In those inscriptions relating to him as Caesar, of course, Julian often features as a formal adjunct to Constantius and has no significant role as actor or honorand himself. A potential complication in analysing the corpus of Julian's inscriptions is that the transition of supreme power from Constantius to Julian was untidy both chronologically and geographically, so that for the twelve months from November 360 to November 361, Julian will have been considered Augustus in some areas while still Caesar in others.[13] On the evidence of coins produced by some mints under Julian's control in 360/1, it is clear that even though Constantius refused to recognise Julian's promotion to Augustus, Julian continued to recognise Constantius as a legitimate Augustus alongside himself.[14] However, no inscription has yet come to light in which both Constantius and Julian are commemorated together as Augusti simultaneously. Furthermore, despite Julian's unorthodox promotion from the rank of Caesar to Augustus and his controversial religious policies, Constantius' death resolved the question of Julian's legitimacy as Augustus. Julian certainly died a legitimate emperor and, indeed, was accorded the respect of the posthumous title of *divus* in the consular dating formula for the later months of 363, even in some Christian epitaphs from Rome.[15] So, while Julian's name has been deleted in half a dozen texts, this does not amount to a centrally directed programme of *damnatio memoriae*; rather it reflects local initiatives of dissociation from declarations that seemed embarrassing in retrospect.[16] Accordingly, it is perhaps not surprising that no epigraphic testimony of Julian's personal involvement in pagan cultic activity should have survived where we might have expected it (e.g. in the sanctuary of the Magna Mater at Pessinus in Galatia, that of Apollo at Daphne outside Antioch, and at the temple of Zeus on Mons Casius near Seleucia Pieria).[17] Nevertheless allusions to his religious enthusiasms do survive in some of the panegyrical dedication and dating formulae authored by his subjects.[18]

Secondly, the choice of physical support for inscribed texts needs some consideration. All the surviving monumental inscriptions are in stone, although we know that bronze was still being used in the Latin west for public documents. A telling example is provided by one inscription that, in fact, documents an action by Julian and is discussed by Conti, but which, since the emperor is neither the honorand or actor in the text, falls outside the parameters of his catalogue.[19] This is the protocol of greeting and schedule of perquisites for officials (*ordo salutationis commodorumque*) that was inscribed on a limestone plaque at Thamugadi (Timgad) in Numidia in 362 or 363.[20] This text reports that it was originally published 'in bronze for the record of perpetuity' (*ad perpetuitatis memoriam aere incisus*) by Ulpius Mariscianus, the consular governor of the province, at Cirta.[21] The emperor features by virtue of the fact that Mariscianus boasts in passing that he was the first to be promoted to the position of *consularis* (sc. *praeses*) *sexfascalis* of Numidia 'by our lord, the unconquered emperor, Julian' (*a domino nostro invicto principe Iuliano*).[22] The survival of the text of the bronze original only via this stone copy reminds us to be conscious of the likelihood of losses of this kind, losses which are likely to have disproportionately affected the survival of official pronouncements in the Latin west.

The chronological, geographic, and generic distribution of the surviving inscriptions is most easily appreciated by mapping out onto a grid the contents of Conti's corpus, along with the new texts and a small number omitted by him (see Table 1). Following Conti's example, the geographical distribution of the inscriptions is analysed by administrative diocese but starting, as did Arce, in the west, with Britain, rather than Oriens, in order to reflect somewhat better the rough trajectory of Julian's progress as Caesar and Augustus across the empire between 355 and 363. Taking the analysis a couple of steps further, the inscriptions are also classified roughly by genre, and those relating to Julian as Caesar are counted separately from those relating to him as Augustus. To aid detection of any effect of the emperor's proximity on the frequency of attestations, the names of the regions through which Julian actually passed as Caesar or Augustus are indicated in **bold** type in the table below. Aside from the usually banal category of milestones (*miliaria*), the inscriptions have been sorted into three categories: texts where, however panegyrical the phrasing, Julian appears essentially only as an incidental element in a dating formula;[23] dedications on behalf of, or directly to, Julian; and miscellaneous others, including acclamations and texts commemorating honours or activities sponsored by Julian. It is in this last category that the more individual and informative texts are usually to be found.

As the table illustrates, in terms of genre, as with most emperors, texts on milestones are best represented, many of them simply dedications added to stones erected under much earlier régimes. In what may simply be conventional praise, Libanius claims, in his funeral oration for Julian, that many cities had erected his image.[33] As it happens, statue-base dedications only survive in significant numbers from Africa.[34] Looking at the geographical distribution, rather against the grain of the general Roman epigraphic habit, in which Greek texts outnumber Latin ones,[35] the dioceses of the Latin west (Britanniae to Daciae) account for 136 texts (or 145, if the uncertain cases are included), those of the Greek east (Macedonia to Oriens) for 61 (or 70), and even there half the milestones are in Latin. Considering the totals for the dioceses through which Julian passed as emperor, there is no discernible correlation between Julian's movements and the distribution of the surviving texts. In fact there is almost an inverse relationship between Julian's presence and his epigraphic legacy. Neither as Caesar nor as Augustus did he visit any provinces of the dioceses occupying the first three positions in terms of number of inscriptions (Africa, Italia Suburbicaria, and Asiana). This distribution is more a reflection of the relative weakness of the epigraphic culture of those regions in which Julian actually spent much of his reign as Caesar and Augustus. After Julian left Milan for Gaul as a newly appointed Caesar in 355, it was only with his arrival in Oriens, in the summer of 362, that his presence again coincided with an area with a prolific epigraphic habit.[36] Overall the geographical distribution of the texts accords with the overall trends for the distribution of inscriptions in the Roman world. As for chronology, although Julian enjoyed a longer period in the public eye as Caesar (355 to 360/1) than as Augustus (360/1 to 363), more inscriptions attest him in the latter phase. That most of these texts belong to milestones suggests that the advent of a new Augustus was more likely to trigger epigraphic commemoration at the roadside than the promotion of a Caesar.

Table 1. Statistical summary of inscriptions relating to the emperor Julian (numbers of texts of uncertain attribution shown in brackets).

Diocese	Rank	*Miliaria*	Dating formulae	Dedications to Julian	other	Totals (+*incertae*)	
Britanniae	Caes.					0	1
	Aug.				1[24]	1	
Galliae	Caes.					0	0
	Aug.					0	
Viennensis	Caes.						1
	Aug.	1				1	
Hispaniae	Caes.						3
	Aug.	3				3	
Italia Annonaria	Caes.					0	22 (+1)
	Aug.	21 (+1)			1[25]	22 (+1)	
Italia Suburbicaria	Caes.				2[26]	2	37 (+1)
	Aug.	25 (+1)		9	1[27]	35 (+1)	
Africa	Caes.		4 (+2)	1 (+1)		5 (+3)	56 (+6)
	Aug.	26 (+2)	5 (+1)	19	1[28]	51 (+3)	
Pannonia/ Illyricum	Caes.						12
	Aug.	11			1[29]	12	
Daciae	Caes.						4 (+1)
	Aug.	4 (+1)				4 (+1)	
Macedonia	Caes.						6 (+1)
	Aug.	5	1	(1)		6 (+1)	
Thraciae	Caes.						3
	Aug.	3				3	
Pontica	Caes.						7 (+1)
	Aug.	6 (+1)		1		7 (+1)	
Asiana	Caes.	1		1		2	26 (+4)
	Aug.	11 (+1)		12 (+2)	1 (+1)[30]	24 (+4)	
Oriens	Caes.	1			2[31]	3	19 (+3)
	Aug.	11 (+3)	1	3	1[32]	16 (+3)	
Totals (+ *incertae*)	Caes.	2	4 (+2)	2 (+1)	4	12 (+3)	197 (+18)
	Aug.	127 (+10)	7 (+1)	44 (+3)	7 (+1)	185 (+15)	

Limiting our sights to those surviving epigraphic documents (i) of which Julian is the ostensible author in the first person or (ii) in which his name is in the nominative case as third-person subject or (iii) that allude directly to his action, we are left with a far smaller number. However, within this select group of just twenty-six artefacts, bearing twenty-two different texts, it is instructive to observe that two texts fall outside the parameters of Conti's corpus, one of them (attested in two surviving copies) of great significance. In addition to the surviving epigraphic examples, it is possible to speculate from surviving literary testimony as to the original number of Julian's writings that were once publicly posted, some of which may once have been inscribed in a permanent medium.

Julian's actions

Turning first to inscribed texts of which Julian is the subject in the third person, there is, of course, one such category of which the content ought to have been at least approved by the emperor, even if it was very largely tralaticious in nature: that is legends on the coinage. However, the traditional demarcations of scholarship mean that treatment of these belongs to my numismatic colleagues, so I shall leave consideration of them aside here.[37] Very similar in nature are the legends on lead seals and weights, where the emperor's titulature is a mark of authority. Two Julianic examples survive. Julian's name appears as Caesar on one side of a lead weight from Summuntorium in Raetia (Mertingen-Burghöfe, Bavaria) that has Constantius as Augustus on the other.[38] Julian as sole Augustus appears on the legend of a group of four lead sealings from Britain (as Augustus), incidentally the only Julianic texts from Britain.[39]

The vast majority (eleven out of eighteen) of the texts bearing Julian's name in the nominative case are on milestones. Up to the third century AD, when an emperor was named on a milestone, it was almost always in the nominative as the builder of the road but from the third century onwards, the predominant formula became one of dedication of the work to the emperor in the dative, as financial responsibility for the upkeep of the roads was devolved downwards to the municipalities.[40] And, indeed, the majority of Julianic milestones conform to this type (e.g. Conti 2004, nos. 84 and 85 = *CIL* 17/4.1.14, 15, and 26). Hence, there may be some significance in those that do give the name in the nominative, indicating perhaps specific imperial intervention. However, this may be pushing the logic of the grammar too far in the absence of any finite verbs describing funding or ordering of construction. Nevertheless, some groups of milestones certainly relate to areas (i) through which Julian passed or (ii) in which his administration may have had an understandable strategic interest or (iii) where he may plausibly have had a personal interest that would precipitate imperial patronage. In the second category are a series of milestones from the Roman province of Arabia, specifically from the roads emanating from Philadelphia (Amman) to Gerasa (Jerash) and Petra respectively. These texts may reflect investment in the infrastructure of this area as part of the preparations for the Persian campaign of 363. Still the most interesting aspect of these texts is the linking of the emperor's name in various combinations with the phrase εἶς θεός ('one god'), a staple of Christian epigraphy of the region of Palestine and Syria Phoenice. These read as acclamations rather than the conventional dedications usually found in this context.[41] For example, from the Gerasa-Philadelphia road, there comes a milestone that declares 'one god, Julian, rules',[42] another with '9 (miles). One god, the emperor Julian',[43] and others looking forward to imperial victory: '8 (miles). May one god be victorious, one Julian, the Augustus' and '9 (miles). One god, the emperor Julian, may he be victorious'.[44] As Glen Bowersock pointed out in his review of Conti's book, these would seem to reflect the monotheistic tendencies in Julian's paganism, rather than being an expression of Christian resistance to Julian's religious policy or self-assertion in response to it.[45]

That the drafters of these texts were aligning themselves closely with Julian's policies is suggested by another formula used in the milestones of the same Gerasa to Philadelphia road: 'Julian has been victorious happily for the universe. 8 miles'.[46] A milestone from the Petra-Philadelphia road has another formula reminiscent of the religious phraseology of the region: [Αὐτο]κρ(άτω[ρ]| Ἰουλια[νὸς | Α]ὔγουστος | εἰς αἰ[ε]ὶ βα[σιλεύς] (i.e. 'Imperator Iulianus Augustus aeternus princeps'),[47] whose formula may be compared with [μ]έγας ἦς (= εἰς) ἀεὶ Ὀλύμπιος Ζεύς ('great for ever Olympian Zeus') on an inscription from Emesa (modern Homs), in Syria Phoenice.[48] Given the relative proximity of the εἶς θεὸς texts and the emphasis placed elsewhere on the solitary nature of Julian's imperial position after Constantius' death – e.g. the dedication to Julian by the consular governor of Macedonia as 'ruler of all and sole emperor of the habitable world' (παντοκράτωρ καὶ μόνος τῆς οἰκουμένης βασιλεύς)[49] – it is tempting to see a pun being made here on εἰς/εἷς: 'for ever emperor/ever one emperor'.

Another milestone text that may indicate imperial investment in a strategically important route comes from the road along the *limes Columnatensis* in Mauretania Caesariensis.[50] This has Julian as Augustus and author in the nominative. Two more nominative texts from the territory of Miletus, one Greek, the other Latin, may reflect imperial patronage attracted by the emperor's interest in the sanctuary of Apollo at Didyma.[51] Nominative texts at Beroia in Macedonia and Gangra in Paphlagonia come from regions past which the imperial entourage travelled, even if not directly through.[52] However, no particular explanation of this sort can be used in relation to two nominative texts on Italian milestones – one with egregiously poor orthography – which suggests that, after all, within the category of milestones, we should not attach too much weight to the choice of grammar.[53]

The reality of response to a specific imperial initiative is more probable in the case of unique compositions. Three such examples, where the appearance of Julian's name in the nominative case really does indicate imperial action, come from Italy. In two of these cases, however, Julian is named as the junior co-author of the activity alongside Constantius in accordance with the fiction of the unison of the imperial college. So there is some doubt as to whether Julian, then campaigning in the northern Gallic provinces, would have been conscious of the activities being ascribed to him. On the other hand, it is perfectly conceivable that protocol dictated that such matters be referred to him as items for information.

The first example is the dedication of the restoration, after the Magnentian interlude (AD 350–353), of the honorific statue for one of the emperor Constans' loyal officials, Eugenius, who had died as consul designate for AD 349:[54]

> To Flavius Eugenius, *vir clarissimus*, ex-Praetorian Prefect, ordinary consul designate, Master of all the Offices, *comes domesticus* of the first rank, who had fulfilled all the Palatine positions, on account of his outstanding merits on behalf of the *res publica*, for him our lords Constantius, victor and triumpher, ever Augustus and Julian most noble Caesar decided to restore, at public expense and on a plot of theirs, the gilded statue in the forum of the divine Trajan that he had merited before under Constans by virtue of his lifestyle and most faithful devotion, with the approval of the most ample senate.[55]

The high-profile location – in Trajan's forum – and lavishness of the statue – gilded bronze – indicate the political significance attached to this honour. The obvious occasion for this rehabilitation to have been announced, or the restored statue to have been unveiled, is that of Constantius' famous visit to Rome from 28th April to 29th May 357, so memorably described by Ammianus Marcellinus (16.10.5–17). In this case, no doubt, the real author of the decision is Constantius. Another epigraphic text of the same genre, for which Julian was solely and directly responsible, we know of only from the report of Ammianus. In the summer of 361, on his march eastward against Constantius, Julian encountered at Sirmium Sextus Aurelius Victor, who may have just recently completed the Roman history for which he is remembered.[56] Later, in the autumn but before he learnt of the death of Constantius (on 3rd November), Julian, now at Naissus, summoned Victor from Sirmium, appointed him consular governor of Pannonia Secunda and ordered a bronze statue to be erected in his honour 'as a man to be emulated on account of his *sobrietas*', that is his frugal, self-restrained, or serious demeanour.[57] While not part of the regular vocabulary of honorific texts,[58] this virtue is plausibly one that Julian would have celebrated and was presumably cited in the text of the statue base.[59] Although supposed by some modern commentators to have been erected at Rome,[60] Victor's statue was most likely located at Sirmium, chief city of the diocese of the Pannoniae and capital of the province over which Julian had appointed him governor.[61] The unparalleled wording of a milestone from nearby Mursa, dedicated to Julian 'on account of the obliteration of the faults of times gone-by', may testify to Victor's reciprocation of the emperor's admiration.[62]

Returning to surviving inscriptions, the second Italian text in which Constantius and Julian are paired records imperial generosity towards Spoletium (Spoleto) in Umbria through the provision of funds to rebuild a set of baths that had been destroyed by fire some time in the past:

> Repairers of the world and restorers of cities, our lords Flavius Iulius Constantius pious, favoured, ever Augustus and Julian most noble and most victorious Caesar for the eternal promotion of the imperial name restored for the people of Spoletium out of their generosity the baths that had in the past been destroyed by fire.[63]

The same imperial visit to Rome will have afforded the Spoletini a convenient opportunity to importune Constantius either on his way southwards along the Via Flaminia in April 357 or on his way back north again in the first week of June.[64] Julian's epithet *victoriosissimus* may be more than mere flattery here, since in mid-357 (or soon after) it would be an appropriate reflection of his early successes against the Franks in 356 and the Alamanni in 357, even before the famous battle of Strasbourg (Argentorate).[65] Still, just as with the honours to Eugenius, Julian will have been a passive partner in this transaction between the Augustus and the Spoletini. Julian as Caesar is similarly cited as a theoretical fellow-commissioner of fortification works undertaken by the provincial governors of Isauria and Cilicia in two commemorative inscriptions dating from 359/361, in the wake of the Isaurian revolt of 359:[66]

> By order of our lords Constantius triumpher Augustus and Julian most noble Caesar, Bassidius Lauricius *vir clarissimus*, *comes* and governor, occupied the fortress for a long time previously held by brigands and a danger to the provinces and, furnished with a stronghold of soldiers for the perpetual establishment of peace, called it 'Antioch'.[67]

> By order of our lords Constantius triumpher Augustuses (*sic*) and Julian
> most noble Caesar, a wall has been built for the city of the Irenopolitans,
> with Aurelius Iustus *comes* and governor taking responsibility.[68]

However, the third Italian inscription, which has Julian, now Augustus, as
its sole nominative subject, does commemorate a genuine initiative of the
emperor. This marble plaque was discovered in the necropolis di Levante
at the site of Iulia Concordia in Venetia in 1873:

> On account of his signal and singular favour towards the *res publica*, our lord
> Julian, most unconquered prince, responsibility having been removed from
> the provincials, ordered that the fiscal post be run with shortened intervals
> between change-overs, with Claudius Mamertinus *vir clarissimus*, Praetorian
> Prefect over Italy and Illyricum organiser, and Vetulenius Praenestius *vir
> perfectissimus*, corrector of Venetia and Histria taking responsibility.[69]

This commemoration of an administrative reform rather than a physical
construction is unusual and suggests a deliberate policy by the Prefect
Mamertinus,[70] if not Julian himself, to publicise this action. Julian's efforts
to reform the imperial state postal system (the *cursus publicus*) were certainly
remembered positively by those sympathetic to his more controversial
religious stance (e.g. Lib. *Or.* 18.145) and may have contributed to the
grudging respect accorded to his non-religious administrative measures
even by ideological enemies (e.g. Greg. Naz. *Or.* 4.75).[71] It is notable that
three of the four laws of Julian preserved in truncated form under the title
de cursu publico in the *Theodosian Code* are addressed to the very same
Mamertinus *praefectus praetorio* (*Cod. Theod.* 8.5.12–14),[72] the earliest of the
series having been issued soon after the death of Constantius in the winter
of 361/362.[73] The opening phrase of the Concordia inscription is
reminiscent of the sort of rhetoric found in the justificatory preambles that
prefaced the official imperial pronouncements formulated by the emperor's
quaestor.[74] It is tempting to imagine that it may echo the wording of the lost
preamble to *Cod. Theod.* 8.5.12 or its sequels. If so, then we are the closest
yet to epigraphic attestation of a text actually authored by Julian, even if in
reality composed by his quaestor, Iovius.[75]

Julian's words
For some eighty years from its discovery at Eleusis in the 1890s a lacunose
Greek text carved on three fragments of a Pentelic marble stēlē was
considered to preserve a pronouncement by Julian.[76] As such it was
registered and discussed by Arce in the addenda to his catalogue.[77]
However, given, on the one hand, that of the author's names and titles
only [- - -]λιανὸς is actually preserved and, on the other, that the

146

palaeography of the script better suits a date in the second or third century, the text has now been more convincingly interpreted as the pronouncement of any one of a number of proconsuls of Achaea whose names end [- - -]lianus.[78] It was, accordingly, rightly ignored by Conti.

Nevertheless, as it happens, the epigraphic record does transmit one text that may confidently be identified as the *ipsissima verba* of the emperor, at least in his official voice, and which, as a legal pronouncement, serves as a minor supplement to Jill Harries' chapter in this volume. For it is the case that one Latin ordinance of Julian is preserved in no less than two verbatim inscribed copies from the province of the Aegean Islands in the diocese of Asiana. Expressed in Latin, this official voice is possibly less reflective of Julian's personal discourse and idiolect than that of his predecessors. For, while Ammianus Marcellinus testifies to Julian's fluency in spoken Latin, it is equally clear that his literary formation was essentially Hellenic.[79] Ironically, perhaps because Julian's name is not preserved, neither version is registered in either the catalogue of Arce or that of Conti, or even included in the latter's discussion of those inscriptions reflecting the emperor's legal activity.[80] The omission is curious since both copies have long been on record as Julianic texts in the *Corpus Inscriptionum Latinarum*.[81] A further fragmentary imperial pronouncement in Latin from Cos may also be attributable to Julian but is probably better assigned to the emperor Valens.[82]

As for the certifiably Julianic pronouncement, the more complete copy of this text (*CIL* 3.459A + B, lines 1–4) was discovered and first recorded at the port of Katapola, ancient Minoa, on Amorgos in August 1841. Here the constitution, which is a letter addressed to a Secundus *parens carissimus atque amantissimus* (in fact, the Praetorian Prefect with Julian in the east, Saturninius Secundus *signo* Salutius),[83] was disposed over two blue/grey-veined marble plaques. On the second plaque (now lost) the imperial letter was followed by another text (*CIL* 3.459B, lines 5–16), most likely an edict of the Prefect, perhaps instructing provincial governors to publicise the measure. The topic is the delegation of legal judgement by governors to so-called *iudices pedanei*. A more fragmentary copy, inscribed in the same fashion (on which see further below), was subsequently identified in the castle at Mytilene on Lesbos (*CIL* 3.14198). Although the text, as presented at Amorgos, is anonymous, it is not actually acephalous. It bears the heading *E S L*, i.e. *e(xemplum) s(acrarum) l(itterarum)*, which may be translated 'a copy of the imperial letter'.[84] Nevertheless the author can confidently be identified as Julian because a severely edited extract was preserved in the fifth-century *Theodosian Code* (1.16.8), with the heading identifying it as issued by Julian to Secundus *p(raefectus) p(raetori)o*.[85] This in turn was taken over by the compilers of the sixth-century Justinianic *Code* (*Cod. Iust.* 3.3.5), which version alone preserves a subscript transmitting a date and place of issue: Antioch on 28th July 362 (*dat(a) V kal(endas) Aug(ustas) Antiochiae, Mamertino et Nevitta cons(ulibu)s*).[86]

The surviving stone (preserved in the Epigraphical Museum in Athens) and the texts have been subjected to a detailed study by Denis Feissel.[87] The survival of two witnesses of this text within the same provincial boundary cannot be mere chance. It shows that the *praeses Insularum* must have ordered the publication in some durable form of this particular constitution. However, as is demonstrated by the Amorgos copy, the existence of multiple texts does not aid dissemination of the content if the text is so garbled as to be almost unintelligible (see fig. 1). It is clear from the orthography that there are at least two layers of distortion to which the text has been subject. First, there are clear symptoms of mistakes arising from phonetic transcription as a reader has dictated to a scribe with imperfect Latinity, such as, simple E for AE (e.g. *controversie*, line 3), E for I (e.g. *admenestren[t]*, line 21), confusion of B and V (e.g. *quivus*, line 7), and loss of H (e.g. *umiliora*, line 13). At Amorgos and, to judge from its more exiguous remains, at Mytilene too, this text has then been carved by a mason illiterate in Latin, who has attempted to reproduce mechanically a facsimile of the half uncial text on the papyrus or parchment in front of him (rather than transforming it into an appropriate monumental script), while also regularly reproducing the superficially similar Latin P and R indifferently as a Greek Rho. The result is certainly no masterpiece of public communication from emperor to subject. It does, however, demonstrate that, while numerous Greek letters and edicts addressed to Greek provincial audiences survive amongst Julian's correspondence as transmitted by the manuscript tradition, official communication between emperor and officials of the imperial government was conducted in Latin. So, when such missives were published and left in their authoritative Latin version, a potentially baffling Latin layer was interposed between Hellenophone emperor and Hellenophone subjects. Nevertheless, even in its garbled state, the Amorgos inscription allows us to recover one of Julian's Latin pronouncements in something close to its authentic version, prior to editing by the compilers of the *Theodosian Code*:[88]

> A copy of the imperial letter:
> Not a few controversies are accustomed to arise that require the attention and scrutiny of a higher judge, but there are still some matters in which it is superfluous to wait for the governor (*moderator*) of the province. Weighing which matter up, it has seemed quite right to us that we should give governors (*praesides*) the power to establish subordinate judges (*pedanei*

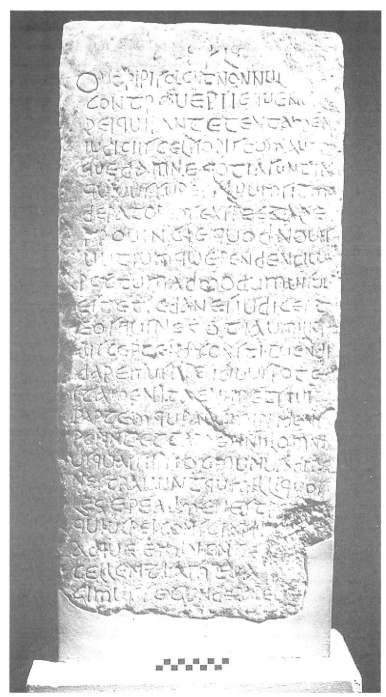

Figure 1. Julian's letter to Secundus on a marble stele from Amorgos, CIL 3.459A (Athens, Epigraphikon Museion, inv. 10401).

iudices), that is, those who decide more humble matters. For thus they will be both relieved of a part of their responsibilities and yet will still be carrying out this obligation when those whom they select carry it out. Conscious (?) of which matter [- - -] we decree that your excellence, Secundus, most dear and beloved relative, [- - -] most agreeable [- - -] that one should take account of the public interest.

In ordering the inscribing of multiple copies of this imperial pronouncement in Latin, the governor of the province of the Islands echoes the practice of some of his early-fourth-century predecessors in the Greek east, most notably under Diocletian, Galerius, and Maximinus.[89] It may be entirely coincidental but it is interesting that Julian's reign should see the last efflorescence of a phenomenon most widely attested under a series of emperors notorious for their anti-Christian stance.

The Amorgos and Mytilene text is a rare example of an intact original pronouncement by Julian but it is not unique, and it is not the best preserved – that honour goes to the stray and acephalous, but otherwise complete, constitution of Julian on advocacy, transmitted in the famous Codex Victorianus of Terence.[90] Still, this epigraphically transmitted text is significant as representing the source material for a later codified text, something that the advocacy law does not. Even though the epigraphic parallel at Amorgos and later Mytilene has long been signposted in the standard editions of the Roman law codes as well as the registers of extraneous legal material, this precious opportunity has been under-exploited by those approaching the legislative material from the direction of the literary tradition.[91] Feissel's comparison of the epigraphic with the codified version reveals the editorial commission of the *Theodosian Code* to have followed their instructions well. The compilers used their authorised powers to excerpt the statements that might be construed as of general applicability and carry out minor grammatical and verbal adjustments to allow the extracts to stand on their own grammatically:[92]

> Emperor Julian Augustus to Secundus Praetorian Prefect.
> There are some matters in which it is superfluous to wait for the governor of the province. And therefore we give governors the power to establish subordinate judges, that is, those who decide more humble matters.
> Given on the fifth day before the kalends of August, Mamertinus and Nevitta being consuls.[93]

Importantly the example of the Amorgos and Mytilene inscriptions shows that there is a chance that any of Julian's utterances, for which public posting is likely to have taken place, may have been recorded in more permanent form by inscribing in stone (in the Greek east) and stone or bronze in the Latin west. But how to identify the possible candidates for these potentially 'lost' inscriptions? The integrated edition of Julian's letters and laws by Joseph Bidez and Franz Cumont greatly facilitates the exercise of identification.[94] Amongst Julian's letters and codified legislation, those texts that (i) are identified as edicts, (ii) are addressed to a general public, (iii) recorded as having been posted (*proposita* or προτεθήτω), or (iv) as received (*accepta*) elsewhere than issued, may have received this treatment. On this basis eighteen certifiably, or very plausibly, publicly-posted writings by Julian can be identified.[95] It is, of course, impossible to know how many, if any of these, might have received permanent inscription. On the other hand, without the Amorgos and Mytilene stones, there would be nothing to indicate that Julian's letter on *iudices pedanei* fell into this category, so there is a high probability that other texts for which there is now no indication were not only publicly posted but actually inscribed.

Conclusion

Within the wider corpus of inscriptions relating to the emperor Julian, there is a relatively narrow range of inscriptions that record some nominal or actual public action by him. More significantly there is actually one text with a genuine claim to be considered a writing of Julian, albeit in his official voice, that was memorialised in a permanent medium for public display. This Latin voice was, however, perhaps somewhat distant from Julian's own personal expression. Nor does any of this surviving epigraphic output specifically reflect his religious views. Moreover, of this meagre collection, it is ironic that this one surviving publicly-inscribed writing of Julian does not, as it was presented to the audience, in fact, name him. Surprising as it may seem in the case of an emperor with such a controversial personality, it appears that for the purposes of information and authority its status as an imperial pronouncement was more important than the individual identity of its author.

Acknowledgements

The author is grateful to Maria Lagogianni, Director of the Epigraphikon Mouseion, Athens, for permission to reproduce the photograph of inv. 10401. Special thanks for advice and helpful criticism are owed to Simon Corcoran, María del Mar Marcos Sánchez, Muriel Moser, and Katerina Panagopoulou, as well as this volume's editors.

Notes

[1] Arce 1975, 35–47, and 1984, 89–176, esp. 97–112 (catalogue); Conti 2004.

[2] Conti 2004, 24. The *c.* 50 epigraphic attestations of Julian's consulates in AD 356, 357, 360, and 363, the vast majority of them on epitaphs from Rome, are registered by Bagnall *et al.* 1987, 246–8, 254, and 260.

[3] *IG* 12.6 1 (Samos) 427 = *SEG* 50 (2000) 810, p. 276: a white marble plaque dedicated to Julian as Augustus.

[4] *SEG* 49 (1999) 2105: a large limestone base. The name of the Prefect is lost but ought to be one of Constantius' Prefects based at Antioch between 355 and 361, i.e. Strategius Musonianus (*PLRE* 1, 611–12, Musonianus), Hermogenes (*PLRE* 1, 423 Hermogenes 3), or Helpidius (*PLRE* 1, 414, Helpidius 4); see Barnes 1992, 259–60.

[5] *AE* 2002, 1710b, in which Julian *semper Augustus* has been added to a dedication to Constantius and Constans as Augusti from AD 340/350 (*CIL* 8.22557).

[6] *AE* 2002, 1413c, in which Julian *nobilissimus Caesar* has been added to a dedication to Constantius and Constans as Augusti from AD 340/350 (*AE* 2002, 1413b).

[7] *AE* 2006, 1570c, in which Julian *perpetuus Augustus* has been overcut onto a text of Constantine and his Caesars of AD 333/335 (*AE* 2006, 1570b, lines 10–11).

[8] Tougher 2007, 102, no. 29.

[9] Cf. the notice at *SEG* 54 (2004), 1838, with concordance between Conti's corpus and *SEG* and other corpora; and review by Bowersock 2006.

[10] Cf. Hadrian, honoured by dedications in Latin and Greek by the Athenians while still a *privatus*: *CIL* 3.550 = *ILS* 308 = *IG* 2².3286 (Athens).

[11] Proclaimed Augustus by his troops in Paris as early as February 360, Julian did not assume the diadem until November in Vienne (Amm. Marc. 21.1.4).

[12] On the chronology see Seeck 1919, 201–10, and Barnes 1992, 224, 226–8.

[13] At the death of Constantius on 3rd November 361, Julian controlled the Rhine and Danube provinces as far east as Dacia but in Italy Aquileia remained loyal to Constantius (Amm. Marc. 21.12.2), as did Africa (Amm. Marc. 21.7.2–5). See Matthews 1989, 105. Julian himself says that Constantius continued to acknowledge him as Caesar, while rejecting his promotion to Augustus: Julian, *Ep. ad Ath.* 286.

[14] Cf. Kent 1981, 225–7, nos. 280–302 (Arles), 192–4, nos. 205–25 (Lyons). Julian continued to refer to himself as merely Caesar in communications with Constantius: Julian, *Ep. ad Ath.* 281a. For Julian's coins see also the chapters by Fernando López Sánchez and Eric Varner in this volume.

[15] *ICUR* suppl. 1515 = *ILCV* 4410; *ICUR* n.s. 5.13314 = *ILCV* 4409; on which see Bagnall *et al.* 1987, 260–1. The Greek dedication *I.Side* (*IK* 43) 50 = Conti 2004, no. 45, addressed Θεὸν Ἰουλιανόν, may be another posthumous honour; but cf. Conti 2004, 46–7.

[16] *CIG* 2744 + add. 1109 and *AE* 1990, 957 = Conti 2004, nos. 32–3 = Roueché 2004, nos. 19–20, with commentary III.4 and III.10 (Aphrodisias, Caria); possibly *AE* 2008, 1408 (Iasos, Caria); *CIL* 3.7088 = *ILS* 751 = Conti 2004, no. 28 (Pergamum, Asia); *CIL* 8.5338 = Conti 2004, no. 136 (Calama, Africa Proconsularis); *CIL* 8.17770 and *AE* 1987, 1075 = Conti 2004, no. 174 and possibly *incerta* 15 (Thamugadi, Numidia). See Bowersock 2006, 704–5.

[17] On Julian's visits to Pessinus, Daphne, and Mons Casius, see Amm. Marc. 22.9.5, the *Passio Artemii* 40, 49–56, and Amm. Marc. 22.14.4 respectively.

[18] Restoration of temples or rites: *ILS* 9465 = Conti 2004, no. 1; *AE* 2000, 1500 and 1503 = Conti 2004, nos. 17–18; *AE* 1983, 895 = Conti 2004, no. 54; *CIL* 8.4326 +18529 = *ILS* 752 = Conti 2004, no. 167; *AE* 1893, 87 = Conti 2004, no. 176. Adherence to philosophy: *I.Ephesos* (*IK* 12) 313a, (*IK* 17.1) 3201 = Conti 2004, nos. 26–7; *CIL* 3.7088 = *ILS* 751 = Conti 2004, no. 28; *CIL* 3.14201[8] = Conti 2004, no. 30; *ILS* 751 = Conti 2004, no. 34. For a limited discussion, see Conti 2004, 46–50.

[19] Conti 2004, 174.

[20] *CIL* 8.17896, cf. *AE* 1948, 118 + *AE* 1949, 133 + *AE* 1978, 892 + *AE* 1979, 667 = *FIRA* 1².64. Thamugadi, Numidia: Ex au[ctori]tate Ulpi Mariscia|ni v(iri) c(larissimi) consularis sexfascalis | promoti primo a domino nostro | invicto principe Iuliano ordo sa|lutationis factus et ita at(!) perpetui|[t]atis memoriam aere incisus, . . . *etc.* (trans. Johnson *et al.* 1961, 242, No 307). See most recently Stauner 2007.

[21] *PLRE* 1, 561, Mariscianus.

[22] Meaning Mariscianus was the first *consularis Numidiae* to be appointed during Julian's reign, not the first ever to that post: see *PLRE* 1, 1086, and Stauner 2007, 155–6.

[23] On these introductory formulae see Chastagnol 1988, 19–28 [141–50]. Following Conti's practice (see above n. 2), inscriptions where Julian only features in the consular date are excluded.

[24] Four examples of a lead sealing stamped with Julian as Augustus (discussed below, under 'Julian's actions').

[25] *CIL* 5.8987 = Conti 2004, no. 87: a plaque commemorating reform of the *cursus publicus* (discussed below, under 'Julian's actions').

[26] A statue base (*CIL* 6.1721 = Conti 2004, no. 114) and a building inscription (*CIL* 11.4781 = Conti 2004, no. 124) erected by Constantius with Julian as junior partner (discussed below, under 'Julian's actions').

[27] *CIL* 11.6711, 2 = Conti 2004, no. 125: a gold brooch with acclamation 'Iuliane, vivas' the same legend as on *CIL* 3.1639 from Pannonia (see below n. 29).

[28] *CIL* 8.17896, the *ordo salutationis*, discussed above (n. 20).

[29] *CIL* 3.1639 = Conti 2004, no. 72: a gold brooch with acclamation 'Iuliane, vivas', the same legend as on *CIL* 11.6711, 2 from Arretium, Italia Suburbicaria (see above n. 27).

[30] Two imperial pronouncements, *CIL* 3.459A and *AE* 1947, 58 = *IG* 12/4.1, 272, discussed below under 'Julian's words' (not registered by Conti 2004).

[31] Two commemorative plaques for fortification works in Cilicia (*AE* 1974, 644 = Conti 2004, no. 12) and Isauria (*CIL* 3.6733 = Conti 2004, no. 15) on the orders of Constantius and (nominally) Julian (discussed below under 'Julian's actions').

[32] *AE* 1948, 137 = Conti 2004, no. 16: a marble column from Ascalon, Palaestina, with an acclamation of the εἷς θεός type, as found on Julianic milestones from Arabia (discussed below, under 'Julian's actions').

[33] Lib. *Or.* 18.304, on which see Nock 1957, 115.

[34] Thirteen out of the nineteen dedications to Julian from Africa are from statue bases.

[35] Trout 2009, 172.

[36] Julian traversed Pontica from Chalcedon to the Taurus in May, arriving in Antioch in the first week of June 362; see Seeck 1919, 210.

[37] For a catalogue, see Kent 1981; for discussion, see Arce 1984, 177–228, and Fernando López Sánchez in this volume.

[38] *AE* 2000, 1136b = Conti 2004, p. 183: [D(ominus) n(oster) Constan]tius [p(ius) f(elix) Aug(ustus)] | | [Fl(avius)] Cl(audius) Iulia[nus nob(ilissimus) C(aesar)].

[39] *AE* 1979, 380 + Hassall and Tomlin 1980, 413, no. 52 = *RIB* 2.2411[25–28] = Conti 2004, no. 188. Ickham, Kent: D(ominus) n(oster) Iulianus Aug(ustus) | | S | RVF.

[40] For the phenomenon see the summary tables of *CIL* 17/2, pp. viii–xxxv, and 17/4.1, pp. ix–xvi.

[41] On acclamations generally see Roueché 1984, 181–8; on these specifically, Petersen 1926, 271–3, and Di Segni 1994, 107.

[42] *AE* 1998, 1445b = *SEG* 48 (1998) 1912 = Conti 2004, no. 3: εἷς θεὸς, | Ἰουλιανὸς | βασιλεύει.

[43] *CIL* 3.14175[1] = Conti 2004, no. 8: VIIII | εἷς θεὸς, | Ἰουλιανὸς | βασιλεύς.

[44] *AE* 1895, 167 = *CIL* 3.14176 = Conti 2004, no. 5: VIII | εἷς θεός ν[ικᾷ] εἷς Ἰουλιανὸς | ὁ Αὔγουστος; Conti 2004, no. 7: VIIII | εἷς θεός, | Ἰουλιανὸς | βασιλεύς, νι[κᾷ].

[45] Bowersock 2006, 703.

[46] Conti 2004, no. 10: Ἰουλιανὸς | ἐνίκησεν εὐ|τυχῶς τῷ κόσ|μῳ. | μίλια θ΄.

[47] *CIL* 3.14149[41–44] = Conti 2004, no. 2.

[48] *IGLS* 5.2455.

[49] *AE* 1983, 895 = *SEG* 31 (1981) 641 = Conti 2004, no. 54. A marble altar, Thessalonica, Macedonia: ἐπὶ τοῦ θεοφιλε|στάτου καὶ ἀνανε|ωτοῦ τῶν ἱερῶν | τοῦ δεσπότου καὶ | νικητοῦ παντὸς | ἔθνους βαρβαρικοῦ | Κλαυδίου Ἰουλια|νοῦ | παντοκράτο|ρος καὶ μόνου τῆς | οἰκουμένης βασι|λέως Καλλιόπι|ος ὁ λαμπρότα|τος ὑπατικὸς | καθιέρωσεν (trans. Tougher 2007, 102; photograph: Conti 2004, Taf. 6).

[50] *CIL* 8.10339 = Conti 2004, no. 162: D(ominus) n(oster) | Iulianus | vict[or ac]| tr<i>um[f(ator)]| sempe[r | Aug(ustus)].

[51] *I.Didyma* 60 = Conti 2004, no. 38: Φλά(ουιος) Κλ(αύδιος) Αὐτοκρ(άτωρ) | Ἰουλιανὸς | Αὔγουστος | ἀπὸ τῆς π[ό](λεως) | vacat μίλ(ια) | IIII; *CIL* 3.14404a = Conti 2004, no. 39, an addendum to a dedication to Constantius Augustus and Julian Caesar: E+ITEI (=? et d. n. Fl.) Cl(audius) Iulia|nus Imp(erator) Aug(ustus). Julian's interest in Apolla at Didyma is documented by Soz. *Hist. eccl.* 5.20.7 (Bidez and Cumont 1922, no. 124).

[52] *AE* 1974, 586 = *SEG* 37 (1987) 546 = Conti 2004, no. 56. Beroia, Macedonia: Ἰο[υλια]|νὸς{νὸς} | [Αὔ]γουστος; *AE* 1991, 1498c = Conti 2004, incerta 4. Gangra, Paphlagonia: Imp(erator) Caes(ar) |[Iulia?]nus | [Augustu]s.

[53] *CIL* 11.6629b = Arce 1984, no. 28 = Conti 2004, incerta 9. Sentinum, Flaminia-Picenum: [D(ominus) n(oster) | Fl. Cl. | Iulianus | pius] f[e]l[i]x [vi]ctor | semper Aug(ustus) | b(ono) r(ei) <p(ublicae)> n(atus) | CXLI; *CIL* 10.6945 = *ILS* 748 = Conti 2004, no. 105. Atella, Campania: D(ominus) n(oster) imp(erator) Cl<a>udi(us) | Silvanus (!) Aug(ustus) | bono rie (!) p(ublicae) na|tus. This is recut over a dedication to Severus Alexander from AD 229/230 (*CIL* 10.6944).

[54] *PLRE* 1, 292, Eugenius 5.

[55] *CIL* 6.1721 + pp. 3173, 3813 = Conti 2004, no. 114. Rome: Fl(avio) Eugenio v(iro) c(larissimo) ex praefecto praetorio | consuli ordinario designato, magistro | officiorum omnium, comiti domestico | ordinis primi omnibusque Palatinis | dignitatibus functo, ob egraegia (!) eius | in rem publicam merita: huic | dd(omini) nn(ostri) Constantius victor ac | triumfator semper Augustus et | Iulianus nobilissimus Caesar | statuam sub auro in foro divi | Traiani, quam ante sub divo |

Costante (!) vitae et fidelissimae | devotionis gratia meruit, adprobante amplissimo senatu | sumptu publico loco suo | restituendam censerunt.

[56] *PLRE* 1, 960, Victor 13. The narrative of his *Liber de Caesaribus* or *Historiae abbreviatae* closes in AD 360.

[57] Amm. Marc. 21.10.6: Ubi (*sc.* Naissum) Victorem apud Sirmium visum, scriptorem historicum, exinde venire praeceptum, Pannoniae Secundae consularem praefecit, et honoravit aenea statua virum sobrietatis gratia aemulandum, multo post urbi praefectum. On the quality of *sobrietas* see den Boeft *et al.* 1991, 140.

[58] It is found in *ICUR* 6.17272b, a Christian epitaph from the cemetery of Marcellinus and Peter outside Rome.

[59] Cf. Julian, *Caes.* 336a–b, where he satirizes his uncle Constantine for his proclivity to indulgence (τρυφή) and debauchery (ἀσωτία).

[60] The site for the statue base is located in Trajan's Forum at Rome by Chastagnol 1962, 232–3, and Matthews 1989, 23–4; cf. the doubts of Hedrick 2000, 292 n. 59.

[61] A provincial location (Naissus or Sirmium) is preferred over an urban one by den Boeft *et al.* 1991, 139.

[62] *CIL* 3.10648b = *ILS* 8946 = *ILCV* 11 = Conti 2004, no. 73. Mursa, Pannonia Secunda: Bono r(ei) p(ublicae) nato, d(omino) n(ostro) | Fl(avio) Cl(audio). Iuliano [princip]|um (?) max(imo) triumf(atori) semp(er) | Aug(usto), ob deleta vitia | temporum pr<a>eteri|torum.

[63] *CIL* 11.4781 = *ILS* 739 = Conti 2004, no. 124. At the temple at the source of the river Clitumnus, Spoletium: Reparatores orbis adque urbium resti|tutores, dd(omini) nn(ostri) Fl(avius) Iul(ius) Constantius p(ius) f(elix) semper Aug(ustus) | et Iulianus nobilissimus ac victoriosissimus Caes(ar) | ad aeternam divi nominis propagationem, | thermas Spoletinis in praeteritum igne consump|tas sua largitate restituerunt.

[64] For Constantius' itinerary see Barnes 1993, 222.

[65] Drinkwater 2007, 217–24.

[66] For the revolt see Amm. Marc. 19.13.1, with Matthews 1989, 364.

[67] *CIL* 3.6733 = *ILS* 740 = Conti 2004, no. 14. Germanicopolis (Ermenek), Isauria: Iussu dd(ominorum) nn(ostrorum) Constantii triumfatoris | Augusti et Iuliani nob(ilissimi) Caesaris, | castellum, diu ante a latronibus | possessum et provinciis perniciosum, | Bassidius Lauricius v(ir) c(larissimus), com(es) et | praeses, occupavit ad[q]ue ad perpe|tuam [q]uietis firmitatem militum | praesidio munitum Antiochiam | nuncupavit. On the date of this activity, see *PLRE* 1, 497, Lauricius.

[68] *AE* 1974, 644 = Conti 2004, no. 12. Irenopolis (İrnebol), Cilicia: [Iuss]u dd(ominorum) nn(ostrorum) Constantii triumfa|tori]s Augg(ustorum) (!) et I[uliani nob(ilissimi) Caesaris,]| murus aedi[ficatus est]| Hirenopolit[anorum civitati,]| Aur(elio) Ious[to] (!), co[m(ite) et praeside, c(uram) a(gente)].

[69] *CIL* 5.8658 and 8987 = *ILS* 755 = Bidez and Cumont 1922, no. 67c = Arce 1984, no. 38 (with pp. 128–32) = Conti 2004, no. 87. Iulia Concordia, Venetia et Histria: Ab (!) insignem singula|remque erga rem publicam | suam faborem, d(ominus) n(oster) Iulianus, invictissimus prin|ceps, remota provincialibus cura, | cursum fiscalem breviatis mutationum spa|tiis fieri iussit, | disponente Claudio Mamertino, v(iro) c(larissimo), per Ita|liam et Inlyricum praefecto praetorio, | curante Vetulenio Praenestio, v(iro) p(erfectissimo), corr(ectore) | Venet(iae) et Hist(riae). Photograph: Conti 2004, Taf. 8.

[70] *PLRE* 1, 541–2, Mamertinus 2, who was also appointed consul prior for 362, for which he wrote his surviving *gratiarum actio* (*Pan. Lat.* 11[3]).

[71] See the discussion by Arce 1984, 128–32.

[72] *Cod. Theod.* 8.5.12: Imp. Iulianus A. ad Mamertinum PPo (22nd February 362); 8.5.13: idem A. ad Mamertinum PPo (20th June 362); 8.5.14: idem A. ad Mamertinum PPo (9th September 362).

[73] The chronology is extrapolated from the recorded receipt of *Cod. Theod.* 8.5.12 at Syracuse on *VIII Kal. Mart.* (22nd February) of 362. Given that Julian was then in Constantinople, having arrived there on 11th December 361, the law was probably issued a month or so prior to its arrival in Sicily. For Julian's movements see Seeck 1919, 209, and Barnes 1993, 228.

[74] For the function of the imperial quaestor see Harries 1988, 151–3.

[75] *PLRE* 1, 464, 'Iovius 2'; Harries 1988, 171.

[76] Skias 1895, cols 103–5, no. 18A: [Αὐτοκράτωρ Καῖσαρ - - - Ἰου]λιανὸς ‖[τῇ βουλῇ καὶ τῷ δήμῳ τῷ Ἀθηναί]ων λέγει, ‖[- - -] εἴη, τῆς τ' ἐξ ἡμῶν ‖[- - -]ε γεινόμεν[ο]ν ἀνά‖[λωμα(?) - - - τ]ῶν γειτονού[ντ]ων κτη‖[μάτων(?) - - -] ε· ἵνα δὲ ὁ χ[ρ]ήζων] τὸ ὕδωρ ‖[- - - ἐ]κ τ[οῦ ἀρχ]αίου χρό‖[νου - - -] οὗ φροντ‖[ίζ- - -].

[77] Arce 1984, 168–9, addendum no. 2.

[78] Kapetanopoulou 1975, 63–4, no. 9.

[79] Amm. Marc. 16.5.7: ...Latine quoque disserendi sufficiens sermo. On Julian's reading and literary models see Bouffartigue 1992, 408–24.

[80] Cf. Conti 2004, 51–5.

[81] Mommsen 1873, pp. 86–7, no. 459; Mommsen *et al.* 1902, p. 2316[32], no. 14198.

[82] *AE* 1947, 58 = *IG* 12/4.1, 272; see Feissel 2009, 314–17.

[83] *PLRE* 1, 814–17, Secundus 3; Barnes 1992, 249.

[84] On the use of this heading see Corcoran 2008, 298–300.

[85] The constitution is restored to the title *De officio rectoris provinciae* in modern editions on the basis of an uncertainly identified and possibly now lost manuscript, where the constitution was actually headed *Idem Aug(ustus) Secundo p(raefecto) p(raetori)o*; see Paul Krüger's apparatus to *Cod. Theod.* 1.16.8 in Mommsen 1904, 57.

[86] The authority for the subscript is the now lost manuscript of Giambattista Egnazio, known only through an early printed edition (Haloander, 1530, 104); see the apparatus to *Cod. Iust.* 3.3.5 in Krüger 1877, 242.

[87] Feissel 2000; *AE* 2000, 1370a–b.

[88] Feissel 2000, 335 [221] = *AE* 2000, 1370a + b, lines 1–4, provides a consolidated and restored text (underlining here indicates the extent of overlap with *CIL* 3.14198, Mytilene): E(xemplum) s(acrarum) l(itterarum). Oboriri solent nonnul[lae] controversiae quae not(ionem) requirant et examen iudicis celsioris, tum autem quaedam negotia sunt in quibus superfluum sit moderatorem exspectare provinciae. Quod nobis utrumque pendentibus rectum admodum visum est ut pedaneos iudices, hoc est eos qui negotia humiliora disceptent, constituendi daremus praesidibus potestatem. Ita enim et sibi partem curarum ipsi dempserint et tamen nihilominus quasi ipsi hoc munus administrabunt cum illi quos legere administraren[t]. Cuius rei conscii ANI[- c. 6 -] atque eminente[m ex]cellentiam tuam [san]cimus, Secunde paren[s cari]ss[ime at]que ama[ntissime, - - -]ICVM E[. .]I CI[. .]I[- c. 8 - g]ratissimum CONC[- c. 10 -]TARE in quo pub[lico commodo] consulatur.

[89] For a catalogue see Corcoran 2007, 224–6.

[90] Florence, Biblioteca Medicea-Laurenziana, pluteus 38.24 (a south German manuscript of the tenth century; on-line at: http://teca.bmlonline.it/TecaRicerca s.v. 'Terentius'), fols 171r–172r; for edition and commentary see Bischoff and Nörr 1963.

[91] *Cod. Iust.*: Krüger 1877, 242; *Cod. Theod.*: Mommsen 1904, 57; and duly registered by Hänel 1857, 212, no. 1115; Seeck 1919, 210; and Bidez and Cumont 1922, no. 113a (codified) and 113b (epigraphic). Ignored by Volterra 1971, 95–101, and Carrié 2009; but cf. Benoist 2009, 115.

[92] Feissel 2000, 334–7 [220–2] confronts the epigraphic with the codified versions in *Cod. Theod.* 1.16.8 = *Cod. Iust.* 3.3.5. On the editorial powers provided by *Cod. Theod.* 1.1.5 (26th March 429) and 1.1.6 (20th December 435), and the procedures of the compilers of the *Theodosian Code* generally, see Matthews 2000, 121–67 and 200–53.

[93] *Cod. Iust.* 3.3.5 (cf. *Cod. Theod.* 1.16.8): Imp(erator) Iulianus A(ugustus) Secundo p(raefecto) p(raetori)o. Quaedam sunt negotia, in quibus superfluum est moderatorem exspectare (expectari *Cod. Theod.*) provinciae: ideoque pedaneos, iudices hoc est qui negotia humiliora disceptent, constituendi damus praesidibus potestatem. Dat(a) V kal(endas) Aug(ustas) Antiochiae, Mamertino et Nevitta cons(ulibu)s.

[94] Bidez and Cumont 1922.

[95] Bidez and Cumont 1922, no. 60 = Socrates, *Hist. eccl.* 3.3: Ἀλεξανδρέων τῷ δήμῳ (προτεθήτω τοῖς ἐμοῖς πολίταις Ἀλεξανδρεῦσιν); no. 65 = *Cod. Theod.* 2.29.1 = *Brev.* 2.29.1: ad populum (dat. C'poli 1st February 362); no. 67 = *Cod. Theod.* 8.5.12: Mamertino PPo (acc. Syracusis 22nd February 362); no. 68 = *Cod. Theod.* 9.42.5: ad Felicem com. s. l. (pp. Romae 9th March 362); no. 47a–d = *Cod. Theod.* 11.16.10 + 10.3.1 + 11.23.2 (dat.) + 12.1.50 = 13.1.4: Secundo/Sallustio PPo (pp. C'poli 13th March 362); no. 75a = *Cod. Theod.* 13.3.4: ad archiatros (dat. C'poli 12th May 362) = Greek letter [no. 75b] *Ep.* 25b [Wright no. 31]; no. 61b = *Cod. Theod.* 13.3.5 (dat. 17th June 362, acc. Spoletio 29th July 362); no. 110 = *Ep.* 26 [Wright no. 24/Tougher 2007, no. 15] described by the *Historia acephala* as an edict that was posted (banishing Athanasius); no. 111 = *Ep.* 51: Ἀλεξανδρεῦσιν (προτεθήτω τοῖς ἡμετέροις πολίταις Ἀλεξανδρεῦσιν); no. 119 = *Cod. Theod.* 12.1.52: ad Iulianum cons. Phoenices (dat. Antiochiae 3rd September 362, acc. Tyro 15th October 362; no. 123 = *Cod. Theod.* 6.26.1: ad Secundum PPo (dat. Antiochiae 25/09, acc. [- - -]isis 9th November 362); no. 126a–d = *Cod. Theod.* 11.28.1 [+ 15.3.2 + 8.5.15 + 8.10.7]: ad Avitianum vic. Africae (dat. 26th October 362, acc. Carthagine 18th March 363); no. 127 = *Cod. Theod.* 12.1.54: ad Iulianum com. Or. (pp. Beryto 1st November 362); no. 128a–b = *Cod. Theod.* 15.1.8 + 15.1.9 [= *Brev.* 15.1.9]: Ecdicio praef. Aeg. (pp. Antiochiae [*sic*] 2nd October 362); no. 132 = *Cod. Theod.* 4.12.5 = *Cod. Iust.* 9.19.5: Secundo PPo (pp. in foro Traiani 6th December 362); no. 136 = *Cod. Theod.* 9.17.5 = *Cod. Iust.* 9.19.5: ad populum (dat. Antiochiae 12th February 363); no. 137b = *Cod. Theod.* 11.3.4: edictum (dat. 27th February 363); no. 141 = *Cod. Theod.* 6.27.2: Secundo PPo (pp. Beryto 28th February 363).

11

JULIAN AND HIS COINAGE:
A VERY CONSTANTINIAN PRINCE

Fernando López Sánchez

Julian: a literary figure in the sources and an emperor in his coinage

As stated in the introduction to Shaun Tougher's *Julian the Apostate*, this emperor has been the object of 'fascination' from antiquity right up to today.[1] It seems the writings of Julian himself have allowed us to get to know the psyche of this Roman emperor much better than that of any other ruler of his time – circumstances which enabled the writing of an *Intellectual Biography* by Polymnia Athanassiadi.[2] Paradoxically, the availability of so much information has contributed to obscuring his political figure. As Fergus Millar has observed, a Roman emperor does not respond to an abstract theory, but to a specific – and usually passive – way of governing.[3] It is therefore legitimate to ask whether Julian, the person, and his writings, are one and the same. The answer given by some historians, such as Glen Bowersock, is simple: Julian lived in an oppressive atmosphere during the rule of his cousin Constantius II, until he was proclaimed Augustus in the midst of a tumult in Paris in February 360.[4] Until then, his writings were false, due to constraint; it was not until later, once he was Augustus, that Julian was able to imprint his particular way of thinking upon his government (e.g. Bowersock's chapters, 'The Mask Removed' and 'The Puritanical Pagan').[5] According to this interpretation of Julian's work and government, the reader must separate his first writings from his later work, which was much closer to reality. Javier Arce's *Estudios sobre el emperador Fl. Cl. Juliano* and Samuel Lieu's *The Emperor Julian: Panegyric and polemic* stress the difficulty in reading *anything* regarding Julian, not just his own works.[6] This emperor has unleashed so many passions, attacks and defences, that it is difficult to assess reality in his reign. Julian, the intellectual, an image that he promoted himself, must be joined to the image of Julian the emperor-soldier, transmitted by Ammianus Marcellinus. An emperor who shared the hardships of his soldiers in Gaul or Persia would certainly be the cause of admiration in his *conmilitones*. Nevertheless, good soldiering qualities have never necessarily implied good political judgement, and Ammianus comments little on the strategic reasons behind Julian's decisions. Other ancient authors, such as Socrates, Zosimus, Gregory of Nazianzus, Festus, Eutropius and Aurelius Victor, focus on Julian's reign from a partisan perspective, such as Paganism vs. Christianity.[7] Therefore, it is very difficult for modern historians to evaluate the relationship this emperor had with Constantius and the army, or even his own undertakings in Gaul and Persia.

The main object of this chapter is to approach Julian as an emperor more than as an intellectual, i.e. the idea is to frame him into the coordinates belonging to Roman rulers of the fourth century. The main source used will be coinage, a written and iconographic record that has been seriously under-exploited.[8] The writings of Julian the Apostate were not all captured on paper and scrolls. There is other writing, concise, but not less important, which spread throughout fourteen imperial mints in eight years (355–363). A. H. M. Jones observed in 1956 that the study of coin types lacked any interest and only led to over-interpretation, which sufficiently excused any serious historian from their study.[9] This negative view of coin iconography and legends has been appropriately termed by Ragnar Hedlund as 'ultra-scepticism',[10] and has been expressed in the past by T. V. Buttrey,[11] Andrew Wallace-Hadrill,[12] and Michael Crawford.[13] However, the recurrence and disappearance of certain legends and coin representations throughout Roman imperial history, including Julian's reign, allow for the piecing together of distinctive and coherent imperial narratives. The following is an attempt at uncovering Julian's narrative and the way it was articulated in his coinage.

Julian as Caesar of Constantius

Julian Caesar's imperial narrative, as represented in his coin series of November 355–Spring 360, was identical to that of Gallus Caesar from mid 351–Winter 354. Gallus, Julian's half-brother, was appointed Caesar by Constantius II in Sirmium, March 351,[14] after the latter was accepted as commander in chief of the Danubian forces by Constantius' spokesman, the general Vetranio.[15] Vetranio was certainly not an unconditional partisan of Constantius, as his uprising in early 350 demonstrated. In fact, Julian (*Or.* 1 30d) considers him a 'traitor' and gives him a status similar to that of the usurper Magnentius. Indeed, Vetranio did not hand over the Balkans to Constantius freely, but examined his leadership capacity beforehand, in case of a western invasion led by Magnentius.[16] The miliarenses with the three standards on the reverse from the mints of Thessalonica[17] (Figs 1 and 2) and Nicaea,[18] although vaguely dated by *RIC* to 351–354, must actually be placed at the beginning of 351, i.e. shortly after the meeting of

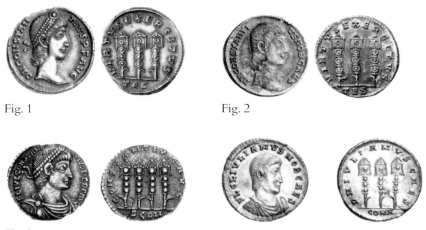

Fig. 1   Fig. 2

Fig. 3   Fig. 4

Fig. 1 Constantius II. Thessalonica, heavy miliarense, 351. Ira & Larry Goldberg Coins & Collectibles. Auction 55. Auction date: 29 October 2009. Lot number 209.
Fig. 2 Constantius Gallus, Thessalonica, heavy miliarense, 351. Numismatica Ars Classica 46. Auction date: 2 April 2008. Lot number 723.
Fig 3 Constantius II, Arles, miliarense, 355. Classical Numismatic Group, Inc. Mail Bid Sale 72, Closing Wednesday, June 14, 2006. Lot number 1792.
Fig. 4 Julian II. Arles, miliarense, 355. Helios Numismatik. Auction 1. Auction date: 17 April 2008. Lot number 595.

Constantius II with Vetranio in Naissus in December 350. Furthermore, these miliarenses testify to the introduction by Constantius II of Gallus as Caesar before the Danubian army. There are other military series linked to the introduction of Gallus to the Illyrian army, such as the gold and bronze *Hoc Signo Victor Eris*.[19] Nevertheless, these miliarenses with the three (or four) standards have been consistent in their typology since Constantine I, unlike the *Hoc Signo Victor Eris*. Therefore, the *Virtus Exercitus* miliarenses struck in Arles that explicitly mention Constantius II (*Constantius Aug*)[20] (Fig. 3) and Julian (*D N Iulianus Caes* or *D N Iulianus Nob Caes*)[21] (Fig. 4) on their reverses must be read as coins introducing Julian to the army of Gaul by Constantius II late in 355.

Gallus and Julian were both protégés of Constantius II and were presented before the army numerous times as members of the Constantinian dynasty. Several series of miliarenses reading *Felicitas Romanorum* with the figures of Gallus and Constantius II under an arch were minted in Sirmium[22] and Nicomedia[23] (and perhaps Thessalonica), which were the probable headquarters of Gallus in the Balkans and the Bosphorus region before his departure for Antioch (Fig. 5).[24] These miliarenses with the arch were typical of the ruling dynasties of the fourth century, which contrast strongly with the purely military types (with no arch) of generals such as Vetranio (Fig. 6), with no lineage to back them.[25] Constantius II also struck miliarenses with Victory and arch for Julian and for himself in Antioch (Fig. 7). They were issued by Constantius II in 355, or more probably in 360/361, and are highly representative of the dynastic plans that this Augustus had for his cousin.[26] The *Victoria Romanorum* miliarenses, minted at Sirmium and Antioch in late 361 or early 362[27] (Fig. 8), are equally of great historical significance, because they prove Ammianus to be right, that Constantius favoured Julian even on his deathbed in Cilicia despite Julian's disposition to confront him in civil war (*successorem suae potestatis statuisse dicitur Iulianum*).[28]

Had Constantius II lived beyond November 361, it is easy to conclude that he would have directed his whole Balkan army against Julian, the invader, much as he did in 351 against Magnentius, with the support of Vetranio.[29] Nevertheless, Julian's advance towards Sirmium, as well as the occupation of strategic points, such as the Succi Pass and the city of Naissus (Amm. Marc. 21.10.1–8), seem to indicate otherwise.[30] Although two legions revolted against Julian in Aquileia in the autumn of 361 they had previously given their loyalty to him in Sirmium (Amm. Marc. 21.11.2). They only rebelled in the Adriatic city when Julian commissioned them to Gaul. Even so, these troops surrendered to the new emperor when the death of Constantius II was made known, thereby recognizing a Constantinian sovereign (Amm. Marc. 21.12.18–19). The difference in Constantius II's reaction to the Balkan advances of Magnentius and Julian is therefore enormous. Great also is the difference in Magnentius' and Julian's attitudes towards Constantius II. Julian did not strike in Aquileia the *adventus* types with the legend *Liberator Rei Publicae* (Fig. 9), as Magnentius had done,[31] nor did Constantius II issue the series *Salvator Rei Publicae* that was struck by Vetranio in Siscia (Fig. 10).[32]

Given these examples, it must be concluded that the dynastic loyalty shown by Constantius II towards Julian played an essential role in the acceptance of the latter by the armies from Gaul and the Danube. Magnentius was well aware of this, as he attempted – with no success whatsoever – to enter the Constantinian house. He offered his daughter to Constantius in marriage, and himself in turn asked to marry Constantia, the emperor's sister.[33] On the other hand, it is also legitimate to ask whether Constantius II was actually the posthumous winner in the political and military dispute between Julian and himself, begun in February 360. After arriving at Sirmium and Naissus, in mid 361, Julian rapidly continued his journey towards Antioch, firmly decided to begin the Persian invasion

Fig. 5

Fig. 6

Fig. 7

Fig. 8

Fig. 9

Fig. 10

Fig. 5 Constantius II, Antioch, light miliarense, 352. Classical Numismatic Group, Inc. Mail Bid Sale 58, Closing Wednesday, September 19, 2001. Lot number 1372.

Fig. 6 Vetranio, Siscia, light miliarense, 350. Numismatica Ars Classica NAC AG. Auction 39. The Barry Feirstein Collection of Ancient Coins. Part I. 16th May 2007. Lot number 195.

Fig. 7 Constantius II, Antioch, light miliarense, 352 or 355 or 359. Freeman & Clear, Mail Bid Sale 15, Closing Date, Friday, June 27, 2008. Lot number 429.

Fig. 8 Julian II, Antioch, light miliarense, Late 361 or early 362. Numismatica Ars Classica. Auction 42. Auction date: 20 November 2007. Lot number. Lot number 219.

Fig. 9 Magnentius, Aquileia, Golden multiple, 350–1. Numismatica Ars Classica NAC AG. Auction 24. A Higly Important Collection of Roman and Byzantine Gold Coins, Property of a European Nobleman. 5th December 2002. Lot number 307.

Fig. 10 Vetranio, Siscia, solidus, 350–1. A. Tkalec AG/ Astarte S.A. Bolla Collection Auction date: 28 February 2007. Lot number 111.

designed by Constantius II.[34] The only discord existing between Constantius II's and Julian's governments was the favour Gauls enjoyed over other Romans and Danubians in the highest positions. The loyalty of Nevitta or Dagalaifus to Julian was recompensed, not without scandal, with the offices of *magister equitum* and *comes domesticorum* respectively (Amm. Marc. 21.8.1).[35]

Julian as successful commander of Constantius II in Gaul

Between 355, when he was named Caesar in Milan,[36] and his proclamation as Augustus in Paris in February 360, Julian's coin series reflects a military programme encouraged by Constantius II. The fallen horseman type, distributed among the reverses of Ae 2, Ae 3 and Ae 4 bronzes from 348 (Fig. 11), originated as a copy of the celebrated pictorial scene of one of Darius III's *corps* guards being lanced by Alexander the Great, known to us thanks to the famous mosaic at Pompeii and the sarcophagus of Sidon (Fig. 12).[37] The adoption of this coin type is linked to the second battle between Constantius II and Shapur at Singara in 348.[38] The victory was Roman, and subsequently exploited as propaganda of Constantius II, which seems to be also the case with the gold series related to the first battle around 344, with Victory, trophy and palm-branch.[39]

The fallen horseman clearly distinguished Constantius II's coins from those of his rival Magnentius during the civil war of 351–353. Constantius II, Gallus, and Julian all struck millions of these coins well after the defeat of Magnentius, until 357, probably as a clear indication that affairs of the eastern empire held primacy over anything occurring in the west. In fact, when Julian informs us that the civil war against Magnentius was only an undesired distraction from Constantius II's campaign in Persia, he was probably right. During the 340s Constantius held very few troops in the east (Jul. *Or.* 1 31a); the Danube and western empire belonged to Constans,

Fig. 11   Fig. 12

Fig 11 Constantius Gallus, Siscia, Ae 2, 351–355, RIC VIII, pl. 17, no 347.
Fig. 12 Sarcophagus of Sidon. Late IVth century. Istanbul. Archaeological Museum. Inv. 370. López Sánchez 2005.

and Constans always denied him the soldiers he needed for his eastern campaigns. The rise of Magnentius in the west in 350 gave Constantius II the chance of grabbing Roman Illyria, and maybe even the west as a whole. If successful, he would not only be recognized as supreme Augustus of the entire empire, but more importantly, he could solve his permanent lack of troops. The need for more soldiers lies at the heart of Constantius' interest in spreading west. The need to transfer troops from west to east also explains the continuity until 357 of the fallen horseman coin type. Why should these coins cease to be struck, precisely in this year? In 357, Constantius, after entering Rome in triumph,[40] decided to march on the Danube (October 357–late 359);[41] he subsequently formally reopened the front against Persia, early in 360 (Amm. Marc. 20.9.1).

The battle of Strasbourg, in which the Roman army commanded by Julian Caesar faced the troops of seven kings of the Alamanni (Amm. Marc. 16.11–12), may be interpreted as an example of Constantius' eagerness to recruit in the west. Although the Roman victory must be credited to Julian, the contribution of Constantius was also essential. After Strasbourg, there was a joint offensive against the Juthungi led by Nevitta, Julian's right-hand man, and Barbatio, a close agent of Constantius,[42] reflecting a close collaboration between the forces of Augustus and Caesar (Amm. Marc. 17.6.1–3). It is even legitimate to ask whether the Roman operation against the Alamanni would have been successful without the forces Constantius sent from Milan. Ammianus is very clear on this, and states that 'from another direction Barbatio...came from Italy at the emperor's order with twenty-five thousand soldiers to Augst' (*Parte alia Barbatio...ex Italia iussu principis cum XXV milibus armatorum Rauracos venit*).[43] Furthermore, Ammianus (16.12.62) names four Roman officials fallen in battle, including Bainobaudes and Laipso, the two tribunes from the palatine troops of *Cornuti* of Constantius II. A third official, called Innocentius, is described by Ammianus as 'commander of the mailed cavalry', which seemingly identifies him as an officer of the cataphracts (heavy cavalry). There is no evidence for the existence of this kind of cavalry in the west, although it is cited by Ammianus as accompanying Constantius during his triumphal entry into Rome in 357.[44]

The Alamanni who fought against the troops of Julian and Constantius II at Strasbourg do not seem to have been staunch Roman enemies. On the contrary, they were allies of Constantius II in 352, when the emperor sent them a message to cross the Rhine from the *barbaricum* to occupy the region that spread between Mainz and Trier. Their mission was to obstruct Magnentius in Gaul and aid the advance of the Balkan forces into the region.[45] Missives between Romans and Alamanni were not only sent by

Constantius. In 361, the Alamannic king Vadomarius sent secret letters to Constantius, without the consent of Julian, informing him of the political situation in Gaul (Amm. Marc. 21.4.1–6). The same king Vadomarius was previously involved in important negotiations with Julian in 359, jointly with three of the seven kings mentioned by Ammianus at the battle at Strasbourg: Urius, Urscinus and Vestralpus (Amm. Marc. 18.2.18). Ammianus does not reveal the content of the negotiations between Julian and the Alamannic kings. Nonetheless, based on Vadomarius' collaboration with different Roman emperors in the east after 361, they were probably centred on supplying Alamanni as auxiliary troops to Julian or Constantius. Everything seems to indicate that the Alamanni mentioned by Libanius in 352, or by Ammianus in 357–365, provided, more or less enthusiastically, military contingents to Rome. Once this is understood, it becomes much easier to explain a Roman offensive precisely in 357. Constantius II needed to pacify the west before moving to the east (Amm. Marc. 17.5.1–5). Nevertheless, it was much more important for him to secure contingents of Alammani for his Persian campaign.

Modern and ancient historiography interprets the events in Gaul in 357 as obvious proof of the ingratitude of Constantius towards Julian. Julian defeated the Alamanni and Constantius intended to take the glory. Not only is this not correct, as we can glean from Ammianus, but the glory seems to have been shared equally between Augustus and Caesar. The series of solidi struck in Arles show on their reverses a palm of victory depicted in the field of the coin (Fig. 13).[46] This victory palm was not a random choice of the coin engravers. After the death of Valens at Adrianople in 378, Gratian also struck a series of solidi in Sirmium with a similar palm (Fig. 14).[47] This palm was depicted on the coin reverse, also showing a winged victory between the seated figures of Gratian and Valentinian II with the legend *Victoria Augg*. On the obverse, Gratian is bearded, a clear symbol of mourning for the death of Valens. The depiction of a palm on the reverse with the legend *Victoria Augg*, clarifies the context in which the coin was issued. It celebrated the launch of Gratian's campaign against the Goths in 379. Julian's series, struck in Arles, commemorates, as in the case of Gratian in 378/9, an important military operation.[48] Since there was only one during Julian's period as Caesar in Gaul (the battle of Strasbourg) it must be this victory to which the 357 solidi series from Arles refers.

The series from Arles is not the only one to celebrate the victory at Strasbourg. In the gold coins issued in Rome with seated Roma and Constantinople, there is a victory palm.[49] This time, it is on the exergue, to the right and left of the mint mark *RSM(P–Z)*. The military component,

Fig. 13   Fig. 14

Fig. 15   Fig. 16

Fig. 13 Julian II, Arles, solidus, 357. Numismatica Ars Classica NAC AG, Auction 28, 21st March 2007. Lot number 258.
Fig. 14 Gratian, Sirmium, solidus, 378/9. Triton IX, January 10–11, 2006, Sessions 2–4. Lot number 1601.
Fig. 15 Julian II, Rome, solidus, 357. Numismatica Ars Classica NAC AG, Auction 28, 21st March 2007. Lot number 257.
Fig. 16 Constantius II, Rome, solidus 357. UBS Gold & Numismatics. Auction 78. Auction date: 9 September 2008. Lot number 1964.

which is very clear in the Arles series, is even more defined in these Roman issues. The *adventus* of Constantius in Rome in 357 (Amm. Marc. 16.10.1–18) may have taken place immediately after the battle of Strasbourg, as it is linked in Ammianus with the construction of a triumphal obelisk in the Circus Maximus of Rome.[50] Furthermore, the Roman series depicts the military busts of Julian with cuirass (Fig. 15) and Constantius II with helmet, cuirass, shield, and spear (Fig. 16).[51] Constantius II most certainly planned and won the battle of Strasbourg jointly with Julian. Subsequently, it was Constantius, who was able to celebrate the victory in person in Rome. Ammianus (17.1.1–2.3) does not suggest in the least that Julian celebrated his own *adventus* in Arles, similar to that of Constantius in Rome. However, the city of Arles held the rank of Italian city since 313, when the mint at Ostia was moved to this city.[52] Therefore, we can consider that there were two joint triumphal celebrations, one in Rome and the other in Arles, and both were directed from Italy on the initiative of Constantius.

Arles and Julian

Julian was invested Caesar by his cousin in Milan in 355 (Amm. Marc. 15.8.8). Nevertheless, the announcement was probably received before this year, and in a city different from Milan. It can be argued that this announcement was probably made late in 353 or early in 354, shortly after the *adventus* of Constantius in Arles (Amm. Marc. 14.5.1, and 14.10.1), once the usurper Magnentius was finally defeated and the situation in Gaul completely calm. The panegyric of Julian in honour of Constantius (*Or.* 1) is thought to have been composed in 355/6, mainly because of the references in it to a military coup in Gaul (*Or.* 1 48c), generally understood as referring to the revolt of Silvanus in Cologne in 355. Nevertheless, the association of this coup in Julian's panegyric with Silvanus' revolt is by no means securely proved. In the panegyric Julian mentions only how someone of military importance, in an isolated position in Gaul, tried to rally some troops to him. From Ammianus 15.6.4 we know that the city of Trier acted independently of Constantius and Magnentius during the war of 351–353. We also know that a certain Poemenius was chosen to protect the city from Decentius (the brother and Caesar of Magnentius) at this time. All this seems to be confirmed by the fact that the mint of Trier struck hybrid coins at the time of the war, mixing features of both Magnentius and Constantius II, thus proclaiming its independence.[53] Poemenius and Silvanus were put to death in 355 as they were considered allies in the plot at Cologne. However, it is just possible that another plot, unknown to us from the literary sources (Ammianus' books before 353/4 are lost), and only partially indicated in some coins of Trier, erupted in post-war northern Gaul in 353.[54] On the occasion of a hypothetical plot to gain the purple in northern Gaul in 353, Poemenius would have adopted a pro-Constantius policy against any possible pretender to the throne. This, and not the plot of Silvanus in 355, could be the coup referred to by Julian in the panegyric. The absence of any definite reference to the fate of Gallus in October 354 (Amm. 14.11.19–23) in Julian's panegyric could also support the case for an earlier date of composition.

Arles in 353/4 would have been chosen as the most suitable place for Constantius to announce for the first time his intentions to proclaim Julian as Caesar. After the defeat of Magnentius in Gaul, Julian's panegyric to Constantius could have been composed in Arles to celebrate the intentions of the Augustus towards him. The panegyric starts and ends with explicit references to the war of Constantius against Magnentius, thus making the year 353/4 the most logical date for its composition. What Constantius did with Gallus at Sirmium, that is, proclaiming him Caesar in the headquarters of the Roman army in the Balkans on 15th March 351, could have been repeated with Julian at Arles in 353/4. To reinforce the special place that Arles had in Julian's career, it can be said that Arles, like no other place in the empire, features the distinctive imperial symbol of the eagle, with a

Fig. 17   Fig. 18

Fig. 17 Julian II, Arles, solidus, 360. Numismatica Ars Classica NAC AG. Auction 49. An interesting selection of Roman Gold Coins from the B.d.B. collection. 21st October 2008. Lot number 507.
Fig. 18 Julian II, Arles, solidus, 363. Triton XIII, January 5, 2010, Sessions 1 and 2. Lot number 396.

wreath in its beak, on its coin issue. (Figs 18 and 24).[55] The first solidi struck at Arles sometime in 360 after the proclamation of Julian as Augustus in Paris still recognized Constantius as his colleague (Fig. 17).[56] The depiction of Rome and Constantinople on the reverse (with the legend *Gloria Rei Publicae*) symbolizes the collaboration between the two emperors. Furthermore, the eagle added to the coin type is highly significant, since it is placed over Constantinople and not over Rome. It is not uncommon in the fourth century for coin legends to communicate a break with the past, such as *Restitutor Rei Publicae*, used by Valentinian in 364,[57] or *Salvator Rei Publicae*, used by Vetranio in 350.[58] The legend *Virtus Exerc Gall*, which Julian adopted in his gold issues of 363 in Arles,[59] would have declared a break with Constantius II had those issues been struck in Arles in 360. It would also have declared the superiority of the army of Gaul over the Danubian army. Nevertheless, the legend *Virtus Exerc Gall* is found on a particular type; the emperor helmeted, advancing right, head to left, holding trophy in left hand and placing right hand on head of crouching captive (Fig. 18), which is associated in other instances with a Roman campaign against Persia.[60] Ammianus tells us that the *Petulantes* and *Celtae*, the elite units that proclaimed Julian Augustus in Paris, did so to avoid being sent to the Persian front, as Constantius planned.[61] Nevertheless, Julian highlights in 361–363 the participation in the Persian campaign of troops that elected him Augustus. What greater indication could there be of his compromise with Constantius' projects than this voluntary incorporation of the Gauls in the Persian campaign?

Arles held great significance for Constantius II and the whole Constantinian dynasty, much more than any other city in the west. The city of Arles was the birthplace of Constantine II in 316 or 317, the firstborn and heir to the Prefecture of Gaul. It was also named *Constantina* in 328 in honour of Constantine. In the political design of the Constantinian dynasty, Arles was destined to perpetuate the memory of

Fig. 19

Magnentius, Arles, Ae 1, 352–353. Classical Numismatic Group, Inc. Mail Bid Sale
72, Closing Wednesday, June 14, 2006. Lot number 1805.

Constantine the Great in the west, as did Constantinople in the east. Even
Magnentius, *protector* of Constantine and *comes domesticorum* of Constans,[62]
also wished to distinguish Arles as a special city in the west. For his issues
of billon Ae 1 in 352, he adopted the Chi-Rho symbol, together with the
Greek letters alpha and omega, which clearly recalled his connection with
Constantine. Additionally, the coin type was circled by a laurel wreath in the
Arles mint (Fig. 19),[63] as a way of signalling the significance of the city.
It is impossible to know the whereabouts of Magnentius before the invasion
of Gaul by Constantius II, because Ammianus' books before 353 are lost.
We can, however, suggest that Magnentius was not on the Rhine, where
Decentius watched over Trier and the surrounding area (the 352 coin series
from this mint also give him the title *Fort(is)* or *Fort(issimus)*).[64] Given the
territorial division normally applied between Augustus and Caesar, and the
fact that Ammianus does not associate Magnentius with Trier, it can be
assumed that this Augustus was in southern Gaul in 352, in the vicinity of
Lyons or Arles. Whatever the case, Magnentius decided in 352 to clarify
that he also respected the link between Arles and the Constantinian dynasty.

In order to dissociate Arles from the memory of Magnentius, and given
that Arles was the 'Rome' of Gaul, Constantius entered the city in triumph
in 353. After defeating Magnentius, according to Ammianus (14.5.1),
Constantius held a formal *adventus* in Arles, which celebrated his *tricennalia*
and his recent military victory.[65] Furthermore, Constantius offered games
in the theatre and erected an obelisk in the circus.[66] The issues
Votis/XXX/Multis/XXXX still keep the mint mark *PAR* from Arles.[67]
Nevertheless, a second series incorporates *Con* in the exergue, the
abbreviation of the city's new name, *Constantina*, in honour of
Constantius II.[68] The first of Julian's solidi from Arles not only recognize
Constantius II as Augustus, but also keep the name *Constantina* for the
city.[69] Finally, the eagle depicted on the reverse signifies that Constantius
was still the *senior* member of the imperial college in 360. Until Julian's

death in Persia, the eagle, or the eagle with wreath in its beak, was a symbol linked to the emperor Julian in Arles.[70] Even if Julian renounced Constantine in his *Caesars*,[71] the truth is that Arles, the chosen-city of the Constantinians in the west, always considered him as a legitimate heir.

After his proclamation as Augustus, Julian crossed the Rhine at Tricensima and attacked the Attuarian Franks in the summer of 360. In autumn, he marched over the left bank of the Rhine to Augst, and later installed himself in Vienne in the winter of 360–1 (Amm. Marc. 20.10, 21.1–2). Meanwhile, he also secured the control of Britannia through Lupicinus. This frenzied military and logistical activity rightly corresponds to the military commander in control of the Prefecture of Gaul. Essentially, it is not that different from what Constantius did on the Danube in 358–9. Julian's arrangements in 360–361, even his proclamation as Augustus, do not necessarily correspond to a meditated confrontation with Constantius, but rather to the concern of an emperor, unwilling to leave a power vacuum in Gaul, before leaving for the east. The issues of siliquae in Lyons, both under Julian's and Constantius II's names, celebrating their joint victory (*Victoria DD NN*) (Figs 20 and 21), as well as their *Vota* (*Vot V Mult XX* for Julian, *Vot XXX/Mult XXXX* for Constantius) (Figs 22 and 23),[72] show two emperors still in institutional and military harmony.[73]

Fig. 20   Fig. 21

Fig. 22   Fig. 23

Fig. 20 Julian II, Lugdunum, Reduced siliqua, 361. Stack's. Stack & Kroisos Collections. Auction date: 14 January 2008. Lot number 2384.

Fig. 21 Constantius II, Lugdunum, Reduced siliqua, 361. Gemini, LLC. Auction III. Auction date: 9 January 2007. Lot number 471.

Fig. 22 Julian II, Lugdunum, Reduced siliqua, 361. Stack's. Stack & Kroisos Collections. Auction date: 14 January 2008. Lot number 2386.

Fig. 23 Constantius II, Lugdunum, Reduced siliqua, 361. Classical Numismatic Group. Mail Bid Sale 72. Auction date: 14 June 2006. Lot number 1791.

Julian's bull coinage

The Ae 1 coins depicting Julian with a reverse type of a bull, standing, crowned by two stars, with the legend *Securitas Rei Publicae*, were minted throughout the empire (except for the mints of Trier, Rome and Alexandria)[74] before the death of the emperor in June 363 (Figs 24 and 25).[75] This is the most original of Julian's coin types, and one of the most studied from Late Antiquity. Theories that ascribe a religious significance to this coin type suggest that the bull pushed Christianity aside, since the bull is a symbol of Mithraic, Neoplatonic or solar religions.[76] Political theories, on the other hand, maintain that the bull type, linked to archaic literature, is a symbol of good state governance.[77] Finally, there are those who suggest that the bull may have carried, partially at least, some kind of military significance, linked to the Persian campaign.[78]

Nevertheless, the true significance of this type may be more traditional than is often assumed. The bull plays two different roles in Roman religion. For one, a bull and a cow are used in the delimitation of the *pomerium* of any Roman city or colony. The furrow created in the process that defined a Roman city (*circumdatio*) was very important in the Roman perception of the world. The bull, a symbol of strength and protection for the city, was always on the exterior side of the furrow. The cow, on the other hand,

Fig. 24

Fig. 25

Fig. 24 Julian II, Arles, Ae 1, Late 362–363. Classical Numismatic Group. Mail Bid Sale 69. Auction date: 8 June 2005. Lot number 1494.

Fig. 25 Julian II, Sirmium, Ae 1, Late 362–363. Classical Numismatic Group, Inc. Mail Bid Sale 69, Closing Wednesday, June 8, 2005. Lot number 1767.

symbolized fertility and peace, and walked inside the boundary of the future city. Beyond the *pomerium*, defined by the bull and cow, was the military world. The Romans, who were very careful in stressing the spatial order existing between *domi* and *militiae*, required sacrifices to Mars to take place beyond the *pomerium*, in the military camp.[79] The bull was the centre of these sacrifices, normally conducted as *suovetaurilia*. The significance of Julian's bull type may be easily explained then by the double character, *domi* and *militiae*, of the Roman spirit, both of which were necessary to preserve the security of the *Res publica*. Thus, it was not coincidental that the bull depicted by the engravers was identical to other legionary bulls. Like the totemic animals of numerous Roman legions, Julian's bull was intentionally invested with martial significance.

Not even the ancient authors dispute the sacrificial character of Julian's monetary bull. It is rare for literary sources to make direct references to coinage, but in his church history Socrates specifically comments on Julian's type (*Hist. eccl.* 3.17.4). He attributes a sacrificial meaning to the animal, even asserting – albeit erroneously – that the bull in these Ae1 was accompanied by a sacrificial altar. Nevertheless, the issue debated by modern scholars is not its sacrificial character, but whether this was the only one, whether there were other meanings embedded in this coin type. Here is where the two stars placed by the monetary engravers above Julian's animal are considered to be important. These stars had never been previously associated with a bull in Roman coinage. For this precise reason, Marco and Vanderspoel interpreted this animal as Mithraic and eastern in character, rather than purely 'Roman': for them the two stars may be identified with Aldebaran and Antares, but also with Cautes and Cautopates.[80] Nevertheless, it may be argued that if Julian's engravers had wanted to depict only a sacrificial, openly Mithraic, bull in this type, it would have been depicted wearing a tiara, with some garlands, or at least with an altar. All these attributes are common to many imperial and provincial sacrificial coin series prior to Julian's rule. Nothing would have been easier for the engravers than to continue with an established iconographic tradition. They could even have depicted the officiating priest next to the animal, as found in a provincial series of Pergamum from the reign of Caracalla.[81] However, the Constantinians did use the double star motif in their coin series, their reading being very 'Roman', as well as very similar to the meaning behind Julian's bull.

Certain medallions and nummi, repeatedly struck by Constantine and his successors since the foundation of Constantinople in 330, depict the legend *Urbs Roma* with the bust of the city on the obverse and the Capitoline wolf with Romulus, Remus, and two stars above them on the reverse.[82] These Roman coin series emphasize the city of Rome and its eternity, and they were struck during the dynastic transition from Constantine I to his sons (330–347/8). Moreover, it is very important to note that they were produced jointly with an imposing series of nummi enhancing the new city of Constantinopolis, founded on the Bosphorus by Constantine.[83] The depiction of the Capitoline wolf with Romulus and Remus is relatively frequent among Roman coin series of all periods. Nevertheless, the two stars above the figures are new in these issues. Most plausibly interpreted as *aeternitas* and *translatio imperii*, the motif of the two stars may be explained in a similar way as Julian's bull. Romulus and Remus are the two mythical founders of Rome, one of them perishing when crossing the trench (*circumdatio*) that bounded the city of Rome.[84] There is an evident sacrificial element in Rome's foundation, but there are also other aspects to be read, relating to continuity and dynastic succession. Foundational and successional references on Rome's nummi must be studied alongside the series struck in honour of Constantinopolis, as both cities are perceived as bound to the emperor. Thus, the two stars situated above the Capitoline wolf can be seen as referring to Romulus and Remus: one stars represents the twin who is sacrificed and dies, the other signals the twin who continues with Rome's *aeternitas*, in the new-founded city of Constantinopolis.

The sacrificial and *renovatio* element gleaned from the *Urbs Roma/ Constantinopolis* series may also be found in Julian's bull. Instead of having two bulls, joined by the foundational yoke, or a bull and a cow, there is only one. Nevertheless, the two stars above the bull, as in the case of Romulus and Remus, refer to two animals. The martial and transgressor bull has crossed the foundational furrow, while the other one, still alive, guarantees Rome's commitment to civilization. A dual *domi* and *militiae* interpretation is therefore valid for the *Urbs Roma* and bull series. The stars found on both series are bound by the same force as an emperor and his ancestors. It is precisely imperial continuity that concerns Julian in the *Caesars* and his *Hymn to King Helios*, in which the emperor synthesizes his views in a religious association with sunlight. One of the stars on the Julian type, placed above the bull's back, must be interpreted as the sacrificed animal. The other star, the one above the bull's horns (sun and moon, the two complementary stellar bodies), recalls that the live bull remains *invictus* and eternal. This second star, representing immortality and orderly succession, can be identified with Helios, the father to whom Apis, and the reigning emperor Julian, look up (Julian *Caes.* 336c). It is not coincidental then that the discovery of the Apis bull in Egypt took place precisely at the time of the first issues of this type by Julian, i.e. late in 362.[85]

If the double star motif is interpreted as an allusion to the orderly succession of power, the legend *Securitas Rei Publicae* can in turn be associated with the delimitation and armed defence of Roman civilization, implied by the bull. Legends like *Securitas Publica*, referring to the territorial scope of the empire, are typical of periods of confrontation between Rome and Persia. It is not strange then that legends like *Securitas Imperii* or *Securitas Orbis* should be frequent in the third century. In this way, *Securitas Imperii* in Caracalla's coins are linked to *Victoria Part(ica) Max(ima)* and to *Restitutio Orbis*.[86] In 193–196 Emesa and Laodicea issued coinage under the name of Julia Domna with the legend *Securitas Imperii*, echoing a military victory in the region.[87] In the same way, the legend *Securit Orbis* is linked in Laodicea with a legend of clear Persian connotations (*Victoriae Parthicae*).[88] On the other hand, *Securit Orbis* in Gallienus' coins shows Securitas raising her hand to her head in salute to Sol; and other coins are also related to Securitas and Valerian's concerns for the Persian frontier.[89] In this respect, Dominique Hollard's theory on Julian's bull type is worth considering seriously. He also sees a reference to orderly succession in association with the sacrificial element, but goes even further, suggesting that the iconography was chosen ad hoc, motivated by Persian dynastic aspirations, not just Roman. According to Hollard, Julian wanted his Persian campaign to secure the Persian throne for Hormisdas, who travelled with the Roman army as an anticipated puppet replacement for Shapur II (Amm. Marc. 24.1.2, 8; 24.2.4, 11, 20; and 24.5.4).[90]

Hoards and casual finds of Julian's bull type indicate that this coin was not struck before late 362.[91] The examination of Julian's texts allows us to fix an exact date, December 25th. For Julian, this date is not linked to a Christian celebration, but on the contrary, to a solar and Mithraic rebirth. On 15th–16th December 362 in Antioch (during the *Banquet* or the *Saturnalia*), Julian pronounced his *Caesars*, which ends with a direct and scandalous attack against Constantine and Christ. Christ encompasses all that is mediocre and criminal, a true reversal of values ('He that is a seducer, he that is a murderer, he that is sacrilegious and infamous, let him approach without fear!', *Caes.* 336b). In the last verses, Hermes reminds Julian that Mithras is his father, and that Mithras should guide his life until he is welcomed to his bosom at death (336c). On 25th December 362, on the occasion of the *Sol Invictus* festival, Julian pronounced his great theological work, his *Hymn to King Helios*, which ends with a prayer asking Helios to admit him to his side at the time of death (*Or.* 4 158 b–c). Therefore, the bull crowned by two stars can be interpreted as the new religious and military symbol that the emperor gave to his elite palatine troops, his *protectores*, on the *dies natalis*, 25th December 362. No doubt this emblem was invested on his troops when he was pronouncing his speech, a true manifestation of the theological ideas of the emperor.

Ammianus records that, after being mocked by the people of Antioch in 362, Julian conducted pagan sacrifices on Mons Casius to annoy Christians (22.14.2–6). Shortly before elaborating on the passage describing the sacrifices at Antioch, Ammianus explains that Julian did not wish to bother anybody with his religious beliefs (*nec quemquam propter religiones gravat*).[92] Julian was only promoting his own religious beliefs, although as emperor he did demand loyalty from his *protectores*. It is towards Constantius' *protectores*, the *Cornuti* and the *Bracchiati*,[93] that the reprisals in late 362 were directed, not towards the rest of the army, who were not affected in any way.[94] On the contrary, the *Petulantes*, together with the *Celtae*, their associate or subordinate unit, made up the Palatine guard, undertaking all of Julian's new policies. Hence, when Ammianus records that there were army units belonging to Julian who prior to the Persian campaign fed abundantly on meat every day (*ut in dies paene singulos milites carnis distentiore sagina*), thanks to the sacrificed bulls (*tauros aliquotiens inmolando centenos*), he is specifically referring to the *Petulantes* and the *Celtae* (*Petulantes ante omnes et Celtae*).[95] These *Petulantes* and *Celtae* are described by Ammianus as uncouth, and are linked to the temple sacrifices and to the consumption of the resulting meat (*per plateas ex publicis aedibus*). Their disposition to participate in traditional rites and eat bull meat greatly contrasts in Ammianus' work with the resistance shown towards these practices by the members of the late guard corps of Constantius II, the *Iovani* and *Herculiani*.[96]

In this respect, Libanius (*Or.* 18.199) speaks of an incident at a celebration in Antioch, in which ten soldiers were accused of criticizing Julian. According to Libanius eight of the ten were exonerated, probably because they agreed to perform sacrifices in Julian's presence, while the remaining two did not.[97] As rightly noted by David Woods, *The Passion of Sergius and Bacchus*, describing the trial and execution of the two military martyrs during the rule of Galerius (305–311), may have been inspired by the trial and deaths of Iuventinus and Maximinus in Julian's reign.[98] The sixth-century chronicler John Malalas, as well as another, Syriac, source, explicitly identified Iuventinus and Maximinus as the martyrs executed by Julian in Antioch; they were part of the *Gentiles* of the *Scholae Palatinae* (*Schola Gentilium Senior*), i.e. they were *Cornuti*.[99] The martyrdoms of the standard-bearers of the cavalry troops of the *Cornuti*, Bonosus and Maximilianus,[100] may also be linked to Julian's purging of pro-Constantian Christian *protectores* in Antioch in late 362.[101] Bonosus and Maximilianus were the standard-bearers of the *Iovani Cornuti Seniores* and *Iovani Cornuti Iuniores* in Antioch in 362. Such testimonies indicate that there was an intentional policy deployed by Julian against Constantius II's *Cornuti*, in favour of his *protectores*, the *Petulantes* and *Celtae*, who had made him emperor in Paris.

The famous passage in Ammianus (20.4.18) narrating how Maurus, the standard-bearer of the *Petulantes*, crowned Julian with a torque in Paris, has been analyzed and commented upon many times. Nevertheless, the commander leading the elite troops of *Petulantes* who invested Julian as Augustus in 360 remains unknown. In this respect, it may not be coincidental that the officer Nevitta and Maurus are both mentioned by Ammianus in relation to military action in the Succi Pass (20.4.18; 21.10.2). If the two men fought in the same unit of *Petulantes*, then Nevitta's promotions after Julian was crowned Augustus are more easily understood. Before leaving for Vienne, to meet Constantius II on the Danube, Julian named Dagalaifus *comes domesticorum* and Nevitta *magister equitum* and consul. Dagalaifus and Nevitta are the only military figures mentioned by Ammianus when explaining Julian's promotions and changes to his close palatine circle and government (21.8.1). This duo appears as staunchly loyal to Julian and opposed to Victor, Arintheus, and other pro-Constantinian officers and previous followers of Constantius II. Moreover, Julian further designated Nevitta no less than consul, despite his lack of culture and Frankish origin (Amm. Marc. 21.10.8). Nevitta was not a Christian; his figure was so attached to Julian's cause that nothing is known of him after the emperor's death. If Julian ultimately owed his imperial mantle to Nevitta, commander of the *Petulantes* in Paris, it would easily explain the soldier's fervent paganism, his elevation to the consulate in 362, and his complete absence from any historical source after Julian's death. Therefore, the bull in Julian's Ae1 can be interpreted as a personal and military pagan symbol of Julian's *Petulantes* and *Celtae protectores*, who furthermore wished to suppress Constantius' Chi Rho emblem and break up the Christian loyalties of the *Cornuti* and the *Bracchiati*.

Julian's religious and military purification, expressed in his adoption of the bull type, was immediately followed by an official declaration of his qualities as supreme commander of the entire Roman army. This is precisely the significance behind the series of solidi *Virtus Exercitum Romanorum*, struck undoubtedly in January 363.[102] Julian is shown on the obverse facing left, bearded and with a diadem, dressed in consular robes, holding *mappa* and sceptre, enthroned facing or standing left (Fig. 26). With this new type, Julian signalled his new consulship, which would coincide with the launching of the Persian campaign, for which the Roman army and palatine troops were already prepared. The gold series that follows this

Fig. 26   Fig. 27

Fig. 26 Julian II, Antioch, solidus, 363. Triton XIII, January 5, 2010, Sessions 1 and 2. Lot number 397.
Fig. 27 Julian II, Sirmium, solidus, 363. Gemini, Numismatic Auctions VI. Sunday, January 10. 2010. Lot number 580.

inauguration of the military campaign is contemporaneous with the campaign itself: *Virtus Exercitus Romanorum*, with the emperor helmeted, advancing right, head to left, holding trophy in left hand and placing right hand on head of crouching captive (Figs 27 and 18).[103]

Neither Heraclea[104] nor Cyzicus,[105] two very important cities specially honoured by the Tetrarchy at the beginning of the fourth century, depict any special symbol on their mint marks. Various symbols were customarily used by Roman engravers in association with mint marks on the exergue. The most common were wreaths and palm branches. As mentioned above, the mints of Arles and Rome represented Julian's – and Constantius II's – victories in Gaul in 357 with wreaths and palms. They may also be found on the gold solidi of Sirmium in 379 at the beginning of Gratian's campaign against the Goths. Palms in the exergue usually represent a city's accommodation with a specific imperial enterprise. On the other hand, wreaths are honorific symbols granted by the emperor to the city in recognition of its support. Wreaths and palms, representing symbolic dialogues between the emperor and his cities, are normally associated with military events, although they may also be depicted for dynastic or logistical reasons. Interestingly, Aquileia, which posed serious resistance to Julian at the end of 361, did not use any of these marks. Arles, on the other hand, displays more of these marks than any other Roman city, probably because of the close connection of the city with the Constantinian dynasty (Fig. 24).[106] Siscia and Sirmium, headquarters of the Danubian army, loyal to Constantius II, also used these symbols on their mint marks, as did many other cities that struck coinage (Fig. 25).[107] These symbols do not seem to be related to any particular advance of Julian's army in Mesopotamia in 363. They are more likely related to the distinction Julian had given some cities over others, perhaps also according to his army's logistical needs, as may be the case with series from Thessalonica, Heraclea and Nicomedia. Together, they help trace the map of cities in the Roman empire that were privileged by Julian, but also those that were favoured by Constantius II and Constantine.

Conclusion

All of Julian's coin series use a clear and concise verbal and iconographic language. Both as Caesar and Augustus, Julian was a good governor of the *Res Republica Romana*, and competently defended the territory as a military commander. From 355 to 363, all of Julian's coin series show an emperor integrated in Constantinian ways and manners, either because he was promoted as Caesar by Constantius II, or because he gained the support of the army and cities that were clearly Constantinian in their loyalties. Nevertheless, the style and typology of Julian's coin series are not identical everywhere. They differ according to mints and the communities among which the coins would be distributed. Julian also changed status in different cities. In Paris, for example, he was invested emperor. Nevertheless, the celebration of his new rank took place in Arles. Furthermore, while Julian was recognized as sole emperor in Sirmium, it was in Antioch that he assumed the consulship and reformed the *Schola Palatina*.

While there is no clear Christian symbol in Julian's coinage, it is equally true that in the mid fourth century, the only Christian symbols used on coins were the Greek letters *Chi* and *Rho*, and even then with many restrictions. Because these letters were the symbol of the elite troops of Constantius' *Scholae Palatinae*, their use was always limited to certain moments and certain people, including Magnentius, first *protector* of Constantine and then *comes domesticorum* of Constans. Julian decided to do without Christian *protectores* before the end of 362. Being in the midst of a difficult military campaign, he wished his *garde de corps* to be unwaveringly loyal to him. It is for this reason, rather than a purely religious one, that Julian decided to purge the *Cornuti* and *Bracchiati protectores* and to give the *Petulantes* and *Celtae* a new military emblem. However, this was no innovation of Julian's. He followed the same Constantinian methods as Constantius and Magnentius before him, and struck the same kind of billon coin Ae1 that Magnentius had already struck in 352–353. In sum, according to his coin series, Julian was a good Roman emperor of the mid fourth century, both as soldier and governor, who interacted with the different people and social groups in his empire.

Notes

[1] Tougher 2007, 3–11. For the reception of Julian see Richer 1981.

[2] Athanassiadi-Fowden 1981.

[3] Millar 1977, 10–1.

[4] All dates are AD unless indicated otherwise.

[5] Bowersock 1978, 55–65, 79–93.

[6] Arce 1984, Lieu 1989 (first published 1986).

[7] Arce 1984, 33–87.

[8] For Julian's coinage see also the chapter by Eric Varner in this volume.

[9] Jones 1956, 15.

[10] Hedlund 2008, 14–39.

[11] Buttrey 1972, 101–9.

[12] Wallace-Hadrill 1981, 36–9.

[13] Crawford 1983, 50–9.

[14] Barnes 1993, 226.

[15] Abdication of Vetranio in Naissus, Barnes 1993, 220–1.

[16] López Sánchez 2002.

[17] *RIC* 8, 417, Thess. nos. 158–159.

[18] *RIC* 8, 477, Nic. no. 76.

[19] *RIC* 8, 369, Sis. nos. 270–292; 386, Sirm. nos. 21–24; 416, Thess. no. 146.

[20] *RIC* 8, 222, Arl. nos. 243–246.

[21] *RIC* 8, 222, Arl. nos. 247–249.

[22] *RIC* 8, 385, Sirm. nos. 11–14.

[23] *RIC* 8, 477, Nic. nos. 77–79.

[24] *RIC* 8, 520, Ant. nos. 102–104. Socrates, *Hist. eccl.* 2.28.22, indicates that Gallus arrived in Antioch 7th May 352. Bleckmann 2003 and López Sánchez 2007 contend that he was not in the Balkans until well into 352.

[25] *RIC* 8, 368, Sis. nos. 262–263.

[26] *RIC* 8, 527, Ant. nos. 181–182.

[27] *RIC* 8, 392, Sirm. no 104; 531, Ant. no. 210.

[28] Amm. Marc. 21.15.2. Malosse 2004, 83 and n. 30; *RIC* 8, 392, Sirm. no. 104.

[29] Barnes 1993, 221.

[30] Malosse 2004, 83; López Sánchez 2007.

[31] *RIC* 8, 326, Aq. nos. 122, 127–128. Other types related to *libertas* in this mint in nos. 123–126.

[32] *RIC* 8, 367, Sis. no. 260.

[33] Peter the Patrician fr. 16. This is discussed by Seeck 1901, 1065, and Ensslin 1930, 448–50, but see now also Chausson 2007, esp. 98–9.

[34] Barnes 1993, 228.

[35] Amm. Marc. 21.10.8, complains that Nevitta had risen too high.

[36] Amm. Marc. 15.8.17, Barnes 1993, 226.

[37] López Sánchez 2005.

[38] Festus, *Brev.* 27. See Dignas and Winter 2007, 89; Barnes 1993, 220.

[39] *RIC* 8, 512, Ant. nos. 3–8.

[40] Amm. Marc. 16.10.20; Barnes 1993, 222.

[41] Barnes 1993, 222–3.

[42] Amm. Marc. 14.11.19 and 24.

[43] Amm. Marc. 16.11.2.

[44] Amm. Marc. 16.10.8.

[45] Lib. *Or.* 18.33–4.

[46] *RIC* 8, 221, Arl. nos. 234–237 *Gloria Rei Publicae/Votis V.*

[47] *RIC* 8, 214–15, Arl. nos. 159–160, *RIC* 9, Sirm. no. 9.

[48] *RIC* 8, 221, Arl. nos. 234–237 *Gloria Rei Publicae/Votis V.*

[49] *RIC* 8, 276, Rom. nos. 290–295.

[50] Amm. Marc. 17.4.14–15.

[51] *RIC* 8, 276, Rom. nos. 290–295.

[52] Depeyrot 1996, 5; Ferrando 1997, 3; Van Heesch 2006, 56.

[53] López Sánchez 2009.

[54] Overbeck and Overbeck 2001, 246: 'Die ungewöhnliche Trierer Münzprägung, die am Beginn der Wiederaufnahme der regulären Prägetätigkeit für Constantius steht, feiert den Sieger Constantius und erklärt sich aus der Situation der Münzstäte direkt nach dem Ende Kampfhandlungen'.

[55] *RIC* 8, 227–9, Arl. nos. 303–312, 318–326.

[56] *RIC* 8, 225–6, Arl. nos. 280–287.

[57] *RIC* 9, 209, Constantinople no. 3.

[58] *RIC* 8, 367, Sis. no. 260.

[59] *RIC* 8, 227, Arl. nos. 303–304.

[60] *RIC* 10, 261, Constantinople nos. 282–284, on the occasion of the Roman-Persian war of 441: Greatrex 1993.

[61] Amm. Marc. 20.4.2.

[62] Zos. 2.42.2; *PLRE* 1, 532, Fl. Magnus Magnentius.

[63] *RIC* 8, 217, Arl. nos. 192–193.

[64] *RIC* 8, 155, 163–4, nos. 313, 314, 316, 316B, 317, 319, 322, 324, 326, 327A.

[65] Ferrando 1997, 20.

[66] Ferrando 1997, 20; Charron and Heijmans 2001, 378.

[67] *RIC* 8, 218, Arl. nos. 203–205.

[68] *RIC* 8, 219, Arl. nos. 207–210.

[69] *RIC* 8, 225–6, Arl. nos. 280–287

[70] *RIC* 8, 227–9, Arl. nos. 303–312, 318–326.

[71] For the *Caesars* see the chapter by Rowland Smith in this volume.

[72] *RIC* 8, 193, Lyons nos. 210–215A, 218–219, and 216–217.

[73] Barnes 1993, 227–8.

[74] *RIC* 8, 47; Vanderspoel 1998, 115.

[75] Socrates, *Hist. eccl.* 3.17, Soz. *Hist. eccl.* 5.19, and also Julian *Misop.* 355d, speak of *nomisma* in reference to this billon coin known today as Ae1.

[76] Woods 2000; Soz. *Hist. eccl.* 5.17.2–3, for images of Jupiter, Mars, and Mercury on Julian's standards. Soz. *Hist. eccl.* 5.19.2, and Socrates, *Hist. eccl.* 3.17.4, link Julian's bull type with anti-Christian pagan sacrifices.

[77] Kent 1954, 217; Arce 1984, 189–90; Tougher 2004, 328, 330.

[78] Tougher 2004, 329 n. 17; Desnier 1985, 406.

[79] Whittaker 1994, 24–5.

[80] Marco 1999; Vanderspoel 1998, 116–17.

[81] Wroth 1892, no. 324 and pl. 31, 5; Von Fritze 1910, pl. 8, no. 8; Levante 2001, no. 2230.

[82] See, i.e. Arles for *Urbs Roma* (*RIC* 7, nos. 343, 351, 356, 362, 368, 373, 379, 385, 392, 400, 407, 415; *RIC* 8, nos. 8, 15, 25, 30, 38).

[83] See, i.e. Arles for *Constantinopolis* (*RIC* 7, nos. 344, 352, 357, 363, 369, 374, 380, 386, 393, 401, 408, 416; *RIC* 8, nos. 9, 16, 26, 31, 39).

[84] Wiseman 1995, 9–11.

[85] Munzi 1996, 299.

[86] *RIC* 4.1, nos. 168, 168a and 166.

[87] *RIC* 4.1, nos. 634 and 634a.

[88] *RIC* 4.1, nos. 351 and 353.

[89] *RIC* 4.1, nos. 278, 237–239 and 240.

[90] Hollard 2010.

[91] Elmer 1937, 29–30; Kent 1959, 116; *RIC* 8, 28, 54; Carson 1981, 58, no. 1411; Carson 1990, 189; Bastien 1985, 94–6; Munzi 1996, 300; Conton 2004.

[92] Amm. Marc. 22.10.1.

[93] Hoffmann 1969, 206.

[94] For the purges of the *protectores domestici* by Julian (or *protectores* and *domestici*), *Cod. Theod.* 6.24.1 (362) indicates evidence for an imperial constitution; see also Jones 1964, vol.1, 129–30 and n. 41, vol. 2, 1093.

[95] Amm. Marc. 22.12.6.

[96] Woods 1995a.

[97] *Ep.* 113 (Norman 1992, vol. 2, 200–3).

[98] Woods 1997.

[99] Mal. 13.19; Peeters 1924, 77–82.

[100] Woods 1995a, 1995b.

[101] See above, n. 94.

[102] *RIC* 8, 530, Ant. nos. 204–206.

[103] *RIC* 8, 529–30, Ant. nos. 195–203.

[104] *RIC* 8, 438, Her. nos. 101–104.

[105] *RIC* 8, 500, Cyz. nos. 125–128.

[106] López Sánchez 2007.

[107] *RIC* 8, 546, Alex. no. 91; 483–4, Nic. nos. 119, 121–122, 124; 422–3, Thess. nos. 217, 218, 223–228; 391–2, Sirm. nos. 94–100, 105–107; 379–80, Sis. nos. 410–413, 415–419, 421–422; 227–9, Arl. nos. 303–313, 318–326.

12

ROMAN AUTHORITY, IMPERIAL AUTHORIALITY, AND JULIAN'S ARTISTIC PROGRAM

Eric R. Varner

Although he reigned as sole emperor for only two years, Flavius Claudius Julianus has left an indelible historiographical imprint as both author and emperor. Despite the brevity of his principate, Julian engineered a distinctive artistic program clearly discernable in his coinage and portraiture which forged a discrete visual identity.[1] His representations fused the authority of *romanitas* and the imperial past with hellenized traditions of *paideia* and philosophy. Julian's written work survives in greater abundance than any other emperor-author and the development of his visual persona follows a trajectory similar to that of his literary output. Like his early panegyrics to Constantius II which conform to established protocols,[2] Julian's initial portraits adhere to Constantinian precedents, whereas his later images are highly individualistic and decidedly confrontational like much of his later writing.

Julian's first numismatic depictions, created during his tenure as Caesar from 355–60, adopt a careful and studied approach, relying on the new portrait orthodoxy established by Constantine and founded on the authority of Augustan and Trajanic imagery. Constantine's second portrait type, introduced to mark the five-year anniversary of his reign (*quinquennalia*) in 311, broke with two centuries of bearded representations of the Roman ruler, a convention established by Hadrian when he ascended to the principate in 117.[3] Constantine becomes the first adult emperor since Trajan to be consistently depicted as clean shaven. In addition, Constantine's images omit the short military hairstyles in vogue during the third century in favor of long comma-shaped locks which intentionally evoke Trajanic and Julio-Claudian coiffures. Furthermore, the style of Constantine's likenesses is also consciously classicizing with idealized and youthful facial features that reject the heightened psychological realism of many third-century portraits or the abstracted and stylized modes employed under the Tetrarchy.[4] All three of Constantine's sons and successors (Constantine II, Constantius II, and Constans) follow similar patterns in their portraiture, and the resulting dynastic homogeneity often makes it notoriously difficult to distinguish between them in sculpted images, or even to differentiate between father and sons, as evident in the colossal bronze head in the Palazzo dei Conservatori which, although a late portrait of Constantine himself, has sometimes been identified as Constantius II (Fig. 1).[5] Similarly, in the codex-calendar of 354 affinities of coiffure and physiognomy are stressed in the depictions of Constantius II and Julian's half-brother, Gallus.[6]

Following the execution of Gallus, Julian succeeded him as Caesar on 6th November 355; at this time, his coin portraits issued at Arles in all denominations show him as cuirassed, clean-shaven, and with a coiffure like those of Constantine and his sons.[7] The smooth, youthful facial features and Constantinian coiffure visually align Julian with the ruling Augustus, Constantius II, and underscore his affiliations with the dynasty. Prior to his acclamation as Caesar, Julian had sported a beard which he reluctantly shaved and he apparently remained beardless until the death of Constantius.[8] During this period, similar beardless portraits of Julian were issued at most of the major mints, including Aquileia, Arles, Siscia, Sirmium, Thessalonica, Heraclea, Constantinople, Nicomedia, Cyzicus, Antioch, and Alexandria (Fig. 2).[9] An *aureus* from Constantinople is noteworthy for its emphatic Constantinian hairstyle.[10] At Rome, a variant portrait was created where the Constantinian inflections are less strong and the coiffure is actually shorter and approximates Tetrarchic and third-century military coiffures, like those of Julian's putative ancestor, Marcus Aurelius Claudius Gothicus.[11] In the Roman coins, Julian appears with cuirass and *paludamentum* (military cloak). In keeping with long-standing numismatic tradition going back to the Claudian portraits of Nero, Julian, as imperial heir, is represented as bare-headed in contradistinction to the reigning emperor who can appear wreathed, or later diademmed, as in the contemporary coin portraits of Constantius II.[12]

Following his salutation as Augustus in February of 360, coins struck at the mints under Julian's control in Gaul (Arles, Lyons and Trier) continued to promote a beardless, Constantinian conception of the new emperor.[13] The portraits add a pearl diadem to signal Julian's new rank of Augustus. These images, however, are decidedly non-confrontational and they maintain a fiction of collaboration and *similitudo* between Julian and Constantius.[14] Julian also continues to mint coinage in honor of Constantius as Augustus. Following prevailing Constantinian conventions in portraiture, the numismatic likenesses of the cousins and co-rulers are almost indistinguishable.[15]

After Julian's occupation of Italy and Illyricum a new bearded portrait type is introduced. At first, Julian's beard is rather short, as seen on issues from Lyons, Arles, Sirmium and Thessalonica (Fig. 3).[16] Like the Roman

Fig. 1 Constantine, Rome, Palazzo dei Conservatori, inv. 1072 (photo author).

Fig. 2 Julian, siliqua, Lyons, 361, *RIC* 8.218 (photo courtesy the Classical Numismatic Group, Inc., cngcoins.com).

Fig. 3 Julian, siliqua, Arles, 361, *RIC* 8.310 (photo courtesy the Classical Numismatic Group, Inc., cngcoins.com).

issues with more military coiffures, the shorter beard also evokes the style of Claudius Gothicus' representations and similar contemporary likenesses, as notably reflected in a series of gilded bronze portraits from Brescia, thus visually substantiating Julian's putative ancestral links to Gothicus.[17] Although Julian's and Constantine's descent from Gothicus is thought to be apocryphal, it is earnestly promoted in ancient sources such as the *Historia Augusta*; Julian himself highlights the connection in his *Caesars* and in his two panegyrics to Constantius II, and there may actually be some basis in fact for this imperial geneaology.[18] Apparently composed for the Saturnalia of 362, the *Caesars* is a biting Menippean satire in the Roman tradition of the *Apocolocyntosis* likely written by Seneca for the Saturnalia of 54.[19] Julian's work eschews the historical tradition of his friend Aurelius Victor's *De Caesaribus* (which had just appeared in 360) in favor of merciless caricatures of many of the emperor's most illustrious predecessors, including Augustus, Trajan, Hadrian and Constantine. His praise of Marcus Aurelius as an intellectual emperor, and his enthusiasm for his putative ancestor Claudius Gothicus and for Aurelian, who promoted a national cult of Sol Invictus, are designed to situate Julian as their true conceptual heir and consolidate an alternative imperial genealogy for himself.[20] The importance of Claudius Gothicus, positioned as the imperial ancestor of the new Flavian dynasty, is also signaled at this time by his appearance in the codex-calendar of 354, where he in fact displaces his homonymous Julio-Claudian predecessor, Claudius, who is omitted from the list of imperial birthdays.[21]

In sculpture, the shorter bearded type is reflected in a bronze bust in Lyons.[22] As on the coins, the bust depicts the emperor wearing the cuirass and *paludamentum* and with the longer Constantinian coiffure and imperial diadem, combined with a shorter, more military beard. The locks over the forehead are slightly parted over the inner corner of the left eye, while the beard is treated as a series of incised decorative curls. The eyes are wide and almond-shaped, and the mouth has a full, slightly receding lower lip, a physical characteristic of Julian actually described by Ammianus Marcellinus (*labro inferiore demisso*).[23] The small scale of the bust may suggest that it was designed for display in a public or private shrine (*sacra publica* or *privata*) or perhaps to travel with the army. A relief portrait on a chalcedony *phalera* similarly represents Julian with his shorter beard, long comma-shaped locks parted near the center of the forehead, *paludamentum* and diadem.[24] Holes carved into the surface of the *phalera* indicate that the diadem, as well as the fibula of the *paludamentum*, were separately-worked metal attachments. The *phalera* was discovered at Antioch in 1897 near the Gate of St. Paul. It is inscribed *ANTONIANAE* likely referring to its owner. Although the beard is slightly longer in a sardonyx intaglio in Paris, it also combines the diadem and the military intonations of the *paludamentum*.[25] The mass production of Julian's portraits in various media confirms an active and thriving dissemination of the new bearded portrait type, with its concomitant messages of military authority and imperial tradition, early in Julian's reign.

Perhaps the best-known ancient images associated with Julian are nearly identical full-length statues in the Louvre (Fig. 4) and Musée Cluny (Figs. 5a–b).[26] Both statues are said to be from Italy where they allegedly formed part of the Millotti collection before their transfer to France in 1787.[27] Both portraits are clearly part of a replica series, which suggests an imperial identity and the coiffure and beard correspond closely with Julian's coin portraits, especially those with longer beard such as the late Antiochene issues celebrating Julian's assumption of the consulate in 363.[28] The long, comma-shaped locks of the coiffure are combed from right to left over the forehead and they reverse their orientation over both temples. The beard also consists of long, curved locks.[29] The eyes are large and almond-shaped and the mouth has a thin upper lip and, like the bronze bust in Lyon, a full, slightly-receding lower lip.

In earlier scholarship, doubts were raised concerning the authenticity of the Musée Cluny statue, while the Louvre statue was generally considered ancient. New archival research, however, as well as close examination of the statues themselves, may indicate that if either of the statues is modern, it is more likely to be the Louvre statue.[30] The Musée Cluny portrait exhibits weathering to its surfaces and breakage consistent for an ancient work of sculpture, while the Louvre statue is far better preserved and has some irregularities in the handling of the drapery which could suggest that it is a late-eighteenth-century copy created in Paris and based on the Musée Cluny portrait. Marble testing of both portraits might help to settle the questions of authenticity.[31]

Fig. 4 Julian, marble statue, Paris, Musée du Louvre, MA 1121 (photo courtesy of Agence photographique de la RMN/Art Resources).

Fig. 5a–b Julian, marble statue, Paris, Cluny Musée National du Moyen Age, inv. Cl. 18830 (photo courtesy of Agence photographique de la RMN/Art Resources).

In both portraits Julian wears the *tunica* (Greek *chitōn*) and the *pallium* (Greek *himation*) rather than the Roman toga, and the statues follow a well-known compositional type, used especially for representations of Greek intellectuals, orators, and statesmen, like the Aeschines from the Villa of the Papyri or the Lateran Sophocles.[32] The right arm is held close to the chest and is covered by drapery, a pose which ultimately may be derived from representations of Solon and designed to communicate self-control.[33] Indeed, Ammianus Marcellinus records Julian's own remarkable self-control and moderation.[34] In sarcophagi, the *pallium* had been increasingly used for portraits in order to showcase the intellectual accomplishments of the deceased throughout the second and third centuries.[35]

The standing palliate statue, however, is virtually absent from the corpus of imperial portrait sculpture, and it is not included in Pliny's account of typical Roman statuary types.[36] As a result, identification of precedents for representations of emperors wearing the *pallium* proves tenuous at best. Although two statues with the *pallium* have been identified as Hadrian, both prove problematic attributions. The facial features and coiffure of a bronze statue from Adana in Turkey do not conform closely enough to Hadrian's accepted typology, making it more likely that the portrait represents a private individual:[37] recent re-examination of a second statue of Hadrian executed in marble from the Temple of Apollo at Cyrene which uses a nearly identical body type to the Julian statues indicates that the head and body were not displayed together in antiquity.[38] The *pallium* is also employed in a marble statue which Margarete Bieber identified as Trajan[39] and as well in a marble statue formerly in Venice, and a bronze statue allegedly from Bubon in Turkey, both associated with Marcus Aurelius.[40] To be sure, Hadrian and Marcus Aurelius are the most self-consciously intellectual and philosophical of all of Julian's imperial predecessors, so it is tempting to associate them with surviving palliate portraits. Both Hadrian and Julian are recorded to have worn the *pallium*, the latter on his journey from Athens to Milan prior to his appointment as Caesar in Gaul.[41] Ammianus also faults Julian for being too much like Hadrian in his over-reliance on portents and omens, and too much like Marcus in his over-spending on sacrifice.[42] During the mutiny in Gaul of 359, the soldiers refer to Julian as 'Graeculus', an epithet also recorded for Hadrian by the late-fourth-century author of the *Historia Augusta*.[43]

By the early third century, Tertullian is able to characterize the *pallium* as the typical *habitus* of rhetoricians, grammarians, philosophers, musicians, astrologers and all practitioners of the liberal arts, but notes that its new incarnation as a Christian garment makes it more dignified than philosophy itself.[44] By the fourth century the *pallium* or *himation* is commonly used in early Christian art for depictions of Christ and the apostles, including the nearly-contemporary sarcophagus of Junius Bassus, itself dated to 359, or the slightly later statuette of the teaching Christ.[45] Julian's adoption of the *pallium* in the Louvre and Cluny portraits may be intended to counter the Christian co-option of the *pallium* and to re-assert its traditional intellectual connotations in much the same way that Julian had wanted a statue of Christ at Caesarea Philippi replaced with his own portrait.[46]

The unusual multi-tiered crown of the Louvre and Cluny statues consists of a lower rolled fillet, surmounted by a stylized laurel or myrtle wreath, itself topped with two additional rolled fillets. Although broken in both statues, the summit of the crown is scalloped. The closest comparanda to these crowns with multiple fillets and vegetal wreath occur in representations of priests, including a Severan portrait in Ephesus with fillet, myrtle (?) wreath and two upper fillets,[47] and a Hadrianic statue from Cyzicus which combines fillets with laurel and also employs an identical body type with *pallium*.[48] Prior to adopting the jeweled diadem which broadcast his elevation to the rank of Augustus, Julian is known to have worn crowns not traditionally associated with imperial insignia and Ammianus derides them as similar to those worn by *xystarchae* (gymnasium officials): 'at the outset of his principate he went around with a tawdry crown just like that of a gymnasium official attired in purple' (*cum inter exordia principatus vili corona circumdatus erat xystarchae similis purpurato*).[49] Julian himself would have encountered such crowns during his brief time at Athens where they were also featured in portraits of the *cosmētai* and other important officials and priests.[50]

Although the crown of the Louvre and Musée Cluny statues has been identified as that of the *pontifex maximus*,[51] and Julian in his letters refers to himself as head of the pontifical college at Rome, the portraits do not follow standard statuary formats for emperors as *pontifex maximus* which always represented them as togate and veiled with the right hand extended and holding the *patera*, as in the well-known portrait of Augustus from the Via Labicana in Rome.[52] By eschewing the traditional togate, cuirassed, divine or heroic body types of imperial statues, as well as the conventional coronae (*civica* [oak], *triumphalis* [laurel], or much more rarely *spicea* [wheat stalk]), Julian is explicitly configured neither as *pontifex maximus* nor *imperator*, but rather as a kind of philosopher-priest who instantiates an amalgamative Graeco-Roman version of *romanitas*; Libanius records that it pleased Julian to be called priest as much as emperor (χαίρει καλούμενος ἱερεὺς οὐχ ἧττον ἢ βασιλεύς).[53] Paul Zanker has noted that fillets and wreaths become a standard feature of late Roman philosopher portraits, underscoring the emerging priestly and theurgistic roles of philosophers.[54]

What is of course missing from the Paris statues are their accompanying inscriptions which would have added Julian's impeccable and allusive imperial nomenclature (*Flavius Claudius Iulianus*), as well as his official titulature. Since the statues are alleged to have originated in Italy, their inscriptions may have been in Latin which together with the intellectual and priestly allusions of the statues would have successfully fused Julian's Hellenic and Roman identities. Indeed, Julian's conflation of Roman and Greek traditions must have been well understood by his contemporaries, as Gregory of Nazianus was able to employ it as an invective strategy against the emperor when he unfavorably compared him to Epaminondas and Scipio.[55]

The imperial attribution of the statues, however, continues to be controversial and John Jakob Bernoulli was the first to suggest that the Louvre statue depicts a private individual, largely as a result of its highly unusual choice of body type and its priestly headgear.[56] More recently, Klaus Fittschen has proposed that the statue and its replicas are in fact representations of a private Hadrianic portrait depicting a priest of Serapis.[57] Fittschen adduces several Hadrianic portraits as comparanda for the Louvre and Musée Cluny statues, but their coiffures are in fact much more plastically modeled, their beards are much shorter and not made up of long curving locks, and none attains the schematized and abstracted style of the Louvre and Musée Cluny images.[58] In the Musée Cluny portrait the drillwork of the hair and beard is extremely linear and inorganic and the drapery is fairly flat; the dryly classicizing style of both portraits also seems more commensurate with a mid-fourth-century date, rather than the Hadrianic period.[59] In addition, the standing body type with *pallium* is unattested for private or imperial portraits in the west, which presupposes very particular, if not idiosyncratic motives for its use in the Louvre and Cluny statues.

An unfinished portrait head in Thasos employs a very similar crown of multiple fillets and it is clearly a replica of the same portrait type as the two statues as it exhibits an identical configuration of the locks over the forehead.[60] The use of recognizably priestly headgear in the two images confirms that it is a programmatic choice intended to underscore Julian's oppositional religious role as restorer of pagan rites and traditions.[61] The unfinished state of the Thasos head may have been caused by Julian's untimely death during the abortive Persian campaign and the subsequent restoration of Christian hierarchy within the imperial administration and throughout the empire.

It is not only the priestly crown in all three portraits and the use of the *pallium* in statues which signal Julian's intellectualized self-presentation, but also the philosophical implications present in the iconography of the hair

Fig. 6 Pythagoras, marble shield portrait, Aphrodisias, Museum (photo courtesy New York University Excavations at Aphrodisias).

and beard, which have close correspondences to later Roman depictions of philosophers and poets. An inscribed shield portrait of Pythagoras from a cycle of philosophers and poets at Aphrodisias exhibits a similar coiffure and beard comprised of long curving locks (Fig. 6).[62] The cycle seems to have been created in the late fourth or early fifth centuries and it is unclear how closely the Aphrodisias portrait may reflect earlier images of Pythagoras, but it has been endowed with a contemporary coiffure 'characteristic of male self-representation in the late 4th century'.[63] The bust-form sports the *pallium* appropriate to Pythagoras' role as philosopher and teacher, but he also wears a rolled diadem (*taenia*) which emphasizes the mystic and priestly attributes with which he was imbued by his late antique interpreters.[64] The long curving locks of Julian's hair and beard

193

also find affinities with late elaborations of Pindar's portraits, including another shield portrait from Aphrodisias.[65] Julian himself famously satirizes his philosopher's beard in the *Misopogon* where he exaggerates his unkempt appearance.[66] Earlier, in his *Letter to the Athenians*, Julian regrets the loss of the beard he had worn in Athens as a student of philosophy which he was forced to shave off when Constantius nominated him as Caesar.[67] Intriguingly, the philosophical and intellectual associations of Julian's portraiture and literary self-presentation may have endured long after his death as evidenced by an ancient portrait of Pindar from Rome which was re-attributed to Julian sometime in the Byzantine or Medieval period when it was given a new inscription identifying the likeness as *Julianus* (Fig. 7).[68] Indeed, the memory of Julian apparently continued to have resonance at Rome as evidenced by the medieval tradition of a palace associated with Julian, the *Palatium Iulianum*, and the *Mirabilia* which record a *Templum Juliani*.[69]

Julian's particular coiffure and beard also share strong formal correspondences with representations of Numa Pompilius. Coins minted in the late Republic depict Numa with coiffure and beard of long curving locks similar to Julian's and also represent the second king of Rome wearing a diadem (Fig. 8).[70] The coins likely reflect the appearance of the portrait of Numa which was included in the group of bronze statues representing Rome's kings displayed on the Capitoline.[71] There, Numa's togate image seems to have been added sometime in the third century BC and a surviving marble statue from the Atrium Vestae may have been based on it (Fig. 9).[72] Like the coins, the marble statue features a diadem, and the coiffure is made up of long curving locks, like the Louvre and Thasos portraits of Julian. The beard was repaired at some point in antiquity with a separately worked piece of marble, but enough survives on the lower face to suggest that it resembled those seen on the Republican coins. The statue was discovered in 1883 together with portraits of the Vestals. The date of the statue has proved problematic and it has been dated into the fourth century, but details of the toga and the form of its plinth suggest a date in the late Hadrianic or early Antonine period for its creation.[73] Its display at the Vestal complex, however, seems to post-date the Severan reconstruction.[74]

Julian's suggestive visual linkages to both Pythagoras and Numa are not coincidental. The two figures are closely aligned in Plutarch who speculates about the historical accuracy of the alleged close friendship between Numa and the philosopher.[75] Like Pythagoras, Numa promotes an aniconic religion devoid of anthropomorphic or zoomorphic images and he practices the 'philosophy of the one'.[76] Pythagoras was also purportedly enrolled as a citizen of Rome.[77] Plutarch underscores the philosophical

Fig. 7 Pindar ('Julianus'), marble bust, Rome, Museo Capitolino, Satanza dei Filosofi, inv. 587 (photo author).

Fig. 8 Numa Pompilius, *denarius*, *RRC* 446, Rome (courtesy Trustees of the British Museum).

Fig. 9. Numa Pompilius, marble statue, Rome, Antiquario Forense (photo author).

resemblances between the two and records that Numa's own twelve books of philosophy were buried with him.[78] Julian read Plutarch closely, and presents Numa as the philosopher king placed by Jupiter at the head of the Roman state.[79] In Julian's *Hymn to King Helios*, Numa is the divine ruler who appoints the Vestals to guard the sacred flame of the sun and reforms the Roman calendar according to solar stages.[80] For Julian, Numa is clearly the ideal Roman *exemplum* of the philosopher-priest-king, credited with founding Roman religion. The conscious references to Numa in the emperor's portraiture and writing seek to position Julian as a new founder or restorer of Roman religion much as he is also referred to as *recreator sacrorum*, *reparator*, *restitutor*, *conservator* and *propagator* in inscriptions.[81] Pythagoras also features prominently in Julian's works as an almost divine philosopher, and, like Julian, an ethical vegetarian.[82] Iamblichus was likely Julian's fullest available source on Pythagoras, and it is also Iamblichus who develops the idea of the philosopher-priest.[83]

The Louvre and Musée Cluny statues, as well as the Thasos portraits, also share the same stylistic and technical anomaly of uncarved pupils and irises. Beginning in the Hadrianic period, pupils and irises were normally carved in most Roman portraits. Later portraits of the second and third centuries can employ uncarved pupils and irises as a deliberate sculptural anachronism designed to link them to the representations of earlier Greek philosophers, poets and statesmen as in the two statues and the Thasos head.[84] Late Roman philosopher portraits, like the Pythagoras from Aphrodisias, also omit the carving of the pupils. In addition, the statue of Numa from the Atrium Vestae exhibits uncarved pupils which would have been an attribute of the Capitoline image created in the third century BC that inspired it. The Louvre, Cluny and Thasos replicas provide dual provenances of Latin west and Greek east for the nexus of references to Numa, priests and philosophers encoded in the basic portrait type again suggesting the possibility of a wide geographic dissemination of its amalgamative messages.

The Louvre, Cluny and Thasos portraits also find strong iconographic and stylistic parallels in a gold likeness of Marcus Aurelius from Avenches.[85] Although the correspondences are not close enough to support Jean Charles Balty's proposal that the Avenches bust actually depicts Julian, they may indicate that it was created during Julian's reign and designed to stress the similarities between the two emperors.[86] In addition to the predominant role Julian awards Marcus in his *Caesars* as the philosopher emperor and *civilis princeps*, Julian states his desire to emulate Marcus in his *Letter to Themistius*.[87] Ammianus Marcellinus highlights Julian's *aemulatio* of Marcus' deeds and character at the outset of Book 16.[88] In Book 22 he positions Julian as *similis* to Marcus in contradistinction to Constantius who is distinctly *dissimilis*, in order to lend historical legitimacy to Julian's accession despite the fact that Julian was technically a usurper who was acclaimed Augustus in opposition to the senior *princeps*.[89] Ammianus also records Julian's use of a saying he attributed to Marcus concerning the Alamanni and the Franks.[90] Eutropius confirms the positive similarities between Julian and Marcus.[91] Marcus was the paradigm of the philosopher emperor, who composed his *Meditations* in Greek, but he also stood as an important *exemplum* of an *imperator* because of his military achievements which had been visually celebrated in major public monuments such as his Column in Rome. Indeed, both emperors shared a principal adversary in the Alamanni.[92] Like Julian, Marcus is simultaneously Roman emperor and Greek philosopher.[93] The Avenches bust of Marcus is created from gold repousse, making it light-weight and easily portable which may suggest its use as military paraphernalia intended for an audience composed of soldiers.[94]

Julian himself implicitly adduces Marcus' military aspects in his *Letter to Themistius*,[95] where Marcus is paired as an *exemplum* to be imitated or surpassed with Alexander the Great. Ammianus compares Julian to

Alexander, as does Libanius in his *Monody* and *Funeral Oration* for Julian.[96] Julian's own extensive allusions to Alexander are well known and his formulations may have been shaped by a work likely completed in 340, the so-called *Alexander Itinerary*, which compared Alexander's Persian exploits with Trajan's campaigns.[97] An unusual contorniate medallion of Alexander whose profile vaguely resembles that of Julian may, in fact, have been issued by the emperor to celebrate the New Year of 363.[98] Similarly, a contorniate with an obverse portrait of Trajan, sometimes identified as Julian, may also have been minted under Julian.[99]

The same general configuration of the hair and beard in the Louvre, Cluny and Thasos likenesses is also featured on a chalcedony intaglio portrait in Paris.[100] The gem presents the emperor with pearl diadem which recalls Numa's flat diadem on the coins and statue from the Atrium Vestae, but Julian also wears the *paludamentum*, thus adding an imperial and military inflection to the image, like the literary allusions to Marcus and Alexander. The military implications are even more explicit in a bronze medallion used as an official weight at the mints (*exagium solidi*).[101] In the *exagium* Julian again wears the pearl diadem and *paludamentum* and also the cuirass, while a figure of Victory on a globe extends a triumphal wreath to Julian. The Louvre, Cluny and Thasos sculptures, *exagium*, the intaglio, and the bearded coin portraits with *paludamentum* and diadem present a complex composite of Julian as priest, philosopher and imperator.

Julian's costumes in visual representations were not limited to the *pallium*, cuirass or *paludamentum*. When Julian greeted the new consuls for 362, Claudius Mamertinus describes the emperor's costume as virtually indistinguishable in form and color from the *togae praetextatae* worn by his new consuls.[102] On this occasion, Julian's costume is a retrospective visual manifestation of his pronounced revival of the concept of the emperor as *civilis princeps*.[103] Julian also features the more elaborate *toga contabulata* on both the obverses and reverses of gold *solidi* minted at Antioch.[104] At Aphrodisias, Julian was also honored with a portrait which reused an earlier imperial togate statue from the mid-second century.[105] The sculpture may originally have depicted an Antonine prince and employs a well known type in which the left hand is extended and holds a scroll. The earlier style of toga, as well as the senatorial shoes (*calcei senatorii*) which the statue wears (as well as a ring) would have been traditional markers of *romanitas*. Although the portrait head of Julian is no longer extant, it was likely of Julian's later type with beard and imperial diadem. Julian's name was subsequently erased on the plinth which was reinscribed for Theodosius I and Theodosius II, and at that time the body was recombined with a recarved Julio-Claudian portrait head.[106] The Theodosian reconfiguration of the monument to Julian underscores the ongoing importance of historic Roman references in imperial ideology and iconography.

With his literary and artistic evocations of Numa, Julian validates his own position as ruler and priest through the authority of Roman history, but he also accesses the military foundations of the city and empire through specific references to Romulus with the *spolia opima* in a series of highly innovative coin reverses. Julian's acclamation as Augustus had been primarily based on his series of spectacular military victories in Gaul, especially Strasbourg, and a series of (solidus) reverses issued throughout the empire at Rome, Sirmium and Constantinople, consciously quote the images of Romulus *tropaiophoros* ('trophy bearer') which celebrated the founder of Rome as warrior king (Fig. 10).[107] In Julian's coins, a cuirassed figure holds a trophy, recalling in particular the well-known depiction of Romulus with the *spolia opima* from the Forum of Augustus in Rome, but known in numerous other versions in sculpture, gems and coins and as recorded by Ovid and Plutarch.[108] Augustus made Romulus and the *spolia opima* a central focus of the sculptural program of his Forum in order to equate the Parthian standards eventually displayed there with Romulus' signal achievement (Fig. 11).[109] Julian's coin reverses depict the soldier moving right and carrying the trophy in his left hand, just as Romulus in the Augustan sculpture, and with a kneeling or crouching captive beneath his right hand, surrounded by the legend *Virtus Exercitus Romanorum* or *Virtus Exercitus Romani*. For Julian, the numismatic evocations of the Romulus composition obviously underscore his military prowess but they also subtly deploy Rome's mytho-historical origins and the traditions of the *spolia opima* in order to legitimate the new emperor's authority.[110]

Julian's desire for military glory is well documented by Ammianus Marcellinus. In particular, Julian viewed the Persian campaign as a way of surpassing Rome's previous exploits in Parthia and he desired the epithet Parthicus, like Trajan, Lucius Verus or Septimius Severus before him.[111] Just as Numa had provided an impeccable regal, philosophical and priestly model, Romulus stood as his military counterpart.[112] In Plutarch, Romulus is fond of war, but he also is described as religious, interested in sacrifice and divination, and an *augur*.[113] Additionally, Romulus plays a role in Julian's *Hymn to King Helios* where he becomes divine Quirinus whose soul is directly derived from Helios.[114] In the *Caesars* it is Romulus who gives the banquet to which all the gods are invited and which allows Julian to satirize most of his imperial predecessors. Julian's presentation of Romulus as Quirinus seems to demonstrate a knowledge of Dionysius of Halicarnassus' account of the foundation of Rome in the *Roman Antiquities*.[115]

Fig. 10 *Solidus* reverse 361–3, Antioch, *RIC* 8.196 (photo courtesy the Classical Numismatic Group, LLC, cngcoins.com).

Fig. 11 Romulus with *spolia opima*, reproduction of a painting from the Fullonica of Fabius Ululutremulus, Pompeii 9.13.5, Rome, Museo della Civiltà Romana 72 (photo author).

Not surprisingly, Aeneas, the other great founding figure from Rome's earliest origins, also features in Julian's writing as well as his visual program. Again, in the *Hymn to King Helios* in the same section that details Romulus/ Quirinus' descent from Helios, Julian describes the current inhabitants of the Roman empire as the sons of Romulus and Aeneas (οἱ Ῥωμυλίδαι τε καὶ Αἰνεάδαι).[116] The story of Aeneas' journey to Italy may also have formed part of a missing section of Julian's *Against the Galileans*, and prior to becoming emperor Julian visited Troy where a statue was erected in his honor.[117]

An extraordinary *Virtus Exercitus Romanorum* reverse from Antioch reconfigures the soldier with trophy and captive in such a way that it also incorporates visually strong allusions to Aeneas fleeing Troy together with his young son Iulus Ascanius (and his father Anchises), which had formed the sculptural pendant to Romulus with the *spolia opima* at the Forum Augustum in Rome (Figs. 12–13).[118] In the Antiochene reverse the captive is now standing and wearing trousers, billowing cloak and Phrygian cap, very similar in appearance to Ascanius/Iulus in the Augustan statuary group.[119] The clever conflation of the sculptural groups from the Forum Augustum creates an unprecedented image which belies J. P. C. Kent's assessment of the 'disappointing character of his (Julian's) coin types'.[120] The use of metropolitan Roman models from the Augustan period is probably not coincidental, and for Julian, Augustus would have been of particular interest because of his well-known associations with Apollo-Helios, also referenced in the *Caesars*.[121] In the same section of the *Hymn to King Helios*, Julian also alludes to Augustus' temple of Apollo Palatinus which may be deliberately intended to invoke 'Augustan order'.[122] Julian was also following well-known Augustan precedents for the exportation of Egyptian obelisks in his planned expropriation of a Heliopolitan obelisk, sacred to the sun, for display at Constantinople.[123]

The apparent incorporations in Julian's coins of motifs first established in the Forum of Augustus were, however, not recondite Roman references, for the Augustan compositions of Romulus and Aeneas had been widely disseminated and diffused in various media and appear in funerary reliefs, medallions, and painting.[124] In fact, the compositions were well enough known, at least in the first century AD, to have inspired caricatures, with Romulus, Aeneas, and Iulus-Ascanius all appearing as macrophallic dogs in a famous fresco from the Masseria di Diego Cuomo at Pompeii.[125] By the fourth century, the motif is resurrected in contorniate medallions not far removed in date from Julian's coins.[126] In the Antiochene *Virtus Exercitus Romanorum* reverse, the transformation of Iulus-Ascanius into a foreigner also has important precedents on the Column of Trajan, where

Fig. 12 *Solidus* reverse, *RIC* 8.201, Antioch (photo courtesy the Classical Numismatic Group, Inc., cngcoins.com).

Fig. 13 Aeneas, Iulus-Ascanius and Anchises, reproduction of a painting from the Fullonica of Ululutremulus, Pompeii 9.13.5, Rome, Museo della Civiltà Romana 22 (photo author).

Dacian father and son groups are modeled on the Aeneas-Iulus/Ascanius composition in scenes of historical repatriation meant to resemble the forced exile of Aeneas himself.[127]

Various reverses also configure *Salus Rei Publicae*, *Securitas Rei Publicae*, or *Gloria Rei Publicae*, and their invocation of the *Res Publicae* again testifies to the authority of Roman tradition. During Julian's tenure as Caesar, bronze issues from all of the major mints at Lyons, Arles, Rome, Aquileia, Siscia, Constantinople, Nicomedia, Cyzicus, Antioch, and Alexandria all featured reverses with *Spes Rei Publicae*.[128] After Julian's acclamation as Augustus, all of the mints, except Rome and Alexandria, issuing the bronzes change the emphasis and *Spes Rei Publicae* becomes *Securitas Rei Publicae*, signaling that the new emperor ensures that hope for the state has strengthened to security.[129] A *solidus* from Trier issued in 360 while Constantius was still living but after Julian's acclamation as Augustus features Julian's beardless Constantinian type with pearl diadem on the obverse and seated representations of Roma and Constantinople surrounded by the legend *Gloria Rei Publicae*.[130] Its reverse imagery and legend echo a series of nearly identical *aureus* reverses issued for Constantius while Julian was Caesar.[131] In Julian's coins, the goddesses hold a shield inscribed *Votis V/Multis X* to mark Julian's *quinquennalia*. The continued references to the Republic revive the glories of the Roman past.

The most enigmatic of the *Securitas Rei Publicae* reverses feature a bull, whose symbolism is clearly multivalent. The unusual imagery appears in issues from all mints except Rome, Alexandria and Trier. The bull melds solar, mithraic and astrological aspects, together with highly literate references to Dio Chrysostom's *Discourses on Kingship* where the author derives the metaphor of ruler as bull from Homer (*Il.* 2.480–3).[132] Julian himself was clearly familiar with Dio's kingship treatises and he may have been involved in developing the new and atypical numismatic imagery.

Another unusual reverse insists on the *romanitas* of its message. The coin represents a Roman military standard flanked by bound captives, surrounded by the legend *Victoria Romanorum*, recalling the *Exercitus Romanorum* legends.[133] The Vexillum itself is decorated with the well-known abbreviation SPQR (*Senatus Populusque Romanus*) which is particularly emblematic of the city of Rome itself and generally absent from the later Roman coinage. There is no evidence that Julian accompanied Constantius on his visit to Rome in 357 (although Julian's wife Helena does seem to have been present) and he is not recorded as having visited the city on any other occasion.[134] Nevertheless, he personally attended to the relief of famine in Rome and the city's histories resonated throughout his writing and artistic program.[135] Ammianus writes that Rome, rather than Tarsus, was the truly fitting burial site for Julian, near to the Tiber and the monuments of earlier deified emperors.[136] In fact in 361 it was to Rome that Julian consigned the remains of his wife Helena to be buried in an imperial mausoleum along the Via Nomentana, the future church of Santa Costanza, named after one of the sisters of Helena, either Constantina (the wife of Julian's half-brother Gallus) or Constantia.[137]

Julian clearly understood the efficacy of images and the immediacy of imperial portraits that transcended their status as works of art created out of stone or bronze.[138] Julian also evinced a willingness to manipulate existing semantic and visual conventions in order to construct an image of himself and his empire that blended Greek and Roman. Because he was born in the east at Constantinople, wrote only in Greek, and was said to have had only passable Latin, Julian is often characterized exclusively in terms of his nostalgic Hellenism, but he ultimately authored his own highly inventive and individual identity in literature and art, founded not only on the philosophical and intellectual precepts of Hellenic *paedeia* and the Second Sophistic, but also on the unassailable authority of Roman tradition.[139]

Notes

[1] For Julian's coinage see also the chapter by Fernando López Sánchez in this volume.

[2] For Julian's panegyrics on Constantius see the chapters by Shaun Tougher and Hal Drake in this volume.

[3] For the range of iconographic, ideological and cultural meanings of Hadrian's beard, see Vout 2003 and D'Ambra 2005.

[4] On Constantinian portraiture and classicism see L'Orange 1984, 37–85, 118–38; Chiesa 2005; Parisi Presicce 2005; Hannestad 2007.

[5] Palazzo dei Conservatori, Sala di Marco Aurelio, inv. 1072, h. 1.77 m.; L'Orange 1984, 135; Fittschen and Zanker 1985, 153–5, no. 123, pls. 153–4; Lahusen and Formigli 2001, 315–7, no. 196; Parisi Presicce 2006, 141–3; Parisi Presicce in La Rocca, Parisi Presicce and Lo Monaco 2011, 3301–31, no. 5.13. In his catalogue for *Das Römische Herrscherbild*, L'Orange 1984, 128–39, does not distinguish between the three sons individually.

[6] Section VII, Salzman 1990, 34–5, figs. 13–14.

[7] Amm. Marc. 15.8.17; *RIC* 8, 220–5, nos. 230, 231, 233a, 235, 237, 239, 240, 242, 247–9, 251, 255–6; L'Orange and Wegner 1984, 159; Fittschen 1997, 33.

[8] Julian *Ep. ad Ath.* 274d; Gilliard 1964, 135.

[9] Aquileia: *RIC* 8, 335–7, nos. 213–14, 216, 218–20, 223, 225, 227, 229, 234, 236, 238, 240; Siscia: *RIC* 8, 377–8, nos. 363, 365–6, 368, 370–1, 373–4, 376, 378, 380; Arles: *RIC* 8, 221, no. 232; Sirmium: *RIC* 8, 389–90, nos. 67, 70, 72, 74, 76, 78, 81, 83–5, 87, 89, 91; Thessalonica: *RIC* 8, 420–2, nos. 194, 197, 200, 202, 204, 206, 209–10, 212, 214, 216; Heraclea: *RIC* 8, 437, nos. 92, 94–5, 97, 99–100;

Constantinople: *RIC* 8, 460–1, nos. 136, 138, 140–1, 143, 145, 145a, 147, 150, 152, 154; Nicomedia: *RIC* 8, 481–2, nos. 102a, 105–6, 108, 111, 113–14; Cyzicus: *RIC* 8, 499, nos. 112, 114, 116, 118, 120, 122; Antioch: *RIC* 8, 526–8, nos. 163–4, 166–7, 169, 171, 176, 178, 180, 182, 185, 187, 189, 192, 194; Alexandria: *RIC* 8, 545, nos. 83, 85–6, 88. See also Fleck 2008, 152–3, nos. 1–7.

[10] Lévêque 1960, fig. 10; Calza 1972, fig. 456.

[11] *RIC* 8, 276–9, nos. 292, 294–5, 306, 308, 311–12, 315, 317, 319, 321; Bastien 1992–94, pl. 203.6–8.

[12] Bastien 1992–94, 42.

[13] Kent 1959, 110–12, pls. 10.1, 4, 6, 8, 9, 10, 11, 14; L'Orange and Wegner 1984, 159; Fittschen 1997, 33.

[14] For the importance of *similitudo* as a kind of 'family fiction' in the late Roman period, see Kampen 2009, 104–22.

[15] Kent 1959, 110–12, pls. 10.2, 3, 5, 7, 12, 13.

[16] Kent 1959, 112–13, pls. 10.15–17. Sirmium: *RIC* 8, 391, no. 94; L'Orange and Wegner 1984, 159; Fittschen 1997, 33.

[17] Musei Civici di Arte e Storia di Brescia, S. Giulia, Museo della Città, inv. nos. MR 350–3; Lahusen and Formigli 2001, 298–301, no. 187 I–IV, figs. 431–5; Morandini in Aillagon 2008, 182.

[18] *Or.* 1 6d; *Or.* 2. 51c; *Caes.* 313d, 336b; MacCormack 1981, 188–9; Chausson 2007, 25–96.

[19] Lacombrade 1962, 47–67. For Julian's *Caesars* see also the chapter by Rowland Smith in this volume.

[20] Bowersock 1982; Smith 1995, 13.

[21] Salzmann 1990, 29 n. 13, notes a missing Divus Claudius in the list and assigns it to Claudius Gothicus. However, the birthday listed is 10th May which is that of Gothicus so it is the first Claudius (whose birthday was on 1st August) who is not in the list.

[22] Palais des Beaux-Arts, inv. L 215; De Loos-Dietz 1983, 116–26 (not ancient); L'Orange 1984, 162, pl. 78a–b; Bastien 1992–94, 150, 408, pl. 204.2; Meischner 1995, 432; Lahusen and Formigli 2001, 322–3, no. 200; Bringmann 2004, 95; Fleck 2008, 93–6, 177–8, no. 51 (Eugenius).

[23] Amm. Marc. 25.4.22; Lévêque 1962, 80.

[24] Paris, Bibliothèque Nationale, inv. 321 a; M. Avisseau-Broustet in Donati and Gentili 2005, 224–5, no. 36; Fleck 2008, 105–7, 181–2, no. 55.

[25] Paris, Bibliothèque Nationale, Cabinet des Médailles, inv. 2106a, 1.2 x 0.9 cm; Calza 1972, 384–5, no. 270, pl. 130.481; Avisseau-Broustet in Donati and Gentili 2005, 225, no. 37.

[26] Paris, Louvre, MA 1121 (MR 246), h. 1.7 m.; L'Orange and Wegner 1984, 162–3, pl. 76 c–d, 77; Kiilerich 1993, 222–3; De Kersauson 1996, 294–5, no. 133; Fittschen 1997, 32–6, pls. 8.1, 9.5, 10.9; Hamiaux 2003; Bringmann 2004, 131; Saragoza 2005; Fleck 2008, 63–73, 163–5, no. 37; Spiedel 2009, 244, fig. 3; Söldner 2010, 240, 344, pl. 323; L. Buccino in La Rocca, Parisi Presicce and Lo Monaco 2011, 198. Paris, Musée Cluny, Musée National du Moyen Âge, inv. CL 18830; L'Orange and Wegner 1984, 162; Kiilerich 1993, 222–3; Fittschen 1997, 32–6, pl. 8.2; Hamiaux 2003; Saragoza 2005; Fleck 2008, 63–73, 165–6, n. 38; L. Buccino in La Rocca, Parisi Presicce and Lo Monaco 2011, 198–9.

[27] Fittschen 1992–93, 478, n. 94.

[28] Carson 1981, 58, no. 1413.

[29] Ammianus records that Julian was ridiculed for having the beard of a billy goat, 22.14.3 (*barbam prae se ferens hircinam*); and that he trimmed his beard into a point, 25.4.22 (*hirsuta barba in acutum desinente vestitus*).

[30] Hamiaux 2003; Saragoza 2005; Buccino in La Rocca, Parisi Presicce and Lo Monaco 2011, 198. Both statues were displayed together in 2003–4 for the exhibition, *Julian l'Apostat ou la double imposture: les statues du Louvre et des thermes de Cluny*.

[31] The marble of the Musée Cluny statue has been characterized as both Naxian (Saragoza 2005) and Thasian (Bardiès-Fronty 2009, 155, no. CL 84); the grayish color of the marble and large crystals are consistent with Greek island marbles.

[32] Naples, Museo Nazionale Archeologico, inv. 6018; Dillon 2006, 61–2, fig. 63; Musei Vaticani, Museo Gregoriano Profano.

[33] Dillon 2006, 61.

[34] Amm. Marc. 25.4.4. On Julian and self-control see also the chapter by Nicholas Baker-Brian in this volume.

[35] Ewald 1999; Borg 2004, 166–71; Fejfer 2008, 200; Hansen 2008.

[36] Plin. *HN* 34.18–19; Borg 2004, 162; Koortbojian 2008, 78–9.

[37] Adana, Istanbul, Archaeological Museum, inv. 5311; Kozloff 1987, 92, figs. 18–19. Evers 1994, 283, 291 (not Hadrian); Lahusen and Formigli 2001, 203–4, no. 122 (not Hadrian).

[38] London, British Museum, no. 1381, inv. 1861.11.27.23; Rosenbaum 1960, 51–2, no. 34, pls. 26.1–2–27.1; Huskinson 1975, 38–9, no. 69, pl. 28; Evers 1994, 125–6, no. 27; Zanker 1995, 208–9; Huskinson 2000, 9, fig. 1.4; Vout 2003, 447–8, pl. 7.1; Borg 2004, 158, n. 6; Fejfer 2008, 395–7, fig. 316; Opper 2008, 70.

[39] Formerly in a German private collection; West 1941, 2, 67, no. 5, pl. 18.67. Bieber 1959, 399 and n. 41.

[40] Marble statue formerly in Venice; Zanetti and Zanetti 1740, pl. XXVII; Dütschke 1882, 25–6; Kozloff 1987, 89, fig. 11; headless bronze statue from Bubon, Cleveland Museum of Art, inv. 86.5, associated with inscription of Marcus Aurelius, Kozloff 1987. Fittschen 1999, 129, has suggested that the portrait is a pastiche of an earlier Hellenistic body that was later combined with a head of Marcus; see also Fejfer 2008, 397. A Hellenistic date for the body is supported by the Greek sandals *trochades* which the statue wears, as opposed to the more usual sandals with *lingulae* worn by most Roman period *palliati* like the Louvre Julian, see Pfrommer 1987. Nevertheless, the overall intellectual and philosophical emphasis of the new agglomerative image would have been the same as the marble likenesses of Trajan and Hadrian.

[41] *SHA, Hadr.* 22.4–5; Fejfer 2008, 395; Amm. Marc. 15.8.1; Gilliard 1964, 135.

[42] Amm. Marc. 25.4.17; Kelly 2005, 409.

[43] Amm. Marc. 17.9.3; *SHA, Hadr.* 1.4.

[44] Tert. *De pallio* 6.2, *De meo vestiuntur et primus informator litterarum et primus enodator vocis et primus numerorum harenarius et grammaticus et rhetor et sophista et medicus et poeta et qui musicam pulsat et qui stellarem coniectat et qui volaticam spectat. Omnis liberalitas studiorum quattuor meis angulis tegitur...Sed ista pallium loquitor...Gaude pallium et exsultat! Melior iam te philosophia dignata est ex quo Christianum vestire coepisti.*

[45] Bieber 1959, 411; Malbon 1990; Mathews 1993, 39, 109–11; Vout 2003, 448–9; Rezza 2010; the statuette of the teaching Christ, Rome, Museo Nazionale Romano,

Palazzo Massimo alle Terme, inv. 61565; M. Sapelli in Donati and Gentili 2005, 298–9, no. 149.

⁴⁶ Soz. *Hist. eccl.* 5.21; Philostorgius, *Hist eccl.* 7.3; *Parastaseis Syntomoi Chronikai* 48; Kristensen 2009, 205–6. Smith 1999a, 452, has suggested that the late philosopher portraits generally can be read as a reaction against the Christian co-option of philosophical imagery for Christ and the apostles.

⁴⁷ Vienna, Kunsthistorisches Museum inv. I 818, h. 0.555 m.; Rumscheid 2000, 122, no. 16, pl. 8.1–2.

⁴⁸ Archaeological Museum, inv. 103, h. 2.05; Rumscheid 2000, 128, no. 28, pls. 5.3, 17.4, 18.1–2; Smith and Ertu 2001, 176, pl. 69.

⁴⁹ Amm. Marc. 21.1.4; Piganiol 1938, 245–6.

⁵⁰ Rumscheid 2000; D'Ambra 2005; Riccardi 2007.

⁵¹ Kiilerich 1993, 222–3; Piganiol 1938, 243–8.

⁵² Julian, *Letter to a Priest* (=B–C *Ep.* 89b), 298c, 302b; and *Ep.* 18 (=B–C *Ep.* 88), 45b. Julian as Pontifex Maximus (Lib. *Or.* 12.33–68); see also Bowersock 1978, 82–3. Via Labicana Augustus, Museo Nazionale Romano, Palazzo Massimo alle Terme, inv. 56.230, h. 2.05 m.; Boschung 1993, 40–2, 142, 146, 151, 162, 170, 177, no. 166, pls. 80, 148.8, 214.1.

⁵³ Lib. *Or.* 12.80.

⁵⁴ Zanker 1995, 310.

⁵⁵ Greg. Naz. *Or.* 4.71; Stertz 1977, 437. On Julian and Gregory see also Elm 2010b, as well as her chapter in this volume.

⁵⁶ Bernoulli 1894, 243; Vout 2003, 448.

⁵⁷ Fittschen 1992–93, 478, 482, 485, figs. 24.1, 25.1, 26.4, 27.1–2; Fittschen 1997, 32–6, pls. 8.1–2, 9.5, 10.9–10; see also Goette 1989, 186, and Papini 2002, 106.

⁵⁸ Portraits in Vienna (Kunsthistorisches Museum, Fittschen 1992–93, fig. 25.3) and the Musei Vaticani (Magazzini, Fittschen 1992–93, fig. 28.2) have much fuller coiffures than the Louvre Julian, while portraits in New York (Metropolitan Museum of Art, Fittschen 1992–93, fig. 28.1), Kansas City (Nelson-Atkins Museum of Art, inv. 34–138 A, Fittschen 1992–93, fig. 284), and Rome (Catacombs of S. Callisto, Fittschen 1992–93, figs. 25.4, 26.3) have full coiffures with layered locks over the forehead that are not comparable to the Louvre Julian. A bust in the Uffizi (Fittschen 1992–93, fig. 28.3) has a much less ordered coiffure and omits the precise regularity of pattern seen in the Louvre statue. None of the Hadrianic portraits has a comparable beard. The Hadrianic portraits that Fittschen gathers are not themselves unproblematic, and Smith has proposed that some are, in fact, Antonine: see Fittschen 2011, 237 n. 63, and Smith 1998.

⁵⁹ Kiilerich 1993, 222.

⁶⁰ Museum, inv. 937; L'Orange and Wegner 1984, 164, pl. 76a–b; Fittschen 1997, 32–6 (Hadrianic priest); Fleck 2008, 88–9, 173–4, no. 46 (Hadrianic priest); see Lévêque 1960, 111, fig. 8, for diagrams of the identical lock formations in the Louvre and Thasos portraits.

⁶¹ Fittschen 1997, 34–5, n. 28, pl. 10.11–12, associates the crown with the cult of Serapis based on a portrait in Alexandria. Although the crown in the Alexandrian portrait is similar, it is not identical and does not have the very prominent vegetal wreath.

⁶² Aphrodisias, Museum; Smith 1991.

⁶³ Smith 1991, 163, and also 164, 167.

⁶⁴ O'Meara 1989; Smith 1991, 163, 167.

⁶⁵ Aphrodisias, Museum; Smith 1990, 132–5, pls. 6–7; Zanker 1995, 322, fig. 176. Prior to its clear association with Pindar, this portrait had also been associated with Julian: see Fleck 2008, 92–3, 176–7, no. 50.

⁶⁶ *Misop.* 338b–339b, 349c, 358a, 364b, 367b; Mayer 2002, 20–2. For the *Misopogon* see the chapter by Nicholas Baker-Brian in this volume.

⁶⁷ *Ep. ad Ath.* 274d. For the *Letter to the Athenians* see the chapter by Mark Humphries in this volume.

⁶⁸ Rome, Museo Capitolino, Sala dei Filosofi inv. 587; *CIL* 6.5 3499*; Bernoulli 1894, 247–8; Andreotti 1931, 49–50.

⁶⁹ De Spirito 1999.

⁷⁰ *RRC* 332, no. 334 (97 BC?); 357, no. 346 (88 BC); 463, no. 446 (49 BC). See also an *as* of 9 BC by Cn. Calpurnius Piso and the triumviri monetali with similar portrait but no inscription.

⁷¹ Plin. *HN* 33.9–10, 24, and 34.22–3; Asconius *Scaur.* 25 (Stangl 29); App. *B. Civ.* 1.16; Dio Cass. 43.45.3–4; *CIL* 16.24 (military diploma *in basi Pompil(i)*; Evans 1990; Richardson 1992, 372 (Statuae Regum Romanorum); Coarelli 1999, 368–9.

⁷² Anti 1919; Becatti 1941; Von Heintze 1963, 42; Goette 1990, 56, 141, no. Ca 6; Coarelli 1999, 369. A chalcedony gem is close enough to the coin images that it, too, seems to represent Numa: Bernoulli 1882, 14 (Cades 5, no. 52), and Anti 1919, 221.

⁷³ Goette 1990, 56, and n. 286.

⁷⁴ Anti 1919, 214.

⁷⁵ Plut. *Num.* 1.2–4; Dion. Hal. 2.58–9.

⁷⁶ Plut. *Num.* 8.3–9; Tertullian also notes the idyllic nature of religion without images under Numa (*Apol.* 25.12).

⁷⁷ Plut. *Num.* 8.9.

⁷⁸ Plut. *Num.* 22.3–4.

⁷⁹ *C. Gal.* 193c–d; on Julian's 'heavy debt' to Plutarch, see Smith 1995, 13.

⁸⁰ *Or.* 4 155a–d. For the *Hymn to King Helios*, see the chapter of Andrew Smith in this volume, as well as that of J.H.W.G. Liebeschuetz.

⁸¹ *reparator orbis romani et restitutor omnium rerum et totius felicitatis recreator sacrorum* (Arce 1984, 110, no. 106, 160); *reparator orbis romani* (*CIL* 9.417; Arce 1984, 103, no. 32, 126); *liberator orbis romani, restitutor libertatis et rei publicae et conservator multum (militum) et provincialium* (*CIL* 11.6669; Arce 1984, 103, no. 29, 125); *restitutor libertatis, restitutor omnium rerum et totius felicitatis* (*CIL* 9.5960, Arce 1984, 102, no. 11, 123); *propagator romani nominis restitutor libertatits* (Arce 1984, 1088, no. 87, 143). For Julian's inscriptions see also the chapter by Benet Salway in this volume.

⁸² *Or.* 6 191b; for Pythagoras and Julian, see Smith 1995, 39, 65–6, 67, 123.

⁸³ Athanassiadi-Fowden 1981, 181–2; Smith 1995, 187–9.

⁸⁴ Uncarved pupils and irises are also an anachronistic feature of two Severan portrait replicas of the same individual with uncarved pupils and irises in the Louvre, inv. MA 4696 (De Kersauson 1996, 294–5, no. 133), and Atlanta, Michael C. Carlos Museum, inv. 2004.13.1. For Roman-period portraits of Greek philosophers, intellectuals and statesmen, see Dillon 2006.

⁸⁵ Avenches, Musée Romain d'Avenches, inv. 1939/34; h. 0.335 m.; L'Orange and Wegner 1984, 161; Lahusen and Formigli 2003, 514, 512; Riccardi 2002, 86;

A. Hochuli-Gysel in Aillagon 2008, 82 (with earlier literature); Fleck 2008, 83–8, 172–3, no. 45.

[86] Balty 1980; for the strong arguments against Balty's identification, see Jucker 1981.

[87] *Ep. ad Them.* 253a; see Stertz 1977, 436–9; Hunt 1995 for Julian's 'conventional' use of Marcus in his writing. For the *Letter to Themistius* see the chapter by John Watt in this volume.

[88] Amm. Marc. 16.1.4 (*rectae perfectaeque rationis indagine congruens Marco, ad cuius aemulationem actus suos effingebat et mores*).

[89] Amm. Marc. 21.16.11–12; Kelly 2005, 411–15; on Julian's illegitimate usurpation of power, see Kolb 2001, 98–9, 208–14.

[90] Amm. Marc. 22.5.4; Hunt 1995, 288, has suggested that Ammianus casts Julian as 'Marcus *redivivus*'.

[91] Eutr. 10.16.3.

[92] Drinkwater 2007.

[93] Stertz 1977, 438.

[94] Riccardi 2002.

[95] *Ep. ad Them.* 253a.

[96] Amm. Marc. 21.8.3; Lib. *Or.* 17.17, 32; 18.260, 261; Lane Fox 1997, 250.

[97] Lane Fox 1997.

[98] Alföldi 1962, 404, pl. 119, fig. 6; Lane Fox 1997, 250; Fleck 2008, 46–8, 160, no. 26.

[99] Alföldi 1976, 40, no. 617, pl. 184.7; Fleck 2008, 45–6, 159, no. 24.

[100] Bibliothèque Nationale, inv. 2106 a; Bastien 1992–94, 253, pl. 203.4; Vollenweider and Avisseau-Broustet 2003, 207, no. 266; M. Avisseau-Broustet in Donati and Gentili 2005, 225, no. 37; Fleck 2008, 134–5, 190, no. 64.

[101] Geneva, Musée d'Art et d'Histoire. Alföldi 1962, 404–5, pl. 119.10; Lévêque 1963, 80–2, pl. 14.4; Bastien 1992–94, 319, pl. 204.1; Bringmann 2004, 173; Fleck 2008, 43–5, 158, no. 23.

[102] Mamert. 29.5.

[103] On Julian's revival of the ideal of the *civilis princeps*, see Wallace-Hadrill 1982, 48.

[104] *RIC* 8, 530, nos. 204–6; Kent 1959; Bastien 1992–94, 425, 538, pl. 203.6.

[105] Museum, inv. 72–131 (statue), h. 1.32 m.; R.R.R. Smith in Smith 2006, 113–14, no. 5; Smith 2001; Smith 1999, 161–2, fig. 2; Smith and Ratté 1998, 243–4, fig. 20.

[106] Smith in R.R.R. Smith 2006, 113; Smith 2001; K. Erim in Inan and Alföldi-Rosenbaum 1979, 134–5, no. 80.

[107] *RIC* 8, 279, no. 323 (solidus, Rome, 361–363); *RIC* 8, 391, no. 95 (solidus, Sirmium, 361–363); *RIC* 8, 391, no. 96 (solidus, Sirmium, 361–63); *RIC* 8, 462, no. 157 (solidus, Constantinople 362). A Constantinian *aureus* minted at Trier *c.* 312–313 featured a figure of Mars similar to the Romulus *tropaiphoros* with the legend *Virtus Exercitus Gall, RIC* 6, 223, no. 820.

[108] Ov. *Fast.* 5.559–66; Plut. *Rom.* 16.8; Small 1994, 640–1.

[109] Flower 2000, 57.

[110] On the *spolia opima* as an 'invented tradition' see Flower 2000.

[111] Amm. Marc. 22.12.1–2; Athanassiadi-Fowden 1981, 196; Julian also addresses the Roman troops in Persia and alludes to earlier Roman victories in Parthia including

those of Lucullus, Pompey, Ventidius, Trajan, L. Verus, S. Severus (and Gordian the Younger?); Browning 1975, 198.

[112] For Numa and Romulus as complementary counterparts, see Rehak 2001, 198.

[113] Plut. *Rom.* 7.2 (sacrifice and divination); 14.1 (fond of war); 22.1 (as religious and an augur).

[114] *Or.* 4 154a–d.

[115] In particular, Dion. Hal. *Ant. Rom.* 1.87 and 2.56.6 (chronicling the eclipses associated with Romulus' birth and death); Lacombrade 1960, 161.

[116] *Or.* 4 154a.

[117] Cyril, *C. Jul.* 6.193a. Statue base: *CIL* 3.7068; *ILS* 751; Arce 1984, 156, no. 103. For Julian's visit to Troy see Julian, *Ep.* 19 (=B–C 79); Bourgeaud 2010, 348–50. For Julian's *Against the Galileans* see the chapter of David Hunt in this volume.

[118] *RIC* 8, 530, no. 201 (solidus, Antioch, 360–363).

[119] Aeneas, Ascanius and Anchises had also been featured on earlier reverses minted in Rome *c.* 327–333, with *Roma* on the obverse: *RIC* 7, 334, no. 317.

[120] Kent 1959, 109.

[121] *Caes.* 309a–c.

[122] *Or.* 4 153d; Smith 1997, 169. Mamert. 9.2, also mentions Julian's restoration of Nicopolis, the city founded by Augustus in honor of his victory at Actium and the site of the Actian Games.

[123] Julian, *Ep.* 48 (=B–C 59), 443b. For the obelisk that Constantine intended for the Circus Maximus in Rome and Constantius eventually erected, see *CIL* 6.1163; Amm. Marc. 17.4.15. The obelisk was actually not moved to Constantinople until the reign of Theodosius I, when it was erected at the circus; on the obelisk, see Mayer 2002, 114, 125.

[124] Cianciani 1981; funerary stēlē of Petronia Grata: Turin, Museo Archeologico. In painting from the House of Fabius Ululutremulus, Pompeii 9.13.5; De Vos 1991, 117, fig. 9; Zanker in Carandini and Capelli 2000, 85, fig. 2.

[125] Naples, Museo Nazionale Archeologico, Gabinetto Segreto, inv. 9899 (with 8588 depicting canomorphic Romulus and a marine thiasos); De Vos 1991, 113–23; R. Capelli in Carandini and Capelli 2000, 222. The painting was erroneously attributed to the Villa at Gargano in the *Le Antichità di Ercolano* 4 (1765), 367, no. 108: see De Vos 1991, 113.

[126] Alföldi and Alföldi-Rosenbaum 1976, 202, nos 90–1; pls. 6.10, 14.9–12, 143.1–4, 145.4; Cianciani 1981, no. 145.

[127] Scenes 30–2; scene 76; scene 154.

[128] Carson, Hill and Kent 1978, 50, nos. 265–7 (Lyons); 55, nos. 461–2 (Arles); 60, nos. 689–92 (Rome); 67, nos. 951–6 (Aquileia); 71, nos. 1244, 1246–51 (Siscia); 78, nos. 1689–92 (Sirmium); 83, nos. 1905–6 (Heraclea Thracica); 87, nos. 2053–5 (Constantinople); 92, nos. 2315–6 (Nicomedia); 97, nos. 2504–7 (Cyzicus); 100, nos. 2638–9 (Antioch); 103, nos. 2850–1 (Alexandria). *Spes Reipubl* also appears on a Constantinian bronze minted at London *c.* 310–312, *RIC* 6, 138, no. 241, and Sirmium and Heraclea issued bronzes for Constantius II, *c.* 355–361, in conjunction with Julian's coins, *RIC* 8, 390, no. 80, and 437, no. 98.

[129] Carson, Hill and Kent 1978, 51, nos. 268–9 (Lyons); 55, nos. 466–71 (Arles); 67, nos. 957–9 (Aquileia); 71, nos. 1244–54 (Siscia); 79, nos. 1693–7 (Sirmium); 83, nos. 1907–10 (Heraclea Thracica); 87, nos. 2056–9 (Constantinople); 92, nos. 2317–19

(Nicomedia); 97, nos. 2508–12 (Cyzicus); 100, nos. 2640–1 (Antioch). Earlier, Constantine had featured *Securitas Rei Publicae* on a solidus minted at Trier in 320 (*RIC* 7, 185, no. 246), and it is used for Constantius II on an unlisted *siliqua*.

[130] Carson 1981, 57, no. 57.

[131] *RIC* 57 (Constantinople, *c.* 341–350); 74, 100 (Nicomedia, *c.* 351–355); 81, 83, 86 (Antioch, *c.* 347–355); 150, 195 (Thessalonica, *c.* 355–361); 172 (Antioch, *c.* 355–361); 179 (Aquileia, *c.* 352–355); 291 (Rome, 355–357); 297 (Siscia, *c.* 350–351).

[132] *Or.* 2.66–7; Tougher 2004; see also Arce 1984, 186–93; Harl 1987, 33–4.

[133] *RIC* 298, no. 468. The obverse features a bearded Julian with the legend *D N Fl Cl Iulianus Pf Aug*; Alföldi 1999, 241, n. 10. A *follis* of Constantine from Rome issued *c.* 312–313 features three military standards surrounded by the legend *SPQR Optimo Principi* (*RIC* 346), and a rare, unlisted solidus of Constantine from Trier featured a reverse with the legend *SPQR Optimo Principi* surrounded by a laurel wreath.

[134] Calza 1972, 365, entertains the possibility that Julian did, in fact, visit Rome, either for the imperial visit of 357, when Julian could have delivered his panegyric for Constantius, or in 361 for the burial of Helena.

[135] On Julian's efforts to relieve the famine, see Mamert. 14.1–2.

[136] Amm. Marc. 25.10.5, *Exindeque egredi nimium properans, exornari sepulchrum statuit Iuliani, in pomerio situm itineris, quod ad Tauri montis angustias ducavit, cuius suprema et cineres, siqui tunc iuste consuleret, non Cydnus videre deberet, quamvis gratissimus amnis et liquidus, sed ad perpetuandam gloriam recte factorum praeterlambere Tiberis intersecans urbem aeternam divorumque veterum monumenta praestringens*; MacCormack 1981, 134.

[137] Amm. Marc. 21.1.5, 25.4.2; Lib. *Or.* 18.179. Archaeological evidence may suggest that the mausoleum in fact post-dates the deaths of Constantina and Constantia, and it is possible that it was actually constructed for Helena: see Stanley 1994. If so, the suggestive pagan imagery of the mausoleum's mosaic decoration may in part be attributed to Julian's influence; on S. Constanza, see also Johnson 2009, 139–56, where he argues against Julian's direct involvement in construction of the mausoleum, as proposed by Mackie 1997, 399, and Holloway 2004, 104. On the genealogical confusion and difficulties surrounding Constantia and Constantina, see Chausson 2007, 100 and n. 9, 105–6, 108, 114–16, 139–41, 151, 162, 166, 171–2, 256 (Constantina wife of Gallus); 99, 108, 112 and n. 34, 115–16, 163, 256 (Constantia).

[138] *Letter to a Priest* 294c–d, 'And indeed we do not say that the statues of the emperors are mere wood and stone and bronze, but still less do we say they are the emperors themselves. He therefore who loves the emperor delights to see the emperor's statue' (καὶ γὰρ οὐδὲ τὰς βασιλικὰς εἰκόνας ξύλα καὶ λίθον καὶ χαλκὸν λέγομεν, οὐ μὴν οὐδὲ αὐτοὺς τοὺς βασιλέας, ἀλλὰ εἰκόνας βασιλέων. ὅστις οὖν ἐστι φιλοβασιλεὺς ἡδέως ὁρᾷ τὴν τοῦ βασιλέως εἰκόνα); Bonfante 1964, 408.

[139] For Julian and Hellenism, see most recently Stenger 2009, 135–64, 333–54. Ammianus (16.5.7) criticizes Julian's Latin as 'merely adequate' (and see Matthews 2010, 203); based on the *Caesars*, Bowersock 1982 assumes that Julian is largely unaware of historiographical writing in Latin including the *De Caesaribus* of his friend and contemporary, Aurelius Victor, but the historical inconsistencies and omissions may be largely the result of the work's satirical genre and rapid composition for the Saturnalia, rather than Julian's ignorance.

13

JULIAN'S *HYMN TO THE MOTHER OF THE GODS*: THE REVIVAL AND JUSTIFICATION OF TRADITIONAL RELIGION

J. H. W. G. Liebeschuetz

Introduction

When Julian came to Constantinople in 361 as sole emperor he was determined to restore the traditional religion to a pre-eminent position in the empire:

> For it is our duty to maintain all the ritual of the temples that the law of our fathers prescribes…neither more nor less than that ritual; for eternal are the gods, so that we too ought to imitate their essential nature in order that thereby we may make them propitious.[1]

So it is not surprising that the two theological writings of Julian were composed on the occasions of two traditional festivals which they are intended to justify. The festivals are that of Cybele (the Mother of the Gods) in March, and that of Helios – the predecessor of Christmas – on 25th December. In editions and translations of Julian's writings, the *Hymn to King Helios* precedes the *Hymn to the Mother of the Gods*, although chronologically the latter was the earlier of the two, dating from March 362.[2]

Being an intellectual, Julian was keen to justify his religious policy intellectually to fellow intellectuals, men like his friend Salutius,[3] whom he appointed Praetorian Prefect of the East, and the famous sophist Libanius. Julian was probably unique among Roman emperors in that he took an active part in intellectual discussions. In his efforts to save and revitalize traditional religion by intellectual argument, Julian's basic reasoning is that the views about the gods presented by traditional religion are compatible with Neoplatonist philosophy, that traditional religion is philosophically sound.[4] Allegorical interpretation serves to bridge philosophy and religion. Allegorical interpretation is more prominent in the *Hymn to the Mother of the Gods* than in the *Hymn to King Helios*. This is no doubt because the myth of Attis was much more prominent in the ritual of the March festival of

Cybele, than the myths concerning Helios were in the festival of Sol Invictus in December.[5]

The *Hymn to the Mother of the Gods* and the *Hymn to King Helios*, together with Julian's response to the lecture of the Cynic Heraclius, are closely linked.[6] They arguably represent a systematic intellectual apology for the paganism that Julian was seeking to revive. Julian was doing for his paganism (though in a much more learned and intellectual way) what Constantine had done for Christianity in his *Oration to the Saints*.[7] In the *Hymn to the Mother of the Gods* Julian argues that the myth of Attis, correctly understood, is an allegory of the Neoplatonist world picture. After validating the myth of Attis, Julian is equally concerned to show that the traditional ceremonies and ritual of the festivals of the Mother of the Gods also symbolize philosophical truths and so remain as valid as ever.

The Neoplatonist world picture

The underlying philosophical idea is that thought, or mind, or spirit precedes matter (as in the opening of John's Gospel: 'In the beginning was the Word'), and that thought or mind gives rise to matter, and shapes it into the myriad forms that make up the world. So the idea of the world existed before the world, and the idea of the world created the world of matter. The Platonic theory of ideas is made the basis of an explanation for the coming into being of everything that exists. So Julian asks:

> For why are there so many kinds of generated things? Whence arise masculine and feminine...if there are not pre-existing and pre-established concepts, and causes which existed beforehand to serve as a pattern?[8]

According to this Neoplatonic world view, the problem arises of how thought or mind can first create, and then interact with matter. This, in truth, insoluble problem is supposedly solved (or in fact only postponed) by positing a hierarchy of intellectuality. This hierarchy proceeds from the original divine unity, comprising in potential everything that is about to be, and descends – via the intelligible gods, the deified ideas of Plato, and the intellectual gods, a grade of divinity introduced by Iamblichus,[9] and the visible gods which are the sun and the stars – finally to our earth and its earthy material. As each stage becomes more distant from the original unity, so its make-up becomes inferior, with earthy matter at the bottom of the hierarchy. But each stage, while inferior to the preceding one, also participates in its predecessor's particular qualities. The visible gods are the stars and their leader is the sun, the indispensable source of all life on earth. Since everything in the visible world is already contained in the invisible world of ideas, there is a sun at each level, at the intellectual and at the intelligible all the way back to the original unity, which has the same generative relationship to the universe coming into existence as our sun has to our planet and everything on it.[10]

So far this account of the origin of the world cannot be called a religion. It is in fact a logical succession of operations that have to be carried out for our world to come into existence. So the philosophical equivalent to Cybele, the Mother of the Gods, is not a personality, but a creative mental process, which leads to the production of the intellectual gods, who are themselves mental processes and ideas. There is no necessity that these abstractions should demand worship or respond to worship. These abstracts are made into the basis of a religion, or rather they are used to give traditional Graeco-Roman religion a philosophical justification on the assumption that Graeco-Roman mythology is actually an allegorical account of the philosophical picture of the world, and that the traditional gods are personifications of the abstract creative processes active in the philosophical cosmogony.

Julian's two so-called 'prose hymns' supplement each other. The *Hymn to King Helios* is essentially about the coming into existence of the intelligible and intellectual gods (that is about the mental world of ideas that models and predates our world, and will eventually generate it), while the *Hymn to the Mother of the Gods* is about the generation of this material world of ours and of mankind itself. On some level, Julian's treatises can be compared with the thirteenth book of Augustine's *Confessions* with its ethical interpretations of the creation narrative of *Genesis*.[11] It will be seen that neither of Julian's pieces is what we would call a hymn, that is a poem (or even a piece of prose) in praise of a god. Rather each is a sermon with the message that the myths of the gods (when properly understood) convey the same view of the gods and their relationship to the world and to mankind as the teachings of the philosophers,[12] as mediated through the Chaldean Oracles.[13]

The Chaldean Oracles

The Chaldean Oracles, as interpreted by Iamblichus, provide the link between the world of philosophy and the world of religion, which makes it possible to introduce the traditional gods into the abstract world picture of the philosophers, and indeed to give them the key dynamic roles in it. These oracles, which are preserved only in fragments, seem to describe the nature of the universe, and show how the divine principle and the human soul are related to the universe as a whole. In this way they explain why man is able to communicate with the gods, and suggest how this communication can be established by ritual invocation. They purport to have been inspired by gods, and their message is in fact related to that of the theological oracles of Apollo of Didyma. Thus they have supernatural authority. What fits them so well for Julian's purpose is that their theology, as far as there is one, is related to that of Middle Platonism.[14] Like the philosophers they are basically monotheistic. They assume a supreme primary divine being. But they also have a role for the traditional gods as derivatives and functionaries of the supreme divinity. They thus provide a link between the divine of the philosophers and the traditional gods. At the same time they insist that individual humans can communicate with the gods by using techniques, formulae and symbolic objects which the gods in their benevolence have given to humans for that very purpose. These rituals and ceremonies – which were thought capable of uniting a human soul with the divine, and of bringing men into the divine presence by animating the statues of gods – were known as theurgy. The Neoplatonist philosopher Iamblichus wrote a commentary on the Chaldean Oracles in which he elaborated on all theurgic techniques that were available. His combination of philosophy and religion immensely impressed Julian. He tells us that the *Hymn to King Helios* summarizes teachings of Iamblichus.[15]

Julian and the Cynic Heraclius

During his stay at Constantinople in 361–362 Julian accepted an invitation to attend a lecture of the Cynic Heraclius.[16] It is clear that Heraclius' lecture was respectful neither of the gods nor of Julian himself. It seems that the lecturer made up an allegory in which Zeus stood for Heraclius himself, while Pan stood for Julian.[17] It is not clear whether his motive was political or academic, or even just a case of a Cynic philosopher practising provocative *parrhēsia* for its own sake.[18] But whatever the motive of Heraclius, Julian was annoyed, or at least professed to be annoyed, and his response was not what one would expect of an emperor but what one would expect of an academic. He replied to one lecture with another. This is his *Against Heraclius the Cynic* (*Or.* 7), which he wrote more or less immediately after hearing the lecture, that is in March 362, and just before he wrote the *Hymn to the Mother of the Gods*, whose opening question: 'Ought I to say something on this subject also?' alludes to the recent earlier work.

Heraclius had veiled his criticism in the allegory of a myth which in some way – we can only conjecture precisely how – mocked Julian's policy of pagan revival, and perhaps even the legitimacy of his rule. In his response Julian gives a careful and full account of his views about the nature and proper uses of mythology, and he ends by replying to the myth of Heraclius with a myth composed by himself, which at the same time justifies both his view of the gods, and the legitimacy of his rule. For in Julian's myth it is the gods who have entrusted Julian with the mission to put right the abuses of the reign of Constantius II, and above all to restore the traditional worship. At the same time the treatise expounds Julian's view of the place of mythology in religion, and so provides a commentary on Julian's treatment of the myth of Cybele and Attis in the *Hymn to the Mother of the Gods*. In the address to the Cynic Heraclius Julian illustrates how myths can be interpreted philosophically by allegorizing traditional myths of Heracles and of Dionysus, and by composing a new myth which would legitimize his own imperial mission. The *Hymn to the Mother of the Gods* is essentially an elaborate philosophical reinterpretation of the myth of Attis. Julian surely wrote the two treatises in close succession, so that each should supplement the other.

Julian and the Cynics

In June 362,[19] Julian wrote a second, and more general diatribe against the Cynics, entitled *To the Uneducated Cynics* (Or. 6).[20] This speech focuses neither on the Cynics' satirical treatment of the gods, nor on what Julian considers their abuse of mythology, but on a particular pamphlet of satire and criticism directed at Diogenes, the founder of Cynic philosophy, which had been composed by a Cynic whose name Julian does not divulge.[21] It seems extraordinary that a Cynic philosopher should have attacked the founder of his own fellowship: this requires an explanation. Heraclius had only been the first of a group of Cynic philosophers to seek contact with Julian's court. These men were wandering preachers who travelled all over the empire.[22] They not only delivered diatribes at street corners for the general public, but they had even targeted the court of the emperor Constantius II when that emperor was in Italy,[23] as they were to target that of Julian at Constantinople.[24] They must have enjoyed considerable prestige. They even seem to have enjoyed the privilege of using the public post.[25] These later Cynics appear to have been agnostics. They did not claim divine authority for their preaching.[26] But they mocked not only the gods, but also Diogenes the founder of their own way of life and philosophy.

At this time Diogenes figured in the controversy between Christians and pagans. The pagans, not least Julian himself, presented Diogenes' way of life as the asceticism of a true philosopher, and they compared it favourably with the perverse asceticism of Christian monks and hermits. Against this, Christian preachers claimed that it was the monks and hermits who were living the one and only truly philosophic life. That is why, a few years later,

John Chrysostom describing how Babylas, the martyred bishop of Antioch, excluded a sinful emperor from his church, insisted that the language used by the bishop had been extremely moderate,[27] contrasting it with the supposedly gratuitous and theatrical rudeness displayed by Diogenes towards Alexander the Great.

It would be tempting to conclude that the Cynic philosopher attacked by Julian was a Christian, who was covertly propagating the Christian ascetic philosophy, just as the Cynic Maximus of Alexandria, who tried to replace Gregory of Nazianzus as bishop of Constantinople, was certainly a Christian.[28] This conclusion could be supported by a few sentences in Julian's pamphlet which seem to assume that Cynics knew the Bible.[29] For it is indeed quite possible that Julian would attack ascetics who were Christians without mentioning their Christianity. Classicizing pagan authors, for instance Libanius and Ammianus,[30] did as far as possible avoid explicit references to Christianity and the use of Christian vocabulary. Moreover it was not only pagans who joined in this conspiracy of silence. Synesius of Cyrene was probably a Christian from birth, but in his capacity of philosopher and literary man he remained altogether a Hellene. So when he wrote some paragraphs which surely amount to a reasoned criticism of Egyptian monks, he left it entirely to the reader to recognize that he was in fact criticizing a Christian movement.[31]

So the conclusion that the Cynic preachers attacked by Julian were covert Christians would be plausible. Nevertheless it is unlikely to be correct. For Julian compares the Cynics unfavourably to another sect of wandering and begging ascetics, a group whom the Christians called *apotaktistai*,[32] and who were in fact a Christian sect. He says that he had invited the latter to his court,[33] while the Cynics were unwanted. So it would seem that Julian showed more favour to sectarian Christians, than to these followers of a traditional school of philosophy.

If these Cynics were not Christians, why was Julian so strongly opposed to them? Julian and the Cynics had after all much in common. He shared the Cynics' rejection of conventional etiquette and care for external appearance.[34] He favoured an extremely austere way of life.[35] His *Caesars* and *Misopogon*[36] are satires, displaying some of the characteristics of the Cynic diatribe. In the *Caesars* he even approaches the religious irreverence of Lucian. There is no evidence that Heraclius or other Cynics were actively hostile to Julian.[37] It looks rather as if they had been drawn to Julian's court because the new emperor was known to be a good patron of philosophers. That Julian attacked these Cynics shows that he could not tolerate even potential supporters if they consistently mocked the traditional gods. That is not surprising because their mockery not only undermined Julian's campaign to restore the old cults, but also offended his own profound piety.[38] Julian may have suspected that these later Cynics secretly sympathized with the Christians,[39] and that there was some kind of unofficial alliance between them.[40]

The attack on the uneducated Cynics reveals a second reason for his dislike of the sect: in Julian's opinion contemporary Cynics did not respect the Hellenic literary education, and the wisdom of the classical philosophers.[41] He saw them as cultural nihilists – like the Christian anchorites and monks[42] – and consequently attacked them, but in writings, as befitted an intellectual, and without using the instruments of coercion at the disposal of an emperor.

Allegorical interpretation

A principal theme of the oration directed against the Cynic Heraclius is the proper use of mythology. Julian criticizes the way Heraclius used, or as Julian thought abused, mythology and he supplements his criticism with an explanation of the ways mythology should correctly be used. Julian explains that most people cannot receive the truth about the gods in their purest form. They can only receive it in the form of allegory, which is conveyed by myths (*Or.* 7 217c–d). Moreover it is precisely the incongruous element in myth that guides us to the truth:

> I mean that the more paradoxical and prodigious the riddle is, the more it seems to warn us not to believe simply the bare words, but to study diligently the hidden truth, and not to relax our efforts until under the guidance of the gods those hidden things become plain.[43]

The fact is that although the Greeks and Romans did not believe that their traditional myths had been directly inspired by the gods, and although they did not consider it to be a religious duty to believe in their truth, the myths provided the evidence on which all ideas about the divine world, and about the characteristics and concerns of individual gods, had to be based. Anybody who was going to talk about the nature of the gods had to start from their myths.[44] So if somebody wanted to emphasize aspects of divine nature that were not conspicuous in the traditional stories, or possibly were even inconsistent with them, which was precisely what Julian was going to do, the stories would have to be reinterpreted. It follows that philosophical pagan reformers like Julian had to treat the myths of the gods, whose authority was merely that of age and tradition, in much the same way as Christian teachers treated the text of the Bible, which they considered to be literally the words of God.

But Julian's use of allegory differed from that of the Christians in an important way. For him the scope of interpretation was not circumscribed by dogma:

> under the guidance of the gods men may be inspired to search out and study the hidden meaning, though they must not ask for any hint of the truth from others, but must acquire their knowledge from what is said from the myth itself.[45]

The myth of Attis and the March festival of Cybele

The myth Julian chose to interpret in his *Hymn to the Mother of the Gods* is the myth of Attis, which was celebrated in the March festival of Cybele, the Mother of the Gods. It is clear that many versions of this myth coexisted, and the cult had a long history.[46] Certainly the surviving narratives diverge considerably, and none of them, it would seem, corresponds exactly to the version interpreted by Julian.[47] Pausanias' version is as follows. The goddess Cybele was originally bisexual. The gods castrated her. Her male organ turns into an almond tree. Nana, daughter of the river god Sangarius, falls in love with the tree, and puts a blossom in her bosom. She finds herself with child. This is Attis. She exposes the child. The child survives, nourished by a she-goat, and grows up into a handsome young man. The goddess Cybele falls in love with the youth who in this version is something like her grandchild. But the young man has an affair with a nymph of the river Sangarius. Cybele is jealous. She drives the young man mad with the result that he castrates himself. He loses blood, leans against a pine tree, and dies. Cybele is desolate and prays to Zeus. Zeus hears her prayer to the extent that he ordains that the dead body of Attis was not to undergo decay, that it should remain capable of moving one finger, and that its hair would continue to grow.

The version of the myth interpreted by Julian was not exactly the same as this. He does not give us a complete narrative, but his myth is likely to have been very close to the version related and interpreted by Salutius, Julian's friend and close collaborator. For according to Salutius, 'the Mother of the gods caused Attis...to cut off his genitals and leave them with the nymph and to return and dwell with her again'.[48] According to Julian, 'after his castration [Attis] is led upwards again to the Mother of the Gods'.[49] One important difference from the versions reported by Pausanias and Arnobius is that neither Julian nor Salutius describes Attis as dying. In their versions of the story Attis castrates himself, and then returns to heaven. Julian gives a role in the story to a certain 'flame-coloured lion' who does not figure in other versions.[50] In Julian's account Helios, who sees everything, observed the love of Attis and the nymph, and straight-away ordered the lion to inform the Mother of the Gods of her lover's unfaithfulness.[51] This is puzzling. It has been suggested that the lion has Mithraic significance, and that his inclusion in the myth reflects Julian's personal devotion to Mithras.[52] But, as Rowland Smith has argued, this is not necessarily so.[53] It is quite possible that the lion already had a place in the version of the myth told at the sanctuary of Cybele at Pessinus. After all there are many images representing Cybele in a chariot drawn by lions, or on a throne which lions are guarding.[54]

One reason why we have different versions of the myth of Cybele and Attis, no doubt, is that the diversity reflects differences in the rituals performed at different localities, and also at different stages of the evolution of the worship.[55] This – in a very simplified form – is how Attis was celebrated at Rome after the reign of Claudius.[56] A series of festivals started on 15th March, with the Cannophori processing through the streets of Rome, carrying reeds harvested from the banks of the Almo to recall the reeds on which the new-born Attis was exposed on the banks of the Sangarius. Neither Julian nor Salutius mentions this ritual. But according to Salutius the ceremonies of 22nd March were preceded by a period when the worshippers abstained from 'bread and all other rich and coarse food', considered 'unsuited to the soul', a kind of Lent.[57] On 22nd March a pine tree was cut and carried in procession through the city to the temple of Cybele (Magna Mater), and displayed for adoration by the public. On the 23rd March the pine tree was mourned. On the 24th March, the day of blood, the Galli mutilated themselves (possibly commemorating the self-castration of Attis), and the pine was ceremoniously buried. The following day, the 25th March, the *Hilaria,* was a day of popular rejoicing at the resurrection (or rebirth) of Attis.

Festival and myth interpreted allegorically

So the festival was one of death and rebirth. It is clear that the festivals and myth originated in Asia Minor as a fertility cult, a festival celebrating the rebirth of vegetation in spring after its death in winter, and calling on the relevant divinities to favour the growing crops, and to allow them to ripen into a good harvest. But in Julian's interpretation myth and ritual are given a cosmological and soteriological meaning.

Attis is both the son and the beloved of Cybele, the Mother of the Gods. But both the birth and the love affair are moved from earth to heaven. Attis breaks off his affair with Cybele in order to descend to earth, where he makes love to a nymph in a cave. Then overcome by shame, a punishment sent by Cybele, he castrates himself. He returns to heaven and to Cybele. Julian interprets Attis' descent to the earth and his affair with the nymph as an allegory of the mingling of divine forms with earthly matter – or rather the lowest immaterial cause which subsists prior to matter[58] – which stimulated it into shaping itself into the infinite variety of our world. Attis' castration marks the end of creative mingling of spirit and matter, and the return of the spirit to heaven. This process is not a once-and-for-all event, but it recurs every year with the cycle of the sun: 'forever [Attis] yearns passionately towards generation; and forever he cuts short his unlimited course through the cause whose limits are fixed, even the cause of the forms'.[59] So Julian is putting forward not a 'big bang' theory, but a theory of continuous creation (unlike John's gospel).

Julian has saved the myth, i.e. he has given it an 'up to date' religious significance by allegorizing it. But by saving the myth, he has also saved the festivals, in connection with which the myth had developed. So Julian explains the significance of the festivals as follows:

> When king Attis stays his limitless course by his castration, the god bids us also root out the unlimited in ourselves, and to imitate the gods our leaders and hasten back to the defined and uniform, and, if it be possible, to the One itself.[60]

Julian points out that at the centre of the March festivals was joy over the resurrection of Attis:

> For what could be more blessed, what more joyful than a soul which has escaped from limitlessness and generation and inward storm, and has been translated up to the very gods? And Attis himself was such a one.[61]

Accordingly he interprets the food laws as intended to remind the worshippers that the resurrection of Attis should give them hope that they too have the possibility of freeing their soul from its earthy entanglements and achieving the return of their spiritual selves to their heavenly home. That is also why participants in the worship are forbidden to eat root crops, and are allowed to eat only fruit and vegetables that grow upwards, that is towards heaven. For as Julian explains:

> He who longs to take flight upwards and to mount aloft...even to the highest peaks of heavens, would do well to abstain from all such food. He will rather pursue and follow after things that turn upwards towards the air.[62]

The ancient, and very earthy, fertility festival has been transformed into a celebration of the hope of personal immortality,[63] like the Christian Easter.[64]

Cybele and Helios

The fact that Julian composed an oration 'to save' Cybele does not mean that he thought that Cybele was to be worshipped rather than the other traditional gods. His theology was syncretistic. All the traditional gods represented aspects of the divine.[65] The fragmentary letter to a priest[66] shows that he wanted the traditional cult of the gods to be continued in its entirety. As we have seen, he wrote the hymns to Cybele and Helios for the respective festivals of these two deities. While at times it may seem as if the roles of Helios and Cybele are alternatives, this is not so. The festival of Cybele straddles the date of the spring equinox. This means that it is determined by the annual course of the sun. So it too is in a sense a sun festival. Attis is dependent on Helios[67] as well as on Cybele, or perhaps both Attis and Cybele are in a sense different aspects (or emanations) of Helios. The December festival of Helios and the March festival of Cybele were both festivals of the Roman state religion which Julian was striving to revive.[68] But it is clear that Julian (like at one time Constantine) also felt a particular personal devotion to the sun god.[69] He had a shrine to 'the god of the day'[70] built in the palace and worshipped there every day. This piety was partly aesthetic,[71] but it was also a tradition of his family.[72]

It so happened that Julian had occasion to compose allegorical interpretations of Helios and Cybele, but he clearly could have allegorized the other gods also. For even though they retain their individuality for the purpose of worship, they are at the same time different but closely related aspects of the single process which is the Neoplatonic cosmogony. It was Julian's policy to revive the cult of all the gods, and all the festivals, even if they ultimately stood for different aspects of a divine unity.

The influence of Christianity

Julian the Apostate wished to reform the traditional religion to enable it to compete successfully with Christianity. But his up-dated paganism shares important features with its rival. It is basically monotheistic. The influence of Christianity on Julian's project is particularly conspicuous in the fragmentary *Letter to a Priest*, and there especially in the importance given to charitable giving, and to the bishop-like role of the priest.[73] The gods are aspects of a single divine power, yet they also retain their own identity. Attis is a saviour figure who descends from heaven, mingles with lower matter, suffers, and rises again, setting an example of how man can rise too.[74] But there is no suggestion that Attis atones for the sins of man. As for Cybele, she is the mother of Attis only in as far as she is the mother of all gods. But at the same time she is described as motherless virgin (*Or.* 5 166b, παρθένος ἀμήτωρ). No doubt in the first place this was to identify her

223

with Athena, but there is also a clear parallel with the Virgin Mary. So too Julian likes to think that Heracles did not cross the sea in a golden cup as a legend has it, but that he walked across the sea – like Jesus on the lake of Tiberias.[75] As we have seen, the whole sequence of religious rites of the 22nd–25th March bears some resemblance to Easter.

Final prayer

The final prayer to Cybele unites all the disparate elements that make up the religion of Julian, the traditional cult of the traditional gods, the philosophic gods of which they are an allegorical image, the Roman state cult of Cybele, and Julian's personal hope for salvation:

> Do thou grant to all men happiness, and that highest happiness of all, the knowledge of the gods; and grant to the Roman people in general that they may cleanse themselves of the stain of impiety... And help them to guide their empire for many thousand years! And for myself, grant me as a fruit of my worship of thee that I may have true knowledge in the doctrines about the gods. Make me perfect in theurgy. And...in the affairs of state and the army, grant me virtue and good fortune, and that the close of my life may be painless and glorious, in the good hope that it is to you, the gods, that I journey![76]

Notes

[1] Julian, *Letter to a Priest* 302b. In this chapter the letters and orations of Julian will be numbered as in the Loeb Classical Library edition of W. C. Wright. All translations are from the same edition, unless otherwise stated.

[2] Lib. *Or.* 18.157. The *Hymn to King Helios* was written around the time of the winter solstice, inspired by the festival of Sol Invictus (cf. Julian, *Or.* 4 131d and 156b–c).

[3] i.e. Saturninius Secundus Salutius 3, *PLRE* 1, 814–17. He is also known as Salustius or Sallustius, which can cause confusion: see also n. 48 below.

[4] This was very much like the strategy used two hundred years earlier by Justin Martyr to defend Christianity in the age of persecutions.

[5] The December festival was essentially a festival of the solstice. It is significant that in the *Hymn to King Helios* Julian hardly, if at all, concerns himself with the myths of Mithras.

[6] See also the chapter by Arnaldo Marcone in this volume.

[7] See Drake 1989; translation in Edwards 2003, 1–62.

[8] *Or.* 5 162d–163a.

[9] On Julian's telescoping of the intellectual and intelligible levels, see the chapter by Andrew Smith in this volume.

[10] The incorporeal light of the sun is the link between our world and the immaterial world or world of ideas; and its life-giving role on earth is analogous to the process by which the higher entities generate the lower in the invisible mental world.

[11] E.g. August. *Conf.* 13.15.16–17.21, though Augustine's use of allegory is

'practical', i.e. ethical, while Julian's is philosophical. But Julian too recognises two uses of allegory in religion, i.e. practical concerning behaviour, and theological (*Or.* 7 216b–c).

[12] See *Or.* 6 184c–185a, on the essential consensus of all the classical philosophers, who represent different routes to the same truth.

[13] *Or.* 5 162c–d: 'For I hold that the theories of Aristotle himself are incomplete unless they are brought into harmony with those of Plato; or rather we must make these also agree with the oracles that have been vouchsafed to us by the gods'.

[14] See the chapter by Andrew Smith in this volume.

[15] *Or.* 4 157c.

[16] Julian was accompanied by Salutius the Praetorian Prefect of the East (*PLRE* 1, 814–17, Secundus 3), Anatolius the Master of Offices (*PLRE* 1, 61, Anatolius 5), and Memorius, soon to be governor of Cilicia (*PLRE* 1, 595, *MEMORIVS* 1): *Or.* 7 223b.

[17] See *Or.* 7 234c–d.

[18] It seems unlikely that Heraclius would have been an opponent of Julian himself, since in 365 Heraclius encouraged the usurpation of Procopius (Eunap. *fr.* 31 = 34.3 Blockley 1983, 50–1), who was a relative of Julian, had commanded an army in Julian's Persian campaign, and was rumoured to be Julian's preferred successor.

[19] *Or.* 6 181a: close to the summer solstice. On the two speeches against the Cynics see Smith 1995, 49–90, and the chapter by Arnaldo Marcone in this volume.

[20] The addressee is an anonymous Egyptian (*Or.* 6 192d).

[21] Probably not Heraclius.

[22] *Or.* 7 224a–d. Others were Asclepiades, Serenianus, Chytron, and an anonymous fair-haired young man.

[23] *Or.* 7 223d.

[24] *Or.* 7 224d–225a.

[25] *Or.* 7 224a: 'I hear that you wear out the mule drivers as well, and that they dread the sight of you Cynics even more than of soldiers'. Mule drivers transporting soldiers as well as philosophers are probably employees of the *cursus publicus*.

[26] *Or.* 7 224b; cf. *Or.* 7 211b–d, which argues that Diogenes and early Cynics did revere the gods.

[27] According to Chrysostom the martyr preserved moderation and rationality, avoided anger and preserved calm (*De S. Babyla* 36–7, 45–6).

[28] Greg. Naz. *Orr.* 25 and 26. Previously Gregory had treated him as a friend, see Asmus 1894. Cf. Bidez 1930, 248–9.

[29] See the use of Gen. 9.3 in *Or.* 6 192d–193a. Also Mt. 6.28 in *Or.* 6 181c.

[30] See e.g. Hunt 1985. Libanius even wrote a panegyric of the Christian emperors Constantius II and Constans (*Or.* 59) without mentioning their Christianity. As late as the sixth century the Christian historian Agathias avoided explicitly Christian language. See Cameron 1970, 89–108, on a Christian world view obscured by a classicising literary convention.

[31] Synes. *Dio* 7–8 (1123–40).

[32] Cf. Basil. *Ep.* 199.47; treated as heretics, *Cod. Theod.* 16.5.7 (381), and 16.5.11 (383).

[33] Cf. *Or.* 7 224c: 'You [Cynics] gave more trouble than they [the Apotaktistai] did at my headquarters, and were more insolent. For they were at any rate invited to come,

but you we tried to drive away'. Perhaps Julian had recalled them, i.e. the Apotaktistai, from exile like other 'heretical' Christians.

[34] *Misop.* 339a–c.

[35] *Misop.* 340b.

[36] See esp. Wiemer 1998, but also Marcone 1984, Fontaine 1987, and Gleason 1986.

[37] Cf. n. 18 above. Would Heraclius have invited Julian to his lecture, and would Julian have come, if Heraclius had been an open opponent?

[38] *Or.* 7 213a–d.

[39] So already Lucian, *De mort. Peregr.* 13, 16.

[40] E.g. Oenomaus (*Or.* 6 199a–b; *Or.* 7 209b, 210d, 212a). He wrote a pamphlet *Against the Oracle* which mocks Apollo of Delphi (Euseb. *Praep. evang.* 5.25).

[41] Athanassiadi-Fowden 1981, 128–31.

[42] Cf. *Letter to a Priest* 288b.

[43] *Or.* 7 217c. This attitude to the traditional myths has an exact parallel in the Christian attitude to the literary meaning and humble language of the Bible, e.g. August. *Conf.* 6.4.6.

[44] In Julian's hymns the gods Helios, Cybele, Attis and the others are personifications of Neoplatonic ideas or forms. But at the same time they retain some of the properties assigned to them in cult and myth. For instance, Cybele's title 'Mother of the Gods', and therefore also mother of Zeus, belongs to her ritual, not to philosophy. That she also is the wife of Zeus must be because she is also Hera, and she is a motherless maiden (*Or.* 5 166a–b) because she is also Athena.

[45] *Or.* 7 219a.

[46] For a clear summary see Turcan 1996, 28–74; and see now also Bowden 2010, 83–104.

[47] Diod. Sic. 3.58.4–59.8; Paus. 7.17.10–12; Arn. *Adv. nat.* 5.5–7.

[48] Salutius, *On the Gods and the Universe* 4, trans. Nock 1926, 7–9. Like Athanassiadi-Fowden 1981, 68 n. 74, and Smith 1995, 33, I identify the author of *On the Gods and the Universe*, known as Sallustius (*PLRE* 1, 796, Sallustius 1), with Saturninius Secundus Salutius 3, *PLRE* 1, 814–17, Praetorian Prefect of the East 361–365, also sometimes Sallustius (though *PLRE* 1, 797–8, suggests that the author is Flavius Sallustius 5, Praetorian Prefect of Gaul 361–363). Salutius took a more positive view of our world than Julian did and he rejected Egyptian theology, which Julian did not: see Athanassiadi-Fowden 1981, 158–60. On the identity of Sallustius/Salutius see also Josef Lössl's chapter in this volume, at pp. 62–3.

[49] *Or.* 5 168a.

[50] *Or.* 5 167b–c.

[51] According to *Or.* 5 167b the lion allegorizes 'the cause that subsists prior to the hot and fiery'. Turcan 1996, 73, interprets this as 'the part of Attis concerned with the celestial fire', that is that part of his nature that looks back to his fiery origin in Helios, 'the third cause'. This Helios was not the visible sun, but its intellectual source, the intellectual god from whom Attis emanated; see *Or.* 5 161d and 168a.

[52] Athanasiadi-Fowden 1981, 145 n. 89.

[53] Smith 1995, 161.

[54] *LIMC* 8.2, 511–12; 514–16.

[55] On evolution of the cult, see Turcan 1996, 35–56, and Sfameni Gasparro 2003, 249–327.

[56] Turcan 1996, 43–9.

[57] Salutius, *On the Gods and the Universe* 4, trans. Nock 1926, 9. At Rome, the prohibited foods included pomegranates, quinces, pork, fish; and probably wine, for only milk was drunk (so Turcan 1996, 44).

[58] The so-called 'fifth matter'.

[59] *Or.* 5 171d. 'The unlimited' is the world of matter, 'the limited' is the intellectual world of ideas (forms); cf. *Or.* 5 169c–d. The process of genesis involves an infinite increase of diversity, its reversal is a return to unity.

[60] *Or.* 5 169c.

[61] *Or.* 5 169d.

[62] *Or.* 5 177b.

[63] *Or.* 5 175b: 'The end and aim of the rite of purification is the ascent of our souls'.

[64] No wonder Firmicus Maternus (*Err. prof. rel.* 3.27.1), the apostate pagan become Christian apologist, considered the resurrection of Attis a parody of the Easter mystery.

[65] *Or.* 4 143d ff: Helios identified with Zeus, Apollo, Dionysus, and Asclepius. *Or.* 5 179a–b: the Mother of the Gods is brought into a close relationship with Athena, Dionysus and Hermes.

[66] See Wright 1913, vol. 2, 296–339.

[67] *Or.* 5 171b–c: 'Attis...after...he has set in order the chaos of our world through his sympathy with the cycle of the equinox, where mighty Helios controls...his motion within due limits, then the goddess [Magna Mater] gladly leads him upwards to herself'. See also *Or.* 5 175a–b: 'Attis...descends to the lowest limits and is checked by the creative motion of the sun so soon as that god reaches the exactly limited circuit of the universe, which is called the equinox'.

[68] The state cult of Helios was that of Aurelian's Sol Invictus (*Or.* 4 155b); the March festivals of the Mother of the Gods were also on the calendar of Roman public festivals.

[69] *Or.* 4 130c: 'From my childhood an extraordinary longing for the rays of the god penetrated deep into my soul'.

[70] Lib. *Or.* 18.126. The 'god of the day' worshipped by Julian here may have been Sol Invictus Mithras who, though favoured by soldiers, was never admitted to the Roman state religion.

[71] Cf. Cic. *Nat. D.* 2.38–9, 98–104.

[72] *Or.* 4 131c–d.

[73] *Letter to a Priest* 289a–293a, 305b–c.

[74] *Or.* 5 179c: Attis is described as the 'Word' (λόγος), a refutation of the 'Word' of John 1.3, 'through whom all things were made and without whom nothing was made that was made'. Cf. Julian, *Ep. ad Alex.* (*Ep.* 47) 434c–d: Helios, not Jesus, is the true Word. It follows that Attis, being an emanation of Helios, can also correctly be described as the Word.

[75] *Or.* 7 219d.

[76] *Or.* 5 180b–c.

14

JULIAN'S *HYMN TO KING HELIOS*: THE ECONOMICAL USE OF COMPLEX NEOPLATONIC CONCEPTS

Andrew Smith

Numerous scholars have attempted to pin down and interpret the complex and elusive metaphysical structure which seems to form the background of Julian's *Hymn to King Helios* (composed December 362) and to identify its source or sources. The latest attempt is by John Dillon, in which I find much to agree with.[1] Thus there might seem little more that can be said about the matter. In what follows I want to explore only a few very precise, but possibly significant, details in Julian's exposition. At the outset a word of caution is in order: Julian does not set out in this hymn to discourse on or expound in a formal way a structure of reality for its own sake but does so only incidentally in his concern to locate the God Helios who is the hymn's main theme. In fact the metaphysical location of Helios becomes one of the main occasions for the incorporation into the work of complex ideas involving the relationship of the standard levels of reality of the Neoplatonic universe: the One, Intellect, Soul, and the physical universe. And it is the version of Iamblichus which Julian exploits in his own presentation.

Hierarchical structures

Probably the most obviously schematic presentation of the structure of reality is to be found in the hymn at 132d onwards, where Julian begins from the lowest level, the earth. From it we may extract the following levels of reality:

> The One
> The intelligible realm
> The physical universe

The omission of Soul is striking. But the concept is not important for this work. That itself is a sufficient indication of the philosophical economy exercised by Julian. But there is another peculiar feature in this exposition of levels of reality and it presents a problem: the highest level is described as the 'total intelligible' (τὸ νοητὸν συμπάν). At first sight this appears to be an odd designation of the Neoplatonic One which is beyond Intellect and Being. It also seems at odds with the other descriptions of the highest principle in this very passage which include the Good, a designation applied to the One rather than to the intelligible realm and also τὸ ἐπέκεινα νοῦ (that which is *beyond* Intellect). A further source of confusion is that Helios, who throughout the hymn, and in this passage too, is identified as holding the second place – here designated clearly as the '*intelligible* realm' – is normally described by Julian as *intellectual* (νοερός), which in the Iamblichean presentation of levels of reality represents a distinct level below the intelligible.

At first sight it would appear that what we have here may be either a simple pre-Neoplatonic schema which neither advocates a totally transcendent One nor distinguishes intelligible from intellectual, or a confused and inaccurate version of Iamblichean Neoplatonism. But possibly neither of these explanations quite captures what Julian is doing. I want to suggest that he is neither confused nor reverting simply to earlier schemas, but using an expression of Neoplatonic structures that is appropriate to the occasion at hand.

We might begin with the first principle. One of the most significant features of Neoplatonism is the development of a completely transcendent One. This is not an easy concept to uphold and the doctrine as presented by Plotinus continued to challenge his successors. Both Porphyry and Iamblichus attended to this issue. The basic problem was to preserve the transcendence of the One without losing its link with its products and more particularly with its first product, Intellect (*nous*). Iamblichus' solution was, to put it simply, to posit a number of intermediaries to bridge the gap. He posited not only a One but an all-transcendent One above this, and also a One-Being, as it were, in third place, to act as a further bridge between the One and Nous. This one being could also be viewed as the Monad or first element in Nous itself.

What we have in Julian is effectively a telescoping of these phases to present us with a One which is at the same time intelligible. Such a telescoping is not necessarily to be regarded as a simplistic version. Plotinus himself had on occasion described the One itself as intelligible and even ascribed a 'kind of thinking' to it (*Enn.* V.4.2). It has been argued that such talk in Plotinus represents either untidy thinking or an early stage of development when he had not yet risen above certain Middle-Platonic ideas. More recently it has been convincingly argued that Plotinus deliberately and skilfully juxtaposed the transcendent or negative concept of the One with a more positive concept which could include statements about its activity in order to project the discussion to something beyond (yet embracing) both.[2] That sounds remarkably like what Iamblichus was later trying to express but without his formalised distinctions. When Julian characterises the One in mainly positive terms (e.g., as intelligible), this is no more than presenting or bringing into the open the 'issue' of what the One is when seen in relation to what it causes. In his own context there is no further need to engage with that issue, that is to find means to express the paradox of its nature, because he is in this hymn concerned primarily not with the utter transcendence of the One but with the mediating nature of Helios, and the description of the One as 'intelligible' brings it closer to Helios.

And so again in 139b Julian's highest principle seems to combine the Neoplatonic properties of the One and of Nous. It is described as 'the intelligible world, totally one, always pre-existing, combining everything together in its oneness'. It is tempting to translate ἐν τῷ ἑνί here as 'in the One' but that would pre-empt interpretation. This highest level is then directly compared with the one living being that is the physical universe. Helios lies between. This description is intended to enlarge on and explain the immediately preceding threefold division of:

> Intelligible gods
> Helios
> Visible gods

The intelligible gods are said to be 'around the Good', which hints at the complexity of this level. For we know that Iamblichus apparently held that the 'intelligible' gods exist not only at the level of Nous proper but also in the lowest aspect of the One.[3] And Julian may reflect that idea here when he neither *identifies* them with the One nor places them at a second level but says that they are linked (around) in some way with the One. Thus, as in 133, we have a telescoping of the Neoplatonic One and Nous, something which is seen once more in 142a:

> This then we must declare, that King Helios proceeds from god who is one,
> [Helios being] one [and derived] from the intelligible universe which is one.

There seems here to be no clear mention of a totally transcendent One nor is the One even just subsumed under Intellect as in 139. But the point is not important. The status of the One is not Julian's concern. What is really central for him in this passage is not the significance of 'oneness' as a transcendent cause, but its presence at each level. Helios, as is emphasised here, is responsible for unifying and bringing together. For Helios

231

> joins what is sundered; and he brings together into one the last and the first,
> having in his own person the means of completeness, of connection...[4]

It is thus appropriate to describe him as 'one' and to assert that he acquires this oneness from a higher source – whether it is Intellect or the One itself, the distinction does not matter.

We have in Julian's *Hymn to King Helios* the same kind of economical presentation of reality as is found, for example, in Plotinus *Enneads* VI 4 and 5 on the omnipresence of being, where he is unconcerned about the distinction between One, Intellect and soul but concentrates on the interface of all true Being and physical reality. A similar presentation is also to be found in Porphyry's *de abstinentia* and his letter to Marcella which – though clearly written after his adoption of Plotinian metaphysics – do not, because of the nature of the subject matter and its level of presentation, require a complex metaphysical framework; so much so in fact that they have often mistakenly been termed Middle-Platonic.

The second level

Complex Iamblichean doctrine may also lie behind what may appear to be a corresponding blurring of the distinction between the 'intelligible' and the 'intellectual'. In our earlier passage 133 the second level, that of Helios, is called the 'intelligible realm' whereas Helios in 139a is described as an 'intellectual substance' and so clearly demarcated from the intelligible gods. In fact, as remarked earlier, Helios is usually designated as 'intellectual'. But there need be no conflict. We have already seen that Iamblichus could refer to the 'intelligible' both at the (lowest) level of the One and as the second Hypostasis. Within the second Hypostasis Iamblichus formalised the Plotinian distinction between Intellect and its object, the Intelligible, by suggesting a kind of internal hierarchy in which the intelligible object took first place and intellect (as observer) a lower place. It is this active noetic, i.e. intellectual, aspect that Julian usually wishes to emphasize as his second Hypostasis. At other times he assigns the more complete designation 'Intelligible realm' to the second Hypostasis. In fact this occurs only once, in 133, understandably in a context in which he begins with the physical realm (κόσμος) from which he ascends to its corresponding model, the intelligible realm (κόσμος). In this context the fuller expression, 'intelligible [world]' which embraces the notion of the objects of thought, the Forms, comes to mind more readily than the more limited notion of active thinking (the intellectual).

Another interesting indication of the underlying subtlety of the schema used by Julian is his comment that the intellectual gods are on a similar level to Helios himself. At 133c they are said to have 'come forth and have been constituted along with him' (συμπροῆλθον αὐτῷ καὶ συνυπέστησαν). In Iamblichean terms this is just what we would expect, that the intellectual gods will be on the same *taxis* as Helios who is 'intellectual', but on a lower *taxis* than the intelligible gods. Julian betrays precision too in that two stages of emanation, procession and being established, are expressed in the terminology, συμπροῆλθον...συνυπέστησαν. The intelligible gods, however, do not seem to have the same relationship to the One as the intellectual gods have with Helios. And in 139d too we can discern a difference between the connecting power of Helios with the intellectual gods on his own level and his connecting power exercised in a vertical sense between the intelligible above him and the physical realm below:

> These existences, therefore, which are two causes of connection, one in the intelligible world, one in the world of sense perception, King Helios combines into one, imitating the synthetic power of the former among the intellectual gods...[5]

Helios then connects (combines into one) the higher and lower levels which are internally connected by their own relevant connecting power, whilst at the same time acting as a connecting power on his own intellectual level. In this sequence of ideas, then, the full deployment of different levels of reality within the Intelligible/intellectual realm is exploited in order to demonstrate the different unifying powers of Helios.

All of these observations of detail demonstrate to us how Julian can recall and make use of quite complex and sophisticated elements of Neoplatonic, and mostly Iamblichean, metaphysics, when and to the extent that it serves the particular purpose at hand, telescoping entities when speaking in general, e.g., of the level of Intellect, and distinguishing when he wants to stress the particular activities of sub-levels.

Neoplatonic procession

Julian can also be quite precise in his observation of basic Neoplatonic concepts employed in the explanation of how Hypostases proceed from each other. In 132d, for example, the highest principle is described as a πρωτουργὸς οὐσία ('being active at the first level'). 'Activity' or 'power' are key concepts in the Plotinian explanation of how the One produces, though Plotinus might want to exclude the notion of οὐσία, which we might excuse here as either an inaccuracy of terminology or a sign of the conflation of the One and Nous. The highest principle is said in this passage to 'remain' whilst producing, a standard term marking the inexhaustibility and impassibility of Hypostases in the production of their inferiors. The product is also said to be 'like' (ὅμοιον) its product. Similarly in 139d Helios is said to 'imitate' the connecting power of the entity above it. Continuity in the transfer of powers is also a characteristic of hypostases. But the inclusion of such detail is not mere ornamentation; these concepts are stressed because they have an important role in this hymn, more particularly with regard to light which as an activity may be seen to represent a likeness – sun image – between intelligible, intellectual and physical 'suns'.

More complex details of procession are found in Iamblichus' use of the concepts of perfection, production (or power), unity and connection. These terms in various forms are found throughout the hymn and are frequently grouped together.[6] It is important to realise that they are not vague imagery but have precise philosophical connotations particularly in the later Neoplatonic expositions of procession. Their origin may be traced back to Plotinus but their formal incorporation into triadic schemes of procession is a development of Iamblichus and thereafter given its fullest expression in Proclus. The basic concept in Plotinus is that each hypostasis has a power or productive capacity. Each hypostasis in turn provides unity to what it produces and connects the multiplicity of its product not only with itself, the producer, but also promotes the internal cohesiveness of the product. **Unity**, in fact, is the essential ingredient for anything to be anything and its ultimate source is the One. Whether or not Iamblichus is the author of the theory of henads, a concept used by Proclus to account for the influence of the One on the whole of being and creation, the transmission of unity right down to the lowest element of the physical universe is an important topic both for the nature of reality and for the dynamic of the spiritual ascent of the soul to the One. **Perfection** is even more complex than I have already intimated since it not only marks the aspect which enables a hypostasis to produce something lower than itself – all that is perfect produces, is a standard metaphysical principle – but is also the stage at which a hypostasis turns back on its producer to perfect itself. The initially imperfect and infinite hypostasis has in itself an innate tendency to stop, revert upon its producer which it contemplates to become bounded, formed and perfected.[7] All three concepts of perfecting/perfection are found in Julian, that of the higher perfecting the lower, that of the lower perfecting itself through the higher, and that of the productive capacity of a hypostasis being dependent on its reaching maturity or its own perfection. **Connectivity**, too, is a key idea which in various guises helps Plotinus to explore more effectively the barely developed Platonic doctrine of the συμπλοκή εἴδων, the interconnectivity of the Forms, and thus the structure of the Intelligible world, as well as the vertical connection of one level of reality with another.

Finally I would like to turn to the doctrine of intelligible light which seems to me to lie behind Julian's whole metaphysical edifice. It is clear that by the time of Proclus there was a developed Neoplatonic metaphysical theory of light which was also deeply intertwined with quasi-religious notions, particularly as expressed in the Chaldean Oracles. Because of the fragmentary nature of our knowledge of the Neoplatonic tradition between Plotinus and Proclus it is difficult to reconstruct the theory before the latter. But there is enough evidence to suggest that in Iamblichus light has an important role metaphysically and in the context of theurgy. And Iamblichus is the most likely source for Julian's ideas. The importance of light metaphysics for our appreciation of Julian's theology lies in the fact that the impact of the 'physical sun' and stars on Julian is not simply a metaphor for divine influence but an expression of its reality, for the light of the sun as incorporeal is in a sense continuous with the intelligible light that constitutes the nature of the transcendent cosmos. Light in this world, then, is not a symbol of divine power but its actual manifestation. Moreover, as we will see, the phenomenon of physically-manifest light also has for Julian an epistemological aspect.

Julian introduces his main discussion of light after his first exposition of the structure of the universe and the central role of Helios. Just as he had commenced his analysis of the universe from the physical world so too his discussion of light begins with the light experienced in the physical world. His starting point is Aristotle, whose theory of the incorporeal nature of light in *de anima* is clearly alluded to.[8] This use of Aristotle as well as the doctrine of the incorporeality of light Julian almost certainly owes to Iamblichus.[9] But the acceptance of this doctrine amongst Platonists goes back at least as far as Plotinus.[10] The most significant feature of Julian's use of the Aristotelian doctrine is the suppression of the term ἐντελέχεια and its replacement with ἐνέργεια which he interprets not in the usual Aristotelian sense of a change from potentiality to actuality, but rather as 'activity', for although Julian begins with the Aristotelian phrase κατ᾽ ἐνέργειαν he goes on to describe light (now in the transcendent realm) as an 'activity' of Intellect. The same change may be found in Plotinus who describes the light of this world as an incorporeal 'activity'. This doctrine of light as an 'activity' is in the end quite different from the Aristotelian doctrine of it as an actualisation. The change is important because it gives light a substantiality which it does not have in Aristotle. It is unlikely that Julian, any more than Plotinus, thought he was misinterpreting Aristotle. But, more importantly, it becomes clear as Julian continues that the incorporeal light of the physical universe is continuous with the light of the sun and with a transcendent form of light above this which forms its source in Intellect:

> And the culmination and flower, so to speak, of light which is itself incorporeal, is the sun's rays. Now the doctrine of the Phoenicians, men wise and learned in divine matters, declares that the ray which goes forth everywhere is the unblemished activity of pure Intellect itself. And our argument is not discordant with this, given that light is in itself incorporeal, if one regards its source not as body, but as the unblemished activity of Intellect shining upon its own seat, which possesses the middle of the whole heavens, from which it shines upon and fills the heavenly spheres with every kind of harmony and shines around all things with divine, unblemished light.[11]

The idea of intelligible light, that is a transcendent light which is not merely a metaphor, was destined to have a long history in later thought. It is clearly present in Proclus and may also be found in Plotinus. This has recently been disputed but careful analysis of the texts demonstrates it to be the case. For Plotinus the main significance of the doctrine lies in its epistemological value in terms of analogy. One of the frequent ways in which he seeks to explain higher realities is by analogy with a similar phenomenon on a lower level of reality. We can thus argue from things in this world to those in the transcendent world. But analogy is more than an illustration. Proper analogy in this sense requires an essential connection between the undisclosed and the disclosed. We can take as an example the principle we have earlier referred to whereby every hypostasis that is perfect produces. This is derived from the empirical observation that all things that are mature produce offspring. This 'pattern' in the physical universe points to some prior causal principle of a similar if not identical nature. Now in the case of light the relationship between light at the physical and the transcendent level is even closer since both are incorporeal. Julian is clearly aware of this function of his light analysis when he bids us to look at the light around us and infer from this to something higher:

> How then can we now fail to believe, in view of this, in respect also to things more divine that the invisible and divine tribes of intellectual gods above the heavens are filled with power that works for good by him...[12]

This 'belief' is not the unreasoned belief of Christians, nor the lowest level of cognition in the Platonic divided line, but the conviction of reasoned discourse. But the light doctrine surely has for Julian another dimension, that of religious experience. It is unlikely that his experience of the sun's rays or the night sky[13] was solely that of the intellectual stimulus of an ordered cosmos. The illumination of light is also a powerful religious image and in the rites of theurgy even a spiritual reality or power.

I have tried to show in this analysis that Julian has a sophisticated knowledge of Neoplatonic metaphysical ideas and, more particularly, knows how to deploy them in a simplified format and one appropriate to the genre in which he is writing. His use of Neoplatonic concepts in this regard serves as a means of expressing his own religious concerns and convictions both in the location of Helios as a mediating force in the hierarchy of reality, and in explaining the illumination that comes from the highest principle.

Notes

[1] Dillon 1999. [Editors' note: on the *Hymn to King Helios* see also the chapter by Wolf Liebeschuetz in this volume.]

[2] Lavaud 2008.

[3] See Dillon 1973, 32 f.

[4] *Or.* 4 142a, trans. Wright 1913, vol. 1, 387.

[5] *Or.* 139d, trans. Wright 1913, vol. 1, 379.

[6] E.g. *Or.* 4 142. Also *Or.* 4 132, 139–40, 151b f., 156c–d.

[7] For perfection in Proclus see *Elements of Theology* propositions 39 and 133, and *Platonic Theology* I.104.

[8] *Or.* 4 133d; *de anima* 419a.

[9] Iamblichus had a strong interest in Aristotle. For Iamblichus' acceptance of the doctrine of the incorporeal nature of light see Priscian, *On Theophrastus* 9, 12–14. See Finnamore 1993.

[10] See Plot. *Enn.* II.1.7, 23–8; IV.5.7, 33–4; VI.4.7, 31.

[11] *Or.* 134a–b.

[12] *Or.* 135a.

[13] *Or.* 130c.

15

THE FORGING OF AN HELLENIC ORTHODOXY: JULIAN'S SPEECHES AGAINST THE CYNICS

Arnaldo Marcone

Asceticism is a theme that has relevance to Julian and his attitude to Cynicism in particular. The various forms of Roman asceticism which developed during the imperial period have many things in common: notably, a typically Roman interest in what modern scholars would call 'lived religion', that is, a concern for the practice as well as the theory of ethical and philosophical living. There was undoubtedly an ascetic side to Cynicism. The Cynic praise of poverty widely resonated through different intellectual circles and social classes.[1] Cynics were known for their ascetic lifestyle, having no possessions except a cloak, staff and wallet: this was the form of Cynicism that furnished the material for countless popular anecdotes. Cynicism was undoubtedly a philosophy with a limited theoretical basis. We could even say that it was 'an easy philosophy'.[2] The option of Cynicism could be attractive on some occasions.[3] Lucian of Samosata's own character and temperament made him sympathetic towards certain aspects of Cynicism since he was seriously interested in constructing an ethical model. But even if he admired the great representatives of early Cynicism, this did not prevent him from giving an extremely burlesque portrait of Diogenes in the *Vitarum auctio*.[4] What is certain is Lucian's irreconcilable hatred for the degenerate and false Cynicism of the empire which under the cover of this name concealed a moral and social corruption.[5]

The Cynics, who traced their intellectual pedigree back to that Diogenes who told Alexander the Great to get out of his light, had not taken part in the fusion of the schools of philosophy in Late Antiquity. They continued to be, as it were, anarchistic drop-outs from ancient society, mockingly critical of all its values and institutions, ostentatiously simple in their style of life, with nothing positive to offer in place of what they demolished, and by now politically and socially ineffectual. Their destructive criticism of traditional religion made them up to a point the natural allies of the Christians.[6]

Cynics could be viewed as the pagan predecessors of the Christians in rejecting human society and living a life of asceticism. The Christian apologist Tertullian in his *De pallio* praises Diogenes and Crates as true lovers of wisdom. Epictetus, when dealing with the personality of the ideal Cynic, draws on anecdotal material about Diogenes.[7] The two movements (Cynicism and Christianity) were closely associated in the minds of their sharpest critics: Lucian, as an enemy of superstition, and Aelius Aristides and Julian, as enemies of religious dissent.[8]

Cynics drew on themselves the wrath of Julian, who saw in them a threat to his own project of religious and moral reform. Heraclius was one of those exhibitionist critics of established order who adopted the outward characteristics of Cynicism – long hair, staff and philosopher's cloak. Heraclius and Cynics in general exploited their freedom to criticize conventional society and conventional paganism. Heraclius had already made something of a name for himself at Constantius II's court in Milan.[9] Early in 362, Heraclius presented himself in Constantinople and asked permission to give a lecture in the presence of Julian.[10] Courts provided opportunities for speakers attempting to impress and persuade large audiences.[11] Julian was shocked by Heraclius' blasphemy and by the conclusion of his paradoxical arguments. He objected to his ridiculing tales about gods, to the confusion that Cynics caused in society, and the discrepancy between their moral pretensions and their conduct. He went on to give his own interpretations of some of the Greek myths, which were probably those current in Neoplatonist circles, and to outline his own intellectual and moral development as a kind of allegory of the descent of the divine sphere to the human sphere, and the corresponding ascent of the soul to God.[12]

Heraclius was not without predecessors. It is enough to mention Menippus from Gadara and, in the 2nd century AD, the Cynic writer Oenomaus (also from Gadara), who dismissed oracles as worthless and opposed prophecy, beliefs and institutions popular in his own age. Oenomaus attacked also one of the principles of Julian's faith: that gods care about the men who rely on them. It is no mere coincidence that this criticism of the gods was welcomed by the Christians and most of Oenomaus' surviving fragments of his *Exposure of Frauds* come from Eusebius in his *Praeparatio evangelica*.[13] Julian, who mentions Oenomaus critically in his writings, abominated him as a 'shameless dog' and claimed that Oenomaus did not reflect the spirit of the true Cynicism of Diogenes and Crates (*Or.* 7 209b–c, 210d–211a).[14] Julian was conscious that Eusebius, writing early in the 4th century, found Oenomaus' polemics useful for dividing pagans, discrediting the old religion and promoting Christianity, which had its own prophetic tradition.[15]

It appears significant that, shortly before 21st March 362, Julian composed his treatise the *Hymn to the Mother of the Gods*,[16] and in early June 362 he published a third treatise on philosophy, occasioned by the lecture of a Cynic on Diogenes, who had been for centuries the typical specimen of the Cynics.[17]

In the Cynic movement – which was without established texts, or settled, recognizable doctrine – reference was regularly made to certain real or mythical personalities who were taken to be the sources of Cynicism as a way of life.[18] Such personalities were the starting point for Cynic reflection and commentary. The mythical characters referred to included Heracles, Odysseus and Diogenes. Diogenes was an actual, historical figure, but his life became so legendary that he developed into a mythical figure, and anecdotes and scandals were added to his historical life. About his actual life we know very little, but it is clear that he became a kind of philosophical hero: for instance, Epictetus, when dealing with the personality of the ideal Cynic, draws on anecdotal material about Diogenes.[19] Most of Julian's speech, *To the Uneducated Cynics* (*Or.* 6), though undoubtedly derivative, is devoted to an examination of Diogenes' life as passed down in the tradition. Julian's immediate object was to show that Diogenes was in fact a devout man, animated by the same principles as Plato, and that the Cynics of the mid-fourth century were hypocrites and charlatans who had misunderstood and distorted the heritage of the great masters. From this argument emerges the important belief in the fundamental unity of all Hellenic philosophy, with the exception of the pseudo-Cynics.

There is an obvious paradox which must be remembered even if it must not be overemphasized. For Julian, who is trying to forge an Hellenic orthodoxy, Cynicism is a natural philosophy that requires no special knowledge. However, he chastises his opponents as 'uneducated', who do not know what they are talking about because they have not read any books. Julian quips: 'I must not detain you even for a moment or hinder you on your way along that shortcut to wisdom by making you embark on books that are long and hard to read'.[20] This is a central issue concerning Julian's views of religion. Julian's 'theology' is in an uneasy relationship with his 'devotional interests and practices'. And in each case there is more than a touch of exaggeration: on the one hand, he can appear bookish and erudite (and polemical) to an extreme, on the other, his behaviour veers towards the irrational.[21]

What Julian undoubtedly condemned in his orations against the Cynics was the enlistment of rhetoric by contemporary Cynics in the service of defending, what Julian considered to be, religious and philosophical errors. As fraudulent versions of true Cynics they appear intolerable to a 'puritanical pagan'[22] like Julian who prescribed sincere piety for worshippers of the gods. He consciously idealizes Diogenes, the founder of the movement, as a model for a universal and divine philosophy and as an exemplar of moral life.[23] A significant precedent of Julian's criticism of vulgar Cynics can be found in Dio Chrysostom's *Or.* 32. Here Dio, who appears in his own person as a Cynic philosopher, launches an attack on the 'so-called philosophers'.[24] These are people who call themselves Cynics but merely work mischief and bring philosophy into discredit and contempt. The practice might be right, at best, but the practice fell short. On the contrary in his *Fourth Discourse on Kingship* he had drawn a picture of Diogenes as the ideal sage which is very similar to that drawn by Julian.[25] The later Cynics, who could not see that Diogenes' scorn for social conventions was an expression of a deep moral purpose, even tried to discredit his principles. We must not forget that Julian never distinguishes between sacred and profane letters. His idea of Hellenism is that of an all-embracing force more complex than the paganism the empire had hitherto known as its official religion.

It is often assumed that one reason for Julian's harsh treatment of the Cynics was their general resemblance to early Christians. There may well have been more than some superficial similarities. Broadly speaking, it is true that Cynic preaching about freedom, the renunciation of luxury, their criticisms of political institutions and existing moral codes, and so on, also prepared the ground for some Christian themes. In fact by the fourth century the word 'philosophy' could embrace a regimen of self-denial without any special requirement for reasoned truths. This ascetic meaning seems obvious in some Christian writers. Eusebius (*Praep. evang.* 12.19.1) describes the old Jewish prophets 'living in deserts, mountains or caves in order to reach the summit of philosophy'. Long before the emergence of Christian asceticism, however, a wide variety of Roman philosophers proposed sophisticated systems of ascetic formation. The ascetic agenda of the Cynics is well attested also in ancient literature.

Julian's variety of asceticism should be seen in combination with his fundamental philosophical conviction, together with his idea of a natural religion whereby through self-knowledge we may become like the gods. This explains why in his opinion:

> [H]e who is entering on the career of a Cynic ought first to censure severely and cross-examine himself, and without any self-flattery ask himself the following questions in precise terms: whether he enjoys expensive food;

whether he cannot do without a soft bed; whether he is the slave of rewards and the opinion of men.[26]

If this is true, this was surely no easy task, at least not for everyone. When Julian wanted to reach the common man, his first step was to restore the gods' traditional public rites: '[B]y plain and formal decrees [he] ordered the temples to be opened, victims brought to the altars, and the worship of the gods restored'.[27]

Julian was notoriously fond of lecturing. But his arguments did not convince, except superficially. Of course he was aware of this. A good example is what happened when Julian was in Beroea at the beginning of March 363, as related by him in a letter to Libanius:

> I stayed there for a day and saw the Acropolis and sacrificed to Zeus in imperial fashion a white bull. Also I conversed briefly with the senate about the worship of the gods. But though they all applauded my arguments very few were converted by them, and these few were men who even before I spoke seemed to me to hold sound views. But they were cautious and would not strip off and lay aside their modest reserve, as though afraid of too frank speech.[28]

The following comment from the letter to Libanius sounds particularly bitter:

> For it is the prevailing habit of mankind, O ye gods, to blush for their noble qualities, manliness of soul and piety, and to plume themselves, as it were, on what is most depraved, sacrilege and weakness of mind and body.[29]

As Julian's letter demonstrates, rituals of social communication undoubtedly required a certain amount of consensus about what constituted sacred values. Julian was disappointed that most of the Cynics were not able to represent ancient Graeco-Roman culture, for he hoped that there would be something like a popular philosophical movement which would compete with Christianity.

For example, a Cynic rejection of engagement in politics called for a positive reinterpretation, if Cynicism, especially among Romans, was not to become suspect and be regarded as a subversive movement.[30] *Parrhēsia* was typical of Cynics. In the classical Greek city *parrhēsia* was the ability to speak one's mind freely. A philosopher could claim an entitlement to *parrhēsia* if he was able to show that he owed nothing to ties of patronage and friendship.[31] Julian observed how contemporary Cynics had failed to live up to these ideals:

> In our day, however, the imitators of Diogenes have chosen only what is easiest and least burdensome and have failed to see his nobler side. And as

for you, in your desire to be more dignified than those early Cynics you have strayed so far from Diogenes' plan of life that you thought him an object of pity (...) [I]f you had the least habit of reading books as I do, though I am a statesman and engrossed in public affairs, you would know how much Alexander is said to have admired Diogenes' greatness of soul (...) You admire and emulate the life of wretched women.[32]

Julian's ideal of Cynicism seems indeed to correspond to his ideal of religion, in which asceticism plays a major role: 'Therefore he who desires to be a Cynic despises all the usages and opinions of men, and turns his mind first of all to himself and the god'.[33]

The reality, however, is different. That is to say, Julian in fact has mixed feelings about the Cynics. Thus he writes:

Though indeed I have nothing but friendly feelings for the really virtuous Cynics, if indeed there be any such nowadays, and also for all honest rhetoricians.[34]

In the pagan society of the fourth and fifth centuries AD, there was a peculiar category of leading philosophers who were prominent, influential, even glamorous figures. They travelled widely, operating in an elevated cultural milieu. Long hair and *himation* usually indicated that they were professional intellectuals. The difference between the sophist (the display orator) and the philosopher (the contemplator of higher things) could become uncertain. A philosopher could turn – which was of course a problem for Julian – into a religious leader.[35] Cities might turn to them as advisers or spokesmen, or to act as ambassadors to the emperor.

Philosophers could bring to their tasks certain carefully nurtured virtues. By a heroic effort of the mind they were supposed to have found freedom from society. The right of *parrhēsia* could entitle them to address men of importance directly because they were not compromised by political attachments. In the later Roman empire the approach of petitioners to the emperor was increasingly associated with the concept of *parrhēsia*. But what about imposture? *Parrhēsia* might not always be a candid speech and not every counsel could be innocent. As Gilbert Dagron has written, 'Philosophers were supposed to be men of the court at one and the same time close to power and independent from it'.[36] This is exactly the attitude that Julian could not accept. At the end of his *Letter to Themistius* he asked all philosophers for their support: 'I need assistance from God above all, and also from you philosophers by every means in your power'.[37] But Themistius apparently did not get the opportunity to associate with Julian in any role of comparable significance to that exercised by himself under Julian's predecessor and successors. It is well known that Julian manifested a higher regard for philosophy than for politics. The exemplary role of philosophy is evident in the following passage from Themistius' letter to Julian, which Julian quotes in his response:

> [The philosopher] does not only direct counsels or public affairs, nor is his activity confined to mere words; but if he confirm his words by deeds and show himself to be such as he wishes others to be, he may be more convincing and more effective in making men act than those who urge them to noble actions by issuing commands.[38]

It may in any case be true, as has been suggested by Rowland Smith, that the analogy Julian drew between Cynics and Christians has been exaggerated.[39] But a precise analogy is drawn by Julian between pseudo-Cynics and monks, because both groups are insolent and pursue a counterfeit asceticism in their wanderings after giving up home and possessions (*Or.* 7 224a–b).

I suspect that in fact Julian had in common with early Christians the problem of how to define paganism and decide what was and what was not pagan, in doctrine and practice, and in inherited culture. On what ground religious affiliation could be defined is obviously doubtful. Religious labelling is notoriously subjective, not least in the case of the derogatory label 'pagan', rejected by a number of scholars in the field today.

When discussing Julian's orations against Cynicism, it should be appreciated that they were composed *ad hominem*: the speech against Heraclius was a public one, whereas the one against the uneducated Cynics seems to have been produced only in written form.[40] Rowland Smith has rightly found in *Orations* 6 and 7 little more than a series of commonplaces.[41] It seems very unlikely that Julian's main source could be, as Asmus and many scholars after him have thought, Iamblichus' commentary on Plato's *Alcibiades* 1.[42] Both speeches are basically 'an oratorical display of learning and skill in the manipulation of a familiar repertoire of literary invective'.[43] *Oration* 6 in particular looks like 'a sermon or rather a scolding addressed to the New Cynics', even if with a positive goal: to demonstrate the essential unity of philosophy.[44]

Thus, Julian was obviously not ready to tolerate either philosophical or religious diversity. We must remember that Heraclius had invited Julian and the intellectuals of his entourage to listen to his lecture, which consisted of an allegory in which the gods were treated irreverently. *Orations* 6 and 7 are both unusual documents. Not so unusual – it is true – as Julian's *Misopogon,* in Glanville Downey's words 'one of the most incredible things that a Roman emperor, supposed to be in his right senses, ever did'.[45] However, in dealing with Julian it is always difficult to distinguish between apologetics and a reasoned (successful or not) argument, a planned and considered effort of propaganda. The answer to Heraclius was the reaction to an individual, whereas *Misopogon* was a retort in prose to scurrilous jibes in verse that had been circulating about him in the city of Antioch in late 362 – early 363. We have to do with the so-called '[r]ituals of social communication in which "the central authority of an orderly society...is acknowledged to be the avenue of communication with the realm of sacred values".'[46] I do not think that Julian's reaction can belong to a traditional pattern of imperial public behaviour, as was suggested by Gleason, who regards Julian's posting of the *Misopogon* as the promulgation of what might be called an edict of chastisement.[47] In the words of the Roman rhetorician Fronto, emperors ought by their edicts to repress the faults of provincials, give praise to good actions, quell the seditious and terrify the riotous.[48] But Julian is not simply rebuking some people (the Cynics) or his subjects (the Antiochenes) in countering noisy demonstrations of opinion. He is an angry emperor who acts in word and writing not only to rebuke but also and above all to defend a philosophical and religious creed.[49]

Something of Julian's ideas about such a creed can be glimpsed in the so-called autobiographical myth in *Oration* 7, where the restoration of the Roman empire is presented as predestined, the work of the fates complying with the will of the father of the gods.[50] Furthermore, in his letter to the high priest Theodorus Julian explained his views about religion, political institutions and laws in the following way:

> I very seldom act offhand, as all the gods know, and no one could be more circumspect; and I avoid innovations in all things, so to speak, but more peculiarly in what concerns the gods. For I hold that we ought to observe the laws that we have inherited from our forefathers, since it is evident that the gods gave them to us.[51]

It is also worthwhile considering Julian's satire at the expense of his predecessors, namely his *Caesars*.[52] As Glen Bowersock opined, Julian was an essentially humourless man, whose efforts at wit quickly degenerated into raillery or bitterness.[53] What emerges from this work is what Julian considered essential in a monarch: the twin virtues of military experience and philosophical austerity. For which reason, Trajan and Marcus Aurelius epitomized the good ruler: the warrior and the sage.[54]

In Julian there was undoubtedly a sort of ostentatious asceticism.[55] Thus he assigned these words to Marcus: 'I nourished my body because I believed, though perhaps falsely, that even your bodies require to be nourished by the fumes of sacrifice'.[56] As imitator of the gods, Marcus adds that in his opinion this would mean 'having the fewest possible needs and doing good to the greatest possible number'.[57] The point is that Julian's quest into the historical past for models for himself was not an easy task. The ascetic side of Cynicism could be attractive to him. But in the Cynic tradition there was also an ostentatious opposition to power which had its foundational myth in the antithesis of Diogenes-Alexander.[58] This political side of Cynicism plays a role in its re-emergence, after two centuries of decline, in the first century AD in the philosophical opposition to the Roman emperor.[59]

The notion that there was a 'Cynic-Stoic' theory of kingship must be discarded even if it is not surprising that a few Stoics could be called *paene Cynici* (Cic. *Off.* 1.128), as Cynicism could be seen as a radical form of Stoicism. It is likely that some Cynics under the Principate did assail monarchy and the whole social order.[60] In this regard, religious affiliation plays no significant role as the Roman emperor is the obvious heir of Alexander and of the idea of the omnipotent king. Heraclius in his fable had cast Julian as Pan and himself as Zeus in a way which predictably irritated the emperor.[61] It should be considered that the Stoa itself was profoundly apolitical, attempting to counteract the loyalties felt towards any political community. It is not surprising that the Stoic idea of 'natural law' provided each human being with a bastion against coercion from any tyrannical power, from public opinion and even from written law.[62]

Julian could not accept any opposition or antipathy of this kind to his project. His reaction against the Cynics as well as that against the Antiochenes derives, in part at least, from the severe regimen he imposed on himself which led him to expect comparable self-control in others.

It had long been a main plank of Christian anti-polytheist propaganda that traditional religious worship was irreducibly chaotic since a plethora of divinities flourished in various parts of the world. A salient feature of late Hellenic religiosity was the concern to link together, into a coherent system, all divinities worshipped in the known world. An aspect of this was the attempt to allegorize disreputable forms of traditional mythology in order to neutralize criticism of the myths; Julian's *Hymn to the Mother of the Gods* is a nice example of this allegorizing tendency.[63]

Religious unity, bound in with culture in a special way, was the main goal for Julian, as it was for Constantine when confronted with religious conflicts inside the Christian church. Cynic radicalism and antagonism could not be tolerated. As he notes in *Oration* 6:

> Therefore, I say, let no one divide philosophy into many kinds or cut it up into many parts, or rather let no one make it out to be plural instead of one. For even as truth is one, so too philosophy is one. But it is not surprising that we travel to it now by one road, now by another.[64]

Furthermore, for Julian there is only one possible shortcut to philosophy:

> Now the true short cut to philosophy is this. A man must completely come out of himself and recognise that he is divine, and not only keep his mind untiringly and steadfastly fixed on divine and stainless and pure thoughts, but he must also utterly despise his body, and think it, in the words of Heracleitus, 'more worthless than dirt'. And by the easiest means he must satisfy his body's needs so long as the god commands him to use it as an instrument.[65]

In Antioch – partly as a response to the provocations of the Antiochenes and in reaction to particular problems elsewhere, partly in his anticipation of the help from the gods required for success against the Persians – Julian's anti-Christian feelings intensified. The Cynics' parrhesiastic technique, their 'provocative dialogue'[66] was for Julian as emperor as unacceptable as the jibes of the Antiochenes. Unfortunately for him shortly afterwards *parrhēsia* would be taken over by other spokesmen. Bishops could deploy the same methods as a civic notable. But the new bearers of *parrhēsia*, who replace the philosophers, were holy men and monks who were not without resemblance to those Cynics whom Julian abominated.[67]

Notes

[1] Cf. Desmond 2006, 172.

[2] The original Cynic impulse 'to deface the idols of the tribe' must be considered: cf. Branham and Goulet-Cazé 2006, 18.

[3] Cf. Moles 1983, 114.

[4] There is an apparent decline of Cynicism between Cercidas (290–220 BC) and Demetrius (1st century AD). Cynic ideology reached its apogee in the 2nd century AD when very little in the way of original Cynic literature was being produced by practising Cynics. Our most important sources (other than Diogenes Laertius) are sophists (such as Dio Chrysostom and Lucian) and Stoic moral philosophers (such as Seneca and Epictetus) who are concerned to reconcile Cynicism with the mainstream of Socratic and Stoic moral philosophy in the empire (Cf. Branham and Goulet-Cazé 2006, 14).

[5] Cf. Nesselrath 1998.

[6] Julian, *Or.* 6 203b, 'You admire and emulate the life of wretched women'. Unless otherwise indicated, all translations of Julian come from the Loeb Classical Library edition by Wright 1913–23.

[7] Cf. Billerbeck 2006, 208.

[8] Branham and Goulet-Cazé 2006, 19.

[9] *Or.* 7 223d. Cf. Smith 1995, 80–1.

[10] See Guido 2000.

[11] Cf. Maxwell 2006, 49.

[12] See Nesselrath 2008.

[13] See Hammerstaedt 1998.

[14] Cf. Hammerstaedt 1998, 28–32.

[15] Cf. Desmond 2006, 42.

[16] For Julian's *Hymn to the Mother of the Gods* see the chapter by J. H. W. G. Liebeschuetz in this volume.

[17] Prato and Micalella 1988 do not pronounce on the identity of the anonymous Cynic of *Or.* 6. Now Goulet-Cazé 2008 shows convincingly, in my view, that the anonymus Cynic is a real person ('en chair et en os'), of Egyptian origin, who appears to have a certain knowledge of Christian texts. The person who most closely corresponds to the characteristics adumbrated by Julian in his discourse is Hero Maximus, a Christian Cynic from Alexandria, friend and later bitter enemy of Gregory of Nazianzus, with whom he contested the episcopal seat of Constantinople in 380.

[18] The study of Cynicism is inseparable from the study of its reception. The intentions of the founders of Cynicism are almost entirely constructed from the imperial sources, particularly our primary source Diogenes Laertius' *Lives and Opinions of Famous Philosophers*, which is itself 'a compilation of compilations'. Julian, however, does not seem to make direct use of Diogenes Laertius.

[19] Cf. Branham and Goulet-Cazé 2006, 208

[20] *Or.* 7 227b. Cf. Smith 1995, 70.

[21] Cf. Hoistadt 1948, 68.

[22] Cf. Bowersock 1978, 79 f.

[23] *Or.* 6 199a: '[L]et not the Cynic be like Oenomaus shameless or impudent, or a scorner of everything human or divine, but reverent towards sacred things, like Diogenes'.

[24] *Or.* 32.8 f. Cf. Epictetus, *Diatr.* 3.22: Περὶ Κυνισμοῦ. Cf. Billerbeck 2006, 207–8 and 211–13.

[25] Cf. Moles 1983.

[26] *Or.* 6 200b–c.

[27] Amm. Marc. 22.5.2, trans Rolfe 1940, 203.

[28] *Ep.* 58 399d–400a (To Libanius).

[29] *Ep.* 58 400a.

[30] Cf. Billerbeck 2006, 208.

[31] This point is stressed by Michel Foucault who devoted his last course at the Collège de France to ancient Cynicism: cf. Galzigna 2009; Brown 1992, 62.

[32] *Or.* 6 202d–203b.

[33] *Or.* 7 225d.

[34] *Or.* 7 236b.

[35] Cf. Smith 1990, 150.

[36] Dagron 1984, 123 (quoted by Brown 1992, 69).

[37] *Ep. ad Them.* 266d. For Julian's *Letter to Themistius* see the chapter by John Watt in this volume.

[38] *Ep. ad Them.* 266b–c. We must not forget Julian's notorious edict on teachers, issued on 17th June 362: *Cod. Theod.* 13.3.5: 'School teachers and professors ought to be distinguished first by character and second by eloquence'. This edict is to be explained in terms of the high regard Julian had for learning, especially for rhetoric. Libanius correctly remarked, after his death, that Julian considered learning and religion to be intimately related and their fortunes intertwined. The sense of the law is explained in Julian *Ep.* 36.

[39] Smith 1995, 89.

[40] As supposed by Prato and Micalella 1988. But see now Goulet-Cazé 2008.

[41] *Contra* Alonso-Núñez 1984, 259.

[42] Asmus 1907.

[43] Smith 1995, 90.

[44] Wright 1913, 2.

[45] Downey 1939, 310 (quoted by Gleason 1986, 106). For the *Misopogon* see the chapter by Nicholas Baker-Brian in this volume.

[46] Shils and Young 1975, 147 (I quote from Gleason 1986, 108).

[47] Gleason 1986, 116.

[48] M. Frontonis ad M. Antoninum *de eloquentia liber* 138.4–9.

[49] Cf. Nicholas Baker-Brian's chapter in this volume.

[50] *Or.* 7 227c–234c. Cf. Athanassiadi 1981, 173–5.

[51] *Ep.* 20 453b.

[52] For the *Caesars* see the chapter by Rowland Smith in this volume.

[53] Cf. Bowersock 1982, 159.

[54] On Trajan, see *Caes.* e.g. 327a–328b. On Marcus Aurelius, see *Caes.* e.g. 333b–335a.

[55] Cf. Bowersock 1978, 14–15: 'a man of ostentatious simplicity'; 'asceticism [was] so integral to his character'.

[56] *Caes.* 333d.

[57] *Caes.* 334a.

[58] Cf. Hoistadt 1948, 204

[59] Cf. Branham and Goulet-Cazé 2006, 12.

[60] Cf. Brunt 1975.

[61] *Or.* 7 234c–d.

[62] Cf. Procopé 1988, 24.

[63] See J. H. W. G. Liebeschuetz's paper in this volume.

[64] *Or.* 6 184c.

[65] *Or.* 7 226b–c.

[66] Cf. Foucault 1985, 45.

[67] Cf. Brown 1992, 71–3.

16

THE CHRISTIAN CONTEXT OF JULIAN'S
AGAINST THE GALILEANS

David Hunt

Of all Julian's literary output his polemic against the Christians, composed at Antioch in the winter of 362–3, is the most elusive for the modern reader.[1] The work survives only in the filtered form in which it has come down to us through the pages of the Christian counter-attack, almost exclusively the *Contra Julianum* of bishop Cyril of Alexandria.[2] Cyril's huge riposte to Julian itself exists in a far from complete state, or (some argue) was never finished: of its supposed thirty books, only ten survive in anything like their entirety.[3] This deficiency means that, although Cyril claimed to be quoting verbatim from Julian (*C. Jul.* 2.2), any attempts at reassembling the text can only ever be a partial reconstruction of what he wrote.[4] We do not even know for sure what title was given to Julian's work, other than to surmise that in a polemic against the Christians he is more than likely to have labelled his opponents with his favoured contemptuous tag of 'Galileans'.[5] Nor is it absolutely clear how many books it ran to: Cyril speaks of three, and the surviving section of his riposte appears to be directed principally at the first of these (at one point Julian is quoted as promising fuller discussion in a 'second book' [261e]); but it is worth observing that Jerome had referred to 'seven' books of Julian against the Christians, even if this now tends to be dismissed by scholars as a mistake arising from Jerome's lack of first-hand acquaintance with Julian's original.[6]

Observing that Julian's onslaught on the faith had been widely influential up to his day and regarded by many pagans as unanswerable, Cyril had embarked on the task of 'dragging down this Hellenic serpent raised up against the glory of Christ'.[7] He summarizes Julian's critique of Christianity as follows:

> He says that we have gone astray and have foolishly abandoned the road that is direct and free from reproach, that we have, as it were, gone down onto the rocks, and render worship to the God who is over all things in a manner which is in every respect ill-considered, for it agrees neither with the laws given by the all-wise Moses, nor with the superstitions of the Greeks, that

is, with their customs and habits, but we have, as it were, invented an intermediate way of life that fails to achieve the goals of either.[8]

There are thus three parties to Julian's argument, Jews as well as pagans and Christians. Julian's 'Galileans' were then doubly at fault in parting company with Greeks *and* Jews, while at the same time retaining the worst features of both: the 'atheism' of the latter combined with the lax and slovenly ways of living into which the Greeks had degenerated.[9] Julian announced a threefold structure to his work (42c–43a) a brief introduction on 'whence and how we first arrived at a conception of God', followed by a comparison of Greek and Jewish views 'concerning the divine', and finally an enquiry into the Christians' abandonment of both these traditions – (a structure) which can be readily detected in the surviving portion as represented by Cyril.[10]

The human race, Julian's argument begins, possesses a universally innate knowledge of an immutable creator God governing the cosmos, knowledge which is not the result of any teaching or a special revelation of the kind claimed by Jews and Christians. He then proceeds to his comparison of Greeks and Jews, beginning (naturally enough) from their respective myths of cosmic origins. While recognizing some of the 'incredible and monstrous stories' (44a) which the Greeks invented about their primeval divinities, Julian contends that these were eclipsed by the absurdities of the Garden of Eden narrative: a god, he claimed, who would 'deny to the human beings whom he had fashioned the power to distinguish between good and evil', and hence deprive them of wisdom 'than which there could be nothing of more value to mankind' (89a; for Julian, the serpent of Genesis was 'a benefactor rather than destroyer of the human race'), and a god who was jealous of human achievements (93e–94a). Such criticisms are the prelude to a comparison of the respective creation myths in Genesis and Plato's *Timaeus* (49a–66a). It is the polytheism of the latter which to Julian's eyes provides the more comprehensively satisfactory account of the natural and human order – above all, of its diversity. For the main thrust of this section of Julian's argument is to focus on what he sees as the inability of a unique creator God exclusive to the Jews to account for the variety of nations and peoples which made up the human kaleidoscope. In truth, the god of the Jews was but one among many divinities responsible for the natural diversity of character and language which marked out the nations of the world, and in worshipping him and him alone as supreme God the people of Moses mistakenly elevate a merely 'sectional' deity ('the lordship over a very small portion') to the status of universal creator (148b–c). Moreover, the unhappy history of the Jewish people as recounted in the Old Testament showed little evidence of their god's care and beneficence when compared with the divine gifts showered on other nations, as for example on the city of Rome (193c–194c), or on the variety of places which experienced the international influence of Asclepius, 'who stretched out over the whole earth his saving right hand' (200a–b).[11] Nor was it only their chronicle of servitude and defeat which discredited the Jews: they – and their writings – showed none of the benefits of learning, education and culture which the gods had dispensed with such generosity on the Greeks.

And so to the Christians, and the third part of Julian's case (which will have formed the bulk of his treatise, though incompletely represented in what survives from Cyril). They have deserted not only the superior wisdom and learning of the Greeks, but even this feeble heritage of the Jews which Julian has denounced in the previous section. In according divinity to Jesus Christ they have misappropriated the scriptural teaching of Moses and the prophets, and defied the injunction to worship one god, and only one god; and despite claiming to embody the fulfilment of the promises of the Old Testament, they have systematically rejected the Jewish Law, and the religious practices and observances which it ordained – sacrifice, dietary rules, circumcision. In abandoning these requirements of the Law, Christians set themselves apart precisely from that common realm of religious ritual which in Julian's eyes Greeks closely shared with Jews (306b): Abraham, after all, had been a Chaldaean (354b), an ancestor of the 'sacred people' of old believed to have given to the Greeks the tradition of theurgy which lay at the heart of Julian's paganism.[12] This rejection of hallowed rites and ceremonies exemplified above all the double apostasy of which the Christians stood accused.

It will be clear from this brief résumé that Julian's case against the Christians owed a great deal to what might be termed 'conventional' pagan polemic, and to its principal practitioners Celsus and Porphyry; and modern scholarship has commonly sought to identify the extent of Julian's debt to his predecessors.[13] On the surface resemblances to Celsus predominate, as (for example) in Julian's focus on the diversity of nations and their gods.[14] Yet it is notable that Libanius, in the only surviving contemporary mention of Julian's anti-Christian polemic,[15] saw it principally as a descendant of the work of Porphyry: in it Julian 'showed himself wiser than the old sage from Tyre; and right pleased and happy may this Tyrian be to accept this statement, beaten as it were by his son'. One of Porphyry's chief targets in his attack on Christianity had been the ascription of divinity to the historical figure of Jesus, and it was this central aspect which, for Libanius, formed the link with Julian's composition: the emperor's winter nights in Antioch were devoted to attacking 'the books in which that fellow from Palestine is claimed to be a god and son of god'. Julian, Libanius continues, 'in a long polemic and by dint of forceful argument proved such claims to be stupid, idle chatter'. It was thus Christian assertions about Jesus which Libanius took to be the main subject-matter of Julian's *Against the Galileans*, and which were the basis of his judgement of its merits in surpassing the work of Porphyry.[16] This emphasis, it has to be said, may at first sight be less apparent to a modern reader of Julian's work than it would have been to his contemporaries, given that all that survives is little beyond the first book, and that only in the excerpted form preserved by Cyril.

My purpose in this chapter is to suggest that modern discussion of *Against the Galileans*, by preferring to focus on the defence of polytheism and cult ritual at the heart of the three-way comparison of Greeks, Jews and Christians (seemingly the dominant motif of the surviving sections),[17] has substantially underestimated both the specific attack on Christ's divinity as a significant feature of Julian's polemic, and also his engagement with contemporary Christian debate on precisely this theme. While a concern with traditional religious observance may well have been the stuff of inherited pagan polemic – and undeniably underpinned much of the emperor's public policy on religion[18] – it was surely not the burning issue of the day likely to ignite the flames around Julian's Christian opponents; whereas the status of Christ's divinity could hardly have been a more topical or contentious subject, and one finely tuned to expose the fault-lines of the Christian church which Julian confronted.

It will be helpful to try to position Julian's polemic against the background of ecclesiastical history of the time. In the late 350s from Sirmium to Constantinople, with the aid of the 'twin' councils of Ariminum and Seleucia, Constantius II had presided over a sustained effort of episcopal creed-making: though much maligned by hostile witnesses as unwarranted state interference in matters of faith, Constantius' actions are susceptible of more generous interpretation as a serious attempt at fulfilling the paramount duty of a Christian ruler, inherited from his father, to ensure the doctrinal unity of God's people on earth.[19] The climax of this process was the official endorsement, at Constantinople in January 360, of a creed which – on the critical question of the relationship of Son to Father in the definition of the Godhead – pronounced that the 'Son is *like* the Father, as the Scriptures say and teach', eschewing any mention of 'being' (or 'essence', *ousia*) as not found in the Bible, and even dispensing with the catch-all qualification '(like) *in all respects*' which had held the ring for a while.[20] Constantius' winning formula, the so-called 'homoean' creed, can be seen as the 'lowest common denominator' of the doctrinal alternatives, a hard-won (not to say enforced) consensus attractive to an emperor with his eye on the prize of formal unity, and designed especially to exclude those of the competing participants who occupied the extremities of the theological spectrum, i.e. those, on the one hand, for whom God the Son was so comprehensively identical with God the Father that he had no separate divine being at all (differentiated only as a *man* in the earthly Jesus of Nazareth), and on the other hand those for whom the Son's divine being was not identical at all with that of the Father (but merely shared *attributes* such as God's will and activity).

Yet these and other ecclesiastical 'casualties' forced out from Constantius' middle ground would become natural allies for Julian, the newly-acclaimed Augustus, as he came to challenge his cousin's government first from his power-base in Gaul, then as he moved to take over the empire.[21] Granting amnesty to Constantius' exiled bishops began life as a political gesture to garner support for a forthcoming civil war; it would later come to be vaunted by Julian as a magnanimous display of religious toleration, although Ammianus would famously attribute to him more sinister motives and an intention to capitalize on the Christians' innate tendency to internecine strife ('experience had taught him that no wild beasts are such dangerous enemies to man as Christians are to one another').[22] However we understand Julian's recall of the banished churchmen, we may surmise that he was surely no stranger to the theological wrangling which divided Christian communities. Back in the days of his own Christian youth his principal 'minders', first bishop Eusebius of Nicomedia and then George of Cappadocia, had been prominent partisans on the Arian wing of the controversy; and when George was lynched by a mob in Alexandria it was his library, including 'numerous books of all kinds by the Galileans', which Julian ordered to be transported to him in Antioch – valuable source material, we might suppose, for his anti-Christian polemic.[23]

Of Constantius' recent ecclesiastical 'victims', one notable figure was singled out for favour by Julian. This was the deacon Aetius, a one-time protégé of George's, who was not merely recalled from exile, but strikingly the only Christian among those special friends invited to join the new emperor's entourage (and granted permission to use the *cursus publicus*); he was also presented, we learn, with the gift of an estate on the island of Lesbos.[24] In paying court to Aetius, Julian was embracing a *bête noire* of Constantius and of establishment figures in the eastern churches, and one whose radical doctrinal views had been a principal target of the settlement of 359–360 – precisely one of those theological extremities alluded to above.[25] Aetius, the founding father of what used to be labelled (inaccurately) as 'neo-Arianism', championed the viewpoint which affirmed that God the Father and God the Son (or rather 'Ingenerate' and 'Generate', i.e. without familial relationship), although sharing in divine will and activity, were actually 'unlike' each other in essence (hence 'anomoeans'). It was a severely intellectualized version of the faith, one which appealed to logic-chopping and metaphysics rather than to the biblical record: and that its chief adherent, alone among the warring factions of the church in the eastern empire, was specifically courted by Julian is surely pertinent to any attempt at establishing the context and rationale of *Against the Galileans*.

Not, it would seem, a presence at his court, but another controversial Christian leader certainly known to Julian was Photinus, former bishop of Sirmium. He represented the other of my 'theological extremities', and had long fallen foul of the mainstream ecclesiastical establishment: he had been ousted from his see as early as 351, on the basis of heretical opinions derived from his teacher Marcellus of Ancyra which stressed the single divinity of God the Father alone ('I am the first and the last; besides me there is no god,' Isaiah 44.6), at the expense of that of the Son, who on this view came into being only in the earthly incarnation of the *man* Jesus.[26] Marcellus, Photinus and their followers had been anathematized by a series of church councils for views purportedly denying the divinity of Christ: a fact which made Photinus a kindred-spirit for Julian in undermining the central tenets of Christian belief. We know nothing of how or in what context Julian came to know of Photinus, but writing to him from Antioch, he openly commended his views: 'you seem to maintain what is probably true ... and do well to believe that he whom one holds to be a god can by no means be brought into the womb', a formulation to which he would return in *Against the Galileans*.[27] This letter to Photinus (which survives only in extracts found in a 6th-century Latin translation) in fact provides the only indication known to us of the particular circumstances which gave rise to the composition of Julian's anti-Christian work, for in it Julian reveals himself at loggerheads with one of Antioch's leading churchmen, Diodorus (Diodore), later to become bishop of Tarsus and an influential ecclesiastical figure in the eastern empire in the early years of Theodosius.[28] In the letter Julian ridicules the Christian orthodoxy of Diodore (in contrast to the more acceptable views of Photinus): he was a 'sorcerer (*magus*) of the Nazarene... attempting to give point to his unreason', and misguidedly deploying his classically-trained skills of rhetoric and argument in defence of the 'folly of base and ignorant creed-making (*theologorum*?) fishermen'; in return for his conduct he has received due and visible punishment from the gods in the painful, wasting illness which has afflicted him 'for many years'. Despite such frailty, the ascetic Diodore was evidently a vocal Christian protagonist who had caught Julian's eye, perhaps even directly confronted him over his religious policies in Antioch: and what is more, it was in response to these same attacks of Diodore, so Julian writes to Photinus, that the emperor planned to demonstrate that 'that new-fangled Galilean god of his, whom he by a myth (*fabulose?*) styles eternal, has been stripped by his humiliating death and burial of the divinity falsely ascribed to him...'. Such, in this problematical Latin transcription of his letter,[29] is Julian's only known programmatic announcement of his own for *Against the Galileans*: it was designed to be a challenge to the orthodox Diodore on the central question of Christ's divinity, and from one whose own view of the subject was very much coloured (I would argue) by association with the heterodox extremes of Aetius and Photinus.

To return to what survives of Julian's polemic, the dismissal of Christ's divinity arises first from his critique of the jealous exclusivity of the national god of the Jews ('Thou shalt have no other gods but me', Exod. 20.2): 'if it is God's will that none other should be worshipped, why do you worship this spurious ('bastard') son of his whom he has never yet recognized or considered as his own?' (159e). By abandoning the one and only god of their forefathers, Christians had transferred their allegiance to a mere mortal, and a dead mortal at that ('the corpse of a Jew'), who only three hundred years before had accomplished nothing of note other than freak instances of healing and exorcism in some up-country villages of Palestine ('Bethsaida and Bethany').[30] That this Jesus was God was a Christian invention, completely at odds with the 'teaching of Moses' which Christians falsely claimed as theirs: the Mosaic law enjoined worship of one supreme god alone, and 'does not assume any god as second, *either like or unlike* him' (253c: note the pointed allusion to current Christian controversy). Nor could Old Testament prophecies of a future saviour for the Jewish people be applied to Jesus Christ born of God, as Christians would have it, but they pointed rather to an earthly descendant of the royal house of David: in the words of the book of Numbers (24.17, in the Septuagint translation), 'there shall arise a star out of Jacob, and a *man* out of Israel' (261e).

With Christian claims about the birth of Jesus, Julian was shifting his focus from Old to New Testament: the gospels of Matthew and Luke, he noticed, could not even agree in their genealogies purporting to provide Joseph with the necessary pedigree (253e), a topic which he says he intends to examine in more detail in the second book of his polemic (261e). But in what survives from the first book, it is the gospel of John onto which Julian now principally turns his attack: 'In the beginning was the Word, and the

Word was with God, and the Word was God' (John 1.1). Despite the Mosaic insistence on 'the Lord our God is one Lord', here were the Christians claiming at least two, if not three, gods (262b–c): besides God himself, the divine Word who was with God from the beginning, and Jesus the son born to Mary. But how could it be that Mary as a human being could give birth to God (276e)? The familiar biblical prophecy always advanced in support ('Behold a virgin shall conceive and bear a son', Isaiah 7.14) makes no mention of a god; and, in any event, how could the son born to Mary be the same as the divine Word which had existed since the beginning? Such theological pluralism was, for Julian, nothing more than an invention of John's gospel. The assertion of Jesus' divinity was not to be found in the synoptic gospels, nor in the letters of Paul: it was, claimed Julian, merely John exploiting the early success of Christianity in 'many of the towns of Greece and Italy', as well as a response to his hearing of the veneration which had already come to surround the tombs of Peter and Paul (327a–b).

Aside from these (hardly convincing) attempts to discredit the authority of St. John's gospel, it is this section focusing particularly on the Johannine prologue which places Julian's polemic securely in the context of the current Christian debates outlined above. He acknowledged as much in explicitly invoking the name of Photinus over the issue of whether the Jesus born to Mary was the Word of God 'or someone else': whereas in his earlier letter addressed to Photinus he had seemingly endorsed the latter's denial of Jesus' divinity, he now preferred to feign indifference to Christian theology ('I leave the dispute to you'), and fall back on the argument from incompatibility with Old Testament teaching and prophecy (262c). But the Christian debate clearly influenced the content and language of Julian's material. Still speaking of John's identification of the Word of God with Jesus Christ – derived, notices Julian, from the claims attributed to John the Baptist – and hence John's seeming contradiction in asserting later in the prologue that 'no one has ever seen God' (John 1.18), Julian referred to what he had 'heard' from 'certain of the impious' (i.e. Christians) who 'think that Jesus Christ is quite different from the Word proclaimed by John', and that 'the only-begotten Son is one person and the God who is the Word another' (333b–d). Julian had evidently been listening to his friend Aetius and his followers, with their insistence on the essential 'unlikeness' of God the Father and God the Son. He had indeed already hinted as much when he had affirmed that the God of Moses would not admit of any duplication 'either like or unlike him' (see above).

In repeatedly challenging, on the one hand, Christian claims about the divinity of Jesus Christ, and, on the other, pointing to the multiplication of gods implicit in current understandings of Christology, Julian was locking into themes which were at the very heart of recent credal controversy in the churches. If this conclusion were not obvious from his own awareness and experience – and we should not forget that during his years as Caesar in Gaul Julian had acted out the part of loyal deputy to Constantius in matters which must have included dealing with current ecclesiastical issues and church councils[31] – then he need only turn to the variety of creeds which council after council had issued in the 340s and 350s, and particularly to the catalogue of anathemas attached to some of them, denouncing those who said in any shape or form that 'Jesus Christ is not God', and equally those who maintained that 'the Father and the Son are two gods', or that 'the Father, the Son and the Holy Ghost are three gods'.[32] Julian does not, it is true, enter into serious intellectual debate on Christian theology, resorting instead to a very literal reading of the Scriptures, casting them back verbatim at his opponents and highlighting their misapplications, inconsistencies and contradictions. But to conclude, as have several recent treatments of *Against the Galileans*,[33] that Julian's polemic was largely indifferent to the current ferment of argument among the churches over essential doctrine is, I have tried to suggest, to ignore its weight of emphasis on the issue of Christ's divinity. This emphasis had been central to the work's professed purpose, and had the promised 'second book' survived (let alone the third), its debt to Christian creed-making might have been even more apparent.

Notes

[1] For modern discussions of *Against the Galileans*, see Malley 1978; Meredith 1980; Wilken 1984, 176–96; Athanassiadi 1992, 161 ff.; Bouffartigue 1992, 379–97; Smith 1995, 189–207; Rosen 2006, 313 ff. On the date of composition: Libanius, *Or.* 18.178.

[2] For some fragments deriving from an earlier response by Theodore of Mopsuestia, see Guida 1994.

[3] On Cyril's work, see Russell 2000, 190–203, with the modern edition of its first two books by Burguière and Evieux 1985.

[4] Modern reconstruction of the text stems from Neumann 1880, followed by Wright 1923; for a new edition organised by fragments, see Masaracchia 1990; for French translation and brief commentary, Gérard 1995.

[5] Burguière and Evieux 1985, 27–9 (hence not 'Against the *Christians*' as favoured by Neumann).

[6] Jer. *Ep.* 70.3, cf. *Comm. In Osee* 3.11 (CCL 76, 121). For Cyril's 'three', see *C. Jul.*, address to Theodosius, 4 (Burguière and Evieux 1985, 106). (The 'third book' mentioned by Socrates, *Hist. eccl.* 3.23.33, is a confusion with Cyril's work.)

[7] *C. Jul.*, address to Theodosius, 5 (Burguière and Evieux 1985, 109).

[8] *C. Jul.* 1.3, trans. Russell.

[9] 'From both religions they have gathered what has been engrafted like powers of evil, as it were, on these nations, atheism from the Jewish levity, and a sordid and slovenly way of living from our indolence and vulgarity; and they desire that this should be called the noblest worship of the gods' (43a–b; cf. 238 b–e). [Refs. to *C. Gal.* use the marginal numbers deriving from the 1696 edition of Cyril, reproduced in Wright's Loeb text.]

[10] For the structure of *C. Gal.*, see Meredith 1980, with the useful scheme (deriving from Neumann) set out in Burguière and Evieux 1985, 30–3.

[11] Cf. 235c, for Julian's own experience of the healing power of Asclepius, with his *Hymn to King Helios* (*Or.* 4), 144b, 153b ('the saviour of the world'). Pagan polemic had long compared Christ unfavourably with the divine skills of Asclepius, e.g. Origen, *C. Cels.* 3.3.

[12] See Smith 1995, ch. 4 'The *Chaldaean Oracles* and Neoplatonist Theurgy'.

[13] Notably Bouffartigue 1992, 380–5, on Celsus and Porphyry. Smith 1995, 191, acknowledges Julian's 'readiness to repeat standard criticisms'.

[14] See Origen, *C. Cels.* 5.25–8. Bouffartigue 1992, Appendix III (685–6), well illustrates the predominance of the debt to Celsus.

[15] Lib. *Or.* 18.178 (cf. Socrates, *Hist. eccl.* 3.23.1–11).

[16] Porphyry's attack on the divinity of Jesus is less apparent from the meagre surviving fragments of his own *Against the Christians* than from what is known of other works, e.g. *Philosophy from Oracles*: Wilken 1984, 148–56.

[17] The view of Smith 1995, 195, 'the pervasive concern to defend polytheism'.

[18] So Bowersock 1978, 79–93, esp. 86 ('Ritual and sacrifice were of paramount importance in the religion of Julian'); Smith 1995, 216–18.

[19] So Hunt 1998, 32–7. Among other narratives of these events, see Hanson 1988, 315–86; Brennecke 1988, 5–86; Barnes 1993, 136–51.

[20] Kelly 1972, 293–5. For the text, see Athanasius, *De Synodis* 30; with Socrates, *Hist. eccl.* 2.41.8–17, and Theodoret, *Hist. eccl.* 2.21.3–7.

[21] For the political context of Julian's making common cause with exiled bishops (and the synod of Paris in 360) see, e.g., Brennecke 1984, 360–7; Barnes 1993, 153–4; Rosen 2006, 205–7.

[22] Amm. Marc. 22.5.4, with Julian, *Epp.* 40 (424c), 41 (436a–b) [Julian's *Letters* are cited according to the numbering of Wright's edition].

[23] Julian, *Ep.* 38 (411c–d), seemingly a follow-up to an earlier request to the Prefect of Egypt, *Ep.* 23 (377d–378c), indicating that Julian's interest in preserving George's library lay principally with the books on 'philosophy and rhetoric': in order that these should not be destroyed in error, the books on 'the teachings of the impious Galileans' were also to be rescued.

[24] Julian, *Ep.* 15, with Sozom. *Hist. eccl.* 5.5.9; Philostorgius, *Hist. eccl.* 6.7. Lesbos: Philostorgius, *Hist. eccl.* 9.4.

[25] Aetius: Kopecek 1979, esp. chs. 1–4 *passim*; Hanson 1988, 603–11. For his surviving *Syntagmation*, see Epiph. *Pan.* 76.11–12, with Wickham 1968. Barnes 1993, 136–8, rejects the 'neo-Arian' label.

[26] On Photinus, see Bardy 1934; Hanson 1988, 235–8; Parvis 2006, 248–9.

[27] Julian, *Ep.* 55 = Facundus of Hermiane, *Pro defensione III capit.* 4.2.61–4 (SChr. 478, 2003), '...nequaquam in utero inducere quem credidisti deum'.

[28] On Diodore of Tarsus, see Abramowski 1960; Schäublin 1981.

[29] See Wright 1923, *ad loc.* '...curious and sometimes untranslatable Latin'.

[30] *C. Gal.* 191e. For Jesus as a 'corpse', see 194d, 335b ('you keep adding many corpses newly dead [i.e. martyrs] to the corpse of long ago').

[31] An obscure passage of Hilary of Poitiers (*Liber II ad Constantium* 2 = CSEL 65, 197) hints at Julian's role in connection with the council of Béziers in 356: see Beckwith 2005, 34–5. He was still publicly attending church at Epiphany 361 (Amm. Marc. 21.2.4–5).

[32] As at the council of Sirmium in 351 (which deposed Photinus): Athanasius, *De Synodis* 27, nos. 2, 9, 23.

[33] e.g. Bouffartigue 1992, 388–9; Smith 1995, 205, 'the Arian colour of his upbringing seems to have left no discernible trace in any of his writings'.

17

THE POLITICS OF VIRTUE IN JULIAN'S
MISOPOGON

Nicholas Baker-Brian

The New Year in Antioch

After a period of some months during which relations between the emperor Julian and the citizens of Antioch on the Orontes had grown very strained, the New Year of 363 held the promise of a fresh start for both the city and its ruler. Antioch, the 'part-time imperial capital'[1] on Rome's eastern frontier, was set to enjoy a high civic honour by hosting the inauguration of Julian, along with the Praetorian Prefect of Gaul Flavius Sallustius,[2] as the serving consuls for the year.[3] The emperor himself appeared to look ahead with enthusiasm to the spring and summer months, anticipating a successful outcome for his plans to engage the armies of the Sasanian monarch Shapur II.[4] However, according to Ammianus Marcellinus, an author conventionally associated with the city,[5] the signs for the year ahead were inauspicious from the very beginning. On the day of the Kalends itself, as Julian was entering the Temple of the Tyche, the divine patroness of Antioch, the officiating priest suddenly died. The incident likely unnerved both consuls, although Sallustius was perhaps led to worry more than Julian since the Antiochenes read the priest's collapse as a sign of his rather than the emperor's imminent demise.[6]

Julian's apparent imperviousness to the numerous ill omens accompanying his time in Antioch and during the early stages of the military campaign in Mesopotamia, in Ammianus' *Res Gestae* (Book 23), serves as a foil to the atmosphere of impending doom conveyed in the narrative of Ammianus.[7] For Ammianus, the only voices of dissent during a time of unalloyed optimism for an emperor seemingly inspired by 'an heroic superabundance of energy and *philotimia*',[8] came from the haruspices accompanying the expeditionary force, and also from Sallustius himself. As far as the soothsayers were concerned, there was little room for ambiguity in the interpretation of events such as the lightning strike which killed a soldier with the portentous name of Jovian and two battle horses (23.5.12–13): to continue with the campaign was to flout recklessly the divine numen. In a 'gloomy letter' received by Julian during a halt at the fortress of Cercusium on the frontier with Persia, Sallustius implored for the expedition's cancellation on the basis that Julian had not yet secured sufficient approval from the gods for the venture to be a success (23.5.4–5). As Ammianus notes, the strength of Julian's ambition and virtue was in itself insufficient to overturn an outcome which had already been ordained by the *ordo fatalis*.[9]

The portrayal of Julian's blindness to the heavenly signs, beginning in Antioch and warning him of the catastrophe awaiting him on Mesopotamian soil, is an important feature in Ammianus' process of rationalising the tragic fate of Julian – an emperor who promised so much and appeared fêted by the gods for the better part of his reign yet who ended up being 'so mistaken about the will of the gods':[10] an outcome which, although inscrutable to Ammianus nevertheless served for that author as an apposite demonstration of the gods' unfathomability. Misplaced optimism emerging from a misreading of the divine will may have been Ammianus' assessment of Julian's state of mind whilst in Antioch, although a contrasting image of Julian's time in the city is provided by the oratory of Libanius, Julian's associate in Hellenic revivalism. As the incumbent of the publicly-funded chair of rhetoric in the city, Libanius was appointed by Julian to deliver a panegyric (*Oration* 12) to mark the appointment of the new magistrates.[11] It is a speech that drips with optimism for the year ahead, Libanius' sanguineness enshrined in his closing prayer to the god Chronos: 'father of the year and the months, extend this year for us as far as you can, as once you extended the night when Heracles was begotten'.[12]

Imagining an imperial style

Libanius placed at the centre of the panegyric Julian's reason for being in Antioch, namely that the city was the staging area for the latest Roman challenge to Shapur on Persian territory. Libanius' optimism was coloured by the willingness of Julian to take the lead in sacrificing to the gods, which Libanius held had not only breathed new inspiration into his own army, but also struck fear into the hearts of the enemy:

> No infantry battle, no cavalry activities, no innovation in armament or invention of engines of war, but it is the many sacrifices (αἱ πυκναὶ θυσίαι), the frequent blood-offering, the clouds of incense, the feasting of gods and spirits that has brought our enemies low.[13]

Libanius' association linking a revived Roman military confidence to the sacrificial activities of the emperor, and the anticipation of imminent success in Persia, was evidently a thinly veiled challenge to the memory of

Constantius II – the previous Augustus and darling of the Antiochenes – and the somewhat indecisive outcome for Rome of his many engagements with the armies of Shapur.[14] Following, arguably, in the footsteps of his father,[15] Constantius himself also issued laws against sacrifice and divination,[16] and the absence from the Roman religious scene of sacrificial activity performed with the intention of securing the gods' goodwill provided Libanius with an adequate explanation for the dearth of Roman success on the eastern frontier.

In *Oration* 12, Julian naturally inhabits the centre of this sacrificial revival, the essentiality of his role characterised by the emperor's own willingness to engage in the practical mechanics of cult worship.[17] Libanius notes that Julian found no less pleasure in the title of priest (ἱερεὺς) than that of emperor, 'and the title is matched by his actions, for he has excelled priests in his performance of services to the gods as he has done emperors in government'.[18] Ignoring the conventions on sacrificial procedure, the emperor greeted every sunrise and every sunset with a blood-offering, many performed from within the imperial palace by Julian himself: 'he busies himself on the preparations, gets the wood, wields the knife, opens the birds and inspects their entrails'.[19] For Libanius, Julian's generous propitiation of the gods was in direct proportion to his desire to secure the welfare of the Roman state, especially during the predictably parlous war that Julian was about to lead the empire into in a few short months' time.[20] Nevertheless, Libanius also stresses that whilst the practical execution of ritual is crucial to Julian and his army's future successes, the fortification (τεῖχος) of assurance that Julian has brought to the empire is based on his participation in the gifts of reason (λόγοι) (*Or.* 12.91–2). Libanius reminds his audience that their emperor's commitment to this guiding principle is prominent in two aspects of Julian's life: his writings, and his choice of lifestyle.[21] Addressing Julian directly, Libanius notes, '[i]n these [writings] you produce works of panegyric, persuasion, injunction and charm. You excel the orators in philosophy, philosophers in oratory, and both alike in poetry'.[22] Julian's literary productivity, his ceaseless work-rate, together with his pious association with the gods – all indications that the emperor allows himself to be guided by reason – are possible only because Julian pursues a life governed by self-control (σωφροσύνη).[23] This apparently candid presentation of Julian by Libanius, conveying the image of an emperor and consul ruled privately by a lifestyle of austerity, was intended by the sophist to elicit public admiration for a ruler whose virtuous conduct 'stops even the mouth of Momus', the god of satire and ridicule.[24] However, the events during the Kalends of January, and the behaviour of the Antiochenes towards the emperor were to prove Libanius sorely mistaken: Julian's manner of life and style of governance could not silence the tongue of satire, but rather appeared to have set it wagging in the first place.

'Big Government'

The people of Antioch were not especially interested in the model of the philosopher priest and ruler that Libanius had in mind when he presented his portrait of Julian to the city. By the time of the Kalends good relations between the emperor and the city had almost wholly crumbled away. Modern discussions that prioritise discrete reasons for this deterioration of affairs arguably misjudge the aggregative nature of the situation.[25] Rather, a complex web of problems had created a very tense relationship on both sides, which meant that almost from the very beginning of Julian's stay in Antioch (he arrived on the 18th July 362), his good intentions were misconstrued by the Antiochenes, whilst their gestures of protest were handled disproportionately by the emperor. For Julian the final straw seems to have been a series of personal criticisms, presented mainly in the form of satirical verse (ἀνάπαιστοι e.g. *Misop.* 345d),[26] which gave voice to the Antiochenes' deep dissatisfaction with Julian's handling of a series of civic crises that had afflicted the city during the year.[27] Profound popular criticism of a ruler's fitness to govern frequently manifests itself in the lampooning of physical appearance, and Julian's appearance seems to have suffered from the ridicule of the citizenry, not least his unfashionably hirsute appearance, which prompted comparisons of the emperor's beard with that of a goat.[28]

Slanderous remarks (βλασφημίαι) against Julian had been circulating both privately and publicly in the city for some time (*Misop.* 364c). However, the flash-point came with a relentless tirade of satire and pantomime directed at Julian as the consuls processed through the market place (*Misop.* 366c), and into the hippodrome for further New Year games and festivities on the 3rd January 363.[29] In the hippodrome, the abuse directed at Julian continued,[30] possibly no longer in ribald verse but rather as acclamations of disapproval addressed to the emperor, and perhaps orchestrated and led by the theatrical claque of Antioch, whose political strength and ability to agitate for whoever had hired them was to grow considerably in the immediate decades.[31] As Maud Gleason has indicated, such behaviour on the part of the citizens was in keeping with the lustral role of the Kalends in easing communal conflict:

> a time for healing social rifts and softening social tensions, when a reversal or temporary suspension of the familiar dichotomies that normally articulate the social structure (male and female, ruler and subject, slave and free) might open the way for the experience of community in a large sense.[32]

However, as far as Julian was concerned, the holiday had exposed his reign and its legacy to an unrestrained and very public form of criticism: in his position, he simply could not afford for the slanders of Antioch to go unchallenged.

Dating from the end of January or early February of 363[33] Julian's invective as a response to the city's bellicosity, the *Antiochikos* or – as it is more commonly known – *Misopogon* ('Hater of the Beard'), certainly qualifies as, in the words of one recent commentator, a work of 'imperial journalism'.[34] Affixed for public consumption to the Tetrapylon of the Elephants, outside the entrance to the city's imperial palace,[35] the topical nature of the 'discourse' between Julian and the Antiochenes had been set from the start of Julian's presence in Antioch, and it was one of sloganeering, satire and self-parody. 'Everything is plentiful, everything is expensive' (πάντα γέμει, πάντα πολλοῦ, *Misop.* 368d) was the acclamation that greeted Julian on one of his first official visits to the theatre in Antioch: a rude awakening for the emperor to the everyday realities of life in an imperial capital, where the already beleaguered populace had been unable to secure sufficient supplies of food as the result of a poor harvest,[36] coupled with the endemic corruption plaguing the highest levels (πλούσιοι, *Misop.* 369c) of Antiochene government and society. Life for the Antiochenes had become even more difficult with the arrival of Julian's Persian invasion force that was using the city as a billet-town prior to engaging in operations.[37] However, Antioch had been burdened previously under Constantius II as his headquarters,[38] and in spite of the events of 362 that placed so much pressure on resources, the city had developed its own methods of transacting business that, whilst not particularly equitable, had nevertheless managed to satisfy the traders and propertied classes, although not always the *vulgi*.[39] A central factor in the ground swell of opinion against the emperor was Julian's well-intentioned attempt to ameliorate these crises, and his introduction of specific measures (e.g. regulation of corn prices, *Misop.* 369a; reform of the βουλή, *Misop.* 368a–b) across the delicate social fabric of the city. This had nevertheless failed to alleviate the situation, and in one way had made matters a great deal worse through the opportunities for hoarding and price-fixing of commodities that the reforms had unintentionally introduced.

Ultimately, however, the city council and the citizens appeared not to appreciate the interference of 'Big Government' – namely, 'the degree to which imperial involvement encroached upon local independence' – in their affairs.[40] It was the traders of the city who articulated clearly the general sense of unease with regard to the imposition of the state in provincial affairs, related by Julian in the voice of *Misopogon*'s antagonist:

'But you [Julian] are hated by the shopkeepers because you do not allow them to sell provisions to the common people and those who are visiting the city at a price as high as they please' (*Misop.* 350a).

Julian's conception of 'Big Government' was also, however, very unwelcome in matters of religion.[41] *Misopogon*'s parodical identification of Antioch's guiding civic principle as one of 'freedom' (ἐλεύθερον, e.g. *Misop.* 355b), and Julian's violation of that principle, also included his bullish attempts to influence the religious rhythms of civic life. In a partially preserved address (*Misop.* 362b–363c), Julian berated the council of Antioch for failing to supply a sacrificial offering appropriate for the festival of Apollo, the tutelary god of the Seleucids,[42] which Julian had attended only a month after his arrival in the city, during August 362. The sight of a solitary priest bearing a single goose as a gift for the 'god of your fathers' (*Misop.* 362c) prompted Julian to contrast the beneficent activities of councillors' wives towards 'the Galileans', and to the city's poor, whilst the gods went without honours. In Julian's opinion, the absence of due regard paid to the gods was a failing of the city, a degradation of civic duty which he contrasted with the noteworthy example of the attendant priest and his goose:

> the duty assigned by the gods to the priests is to do them honour by their nobility of character and by the practice of virtue, and also to perform to them the service that is due; but it befits the city, I think, to offer both private and public sacrifice.[43]

However, *Misopogon*'s damning of Antioch's civic failings in epideictic form was nothing new. Dio Chrysostom under Trajan had made similar-sounding complaints against the Alexandrians in his *Oration* 32, a work likely known to Julian.[44] Furthermore, from the point of view of *Misopogon*'s role as an 'edict of chastisement' – a publicly disseminated document indicating Julian's displeasure about the events of the New Year – precedents can be found among the replies of earlier emperors responding to popular lampoons;[45] and, in line with the many satirical episodes and performances which took place during the holiday, Julian was providing his own barbed satire which, cast in traditional forms of invective, amounted to the 'memorable cry of an outraged and helpless man'.[46]

Sōphrosynē and the inversion of virtue

Julian's brief statement in *Misopogon* (362d) concerning the seemly conduct of priests and the responsibilities of cities in relation to the honours (τιμαί) owed to the gods, alerts us to the role played by virtue in shaping Julian's own imperial identity, and in damning the behaviour of the Antiochenes.

However, Julian's ascription of virtues to himself as emperor in that work is far from straightforward. Whilst a number of commentators have noted *Misopogon*'s satirical orientation, and in particular Julian's skilful manipulation of ancient invective (cf. Amm. Marc. 22.14.2),[47] it was Arnaldo Marcone who first showed how Julian in *Misopogon* bled different literary and rhetorical styles into one another, and upset the conventions of epideictic rhetoric.[48] The result is a work in which Julian's virtues, his restraint (σωφροσύνη) towards private and public excess and his accompanying boorishness (ἀγροικία), continually clash against the indulgence (τρυφή) and the libertinism (ἐλεύθερον λίαν) of the Antiochenes: a conventional antithesis that in other circumstances would commend the philosophically-inspired, moderate lifestyle of the ruler, but which in *Misopogon* operates subversively. In it imperial restraint evokes censure, whilst civic excess is commended. Julian, in acknowledging the spirit of deviancy granted by the Kalends in allowing citizens to transgress societal boundaries, maintained the subversive spirit of the New Year by inverting encomium and invective, the two components of epideictic, through the deployment of irony.

As Jacqueline Long has demonstrated,[49] irony plays a central role in *Misopogon*, which Julian used principally to convey criticisms of Antioch. Thus, irony directed towards the Antiochenes is entirely deprecatory, although almost certainly exaggerated: Julian's observation regarding the freedoms of Antiochene civic life recycled *topoi* – e.g. women acting independently of men, hired animals being treated as if they were brides (*Misop.* 355b–356d) – which in *Misopogon* elicited praise, but according to encomiastic and philosophical convention were characteristics of a dissolute society.[50] More complex strategies of irony, however, emerge from the self-deprecatory remarks of the author, transforming Julian's invective against himself.[51] His critical assessment of his own appearance and virtues, becomes a blazing condemnation of Antioch's treatment of him, a 'moderate and mild' ruler (*Misop.* 365d, πραότης ἀρχόντων μετὰ σωφροσύνης).[52]

Identifying the role of irony in *Misopogon* and indeed its wider 'subversion of rhetoric',[53] helps us to understand the literary purport of the work. But other issues remain unaddressed. One untapped area of interest is Julian's own understanding in *Misopogon* of imperial governance, and his implicit criticism of Constantius II, his imperial style, and his relations with Antioch. Marcone seminally observed in his article of 1984, that the rhetoric of *Misopogon* implies that when Julian writes autobiographically, he is also fulfilling certain apologetical and propagandist ambitions.[54] Little was said about the exact nature of these ambitions by Marcone, but a clue as to what they were may emerge from the delineation of virtues and the autobiographical portrait of Julian's imperial persona in the work. *Misopogon* is arguably more than an attack on Antioch. It is part of Julian's efforts to legitimise his rule. Like other examples of his writings, such as *Letter to the Athenians*, *Misopogon* helps to justify what was an act of usurpation in the early months of 360.[55] Although just over a year separates the composition of the *Letter* from *Misopogon*,[56] and the memory of Julian's usurpation continued to fade by the time of *Misopogon*'s composition some three years after the acclamation in Paris, Antioch nevertheless presented a special case in point: its citizens continued to hold Constantius posthumously in very high esteem (see below), which surely affected their reception of Julian from July 362 onwards.

Thus, beyond the emperor's desire to chastise deviant behaviour by his subjects, *Misopogon* reflects Julian as author of imperial encomia, who had spent a good portion of his time creating and consolidating the reputations of his 'elders and betters' (*Orations* 1 and 2 to Constantius; *Oration* 3 for Eusebia), and on occasions tacitly undermining those same reputations (*Oration* 2).[57] Julian understood clearly the inveigling nature of encomia, especially the building blocks of such speeches (ancestry, upbringing, character, virtues), and therefore knew how such commonplaces could be manipulated by panegyricists in representing people and places. At one level, *Misopogon* represents Julian's encomiastic portrayal of himself, and his mastery of encomium as a literary form is triumphantly signalled by his capacity to invert the genre.

Important here is the emperor's appropriation of temperance as his own personal virtue. It appears throughout *Misopogon* as a 'synthetic' virtue,[58] guiding both his private life and his public affairs.[59] In his irony, Julian most frequently employs the word σωφροσύνη (or, less often, ἐγκράτεια) to describe his personal austerity. Temperance becomes his defining moral quality. He exercises self-control over luxury and indolence,[60] whilst the work portrays these as principal habits of the Antiochenes. In an 'autobiographical' passage that stands between criticism of Constantius, Gallus, and Count Julian's immoderate endorsement of Antioch's penchant for horse-racing (340a–b), and a contrasting, comedic description of the absolute austerity of Julian's existence as Caesar in Paris (340d–342a),[61] Julian begins to explain his own ascetic inclinations:

> [s]leepless nights on a pallet and a diet that is anything rather than surfeiting make my temper harsh and unfriendly to a luxurious city like yours. However it is not in order to set an example to you that I adopt these habits. But in my childhood a strange and senseless delusion came over me and persuaded me to war against my belly, so that I do not allow it to fill itself with a great quantity of food.[62]

However, on other occasions in the work Julian also demonstrates an awareness of the *polysemy* of temperance (now well analysed by Adriaan Rademaker).[63] Moderate behaviour not only aids appetitive and emotional control, as in management of anger, but also less conventionally it defines piety, portrayed negatively as an 'enslavement' (δουλεύειν) to the gods and the laws, in contrast to the freedom enjoyed by the citizens of Antioch (e.g. *Misop.* 343a–c). Julian's austere tendencies are criticised by *Misopogon*'s interlocutor, an imagined Antiochene respondent who, as the voice of the city's excess, serves as the foil for the austerity of the emperor:

> Did you really suppose that your boorish manners and savage ways and clumsiness would harmonise with these things [i.e. the lifestyle of the Antiochenes]? O most ignorant and most quarrelsome of men, is it so senseless then and so stupid, that puny soul (ψυχάριον) of yours which men of poor spirit called temperate, and which you forsooth think it your duty to adorn and deck out with temperance? (ὃ δή σὺ κοσμεῖν καὶ καλλωπίζειν σωφροσύνῃ χρῆναι νομίζεις;) You are wrong; for in the first place we do not know what temperance is and we hear its name only, while the real thing we cannot see (οὐκ ὀρθῶς, ὅτι πρῶτον μὲν ἡ σωφροσύνη ὅ τι ποτ' ἔστιν οὐκ ἴσμεν, ὄνομα δὲ αὐτῆς ἀκούοντες μόνον ἔργον οὐχ ὁρῶμεν).[64]

The rhetorical orientation of *Misopogon*, the inversion of encomium as invective in the work, meant that Julian's portrayal of his own virtues, especially temperance, required his audience to judge the temperate character of the emperor as a failing rather than as something meritorious. However, in appropriating temperance as the mark of his moral being, Julian was acknowledging at the very least the cardinal nature of the virtue in the Imperial Oration (βασιλικὸς λόγος), the speech in praise of the emperor, and its role within imperial panegyric as a value term for idealised kingly rule.[65] The deployment of particular virtues (ἀρεταί), as criteria for fair or tyrannical rule within imperial encomia, most obviously derived from the Greek philosophical tradition, especially from the works of Plato and Aristotle. However, the historiographical tradition, by supplying panegyricists with literary and historical examples of virtuous or depraved rulers, arguably also helped to shape both philosophical and panegyrical perceptions of the relationship between the virtues and the laudation of rulers.[66]

Competing virtues

To demonstrate that an emperor was the living incarnation of all known ἀρεταί, especially the four so-called cardinal virtues of courage (ἀνδρεία), justice (δικαιοσύνη), temperance (σωφροσύνη) and wisdom (φρόνησις), was the stock-in-trade of the writer of imperial orations. But from the fourth century many panegyricists sought to realign the utility of these and other virtues (e.g. φιλανθρωπία, 'love of mankind') with philosophically-guided reflections on the nature of the ideal ruler, viz. the philosopher-king.[67] Part of the explanation for this shift was the increased presence of philosophically-minded rhetoricians (or indeed, rhetorically-minded philosophers) aligned with the imperial court. Their panegyrics seem absorbed with presenting their subjects as the 'philosophical ideal incarnate'.[68] In this regard, Constantius II is particularly well served, often presented as the virtuous ruler with conduct most suggestive of the philosopher-king. The *tour de force* is Themistius' first oration, 'Philanthropy, or Constantius'. Delivered before the emperor in Ancyra *c.* 347,[69] *Oration* 1 is a speech in which Themistius made the bold yet conflicted claim to uphold the independent and truth-telling stance of a philosopher, whilst nevertheless delivering a laudation in honour of Constantius: 'for nothing is more inimical to truth than flattery, but praise is virtue's witness'.[70] Praising Constantius as part of a discussion of the virtues most appropriate for kingly rule, Themistius moves through the cardinal character-istics as they are perfected in the actions of the emperor, himself guided overall by φιλανθρωπία.[71] Themistius' philosophical reception of ἀρεταί in his portrayal of Constantius is perhaps most apparent when he presents the emperor as tempering the passionate element (θυμοειδές) of his soul. Rather than yielding to anger (*Or.* 1 7b) and passion (7c), the emperor

> has softened all the passionate element of the soul as if it were iron and rendered it useful instead of useless, and beneficial instead of harmful. For he does not allow it to rush ahead of reason, not permit it, like a horse champing on its bit, to ignore the charioteer, who alone is the preserver of virtue in the soul and dwells in the man who possesses it throughout his life.[72]

The value for the soul whose appetitive element has been restrained is akin to tempered iron or the horse obedient under the whip hand of the charioteer: clear Platonic allusions one and all (*Resp.* 411b, and *Phdr.* 246a respectively), which Themistius employs for the self-control of Constantius. After Plato, the virtue came to be regarded in some quarters as 'the exclusive property of the leaders rather than their subjects';[73] the great power enjoyed by rulers made it necessary that they manage their appetites, including anger, through temperance (cf. Them. *Or.* 1 7b), in order to ensure the safety of the state and its citizens. Personal self-control, revealed in the *topoi* of moderation which included restraint in sleeping, eating, continence and the acquisition of private wealth, thus equated with fitness to govern.[74] As John Vanderspoel has noted, it was likely that Themistius was 'adopting the imperial view'[75] of Constantius as the philosophically-minded ruler whose appetites and emotions were governed by an austere self-determination, a view which was also regarded as informing Constantius' ceremonial demeanour in displays witnessed by the citizens of the empire. However, if this was the case, then it is no mere slavish artifice on Themistius' part: that moderation and philanthropy in a sense became *the* virtues most readily associated with Constantius in both the panegyrical and historiographical traditions of the fourth century,[76] suggests the intellectual influence that Themistius had over the emperor, particularly as both men attempted to reconcile the speculative nature of philosophy with its practical application in the act of government.[77]

However, the portrait offered in encomia had also to be realised in ceremony. Alongside the panegyrical use of philosophy portraying Constantius as an emotionally restrained figure, there were also imperial displays of exquisite self-control. Typical is the description of Constantius' *adventus* into Rome in April 357 in Book Sixteen of Ammianus' history, the central image of which the author repeated in his obituary notice on Constantius in Book Twenty-One: '[Constantius] was never seen in public wiping his face or nose or spitting or turning his head to either side'.[78] Constantius' reputation ultimately fell foul of the struggle for dynastic supremacy, as Julian and his thurifer Ammianus[79] sought to justify their own ambitions. However, for a considerable period Constantius stood well within the boundary of virtues that defined the good ruler, regarded widely as an emperor who governed his soul and his demeanour through estimable displays of self-control.

The loss of control ascribed to Constantius by both Julian and Ammianus, his universal malice[80] and his displays of anger and bitterness towards his real or imagined opponents,[81] all driven by a fury surpassing even Caligula, Domitian, and Commodus,[82] undid his reputation for temperance and philanthropy, and forced on Constantius the image of a tyrant, which has remained ever since.[83] The historical underpinning of this image evidently derived from the apportioning of blame to Constantius II for the assassination of the male relatives (including Julian's father Julius Constantius) of Constantius I and Theodora in 337.[84] The branding of Constantius as a dynastic murderer may very well have been completely justified,[85] but it certainly enabled Julian and his coterie to begin the dissolution of Constantius' reputation as a temperate ruler, in favour of an alternative image of Constantius as a furious tyrant, whose lack of self-control marked him out as the opposite of the philosophical ideal.[86]

Libanius (e.g. *supra Or.* 12), Claudius Mamertinus[87] and Ammianus[88] all played their part in aligning Julian squarely with the virtue of σωφροσύνη/*temperantia*, the philosophical meaning of which was clearly paramount in forming Julian's imperial style. However, temperance as legitimising Julian's reign was a matter of equal concern to Julian and his promoters, and went hand-in-hand with the posthumous dismantling of Constantius' reputation. *Misopogon* clearly had its own role to play in this regard. At Antioch, making a favourable impression on its citizens became urgent for Julian, not simply because of the city's strategic importance for his planned invasion of Persian territory, but also because Constantius' own posthumous reputation among the Antiochenes remained very high indeed, thereby presenting an obvious impediment to Julian's ambitions for the future of the empire. Indeed, it seems that Constantius' reputation within the city did not derive from thoughts of fair government under a virtuous and moderate ruler, but rather from the extensive patronage which the city had enjoyed at the expense of Constantius and his court. There were entertainments that Constantius not only generously funded but had been more than happy to attend (unlike Julian: *Misop.* 340b), and the development of the harbour in Seleucia Pieria, Antioch's principal port.[89] As Pierre-Louis Malosse has lately reminded us, 'Constantius' life was linked to Antioch more than to any other city',[90] and Antioch inevitably benefited from the presence of the emperor who based himself there for just over half of his twenty-four year reign as Augustus.[91]

An oblique challenge

It was therefore Julian's fate, even before the disastrous events of the Kalends, to be received unfavourably by a city which missed its imperial patron. In Constantius' memory the Antiochenes were in the habit of recalling, via a quotation from Cratinus, 'that noble youth and genial spirit' (*Misop.* 339d: ἥβης ἐκείνης νοῦ τε ἐκείνου καὶ φρενῶν). Comparisons unfavourable to Julian included a riddle (αἴνιγμα) which also did the rounds during his stay in the city,

> '[T]he *chi*' say the citizens 'never harmed the city in any way, nor did the *kappa*'. Now the meaning of this riddle which your wisdom has invented is hard to understand, but I obtained interpreters from your city and I was informed that these are the first letters of names, and that the former is intended to represent Christ, the latter Constantius.[92]

Misopogon rarely, however, takes a direct aim at Constantius and the reputation for civic munificence which he undoubtedly enjoyed among the Antiochenes.[93] Julian does refer to Constantius' interest in horse-racing (*Misop.* 340b), although his uncle Julian's[94] and his half-brother Gallus' penchant for festival games are mentioned at the same point, thus in a sense diluting the criticism of Constantius, and serving instead to draw attention to Julian's own extreme disposition (τρόπος) in a civic context.

274

Nevertheless, indirect criticism of Constantius by Julian is arguably to be found in *Misopogon*'s exegesis of Plato's *Laws* (*Misop.* 354b–c). Before offering a defence of his own austere governance of the city, in the theatrical, religious, judicial, and economic spheres (e.g. *Misop.* 354c–d; cf. 365c–d), Julian presented the philosophical basis for his approach, via a direct quotation from Plato's *Laws* (730d), together with a paraphrase of the preceding section (*Leg.* 729b sqq.), at *Misop.* 354b. Julian's choice of passages from *Laws* is telling, providing as it does an unambiguous insight into his 'philosophical approach' to ruling the empire. Indeed, it is here that the limits of irony within *Misopogon* become apparent. As Long has noted, Julian's 'ironic mask' breaks very occasionally in *Misopogon*,[95] not least when the emperor is offering a defence of his approach in handling the city's civic affairs. The first, relatively lengthy quotation from Plato's work (730d) in *Misopogon* describes, in explicit terms, the ideal of the ruler who not only does no wrong himself, but also prevents others under his charge from doing wrong. And, whilst he may be the most powerful man in the city and could therefore punish recalcitrant citizens on his own, he nevertheless follows judicial procedure by reporting wrong-doers to the city's magistrates. Such a man, opines Plato's 'Athenian stranger', has full claim to the virtues of temperance, and wisdom, and on account of possessing these virtues, he seeks 'to impart them to other men' also.[96] Serving as a commentary on this passage, Julian proceeds to his own, irony-tinged philosophical justification for his manner of rule (354b):

> But I, because I was ashamed to be less virtuous as a ruler than I had been as a private citizen, have unconsciously given you the benefit of my own boorishness (ἀγροικία) though there was no necessity. And another of Plato's laws (νόμοι) has made me take thought for myself and so become hateful in your eyes: I mean the law which says that those who govern (ἄρχοντες), and also the older men, ought to train themselves in respect for others and in self-control (σωφροσύνη), in order that the masses may look at them and so order their lives aright.[97]

In *Laws*, the 'maxim' handled by Julian above is adapted from the speech of the Athenian stranger in the work's fifth book (729b) concerning the role of the lawgiver (νομοθέτης) in advising citizens on the nature of honour.[98] A dilemma emerges during the speech as to whether or not parents' financial bequests provide a suitable legacy for children. According to the Athenian, the lawgiver should admonish,

> ...let no man love riches for the sake of his children, in order that he may leave them as wealthy as possible; for that is good neither for them nor for the State. For the young the means that attracts no flatterers, yet is not lacking in things necessary, is the most harmonious of all and the best; for

it is in tune with us and in accord, and thus it renders our life in all respects painless. To his children it behoves a man to bequeath modesty, not money, in abundance.[99]

Julian's adaptation of the passage is telling. The replacement of 'children' with 'the masses' (τὰ πλήθη) who, inspired by their rulers' displays of virtue, order (κοσμῆται) themselves accordingly, is a sign of Julian's appreciation of the passage from *Laws* not only for its philosophical (moral) meaning, but also its use as an aspect of his wider critique of the Antiochenes' alleged profligacy, and Constantius' 'poisoned' legacy to Antioch. The epitome at *Misopogon* 354b conflates *Laws* 729b with *Laws* 729c and the sentiment that

> the most effective way of training the young – as well as the older people themselves – is not by admonition, but by plainly practising throughout one's own life the admonitions which one gives to others.[100]

Thus, Julian turns Plato's 'law' into a proof-text for the guidance of the emperor acting as an exemplary figure, manifesting virtuous qualities for citizens under his charge. In *Misopogon*, the importance of Julian's epitome of Plato's *Laws* is in the link which it suggests between, on the one hand, the immodesty of the Antiochenes and the template for their behaviour in the prior rule – i.e. Constantius' generous patronage – of the city; and, on the other, the promotion of Julian's modest style, and his expectation that the citizens will respond in kind by behaving with restraint and responsibility in the management of their affairs.

An association between the generosity of Julian's predecessor and the intemperance of Antioch is not made directly in *Misopogon*. However, it is suggested in the choice of texts from *Laws,* and also in the remark (see above) placed in the mouth of the Antiochene interlocutor at 343a: '...in the first place we do not know what temperance is and we hear its name only, while the real thing we cannot see'. At a fundamental level, Julian's intimation to Antioch is that as emperor, he can offer something better than what had gone before: whilst Constantius' relations with the city may have been more benevolent and therefore encouraged the cultivation of greater freedoms, Julian's are more restrained (e.g. *Misop.* 354c–d; 365c–d) yet of sounder civic sense, since he is offering virtuous government. However, a more stinging attack on Constantius and the edifice of his reign can also be detected in the work, in the claim of the Antiochene to hear 'the name of [temperance] only, while the thing itself we have not seen'. This was evidently an attempt on Julian's part to challenge the image of Constantius as philosophically-inspired and temperate; an image which, as the statement intimates, was never actually realised during his time in residence in Antioch. Indeed, the distinction seems to be between the ruler who governs in accordance with the virtues celebrated in his encomia, and the one for whom they are simply 'window-dressing' to his reign. In this sense, the ultimate ironical intent of *Misopogon* can be glimpsed. By emphasising the need for the emperor to behave and be seen to behave virtuously, rather than simply being heard to do so, Julian was undermining an assumption of encomiastic composition, that people will automatically adopt the manner of conduct of their rulers which they hear promoted in panegyric.[101] In the case of Antioch and Constantius, Julian seems to be arguing that this was not the case. In *Misopogon*, Julian was not only presenting his critique of the city via a reimaging of the rules of encomia, but in its veiled challenge to Constantius' memory he was also arguing that the business of praise had little to do with the real business of government.

Acknowledgements

My thanks to Dr. Alberto Quiroga, Prof. Hans Teitler, and Dr. Shaun Tougher, for assistance with the composition of this paper.

Notes

[1] Matthews 2007, 413.

[2] i.e. Flavius Sallustius 5, *PLRE* 1, 797–8.

[3] Amm. Marc. 23.1.1. All translations of Ammianus are taken from the Loeb Classical Library edition by J.C. Rolfe 1935–40.

[4] For an indication of Julian's eagerness whilst in Antioch to engage Shapur, see Lib. *Or.* 12.76–7 (*Or.* 17.19; *Or.* 18.163–165), and Julian's dismissal of the prelude to an embassy sent by Shapur II. Cf. Amm. Marc. 22.12.1–2.

[5] See Kelly 2008, 110–18.

[6] Amm. Marc. 23.1.6.

[7] See esp. Smith 1999, 100–1.

[8] Smith 1999, 93.

[9] Amm. Marc. 23.5.5.

[10] Smith 1999, 102.

[11] For Libanius' account of the speech, see *Or.* 1.127–9. For commentary on *Or.* 12, see Wiemer 1995, 151–88.

[12] Lib. *Or.* 12.99 (trans. Norman 1969, 95–7).

[13] Lib. *Or.* 12.79 (trans. Norman 1969, 83).

[14] Cf. Amm. Marc. 21.16.15; see Whitby 1999, 81–2. For reappraisals of Constantius' wars with Persia, see esp. Blockley 1989, and 1992, 12–24.

[15] On the law of 324 in Euseb. *Vit. Const.* 2.45.1, see Cameron and Hall 1999, 243–4; and Bradbury 1994.

[16] e.g. the law of 341 (*Cod. Theod.* 16.10.2); for the ascription of the law to Constans, see Barnes 1981, 377, and Corcoran 1996, 315–16; and the laws of 354 (*Cod. Theod.* 16.10.4) and 356 (*Cod. Theod.* 16.10.6); cf. Lib. *Or.* 30.6 (trans. Norman 1977, 106–7).

[17] Cf. Bradbury 1995.

[18] *Or.* 12.80 (trans. Norman 1969, 85). For an epigraphic representation of Julian as *pontifex maximus*, see Bowersock 1978, 123–4.

[19] *Or.* 12.82 (trans. Norman 1969, 85).

[20] Cf. Smith 1995, 168–9.

[21] See Bouffartigue 1992, 653–8.

[22] *Or.* 12.92 (trans. Norman 1969, 91).

[23] *Or.* 12.95 (Norman 1969, 92–3): τί δὴ θαυμαστόν, εἰ σωμάτων ὠλιγώρηται, κάλλος ἐν τεττίγων μὲν τροφῇ, λόγων δὲ ἀπεργασίᾳ, θεῶν δὲ συνουσίᾳ, πόνῳ δὲ συνεχεῖ;

[24] *Or.* 12.96 (trans. Norman 1969, 95).

[25] Cf. Sandwell 2007, 172f. For a convenient summary of scholars' opinions prior to 1979 regarding relations between Julian and Antioch, see Alonso-Núñez 1979.

[26] Translations of *Misopogon* are taken from the Loeb Classical Library edition by W. C. Wright 1913, vol. 2, 421–511.

[27] A still valuable reconstruction of the events and circumstances of the economic crisis affecting Antioch prior to and during Julian's visit may be found in Downey 1951.

[28] *Misop.* 339a. Cf. Amm. Marc. 22.14.3: 'For he was ridiculed as a Cercops, as a dwarf, spreading his narrow shoulders and displaying a billy-goat's beard, taking mighty strides as if he were the brother of Otus and Ephialtes, whose height Homer describes as enormous' (*Ridebatur enim ut Cercops, homo brevis humeros extentans angustos et barbam prae se ferens hircinam, grandiaque incedens tamquam Oti frater et Ephialtis, quorum proceritatem Homerus in immensum extollit*). See Zanker 1995, 198–266.

[29] See Gleason 1986, 109–11.

[30] Lib. *Or.* 15.75 (trans. Norman 1969, 199).

[31] On the Antioch claque, see Liebeschuetz 1972, 208–19 and 278–80, who nevertheless regards it as unlikely that the claque was responsible for the abusive treatment of the emperor; cf. Gleason 1986, 110–11. Also see Cameron 1976, 234–49.

[32] Gleason 1986, 111.

[33] See Long 1993, 15.

[34] Janka 2008, 179. Although publication came too late for its findings to be noted in this paper, I note here the recent article by van Hoof and van Nuffelen 2011.

[35] Mal. 13.19 (328) (trans. Jeffreys, Jeffreys, Scott *et al.* 1986, 178).

[36] Lib. *Or.* 18.195 (trans. Norman 1969, 409). See Downey 1951, 315 n.15.

[37] See Matthews 2007, 409.

[38] Lib. *Or.* 11.177–9 (trans. Norman 2000, 42–3) gives an encomiastic portrayal of Antioch's accommodation of the army and retinue of Constantius in the late 350s.

[39] Amm. Marc. 14.7.5–8 on the crisis of 354; see Matthews 2007, 406–9.

[40] Hunt 1998b, 66.

[41] 'Big Government' leading, however, to Julian's ambitions for the decentralisation of government, and the reinvigoration of the cities of the empire; see Athanassiadi 1992, 87–120; also Hunt 1998b, 64–7.

[42] Lib. *Or.* 11.94 (trans. Norman 2000, 24).

[43] *Misop.* 362d.

[44] See Marcone 1984, 237–8; Salmeri 2000, 82–3; also Webb 2009, 136.

[45] See Gleason 1986, 116–19.

[46] Bowersock 1978, 104, speaking about Julian's complaint in *Misop.* 370c.

[47] Cf. Long 1996, 82–3.

[48] Marcone 1984, *passim*. Cf. Browning 1975, 158, and his assessment of *Misopogon* as typifying 'the pseudo-speeches of late antiquity that were never delivered nor meant to be delivered'.

[49] Long 1993, *passim*.

[50] Pl. *Resp.* 563b–d; Men. Rhet. 363.27–364.7 (ed. Russell and Wilson 1981, 66–9). See Athanassiadi 1992, 216–19.

[51] Cf. Long 1993, 19: 'Irony transmutes the praise and the dispraise'.

[52] See Wiemer 1998.

[53] See Quiroga 2009, *passim*.

[54] Marcone 1984, 238. Cf. Long 1996, 203 f., for an insightful discussion of the issues raised in applying the term 'propaganda' to literature.

[55] Amm. Marc. 20.4.1–5.10; see Matthews 2007, 93–100, and also Mark Humphries' chapter in this volume. Although as Barnes 2011, 63, notes, Ammianus (21.15.2) relates the claim that Constantius appointed Julian his successor while on his death-bed (*successorem suae potestatis statuisse dicitur Iulianum*).

[56] See Bowersock 1978, 60.

[57] See the chapters by Shaun Tougher, Hal Drake and Liz James in this volume.

[58] Fontaine, Prato and Marcone 1987, 326.

[59] See North 1966, 250–2; 'His *Misopogon* is a *sophronizon logos* in the manner of the Cynic diatribe...' (250); see also Marcone 1984, 228f; cf. the sceptical response of Bouffartigue 1992, 541.

[60] Cf. North 1966, 251.

[61] See Janka 2008, 198–201.

[62] *Misop.* 340b. For Julian and asceticism see also the chapter by Arnaldo Marcone in this volume.

[63] Rademaker 2005, *passim*.

[64] *Misop.* 342d–343a.

[65] Cf. Men. Rhet. 376.2–11 (ed. and trans. Russell and Wilson 1981, 90–1).

[66] See Drake 2002, 44f.

[67] See MacCormack 1976; also Seager 1984.

[68] Heather and Moncur 2001, 20.

[69] See Heather and Moncur 2001, 69–73.

[70] *Or.* 1 4c (trans. Heather and Moncur 2001, 80). On this see also the remarks of Shaun Tougher in this volume.

[71] For a fair summary of *Or.* 1 see Vanderspoel 1995, 77–83. See Julian, *Ep. ad Ath.* 270c: ὁ φιλανθρωπότατος οὗτος βασιλεύς.

[72] *Or.* 1 7c (trans. Heather and Moncur 2001, 84); ed. Schenkl and Downey 1965, 11.

[73] Rademaker 2005, 343.

[74] See Harris 2001, 229–63.

[75] Vanderspoel 1995, 79.

[76] Cf. Lib. *Or.* 59.121–5 (ed. and French trans. Malosse 2003).

[77] See Heather and Moncur 2001, 100f.; and also John Watt's chapter in this volume.

[78] Amm. Marc. 21.16.7. See Amm. Marc. 16.10.10 for Constantius' *adventus*. Ammianus may have wished, however, to impute tendencies other than 'self-control'

to Constantius in the passage: n.b. his description of Constantius' sight as 'fixed' at 16.10.10 (*velut collo munito, rectam aciem luminum tendens, nec dextra vultum nec laeva flectebat...*), and the suspicion in physiognomic literature of eyes which are fixed, being a sign of inimical character; cf. versions of Polemon's *Physiognomy*, e.g. Adamantius A6 (ed. and English trans. Ian Repath in Swain 2007, 500–1), and *Anon. Lat.* 22 (Repath in Swain 2007, 570–1); see also Gleason 1995, 56. On the *adventus*, see MacCormack 1981, 40f.

[79] Cf. Malosse 2004, 92.

[80] Julian, *Ep. ad Ath.* 286d: καὶ οὔπω φημί τὴν πανταχοῦ γῆς γυμναζομένην πικρίαν.

[81] e.g. Amm. Marc. 21.16.9.

[82] Amm. Marc. 21.16.8.

[83] See Teitler 1992. Other recent reappraisals of Constantius and his reign include Vogler 1979; Henck 2001a; Henck 2001b; Barceló 2004; Henck 2007.

[84] See esp. Burgess 2008.

[85] e.g. Julian, *Ep. ad Ath.* 281b; Lib. *Or.* 18. 31; Amm. Marc. 21.6.18.

[86] To say nothing of the Nicene-Christian branding of Constantius as tyrant and anti-Christ in response to Constantius' apparent support for the 'Arian' cause in, e.g. Athanasius' *History of the Arians* and Hilary of Poitiers' *Against Constantius*; see Barnes 1993, 129 f., and Humphries 1998.

[87] Mamert. 12 and 14 (*Pan. Lat.* 11.3, trans. Marna M. Morgan in Lieu 1989, 23, 25–6); see esp. García Ruiz 2008b.

[88] e.g. the obituary notice for Julian in Amm. Marc. 25.4.1–27; cf. the notice for Constantius, Amm. Marc. 21.16.1–19; however, Ammianus' portrayal of Julian's virtues and emotions is complex, as discussed recently by Sidwell 2008.

[89] For Constantius' involvement in the development of Antioch's built environment, see esp. Henck 2001a, 293–7.

[90] Malosse 2004, 84.

[91] See Barnes 1993, 219–24.

[92] *Misop.* 357a.

[93] See esp. Henck 2007.

[94] See Amm. Marc. 23.1.4.

[95] Long 1993, 15.

[96] Pl. *Leg.* 730d (ed. and trans. Bury 1926).

[97] *Misop.* 354b.

[98] See Strauss 1975, 66–81.

[99] Pl. *Leg.* 729a–b (trans. Bury 1926, 329).

[100] Pl. *Leg.* 729c (trans. Bury 1926, 331).

[101] Cf. Men. Rhet. 376.8–9 (ed. and trans. Russell and Wilson 1981, 90–1): οἷον γὰρ ὁρῶσι τὸν βασιλέως βίον, τοιοῦτον ἐπανῄρηνται.

18

THE *CAESARS* OF JULIAN THE APOSTATE IN TRANSLATION AND RECEPTION, 1580–ca.1800

Rowland Smith

Introduction

Gibbon prefaces his account of Julian's stay at Antioch with high praise of an 'ingenious fiction' the emperor devised there late in 362, to mark the annual Saturnalia: 'The philosophical fable which Julian composed under the name of the *Caesars*, is of the most agreeable and instructive productions of ancient wit'.[1] Some modern expert readers have judged the fable's wit less generously[2] – but none would dispute its singular interest within the Julianic oeuvre. Even to call it '*Caesars*' raises questions: that title, adopted in Cantoclarus' *editio princeps* of 1577, and long familiar now, was not its original one. The manuscript tradition implies that Julian had signalled its principal literary models by naming it '*Symposium or Kronia*': the double title nods to Plato, partly, but also to the humorist Lucian, many of whose pieces' titles (among them, a *Symposium or Lapiths*) took the '*x* or *y*' form.[3] '*Caesars*', though, had already won currency as a popular name for the piece by the mid-fifth century: the church-historian Socrates Scholasticus casually refers to it as such.[4] Socrates represents it as an indiscriminate rant, the Apostate's jaundiced abuse of every earlier emperor. A brief resumé of its content and 'plot' will disclose the absurdity of that insinuation.

I. A prologue (306a–307a) announces that the text is intended to contribute to the jollities of the Kronia (i.e. the Saturnalia): in dialogue with a friendly interlocutor, the author/narrator proposes to recount a myth that Hermes has taught him – an aptly entertaining one for the occasion, he hopes, but also one in which a serious lesson, as in Plato's myths, is contained beneath the surface.

II. The bulk of the text narrates the myth. To celebrate the Saturnalia, the deified Romulus invites the gods and all the deceased *kaisares* of Rome to a banquet on Olympus. The gods sit in the heavens above its summit

(307b–308d); the 'Caesars' arrive in chronological order of rule, from Julius Caesar to Constantius II, taking their places on its slopes (308d–315d). As they arrive (and sporadically throughout the subsequent action), Dionysus' friend, the satyr Silenus, offers deflating jokes about their deeds and characters; several infamous monsters among their number are refused entry by Justice, or even summarily despatched to Tartarus. Hermes then proposes a contest to amuse the gods: the merits of each Caesar will be scrutinized and tested. Heracles insists that Alexander the Great be summoned to join the competition: a solitary Greek to contend with all the Roman protégés of Romulus (316a–d). A short-list of six is quickly agreed: three martial Caesars (Julius Caesar, Octavian, Trajan); a philosophic one (Marcus Aurelius); at Dionysus' suggestion, a notable 'hedonist' (Constantine); and Alexander. Hermes makes a proclamation in anapaestic verse to initiate the contest (318d–319d), and each contestant delivers a speech (320a–329d). After all six have spoken, each is questioned in turn by Hermes, and a secret ballot of the gods is held: Marcus wins, by majority vote (329d–335b). At Zeus' command, Hermes announces that each of the six should now choose a model or protector. Alexander goes to Heracles, Octavian to Apollo, Marcus to Zeus and Cronos; Trajan decides to join Alexander; Julius Caesar wanders confused, until summoned by Ares and Aphrodite. Constantine runs off to 'Mistress Pleasure' (*Truphē*) who leads him to 'Incontinence' (*Asōtia*), in whose company he encounters Jesus, preaching the forgiveness of all sins through baptism (335d–336b). The avenging deities now intervene, punishing Constantine and his sons as impious murderers of their kin; but Zeus finally suspends the penalty, out of regard for two of their dynasty's better, earlier, rulers (its putative founder, Claudius Gothicus, and Constantine's father, Constantius Chlorus).

III. A short epilogue (336c) reports Hermes' closing words to the narrator: they enjoin him to follow the commandments of Father Mithras, of which Hermes has granted him knowledge, and thus secure for himself a safe anchor during his earthly lifetime, and a god whom he can trust to protect him when he passes beyond it.

For modern scholars, various lines of interest converge in *Caesars*. Historians comb it to appraise the sources, depth and idiosyncrasies of Julian's own knowledge of Roman history;[5] potentially, his verdicts on his predecessors constitute a covert manifesto for his own reformist politics. Or they reflect on its touches of Neoplatonic allegory, or its author's putative self-identification with Alexander and Marcus, looking for insights into Julian's inner state of mind in the months immediately preceding his Persian expedition.[6] Classical scholars and literary theorists debate its intertextual affinities and narratology,[7] or its generic standing as Menippean satire, or Banquet-literature, or a 'hybrid' blending both;[8] some ask what postclassical writers working in the 'Menippean' tradition may have drawn from it.[9] We shall not, though, be dilating on any of these topics here: our particular concern lies not with current historical or literary-critical interpretations of *Caesars*, but with its readership at an earlier period – and the question of its influence on the satirical literature of the period is only tangentially relevant, for our purposes. We focus on a more basic aspect of its reception: its publication and circulation in translation over two centuries, from its first rendering into any modern language (1580) to its first appearance in an English version (1784). During this period, we shall see, *Caesars* would come to appeal to a wider readership than an expert circle of antiquaries and scholars, and not just for its literary piquancy; contemporary political considerations contributed too.

Caesars in translation, 1580–1784

It is an easy guess that *Caesars*' humour, 'potted-history' theme and quick-paced narrative will have made it the most widely read of Julian's works within the period we are treating. Reflection on its circulation in early printed translations confirms the point. Of all his literary pieces, *Caesars* resonated earliest beyond the confines of a learned circle accustomed to read Julian in the Greek (or else the parallel Latin cribs) of the early editions of the 'collected works'.[10] It was first published in a modern language at Paris in 1580, as *Discours de l'Empereur Julian sur les faicts et deportemens des Caesars, avec un abrégé de la vie de Julien et annotations*.[11] The translator, Balthasar Grangier, is better known for a subsequent work: he composed the first complete French version of Dante's *Commedia* [1596]. The immediate stimulus for his 1580 *Caesars* was the publication at Paris, three years previously, of the *editio princeps* of the text as a 'stand-alone' piece in Greek and Latin;[12] but the readership he envisaged was clearly not exclusively a scholarly one. Grangier was well-connected at the court of Henri III; at the time he published his *Caesars*, he was serving as a royal chaplain, and ranked as a *conseiller du roi*. Not least, then, he was hoping to impress some very grand readers – and on that score, the publication of a French *Caesars* at Paris in 1580 had a pleasing aptness: it was at Paris, twelve hundred and twenty years earlier, that Julian had been acclaimed as Augustus. But a more recent, literary, precedent – Amyot's Plutarch – will have prompted Grangier to anticipate readers beyond the court as well, and may have encouraged his choice of *Caesars* as a text on which to work. Amyot's

French version of Plutarch's *Lives*, first published in 1559 with a dedication to Henri II, had gone on to win a wide and varied readership,[13] and Grangier may have hoped that his translated *Caesars* could tap into it: *Caesars*' cameos of Rome's famous (and infamous) emperors could appeal to the kind of reader who had relished 'les vies des hommes illustres grecs et romains' in Amyot's pages. And for readers who preferred lighter-hearted fare than Amyot's Plutarch offered, *Caesars* mixed its Roman history with humorous banter. On that score, it will have been a further encouragement for Grangier that French translations of Lucian were finding a popular audience: by the time he started on his *Caesars*, French versions of several Lucianic texts were already circulating widely; and at the very time he was translating it, the first 'complete Lucian' in French was in the offing (it was published a year after Grangier's *Caesars*).[14] Not the least part of Lucian's appeal for sixteenth-century readers was his deflating treatment of eminent names in classical mythology and history: it chimed with an 'anti-courtier trend' in contemporary French satire that ridiculed royalty's haughtiness and pomp.[15] The teasing representations of the emperors on parade in *Caesars* strike a similar chord, and Grangier will have sensed its potential breadth of appeal in translation on that count.

Grangier's *Caesars* was the first rendering of any Julianic work into a modern language. Throughout the seventeenth century, moreover, *Caesars* would remain the only Julianic text to be so rendered,[16] except for the so-called 'letter to the Bostrans' – and that is a rather special case (to which we shall later return).[17] *Caesars*, by contrast, was to be often retranslated over the century's course.[18] In 1612, when Cunaeus (i.e. Pieter Kuhn, a professor at Leiden) published his neo-Latin Menippean satire *Sardi Venales* ('Mad Scholars for Sale'), he included within the same volume his own elegant Latin version of *Caesars* – and in this particular version *Caesars* was to circulate quite widely, because Cunaeus' *Sardi Venales*, for reasons that we need not dwell on here, was itself to win enduring popularity;[19] it was republished ten times before 1700, and in four of those editions[20] Cunaeus' *Caesars* retained its place. The two pieces also figured together in a large collection of satires published at Leiden in 1655, the *Elegantiores Praestantium Virorum Satyrae*;[21] and it is a testimony to *Caesars*' growing appeal over the ensuing decades that German and Dutch translations of it appeared in 'stand-alone' editions.[22] Moreover, between the 1660s and 1680s, no fewer than three translators offered new 'stand alone' French versions of *Caesars*. Two of these translators we can set aside here;[23] the important man, for our purposes, is the German scholar-diplomat Ezechiel Spanheim.

Half of Spanheim's ancestry was Bavarian, but he was a Frenchwoman's son and had learned French at an early age.[24] Renowned in his day as an immensely erudite antiquarian, he is best remembered now as a pioneer in numismatics.[25] His interest in Julian was to culminate in his publication of a Greek edition of the collected works at Leipzig in 1696;[26] but its origin ran back three decades to the 1660s, and to *Caesars*. He published his translation of it twice, in markedly different formats. In his thirties, he published a lightly annotated French version of the text at Heidelberg (1666). It was dedicated to his friend Sophie, Duchess of Brunswick (the future Electress of Hanover), as a fellow-devotee of satirical literature: they had recently enjoyed reading Rabelais together.[27] Later, while serving in the 1680s as the Elector of Brandenburg's ambassador at Paris and Versailles, he revised and republished this translation (now dedicated to the Elector) in a greatly enlarged edition, as *Les Césars de l'Empereur Julien, traduits du grec avec des remarques et des preuves, illustrées par les médailles et autres anciens monumens* (Paris 1683): a quarto volume of over 600 pages, with a massive running commentary, expansive end-notes, and several hundred engraved illustrations, mostly of imperial coins.

In the eighteenth century, *Caesars* continued to circulate in Spanheim's version: his 1683 commentary was posthumously republished at Amsterdam in 1728, this time with a flattering dedication by the publisher, François l'Honoré, to an eminent field-marshal in the Habsburgs' service; and his French version of the text, shorn of all notes, was reprinted at Gotha in 1736 as an appendage to an edition of the Greek text, along with Cunaeus' Latin version.[28] Several new translations also appeared in the course of the century. In German, *Caesars* featured among the items offered in a volume published by an academic society at Leipzig in the 1730s, and again in two publications of the 1770s: one paired it with the *Misopogon*; the other was a 'stand-alone' edition.[29] There was a stand-alone edition in Italian, too[30] – but more importantly, for our purposes, there was a new rendering of *Caesars* into French: it was one of several Julianic texts translated by the author of a classic early biography of Julian, the abbé Jean Philippe René de La Bletterie, in a work first published in 1748, and posthumously reissued in 1776.[31] That raised the tally of the French translations up to five.[32] By contrast, even when La Bletterie's book was reissued, there was still no English version of *Caesars* in existence. It was only in 1784 that an English translation finally appeared, in a 'selected works' of Julian translated by one John Duncombe. In what follows, we shall be concerned especially with the contexts, relationship and circulation of Spanheim's and La Bletterie's versions of *Caesars*, and with aspects of their reception in Anglophone circles: in particular, with the echoing of their judgements of the piece in Gibbon's *Decline and Fall*; with the significance of La Bletterie's version as a model for *Caesars*' first English translator, Duncombe; and with the bearing of Spanheim's 1683 edition on a propagandizing work of court art produced c. 1700.

Julian's 'masterpiece', 1583–ca.1800: *Caesars*' passage from French into English

Spanheim may have represented his *Caesars* as first published in 1666 as a literary connoisseur's *divertissement*, but he had already, two years previously, published the first edition of his *magnum opus*, a treatise on the utility of coins as historical evidence; and it is plain from the scale and detailed content of the commentary and illustrative matter in his 1683 edition that, by then, the text had come to serve him partly as peg from which he could hang the fruits of his extraordinary antiquarian and numismatic learning. That said, the dedicatory epistle and preface in the 1683 edition still insisted that a unique interest and utility attached to 'a satire fashioned by an emperor...[about] men who, like him, had occupied the greatest and most august throne in the world – a *jeu d'esprit*, accordingly, on a most noble and refined subject, in which he could amuse himself and instruct us':

> Whatever view may be taken about the value of Julian's works in general, no one could justifiably deny that *Caesars* takes the prize among them. Its advantage lies in equal measure in the importance of its subject, and in the manner in which the subject is treated. There could be no nobler, or more agreeable, or more useful; the very title the work bears itself suffices to establish that. Moreover, in this particular case the value is enhanced for the fact that the work expresses the thoughts of an author who was himself a CAESAR, a man of the same rank and station in life, so to say, as those of whom he speaks... It must be acknowledged, then, that Julian could not have conceived of a more appropriate way to exercise his fine wit; to disclose the excellence of his guiding lights; to instruct the public and his successors; and to bestir himself, through noble emulation [of his better predecessors], to heroic actions, and to the practice of the virtues worthy of an emperor.[33]

In sum, Spanheim avowed, 'nothing could conform better to the taste of our times' and to the 'divertissement du Public' than a translated *Caesars*. It could scarcely be bettered as a text 'to amuse and instruct princes', and it could appeal to 'Gentlemen of the Court and to [its] Ladies as much as to scholars; it could satisfy 'un goût assez universel', indeed, and he hoped that his translation of it – albeit the work of an 'étranger' whose ambassadorial duties had restricted his time for the task – would win the approval of its readers as an accurate and intelligible rendering of the original.

Some sixty years later, Spanheim's assessment of *Caesars* as Julian's best work was emphatically endorsed by the Abbé de La Bletterie. The idea of making a new translation of it had come to La Bletterie long before he finally published his version in 1748. In the prefatory *avertissement* to his earlier *Vie de l'Empereur Julien* (1735), he had indicated that the biography was to serve as a kind of 'introduction' to a larger project already under way – a collected edition of Julian's works in French that would commemorate 'les productions de son esprit', and retrieve them from 'l'obscurité des langues savantes'. And he had acknowledged Spanheim's partial anticipation of the project:

> Petavius' fine Latin version has long ago put Julian within the reach of those who do not know Greek well enough to read him in the original, and the celebrated *Satire of the Caesars,* as rendered into French by Mr. Spanheim with a long and learned commentary, has instructed the most expert [scholars in the field] without scandalizing the most ignorant [laymen].[34]

In the event, La Bletterie published only a small selection of Julian's works, and only thirteen years later. They were appended to a compact narrative of the reign of Julian's successor that he published in 1748, under the title *Histoire de l'Empereur Jovien, et traductions de quelques ouvrages de l'Empereur Julien.* The book gave *Caesars* pride of place among the texts translated,[35] and its preface echoed Spanheim's earlier praises of it:

> [It] is indisputably Julian's masterpiece... I cannot think of any other work of comparable brevity in which one finds so much elegance and substance, or so much instruction provided without the author ever adopting a dogmatic tone, or so much witty amusement provided without his ever ceasing to instruct. In a word, it seems to me that *Caesars* ought to forestall, or at least embarrass, those who reserve their praises solely for the works of classical Greece [without considering imperial Rome].[36]

La Bletterie proceeded, though, to offer a distinctly double-edged verdict on Spanheim's 1683 translation and commentary:

> It is over sixty years since Monsieur Spanheim, whose name is so familiar within the world of letters, undertook the translation of *Caesars* into French. That learned foreigner did not grasp the delicacies of our language and his version only resembles the original in the sense that a skeleton resembles a human body. He added to the text a commentary, and a buttress of remarks and proofs, both adorned with illustrations – in such great profusion, overall, that Julian's little work was lost to sight, in a way, within a Quarto of over six hundred pages. [His version] is a masterpiece of the printer's art, a treasure-house of inadequately digested ancient literature and numismatic erudition. Such a book is a fine adornment for libraries, but it scares off the common herd of readers; for them, the sight of such a prolix commentary inspires indifference, or worse, towards a text which, they suppose, stands in such great need of elucidation.[37]

It was not simply, then, that the 'savant étranger' had not always conveyed the original's literary delicacy in French; his inelegant prose had made a grotesque 'skeleton' out of a charming body. And for general readers, La Bletterie objected, Spanheim's 1683 commentary was more bamboozling than enlightening: rambling far beyond explication of the text itself, it expatiated on topics quite extraneous to it, while often neglecting to clarify basic salient points. La Bletterie proposed a version of *Caesars* that would clear the mists in which Spanheim's prolix notes had shrouded it, and which could better transmit its literary elegance:

> My thought has been to give pleasure to those who do not care for heavy tomes, by presenting them with a translation accompanied only by comments that are strictly necessary, or at least of some relevant interest, and in which I could try to preserve, as far as possible, the spark and charm and cleverness of the original.[38]

Both Spanheim (1629–1710) and La Bletterie (1696–1772) were admired in Anglophone circles as learned savants within their lifetimes. In Spanheim's case, diplomatic service enhanced the fame:[39] in 1685, two years after publishing his *Caesars* commentary, he was ennobled by its dedicatee, the Elector of Brandenburg. As Baron Spanheim, he visited London that year to convey the Elector's congratulations to James II on his accession, and he was later to become an esteemed name in its elite society: from 1702 until his death in 1710 (he was buried in Westminster Abbey) he served as Frederick I of Prussia's Ambassador at London. His antiquarian interests were well known at Anne's court, and assisted by acquaintances he made there;[40] and it was at London in 1706 that he published the third, augmented, edition of his *De praestantia et usu numismatum antiquorum*.[41] Spanheim's fame as a scholar was to rest chiefly on that magnum opus – but a few years before his arrival in London in 1702, someone well placed in its elite circles had been particularly interested in his *Caesars*, too. We shall be amplifying on this episode later.[42]

La Bletterie was a more retiring sort; he had published his 1735 *Vie de Julien* anonymously.[43] In 1746, though, a second edition advertised its author as 'M. l'Abbé de La Blet[t]erie, Professeur d'Eloquence au Collège Roïal', and between 1753 and 1761 he published a series of *Dissertations* on Roman history in the internationally circulating *Mémoires* of the Académie des Inscriptions.[44] On both counts, La Bletterie's name became well known abroad to the *cognoscenti* – and not least among them, to the young Edward Gibbon. Gibbon first read the *Vie de Julien* when he was about twenty, ca. 1758, at Lausanne. For him, it was a golden book: 'it first introduced me to the man and his times'.[45] A few years later, after meeting La Bletterie personally in Paris, he read the 'selected Julian' translations too, and was no less impressed; an entry in his journal in 1764 records his admiration for the translator's exquisite scholarship and generous spirit: 'Quelle littérature, quel goût, et quelle élégance! J'ajoute, et quelle modération! Julien étoit païen, et l'Abbé ne haït que les jésuites!'[46]

Gibbon also immersed himself in Spanheim's scholarship in these years, and it will be plain from the passages we have quoted from Spanheim's and La Bletterie's prefaces that Gibbon's own tribute to *Caesars* in *Decline and Fall* – the tribute with which our chapter opened – was informed by these earlier connoisseurs' verdicts. Gibbon's very phrases there carry echoes of theirs[47] – and La Bletterie's promise in the biography to retrieve Julian's writings 'de l'obscurité des langues savantes' surely inspired the wording of a famous remark about *Decline and Fall* in Gibbon's autobiography: 'all licentious passages are left in the obscurity of a learned language'.[48] When Gibbon himself came to narrate the history of Julian's reign, he naturally consulted Spanheim's 1683 edition of *Caesars* – but he took care to signal in a footnote his concurrence with La Bletterie's criticisms of its defects:

> The French version of the learned Ezechiel Spanheim is coarse, languid, and correct; and his notes, proofs, illustrations &c. are piled on to each other till they form a mass of 557 close-printed quarto pages. The Abbé de La Bletterie [...] has more happily expressed the spirit, as well as the sense, of the original, which he illustrates with some concise and curious notes.[49]

Gibbon himself wrote French elegantly; he was entirely fluent in the language, and when he first encountered La Bletterie's *Vie de Julien c.* 1758 he could savour it in the original. By then, though, the biography was already also circulating in an English version. In 1746, it had been republished not just in a second French edition, but also for a general English readership, as *The Life of the Emperor Julian*. The idea for this book had been put to a leading London printer of the day, William Bowyer (so Bowyer's prefatory advertisement announces), by 'an eminent Writer who has had the good fortune to please the world, and is therefore best entitled to judge of its taste'; the translation itself was done under Bowyer's supervision by a team of three, 'Miss Anna Williams, a blind lady, assisted by two sisters of the name of Wilkinson'.[50] Aficionados of Boswell's *Life of Johnson* will recognize the chief translator as the impecunious and cataract-afflicted bluestocking who joined Johnson's household as a lodger a few years after her translation of the *Vie de Julien* came out: she was to live out her last thirty years there as a regular tea-companion of Johnson; she died at his house in her late seventies, in 1783.[51] By that time, an apt companion for her *Life of Julian* – a version of Julian's own works in English – was finally in the offing: Duncombe's *Select works of the Emperor Julian, and some pieces of the sophist Libanius, translated from the Greek* was published in 1784.[52] Dumcombe's book offered roughly half of Julian's extant oeuvre, in two volumes.[53] The first contained (in this order) *To Themistius*, the *Consolation on Sallust's Departure*, the *Letter to the Athenians*, the Helios myth (extracted from *Against Heraclius*), *To a Priest, Caesars, Misopogon*, and sixteen letters from Libanius to Julian. The second contained seventy-seven letters of Julian and two Libanian orations, (the monodies on Nicomedia and the Temple at Daphne), with a translation of La Bletterie's *Histoire de Jovien* and an abstract in English of one of his *Dissertations*[54] appended.

A word on the personality and social milieu of the author of this work can help to clarify its intellectual pitch and envisaged readership. The Revd. John Duncombe [1729–86] was an M.A. of Corpus Christi, Cambridge; he was successively a minister at parishes in Essex, Soho and Kent, and in his later years he obtained a chaplaincy at Canterbury. He was also a popular man of letters – a published poet and parodist, and a friendly acquaintance in the 1750s of the novelist Samuel Richardson. Under the penname 'Crito', he was a frequent contributor to, and a review-editor for, *The Gentleman's Magazine*. His wife was Susanna Highmore, a celebrated beauty of the day, a daughter of the portrait painter Joseph Highmore, and an habituée of Richardson's literary circle; Duncombe sometimes co-wrote verses with her, and his obituarist dwells on his devotion to their only child, a daughter. He sounds a congenial sort. To catch the flavour of his writings, we can name some of his publications from the 1750s onwards: *Horace Satire 2. 7 imitated by Sir Nicolas Nemo* (1754); *The Feminiad, a poem* (in praise of contemporary female writers, 1754); *Select English letters from Henry VIII to the present*, ed., 2 vols. (1755); and *The Poems of Horace translated* (ed. W. Duncombe, assisted by his son [John], 1755); *Letters by eminent persons deceased*, ed., 2 vols. (1772); *Surry Triumphant, or the Kentish-mens' Defeat: a new ballad, being a parody on Chevy-chase* (a mock Border Ballad recounting a cricket match, 1773); *Elegy written at Canterbury Cathedral* (1778); *from an English Traveller* (translated from the French, 1780); *Fishing: a translation from the Latin of Vanière*(c. 1755, posthumously printed in 1809).[55]

Duncombe's 1784 'selected Julian', published two years before his death in his mid-fifties, was his last solely authored work.[56] The epigraph on its title page set the requisite mood with a verse by the Viscountess Irwin, Anne Ingram (one of the contemporary muses whom Duncombe's *Feminiad* had earlier lauded):

Him Poesy, Philosophy, deplore,
The scepter'd Patriot, who distinctions wav'd,
Lord of himself, by Pagan rites enslaved;

Whom all, but Christians, held their common friend,
Whose very errors had a virtuous end. – *Irwin.*

The poet's *topos* of Julian as a perversely self-ruined soul was echoed in prose on the facing page, in a second epigraph which awkwardly conjoined extracts from the rambling Latin of Spanheim's dedicatory epistle in his 1696 edition of Julian's works:

> The inauspicious name of JULIAN is stamped on the memory of all ages, not more by the extent of his dominions than by the infamy of his deserting the Christian religion: that great and eternal blot, that single stain, which has totally sullied his other graces and accomplishments... It was [...] my intention, I will not say to erase or remove (for what Christian would attempt that?), but [rather at] the least to disguise and extenuate the blemish that his name had thus contracted, by paying some respect to his other virtues: so that [the] elogium of uncommon erudition and elegance which his lucubrations in various branches of literature have received from so many past ages should not, I thought, on that account be with-held from them.

Duncombe himself, of course, had no need to look to 'past ages' to find an eloquent admirer of the learning and literary polish of Julian's writings. At the end of his preface (p. xxxiv), he avows himself 'much indebted to the elegant (I am sorry I cannot say, unexceptionable)[57] *History of the Decline and Fall...*, as will appear by the frequent quotations from that work in the notes', and Duncombe will certainly have been encouraged during the preparation of his translations by the puff that Gibbon's special praise of *Caesars* had given to Julian as a writer: he quotes the passage in a note.[58] It is quite conceivable that Duncombe had not even started work on his 'selected Julian' before the publication, in March 1781, of the relevant volume (vol. 2) of *Decline and Fall*; for a reason that will soon become apparent, the project need not have required many years of labour from him. Or perhaps the idea for it came to him a little earlier, in the late 1770s: one cannot say for sure. But whenever he began work on it, and whatever he may have owed to Gibbon, Duncombe acknowledged that he owed a broader debt to La Bletterie: his preface opens with the statement that La Bletterie's 1735 biography and 1748 'selected Julian' 'have been very serviceable to me in the following translations'.[59] That brief formulation rather understates the debt's extent. The selection of Julianic texts that Duncombe translated largely replicates, in an altered order, La Bletterie's 1748 selections,[60] and the bulk of his footnotes are drawn directly from (most of them simply translate) those of La Bletterie. So too, the greater part of Duncombe's preface, some 25 pages of it, self-avowedly translates La Bletterie's: 'the occasion and the motives that encouraged me in this undertaking being the same with those of the French Academician, I cannot so well express them as in the same words'. Duncombe's readers are accordingly told the following of *Caesars* (pp. xxiii–xxv):

> [It is] deemed unquestionably the master-piece of Julian... I venture to say profane antiquity does not afford any piece which is comparable to it for the merit of the subject, and very few which ought to be preferred to it for the merit of the execution... A Roman emperor with much taste and genius for raillery, ready to seize on the ridiculous and never letting it escape in others, not even in himself, knowing how to distinguish those light clouds which constitute the difference between the middling and the good, the excellent and the perfect, and nourished with reading of Plato and Aristotle and speaking their language like themselves, here assembles in one piece all the emperors who reigned before him for about 400 years... It is a moving picture, in which the spectator sees moving rapidly before his eyes, but without confusion, those masters of the world despoiled of their grandeur, and reduced to their vices and virtues... I do not think that in any work so short are to be found so many characters and manners, so much refinement and solidity, so much instruction without the author adopting a dogmatical (*sic*) tone, so much wit and pleasantry, without his ever ceasing to instruct. In a word, the *Caesars*, it seems to me, ought to undeceive, or at least embarrass, those who have voted an exclusive esteem to the productions of ancient Greece [over those of imperial Rome].

All that, and much more in the preface, is simply La Bletterie parroted in English – which raises a question about Duncombe's translations of the Julianic texts themselves. Just how 'very serviceable' had La Bletterie's versions been to him in that connexion? Duncombe's preface opens by praising them as 'executed with uncommon elegance and judgement', and observes that, while the 1735 *Vie de Julien* had already been Englished by 'some ladies', La Bletterie's 1748 book of translations had never been translated: '[it] has till now been to our country "a fountain sealed".' That might seem to imply that Duncombe was simply aiming to open its contents for English readers who could not read Julian easily in French, still less 'the learned languages' – but Duncombe goes on to append a proviso to his praise: he finds La Bletterie's versions 'too free and periphrastical', 'beautiful but flattering'; he himself will prefer a middle course between them and the 'literal versions' whose stylistic awkwardness La Bletterie had criticized, '[so as] to represent this imperial author just as he is, as far as the idiom of the two languages [Greek and English] will admit, in which the English, in point of analogy with the Greek, has the advantage over the French' (pp. iv–vi). The proviso might suggest (no doubt, it was meant to suggest) a fair measure of scholarly independence on Duncombe's part; but certain countervailing facts are telling. For one thing, Duncombe never discusses textual variants in the manuscripts, and gives no clear statement of what particular editions of the Greek he was using or preferring. The occasional references in his notes to the earlier editors Cantoclarus, Petavius and Spanheim all come at second hand from La Bletterie's own notes – and anyway, none of them attends to matters of textual criticism. There is no sign of serious consultation at first hand by Duncombe of Spanheim's learned 1683 commentary and 'proof' notes, and on the (very few) occasions when a note in Duncombe queries La Bletterie's translation on a detail, it is never in connexion with a MS reading; it is always a question of how to construe the Greek (and unintentionally, Duncombe's notes on these occasions disclose the Frenchman's superior scholarship; Duncombe's ear for Julian's Greek was no match for La Bletterie's).[61]

Moreover, there is a clear proof in Duncombe's translation of the close of *Caesars* that he lacked expert acquaintance with the state of play in Julianic textual scholarship in his day. At the end of the emperors' contest in *Caesars*, the humiliated Constantine runs off and finds an apt supporter, a preacher offering pardon for all sinners through the rite of baptism (366a). The preacher in question is certainly Jesus – but Duncombe (and La Bletterie before him, and Spanheim likewise) did not realize that; all three misidentified the preacher as a son of Constantine. Their shared error had a simple cause. In preparing the 1577 *editio princeps* of *Caesars*, Cantoclarus had misread the Greek text in manuscript at this point; he had mistaken an abbreviated form of Jesus' name (Ἰησοῦν) for υἱόν, 'son', and the false reading persisted in all the early editions of Julian's collected works.[62] It was only in 1736 that Heusinger, in his Gotha edition of *Caesars*, detected the error, and argued that the true reading must be 'Jesus'.[63] La Bletterie, when he published his French *Caesars* in his 1748 'selected Julian', was still unaware of the existence of Heusinger's edition – and hence of this correction.[64] His ignorance of it is disquieting at first sight, but understandable at a pinch; in his 1735 *Vie de Julien* La Bletterie had spoken of his translations as a project already under way, and *Caesars* in his view, the best of all Julian's works, and one badly in need of rescue from Spanheim's coarse French prose – was surely one of the works he tackled first. La Bletterie's translation of *Caesars*, then, though only published in 1748, may well have been already completed in draft a good decade earlier, by the late 1730s – a time when Heusinger's 1736 edition of *Caesars* had only very recently come out. Duncombe, by contrast, was translating *Caesars* almost half a century later – and yet he still remained completely ignorant of Heusinger's correction (his footnote on the relevant passage simply translates that of La Bletterie). La Bletterie's unawareness in 1748 of Heusinger's correction is a minor blemish on his scholarship;

Duncombe's unawareness of it in the 1780s marks him out as distinctly an amateur in Julianic textual matters.

The bibliographical evidence for Duncombe's earlier publications tells a similar story. It discloses translations of a few selected items of Latin poetry, and from two books by French prose authors,[65] but it gives no indication that he had ever translated any text composed in Greek before embarking on Julian. To be clear, the title page of Duncombe's 'selected Julian' announces a translation 'from the Greek' (and his Greek was quite passable, no doubt); but all things considered, it looks much likelier that in the case of *Caesars* and the other Julianic works that La Bletterie had translated, Duncombe was usually working mainly from La Bletterie's French, casually checking it against the Greek (and parallel Latin) columns in a standard editions of the collected works.[66] His late-developing interest in Julian was that of a cultivated Anglican clergyman writing with a general readership in mind – a clergyman who well sensed that Gibbon's 'elegant' account of Julian entailed a hostile judgement on the early Church, and to whom a learned French abbé's capacity to admire Julian within the limits of piety was reassuring. His 'selected Julian' looks to have found, for a time, the readers he had in view: *The Gentleman's Magazine*, which circulated at the time in around 10,000 copies, reviewed it over four pages (three of which discussed and excerpted *Caesars*) and printed further excepts; and by 1798 it had gone into a third edition.[67] Arguably, it was also a stimulus to the production of English versions of Julianic texts which Duncombe had not translated, but which he had mentioned in his preface (parroting La Bletterie, again) as likely to interest the philosophically inclined: the Neoplatonist Thomas Taylor's rendering of the *Hymns*, at any rate, was published in nine years after Duncombe's volume had first appeared.[68] On the other hand, it seems a pointer to changing literary taste at the end of the eighteenth century that Duncombe's (and more significantly, Gibbon's) advocacy of *Caesars* as a masterpiece of learned wit would fail to induce anyone later to provide in English what had long since been available in French and German – a 'stand-alone' version of *Caesars* translated and annotated for a general readership in search of literary diversion. No such book has ever appeared in English, to this day.

The 'instructiveness' of *Caesars*

For Gibbon, and likewise for Spanheim and La Bletterie, the literary polish and humour of *Caesars* was only a part of its appeal: all of them valued it highly, too, as a text that could 'instruct' readers in serious connexions – historical, or political, or moral. No other classical opuscule, La Bletterie declared, supplied 'much instruction without ever adopting [...] a dogmatic tone, so much wit and pleasantry, without [...] ever ceasing to instruct';[69] and on Spanheim's reckoning, 'no nobler, or more agreeable, or more useful subject' could be wanted in a book than the testing of the merits of history's mighty rulers, 'les Maîtres du Monde' – a still 'more valuable' subject, he added, when addressed by 'an author [who] was himself a Caesar, himself of the same rank and station in life [...] as those of whom he speaks'.[70] Spanheim's and La Bletterie's phrases were manifestly in Gibbon's mind when he so fulsomely commended *Caesars* in *Decline and Fall*:

> [It] is one of the most agreeable and instructive productions of ancient wit... [and its] value is enhanced by the rank of its author. A prince, who delineates with freedom the vices and virtues of his predecessors, subscribes, in every line, the censure or approbation of his own conduct.[71]

In Gibbon's mind, that is to say, *Caesars* was chiefly 'instructive' for a historian of the Roman empire – and especially, for a historian of Julian: its insider's review of the virtues (and crimes and follies) of a line of monarchs that ran from Julius Caesar to Constantine, and its elevation of Marcus as the perfect ruler in the estimation of the gods, could illuminate Julian's own guiding ideals and aspirations as a Roman emperor. Spanheim and La Bletterie had also appreciated its 'utility' on that score – but there is a difference to observe between Gibbon's case and theirs. In its closing scene, *Caesars'* hostile representation of Constantine takes on a patently anti-Christian edge: it mocks the baptismal rite. For the 'philosophic historian' Gibbon, that was no obstacle to unstinting praise of *Caesars*: on the contrary, it chimed with his own judgement that Constantine was a hypocritical convert, that the Church he promoted was an enfeebling influence within the empire – and that Christianity itself was '[a] mode of superstition'.[72] Spanheim and La Bletterie, by contrast, were both devout believers, and the anti-Christian element in *Caesars* necessarily complicated their responses to it; for them, it was a significant obstacle to praise that needed to be negotiated somehow, if one wished to commend *Caesars* to Christian readers as an 'instructive' masterpiece.[73] On that score, the religious affiliations of Spanheim and La Bletterie arguably predisposed them to discover moral lessons in *Caesars* that could help to compensate for the anti-Christian element in it; and in Spanheim's case, at least, there were also political affiliations in the background of which we need to take account.

Spanheim was the son of a celebrated Calvinist theologian, and devoutly Protestant throughout his life.[74] In his twenties he himself had been appointed to a chair in theology at Geneva, Calvinism's heartland; and his long career as a diplomat, from its beginnings at Rome (1661–65) to his final posting as Prussian Ambassador at London (1702–10), was spent in the service of three firmly Protestant rulers. He began it as the agent at Rome of the Elector Palatine, Charles-Ludwig (the brother of the Duchess Sophie to whom Spanheim was to dedicate his early [1666] edition of *Caesars*). He went on to serve two Electors of Brandenburg successively: firstly, Frederick-Wilhelm (to whom he would dedicate his 1683 *Caesars*); and after Frederick-Wilhelm's death in 1688, his son Frederick (who in 1701 would take the title 'King of Prussia'). He was Frederick-Wilhelm's envoy in London from 1678–80, at a critical point in British politics: the formation around the First Earl of Shaftesbury of a 'Whig' faction determined to exclude the Catholic Duke of York (the future James II) from the succession. Spanheim will certainly have encountered members of this circle in the course of his duties at this time. In April 1680 he was transferred to Paris as Brandenburg's Ambassador at the court of Louis XIV, and he remained in post there until April 1689. He was there in October 1685 to witness a major turn in the decade's politics: the outlawing of the Huguenots (that is to say, French Calvinists) by the Revocation of the Edict of Nantes. In the immediate wake of the edict, Spanheim's actions disclosed his Protestant loyalties: he sheltered Huguenot fugitives in his ambassadorial residence, and worked to win them a permanent refuge in Berlin. His loyalty to the Protestant cause in politics is clearly discernable, too, in the *Relation de la cour de France en 1690*, a text submitted privately to the Elector Frederick after Spanheim's recall from Paris to Berlin in 1689. The *Relation* is a long, descriptive report on the court of Louis XIV by an expertly informed observer.[75] Its purpose was advisory, and it avoids polemic – but nonetheless, it finds occasion to lament the plight of the French Protestants and the 'cruel' sufferings inflicted on them by Catholic intolerance,[76] and its survey of the pomp and 'absolutist' style of court-life at Versailles is coloured by Spanheim's Calvinist moral ethos. It itemizes certain proclivities of Louis as especially reprehensible for their pernicious influence on his court and government: his 'limitless passion' for self-glorification, and for the veneration of his person as a perfect and all-powerful monarch; his 'criminal passion' for adulterous sexual liaisons; and his 'blindly superstitious devotion' to the rituals and ceremonial pomp of Roman Catholicism.[77]

Spanheim's Calvinist morality and his Protestant political loyalties were inseparable – and his attraction to *Caesars* as a text imparting serious instruction within a humorous frame should be appraised with an eye to their conjunction. *Caesars*' satire deflates the pretensions of the high and mighty: it summons the vainglorious ghosts of rulers who had once appeared all-powerful and exposes their crimes and follies before a court in which readers, as well as gods, are judges. For Spanheim, one suspects, the Roman emperors teased in *Caesars* for their vanity and hypocrisy found their modern counterparts in two institutions especially: the Papacy, and the court of the Sun King at Versailles. It is more than a coincidence, perhaps, that his translation of *Caesars* originally appeared in 1666, the year after his return to Germany from his service as a fledgling diplomat at Rome – and when he re-published it in 1683, of course, he was three years into his stint as Brandenburg's Ambassador at the court of Louis XIV. By then, Spanheim was a shrewd observer of the intrigues at play beneath the Bourbon court's surface glitter – and the 1683 commentary's opening matter is suggestive in this connexion: it hints that when Ambassador Spanheim chose *Caesars* as a text to work on in his leisure-hours, the choice owed something to a Calvinist's distaste for the absolutist pretensions emblazoned in the pomp and Catholic ritual of the court of Louis XIV.[78] A clue lies in the dedicatory letter addressed to Spanheim's employer, the Elector Frederick-Wilhelm. The 'Great Elector' was a fellow-Calvinist, and was genuinely revered by Spanheim as a model of Protestant virtue and moderation[79] – but that did not preclude the flatteries conventional on such occasions, and the dedicatory letter lauds him as a ruler superior to any of the emperors he will discover in *Caesars*' pages:

> In you, Sire, one finds a hero in whom there is no weak point for satire to fix upon, and in whom it can discover nothing to condemn – no debaucheries, no rages, no injustices, no character-flaws, nor any other derangements of soul or mind; in short, [it cannot discover in you] any of the vices and blemishes that it so bountifully unmasks here [i.e. in *Caesars*] in an Alexander, a Julius, an Augustus, a Trajan, a Marcus Aurelius, a Constantine – which is to say, in even the greatest, wisest, or most virtuous heroes of Greek and Roman antiquity.[80]

The flattery in this passage surely also hints to the dedicatee (very delicately, of necessity, in a work published 'avec privilège du Roi' at Paris) that another comparison could have been drawn: a comparison between the virtuous and modest Protestant Elector at Berlin and the Roman Catholic reigning at Versailles. Louis' 'criminal' sexual incontinence, and his 'blind devotion' to Catholic ritual, would clearly count as 'derangements of soul' for Spanheim; and as for his 'limitless passion' for self-glorification, he was routinely hailed by his panegyrists as a 'new Alexander', a 'new Augustus' and a 'new Constantine'.[81] His identification with Constantine will have been especially unappealing to a learned Calvinist for its Catholic associations: Spanheim knew that it had an earlier parallel in the efforts of counter-Reformation propagandists to appropriate Constantine as a vindicator of the Papacy's ancestral temporal authority, and a model for contemporary Catholic monarchs to emulate.[82] When he wrote his dedication to the Elector, moreover, Spanheim will also almost certainly have known that a high minister at Versailles had commissioned a statue of Louis from Bernini, to be modelled loosely on the equestrian statue of Constantine that Bernini had earlier made to adorn the Scala Regia at the Vatican Palace.[83]

In our view, then, there is reason to suspect that *Caesars'* aptness as a frame on which Spanheim could hang his prodigious antiquarian learning will not have been the whole of its attraction for him at Paris in the early 1680s. Its satirical vision of kings as (mostly) erring figures with feet of clay made it a text that could also offer Spanheim a private refuge from the pressures that diplomatic politesse imposed on him as a Calvinist envoy at a glittering Catholic court. If this line of argument were pressed further, it might be postulated that Julian himself, inasmuch as he had signalled in *Caesars* the pretensions and delinquencies of a line of Roman emperors stretching back for centuries, possessed an affinity of sorts in Spanheim's mind with contemporary Protestant opponents of (could we say, 'apostates from'?) the Papacy. But nothing Spanheim says suggests that much, and in relation to his own case such an argument would be entirely hypothetical. There is a parallel case, though, very close in time to him, for which there is quite decisive evidence, and which allows us to connect the publication of Spanheim's 1683 commentary with an English politician's estimate of *Caesars'* potential 'instructiveness' around 1700. The evidence lies not in a text, but in a visual image: *Caesars* was to be translated into paint as well as print.

Caesars on a wall: the Hampton Court Palace fresco and Spanheim's *Caesars*

Between 1700 and 1702, the court painter Antonio Verrio was working at Hampton Court Palace in the employment of William III; a major renovation of the Palace was in progress, and Verrio was commissioned to decorate the walls surrounding the newly created King's Staircase. The fresco he produced for the occasion evokes classical antiquity in its subject-matter, and seems designed to impart an allegorical message – but no extant document from the time specifies the subject depicted in the fresco, and for a long time no art historian correctly construed the allegory contained within it. It was only in 1939 that Edgar Wind saw what underpinned the fresco's programme; in a classic paper published the next year, he showed that it was fundamentally inspired by *Caesars*.[84] On one wall, Julian sits at a writing desk, with Hermes hovering close by (Fig. 1). The gods are at

Fig. 1
By gracious permission of Her Majesty the Queen.

Fig. 2
By gracious permission of Her Majesty the Queen.

tables on the ceiling above, feasting in the heavens. Julian is looking towards the adjoining wall, which depicts the story that Hermes is recounting in an intricate Olympian scene (Fig. 2). At the top, just left of centre, one sees Dionysus reclining on a cloud, and Silenus next to him; on the lower reaches of the cloud, to the left and right respectively, Heracles and Romulus plead for their respective protégés to be allowed to ascend to a table on the crest of Olympus; on the ground, below Heracles, stands Alexander; and below Romulus, a dozen Caesars are bunched in a line, with Nemesis descending threateningly from the sky above them. Having identified the fresco's basic subject, Wind went on to explicate its programme with reference to the political crisis that had brought Verrio's royal employer to England a dozen years before the fresco was painted. On his reading, it celebrates the 'Glorious Revolution' of 1688: the collapse of the Stuart dynasty with the flight of the Catholic James II to France, and his replacement by the Protestant Prince of Orange, subsequently crowned as William III. The line of Caesars, championed by Romulus, represents the dethroned James, and more generally, the Roman Catholic dynasts of Europe – and by implication, the Papacy. The solitary figure of Alexander, the late-arriving Greek championed by Heracles in *Caesars*, represents the Dutchman William, England's Protestant saviour.

At first sight, there is a major obstacle (one that Wind did not address) to the identification of Alexander with William: the Alexander of *Caesars* is no spotless paragon – and he does not win the contest. On those counts, William ought surely to have been represented by Marcus Aurelius, rather – and an intricate case along those lines has been fascinatingly argued lately.[85] In our view, the new argument rather overplays the obstacle's seriousness, and does not decisively disprove Wind's reading.[86] But for our purposes, it does not matter whether Wind was right or wrong in this particular connexion; for us, the essential point Wind made (and it is indisputable) is that whoever devised the fresco's programme – not Verrio himself, one assumes, but a highly placed advisor or supporter of William – clearly had Julian's *Caesars* in his mind. Just what had prompted the deviser to exploit this particular text as an item of visual propaganda? The answer to that question takes us back to the early 1680s – and *en passant*, to a text that we have identified earlier as the only Julianic work, apart from *Caesars*, to have been published in a modern language throughout the seventeenth century.

In 1681, two years before Spanheim published his *Caesars* commentary, a pamphlet circulated in London under the title *Seasonal Remarks on the Deplorable Fall* [i.e., the apostasy] *of the Emperour Julian, with an epistle of his to the Citizens of Bostra.* The political atmosphere in London was exceptionally volatile: 1681 was the year in which the efforts of the First Earl of Shaftesbury to exclude the Catholic James of York from the succession earned him imprisonment in the Tower on a charge of high treason. The pamphlet was subtle propaganda in support of Shaftesbury's cause, composed by a highly learned author who styled himself 'Philaretus Anthropopolita'.[87] Ingeniously, the author did not mention Shaftesbury's name or case at all; instead, he found an ancient precursor to them in Julian, an 'excellent person' (so the argument ran) whose 'tragical Apostasy' would never have occurred in better times; its root cause had been 'the Avarice and Ambition of Bishops', whose 'modelling [of] Religion on Court-Intrigues' had 'metamorphos'd [the Church] into an Absolute Tyranny' under Constantine.[88] The pamphleteer thus idealised the Apostate as akin to a virtuous Whig – a Protestant champion of moderation and religious toleration standing resolute against Catholic authoritarianism. To document his argument for the 'impartial Charity' of this 'discerning Prince', he offered an English version of the so-called *Letter to the Bostrans* (strictly speaking, an imperial edict issued in 362), in which Julian ordered the pagan and Christian communities of Bostra to desist from mutual violence and henceforth share their city more harmoniously.[89] And to illustrate the debauched condition of the Church which Julian had abandoned, he also offered a lively rendering of the passage at the close of *Caesars* in which Constantine's son (or so the pamphleteer supposed – really, we have noted earlier, it was Jesus)[90] promises a general amnesty for all sinners through the mechanism of baptism (pp. 18–19):

> Ho! Whoever is either Sodomite, Murderer, Rogue or Villain, let him dread nothing but repair hither, with this water I'll make him clean in a trice: And if he shall happen to repeat the same Crimes, if he will but thump his breast, and box his noddle, I'll warrant him as innocent as the Child unborn.

For the pamphleteer, this advertisement for the automatic pardoning of inwardly unrepentant repeat-offenders with a splash of water nicely epitomized the excesses of Catholic ritualism. He pointedly observed that the Jesuit Petavius, in the Latin crib he had provided in his 1630 edition of Julian's works, 'durst not translate [this passage] to his Catholick friends'; the pamphleteer, though, could consult the Greek original and offer the passage in English 'to pious Protestants without the least offence, since they derive not their religion from Constantine's bishops, but from Christ immediately'. Julian, he implied, was a Protestant *avant la lettre* – an apostate not from the true faith, but from a travesty of it inflicted on the Roman empire under Constantine, and perpetuated subsequently by the Papacy.[91]

The real name of the learned pamphleteer 'Philaretus Anthropopolita' remains unknown. Wind conjectured that he may have been the philosopher John Locke, an intimate friend and supporter of Shaftesbury. The idea is not implausible in itself, and potentially has a bearing on the commissioning of the Hampton Court fresco *c.* 1700: Locke was later a fervent supporter of William III, and a friend in the late 1690s of two high-ranking Whig politicians who both were notable patrons of the arts – John Somers (William's Lord Chancellor); and the Third Earl of Shaftesbury (the First Earl's grandson, whose education Locke had supervised in the early 1680s).[92] But 'Philaretus' could just as easily have been some other learned man who moved, like Locke, in the First Earl's intellectual circle. For Wind's argument, that would not matter; in either case, on his view, a memory of the 1681 pamphlet's image of Julian as a model Protestant prince *avant la lettre* was to be preserved for two decades within a close circle of Whig intellectuals, and was to inspire someone influential in high politics *c.* 1700 to press Julian's *Caesars* into service in an allegorical fresco celebrating William's accession as the salvation of English liberty.[93] As an explanation of a route by which the idealized image of Julian propounded in the pamphlet could persist in Whiggish memory, Wind's argument is entirely persuasive; it certainly does not suffice, though, to explain the specific choice of the emperors' contest narrated in *Caesars* as the programme for the fresco. In the pamphlet, one should be clear, the central subject is Julian, not his *Caesars*: 'Philaretus' only quotes *Caesars* once, and only for a single detail – the proclamation uttered near its close by Constantine's baptiser. There is not a word said in the pamphlet to hint at the central narrative of *Caesars*, the parade and competition of the monarchs; the pamphlet itself, then, cannot have been the chief source of inspiration for the programme of the fresco. On that score, Wind's argument needs a supplement – and the extra ingredient needed is Spanheim's *Caesars*.

We have observed earlier that Spanheim was serving as an envoy at London from 1678 to early 1680, and that his duties will have brought him into casual contact, at least, with some of Shaftesbury's elite associates.[94] It is also clear that he was already working on his *Caesars* commentary at this time; he mentions, for instance, that when diplomatic business took him to Windsor he took the chance to visit the eminent scholar Isaac Vossius, who lived nearby, to inspect 'the best and oldest manuscript' of *Caesars* (a volume which Vossius allowed him to take to France when he was transferred to Paris in April 1680).[95] It is conceivable that the future 'Philaretus' had heard of Spanheim's *Caesars* project indirectly, or even had met him, at this time – but for our purposes, neither of these possibilities matters. When Spanheim arrived in England in 1678, he was already famous for his antiquarian erudition (the second edition of his *De praestantia et usu numismatum antiquorum* had appeared in 1671), and during his two-year sojourn there he will certainly have conversed with other learned men about his *Caesars* project (Vossius is a case in point). After his move to Paris, he continued to correspond with English scholars in the early 1680s;[96] and in 1685, two years after his *Caesars* commentary appeared, he could renew some old acquaintances in London: he made a brief visit there in April, ennobled now as Baron Spanheim, as Brandenburg's representative at the coronation of James II. The 1683 commentary, one can be sure, will have found some scholarly readers in England from the year of its publication onwards, and within a few years a fair number of cultivated men will have at least admired its opening pages and engraved illustrations: the book became famous also as a masterpiece of the printer's art, an 'ornement des bibliothèques'.[97]

For us, a special interest attaches to one particular illustration in the 1683 commentary: the handsome frontispiece designed for it by Pierre le Pautre (Fig. 3). At the top of the quarto page, the gods are feasting at tables in a cloudy heaven. A solicitous Romulus is standing close to Zeus; below them, to the left, Dionysus and Silenus are reclining on a cloud. Further downwards, to the right, stands Alexander (responding to a jest of Silenus, it appears); five Roman Caesars, his rivals in the contest, are bunched in a line behind him. In the foreground, at the bottom left, Julian sits at a writing desk, conversing with Hermes; at the bottom right, in the distance, a couple of villainous emperors are being hauled off to the depths of Tartarus.

Fig. 3
By permission of Syndics of Cambridge University Library.

The parallels between le Pautre's image and Verrio's at Hampton Court are not exact: le Pautre's image lacks Heracles, and Verrio's lacks the villainous pair descending to Tartarus – and Verrio expanded the line of Caesars from five to twelve, evoking the familiar Suetonian number.[98] But they are close enough to establish for sure that whoever devised the programme for the fresco had pondered on the scene depicted in the frontispiece of Spanheim's *Caesars*, and had made its existence known to Verrio;[99] the fresco manifestly echoes the frontispiece not only in its choice of subject, but in some essential compositional details.[100] In the deviser's mind, the scene that he observed in the engraving fused with the Whiggish intellectuals' idealizing of Julian as a cipher for princely moderation, and he conceived the idea of commissioning a visual representation of *Caesars* on a scale far grander than a page in a quarto book. Whether he himself had ever read the 1681 pamphlet of 'Philaretus' is best left an open question; he could easily have picked up on its praises of Julian indirectly, in conversation with some learned Whig. By contrast, the programme that he devised for the Hampton Court fresco required direct knowledge not simply of *Caesars*, but of *Caesars* in a specific illustrated edition – the 1683 commentary by Spanheim, with the frontispiece by le Pautre. Moreover, there is a telling hint in the fresco that its deviser (or else Verrio himself) had looked not only at the frontispiece in Spanheim's book, but also at the French translation he supplied. Of the twelve Caesars depicted in the fresco, one holds a stringed instrument. He is the music-loving Nero, who figures briefly in a walk-on part in *Caesars*: Julian's Nero arrives for the feast on Olympus with a *kithara* in his hand, but is summarily thrown into the river Cocytus for punishment in Tartarus (311c). In French, the traditional rendering of *kithara* would be either 'lyre' or 'harpe', but Spanheim, for a reason he explained at length in a note, preferred to render the word as 'guitarre' – and the Nero of Hampton Court fresco, one finds, is not holding a lyre or a harp: he is playing a kind of guitar.

Verrio's fresco was completed in 1702. As it happened, Spanheim returned to London that same year, in June, as Prussian Ambassador at the Court of Anne (William III having died in March); he would be based there till his own death, eight years later. We cannot be sure that he ever viewed the fresco whose theme his 1683 *Caesars* had helped to inspire; but it is hard to believe that he never came to hear of its existence. On our argument, he could have contemplated the Protestant propaganda of its subtext with equanimity: the Dutch prince glorified in the fresco had been raised as a Calvinist, and had steadfastly supported the persecuted Huguenots – and on our view, Spanheim's own sense of *Caesars*' 'instructiveness' was bound up with his firmly Calvinist moral outlook and his loyalty to the Protestant cause in politics.

The virtuous writer: La Bletterie, Gibbon and Voltaire on Julian as *Caesars*' author

Personal religious allegiances, we have suggested earlier, were also to colour the Abbé de La Bletterie's perception of *Caesars*' moral value. The argument we have formulated for Spanheim's case is plainly not applicable to La Bletterie as it stands: La Bletterie was a Catholic priest. It is not hard, though, to construct a variant on the argument that *is* applicable to him. In his own eyes, La Bletterie was a pious Catholic – but he adhered to Jansenism, a movement with mystical tendencies which had developed within Catholicism over the seventeenth century, and which both the ecclesiastical and the secular authorities had come to distrust. To an outsider's eye, Jansenism could evoke a Protestant ethos; it privileged inner faith and piety over the outward forms of religious observance; it commended an uncompromising moral rigour, as against what was perceived to be the laxness of Jesuit theory and practice on that score; and its theology of predestined salvation had an affinity with Calvinist doctrines. From the 1650s onwards, its teachings had been declared heretical in a series of Papal Bulls: the Jesuits, especially, were keen to eradicate the movement. Louis XIV had sensed a challenge to Bourbon absolutism in it, and its adherents in France had been sporadically penalized with some vigour in his reign. They were under attack again in the period 1715–*c*.1730[101] – which is to say, the 'persecution' extended well into the lifetime of La Bletterie. His own career as a scholar-priest had suffered setbacks on this count. In the 1740s, his learning was to earn him membership of the Académie des Inscriptions (1742) and a chair of rhetoric at the Collège Royal (1746). Nonetheless, in 1743 his election to the Académie Française was personally vetoed by Louis XV; and at an earlier point in his career, in 1730, he had been expelled from the Oratoire de France and had needed to eke out a living for several years as a children's tutor.[102] Against that background, the journal entry in which Gibbon praises La Bletterie's Julianic scholarship is worth recalling: 'What moderation! Julian was a pagan, and [yet] the abbé hates only the Jesuits!'[103] Gibbon here ascribes to La Bletterie an antipathy to religious intolerance that could be traced back to his personal experience as a Jansenist assailed by Catholic zealots; and he implies that the experience was not irrelevant to La Bletterie's undertaking a prolonged and careful study of the reign and writings of Julian – an emblem, in the popular Catholic tradition, of devilish persecution, as well as apostasy. The point is hard to doubt: the *Vie de l'Empereur Julien*, first published anonymously in 1735, was written in the lean years after La Bletterie's expulsion from the Oratoire; and its *avertissement* announced that the author had already conceived a project for a French translation of Julian's own writings that could convey their 'spirit' to a broad readership unable to peruse them in 'the learned languages'.

La Bletterie's personal antipathy to authoritarian zeal, and to the *folie de grandeur* it could instil in high places, has a particular bearing on his estimate of *Caesars*. We recall the specific terms in which he praised it as Julian's masterpiece: it 'imparted much instruction, without the author ever adopting a dogmatic tone'; it 'stripped the masters of the world of their grandeur, reducing them to their vices and virtues'; its author was 'quick to grasp the ridiculousness [of grandeur], never it escape his notice in the case of others, nor even in himself'. There is a paradox, though, to be observed in this connexion. What La Bletterie says of Julian as *Caesars'* author differs markedly from his earlier characterization of him as emperor at the start of his 1735 biography; there, he represents Julian as a ruler driven by 'an uncontrolled passion for glory' – one who pursued his policies with 'a kind of fanaticism', and who was not free of 'the faults which [his] *amour propre* perceive[d] only in others'.[104] Just what La Bletterie was thinking of, on that last count, can be inferred from his note on the passage in *Caesars* in which Hadrian is teased as a star-gazer who was forever prying into ineffable mysteries (311d). La Bletterie was prompted to remark that much the same could be said of Julian: he and Hadrian were both 'full of zeal for idolatry', 'superstitious [...] astrologers wanting to know everything, so constantly inquisitive as to be accused of magic'. And the likeness did not end there: Julian, assuredly, 'did not have the infamous [homosexual] vices of Hadrian [...], but he had almost all his [other] faults and absurdities'; both of them were 'fickle, obstinate, and vain of soul'.[105]

Moreover, at one point in his comparison of Julian with Hadrian, La Bletterie entertains a possibility which would imply a very hostile view indeed of Julian: 'they both passed very wise laws and performed many merciful actions; but Hadrian seemed cruel sometimes, and some say that ["l'on dit que"] Julian was only humane out of vanity'. La Bletterie was here touching on two polarized images of Julian generated by a contemporary ideological debate about religious tolerance. Enlightenment savants in France had argued that the Church Fathers' representation of Julian as a bloody persecutor was a gross calumny, and that in truth he had been a model of tolerance. Voltaire, for instance (like 'Philaretus Anthropopolita' before him), had directed those interested to know the facts to the *Letter to the Bostrans*: 'Read [it], and respect his memory'.[106] To save the Fathers' fantasies of the Apostate's masterminding of clandestine séances at which Christian youths and virgins were ritually disembowelled, a Jesuit author had offered a strained counter-argument:

Julian, he insisted, merely assumed 'le masque de la virtu' in public, to protect his reputation. La Bletterie's own view was far more nuanced; he discounted the lurid fantasies, and he did not believe that Julian had only affected to be humane out of a sense of vanity – but he did think that the emperor's humanity had failed him in his dealings with the Christians. He was in no doubt that Julian should be called a 'persecuteur', notwithstanding the ostensibly tolerant tone of the *Letter to the Bostrans*; his notes on it anticipate Gibbon's pithy summation of its import: 'Julian professes his moderation, and betrays his zeal'.[107] If Julian had returned victorious from Persia, La Bletterie surmised, 'all who remained true to the Christian religion would undoubtedly have perished, unless' – and here, the Huguenots' case was plainly in the writer's thoughts – 'unless they went off to seek asylum among foreigners'.[108]

La Bletterie, then, was quite clear in his mind that Julian's own actions as emperor had fallen short of the imperial ideals he commended in *Caesars*. But as a Jansenist historian, he was also well aware that there were Catholics whose ingenuity and zeal in engineering persecution easily matched Julian's; and as a Jansenist priest, he was inclined to look for personal qualities in Julian that could partially redeem him. Once the glaring exception of his dealings with Christians had been duly registered and deplored, Julian could be credited with some compensating merits: the austere simplicity of his private life (not least, his studiousness and virtual celibacy) appealed to La Bletterie; so did the affable style that Julian had cultivated in public settings, and the distaste for pretentious grandiosity evinced in his pruning of the bloated imperial court at Constantinople.[109] La Bletterie judged that in these respects, and in many of his laws, Julian had exhibited a sense of moderation rarely found in emperors – and as a connoisseur of Julian's writings, he found its most eloquent expression in *Caesars*. The piece could not be unqualifiedly praised, of course; the mockery of baptism at the close of its narrative could only be deplored by Christian readers, and La Bletterie devoted a note to the point that runs for several pages.[110] We have already observed earlier, though, that he never comprehended the real magnitude of Julian's blasphemy in this brief passage, because he did not realize that the preacher it depicts is Jesus Christ in person.[111] As La Bletterie construed the passage, its insult was directed at Constantine, not Christ: its purpose was to damn the emperor as a criminal and hypocritical convert. He treated the slur as an aberration that a substantial footnote could suffice to rebuke – an angry blip within a text that could nonetheless be commended as a gem of moral instruction. In La Bletterie's mind, in the end, *Caesars* was Julian's best work because it disclosed him *in potentia* at his moral best; he idealized its author accordingly, with an eye to the shining emperor he believed that Julian could and might have been – if only 'une espèce de fanatisme' had not overcome his 'bon sens' and turned him into a subtle persecutor.[112] On that score, La Bletterie's view again anticipates Gibbon's: 'the deadly spirit of fanaticism', Gibbon would judge, 'perverted the heart and understanding of a virtuous prince... [who] in the exercise of his uncommon talents [...] often descended below the majesty of his rank' – and in Gibbon's view, we can recall, La Bletterie's *Caesars* had 'happily expressed the spirit' of the 'most agreeable' work that Julian ever wrote; for Gibbon, too, it was the work that showed him at his most attractive.[113]

Some thirty years after Gibbon first read La Bletterie's *Vie de Julien* as a young man at Lausanne, he was to pay it a notable compliment: he named it in his Memoirs as one of 'three particular books [which] may have remotely contributed to form the historian of the Roman empire'.[114] His high regard for its author's scholarship is evident in the footnotes to the chapters treating Julian in *Decline and Fall*, which quite often cite it. On some religious topics, of course, 'superstitious complacency' had clouded the Abbé's judgement – but most of the citations implicitly commend his treatment of some particular historical issue:[115] in the round, Gibbon respected La Bletterie as an acute and essentially honest historian whose writings on Julian had engaged sympathetically, and elegantly, with the subject. It is well known, of course, that the ambivalent picture drawn in the *Vie de Julien* had earlier made a very different impression on another of La Bletterie's stellar contemporaries. In Voltaire's eyes, Julian was a heroic *philosophe* – an emperor untouched by the fanatical spirit, and judiciously tolerant of the Christians in his public dealings with them. Voltaire had read the *Vie de Julien* in 1735, as soon as it was published, and much disliked it; criticisms of its author's Christian bias would recur in his letters and publications over the next four decades. He particularly disliked its underlying assumption that Julian had sincerely revered the traditional pagan gods. To suppose that the philosophic emperor could have done any such thing seemed utterly ludicrous to Voltaire: 'Le père de La Bletterie...a fait un superstitieux de ce grand homme'.[116] But on one point – the merit of *Caesars* – Voltaire concurred with the Jansenist priest, in a fashion. In a letter written four months after La Bletterie's biography came out, he cast about for an argument that could convince a friend of the wrong-headedness of its notion of a devoutly pagan Julian:[117]

> The idea that he seriously believed in paganism simply does not enter my head. Someone may tell me, rightly enough, that he attended in processions, and sacrificed... [I would reply that] he was obliged to appear to be a devotee of paganism. But I can only judge a man by his writings; I read his *Caesars*, and I find nothing in that satire that smacks of superstition.

For Voltaire, then, as for La Bletterie, Julian's best qualities were eloquently inscribed in *Caesars*. But La Bletterie's conception of just what constituted its author's 'best qualities' was not one that Voltaire was inclined to endorse; and for Voltaire it was a philosophic article of faith to believe that the admirable ideals evinced in *Caesars* had been consistently exemplified in practice in the emperor Julian's deeds. He came to regard the piece, just as Spanheim earlier had, as a text that could be commended as instructive reading for a monarch (and by a nice coincidence, the monarch that Voltaire particularly had in mind was a grandson of both Sophie the Duchess of Brunswick and the 'Great Elector' Frederick-Wilhelm, the dedicatees of Spanheim's *Caesars* in its two editions): in a letter of 1740, he commended *Caesars* to Frederick II, on the occasion of Frederick's accession as king in Prussia.[118]

'Mr. Julian the Apostate': *Caesars* transmogrified in a fiction

Voltaire's idealization of Julian as a model of enlightened tolerance was encapsulated in the article 'Julien le philosophe' that he published in the 1767 (sixth) edition of his *Dictionnaire philosophique*. La Bletterie's name crops up five times in it, caricatured as an emblem of Christian credulity and 'mauvaise foi'. By the time Gibbon wrote his chapters on Julian, a decade later, the article was famous; tellingly, Gibbon disdained to refer to it. One can be sure that the jibes it aimed at La Bletterie will have struck Gibbon as crass and meretricious; a distaste for them probably contributed something to the tartness of a remark about Voltaire made much later in *Decline and Fall*: 'in his way, [he] was a bigot, an intolerant bigot'.[119] Nor would Gibbon have cared for Voltaire's ungenerous remarks about another near-contemporary author in a different literary sphere. Voltaire affected to find the fiction of Henry Fielding trivial (notwithstanding the fact that it indisputably influenced Voltaire's own satire).[120] Gibbon never disputed Voltaire's genius as a satirist, but he reckoned the 'Genius of Fielding' fully its equal – and he applauded the latter, not least, in the second volume of *Decline and Fall*: 'I am almost tempted to quote the romance of a great master [Fielding], which may be considered as the history of human nature'.[121] The 'romance' in question is *A Journey from this World to the Next*, a short fiction that Fielding had published in 1743 in a volume of his *Miscellanies* – a couple of years, that is to say, before the printer William Bowyer commissioned an English translation of La Bletterie's *Vie de Julien*.[122] *A Journey* offers us an apt text to round off a discussion of *Caesars'* reception within our selected period: it discloses a brilliant English eighteenth-century novelist – the great rival of Samuel Richardson, whose circle had briefly included the Revd. John Duncombe[123] – as a creative reader of Julian's satire.

Fielding's *A Journey* is a Menippean fiction on a perennial satirical theme – the exposure of the vanity and hypocrisy underlying claims to glory in 'this world'. Its principal narrator is a spirit-author who dies at Cheapside in 1741: he wakes up to be greeted by a dandily waist-coated Mercury and sets out on a coach-tour of the 'next world', in the course of which he meets an assortment of historical figures, ancient and modern. In its early chapters, Plato's Myth of Er and the *Dialogues of the Dead* of Lucian (Fielding's favourite classical author) are clearly the formal literary models;[124] but a complicating twist occurs at Chapter X. The narrator is now visiting the Elysian fields; he has just witnessed the historian Livy brusquely informing the recently arrived Alexander that he 'would have made no Figure against the Romans', when he observes 'a Spirit by the name of Mr. Julian the Apostate' enjoying the pleasures of Elysium:

> This exceedingly amazed me, for I had concluded that no Man ever had a better Title to the Bottomless Pit than he. But I soon found that this same Julian the Apostate was the very [same] individual [as] Arch-Bishop Latimer. He told me that several Lyes had been raised on him in his former Capacity, nor was he so bad a Man as he had been represented. However, he had [originally] been denied Admittance [to Elysium], and forced to undergo several subsequent Pilgrimages on Earth, and to act in the different Characters [of a good score of men], before his Martyrdom [...] in [his] last Character [Latimer] satisfied the Judge [Minos], and procured him a Passage to the blessed Regions.

The spirit-author is keen to hear the details of this story, and 'Mr. Julian the Apostate' now becomes an internal narrator; in the next fifteen chapters of *A Journey* he gives a first-person account of his successive re-incarnations over a millennium of historical time as (*inter alia*) a eunuch slave of John Chrysostom, a Jew, a carpenter's son, a monk, a statesman, a courtier ('in other words, a most prostitute Flatterer'), a court-jester, a king, a beggar, a poet, and 'three times a bishop'.

'Mr. Julian' does not explicitly mention *Caesars* in his story, but it is quite safe to assume that Fielding himself knew the piece and was playing on it when he wrote *A Journey*:[125] he had been well trained in the classical languages, especially Latin; he read widely in classical literature and history throughout his life; and he is known to have owned a bilingual Greek and Latin edition of *Caesars*.[126] Fielding probably had a general historical interest in Julian and his times (Ammianus and Socrates Scholasticus also figured in his library); but as an aficionado of Lucian, he will have been especially interested in Julian's variant on a Menippean satire – and in the possibilities it offered to a satirist of the 1740s. The final, redeeming, incarnation of 'Mr. Julian' as the Anglican Hugh Latimer, burned at the stake at Oxford in 1555 under Mary Tudor, is intriguing on this score: it hints that Fielding had heard something about the Whiggish propaganda that had pictured Julian as a champion of Protestant moderation half a century or so before *A Journey* was written. Most of the earlier existences of 'Mr. Julian', too, have embroiled him in the intrigues and dangers of high politics. His narrative (like that of *Caesars*) dwells often on the folly of mistaking a glorious show for something lasting – and part of the purpose of *A Journey* was to satirize the political career of Walpole, who had been forced to resign from government a year before *A Journey* was published.[127] But in the chapters of *A Journey* narrated by 'Mr. Julian', the underlying joke at play is surely intertextual. The story of his posthumous adventures has moments of mischief that a reader who knew Julian's *Caesars* could particularly relish. In *Caesars*, for instance, the winning contestant Marcus is especially esteemed for his pious spirituality and his dietary austerities: 'his body, diaphanous from lack of food, gleamed like the purest light'; Fielding's 'Mr. Julian', by contrast, grows plump from four years' feasting on meats that he purloins by night from sacrificial altars, '[meats] which the People thought the Deities themselves devoured'. Or take the reviling of Constantine in *Caesars* as a slave to bodily pleasures who is only admitted to the emperors' contest on a whim of the hedonist Dionysus; in his incarnation as a second-time king in *A Journey*, 'Mr. Julian' himself succumbs to just such 'Constantinian' and Dionysian temptations, conceiving an overwhelming passion to seduce 'a young Neapolitan Lady, whose name was Ariadne', and using his regal power '[to] enjoy the most delicious Creatures, without the previous and tiresome Ceremonies of Courtship'.[128] But the joke went deeper than incidentals of this sort: *A Journey* wittily subverts both the guiding premise of Julian's satire, and Hermes' promise to him at its close. In *Caesars*, a Roman emperor passes judgement in the name of the gods on his imperial predecessors, admitting them to Olympus, or consigning them to Tartarus, as he sees fit; in Fielding's satire, *Caesars*' author himself comes repeatedly to face the judgement of Minos, and is repeatedly found wanting. So too, the happy fate predicted for Julian by Hermes at *Caesars*' end – the assurance that when his time comes to leave this world, he will pass 'in good hope' to an afterlife among the Mithraic blessed – is teasingly postponed and deflated in *A Journey*. Fielding's Julian must extend his acquaintance with humanity by living out a score of messy lives over a good millennium before he wins admission to Elysium, and his Mithraic faith does not survive his metamorphoses: the quondam Apostate will finally depart 'this world' as a fervent Christian, in the flesh of an martyred Anglican bishop.

Notes

[1] Gibbon 1994 (ed. Womersley), 1.909 (the opening of ch. xxiv of *Decline and Fall*); cf. 1.96, n. 26 ('ingenious fiction'). We concur with the majority opinion of moderns (see Lacombrade 1964, 27–30, and most recently Sardiello 2000, vii–ix) on the date and place of Caesars' composition: December 362 at Antioch is much likelier than 361 at Constantinople. Gibbon obliquely linked its composition to an Antiochene 'festivity' (1.912), but did not press the point: his earlier remark on Julian's writings at 1.852–3 would allow for composition in either year.

[2] E.g. Witke 1970, 164; Baldwin 1978, 449–51; Bowersock 1982, 159. More recent scholarship has persuasively rehabilitated the text's literary sophistication and wit; see Relihan 1993; Long 2006. On its jokes, see Smith 1995, 13–14.

[3] For *Caesars*' echoes of Platonic dialogue and myth, cf. Caes. 306c with Pl. *Symp.* 215b and 189a–191d; on its Lucianic echoes, see Relihan 1993, 119–22, 127, 132–3, Nesselrath 1994, 30–44, cf. Smith 1995, 58–61. For Lucian's double titles, see Robinson 1979, 239–41.

[4] Socrates, *Hist. eccl.* 3.23.14; cf. 3.1.57.

[5] Kaegi 1964, esp. 33–4; Baldwin 1978; Bowersock 1982.

[6] Pack 1946; Wirth 1978, 483–90; Bowersock 1978, 101–2; Bowersock 1982, 161 and 172; Hunt 1995.

[7] Nesselrath 1994; Sardiello 2000; Long 2006.

[8] Relihan 1993, 3–11 and 119–34 reads *Caesars* with an eye to Northrop Frye's and Bakhtin's theorizing of Menippean satire as a broad 'anatomical' or generic tendency in literature.

[9] Weinbrot 2005, 50–61.

[10] I.e. Cantoclarus (Paris 1583); Petavius (Paris 1630); Spanheim (Leipzig 1696).

[11] Julian's first appearance in the vernacular in 1580 makes him a relatively late arriviste on this score; during the 1500s, the translation of classical authors into vernacular languages had boomed. For the general picture, see Febvre and Martin 1984, 272–4; Mandrou 1978, 21–32, 124–5, 130–2; Bolgar 1954, 317–30 and 508–41.

[12] Cantoclarus 1577; to be distinguished from Cantoclarus 1583 (see above, n. 10).

[13] See Billault 2002, 224–37; Russell 1973, 150–1.

[14] F. Bretin, *Les Oeuvres de Lucien de Samosate*, Paris 1681 [2nd edn. 1583].

[15] See Smith 1966. For a similar 'trend' in German anti–Papal satire, see Robinson 1979, 109–117. For Lucianic influence on Rabelais, Robinson 1979, 134–5, with Screech 1979, 166–7, on *Gargantua* ch. 33 (especially apt, for us: Rabelais satirizes the pretensions of the Holy Roman emperor Charles V in the figure of King Picrochole, flattered by his courtiers as a conqueror as rivalling Alexander and Augustus (and warned by them to avoid the fate of Julian in Persia)).

[16] We infer this from the absence of relevant entries in Harless 1796, 724–32, in the tables in Bolgar 1954, 518–19, and in the on–line catalogues of major European research libraries that we have trawled. The 'version' of the *Hymn to King Helios* published at Madrid in 1625 to which Harless (p. 727) ambiguously refers is a translation into Latin, not Castilian (the author was Vicente Mariner, Librarian of the Escorial under the 'Planet king' Philip IV). We discount the French translation of *Ep. ad Sarapion* (= Jul. *Ep.* 80 Wright) by F. Morel (Paris 1610; *BnF* cat. no. FRBNF30667022): the letter is definitely spurious.

[17] The 'letter' *To the Bostrans* (=*Ep.* 41 Wright) is an imperial edict (*diatagma*), issued

by Julian on 1st August 362, which came to elicit interest in the 17th and 18th centuries in connexion with an intellectual debate about religious tolerance: on its translation into English in a 1681 political pamphlet and subsequently, and the citations of it by Voltaire, see below pp. 301, 307–8.

[18] The remarks on bibliographic matters that follow are drawn from data in Harless 1796 and Sardiello 2000, xxxvii–xl.

[19] For *Sardi Venales'* 17th-century publication history, see Matheeusen and Heesakkers 1980, 19–21. It was a controversial work partly for its bearing on a contemporary Arminian–Calvinist theological debate, partly for its praise of Julian (see Matheeusen and Heesakkers 1980, 10–15, esp. the end of the letter of Cunaeus cited at p. 15, n. 19: 'I also gave my judgement of Julian [in *Sardi*], not without displeasing many an eminent person'.) Cunaeus' high estimate of *Caesars* in the preface of his 1612 volume anticipates the later verdicts of Spanheim and La Bletterie (see below, pp. 286–7): he judged the author 'profoundly erudite'; '[il] a écrit un livre très–savant, dans lequel il touche avec une dextérité incomparable tous les Empereurs, qui avoient commandé aux Romains avant lui...et pendant qu'il fait [sa] censure de ceux, qui ont régné avant lui, il me semble qu'il fait quelque chose de plus noble que de régner...quoi que je fois assuré, qu'il n'a jamais rien écrit, qui doive être préféré à ses *Césars*'.

[20] The editions of 1620, 1627, 1632, and 1693.

[21] Matheeusen and Heesakkers 1980, 1–2. Martinius' Latin translation of *Misopogon* (Paris 1567) was paired with Cunaeus' *Caesars* in this volume.

[22] Anonymous (Hamburg 1663); N. Borremans (Rotterdam 1675), translated from Cunaeus' Latin.

[23] Des Hayons (Liège 1670) and Moret (Paris 1682).

[24] On Spanheim's life and works see *Allgemeine Deutsche Biographie* Band 35 (1893), s.v. 'Spanheim, E'; Loewe 1924; Bourgeois 1900, 3–30. See also below at pp. 288, 295–6 and 303.

[25] For a new study of Spanheim see Ogilvie (forthcoming).

[26] The 'standard' edition of Julian's collected works until Hertlein 1875–6; n.b. La Bletterie (1748, lix), observing that 'the text of Julian is defective "even" as given in Spanheim's 1696 edition'. Spanheim's reputation *qua* textual critic has not lasted: Wilamowitz 1982, 74, was harshly critical ('There is no profit in him except as a numismatist: his [1696] Julian is negligible').

[27] Bourgeois 1900, 6. Spanheim conceivably sensed an affinity of sorts between *Caesars* and Rabelais; for Rabelais as a satirist of regal pretension, see above, n. 15.

[28] Heusinger (Gotha 1736, repr. 1741). Harless' Greek edition (Erlangen 1785) appends Cunaeus' Latin version only, on facing pages.

[29] Lottern, in *Schriften der Deutschen Gesellschaft*, vol. 2, Leipzig 1734 (re-issued 1742); Lasius (Greifswald–Leipzig 1770, with *Misopogon*); Bardili (Halle 1778).

[30] Zanetto (Treviso 1764).

[31] On the career of La Bletterie (or 'La Bléterie': both spellings occur in his publications), see below at pp. 288 and 306–7.

[32] Or six, if Spanheim's 1666 and 1683 versions are differentiated.

[33] Spanheim 1683, preface, sects. 1 and 4, unpaginated [= pp. ii–iv in the 1728 edn.]: 'Quelque mérite qui recommande en général les ouvrages de Julien, on ne sçauroit nier avec justice, que ces Césars n'en remportent le prix. C'est un avantage, qu'ils tirent

également de la dignité du sujet, et de la manière dont il est traitté. Celuy-là ne pouvoit estre ni plus noble, ni plus agréable, ni plus utile; et le titre seul, qu'il porte, suffit pour le faire avoüer sans peine. Aussi, n'y on avoit-il point sans doute, qui fut plus digne de reflections d'un Auteur, qui estoit luy-même CÉSAR, luy-même du rang et du mêtier, pour ainsi dire, de ceux dont il parle...Il faut donc avoüer, que Julien ne pouvoit rien imaginer de plus propre à exercer son bel esprit; à découvrir l'excellence de ses lumiéres; à instruire le Public et ses Successeurs; et à s'esciter luy-même, par une généreuse émulation, à des actions héroïques, à la pratique des vertus dignes d'un Empereur'. (The quotes that follow are from the start and end of the preface [= pp. i and xxxv in the 1728 edn]). Here and in subsequent notes, our French quotations from the volumes of Spanheim and La Bletterie retain idiosyncrasies in spelling, accentuation and capitalization found in the originals.

[34] La Bletterie 1735, iii –iv: 'L'excellente version latine du P. Petau [Petavius] a déjà mis Julien à la portée de ceux qui n'entendent pas assez le Grec pour lire l'original, et la célèbre *Satire des Césars*, donnée en François par M. Spanheim avec un long et docte commentaire, a instruit les plus habiles sans scandaliser les plus ignorans'.

[35] The original (1748) edition of the *Histoire de Jovien* comprised two volumes: the first contained the narrative of Jovian's reign, followed by *Caesars*; the second contained *Misopogon*, a selection of 46 letters (including *To Themistius*), and the 'Helios myth' culled from *Against Heraclius*. The 2nd edition (Paris 1776) retains the order within a single volume, differently paginated.

[36] La Bletterie 1748, xxxiii–xxxvii: '*Les Césars* passent sans contredit pour le chef-d'oeuvre de Julien... Je ne crois pas que dans aucun ouvrage aussi court, on trouve à la fois tant de caractères et de mœurs, tant de finesse et de solidité, tant d'instruction, sans que l'auteur prenne jamais le ton dogmatique, tant de sel et d'enjoûment, sans qu'il cesse jamais d'instruire. En un mot, il me semble que *Les Césars* devraient ou déprévenir, ou du moins embarrasser, ceux qui ont voüé une estime exclusive aux productions de l'ancienne Grèce'.

[37] La Bletterie 1748, xliv–xlv: 'Il y a plus de soixante ans que M. Spanheim, si connu dans la république des lettres, entreprit de traduire les CÉSARS en françois. Ce savant étranger ne possédoit pas les finesses de notre langue et sa version ne ressemble à l'original que comme un squélette à un corps humain. Au texte il a joint des remarques, appuyé les remarques de preuves, enrichi les unes et les autres de médailles; le tout avec tant de profusion que le petit ouvrage de Julien disparoît en quelque sorte dans un Quarto de plus de six cens pages. C'est un chef–d'œuvre d'impression, un trésor de littérature ancienne peu digérée et d'erudition numismatique. Ce livre fait l'ornement des bibliotheques: mais il effraie le commun des lecteurs, à qui la vue d'un commentaire si prolixe inspire au moins l'indifférence pour un texte qu'ils supposent avoir besoin de tant d'éclaircissemens'.

[38] La Bletterie 1748, xlvi–xlviii: 'J'ai donc cru faire plaisir à ceux qui n'aiment point les gros livres de leur présenter une traduction accompagnée de remarques ou purement nécessaires ou du moins intéressantes; et dans laquelle je tâcherois de conserver le plus qu'il seroit possible le feu, les graces et la légèreté de l'original'. La Bletterie subsequently (p. lix) states his purpose as being to render the meaning of Julian's Greek 'as he would have done, if he had composed in French' ('j'ai tâché de rendre son idée, comme je présume qu'il l'auroit rendue s'il avoit écrit en François').

[39] For the details that follow, see Bourgeois 1900, 3–30.

[40] He received copies, for instance, of epigraphic texts newly transcribed at Aphrodisias by an Italian scholar who had accompanied William Sherard, the British consul at Smyrna, on a visit there in 1705: see the admirable 'Aphrodisias Inscriptions' website at http://www.insaph.kcl.ac.uk

[41] 1st edn. Rome 1664; 2nd edn. Amsterdam 1671.

[42] See below, esp. pp. 301–5.

[43] For the context, see below, pp. 306–7.

[44] See Neveu 2000, 100–1. The themes of the earlier *Dissertations* relate closely to La Bletterie's work on Julian: see Ferrary 2007, 314–15.

[45] Murray 1896, 143.

[46] Bonnard 1945, Lausanne journal entry for 25th February 1764: ('What literature, what taste, what elegance! And I add, what moderation! Julian was a pagan, and [yet] the Abbé hates only the Jesuits!').

[47] See below, pp. 294–5.

[48] La Bletterie 1735, iii; Murray 1896, 338; cf. Gibbon 1994, 2.565, on the empress Theodora ('her arts must be veiled in the obscurity of a learned language').

[49] Gibbon 1994, 1.909 n. 1, clearly borrowing from La Bletterie 1748, xix–xx (quoted above, p. 287).

[50] See Nichols 1782, 185–6. The drafts of the translation were checked and revised by two scholarly friends of Bowyer, Jeremiah Mortland and William Clarke (on whom, see Nichols 1782, 19–28). In the 1748 English edition, as in the 1735 French edition, La Bletterie's name was suppressed. Nor does Bowyer's advertisement ever name the 'eminent writer' who had inspired the translation. Nichols' conjecture (p. 186) that it was William Warburton is quite likely right, but in our view another possibility deserves attention: Henry Fielding had a professional connexion with Bowyer in the early 1740s, and a demonstrable interest in Julian: see Fielding 1993, xxxii, 237 and 285, and below at pp. 310–12.

[51] On Anna Williams, see Hyde 1973, 7 and 83 n. 42; Boswell 1976, 735, 755 and 1245.

[52] The printer was John Nichols, Bowyer's partner and successor (and biographer [=Nichols 1782]). Nichols was a friend of Duncombe (and his future obituarist: see below, n. 55); but nothing Duncombe says indicates that he had been commissioned by Nichols to make the translation in the manner that Anna Williams had been by Bowyer.

[53] Duncombe omitted the following: the three panegyrics; the two prose hymns; the two 'anti-Cynic' treatises (bar the 'Helios myth' from *Against Heraclius*); and the fragments from *Against the Galileans*.

[54] See above, n. 44.

[55] On Duncombe's life and writings, see the obituary by John Nichols in *Gentleman's Magazine* 59 (March /June 1786), 187–9 and 451–2; and (briefly) the entry for him in *DNB*. For the social milieu of Duncombe and his wife, see Mild 1978, 377–384, with Turner 1992, 107.

[56] Duncombe is credited as the main author of a sixty-page *History of the Antiquities of the Parishes of Reculver and Herne*, also published in 1784, in a volume in Nichols' series *Bibliotheca Topographica Britannica*; his work on this item, however, was done mainly in the 1770s.

[57] Gibbon's ironic account of early Christianity was distressing to Duncombe's Anglican piety.

[58] Duncombe 1784, 1.146; see also below at n. 66.

[59] Duncombe was apparently unaware of the recent posthumous republication of these books (Paris 1775 and 1776 respectively); he refers only to the original editions.

[60] Duncombe's only additions to La Bletterie's 1748 selection of Julian's texts are the *Consolation*, the fragment *To a Priest, the Letter to the Athenians* (the bulk of which, however, La Bletterie had already earlier rendered either in direct translation or précis in his 1735 biography, and which he expressly omitted [see 1748, 1. xxv–vi] from the 1748 translations for that reason), and thirty additional letters.

[61] See the notes of Duncombe 1784, 1.179, 189 and 208, on details at *Caes.* 317d and 323b that were in fact better understood and conveyed by La Bletterie; cf. Duncombe 1784, 2.129, mistakenly diverging on a passage in Julian's letter to Arsacius (*Ep.* 22 Wright).

[62] Cantoclarus 1577 and 1583; Petavius 1630; Spanheim 1696. On the complexity of the manuscript tradition relating to this passage, see Lacombrade 1964, 30–1.

[63] Heusinger 1736, 142–6, argues the point in a long note. The issue was delicate, because the correction entailed the printing of a highly blasphemous assault on Jesus' person (see below, n. 73 and pp. 293 and 301–2); in order to minimize the distress arising for his Christian readers, Heusinger chose to retain υἱόν, 'son', in the actual text he published. So too, later, did Lasius (Greifswald-Leipzig 1770) and Harless (Erlangen 1785) in their editions of *Caesars*; but they both knew Heusinger's note on the passage and discussed it in their own notes (at pp. 139–41 and p.170, respectively). Duncombe's case (see below) differed from theirs: he was simply ignorant of the textual problem.

[64] La Bletterie 1748, lix–lx, indicates the Greek editions he had consulted; Heusinger's is not mentioned there (nor elsewhere in the book).

[65] From Latin, Duncombe had translated some poems of Horace and part of the neo-Latin *Praedium Rusticum* of the Jesuit Vanière (1664–1739); from French, the *Letters of an English Traveller* (a French work, despite its title), and (in the *Gentleman's Magazine* in 1771) parts of the *Huetiana, ou Pensées diverses* of the scholarly bishop Huet (1630–1721).

[66] Most likely, Spanheim 1696 (from whose Latin dedication Duncombe culled his epigraph; see above, p. 291). Of course, Duncombe's book contained some Julianic works (not many; see above, n. 60) and two short Libanian monodies (*Orr.* 60 and 61) and sixteen letters of Libanius which had not figured in La Bletterie's 1748 book. But all of these items were to hand in editions with parallel Latin versions, and some of the Julianic letters added were extant *only* in Latin; and in the case of the Libanian items, it is suggestive that Duncombe acknowledges (2.242) an unnamed 'learned friend' as the author of the notes. Duncombe's initial decision to include material by Libanius in his book was perhaps prompted by Gibbon's pen-portrait of him in *Decline and Fall* (1.916–7), a footnote which (1.917 n. 28) alerted its readers to Fabricius' edition and Latin translations of Libanius, and to Lardner's translation of Libanian excerpts in his *Heathen Testimonies* (vol. 4, 1767); Duncombe (2.224) quotes this footnote in full. In any event, Lib. *Orr.* 60 and 61 were chosen for inclusion by Duncombe as congenial 'padding'; they offered Duncombe's readers testimonies to

a pagan's discomfiture in the face of the failure of his gods to protect their worshippers and temples from natural catastrophe.

[67] A second edition had appeared in 1792. For the review of the first edition, see *Gentleman's Magazine* 54 (1784), 444–7 and 600–3. For the *Magazine*'s circulation-figure, Porter 1982, 252. Its editor at the time, we may add, was Duncombe's friend John Nichols, the printer of his 'Julian' (see above, n. 52).

[68] *Two Orations of the Emperor Julian, One to the Sovereign Sun and the Other to the Mother of the Gods; translated by T.T.* [London 1793].

[69] See above, p. 287.

[70] See above, p. 286; cf. Cunaeus' praise of *Caesars* in 1612 (quoted above, n. 19).

[71] Gibbon 1994, 1.909–10.

[72] A note in Gibbon (1.910 n. 4) teasingly distinguishes the view that 'the impartial reader' will take of the hostility to Constantine and his religion disclosed in *Caesars* from that which 'the [Christian] interpreters are compelled, by a more sacred interest' to take of it; cf. 1.448–9. Gibbon's own view of the matter is admirably discussed by Womersley (Gibbon 1994, 1.xxxii–xxxvi and xlii–xlv).

[73] One wonders whether either the fervently Calvinist Spanheim or the Catholic priest La Bletterie (or for that matter, the Anglican minister Duncombe) would have so readily commended *Caesars* to a general readership as a congenial masterpiece, if they had realized that 'Jesus', not 'son', was the word that Julian had written at *Caes.* 366a (on which see above, p. 293). Once the true reading is restored, *Caesars* culminates in a spectacularly blasphemous scene: Jesus consorting wantonly with Pleasure and Incontinence, and arbitrarily pardoning seducers and murderers of every stripe (see below, pp. 301–2). It should be noted that in Julian's extant works, outside *C. Gal.*, *Caes.* 366a is one of only two passages to refer directly to Jesus' person; and that the import of the second passage (*Ep.* 47 Wright, at 435c) is not overtly blasphemous.

[74] On his piety, Bourgeois 1900, 21, and for the details of his diplomatic career here summarized, 5–30.

[75] In Bourgeois 1900, the standard modern edition of the *Relation*, Spanheim's report runs beyond 500 pages. For his sheltering of Huguenots at Paris in 1685, Bourgeois 1900, 21–2, 388–9. (It is relevant to add that in 1710, a few months before Spanheim's death in London, his daughter Marie-Anne Spanheim was to be married there to the Marquis de Montendre, a Huguenot aristocrat who had fled to the Netherlands, joined the army of William of Orange, and settled in England in the 1690s.)

[76] Bourgeois 1900, 98–9 and 441–2.

[77] Bourgeois 1900, 70–4 and 93–9.

[78] To be clear, we do not mean to suggest that Spanheim only *began* work on the commentary at Paris in the 1680s: a remark in the preface of his commentary (see below, n. 90) indicates that he was already at work on it during his first period of diplomatic service in England (1678–April 1680).

[79] On the Calvinist Elector's 'toleration' of the Lutheran communities in Prussia, see Clark 2006, 120–4.

[80] Spanheim 1683, *in dedic.* (unpaginated): 'C'est, Monseigneur, qu'on trouve en Vous un Héros, sur lequel la Satyre n'a point de prise; en qui elle ne peut blâmer, ni

ces débauches, ni ces emportemens, ni ces injustices, ni ces foiblesses, ni ces autres deréglamens de l'Ame ou de l'Esprit; ces vices enfin et ces taches, qu'elle dévoile icy librement dans un Alexandre, dans un Jule, dans un Auguste; dans un Trajan; dans un Marc Aurèle; dans un Constantin; c'est à dire dans les plus grands, les plus sages, ou les plus vertuëux Héros de l'Antiquité Grècque et Romaine'.

[81] Burke 1992, 26–37, and 193–7.

[82] See e.g. Barnes 1981, 274 on Cardinal Baronius' 1588 account of Constantine.

[83] On this statue, see Wittkower 1975, 84–102. First commissioned in 1669, it was only completed nearly a decade later, and its transportation from Italy to Versailles was further delayed; it eventually arrived there in 1685 (and famously failed to please Louis). Spanheim, it should be noted, had personal contacts in the early 1680s with the commissioner of the statue, Louis' high minister, Colbert; see Bourgeois 1900, 303, 308–10 and 317 n. 1.

[84] Wind 1939/40, 127–37.

[85] Langley 2001, chs. 19 to 22 *passim*; see esp. 132–3, 139, 144–50, 162.

[86] One needs to allow that the propagandist who devised the programme may well have been less concerned to be faithful to the letter of *Caesars*' plot than to manipulate one particularly striking image in it: a single energetic outsider (the proverbially 'invincible' Alexander, the triumphant Protestant William) answers the call to challenge a complacent crew of Roman (and by extension, Catholic) dynasts. It should be observed that the deviser (or Verrio himself) was certainly prepared to depart from the letter of the text in another significant particular: in *Caesars*, Alexander competes against five Roman monarchs; in the fresco, there are twelve. In this case, the discrepancy arose from the deviser's wish to evoke an antique account of the Roman emperors much more widely read than Julian's Caesars in the deviser's day. For Whig critics of the later Stuarts, the reports of tyrannical excesses in Suetonius' imperial biographies had held a special appeal (see Patterson 2000, 463–4); under the title *The Lives of the XII Caesars*, at least four editions of Suetonius' *Lives* had been published in English between 1670 and 1698.

[87] On the pamphlet and its context and sequel, see Wind 1939/40, 130–6; Langley 2001, 130–1, 140–1; Spink 1967, 1404–6.

[88] 'Philaretus Anthropopolita' 1681, 1, 14, 16 and 18.

[89] On eighteenth-century disputes about the reality or speciousness of the edict's 'tolerance', see below, pp. 307–8.

[90] See above, pp. 293.

[91] 'Philaretus', we may note, was not the first English Protestant writer to select this particular passage from *Caesars* for translation; Marvell had already done so in 1673, in his *Rehearsal Transpros'd II* (he read *Caesars* in Cantoclarus' 1583 edition: see A. Grosart, ed., *Complete Works of Andrew Marvell*, London 1873 vol. 3, 445–6). Marvell, though, construed the passage as a villainous pagan slur on a Christian emperor.

[92] Wind 1939/40, 133–4. So far as we know, Locke specialists have not tested the conjecture (a stylometric analysis comparing the 1681 pamphlet and near-contemporary writings of Locke might be decisive). Cranston 1957, a classic biography of Locke, makes no mention of Wind's suggestion, but has incidental details that could be adduced to support it: Locke had a hand in the production of another pro-Shaftesbury pamphlet late in 1681 (p. 202); he used the pseudonym 'Philander' in 1681/2 correspondence (pp. 215–19); and in the late 1670s he had ingeniously

mistranslated a passage in a French essay attacking Protestantism to represent it as an attack on the Papacy (pp. 177–8).

[93] Langley 2001, 129–30 and 162, speculates that the scholarly theologian Gilbert Burnet (from 1689 onwards, bishop of Salisbury) may have had a part in the inspiration of the programme; in the early 1680s, he had corresponded with (and visited) Spanheim in Paris.

[94] See above, p. 296. One presumes that Spanheim privately wished them well in their efforts to exclude James from the succession. There is a hint, at any rate, that during his second stint at London (1702–10) his name was popular in elite Whiggish circles: before her marriage (see above, n. 75), his daughter, Mlle. Marie-Anne Spanheim, had been famously toasted as a reigning beauty at the Whiggish Kit-Cat Club (Ashton 2005, 22).

[95] Spanheim 1683, pref., unpaginated [= pp. xxxvi–vii in the posthumous 2nd edition of 1728]; cf. Spanheim 1696, preface (pp. xxxiv).

[96] Among them, Gilbert Burnet (on whom, see above, n. 93).

[97] See above, p. 287.

[98] See above, n. 86.

[99] Compare Langley 2001, 129: 'the frontispiece may conceivably be what suggested to Verrio, or [the deviser], that the subject had pictorial possibilities'. In our view, the connexion is virtually certain.

[100] On the fresco, see above, pp. 298–300, and compare Fig. 3 with Figs. 1 and 2 in key details: e.g. the 'supporting cloud' motif; the stance and arm-gesture of Alexander; the arrangement of Julian's cloak, the position of his writing-arm and hand, his eye-contact with Hermes, and the curved legs of his writing-table.

[101] Jones 2002, 21–3, 45, 99–110, 119.

[102] Neveu 2000, 93–133, is excellent on La Bletterie's intellectual milieu and the vicissitudes of his career; for the expulsion from the Oratoire, see esp. 94–5. See also Moatti 1995.

[103] See above, p. 289.

[104] La Bletterie 1735, 2–3: 'Une passion déréglée pour la gloire le porta avec une espèce de fanatisme à tout ce qui lui parut estimable…il eut les défauts qui le flatent, et ceux que l'amour propre n'apperçoit que dans les autres'.

[105] La Bletterie 1748, 1.326–8.

[106] Voltaire, *Questions sur l'Encyclopédie* (1770), s.v 'Apostat'; cf. the article on 'Julien le philosophe' in his *Dictionnaire philosophique* (1767 edition), with Moureaux 1994, 235. On the development of this debate in French authors, and Julian's symbolic importance in it, see Spink 1967, esp. 1409, 1411–13. There was an Anglophone parallel; the Third Earl of Shaftesbury translated *To the Bostrans* in his *Characteristicks* (1711) as proof of Julian's tolerance; Warburton would cite it in his *Julian* (1750, 29–30) to prove him a persecutor.

[107] Gibbon 1994, 1.876 n. 33.

[108] La Bletterie 1735, viii and 488 (persecution).

[109] Neveu 2000, 106–9.

[110] La Bletterie 1748, 1.385–94.

[111] See above, p. 293 and n. 73.

[112] La Bletterie 1735, 2–3.

[113] Gibbon 1994, 1.906 and 958, with 909.

[114] Murray 1896, 143.

[115] Gibbon 1994, 1.900, n. 115 ('complacency'); but compare, e.g., the favourable citations at 1.846, n. 37; 1.851, n. 50; 1.855, n. 60; 1.859, n. 73; 1.871, n. 23; 1.956, nn. 128 and 129. A remark at 1.915, n. 20, is emblematic: 'I have essential obligations to the translation and notes of [...] La Bletterie'.

[116] On Voltaire's idealization of Julian and associated criticisms of La Bletterie, see Spink, 1967, 1411–13; Mervaud 1976, 733–5; Moureaux 1994, 58–60 and 234.

[117] Besterman 1954, 50 (*Ep.* 839, to Nicolas Formont, April 1735).

[118] Mervaud 1976, 726–7 and *passim*, for other references to Julian in the correspondence of Voltaire and Frederick II. An awareness of Frederick's admiration for Julian perhaps inspired a curious note in Duncombe's 'selected Julian' (1.158–9), which insists on a close character-affinity between Julian and 'the royal philosopher of Sans-souci', but which ends by differentiating their religious views: Julian, albeit a pagan, 'believed in the immortality of the soul, which it appears...*the latter does not*'.

[119] Gibbon 1994, 3.916 n. 13. Compare the mischievous formulation at 3.959 n. 54: 'the *pious zeal* of Voltaire is excessive, even ridiculous' (our italics).

[120] See most recently Langille 2010, 85–108 (citing Voltaire's dismissive remark on *Tom Jones* at p. 86 n. 6).

[121] Gibbon 1994, 2.242 n. 13, with the remark in the Memoirs (Murray 1896, 347 n. 71): the 'Genius of Fielding' produced *Tom Jones*, 'the first [among] ancient or modern romances'.

[122] For a possible connexion between the two books, see above, n. 50. *A Voyage* was translated into French as *Julien l'Apostat, ou un Voyage dans l'autre Monde*, Paris 1768. We do not know whether Voltaire ever read it.

[123] See above, p. 290.

[124] Fielding 1993, xxix–xxx; Robinson 1979, 198–9 and 211–18.

[125] On Julian's role in *A Journey*, see Fielding 1993, xxxii; Goldgar 1986, 241–3.

[126] On Fielding's classical learning, see Mace 1991, 234–60. His personal library included Sylburg's *Romanae Historiae Scriptores Graeci Minores* (3 vols., 1588–90), vol. 3 of which contains *Caesars* reprinted from Cantoclarus' 1583 Greek and Latin version: Ribble 1996, entry no. S78 attests his ownership of. (For his Ammianus, Ribble 1996, entry no. A12 [=Ammianus, ed. Gronovius, 1693].)

[127] Fielding 1993, xxiv–xxvi; Clearey 1984, 184–90.

[128] See Fielding 1993, 49, with Caes. 317c and 333d (on Marcus); 67 and 72, with Caes. 318a and 335b (on Constantine)

19

AFTERWORD:
STUDYING JULIAN THE AUTHOR

Jacqueline Long

Ammianus Marcellinus relates that when the emperor Constantius II elevated his cousin Julian to the rank of Caesar on 6th November 355 the troops scrutinized their new ruler as if they were studying physiognomic primers (Amm. Marc. 15.8.16). Whether or not the soldiers truly gazed so bookishly, Ammianus clearly expected his readers to understand and accept his comparison. In his and Julian's world, appearances made a kind of text. Ammianus regularly suggests they might be read to see what principles informed the outward shapes; he holds up a lens of Roman heritage. Even the relatively straightforward visual picture in Ammianus' obituary review of Julian nets together physical image, interpretation, and literary echo:

> Shape and arrangement of the limbs thus: he was of moderate height. His hair fell neat and soft. He wore a bristly beard tapering to a point. His flashing eyes, which declared the liveliness[1] of his mind, lit up his face with charm. His eyebrows were becoming and his nose very straight. His mouth was a little too big, with the lower lip drooping. His neck was plump and bent,[2] his shoulders enormous and broad.[3] From his very head to the tips of his nails his frame was put together right, which made him strong physically and a good runner.[4]

Visual detail immediately gives way to inference and evaluation. From Julian's eyes Ammianus read charm, intensity, and intelligence (*venustate... flagrans*; *mentis argutias*). He invoked standards of appearance (*superciliis decoris*; *ore paulo maiore*). He appraised Julian's body as the instrument of action (*liniamentorum recta compage unde viribus valebat et cursu*). The tag introducing the description immediately echoes Ammianus' use of the same four words to introduce his corresponding obituary-portrait of Constantius (*figura tali situque membrorum*, 21.16.19). More remotely, but aptly, it also echoes Cicero's *De Natura Deorum*.[5] Cicero connected bodies, understanding, character and mortality within cosmic order: he declared that since humanity's unique members and capacities climax in apprehension of divinity, provoking piety and other virtues that make humanity like divinity except for exemption from death, 'it should be understood that neither the shape and arrangement of the limbs, nor such force of temperament and mind, can have been brought about by fortune' (*debet intellegi nec figuram situmque membrorum nec ingenii mentisque vim talem effici potuisse fortuna*). Body measured man individually, and Ammianus' obituary-portraits of emperors each appear plausibly observed as well as characterizing.[6] The Ciceronian tag reinforces the iconic value the portraits derive from being placed in obituary summaries of the emperors' lives. Verbal ancestor-masks, their embodiment attaches enduring form to memory of the ruler's achievements.[7]

Other contemporaries' images of Julian similarly made of his visible physical features a telling discourse. Claudius Mamertinus dynamically set Julian in the view of the people of Illyricum. As he approached, the 'vindicator of Roman liberty' against 'rebelling' Alamanni:

> Maidens, boys, <men>, women, trembling old women, tottering old men, with great dread, thunderstruck, began to discern the emperor running the long road under the weight of heavy arms. His breath came faster as he hurried without awareness of fatigue. Streams of sweat were pouring over his strong neck. Amidst that shock of the dust that loaded his beard and hair, his eyes flashed like starry fires.[8]

Gregory of Nazianzus depicted Julian the student as a quivering mess:

> A sign of no good seemed to me his unsteady neck, his shoulders shaking and rebalancing, his wild eye wandering around and looking mad, unstill feet forever shifting, nose breathing outrage and contempt, the ridiculous expressions of his face bearing the same message, his uncontrolled heaving laughter, nods down and up with no reason, speech halted and chopped by a breath, disorderly stupid questions, answers no better, tumbling over one another and not well-based, not proceeding in the order of education.[9]

Education was the setting in which Gregory encountered Julian, education and the culture with which it equipped young men the stake in his denunciation.[10] His picture of Julian points to his argument. But while mental discipline was most at issue, Gregory explicitly presented himself as divining Julian's character from bodily signs. His verbal description, re-animating the perception he claimed, in turn made his assessment compelling.

Julian too placed his person as a text before his citizens' consideration. His self-projected image in *Misopogon* aggressively confronted the wits of Antioch:

> To this face (I think it is not naturally too fair, good-looking, or blossoming), I myself from peevishness and ill temper have added this long beard... You say I ought to braid ropes from it. And I'm ready to provide, if only you're able to pull them and their roughness doesn't do terrible things to your

'unworn, soft hands.'[11] ...You make your manhood barely visible, indicating it by the brow, not like me from the jaws. But the elongation of my chin wasn't enough for me. Additionally my head is seriously under-groomed. I seldom get my hair and nails cut. Often my fingers are black from using a pen. And if you want to learn one of the unspeakable secrets, I've got a chest rough and shaggy like the lions' who are kings of the beasts. Out of ill temper and awkwardness I have never made it smooth, nor made any other part of my body smooth and soft. I'd tell you if I had a wart, like Cicero, but I don't.[12]

The visual was a personal, political, and public language. It wrote a historical record. The contemporary verbal images of Julian gloss his development of an individual iconography in real time and ideological space. Mamertinus' description confirms the implication of solidi issued from two Gallic mints for Julian as Augustus and not for Constantius, with a bearded obverse portrait and the reverse legend *Virtus Exerc Gall*, that Julian broke from clean-shaven Constantinian iconography as soon as he moved into military rebellion against Constantius; it also suggests that to contemporaries Julian's beard initially looked martial, like the beards of the Tetrarchs from whom Constantine broke when he first shaved.[13] Late antique textual perception of the visual also interacted with history. Julian cited Cicero, wart and all, as an iconic Roman statesman. Ammianus invoked Cicero for his cultural authority; in the same way Julian called on Homer for the threat of Odysseus' bow-string to the suitors' hands, claiming against the Antiochenes a cultural standard for which Gregory would fight him back. The portraits were drawn separately, but they utilized the same media. Fl. Claudius Julianus, 332–363, Caesar of the Roman empire from 355, Augustus from 360 or 361 according to the allegiances of different parts of the empire, remains constituted by texts.

The conference whose fruits are published here took on the challenge of recognizing Julian in this same field of culture. It thus redressed an irony: although Julian's writings are better preserved than many another classical author's, they long were studied as if they were inert vessels of historical facts. Walter Kaegi looked at Julian's knowledge and interpretive judgment of Roman imperial history as early as 1964,[14] but focally literary studies of Julian's artistry largely waited for the 80s and 90s. Arnaldo Marcone showed the *Misopogon* incorporated a 'panegirico rovesciato', turning inside out elements of the rhetorical formula for praise of a city in order to indict clean-shaven Antioch;[15] the procedure corresponded exactly to late antique schoolroom *progymnasmata*'s instructions to compose invectives with the same topics as panegyrics, reversing the topics from praise to blame.[16] Jean Bouffartigue in a giant, fundamental study anatomized Julian's invocations of classical texts so as to determine what of his reading Julian judged worth holding up to view so as to certify his erudition and endow his views with authority.[17] Maud Gleason interpreted *Misopogon* in relationship to its Carnivalesque context at the Antiochene winter festival, and identified it as an imperial 'edict of chastisement'.[18] Joel Relihan aligned Julian's *Caesars* with its formal genre, Menippean satire.[19]

Polymnia Athanassiadi, *à propos* of Gleason, claimed to find the approach through literary form 'baffling'. She maintained the dynamism of genre is too slippery to give study purchase; she sought rather to read Julian with 'empathy' and to 'explore his intentions and feelings'. Her preferred criterion was 'common sense'.[20] Athanassiadi formulated her method expressly and earned criticism for endeavoring to study Julian's subjectivity by it, but other historians' practice differed more in objective than means. Thus, for example, Glen Bowersock in his acute biography read the *Misopogon* as a direct statement of emotion: '[Julian's] cry at the end is that memorable cry of an outraged and helpless man: "Why, in the name of the gods, are you ungrateful to me?"'[21] Julian's writings can compel modern readers because his words evoke emotions which we feel we recognize. It tempts common sense to suppose that Julian wrote them in order to express the same feelings we think we might have felt in something like the circumstances he occupied.

But it is a question, at best a hypothesis biography should demonstrate, not beg, whether Julian did bring twentieth- or twenty-first-century emotions to the circumstances of the mid-fourth century. As literary critics and cultural historians have proven, writers work not only within the vocabulary and syntax of the languages they write, but also within literary and social languages every bit as inflected by tacit consensus of the groups that use them.[22] One of the delights of good writing is to extend familiar usages into new expressiveness. So too generic innovation keeps literary forms supple.[23] Panegyric could be turned inside out, in an exercise late antique pupils practiced. A holiday might see it woven into imperial rebuke with structured, festival irony. Julian was not helpless, although the *Misopogon* does register a failure of his religious activities to stir enthusiasm: he made his frustration part of a performance that recontextualized his endeavors.[24] Both historical and literary contexts inform communication. A reader must be able to recognize a writer's forms and appreciate how they are being manipulated, or their contribution to meaning will be lost. Disregarding the artfulness under a text's surface flattens it. Its potential to reward attention is crushed. Literary study identifies instruments of meaning known to a community, more securely than the common sense of a different era. It gives to empathy lenses through which to see what happens in the space where case-specific content is set in a conventional form; this process corresponds to the way fluency in contemporary literary practices gives an author tools to set his content in their matrix. Understanding the means permits the analysis. Philology, as historicized literary investigation, collects the standard and attested variant tactics by which authors of the period expressed emotion, or logic, or social position, or anything else. Its index can verify the use of recognized means to evoke emotional and other responses: comparison to a literary-historical record confirms, better than anything else can, what intuition may divine of a departed author's intentions. Moreover, the abstract structure of critical literary study makes it possible to ask new questions of a text, how it functioned in ways not necessarily consciously recognized by the author and his contemporaries. Their literary interaction can yield new insights without having to swallow anachronism. The literary discipline is as vital as the living word. And for historical inquiry too, it is powerful.

Even before literary inquiry began to make significant inroads into Julian's corpus, historians recognized his panegyrics did something other than voice feelings. Indeed the challenge was to recognize in panegyrics any contact with genuine emotions other than ennui (e.g. Aug. *Conf.* 6.6.9). Great advances in the understanding of this genre have been made: crucial impetus was imparted by Sabine MacCormack's research into late Roman imperial ceremony.[25] MacCormack located for modern scholarship the excitement of massy ritualized performances of an emperor's presence and power. As convention-articulated visual signs and lengthy speeches indicated, these rulers could transcend the terms of their subjects' lives with a gesture and change everything. They embodied the power of a god on earth. Panegyrists who spoke on the occasions when this ineffable ruler manifested himself before his citizens had the job of giving such occasions verbal form. They interpreted the emperor's being into utterance. They might also conciliate the emperor to the interests of a home-community. They might discuss recent events. They might align their speeches with imperial ideology or current policies, in order to harmonize with the honorand's interests; modern historians seize on the contemporary commentary. But above all panegyrists had to entertain condignly with the ceremony.[26] They had to delight audiences many of whose members had heard hundreds of such speeches before. All those attending were currently engaged in a time-eating pageant: they needed to be inspired with continuing pleasure in it.

Panegyrics accordingly demanded virtuosity. Shaun Tougher discusses here the relationship that Julian's first speech in praise of Constantius owes to its formal model and generic predecessors. Athanassiadi declared Julian's 'slavish imitation' of generic standards distanced him from his own praise.[27]

Tougher's analysis better reveals Julian's subtlety. As he notes, Julian claimed for his speech the perspective of a philosophical outsider, signaling a critical superiority to rhetorical conventions and inviting comparison with Themistius' earlier speech in praise of Constantius (Them. *Or.* 1.1a, 3d, 18a–b). Themistius drew on Dio Chrysostom's orations on kingship.[28] Pedigree validated Julian, whereas his junior rank might have undercut his authenticity praising Constantius from the context of their partnership. At the same time, the intellectual authority Julian assumed competed tacitly with Constantius' temporal authority. Tougher rightly highlights points at which Julian broke from the seamlessness of rhetorical encomium[29] by excusing Constantius small failures from an ideal ruling power. These catches raise questions. Did Julian's preamble sufficiently contrast philosophy with rhetorical flattery (*Or.* 1 1-4c) so that ostensible breaks in rhetorical smoothness seemed to validate Julian's pose and his praise with it? Did the theory of imperial ideals Julian showed off imply he might do better than Constantius, despite his present relative inexperience (*Or.* 1 56b)? How much was his control of his literary medium itself the message? No evidence survives to settle these doubts. Julian need not have intended a single answer. He presumably did not perform his panegyric but sent it to Constantius' court in written form, to be read out if at all by another. He did send a copy to Libanius (Lib. *Ep.* 30), demonstrating that even ostensibly occasional literature like praise-speeches circulated as literary texts. Their polysemic character served multiple audiences.

The parody with which Hal Drake introduces his discussion of Julian's second panegyric for Constantius demonstrates that even making a point did not have to be the point of a ceremonial speech: virtuosity brings its own pleasure. In this speech Julian showed himself manically adept in Homeric comparison. Julian surely was not thinking of how, in erotic verse of the Augustan period, Ovid simultaneously celebrated and exhausted military metaphors for a lover (*Am.* 1.9), but the dazzling overload worked similarly. Julian claimed mastery of a literature and its pattern of thinking. Several of the conference presentations incidentally demonstrated that Julian straight-facedly planted various jests whose wit cannot have escaped him. They are still funny.[30] This boon alone could vindicate literary study. Drake further observes that Julian's sendup of panegyric's conventional exploitation of Homer encased anodyne enough presentation of traditional imperial ideals, but also more pointed advocacy of an aggressive military policy. It corresponded strikingly to what Ammianus Marcellinus portrayed as the great strength of Julian's Caesarship in Gaul and the great folly of his Persian campaign as Augustus (e.g. Amm. Marc. 16.2.1–13, 24.7.3–8). Drake argues this panegyric was parodic, directed to Julian's supporters as diversion, but that it promoted a Roman ideal of military dominance Julian sincerely embraced. As Drake wisely suggests, attention to both sides of differences in policy between Julian and Constantius could produce a more accurate and just picture of their relationship. It is but one way in which the fruits of this collection lay seed for new inquiries.

Liz James dissects Julian's encomium of Eusebia with a scalpel absolutely not part of Julian's conceptual equipment but deft in her hands to reveal integral workings of his text: feminist criticism. Tougher argued in an earlier paper that Eusebia was cast by Constantius' image-management in the role of Julian's patroness.[31] James anatomizes how blandly Julian's praise for Eusebia conformed to rhetorical models and other late Roman encomia of women, demonstrating they shared a template for female virtues that occluded the women's individuality. Gender has been neglected in study of Julian. It is as if his chastity – Ammianus asserted that after the death of Julian's wife he never thought about sex (Amm. Marc. 25.4.2; cf. Lib. *Or.* 18.179) – barred researchers from thinking about the other ways maleness and femaleness functioned in his life. Masculinity is surely a fertile topic all around the bearded, shaggy lion of *Misopogon*, who neglects niceties but not his pen, and has no wart. Late antique holy men, both pagan and Christian, conscientiously embodied a self-mastery identified as masculine and developed out of classical paradigms.[32] Julian emulated that tradition and united it with Roman militarism. His *Caesars* carries these themes further.

The relationships of men can be investigated profitably in Julian's *Consolation on the Departure of Salutius* and in many of Julian's more personal letters. Josef Lössl aligns the *Consolation* with Cicero's self-consolation at the death of his daughter Tullia: not that Julian clearly drew on a Latin model, but that both authors made a distinctly philosophical move by connecting personal occasions to universal reflection. Likewise in the *Consolation*'s use of *topoi* of friendship, Lössl finds Julian showed closer kinship with Cicero's *Laelius* than with Greek sources. On the other hand, Lössl also identifies a popularized Neoplatonic psychology and non-Christian monotheism in Julian's arguments. The *Consolation* bridged Julian's personal and his philosophical work.

Prosopography, drawing with profit from ancient letter-collections among other sources, has established its importance in historical research.[33] Literary scholarship has begun to assay the medium's diversity.[34] Allowing for the considerable differences in technology, twenty-first-century social networking is demonstrating continually, and ever more clearly, that correspondence serves purposes in addition to transmitting news about the correspondents' activities. Historians eager for information about events and persons have not always valued these other functions, and so have missed part of the significance of their evidence. It can be hoped that as the modern analogue inspires further study, ancient letter-texts too will return ever richer results to more sympathetic inquiry.[35] Michael Trapp ably surveys the corpus attributed to Julian. Julian documented his own activities more newsily than Symmachus. His range varied more than Libanius'. Zosimus referred to Julian's letters as a source (Zos. 3.2.4), and modern historians too find vital material there. Literarily, as Trapp notes, Libanius and Ammianus both praised Julian's epistolary style (Lib. *Ep.* 716, *Or.* 18.302; Amm. Marc. 16.5.7). Apart from the sympathies of their religious affinities, the adherence they shared with Julian to classical *paideia* enabled them to appreciate Julian's cultural performance. Julian well deserves to be integrated into study of the late Roman sophistic.[36] Trapp offers illuminating sample analyses.

Setting the study of Julian thus in engagement with the literary and intellectual trends of his era will enrich understanding of his own cultural projects, as several chapters demonstrate. John Watt analyzes Julian's *Letter to Themistius* not only in relationship to the evidence it gives for the exhortation Themistius initially addressed to Julian, but also as a rejoinder in debate. That Themistius so understood it, he argues, is shown by the letter two Arabic manuscripts attribute to Themistius: this treatise on the philosophy of kingship accommodated Julian's contentions but resolved them in favor of resolutely Themistian interpretations of the Platonic and Aristotelian texts which Julian placed at stake. Themistius and Julian engaged dialogically around their disagreement. This fact is an important correction to the impression of isolation Julian's intellectual aggressiveness can suggest.[37] If his texts do not always mark the limits of conversations, if even disagreements could be pursued productively, it becomes possible to deduce if not to recover fully a more participatory exchange, at Julian's court and beyond it.

Not that easy comity embraced all. Julian riposted harshly to Cynics who took it as a prerogative of their sect to challenge him. Arnaldo Marcone draws the intellectual history of Cynic obstreperousness together with the web of Julian's concerns which contemporary Cynics affronted. With the speeches *Against Heraclius the Cynic* and *To the Uneducated Cynics* Marcone connects also Julian's letters to Themistius and the high priest Theodorus, the *Hymn to the Mother of the Gods*, the *Caesars*, and the *Misopogon*. Julian endeavored to revitalize traditional religions under a unified philosophical rationale. Had Cynics been willing to harmonize with this project, they might have embodied principled asceticism in an accessible manner and served Julian's ends. But instead their outspoken questioning of all received ideas incensed him. Marcone points to Julian's comparison of homeless Cynics to Christian monks, not as a valid analogy, but an index of the hostility they generated in him by their refusal to fall into step (*Or.* 7 224a–c).

Whereas Marcone concurs in Rowland Smith's judgment that Julian's orations against Cynics employed mostly commonplace ideas in oratorical fashion,[38] Andrew Smith demonstrates that Julian in his *Hymn to King Helios* followed Iamblichan metaphysics accurately. The apparent departures from Iamblichus' fully-articulated scheme result, he argues, from economical telescoping of expression in accordance with the attention that the hymn focuses on Helios. This targeting is a notable feature of Julian's literary operation. By not recapitulating the entire Neoplatonic cosmology, but celebrating Helios' unique position within it, Julian deferred to his *Hymn*'s festival occasion and specifically honored the god. Likewise in the *Caesars* Julian established his celestial setting in terms of a Neoplatonic incorporeal hierarchy, but thereafter left it to contextualize the ensuing dialogue tacitly.[39] While referring his works to a cohesive religious and philosophical system, maintaining his intellectual commitment, Julian focused within his texts on the particular topic at hand. Smith's finding that Julian maintained philosophical sophistication while being exoterically selective not only vindicates Julian's understanding, it also points the way to a new dimension of study. While philosophical originality and rigor deserve esteem for extending or refining intellectual systems,[40] the complementary endeavor of working out how systems apply to specific concerns also illuminates the system and exercises a writer's acumen.

Wolfgang Liebeschuetz observes that Julian laid claim to originality for his interpretation of the myth of Attis in his *Hymn to the Mother of the Gods* (*Or.* 5 161c). Like Smith, Liebeschuetz centers this *Hymn* on its festival occasion, and like Marcone he explores Julian's interest in religious revival. He identifies more room for common ground between Julian and contemporary Cynics than Marcone: it would be worth considering whether, as Watt suggests of the *Letter to Themistius*, the *Orations* concerned with the Cynics and the *Hymn to the Mother of the Gods* reflect not impervious hostility but an engaged intellectual confrontation. The extent to which Julian's texts stage conflict in order to highlight ideas before a broader audience or to appeal for sympathy is also worth examining. Reading Julian within the succession of Neoplatonic interpreters of Homer, Robert Lamberton found his versions restrictive and ineffective,[41] yet Smith's and Liebeschuetz's chapters suggest that Julian's *Hymns* might be more appropriately compared to homilies as interpretive texts tied to occasions of worship. There is also the question of what status the text interpreted possessed, separate from the interpretation. Whereas Heraclius and Julian competed through allegories of Julian's own reign, the *Hymn to the Mother of the Gods* took up a traditional story and allegorized the scandal it posed to Neoplatonic sensibility. Liebeschuetz authoritatively identifies the significance of myth in traditional Greek and Roman religious discourse, and sets Julian's interpretation in its relationship to Christian allegory and Iamblichus' reading of the Chaldaean oracles.

Susanna Elm had argued before this conference that Julian's rejection of Christian religious beliefs made him a productive opponent for Christian theologians, Gregory of Nazianzus in particular: separating the two sides in the conflict could only limit understanding of either.[42] In her chapter she again calls scholars to probe how Julian instigated Christian responses that became foundational. She analyzes Gregory's *Orations* 4 and 5, the famously fierce Christian counter-claim on the religious affiliation of Hellenism.[43] As Elm shows, the *stēlographia* which Gregory chose as his form (*Or.* 4.20, cf. 5.42), rather than rhetorical *psogos*, integrated *paideia* and politics within a theological vision. Pillorying Julian thus addressed the components of social prestige of the Christian elite who survived him. Through these nobles' attitudes, Julian's cultural program might have posed a tremendous threat. Although Gregory's literary strategy delegitimized Julian's endeavors to associate Greek culture with traditional religion exclusively of Christianity, his vehemence indelibly marked the danger as large. And much as Gregory wrote over Hellenic poetry with Christian content (cf. Zonaras 13.12), his figure of the Apostate created a Christian future of interpretation for Julian's works and policies.

Julian's direct assault on Christian theology is partially preserved. The extant text embedded in Cyril of Alexandria's *Contra Julianum* suggests Julian chiefly followed Celsus in characterizing Christianity as a double apostasy retaining only the worst elements of both Judaism and Hellenic beliefs (*C. Gall.* 43a).[44] David Hunt, however, uses Julian's letter to Photinus, deposed bishop of Sirmium (*Ep.* 55), to help substantiate Libanius' statement that Julian successfully refuted Christian claims for the divinity of Jesus, surpassing Porphyry (Lib. *Or.* 18.178). Hunt demonstrates that Julian indeed took on the hottest debates then current in the church. Even though Julian stuck to eristic fault-finding in his critique, he struck at a cardinal point of Christian belief with calculated understanding of Christian vulnerabilities: his attack was just as seriously contemporary as Elm reveals was Gregory's assault on Julian's Hellenism. Hunt's insight permits a more integrated understanding of *Against the Galileans* as a whole. Not only did Julian contend knowledgeably with ideological opponents (incidentally, an important finding of several of the conference's papers), this treatise in particular also bore a positive purpose. Its defense of polytheism[45] advocated aggressively against the religious alternative that had proven most robust in the Roman empire over the preceding generations. Had Julian been able to return victorious from the campaign in Persia he was also preparing when he composed *Against the Galileans*, he meant to carry through uprooting the opposed faith and replacing it with a rationalized transcendent paganism he considered better respectful of human nature and of local traditions.

Mark Humphries dissects Julian's *Letter to the Athenians* with acute attention to its political eristic. It is the one surviving example of the letters Zosimus reports that Julian wrote from the Danube region to cities of the empire justifying his rebellion against Constantius.[46] Humphries underlines the challenges which a manifesto for civil war had to surmount. He demonstrates how insistently Julian sounded his theme of justice. He reversed the most obvious reading of circumstances to portray Constantius rather than himself as initiating all conflict between them and implicitly threatening the whole empire with misrule. The *Letter* contains Julian's earliest extant references to a plurality of gods but as Humphries emphasizes they too underscored the legitimacy of Julian's claims rather than suggesting any religious program. By comparing the *Letter* to Mamertinus' panegyric for Julian on the following New Year, he displays how closely these political documents served rapidly-changing historical moments. Although the basic message of the parallel letters must have been similar, the fragment of Julian's letter to the Corinthians quoted by Libanius connected the city with himself by his father's having lived there (Lib. *Or.* 14.30); it is tantalizing to wonder whether Julian turned the Homeric idea of guest-friendship he evoked in that letter also to justice, or how much his strategies of personalization reconfigured his arguments. Both literarily and as a matter of policy, these letters together with the *Misopogon* suggest Julian expected cities to be communities of public opinion relevant to imperial administration. This conception would repay evaluation.[47]

Nicholas Baker-Brian reveals how much Constantius was implicitly a figure of the *Misopogon* as well as of the *Letter to the Athenians*. He sifts through the *Misopogon*'s loosely associative structure to identify temperance as the central pole of its contrasts. Not only did Julian position himself in bristly difference from the swish Antiochenes; Baker-Brian argues that Julian appropriated to himself the cardinal virtue developed in famous panegyrics of Constantius. He thus uncovers a new poignancy in Julian's exhibition of superior probity, a rivalry for the Antiochenes' affections. He remarks that Julian's literary expertise gave him the versatility to combine and invert panegyric forms; his own analysis of Julian's negotiation with texts of Themistius and Plato drives the point home.

Four chapters address textual presentations of Julian's work as emperor in media not typically assessed as literary. Jill Harries explains the corporate process by which the late Roman imperial administration produced laws. Julian's, like all imperial laws, amalgamated contributing bureaucrats' voices into the one utterance officially his. Routinely, they argued justification of their provisions, persuading by preference to exerting the state's power so as to compel compliance. This discourse of principles also implicitly aligned Julian with ideals of kingship. He pursued this line of self-justification more directly in the letters to the Athenians and to Themistius, the oration to Heraclius, and the *Misopogon*: a comprehensive rhetoric of justice and authority could be recovered and integrated with panegyric, biographical, and historiographical portraits of Julian and other emperors.[48] Notably, Harries observes that Julian opposed legislation of Constantine as improperly innovative, even on questions separate from religion. He followed the implementation of laws closely, from personally writing out warrants which *vicarii* might issue for the *cursus publicus* to chivvying laggard bureaucrats: Harries surveys the rich breadth of historical information the laws provide. She contrasts Ammianus' emphasis on the distinctive elements of Julian's legislation with the predominance of normal enactments attested in the Theodosian and Justinianic Codes: the laws display rulers' regular work more proportionately. She also demonstrates how the Codes' redactors flattened laws, even to the point of denaturing Julian's most notoriously anti-Christian initiatives.

Benet Salway surveys the known inscriptions that name Julian. He acknowledges and updates Stefano Conti's corpus of 2004.[49] Focusing in greater detail on texts that reflect Julianic authorship or initiatives, he highlights a subset of milestones in the province of Arabia, presumably associated with preparations for the Persian campaign of 363, which link Julian's name in various acclamations and wishes for victory with the phrase εἷς θεός, 'one god': the monotheistic formula standard in Christian inscriptions of the region evidently accommodated Julian too. An unusual formula in the dedication to Julian of a milestone near Mursa (*ILS* 8946, cf. Amm. Marc. 21.10.6) may reflect reciprocation of honor by Aurelius Victor, whom Julian had appointed governor of Pannonia Secunda and honored with a statue. Salway also discusses the fragmentary and garbled inscriptions of a law extracted in the Theodosian and Justinianic Codes, in which Julian authorized provincial governors to appoint subordinate judges to relieve them of some of the burden of minor cases.[50] As a body, this material, like Julian's legislation, displays how much of his reign attended to normal imperial business. It left room for individual touches. Above all, it marked the penetration of the emperor's official concern across the space of the empire.

Eric Varner considers the visual text of Julian's surviving portraiture. He tracks its progression from the clean-shaven Caesar very much in the Constantinian dynastic style to the markedly individual bearded sole Augustus. He discusses the controversy over identifying as Julian the famous full-length statue in the Louvre, and points to an unfinished portrait head in Thasos as confirmation that the images were a deliberately chosen type for Julian. The statue's *pallium* aligned him with images of intellectuals; the crown identified priestly activity, although not the conventional imperial insignia of the *pontifex maximus*. Varner also connects Julian's beard with representations of philosophers and, of particularly Roman note, Numa Pompilius: Julian in the hymn to Helios dated Rome's traditional reverence for the sun from Numa's reign (identifying it also with the undying flame of Vesta: *Or.* 4 155a-d), so that he would have welcomed this connection's tying in with his religious revival. Varner points to Julian's *Virtus Exercitus* coin-reverses as appropriating the visual tradition of Romulus and the *spolia opima* in order to proclaim military virtues.

Fernando López Sánchez advocates for treating Julian's coins as verbal and visual works bearing messages for viewers.[51] He correlates types from the period Julian was Caesar with Constantius' military policies. The victory at Strasbourg, which Julian led but in which Constantius' troops participated too, was marked by a palm on the reverse of solidi minted at Arles.[52] Even when Julian moved to claim the title Augustus by force, Constantius' mints maintained continuity of types in issues naming Julian as Caesar. While Constantius insisted on being the one to determine Julian's rank (Amm. Marc. 20.9.4), he held back from treating him as a rebel: his side of their relationship deserves a more sympathetic assessment than Julian's hostile propaganda allows.[53] López Sánchez also considers Julian's *Securitas Rei Publicae* large bronzes with their famously novel type of a bull and two stars. He proposes that Julian devised the image as a new military-religious emblem and conferred it on the elite units of the *protectores* at the 25th December festival of Sol Invictus in 362: Julian took advantage of the recent discovery of a new Apis bull in Egypt (Amm. Marc. 22.14.6), but also the protective military and sacrificial associations of the bull in the team with which the Romans ritually delimited a city's sacred boundary (*pomerium*). As López Sánchez remarks, Julian's method, using a special symbol to bind his elite troops to himself before a major campaign, was exactly what Constantine had done with the *Chi-Rho* of the *labarum*.[54] Even overwriting an image that had become commonly identified as Christian, Julian used a Constantinian syntax of imperial allegiance.

Finally, Rowland Smith brings Julian's *Caesars* forward to its reception in northern Europe in the sixteenth to eighteenth centuries. He traces the telling details that source-critically connected the translations and comments of Balthasar Grangier, Ezechiel Spanheim, the Abbé de La Bletterie, Edward Gibbon, John Duncombe, Voltaire, the fresco by Antonio Verrio at Hampton Court Palace, and even the fiction of Henry Fielding. He illuminates the contemporary religious politics shaping their various responses to Julian and to the *Caesars*, particularly the idea that this text uniquely instructs readers.[55] The readers' perceptions of a text complement the writer's work producing it. On both sides of this relationship a variety of circumstances – e.g. literary conventions, aesthetics, ideology, attachments, credentials of prestige, structures of authority – color all that is placed in consideration; Smith's chapter too marks a valuable field for future research.

The papers of the Cardiff conference, now the chapters of this volume, individually advance scholarship on the different facets of Julian's authorship. I have tried here to indicate directions for further investigation in which they point. Collectively these studies flesh out Julian's image as a person much more integrally connected with others than historical study of his frustrated reign has always done, or even literary study of his individual works. The confluence of chapters again and again shows Julian fluently manipulating the standards of the different genres in which he produced texts, from panegyric to letters and from treatises to laws. He interacted with the expectations of his audiences, both to entertain and to suggest new ideas. He challenged intellectuals directly as he sought to ground his projects in a system of ideas: he cherished sympathy, like Salutius', and he rebuked religious and philosophical dissenters. He consistently revered traditional Hellenic culture, particularly literature and education. No less consistently he expected others to share the values he found in classical texts. His cultural performance shared its pleasures. As Julian's laws show, he rejected the Constantinian revolution because of its breaks with tradition (including, but not just, religion), yet he repeated Constantinian gestures when he judged they could help secure support. Similarly Julian praised heterodox Christians whose views coincided with parts of his Neoplatonic theology; Julian's Christian opponents, like Gregory, sunk their whole understanding of him in his paganism and reacted with unremitting fierceness. Nevertheless, at the level of ideas their engagement was substantive too. Julian pursued the myriad duties of an emperor, even while trying to advance religious revival and Persian conquest in particular. His repeated efforts to promote his contentions suggest he was not willing to cease trying to turn around people who disagreed with him. No one approach can encompass Julian's reign. His many different works surviving, however, open up a web of opportunities to learn more.

Acknowledgements

I am most grateful to Shaun Tougher and Nicholas Baker-Brian for organizing this conference, to the institutional support and graduate student assistance that helped it to run smoothly, and to all the participants.

Notes

[1] Den Boeft, Drijvers, Den Hengst, and Teitler 2005, 160-61 *ad* Amm. Marc. 25.4.22, very reasonably accept Lindenbrog's *argutias* for V's *angustias*.

[2] Concerning this feature see Bruun 1995, esp. 474-8.

[3] *Pace* Den Boeft, Drijvers, Den Hengst, and Teitler 1995, 243 *ad* Amm. Marc. 22.14.3, and 2005, 159 *ad* Amm. Marc. 25.4.22, it was Antiochene caricaturists who described Julian *ut Cercops homo brevis umeros extentans angustos*; Ammianus here delivered his own contrary appraisal.

[4] Amm. Marc. 25.4.22.

[5] Cic. *Nat. D.* 2.153. See generally Kelly 2008, though he does not discuss this passage.

[6] Matthews 1989, 238; Sabbah 1978, 425–8.

[7] Kelly 2008, 296–317, discusses how the funerary monument Ammianus says Julian should have had at Rome (25.20.5) similarly fixed Ammianus' theme of Julian's significance for the state.

[8] Mamert. 6.1–5.

[9] *Or.* 5.23.

[10] See Susanna Elm's chapter.

[11] τὰς ἀτρίπτους ὑμῶν καὶ μαλακὰς χεῖρας, for the Homeric χεῖρας...ἀτρίπτους ἁπαλάς, *Od.* 21.150–151.

[12] *Misop.* 338b–339c.

[13] For Julian's coinage see also the chapter by Fernando López Sánchez in this volume. Julian's bearded *Virtus Exerc Gall* solidi were issued at Lyon (*RIC* 8, 226) and Arles (*RIC* 8, 303 and 304). They were dated to the rebellion already by Kent 1959, 112–13. Gilliard 1964, 136, objected that Julian's beard was associated with philosophy and paganism, but this interpretation must look anachronistically forward to Julian's later reign or back with blinkers, past the bearded military emperors of the third century, all the way to Marcus Aurelius.

[14] Kaegi 1964.

[15] Marcone 1984.

[16] Kennedy 2003 includes several discussions of panegyric and invective.

[17] Bouffartigue 1992.

[18] Gleason 1986.

[19] Relihan 1993, 119-34.

[20] Athanassiadi 1992, respectively xii, vii, ix, xi.

[21] Bowersock 1978, 104, and even more directly, 'This petulant and self-righteous cry is a clue to Julian's character' (14).

[22] Generally, e.g., Potter 1999, and cf. Bowersock 1994.

[23] Generally, e.g., Fowler 1982; Cairns 1972; Conte 1994.

[24] Long 1993.

[25] MacCormack 1972, 1976 and 1981.

[26] A vital insight of Nixon 1983.

[27] Athanassiadi 1992, 61.

[28] Philosopher's stance: Dio Chrys. *Or.* 1.9–10; paths to kingship and tyranny, Them. *Or.* 1.3b, Dio Chrys. *Or.* 1.67; flattery and praise, Them. *Or.* 1.3c, Dio Chrys. *Or.* 3.17–18.

[29] Cf. Men. Rhet. 370.9–14, 370.30–371.3, 372.27–373.1.

[30] *Pace* Bowersock 1982, 159, 'essentially humorless'.

[31] Tougher 1998b.

[32] Kuefler 2001; he touches on Julian briefly, 78–81, 170–78.

[33] E.g., Averil Cameron (ed.) 2003.

[34] Morello and Morrison 2007.

[35] Matthews 1974 shone crucial insight on a correspondence that earlier scholars had found maddeningly jejune.

[36] Whether it is considered as a part of the Second Sophistic or distinguished as a third, e.g., Amato (ed.) 2006.

[37] E.g., Bowersock 1978, 12-20.

[38] Smith 1995, 49–90.

[39] Pack 1946, and Long 2006, 63–4.

[40] E.g., Dillon 1999; cf. Smith 1995, 40.

[41] Lamberton 1986, 134–43.

[42] Elm 2003. Cf. also Elm 2012.

[43] E.g., Tougher 2007, 60; Alan Cameron 1993.

[44] Bouffartigue 1992, 685–6, details connections with Celsus.

[45] Identified by Smith 1995, 190-206, as the chief thrust of *C. Gall.*

[46] Zos. 3.10.3–4; cf. Mamert. 9.4, Lib. *Or.* 14.29, Amm. Marc. 21.16.7–8. Humphries follows Kaegi 1975 in preferring Ammianus' location at Naissus to Zosimus' at Sirmium.

[47] Jill Harries discusses many of Julian's laws concerning the administration of cities.

[48] Athanassiadi 1992, 89–120, reads Julian's laws simply as expressing idealistic policies.

[49] Conti 2004.

[50] *CIL* 3.459A, 3.14198; *Cod. Theod.* 1.16.8, *Cod. Iust.* 3.3.5; cf. Feissel 2000.

[51] As he remarks, this contention takes one side of a debate among numismatists; the sceptical position is argued by, e.g., Crawford 1983.

[52] *RIC* 8, Arl. nos. 234–237.

[53] Cf. Mark Humphries' chapter. Julian's view swayed others: e.g., Thompson 1947 analyzes Ammianus' hostility to Constantius; cf. Barnes 1998, 129–38.

[54] Drake 2000, 201–4.

[55] 'Instructive' and like terms recur in several of the assessments Smith quotes.

BIBLIOGRAPHY

Abramowski, L.
  1960   'Diodore de Tarse', *Dictionnaire d'Histoire et de Géographie Ecclésiastiques* 14, 496–504.
Adler, A.
  1928–38 *Suidae Lexicon*, Leipzig.
Aillagon, J. J. (ed.)
  2008   *Roma e i Barbari*, Milan.
Alföldi, A.
  1962   'Some portraits of Julianus Apostata', *AJA* 66, 403–5.
Alföldi, A. and Alföldi-Rosenbaum, E.
  1976   *Die Kontorniat-Medaillons. Antike Münzen und geschnittene Steine* 6.1, Berlin.
Alföldi, M. R.
  1999   *Bild und Bildersprache der römischen Kaiser: Beispiele und Analysen*, Mainz am Rhein.
Alonso-Núñez, J. M.
  1979   'The emperor Julian's *Misopogon* and the conflict between Christianity and Paganism', *Ancient Society* 10, 311–24.
  1984   'L'empereur Julien et les Cyniques', *Les Études Classiques* 52, 254–60.
Amato, E. (ed.)
  2006   *Approches de la troisième sophistique*, Brussels.
Andreotti, R.
  1931   'L'iconografia dell'imperatore Giuliano', *Bulletino del Museo dell'Impero Romano* 2 (published with *Bulletino della Commissione Archeologica Communale di Roma* 59 [1931]), 48–53.
Angelov, D. G.
  2004   'Plato, Aristotle and "Byzantine political philosophy"', *Mélanges de l'Université Saint-Joseph* 57, 499–523.
Angiolani, S.
  2008   *Giuliano l'Apostata, Elogio dell'imperatrice Eusebia (Orazione II)*, Naples.
Anti, C.
  1919   'Una statua di Numa nella Casa delle Vestali', *Bulletino della Commissione Archeologica Communale di Roma* 47, 211–24.
Arce, J.
  1975   *Estudios sobre las fuentes literarias, epigráficas y numismáticas para la historia del Emperador Fl. Cl. Juliano*, Granada.
  1984   *Estudios sobre el emperador Fl. Cl. Juliano: Fuentes literarias, epigrafia, numismática*, Madrid.
Ashton, J.
  2005   *Social Life in the Reign of Queen Anne*, London [reprint; 1st edition 1883].
Asmus, J. R.
  1894   'Gregorius von Nazianz und sein Verhältnis zum Kynismus', *Theologische Studien und Kritiken* 67, 314–39.

1895   *Julian und Dion Chrysostomus*, Tauberbischofsheim.

1896   'Eine Enzyklika Julians des Abtrünnigen und ihre Vorläufer', *Zeitschrift für Kirchengeschichte* 16, 45–71, 220–52.

1907   *Der Alkibiades-Kommentar des Jamblichos als Hauptquelle für Kaiser Julian*, Leipzig.

Athanassiadi, P.

1992   *Julian: An intellectual biography*, London and New York [reprint with updated bibliography of Athanassiadi-Fowden 1981].

Athanassiadi-Fowden, P.

1981   *Julian and Hellenism: An intellectual biography*, Oxford.

Aujoulat, N.

1983a 'Eusébie, Hélène et Julien. I. Le témoignage de Julien', *Byz* 58, 78–103.

1983b 'Eusébie, Hélène et Julien. II. Le témoignage des historiens', *Byz* 58, 421–52.

Babelon, E.

1903   'L'iconographie monétaire de Julien l'Apostat', *Revue Numismatique* 7, 130–63.

Bagnall, R. S., Cameron, A. D. E., Schwartz, S. R. and Worp, K. A.

1987   *Consuls of the Later Roman Empire*, Atlanta.

Baldwin, B.

1978   'The *Caesares* of Julian', *Klio* 60, 449–66.

Balty, J. C.

1976   'Pour une iconographie de Pythagore', *Bulletin des Musées Royaux d'Art et d'Histoire* 48, 5–33.

1980   'Le prétendu Marc-Aurèle d'Avenches', in *Eikones. Festschrift H. Jucker*, Berne, 57–63.

Banaji, J.

2001   *Agrarian Change in Late Antiquity: Gold, labour and aristocratic dominance*, Oxford.

Banchich, T. M.

1993   'Julian's School Laws: *Cod. Theod.* 13.3.5 and *Ep.* 42', *AncW* 24, 5–14.

Barceló, P.

2004   *Constantius II und seine Zeit. Die Anfänge des Staatskirchentums*, Stuttgart.

Bardiès-Fronty, I.

2009   *Le bain et le miroir*, Paris.

Bardy, G.

1934   'Photin de Sirmium', *Dictionnaire de Théologie Catholique* 12, 1532–6.

Barnes, T. D.

1978   'A correspondent of Iamblichus', *GRBS* 19, 99–106.

1981   *Constantine and Eusebius*, Cambridge Mass.

1987   'Himerius and the fourth century', *Classical Philology* 82, 206–25.

1992   'Praetorian prefects, 337–361', *Zeitschrift für Papyrologie und Epigraphik* 94, 249–60.

1993   *Athanasius and Constantius: Theology and politics in the Constantinian empire*, Cambridge, Mass.

1996   'Oppressor, persecutor, usurper: The meaning of *tyrannus* in the fourth century', in G. Bonamente and M. Mayer (eds) *Historia Augusta Colloquium Barcinonense*, Bari, 55–65.

1998   *Ammianus Marcellinus and the Representation of Historical Reality*, Ithaca and London.

2011   *Constantine. Dynasty, Religion and Power in the Later Roman Empire*, Chichester.

Barnes, T. D. and Vanderspoel, J.

    1981   'Julian and Themistius', *GRBS* 22, 187–9.

    1984   'Julian on the sons of Fausta', *Phoenix* 38, 175–6.

Bastien, P.

    1985   *Le monnayage de l'atelier de Lyon de la mort de Constantin à la mort de Julien (337–363)*, Wetteren.

    1992–94 *Le buste monetaire des empereurs romains*, vols. 1–3, *Numismatique Romaine. Essais, recherches, et documents* 19, Wetteren.

Baynes, N. H.

    1929   'Constantine the Great and the Christian Church', *Proceedings of the British Academy* 15, 341–442 [issued separately 1931; 2nd ed. 1972].

Becatti, G.

    1949   'Ritratto di un vate antico', *Bolletino d'Arte* 34, 97–110.

Beckwith, C. L.

    2005   'The condemnation and exile of Hilary of Poitiers at the Synod of Béziers (365 CE)', *JECS* 13, 21–38.

Beeley, C.

    2008   *Gregory of Nazianzus on the Trinity and the Knowledge of God: In your light we shall see light*, Oxford.

Benoist, S.

    2009   'Identité du prince et discours impérial: le cas de Julien', *AntTard* 17, 108–17.

Béranger, J.

    1948   'Le refus du pouvoir', *Museum Helveticum* 5, 178–96.

Bernardi, J.

    1978a   'Un réquisitoire: les *Invectives contre Julien* de Grégoire de Nazianze', in Braun 1978, 89–98.

    1978b   *Grégoire de Nazianze. Discours 1–3*, Paris.

    1983   *Grégoire de Nazianze. Discours 4–5 Contre Julien*, Paris.

Bernoulli, J. J.

    1882   *Römische Ikonographie* 1, Stuttgart.

    1894   *Römische Ikonographie* 2.3, Stuttgart.

Besterman, T.

    1954   *Voltaire's Correspondence*, vol. 4, Geneva [107 vols in total, 1953–65].

Bidez, J.

    1924   *L'empereur Julien, Oeuvres complètes* 1.2, *Lettres et fragments*, Paris.

    1929   *La tradition manuscrite et les éditions des discours de l'empereur Julien*, Paris.

    1930   *La vie de l'empereur Julien*, Paris.

    1932   *L'empereur Julien, Oeuvres complètes* 1.1, *Discours de Julien César (I–V)*, Paris.

Bidez, J. and Cumont, F.

    1898   *Recherches sur la tradition manuscrite des lettres de l'empereur Julien*, Brussels.

    1922   *Imp. Caesaris Flavii Claudii Iuliani epistulae, leges, poematia, fragmenta varia*, Paris and London.

Bieber, M.

    1959   'Roman men in Greek himation (Roman palliati). A contribution to the history of copying', *Proceedings of the American Philosophical Society* 103, 274–417.

Billault, A.
  2002   'Plutarch's *Lives*', in G. Sandy (ed.) *The Classical Heritage in France*, Leiden, 219–37.

Billerbeck, M.
  2006   'The ideal Cynic from Epictetus to Julian', in R.Br. Branham and M.-O. Goulet-Cazé (eds) *The Cynics: The Cynic movement in antiquity and its legacy*, Berkeley, 205–21.

Bischoff, B. and Nörr, D.
  1963   *Eine unbekannte Konstitution Kaiser Julians (c. Iuliani de postulando)* (Bayerische Akademie der Wissenschaften, philosophisch-historische Klasse, Abhandlungen, neue Folge 58), Munich.

Bleckmann, B.
  2003   'Gallus, César de l'Orient?', in F. Chausson and E. Wolff (eds) *Consuetudinis Amor. Fragments d'histoire romaine (IIe-VIe siècles) offerts à Jean-Pierre Callu*, Rome, 45–56.

Blockley, R. C.
  1972   'The panegyric of Claudius Mamertinus on the emperor Julian', *American Journal of Philology* 93, 437–50.
  1983   *The Fragmentary Classicising Historians of the Later Roman Empire: Eunapius, Olympiodorus, Priscus and Malchus*, vol. 2, *Text, Translation and Historiographical Notes*, Liverpool.
  1989   'Constantius II and Persia', in C. Deroux (ed.) *Studies in Latin Literature and Roman History*, Brussels, 465–90.
  1992   *East Roman Foreign Policy: Formation and conduct from Diocletian to Anastasius*, Leeds.

Bolgar, R. R.
  1954   *The Classical Heritage and its Beneficiaries: From the Carolingian age to the end of the Renaissance*, Cambridge.

Bonfante, L. W.
  1964   'Emperor, god and man in the IVth century: Julian the Apostate and Ammianus Marcellinus', *La Parola del Passato* 19, 401–27.

Bonnard, G.
  1945   *Le journal de Gibbon à Lausanne*, Geneva.

Borg, B.
  2004   'Glamorous intellectuals: Portraits of *pepaideumenoi* in the second and third centuries AD', in Borg (ed.) 2004, 157–78.

Borg, B. (ed.)
  2004   *Paideia: The world of the Second Sophistic*, Berlin and New York.

Borgeaud, P.
  2010   'Trojan excursions: A recurrent ritual, from Xerxes to Julian', *History of Religions* 49, 339–53.

Boschung, D.
  1993   *Die Bildnisse des Augustus. Das römische Herrscherbild* 1.2, Berlin.

Boswell, J.
  1976   *Life of Johnson*, ed. R. W. Chapman (3rd edition, revised), Oxford.

Bouffartigue, J.
  1978   'Julien par Julien', in Braun and Richer (eds) 1978, 15–30.

1992   *L'empereur Julien et la culture de son temps*, Paris.

2006   'La lettre de Julien à Thémistios: histoire d'une fausse manœuvre et d'un désaccord essentiel', in A. Gonzalez Galvez and P.-L. Malosse (eds) *Mélanges A. F. Norman*, *Topoi* Suppl. 7, Lyon-Paris, 113–38.

Boulenger, F.

1927   'L'empereur Julien et la rhétorique grecque', *Mélanges de Philosophie et d'Histoire publiés à l'occasion de la Faculté des lettres de l'Université catholique de Lille*, 32, 17–32.

Bourgeois, E.

1900   *Ézéchiel Spanheim: Relation de la Cour de France en 1690* [= *Annales de l'Université de Lyon*, n.s. II, fasc. 5], Paris and Lyon.

Bouyges, M.

1924   'Notes sur des traductions arabes III. Epître de Thémistius à Julien sur la politique', *Archives de philosophie* 2, 15–23 [363–71].

Bowden, H.

2010   *Mystery Cults in the Ancient World*, London.

Bowersock, G.

1978   *Julian the Apostate*, London.

1982   'The emperor Julian on his predecessors', *Yale Classical Studies* 27, 159–72.

1994   *Fiction as History*, Berkeley and London.

2006   'The epigraphy of the emperor Julian', *JRA* 19, 703–5.

Bradbury, S.

1987   'The date of Julian's *Letter to Themistius*', *GRBS* 28, 235–51.

1994   'Constantine and the problem of anti-pagan legislation in the fourth century', *Classical Philology* 89, 120–39.

1995   'Julian's pagan revival and the decline of blood sacrifice', *Phoenix* 49, 331–56.

2004   *Selected Letters of Libanius: From the age of Constantius and Julian*, Liverpool.

Brague, R

1999   *Thémistius. Paraphrase de la Métaphysique d'Aristote, Livre Lambda*, Paris.

Brauch, T.

1980   *The Political Philosophy of the Emperor Julian as Found in His Writings, Administration, and Propaganda*, PhD Diss., University of Minnesota.

1993   'Themistius and the emperor Julian', *Byz* 63, 79–115.

Braun, R. and Richer J. (eds)

1978   *L'Empereur Julien. De l'histoire à la légende (331–1715)*, Paris.

Braund, S. M.

1998   'Praise and protreptic in early imperial panegyric', in Mary Whitby (ed.) 1998, 55–75.

Bregman, J.

1997   'The emperor Julian's view of classical Athens', in C. D. Hamilton and P. Krentz (eds) *Polis and Polemos: Essays on politics, war, and history in ancient Greece in honor of Donald Kagan*, Claremont, 347–61.

Brennecke, H. C.

1984   *Hilarius von Poitiers und die Bischofsopposition gegen Konstantius II*, Berlin.

1988   *Studien zur Geschichte der Homöer*, Tübingen.

Bringmann, K.
  2004   *Kaiser Julian*, Darmstadt.
Brown, P.
  1992   *Power and Persuasion in Late Antiquity: Towards a Christian empire*, Madison.
Browning, R.
  1975   *The Emperor Julian*, London.
Brunt, P. A.
  1974   'Marcus Aurelius in his *Meditations*', *JRS* 64, 1–20.
  1975   'Stoicism and the principate', *Papers of the British School at Rome* 43, 3–75.
Bruun, C.
  1995   'The thick neck of the emperor Constantine: Slimy snails and
          "Quellenforschung"', *Historia* 44, 459–80.
Burgess, R. W.
  2008   'The summer of blood: The 'great massacre' of 337 and the promotion of
          the sons of Constantine', *DOP* 62, 5–51.
Burguière, P. and Evieux, P.
  1985   *Cyrille d'Alexandrie: Contre Julien*, vol. 1, Paris.
Burke, P.
  1992   *The Fabrication of Louis XIV*, Cambridge.
Bury, R. G.
  1926   *Plato,* Laws, vol. 1, London.
Buttrey, T. V.
  1972   'Vespasian as moneyer', *Num. Chron.* 12, 89–109.
Cadario, M.
  2011   'Il linguaggio dei corpi nel ritratto romano', in E. La Rocaa, C. Parisi Presicce
          and A. Lo Monaco (eds) *Ritratti. Le tante facce del potere*, Rome, 209–21.
Cairns, F.
  1972   *Generic Composition in Greek and Roman Poetry*, Edinburgh; rev. ed. 2007, Ann
          Arbor.
Caltabiano, M.
  1991   *L'epistolario di Giuliano imperatore*, Naples.
Calza, R.
  1972   *Iconografia Romana Imperiale da Carausio a Giuliano (287–363 d.C.)*, Rome.
Cameron, Alan
  1976   *Circus Factions: Blues and greens at Rome and Byzantium*, Oxford.
  1993   'Julian and Hellenism', *AncW* 24, 25–9.
Cameron, Averil
  1970   *Agathias*, Oxford.
  1976   *Flavius Cresconius Corippus,* In laudem Iustini Augusti minoris, London.
  1985   *Procopius and the Sixth Century*, London.
  1991   *Christianity and the Rhetoric of Empire*, Berkeley.
  1993   *The Later Roman Empire AD 284–430*, London.
Cameron, Averil (ed.)
  2003   *Fifty Years of Prosopography: The later Roman empire, Byzantium, and beyond*,
          Oxford and New York.
Cameron, Averil and Garnsey, P. (eds)
  1998   *The Cambridge Ancient History*, vol. 13, *The Late Empire, AD 337–425*, Cambridge.

Cameron, Averil and Hall, S. G.
   1999   *Eusebius,* Life of Constantine. *Translated with Introduction and Commentary,* Oxford.

Campenhausen, H. von
   1953   *Kirchliches Amt und geistliche Vollmacht in den ersten drei Jahrhunderten,* Tübingen.

Cantoclarus, C. [= Chantecler, C.]
   1583   *Ta Sōzomena: Juliani Imperatoris opera quae extant,* Paris.

Carandini, A. and Capelli, R. (eds)
   2000   *Roma, Romulo, Remo e la fondazione della città,* Rome.

Carrié, J.-M.
   2009   'Julien législateur: un mélange des genres?', *AntTard* 17, 175–84.

Carson, R. A. G.
   1981   *Principal Coins of the Romans,* vol. 3, *The Dominate AD 294–498,* London.
   1990   *Coins of the Roman Empire,* London and New York.

Carson, R. A. G., Hill, P. V. and Kent, J. P. C.
   1978   *Late Roman Bronze Coinage, AD 324–498,* London.

Castelfranchi, M. F.
   2005   'Costantino e l'edilizia cristiana in Oriente', in Donati and Gentile (eds) 2005, 106–23.

Charron, A. and Heijmans, M.
   2001   'L'obélisque du cirque d'Arles', *JRA* 14, 373–80.

Chastagnol, A.
   1962   *Les fastes de la Préfecture de Rome au Bas-Empire,* Paris.
   1988   'Le formulaire de l'épigraphie latine officielle dans l'antiquité tardive', in A. Donati (ed.) *La terza età dell'epigrafia,* Faenza, 11–65 [reprinted in S. Benoist and S. Demougin (eds) A. Chastagnol, *Le pouvoir impérial à Rome: Figures et commemorations. Scripta varia IV* (Hautes études du monde gréco-romain 41), Paris, 2008, 133–87].

Chausson, F.
   2007   *Stemmata Aurea. Constantin, Justine, Théodose. Revendications généalogiques et idéologie impériale au IVe siècle ap. J.-C.,* Rome.

Chiesa, G. S.
   2005   '*Felicia tempora*: la riconquista del classico', in Donati and Gentile (eds) 2005, 130–7.

Cianciani, F.
   1981   'Aineas', *LIMC* 1, 381–96.

Clark, C.
   2006   *Iron Kingdom: The rise and downfall of Prussia, 1600–1947,* Harmondsworth.

Classen, J.-M.
   1999   *Displaced Persons: The literature of exile from Cicero to Boethius,* London.

Clearey, T. R.
   1984   *Henry Fielding: Political writer,* Ontario.

Coarelli, F.
   1999   'Statuae Regum Romanorum', in M. Steinby (ed.) *Lexicon Topographicum Urbis Romae,* Rome, 368–9.

Cohoon, J. W.
   1932   *Dio Chrysostom, Orations,* vol. 1, London and New York.

Consolino, F. E.
    1986   *Elogio di Serena*, Venice.

Conte, G. B.
    1994   *Genres and Readers*, trans G. W. Most, Baltimore.

Conti, S.
    2004   *Die Inschriften Kaiser Julians*, Stuttgart.

Conton, R.
    2004   'Il rovescio con il toro nei bronzi di Giuliano', *Rivista italiana di numismatica* 105, 135–47.

Corcoran, S. J. J.
    1996   *The Empire of the Tetrarchs: Imperial pronouncements and government AD 284–324*, Oxford [rev. ed. 2000; repr. 2007].
    2007   'Galerius' jigsaw puzzle: The Caesariani dossier', *AntTard* 15, 221–50.
    2008   'The heading of Diocletian's Prices Edict at Stratonicea', *Zeitschrift für Papyrologie und Epigraphik* 166, 295–302.

Cranston, M.
    1957   *John Locke: A biography*, London.

Crawford, M. H.
    1983   'Roman imperial coin types and the formation of public opinion', in C. N. L. Brooke *et al.* (eds) *Studies in Numismatic Method Presented to Philip Grierson*, Cambridge, 47–64.

Cribiore, R.
    2007   *The School of Libanius in Late Antique Antioch*, Princeton.

Criscuolo, U.
    1983   'Sull' epistola di Giuliano imperatore al filosofo Temistio', *Koinonia* 7, 89–111.
    1987   'Gregorio di Nazianzo e Giuliano', in U. Criscuolo (ed.) *Talariscos. Studia Graeca Antonio Garzya sexagenario a discipulis oblata*, Naples, 165–208.

Croissant, J.
    1930   'Un nouveau discours de Thémistius', *Serta Leodiensia, Bibliothèque de la faculté de philosophie et lettres de l'université de Liège* 44, Liège-Paris, 7–30.

Cürsgen, D.
    2008   'Kaiser Julian über das Wesen und die Geschichte der Philosophie', in Schäfer (ed.) 2008, 65–86.

Curta, F.
    1995   'Atticism, Homer, Neoplatonism, and *Fürstenspiegel*: Julian's second panegyric on Constantius', *GRBS* 36, 177–211.

D'Ambra, E.
    2005   'Kosmetai, the Second Sophistic and portraiture in the second century', in J. M. Barringer and J. M. Hurwitt (eds) *Periklean Athens and its Legacy: Problems and perspectives*, Austin, 201–16.

Dagron, G.
    1968   'L'empire romain d'Orient au IVème siècle et les traditions politiques de l'hellénisme: Le témoignage de Thémistios', *Travaux et Mémoires* 3, 1–242.
    1984   *Constantinople imaginaire: Études sur le recueil des* Patria, Paris.

Daley, B. E.
    2006   *Gregory of Nazianzus*, New York.

Daly, L. J.
    1980   '"In a borderland": Themistius' ambivalence toward Julian', *BZ* 73, 1–11.
De Kersauson, K.
    1996   *Musée du Louvre. Catalogue des portraits romains*, vol. 2, Paris.
De Loos-Deitz, E. P.
    1983   'Le bronze de Lyon supposé de Julian l'Apostat', *Bulletin Antieke Beschaving* 58, 116–26.
De Spirito, G.
    1999   'Palatium Iulianus', in. M. Steinby (ed.) *Lexicon Topographicum Urbis Romae*, Rome, 44.
De Vos, M.
    1991   'La fuga di Enea in pitture del I secolo d.C.', *Kölner Jahrbuch für Vor- und Frühgeschichte* 24, 113–23.
Den Boeft, J., Den Hengst, D. and Teitler, H. C.
    1991   *Philological and Historical Commentary on Ammianus Marcellinus XXI*, Groningen.
Den Boeft, J., Den Hengst, D. and Teitler, H. C. (eds)
    1992   *Cognitio Gestorum: The historiographic art of Ammianus Marcellinus*, Amsterdam.
Den Boeft, J., Drijvers, J. W., Den Hengst, D. and Teitler, H. C.
    1995   *Philological and Historical Commentary on Ammianus Marcellinus XXII*, Groningen.
    2005   *Philological and Historical Commentary on Ammianus Marcellinus XXV*, Leiden and Boston.
Depeyrot, D.
    1996   *Les émissions monétaires d'Arles (quatrième-cinquième siècles)*, Wetteren.
Des Places, E.
    1971   *Oracles Chaldaïques, avec un choix des commentaires anciens*, Paris.
Desmond, W.
    2006   *The Greek Praise of Poverty: Origins of ancient Cynicism*, Notre Dame.
Desnier, J.-L.
    1985   'Renaissance taurine', *Latomus* 44, 402–9.
Di Segni, L.
    1994   'Εἶς Θεός in Palestinian inscriptions', *Scripta Classica Israelica* 13, 94–115.
Dignas, B. and Winter, E.
    2007   *Rome and Persia in Late Antiquity: Neighbours and rivals*, Cambridge.
Dillon, J. M.
    1973   *Iamblichi Chalcidensis in Platonis dialogos commentarium fragmenta*, Leiden.
    1999   'The theology of Julian's *Hymn to King Helios*', *Quaderns Catuluns de Cultura Clàssica* 14–15, 103–15.
Dillon, S.
    2006   *Ancient Greek Portrait Sculpture*, Cambridge.
DiMaio, M.
    1978   'The transfer of the remains of the emperor Julian from Tarsus to Constantinople', *Byz* 48, 43–50.
DiMaio, M. and Arnold, Duane W.-H.
    1992   '*Per vim, per caedem, per bellum*: A study of murder and ecclesiastical politics in the year 337 AD', *Byz* 62, 158–211.
Donati, A. and Gentili, G. (eds)
    2005   *Costantino Il Grande. La civiltà antica al bivio tra Occidente e Oriente*, Milan.

Downey, G.

1939   'Julian the Apostate at Antioch', *Church History* 8, 303–15.

1951   'The economic crisis at Antioch under Julian the Apostate', in P. R. Coleman-Norton (ed.) *Studies in Roman Economic and Social History in Honor of Allan Chester Johnson*, New York, 312–21.

Drake, H. A.

1989   'Policy and belief in Constantine's *Oration to the Saints*', *Studia Patristica* 19, 43–51.

2000   *Constantine and the Bishops: The politics of intolerance*, Baltimore and London; paperback edition 2002.

2009   'Solar power in late antiquity', in A. Cain and N. Lenski (eds) *The Power of Religion in Late Antiquity*, Aldershot, 215–26.

Drijvers, J. W. and Hunt, D. (eds)

1999   *The Late Roman World and its Historian: Interpreting Ammianus Marcellinus*, London and New York.

Drinkwater, J. F.

1983   'The "Pagan Underground", Constantius II's "Secret Service", and the usurpation of Julian the Apostate', in C. Deroux (ed.) *Studies in Latin Literature and Roman History* 3, Brussels, 348–87.

2007   *The Alamanni and Rome 213–496 (Caracalla to Clovis)*, Oxford.

Duncombe, J.

1784   *Select Works of the Emperor Julian, and Some Pieces of the Sophist Libanius, Translated from the Greek*, 2 vols., London [2nd edn. 1792; 3rd edn. 1798].

Dütschke, H.

1882   *Antike Bildwerke in Vicenza, Venedig, Catajo, Modena, Parma und Mailand*, Leipzig.

Dvornik, F.

1955   'The emperor Julian's "reactionary" ideas on kingship', in K. Weitzmann *et al.* (eds), *Late Classical and Medieval Studies in Honor of Albert Mathias Friend*, Princeton, 71–81.

1966   *Early Christian and Byzantine Political Philosophy: Origins and background*, vol. 2, Washington DC.

Edwards, M.

2003   *Constantine and Christendom*, Liverpool.

Elm, S.

2003   'Hellenism and historiography: Gregory of Nazianzus and Julian in dialogue', *Journal of Medieval and Early Modern Studies* 33, 493–515.

2005   'Hellenism and historiography: Gregory of Nazianzus and Julian in dialogue', in D. B. Martin and P. Cox Miller (eds) *The Cultural Turn in Late Ancient Studies: Gender, asceticism, and historiography*, Durham NC and London, 258–77.

2009   'Family men: Masculinity and philosophy in Late Antiquity', in P. Rousseau and M. Papoutsakis (eds) *Transformations of Late Antiquity: Essays for Peter Brown*, Farnham, 279–302.

2010a   '"Translating culture": Gregory of Nazianzus, *Hellenism*, and the claim to *Romanitas*', in A. Kleihues, B. Naumann and E. Pankow (eds) *Intermedien: Zur kulturellen und artistischen Übertragung*, Zürich, 17–26.

2010b 'Gregory of Nazianzus's life of Julian revisited (*Or.* 4 and 5): The art of governance by invective', in S. McGill, C. Sogno and E. Watts (eds) *From the Tetrarchs to the Theodosians: Later Roman history and culture, 284–450 CE*, Cambridge and New York, 171–84.

2012 *Sons of Hellenism, Fathers of the Church: Emperor Julian, Gregory of Nazianzus, and the vision of Rome*, Berkeley.

Elmer, G.

1937 'Die Kupfergeldreform unter Julianus Philosophus', *Numismatische Zeitschrift* 70, 25–34.

Emerson, H.

1934 'Wilmer Cave Wright, PhD. 1865–1951', *Bulletin of the New York Academy of Medicine* 30 (3), 223–6.

Ensslin, W.

1930 'Constantius (4)', in W. Kroll (ed.) *Paulys Real-Encyclopädie der Classischen Altertumswissenschaft. Neue Bearbeitung. Unter Mitwirkung Zahlreicher Fachgenossen*, vol. 14, Stuttgart, 444–52.

Evans, J. R.

1990 'Statues of the kings and Brutus on the Capitoline', *Opuscula Romana* 18.5, 99–105.

Evers, C.

1994 *Les portraits d'Hadrien: typologie et ateliers*, Brussels.

Ewald, B.

1999 *Der Philosoph als Leitbild. Ikonographische Untersuchungen an römischen Sarkophagreliefs*, Mainz.

Febvre, L. and Martin, H.-J.

1984 *The Coming of the Book: The impact of printing 1450–1800*, trans. D. Gerard, London.

Feissel, D.

2000 'Une constitution de l'empereur Julien entre texte épigraphique et codification (*CIL* III, 459, et *CTh* I, 16, 8)', in E. Lévy (ed.) *La codification des lois dans l'Antiquité. Actes du Colloque de Strasbourg, 27–29 novembre 1997*, Paris, 315–37 [reprinted in D. Feissel, *Documents, droit, diplomatique de l'Empire romain tardif*, Paris, 2010, 205–22].

2009 'Une inscription de Kos et une loi de Valens (Iscrizioni di Cos ED 90 et CTh 13, 10, 7)', *Chiron* 39, 299–317.

Fejfer, J.

2008 *Roman Portraits in Context, Image and Context*, vol. 2, Berlin.

Ferrando, P.

1997 *Les monnaies d'Arles. De Constantin le Grand à Romulus Augustule (313–476)*, Paris.

Ferrary, J.-L.

2007 'L'abbé de la Bletterie et Gian Vincenzo Gravina à propos du gouvernement romain sous les empereurs', in J.-L. Quantin and J.-C. Waquet (eds) *Papes, princes et savants dans l'Europe moderne: Mélanges à la mémoire de Bruno Neveu*, Geneva, 313–32.

Fielding, H.

1993 *A Voyage from this World to the Next*, ed. B. Goldgar and H. Amory in *Henry*

Fielding: Miscellanies, vol. 2, Oxford [originally published as *Miscellanies*, London 1743].

Filges, A.
2000 'Himationträger, Palliaten und Togaten. Der männliche Mantel-Normaltypus und seine regionalen Varianten in Rundplastik und Relief', in T. Mattern and D. Korol (eds) *Munus. Festschrift für Hans Wiegartz*, Münster.

Finnamore, J. F.
1993 'Iamblichus on light and the transcendent', in H. J. Blumenthal and E. G. Clark (eds) *The Divine Iamblichus: Philosopher and man of gods*, London, 55–64.

Fisher, E. A.
1984 'Theodora and Antonina in the *Historia Arcana*: History and/or fiction?', in J. Peradotto and J. P. Sullivan (eds) *Women in the Ancient World: The Arethusa papers*, New York, 287–313.

Fittschen, K.
1992/1993 'Ritratti maschili privati di epoca adrianea. Problemi della loro varietà', *Scienze dell'antichità. Storia, archeologia, antropologia* 6/7, 445–85.
1997 'Privatporträts hadrianischer Zeit', in J. Bouzek and I. Ondrejová (eds) *Roman Portraits: Artistic and literary*, Mainz, 32–6.
1999 *Prizenbildnisse Antoninischer Zeit. Beiträge zur Erschliessung hellenistischer und kaiserzeitlicher Skulptur und Architectur* 18, Mainz.
2011 'The portraits of Roman emperors and their families', in B. Ewald and C. Noreña (eds) *The Emperor and Rome: Space, representation, and ritual* (*Yale Classical Studies* 35), Cambridge, 221–46.

Fittschen, K. and Zanker, P.
1985 *Katalog der römischen Porträts in den Capitolinischen Museen und den anderen kommunalen Sammlungen der Stadt Rom 1. Kaiser-und Prinzenbildnisse. Beiträge zur Erschliessung hellenistischer und kaiserzeitlicher Skulptur und Architektur* 3, Mainz.

Fleck, T.
2008 *Die Porträts Julianus Apostatus. Antiquitates Archäologische Forschungsergebnisse* 44, Hamburg.

Flower, H. I.
2000 'The tradition of the spolia opima: Marcus Claudius Marcellus and Augustus', *Classical Antiquity* 19, 34–64.

Fontaine, J.
1987 'Un insuccesso ambiguo: la diatriba del Misopogon', in Fontaine, Prato and Marcone 1987, lx–lxx.

Fontaine, J., Prato, C. and Marcone, A.
1987 *Giuliano Imperatore, Alla Madre degli dei e altri discorsi*, Milan.

Foucault, M.
1985 *Discourse and Truth: The problematization of parrhesia. Six Lectures given by M. Foucault at Berkeley (Oct.–Nov. 1983)*, ed. J. Pearson, Evanston.

Fowler, A.
1982 *Kinds of Literature*, Cambridge, Mass.; repr. 1985, Oxford.

Frantz, A.
1979 'Did Julian the Apostate rebuild the Parthenon?', *AJA* 83, 395–401.

Gallay, P.
1964–7 *Saint Grégoire de Nazianze. Lettres*, Paris.

Galzigna, M.
2009 'La vérité-événement', *Critique* 749, 860–71.

García Garrido, M. D.
2000 *Las homilias In hexaemeron de Basilios de Cesarea:¿Una respuesta a la política religiosa del emperador Juliano?*, Louvain-la-Neuve.

García Ruiz, P.
2008a 'La evolución de la imagen política del emperador Juliano a través de los discursos consulares: Mamertino, *Pan.* III [11] y Libanio, *Or.* XII', *Minerva* 21, 137–53.
2008b 'Una lectura de la *Gratiarum Actio* de Claudio Mamertino a la luz de los primeros escritos de Juliano', *Emerita* 76, 231–52.

Gautier, F.
2002 *La retraite et le sacerdoce chez Gregoire de Nazianze*, Turnhout.

Geffcken, J.
1914 *Kaiser Julianus*, Leipzig.

Gérard, C.
1995 *L'empereur Julien, Contre les Galiléens: une imprécation contre le christianisme*, Brussels.

Germino, E.
2004 *Scuola e cultura nella legislazione di Giuliano l'Apostata*, Naples.

Gibbon, E.
1994 *The History of the Decline and Fall of the Roman Empire*, ed. D. Womersley, 3 vols., Harmondsworth [originally published in 6 vols, London 1776–88].

Gilliard, F.
1964 'Notes on the coinage of Julian the Apostate', *JRS* 54, 135–41.

Gleason, M. W.
1986 'Festive satire: Julian's *Misopogon* and the New Year at Antioch', *JRS* 76, 106–19.
1995 *Making Men: Sophists and self-presentation in ancient Rome*, Princeton NJ.

Goette, H. R.
1989 'Kaiserzeitliche Bildnisse von Sarapis-Priestern', *Mitteilungen des Deutschen Archäologischen Instituts, Abteilung Kairo* 45, 173–85.
1990 *Studien zu römischen Togadarstellung. Beiträge zur Erschliessung hellenistischer und kaiserzeitlicher Skulptur und Architektur* 10, Mainz.

Goldgar, B.
1986 'Myth and history in Fielding's *From this World to the Next*', *Modern Language Quarterly* 47, 235–52.

Goulet-Cazé, M.-O.
2008 'Qui était le philosophe cynique anonyme attaqué par Julien dans son *Discours* IX?', *Hermes* 136, 97–118.

Greatrex, G.
1993 'The two fifth-century wars between Rome and Persia', *Florilegium* 12, 1–13.

Gregory, T. E.
1983 'Julian and the last oracle at Delphi', *GRBS* 24, 355–66.

Grierson, P., Mango, C. and Ševčenko, I.
    1962   'The tombs and obits of the Byzantine emperors (337–1042); with an additional note', *DOP* 16, 3–63.

Grisar, H.
    1908   *Roma alla fine del mondo antico*, Rome.

Grivaud de la Vincelle, C. M.
    1807   *Antiquités gauloises et romaines*, Paris.

Guida, A.
    1994   *Teodoro di Mopsuestia. Replica a Giuliano Imperatore*, Florence.

Guido, R.
    2000   *Giuliano Imperatore, Al cinico Eraclio*, Galatina.

Gwynn, D. M.
    1999   'Constantine and the other Eusebius', *Prudentia* 31, 94–124.

Haines, C. R.
    1916   *Marcus Aurelius Antoninus. Communings with himself*, Cambridge, Mass.

Haloander, Gregorius
    1530   *Codicis D. N. Iustiniani sacratiss(imi) principis ex repetita praelectione libri XII*, Nuremberg.

Hamiaux, M., with Metzger, C. and Saragoza, F.
    2003   *Julien l'Apostat ou la double imposture: les statues du Louvre et des thermes de Cluny. Actualité du département des Antiquités grecques, étrusques et romaines no 11, du 24 septembre 2003 au 12 janvier 2004*, Paris.

Hammerstaedt, J.
    1988   *Die Orakelkritik des Kynikers Oenomaus*, Frankfurt.

Hänel, G.
    1857   *Corpus legum ab imperatoribus Romanis ante Iustinianum latarum quae extra constitutionum codices supersunt*, Leipzig.

Hannestad, N.
    2007   'Die Porträtskulptur zur Zeit Konstantins des Grossen', in A. Demandt and J. Engemann (eds) *Konstantin der Grosse. Imperator Flavius Constantinus*, Trier, 96–116.

Hansen, I. L.
    2008   'Muses as models: Learning and the complicity of authority', in S. Bell and I. L. Hansen (eds) *Role Models in the Roman World: Identity and assimilation, Memoirs of the American Academy in Rome* supplemental volume 7, Ann Arbor, 273–86.

Hanson, R. P. C.
    1988   *The Search for the Christian Doctrine of God: The Arian controversy 318–381*, Edinburgh.

Hardy, B. C.
    1986   'The emperor Julian and his School Law', *Church History* 37, 131–43.

Harl, K.
    1987   *Civic Coins and Civic Politics in the Roman East, 180–275 AD*, Berkeley.

Harless, G. C.
    1796   *Bibliotheca Graeca* (3rd edition), vol. 5, Hamburg.

Harries, J.
    1988   'The Roman imperial quaestor from Constantine to Theodosius II', *JRS* 78, 148–72.

1999   *Law and Empire in Late Antiquity*, Cambridge.

2007   *Law and Crime in the Roman World*, Cambridge.

Harris, W. V.

2001   *Restraining Rage: The ideology of anger control in classical antiquity*, Cambridge, Mass.

Hassall, M. W. C. and Tomlin, R. S. O.

1980   'Roman Britain in 1979, II. Inscriptions', *Britannia* 11, 403–17.

Haury, J. and Wirth, G.

1964   Procopius Caesariensis *Peri ktismaton libri 6 sive De aedificiis*, Leipzig.

Heather, P.

1998   'Themistius: A political philosopher', in Mary Whitby (ed.) 1998, 125–50.

1999   'The barbarian in late antiquity: Image, reality, and transformation', in R. Miles (ed.) *Constructing Identities in Late Antiquity*, London, 234–58.

Heather, P. and Moncur, D.

2001   *Politics, Philosophy, and Empire in the Fourth Century: Select orations of Themistius*, Liverpool.

Hedlund, R.

2008   '... *Achieved Nothing Worthy of Memory': Coinage and authority in the Roman empire c. AD 260–295*, Uppsala.

Hedrick, C.

2000   *History and Silence: Purge and rehabilitation of memory in late antiquity*, Austin, Texas.

Hekster, O.

2007   'Fighting for Rome: The emperor as military leader', in L. De Blois and E. Lo Casio (eds) *The Impact of the Roman Army (200 BC–AD 476). Proceedings of the Sixth Workshop of the International Network Impact of Empire (Capri, March 29–April 2, 2005)*, Leiden, 91–105.

Henck, N.

2001a   'Constantius ὁ φιλοκτίστης', *DOP* 55, 279–304.

2001b   'Constantius' *paideia*, intellectual milieu and promotion of the liberal arts', *Proceedings of the Cambridge Philological Society* 47, 172–86.

2007   'Constantius II and the cities', in J. Drinkwater and B. Salway (eds) *Wolf Liebeschuetz Reflected: Essays presented by colleagues, friends, and pupils*, London, 147–56.

Hercher, R.

1873   *Epistolographi Graeci*, Paris.

Hertlein, F. C.

1875–6   *Iuliani Imperatoris quae supersunt praeter reliquias apud Cyrillum omnia*, 2 vols, Leipzig.

Hoffmann, D.

1969   *Das spätrömische Bewegungsheer und die Notitia dignitatum*, Düsseldorf.

Hoistadt, R.

1948   *Cynic Hero and Cynic King: Studies in the Cynic conception of man*, Uppsala.

Hollard, D.

2010   'Julien et Mithra sur le relief de Taq-e-Bostan', *Sources for the History of Sasanian and Post-Sasanian Iran, Res Orientales* 19, 147–63.

Holloway, R. R.
2004   *Constantine and Rome*, New Haven.

Honoré, T.
1986   'The making of the Theodosian Code', *Zeitschrift der Savigny-Stiftung für Rechtsgeschichte* 103, 133–222.

1998   *Law in the Crisis of Empire, 379–455 AD: The Theodosian dynasty and its quaestors*, Oxford.

Humphries, M.
1998   'Savage humour: Christian anti-panegyric in Hilary of Poitiers' *Against Constantius*', in Mary Whitby (ed.) 1998, 201–24.

2008   'From usurper to emperor: The politics of legitimation in the age of Constantine', *JLA* 1, 82–100.

Forthcoming a 'Emperors, usurpers, and the city of Rome: Performing power from Diocletian to Theodosius', in J. Wienand (ed.) *Contested Monarchy: Integrating the Roman empire in the 4ᵗʰ Century AD*, New York.

Forthcoming b *Emperors and Usurpers: Civil war, tyranny, and the fall of the Roman empire, AD 200–500*.

Humphries, M. and Gwynn, D.
2010   'The sacred and the secular: The presence or absence of Christian religious thought in secular writing in the late antique west', in D. Gwynn and S. Bangert (eds) *Religious Diversity in Late Antiquity*, Leiden, 493–509.

Hunt, A. S. and Edgar, G. C.
1934   *Select Papyri*, vol. 2, London.

Hunt, E. D.
1985   'Christians and Christianity in Ammianus Marcellinus', *CQ* 35, 186–200.

1995   'Julian and Marcus Aurelius', in D. Innes, H. Hine and C. Pelling (eds) *Ethics and Rhetoric: Classical essays for Donald Russell on his 75ᵗʰ birthday*, Oxford, 287–98.

1998a   'The successors of Constantine', in Cameron and Garnsey (eds) 1998, 1–43.

1998b   'Julian', in Cameron and Garnsey (eds) 1998, 44–77.

1999   'The outsider inside: Ammianus on the rebellion of Silvanus', in Drijvers and Hunt (eds) 1999, 51–63.

Huskinson, J.
1975   *Roman Sculpture from Cyrenaica in the British Museum*, London.

2000   *Experiencing Rome: Culture, identity and power*, London.

Hyde, M.
1973   *The Impossible Friendship*, London.

Inan, J. and Alföldi-Rosenbaum, E.
1979   *Römische und frühbyzantinische Porträtplastik aus der Turkei: Neue Funde*, Mainz.

James, L.
2001   *Empresses and Power in Early Byzantium*, Leicester.

Janka, M.
2008   '*Quae philosophia fuit, satura facta est*: Julians *Misopogon* zwischen Gattungskonvention und Sitz im Leben', in Schäfer (ed.) 2008, 177–206.

Janssen, H.

1953   *Kaiser Julians Herrscherideal in Theorie und Wirklichkeit*, Cologne: Phil. F., Diss. v. 3.

Jeffreys, E. (ed.)

2003   *Rhetoric in Byzantium*, Aldershot.

Jeffreys, E., Jeffreys, M., Scott. R. *et al.*

1986   *The Chronicle of John Malalas*, Melbourne.

Johnson, A.C., Coleman-Norton, P.R. and Bourne F.C. (eds)

1961   *Ancient Roman Statutes*, Austin.

Johnson, M. J.

2009   *The Roman Imperial Mausoleum in Late Antiquity*, Cambridge.

Jones, A. H. M.

1956   'Numismatics and history', in R. A. G. Carson and C. H. V. Sutherland (eds) *Roman Coinage: Essays presented to Harold Mattingly*, Oxford.

1964   *The Later Roman Empire 284–602: A social, economic and administrative survey*, 3 vols, Oxford.

Jones, C.

2002   *The Great Nation: France from Louis XV to Napoleon*, Harmondsworth.

Jones, C. P.

1978   *The Roman World of Dio Chrysostom*, Cambridge, Mass. and London.

Jucker, H.

1981   'Marc Aurel bleibt Marc Aurel', *Bulletin de l'Association Pro Aventico* 26, 5–35.

Kaegi, W. E.

1964   'The emperor Julian's assessment of the significance and function of history', *Proceedings of the American Philological Society* 108, 29–38.

1967   'Domestic military problems of Julian the Apostate', *Byzantinische Forschungen* 2, 247–64.

1975   'The emperor Julian at Naissus', *L'antiquité classique* 44, 161–71.

Kahlos, M.

2009   *Forbearance and Compulsion: The rhetoric of religious tolerance and intolerance in late antiquity*, London.

Kaldellis, A.

2005   'Julian, the Hierophant of Eleusis, and the abolition of Constantius' tyranny', *CQ* 55, 652–55.

Kampen, N.

2009   *Family Fictions in Roman Art*, Cambridge.

Καπετανοπούλου, E. A.

1975   "Ἐπιγραφαὶ ἐξ Ἐλευσῖνος', *Ἀρχαιολογικὴ Ἐφημερίς*, 59–65.

Kelly, C.

2009   *The End of Empire: Attila the Hun and the fall of Rome*, New York.

Kelly, G.

2005   'Constantius II, Julian, and the example of Marcus Aurelius (Ammianus Marcellinus XXI, 16,11–12)', *Latomus* 64, 409–16.

2008   *Ammianus Marcellinus: The allusive historian*, Cambridge and New York.

Kelly, J. N. D.

1972   *Early Christian Creeds*, 3rd edn., London.

Kennedy, G. A.
1983   *Greek Rhetoric under Christian Emperors*, Princeton.
2003   *Progymnasmata: Greek textbooks of prose composition and rhetoric*, Atlanta.
Kent, J. P. C.
1954   'Notes on some fourth-century coin types', *Num. Chron.* 14, 216–17.
1959   'An introduction to the coinage of Julian the Apostate (AD 360–363)', *Num. Chron.* 19, 109–17.
1981   *The Roman Imperial Coinage*, vol. 8, *The Family of Constantine I, AD 337–364*, London.
Kiilerich, B.
1993   *Late Fourth Century Classicism in the Plastic Arts*, Odense University Classical *Studies* 18, Odense.
Klein, R.
1977   *Constantius II und die christliche Kirche*, Darmstadt.
Kolb, A.
1998   'Kaiser Julians Innenpolitik: grundlegende Reformen oder traditionelle Verwaltung? Das Beispiel des *cursus publicus*', *Historia* 47, 342–59.
Kolb, F.
2001   *Herrscherideologie in der Spätantike*, Berlin.
Koortbojian, M.
2008   'The double identity of Roman portrait statues. Costumes and their symbolism at Rome', in J. Edmondson and A. Keith (eds) *Roman Dress and the Fabrics of Roman Culture*, *Phoenix* suppl. vol. 46, Toronto, Buffalo, and London, 71–93.
Kopecek, T. A.
1979   *A History of Neo-Arianism*, Cambridge, Mass.
Koster, S.
1980   *Die Invektive in der griechischen und römischen Literatur*, Meisenheim am Glan.
Kozloff, A.
1987   'The Cleveland bronze: The emperor as philosopher', *Bulletin of the Cleveland Art Museum* 74, 84–99.
Kristensen, T. M.
2009   *Archaeology of Response: Christian destruction, mutilation and transformation of pagan sculpture in late antiquity*, Dissertation, Aarhus University.
Krüger, P.
1877   *Codex Iustinianus*, Berlin.
Kuefler, M.
2001   *The Manly Eunuch: Masculinity, gender ambiguity, and Christian ideology in late antiquity*, Chicago and London.
Kurmann, A.
1988   *Gregor von Nazianz: Oratio 4 gegen Julian. Ein Kommentar*, Basel.
L'Orange, H. P. and Wegner, M.
1984   *Das spätantike Herrscherbild von Diokletian bis zu den Konstantin-Söhnen (284– 361 n. Chr.), Das Römische Herrscherbild* 3.4, Berlin.
La Bletterie, J. P. R. de
1735   *La Vie de l'Empereur Julien*, Paris and Amsterdam [2nd edition Paris 1746; 3rd edition Paris 1775; translated as *The Life of the Emperor Julian,* London 1746].

1748   *Histoire de l'empereur Jovien, et traductions de quelques ouvrages de l'empereur Julien*, Paris [2ⁿᵈ edition Paris 1776].

La Rocca, E., Parisi Presicce, C. and Lo Monaco, A. (eds)

2011   *Ritratti. Le tante facce del potere*, Rome

Labriola, I.

1975   *Giuliano l'Apostata: Autobiografia. Messaggio agli ateniesi*, Florence.

1991–92 'La lode di Atene nella Lettera agli Ateniesi dell'imperatore Giuliano (tradizione e attualità)', *Invigilata Lucernis* 13–14, 179–204.

Lacombrade, C.

1960   'L'empereur Julien et la tradition romaine', *Pallas* 9, 155–64.

1962   'Notes sur *Les Césars* de l'empereur Julien', *Pallas* 11, 59–60.

1964   *L'empereur Julien, Oeuvres complètes* 2.2, *Discours de Julien l'empereur (X–XII)*, Paris.

Lahusen, G. and Formigli, E.

2001   *Römische Bildnisse aus Bronze. Kunst und Technik*, Munich.

Lamberton, R.

1986   *Homer the Theologian*, Berkeley and London.

Lamberton, R. and Keaney, J. J. (eds)

1992   *Homer's Ancient Readers: The hermeneutics of Greek epic's earliest exegetes*, Princeton.

Lanciani, R.

1883   *Notizie degli Scavi*, Rome

1888   *Ancient Rome*, London.

1897   *Ruins and Excavations of Ancient Rome*, London.

Lane Fox, R.

1986   *Pagans and Christians: Religion and the religious life from the second to the fourth century AD*, New York.

1997   'The itinerary of Alexander: Constantius to Julian', *CQ* 47, 239–52.

Langille, E.

2010   '*Candide* and *Tom Jones*: Voltaire perched on Fielding's shoulders', in A. W. Lee (ed.) *Mentoring in Eighteenth Century British Literature*, Farnham, 85–108.

Langley, T. R.

2001   *Image Government: Monarchical metamorphoses in English literature and art, 1649–1702*, Cambridge.

Lavaud, L.

2008   *D'une métaphysique à l'autre: figures d'altérité dans la philosophie de Plotin*, Paris.

Leppin, H. and Portmann, W.

1998   *Themistios Staatsreden*, Stuttgart.

Levante, E.

2001   *Sylloge Nummorum Graecorum (SNG). France 5: Mysie*, Paris.

Lévêque, P.

1960   'Observations sur l'iconographie de Julien dit l'Apostat d'après une tête inédite de Thasos', *Fondation Eugène Piot, Monuments et Mémoirs* 51, 105–28.

1962   'De nouveaux portraits de l'empereur Julien', *Latomus* 22, 74–84.

Levine, L.

2000   *The Ancient Synagogue: The first thousand years*, New Haven.

Leyerle, B.

2001   *Theatrical Shows and Ascetic Lives: John Chrysostom's attack on spiritual marriage*, Berkeley.

357

Liebeschuetz, J. H. W. G.

1972   *Antioch: City and imperial administration in the later Roman empire*, Oxford.

2008   'The view from Antioch: from Libanius via John Chrysostom to John Malalas and beyond', in P. Brown and R. Lizzi Testa (eds) *Pagans and Christians in the Roman Empire: The breaking of a dialogue (IVth–VIth century AD)*, Berlin and Vienna, 309–38.

Lieu, S. N. C.

1989   *The Emperor Julian: Panegyric and polemic*, 2nd edition, Liverpool [orig. pub. 1986].

Lieu, S. N. C. and Montserrat, D. (eds)

1996   *From Constantine to Julian: Pagan and Byzantine views. A Source History*, London and New York.

Lim, R.

2003   'Converting the un-Christianizable: The baptism of stage performers in late antiquity', in K. Mills and A. Grafton (eds) *Conversion in Late Antiquity and the Early Middle Ages: Seeing and believing*, Rochester NY, 84–126.

Loewe, V.

1924   *Ein Diplomat und Gelehrter: Ezechiel Spanheim*, Berlin.

Long, J.

1993   'Structures of irony in Julian's *Misopogon*', *AncW* 24, 15–23.

1996   *Claudian's* In Eutropium*: Or, how, when, and why to slander a eunuch*, Chapel Hill and London.

2006   'Julian Augustus' Julius Caesar', in M. Wyke (ed.) *Julius Caesar in Western Culture*, Oxford, 62–82.

López Sánchez, F.

2001   'Le chrisme et la stratégie idéologique de Magnence (350–353 apr. J.-C.)', *Cahiers Numismatique* 147, 43–58.

2002   'La tutelle de l'armée danubienne sur la dynastie constantinienne (337–361 apr. J.-C.)', *Cahiers Numismatiques* 151, 39–56.

2005   'Le revers au cavalier tombant (348–357/8 ap. J.-C.) comme référence aux batailles de Singara (344 apr. J.-C.) et Gaugamèle (331 av. J.-C.)', *Cahiers Numismatiques* 151, 39–56.

2007   'Arles, la Constantinople gauloise (328–363 apr. J.-C.)', *Cahiers Numismatiques* 174, 23–48.

2009   'A discussion of the "Poemenius" coins in the Welbourn hoard', in R. Abdy, E. Ghey, C. Hughes and I. Leins (eds) *Coin Hoards from Roman Britain*, vol. 12, 302–3 and pl. 30.

Lössl, J.

2007   'Bildung? Welche Bildung? Zur Bedeutung der Ausdrücke "Griechen" und "Barbaren" in Tatians *Rede an die Griechen*', in F. R. Prostmeier (ed.) *Frühchristentum und Kultur*, Breisgau, 127–53.

Luchner, K.

2008   '"Grund, Fundament, Mauerwerk, Dach"? Julians φιλοσοφία im Netzwerk seiner Briefe', in Schäfer (ed.) 2008, 221–52.

Lugaresi, L.

1993   *Gregorio di Nazianzo. Contro Giuliano l'Apostata: Orazione 4*, Florence.

1997   *Gregorio di Nazianzo. La morte di Giuliano l'Apostata: Orazione 5*, Florence.

2003 'Ambivalenze della rappresentazione: Riflessioni patristiche su riti e spettacoli', *Zeitschrift für Antikes Christentum/Journal of Ancient Christianity* 7, 281–309.

MacCormack, S. G.

1972 'Change and continuity in late antiquity, the ceremony of *adventus*', *Historia* 21, 721–52.

1976 'Latin prose panegyrics: Tradition and discontinuity in the later Roman empire', *Revue des études augustiniennes* 22, 29–77.

1981 *Art and Ceremony in Late Antiquity*, Berkeley.

Mace, N. A.

1991 'Henry Fielding's classical learning', *Modern Philology* 88, 243–60.

Mackie, G.

1997 'A new look at the patronage of Santa Costanza, Rome', *Byz* 67, 383–406.

Maguiness, W. S.

1932 'Some methods of the Latin panegyrists', *Hermathena* 47, 42–61.

Malbon, E. S.

1990 *The Iconography of the Sarcophagus of Junius Bassus*, Princeton.

Malley, W. J.

1978 *Hellenism and Christianity*, Rome.

Malosse, P.-L.

1997 'Libanius on Constantine again', *CQ* 47, 519–24.

2003 *Libanios. Discours*, vol. 4, *Discours LIX*, Paris.

2004 'Antioche et le kappa', *Topoi* 5, *Antioche de Syrie: Histoire, images et traces de la ville antique*, 77–96.

Mandrou, R.

1978 *From Humanism to Science, 1480–1700*, trans. B. Pearce, Harmondsworth.

Marco, F.

1999 'Ambivalencia icónica y persuasión ideológica: las monedas de Juliano con representación del toro', *Athenaeum* 87/1, 201–14.

Marcone, A.

1984 'Un panegirico rovesciato: Pluralità di modelli e contaminazione letteraria nel <Misopogon> giulianeo', *Revue des études augustiniennes* 30, 226–39, reprinted in Marcone 2008, 15–28.

2008 *Di Tarda Antichità. Scritti scelti*, Florence.

Marcovich, M.

1995 *Clementis Alexandrini Protrepticus*, Leiden and New York.

Martin, J.

2009 'Julien dit L'apostat, écrits autobiographiques', *AntTard* 17, 27–49.

Marucchi, O.

1887 *Nuova descrizione della Casa delle Vestali*, Rome.

Masaracchia, E.

1990 *Giuliano Imperatore, Contra Galilaeos*, Rome.

Matheeusen, C. and Heesakkers, C.

1980 *Two Neo-Latin Menippean Satires. Justus Lipsius: Somnium. Petrus Cunaeus: Sardi Venales*, Leiden.

Mathews, T. F.

1993 *The Clash of the Gods: A reinterpretation of early Christian art*, Princeton.

Matthews, J.
 1974 'The letters of Symmachus', in J. W. Binns (ed.) *Latin Literature of the Fourth Century*, London and Boston, 58–99.
 1989 *The Roman Empire of Ammianus*, London.
 2000 *Laying Down the Law: A study of the Theodosian Code*, New Haven.
 2007 *The Roman Empire of Ammianus: With a new introduction*, Ann Arbor.
 2010 *Roman Perspectives*, New Haven.

Mattingly, H. and Sydenham, E. A.
 1936 *The Roman Imperial Coinage*, vol. 4.1, *Pertinax to Geta*, London.

Mattingly, H., Sydenham, E. A. and Webb, P. H.
 1927 *The Roman Imperial Coinage*, volume 5.1, *Valerian to Interregnum*, London.

Mauldon, M.
 2008 *Montesquieu: Persian Letters*, Oxford.

Maxwell, J. L.
 2006 *Christianization and Communication in Late Antiquity: John Chrysostom and his congregation in Antioch*, Cambridge.

Mayer, E.
 2002 *Rom ist dort, wo der Kaiser ist. Untersuchungen zu den Staatsdenkmälern des dezentralisierten Reiches von Diocletian bis zu Theodosius II, Römisch-Germanisches Zentralmuseum Forschungsinstitut für Vor-und Frühgeschichte Monographien 53*, Mainz.

Mazza, M.
 1998 'Giuliano o dell'utopia religiosa: il tentativo di fondare una chiesa pagana?', *Rudiae* 10, 19–42.

McCormick, M.
 1986 *Eternal Victory: Triumphal rulership in late antiquity, Byzantium, and the early medieval west*, Cambridge.

McGuckin, J.
 2001 *St Gregory of Nazianzus: An intellectual biography*, New York.

McLynn, N.
 2004 'The transformation of imperial churchgoing in the fourth century', in S. Swain and M. Edwards (eds) *Approaching Late Antiquity: The transformation from early to late empire*, Oxford, 235–70.
 2006 'Among the hellenists: Gregory and the sophists', in J. Børtnes and T. Hägg (eds) *Gregory of Nazianzus: Images and reflections*, Copenhagen, 213–38, repr. McLynn 2009, no. 8.
 2009 *Christian Politics and Religious Culture in Late Antiquity*, Farnham.

Meischner, J.
 1995 'Studien zur spätantiken Kaiserikonographie', *Jahrbuch des Deutschen Archäologischen Instituts* 110, 431–46.

Meredith, A.
 1980 'Porphyry and Julian against the Christians', *Aufstieg und Niedergang der römischen Welt* 2.22, Berlin, 1119–49.

Mervaud, C.
 1976 'Julien l'Apostat dans la correspondance de Voltaire et Frédéric II', *Révue d'histoire littéraire de la France* 76, 724–42.

Michaels-Mudd, M.
:   1979   'The Arian policy of Constantius II and its impact on church-state relations in the fourth-century Roman empire', *Byzantine Studies* 6, 95–111.

Mild, W.
:   1978   'Susanna Highmore's literary reputation', *Proceedings of the American Philosophical Society* 122, 377–84.

Millar, F.
:   1977   *The Emperor in the Roman World (31 BC–AD 337)*, London.
:   2006   *A Greek Roman Empire: Power and belief under Theodosius II*, Berkeley.

Moatti, C.
:   1995   'L'Abbé de la Bleterie, 1697–1772: de l'érudition à la politique', *Mélanges de l'École Française de Rome* 107, 121–43.

Moles, J.
:   1983   '"Honestius quam ambitiosius"? An exploration of the Cynic's attitude to moral corruption in his fellow men', *JHS* 103, 103–23.
:   1990   'The kingship orations of Dio Chrysostom', in F. Cairns and M. Heath (eds) *Papers of the Leeds International Seminar* 6, 297–375.

Mommsen, T.
:   1873   *Corpus Inscriptionum Latinarum*, vol. 3. *Inscriptiones Asiae, provinciarum Europae Graecarum, Illyrici, Latinae, pars prior*, Berlin.
:   1904   *Theodosiani libri XVI cum constitutionibus Sirmondianis, pars posterior: Textus cum apparatu*, Berlin [= T. Mommsen and P. M. Meyer (eds), *Theodosiani libri XVI cum constitutionibus Sirmondianis et Leges novellae ad Theodosianum pertinentes*, 2 vols, Berlin, 1905, vol. I.2].

Mommsen, T., Hirschfeld, O. and Domaszewski, A. von
:   1902   *Corpus Inscriptionum Latinarum*, vol. 3. *Inscriptionum Orientis et Illyrici Latinarum Supplementum, pars posterior*, Berlin.

Morello, R. and Morrison, A. D.
:   2007   *Ancient Letters: Classical and late antique epistolography*, Oxford.

Moureaux, J.-M.
:   1994   *Voltaire: Discours de l'empereur Julien contre les chrétiens*, Oxford [SVEC vol. 332].

Müller, F. L.
:   1998   *Die beiden Satiren des Kaisers Julianus Apostata* (Symposion *oder* Caesares *und* Antiochikos *oder* Misopogon*)*, Stuttgart.

Munzi, M.
:   1996   'Considerazioni sulla riforma monetaria dell'imperatore Giuliano', *Annali dell'Instituto Italiano di Numismatica* 43, 295–305.

Murray, J.
:   1896   *The Autobiographies of Edward Gibbon*, London.

Nesselrath, H. G.
:   1994   'Menippeisches in der Spätantike: Von Lukian zu Julians Caesares und zu Claudians In Rufinum', *Museum Helveticum* 51, 30–44.
:   1998   'Lucien et le Cynisme', *Antiquité Classique* 67, 121–35.
:   2008   'Mit „Waffen" Platons gegen ein christliches Imperium: Der Mythos in Julians Schrift „Gegen den Kyniker Herakleios"', in Schäfer (ed.) 2008, 207–20.

Neumann, K. J.
  1880   *Juliani librorum contra Christianos quae supersunt*, Leipzig.
Neveu, B.
  2000   'Un académicien de XVIII siècle, traducteur et biographie de l'empereur
          Julien: L'abbé de la Bletterie', *Comptes rendus/Académie des inscriptions et belles-
          lettres* 144, 93–133.
Nichols, J.
  1782   *Biographical and Literary Anecdotes of William Bowyer*, London.
Nixon, C. E. V.
  1983   'Latin panegyric in the Tetrarchic and Constantinian period', in B. Croke and
          A. M. Emmett (eds) *History and Historians in Late Antiquity*, Sydney, 88–99.
  1991   'Aurelius Victor and Julian', *Classical Philology* 86, 113–25.
Nixon, C. E. V. and Rodgers, B. S.
  1994   *In Praise of Later Roman Emperors: The Panegyrici Latini. Introduction, translation
          and historical commentary with the Latin text of R. A. B. Mynors*, Berkeley and Los
          Angeles.
Nock, A. D.
  1926   *Sallustius, Concerning the Gods and the Universe*, Cambridge.
  1957   'Deification and Julian: I', *JRS* 47, 115–23 [reprinted in Nock, *Essays on
          Religion and the Ancient World*, ed. Z. Stewart, Oxford, 1972, 833–46].
Noga-Banai, G.
  2008   'Between the Menorot: New light on a fourth century Jewish representative
          composition', *Viator* 39, 21–48.
Norman, A. F.
  1969   *Libanius, Selected Works*, vol. 1, *The Julianic Orations*, Cambridge, Mass. and
          London.
  1977   *Libanius, Selected Works*, vol. 2, *Selected Orations*, Cambridge, Mass. and
          London.
  1992   *Libanius, Autobiography and Selected Letters*, vol. 1, Cambridge, Mass. and
          London.
  2000   *Antioch as a Centre of Hellenic Culture as Observed by Libanius*, Liverpool.
North, H.
  1966   *Sophrosyne: Self-knowledge and self-restraint in Greek literature*, New York.
O'Meara, D. J.
  1989   *Pythagoras Revived: Mathematics and philosophy in late antiquity*, Oxford.
  2003   *Platonopolis: Platonic political philosophy in late antiquity*, Oxford.
Ogilvie, B.
  Forthcoming *Ezechiel Spanheim (1629–1710) and the Learned Culture of Seventeenth-
          Century Europe*.
Opper, T.
  2008   *Hadrian: Empire and conflict*, London.
Overbeck, M. and Overbeck, B.
  2001   'Die Revolte des Poemenius zu Trier – Dichtung und Wahrheit', *Humanitas*
          65, 235–46.
Pack, E.
  1986   *Städte und Steuern in der Politik Julians. Untersuchungen zu den Quellen eines
          Kaiserbildes*, Brussels.

Pack, R.
  1946   'Notes on the *Caesars* of Julian', *Transactions of the American Philological Association* 77, 151–7.

Papini, M.
  2002   'Una statua di Sol a Palazzo Barberini', *Mitteilungen des Deutschen Archäologischen Instituts Römische Abteilung* 109, 83–108.

Parisi Presicce, C.
  2005   'L'abbandono della moderazione. I ritratti di Costantino e della sua progenie', in Donati and Gentile (eds) 2005, 138–53.
  2006   'Costantino come Giove. Proposta di ricostruzione grafica del colosso acrolitico dalla Basilica Costantiniana', *Bulletino della Commissione Archeologica Communale di Roma* 107, 127–61.

Parvis, S.
  2006   *Marcellus of Ancyra and the Lost Years of the Arian Controversy 325–345*, Oxford.

Paschoud, F.
  1979   *Zosime. Histoire nouvelle*, vol. 2.1, Paris.
  1994   'Les fragments 8, 8a et 9 de l'ouvrage historique d'Eunape', in *Scritti classici e cristiani offerti a Francesco Corsaro*, Catania, 549–60.
  2000   *Zosime. Histoire nouvelle*, vol. 1 (rev. ed.), Paris.

Patterson, A. M.
  2000   'A Restoration Suetonius: A new Marvell text', *Modern Language Quarterly* 61, 463–80.

Pearce, J. W. E.
  1951   *The Roman Imperial Coinage*, vol. 9, *Valentinian I to Theodosius I*, London.

Peeters, P.
  1924   'La date de la fête des SS. Iuventin et Maximien', *Analecta Bollandiana* 42, 77–82.

Penella, R. J.
  1990   *Greek Philosophers and Sophists in the Fourth Century AD: Studies in Eunapius of Sardis*, Leeds.
  1993   'Julian the persecutor in fifth century church historians', *AncW* 24, 31–43.
  2000   *The Private Orations of Themistius*, Berkeley.
  2007   *Man and the Word: The orations of Himerius*, Berkeley.

Pernot, L.
  1993   *La rhétorique de l'éloge dans le monde gréco-romain I: histoire et technique*, Paris.

Pétau, D. (Petavius)
  1630   *Iuliani imperatoris opera quae quidem reperiri potuerunt omnia*, Paris.

Petersen, E.
  1926   Εἷς Θεός. *Epigraphische, formgeschichtliche und religionsgeschichtliche Untersuchungen*, Göttingen.

Pfrommer, M.
  1987   'The emperor's shoes: Hellenistic footwear in Roman times', *Bulletin of the Cleveland Museum of Art* 74, 124–9.

'Philaretus Anthropopolita'
  1681   *Seasonal Remarks upon the Deplorable Fall of the Emperour Julian, with an epistle of his to the Citizens of Bostra*, London.

Piganiol, A.
  1938   'La couronne de Julien César', *Byz* 13, 243–8.

Polaschek, K.
   1969   *Untersuchungen zu griechischen Manteldarstellungen. Der Himationtypus mit Armschlinge*, Berlin.
Porter, R.
   1982   *English Society in the Eighteenth Century*, Harmondsworth.
Potter, D. S.
   1999   *Literary Texts and the Roman Historian*, London and New York.
Prato, C. and Fornaro, A.
   1984   *Giuliano Imperatore, Epistola a Temistio*, Lecce.
Prato, C. and Micalella, D.
   1979   *Giuliano Imperatore, Misopogon*, Rome.
   1988   *Giuliano Imperatore, Contro i Cinici ignoranti*, Lecce.
Préaux, J.
   1969   'Les quatre vertus païennes et chrétiennes: Apothéose et ascension', in J. Bibauz (ed.) *Hommages à Marcel Renard*, vol. 1 (*Collection Latomus* 101), Brussels, 639–57.
Procopé, J.
   1988   'Greek and Roman political theory', in J. H. Burns (ed.) *The Cambridge History of Medieval Political Thought*, Cambridge, 21–36.
Quasten, J.
   1974   *Patrology*, vol. 3, Utrecht.
Quiroga, A.
   2009   'Julian's *Misopogon* and the subversion of rhetoric', *AntTard* 17, 127–35.
Rademaker, A.
   2005   *Sophrosyne and the Rhetoric of Self-Restraint: Polysemy and persuasive use of an ancient Greek value term*, Leiden.
Radice, B.
   1968   'Pliny and the *Panegyricus*', *Greece and Rome* 15, 166–72.
Radoševi , N.
   1995   'The division of rule in the Greek *basilikoi logoi* from the fourth century', *Recueil des travaux de l'Institut d'Études Byzantines* 34, 1–20 (in Serbo-Croat; English summary 18–20).
Rambaud, M.
   1966   *L'art de la défamation historique dans les Commentaires de César*, 2nd ed, Paris.
Rapp, C.
   1998   'Comparison, paradigm and the case of Moses in panegyric', in Mary Whitby (ed.) 1998, 277–98.
   2005   *Holy Bishops in Late Antiquity: The nature of Christian leadership in an age of transition*, Berkeley.
Rees, R.
   2002   *Layers of Loyalty in Latin Panegyric, AD 289–307*, Oxford and New York.
   2004   *Diocletian and the Tetrarchy*, Edinburgh.
Rehak, P.
   2001   'Aeneas or Numa? Rethinking the meaning of the Ara Pacis Augustae', *Art Bulletin* 83, 190–208.
Relihan, J. C.
   1993   *Ancient Menippean Satire*, Baltimore.

Renucci, P.
  2000   *Les idées politiques et le gouvernement de l'empereur Julien*, Brussels.
Reynolds, J.
  1982   *Aphrodisias and Rome*, London.
Rezza, D.
  2010   *Un neofita va in Paradiso: il sarcofago di Giunio Basso*, Rome.
Ribble, F. G. and Ribble, A. G.
  1996   *Fielding's Library: An annotated catalogue*, Charlottesville.
Riccardi, L. A.
  2002   'Military standards, imagines, and the gold and silver imperial portraits
          from Aventicum, Plotinoupolis, and the Marengo treasure', *Antike Kunst*
          45, 86–99.
  2007   'The bust-crown, the Panhellenion, and Eleusis. A new portrait from the
          Athenian agora', *Hesperia* 76, 365–90.
Richardson, L.
  1992   *A New Topographical Dictionary of Ancient Rome*, Baltimore.
Richer, J.
  1981   *L'empereur Julien. De la légende au mythe (De Voltaire à nos jours)*, Paris.
Ring, A.
  2004   'Julian', *Suda On Line*, accessed 1 April 2012 <http://www.stoa.org/sol-
          entries/iota/437>.
Robinson, C.
  1979   *Lucian and his Influence in Europe*, London.
Rochefort, G.
  1963   *L'empereur Julien, Oeuvres complètes* 2.1, *Discours de Julien l'empereur (VI–IX)*,
          Paris.
Rodgers, B. S.
  1989   'The metamophosis of Constantine', *CQ* 39, 233–46.
Rolfe, J. C.
  1935–40 *Ammianus Marcellinus*, 3 vols, vol. 1 1935, vol. 2 1940, vol. 3 1939 (vol. 1
          revised and reprinted 1950, vol. 3 revised and reprinted 1952), Cambridge,
          Mass. and London.
Rosen, K.
  2006   *Julian: Kaiser, Gott und Christenhasser*, Stuttgart.
Rosenbaum, E.
  1960   *A Catalogue of Cyrenaican Portrait Sculpture*, London.
Rosenmeyer, P.
  2001   *Ancient Epistolary Fictions: The letter in Greek literature*, Cambridge.
Rosenthal, F.
  1940   'On the knowledge of Plato's philosophy in the Islamic world', *Islamic
          Culture* 14, 387–422 [reprinted Rosenthal, *Greek Philosophy in the Arab World*,
          1990, no. 2].
Roueché, C. M.
  1984   'Acclamations in the later Roman empire: new evidence from Aphrodisias',
          JRS 74, 181–99.
  2004   *Aphrodisias in Late Antiquity, revised second edition. The late Roman and Byzantine
          inscriptions* (http://insaph.kcl.ac.uk/ala2004), London.

Rousseau, P.
1994   *Basil of Caesarea*, Berkeley, Los Angeles, and London.

Rumscheid, J.
2000   *Kranz und Krone. Zu Insignien, Siegespreisen und Ehrenzeichen der römischen Kaiserzeit, Istanbuler Forschungen* 43, Tübingen.

Runyon, R.
2005   *The Art of the Persian Letters: Unlocking Montesquieu's 'secret chain'*, Newark NJ.

Russell, D. A.
1973   *Plutarch*, London.
1998   'The panegyrists and their teachers', in Mary Whitby (ed.) 1998, 17–50.

Russell, D. A. and Wilson, N. G.
1981   *Menander Rhetor. Edited with translation and commentary*, Oxford.

Russell, N.
2000   *Cyril of Alexandria*, London.

Sabbah, G.
1978   *La Méthode d'Ammien Marcellin: Recherches sur la construction du discours historique dans les* Res Gestae, Paris.
1992   'Présences féminines dans l'*Histoire* d'Ammien Marcellin', in den Boeft, den Hengst and Teitler (eds) 1992, 91–105.

Salim, M. S.
1970   *Risālat Thāmistiyūs ilā Yūliyān al-mālik fī al-siyāsa wa-tadbīr al-mamlaka*, Cairo.

Salmeri, G.
2000   'Dio, Rome, and the civic life of Asia Minor', in S. Swain (ed.) *Dio Chrysostom: Politics, letters, and philosophy*, Oxford.

Salzman, M.
1990   *On Roman Time: The Codex-Calendar of 354 and the rhythms of urban life in late antiquity*, Berkeley, Los Angeles and Oxford.

Sandwell, I.
2007   *Religious Identity in Late Antiquity: Greeks, Jews and Christians in Antioch*, Cambridge.

Saragoza, F.
2005   *Un prêtre romain aux thermes de Cluny. Musée National du Moyen Age, février 2005*, Paris.

Sardiello, R.
2000   *Giuliano Imperatore, Simposio I Cesari*, Lecce.

Sarris, P.
2004   'Managing the great estate: Aristocratic property and economic growth in the late antique east', in W. Bowden, L. Lavan and C. Machado (eds) *Recent Research in the Late Antique Countryside*, Leiden, 55–71.

Schäfer, C.
2008   'Julian "Apostata" und die philosophische Reaktion gegen das Christentum', in Schäfer (ed.) 2008, 41–64.

Schäfer, C. (ed.)
2008   *Kaiser Julian 'Apostata' und die philosophische Reaktion gegen das Christentum*, Berlin-New York.

Schamp, J., Todd, R. B. and Watt, J. W.
Forthcoming 'Thémistios', in R. Goulet (ed.) *Dictionnaire des philosophes antiques 6*, Paris.

Schäublin, C.
1970   'Diodor von Tarsus gegen Porphyrios ?', *Museum Helveticum* 27, 58–63.
1981   'Diodor von Tarsus', *Theologische Realenzyklopädie* 8, 763–7.
Schenkl, H. and Downey, G.
1965   *Themistii Orationes*, vol. 1, Leipzig.
Schneider, H.
1966   *Die 34. Rede des Themistios. Einleitung, Übersetzung und Kommentar*, Winterthur.
Schofield, M.
2000   'Epilogue', in C. Rowe and M. Schofield in association with S. Harrison and M. Lane (eds) *The Cambridge History of Greek and Roman Political Thought*, Cambridge, 661–71.
2005   'Julian and Themistius', in C. Rowe and M. Schofield (eds) *The Cambridge History of Greek and Roman Political Thought*, Cambridge, 661–5.
Scott, R.
2010   'Text and context in Byzantine historiography', in L. James (ed.) *Companion to Byzantium*, Oxford.
Screech, M. A.
1979   *Rabelais*, London.
Seager, R.
1984   'Some imperial virtues in the Latin prose panegyrics', in F. Cairns (ed.) *Papers of the Liverpool Latin Seminar*, vol. 4, Liverpool, 129–65.
Seeck, O.
1901   'Constantius (4)', in G. Wissowa (ed.) *Paulys Real-Encyclopädie der Classischen Altertumswissenschaft. Neue Bearbeitung. Unter Mitwirkung Zahlreicher Fachgenossen*, vol. 4, Stuttgart, 1044–94.
1919   *Regesten der Kaiser und Päpste für die Jahre 311 bis 476 n. Chr.: Vorarbeit zu einer Prosopographie der christlichen Kaiserzeit*, Stuttgart.
Sfameni Gasparro, G.
2003   *Misteri e Teologie. Per la storia dei culti mistici e misterici nel mondo antico*, Cosenza.
Shahid, I.
1974   'Epistula de re publica gerenda', in H. Schenkl, H. Downey and A. F. Norman (eds) *Themistii Orationes quae supersunt* 3, Leipzig, 73–119.
Shils, E. and Young, M.
1975   'The meaning of the British coronation', in E. Shils (ed.) *Center and Periphery: Essays in macrosociology*, Chicago, 135 52.
Sidwell, B.
2008   'Ammianus Marcellinus and the anger of Julian', *Iris* 21, 56–75.
Skias, A. N.
1895   'Ἐπιγραφαὶ ἐξ Ἐλευσῖνος', *Ἀρχαιολογικὴ Ἐφημερίς*, cols. 83–124.
Small, J. P.
1994   'Romulus and Remus', *LIMC* 7, Munich, 639–44.
Smith, A.
2004   *Philosophy in Late Antiquity*, London and New York.
Smith, P.M.
1966   *The Anti-Courtier Trend in Sixteenth Century French Literature*, Paris.

Smith, R.
  1995   *Julian's Gods: Religion and philosophy in the thought and action of Julian the Apostate*, London and New York.
  1999   'Telling Tales: Ammianus' narrative of the Persian expedition of Julian', in Drijvers and Hunt (eds) 1999, 89–104.

Smith, R. R. R.
  1990   'Late Roman philosopher portraits from Aphrodisias', *JRS* 80, 127–55.
  1991   'A new portrait of Pythagoras', in R. R. R. Smith and K. T. Erim (eds) *Aphrodisias Papers 2. The Theater, A Sculptor's Workshop, Philosophers and Coin-Types (Journal of Roman Archaeology, Supp. Series* 2), Ann Arbor, 159–67.
  1998   'Cultural choice and political identity in honorific portrait statues of the Greek east in the second century AD', *JRS* 88, 56–93.
  1999a   'Late antique portraits in a public context; Honorific statuary at Aphrodisias in Caria, AD 300–600', *JRS* 89, 155–89.
  1999b   review of P. Zanker, *Die Maske des Sokrates, Gnomon* 71, 448–57.
  2001   'A portrait monument for Julian and Theodosius at Aphrodisias', in C. Reusser (ed.) *Griechenland in der Kaiserzeit; Neue Funde und Forschungen zu Skulptur, Architektur und Topographie*, Berne, 125–36.
  2006   *Roman Portrait Statuary from Aphrodisias. Aphrodisias II. Results of the Excavations at Aphrodisias in Caria Conducted by New York University*, Mainz.

Smith, R. R. R. and Ertuǧ, A.
  2001   *Sculptured for Eternity. Treasures of Hellenistic, Roman and Byzantine Art from the Istanbul Archaeological Museum*, Istanbul.

Smith, R. R. R. and Ratte, C.
  1998   'Archaeological research at Aphrodisias in Caria, 1996', *AJA* 102, 225–50.

Söldner, M.
  2010   'Die Bildhauerkunst während der Regierungszeit des Hadrian (117–138 n.Chr.). Die Gesichter der Privatpersonen', in D. Kreikenbom, C. Maderna, J. Raeder, P. Schoolmeyer, F. Sinn, and M. Söldner, *Die Geschichte der antiken Bildhauerkunst IV. Plastik der römischen Kaiserzeit bis zum Tode Kaiser Hadrians*, Mainz, 237–44.

Sorabji, R.
  1990   *Aristotle Transformed. The ancient commentators and their influence*, London.

Spanheim, E.
  1666   *Les Césars de l'empereur Julien, traduits nouvellement de grec*, Heidelberg.
  1683   *Les Césars de l'empereur Julien, traduits du grec avec des remarques et des preuves, illustrées par les médailles et autres anciens monumens*, Paris.
  1696   *Ioulianou Autokratoros Ta sozomena = Iuliani Imperatoris opera quae supersunt omnia*, Leipzig.

Spawforth, A. J. S.
  1994   'Corinth, Argos and the imperial cult: Pseudo-Julian, *Letters* 198', *Hesperia* 63, 211–32.

Speidel, M. A.
  2009   '"Franke bin ich..." Germanische Verbände in römischen Heer', in *2000 Jahre Varusschlacht. Konflikt*, Stuttgart, 241–7.

Spink, J. S.
  1967   'The reputation of Julian the Apostate in the Enlightenment', *Studies on Voltaire and the Eighteenth Century* 57, 1399–1415.

Stanley, D. J.
  1994   'New discoveries at Santa Costanza', *DOP* 48, 257–61.

Stauner, K.
  2007   'Wandel und Kontinuität römischer Administrationspraxis im Spiegel des *ordo salutationis commodorumque* des Statthalters von Numidien', *Tyche* 22, 151–88.

Stenger, J.
  2009   *Hellenistische Identität in der Spätantike. Pagane Autoren und ihr Unbehagen an der eigenen Zeit. Untersuchungen zur antiken Literatur und Geschichte* 97, Berlin and New York.

Sterk, A.
  2004   *Renouncing the World yet Leading the Church: The monk-bishop in late antiquity*, Cambridge, Mass.

Stertz, S. A.
  1977   'Marcus Aurelius as ideal emperor in late-antique Greek thought', *Classical World* 70, 433–9.

Strauss, L.
  1975   *The Argument and the Action of Plato's* Laws, Chicago.

Sutherland, C. H. V. and Carson, R. A. G.
  1966   *Roman Imperial Coinage*, vol. 7, *Constantine and Licinius* AD *313–337*, London.

Swain, S. (ed.)
  2007   *Seeing the Face, Seeing the Soul. Polemon's Physiognomy from Classical Antiquity to Medieval Islam*, Oxford.

Syme, R.
  1958   *Tacitus*, Oxford.

Szidat, J.
  1997   'Die Usurpation Julians. Ein Sonderfall', in F. Paschoud, J. Szidat and T. Barnes (eds) *Usurpationen in der Spätantike*, Stuttgart, 63–70.

Tantillo, I.
  1997   *La prima orazione di Giuliano a Costanzo: introduzione, traduzione e commento*, Rome.

Teitler, H. C.
  1992   'Ammianus and Constantius: Image and reality', in den Boeft, den Hengst and Teitler (eds) 1992, 117–22.

Thome, F.
  2004   *Historia contra mythos: die Schriftauslegung Diodors von Tarsus und Theodors von Mopsuestia im Widerstreit zu Kaiser Julians und Salustius' allegorischem Mythenverständnis*, Bonn.

Thompson, E. A.
  1947   *The Historical Work of Ammianus Marcellinus*, Cambridge; repr. 1969, Groningen.
  1956   'Constantine, Constantius II, and the lower Danube frontier', *Hermes* 84, 372–81.

Tougher, S.

    1998a   'In praise of an empress: Julian's *Speech of Thanks* to Eusebia', in Mary Whitby (ed.) 1998, 105–23.

    1998b   'The advocacy of an empress: Julian and Eusebia', *CQ* 48, 595–9.

    1999   'Ammianus and the eunuchs', in Drijvers and Hunt (eds) 1999, 64–73.

    2000   'Ammianus Marcellinus on the empress Eusebia: a split personality?', *Greece and Rome* 47, 94–101.

    2004   'Julian's bull coinage: Kent revisited', *CQ* 54, 327–30.

    2007   *Julian the Apostate*, Edinburgh.

    2012   'Imperial blood: family relationships in the dynasty of Constantine the Great', in M. Harlow and L. L. Lovén (eds) *Families in the Roman and Late Antique World*, London and New York, 181–98.

Trapp, M. B.

    2003   *Greek and Latin Letters. An Anthology with Translation*, Cambridge.

Trout, D.

    2009   'Inscribing identity: the Latin epigraphic habit in late antiquity', in P. Rousseau (ed.) *A Companion to Late Antiquity*, Oxford & Malden, Mass., 170–86.

Turcan, R.

    1996   *The Cults of the Roman Empire*, Oxford.

Turner, C.

    1992   *Living by the Pen: Women writers in the eighteenth century*, London.

Ugenti, V.

    1992   *Giuliano Imperatore, Alla Madre degli dei*, Lecce.

Urbainczyk, T.

    1998   'Vice and advice in Socrates and Sozomen', in Mary Whitby (ed.) 1998, 299–319.

Van Dam, R.

    2002a   *Families and Friends in Late Roman Cappadocia*, Philadelphia

    2002b   *Kingdom of Snow: Roman rule and Greek culture in Cappadocia*, Philadelphia.

    2003   *Becoming Christian: The conversion of Roman Cappadocia*, Philadelphia.

Van der Poll, C.

    2001   'Homer and Homeric interpretation in the *Protrepticus* of Clement of Alexandria', in F. Budelmann and P. Michelakis (eds) *Homer, Tragedy and Beyond: Essays in honour of P. E. Easterling*, London, 179–99.

Van Heesch, J.

    2006   'Transport of coins in the later Roman empire', *Revue de Numismatique Belge* 152, 51–61.

Van Hoof, L. and van Nuffelen, P.

    2011   'Monarchy and mass communication: Antioch AD 362/3 revisited', *JRS* 101, 166–84.

Van Nuffelen, P.

    2002   'Deux fausses lettres de Julien l'Apostat (*La lettre aux Juifs, Ep.* 51 [Wright], et *La lettre à Arsacius, Ep.* 84 [Bidez])', *Vigiliae Christianae* 56, 131–50.

Vanderspoel, J.

    1995   *Themistius and the Imperial Court: Oratory, civic duty, and paideia from Constantius to Theodosius*, Ann Arbor.

1998 'Julian and the Mithraic bull', *Ancient History Bulletin* 12.4, 113–19.

Unpublished paper 'Some attitudes to the philosophic life in the 4th century AD'.

Unpublished paper 'The early life of Julian the Apostate'.

Vatsend, K.
 2000 *Die Rede Julians auf Kaiserin Eusebia: Abfassungszeit, Gattungszugehörigkeit, panegyrische Topoi und Vergleiche, Zweck*, Oslo.

Vidal, G
 1964 *Julian*, London.

Vinson, M.
 2003 'Rhetoric and writing strategies in the ninth century', in Jeffreys (ed.) 2003, 9–22.

Vitelli, H.
 1888 *Ioannis Philoponi in Aristotelis Physicorum libros quinque posteriores commentaria, Commentaria in Aristotelem Graeca* 17, Berlin.

Vogler, C.
 1979 *Constance II et l'administration impériale*, Strasbourg.

Vollenweider, M. and Avisseau-Broustet, M.
 2003 *Camée et intailles 2. Les portraits romains du Cabinet des médailles*, Paris.

Volterra, E.
 1971 'Il problema del testo delle costituzioni imperiali', in *Atti del II Convegno Internazionale della Società Italiana di Storia e Diritto (Venezia, 1969)*, Florence, 821–1097 [reprinted in E. Volterra, *Scritti giuridici 6. Le fonti* (Antiqua 64), Naples, 1993].

Von Fritze, H.
 1910 *Die Münzen von Pergamon*, Berlin.

Von Heintze, H.
 1963 '*Vir sanctus et gravis*: Bildniskopf eines spätantiken Philosophen', *Jahrbuch für Antike und Christentum* 6, 35–53.

Vout, C.
 2003 'A revision of Hadrian's portraiture', in L. De Blois, P. Erdkamp, O. Hekster, G. De Keijn and S. Mols (eds) *The Representation and Perception of Roman Imperial Power. Proceedings of the Third Workshop of the International Network Impact of Empire (Roman Empire, c. 200 BC–AD 476) Netherlands Institute in Rome March 20–23, 2002*, Amsterdam, 442–57.

Wallace-Hadrill, A.
 1981 'Galba's acquitas', *Num. Chron.* 141, 20–39.
 1982 'Civilis princeps. Between citizen and king', *JRS* 72, 32–48.

Warburton, W.
 1750 *Julian, or a Discourse concerning the Earthquake and fiery Eruption, which defeated that Emperor's Attempt to rebuild the Temple at Jerusalem*, London.

Ward-Perkins, B.
 2005 *The Fall of Rome and the End of Civilization*, Oxford.

Wardman, A. E.
 1984 'Usurpers and internal conflicts in the 4th century AD', *Historia* 33, 220–37.

Waters, P.
 2009 *Cast Not the Day*, London.
 2010 *The Philosopher Prince*, London.

Watt, J. W.

2004 'Syriac and Syrians as mediators of Greek political thought to Islam', *Mélanges de l'Université Saint-Joseph* 57, 121–49.

Watts, E. J.

2006 *City and School in Late Antique Athens and Alexandria*, Berkeley.

Webb, R.

2003 'Praise and persuasion: argumentation and audience response in epideictic oratory', in Jeffreys (ed.) 2003, 127–36.

2009 *Ekphrasis, Imagination and Persuasion in Ancient Rhetorical Theory and Practice*, Farnham.

Weinbrot, H. D.

2005 *Menippean Satire Reconsidered*, Baltimore.

Weis, B. K.

1973 *Julian, Briefe*, Munich.

Weitzmann, K.

1977 *Late Antique and Early Christian Book Illumination*, London.

West, R.

1941 *Römische Porträtplastik*, Munich.

Whitby, Mary

2003 'George of Pisidia and the persuasive word: words, words, words...', in Jeffreys (ed.) 2003, 173–86.

Whitby, Mary (ed.)

1998 *The Propaganda of Power: The role of panegyric in late antiquity*, Leiden.

Whitby, Michael

1998 'Evagrius on patriarchs and emperors', in Mary Whitby (ed.) 1998, 321–44.

1999 'Images of Constantius', in Drijvers and Hunt (eds) 1999, 77–88.

Whitmarsh, T.

2001 *Greek Literature and the Roman Empire: The politics of imitation*, New York.

Whittaker, C. R.

1994 *Frontiers of the Roman Empire*, Baltimore.

Wickham, L. R.

1968 'The *Syntagmation* of Aetius the Anomoean', *Journal of Theological Studies* 19, 532–69.

Wiemer, H.-U.

1994 'Libanius on Constantine', *CQ* 44, 511–24.

1995 *Libanios und Julian: Studien zum Verhältnis von Rhetorik und Politik im vierten Jahrhundert n. Chr.*, Munich.

1998 'Ein Kaiser verspottet sich selbst: Form und historische Bedeutung von Kaiser Julians *Misopogon*', in P. Kreissl and V. Losemann (eds) *Imperium Romanum: Studien zu Geschichte und Rezeption. Festschrift für Karl Christ zum 75. Geburtstag*, Stuttgart, 733–53.

Wilamowitz-Moellendorff, U. von

1982 *History of Classical Scholarship*, trans. H. Lloyd-Jones, London.

Wilken, R. L.

1984 *The Christians as the Romans Saw Them*, New Haven.

Wind, E.
1939/40 'Julian the Apostate at Hampton Court', *Journal of the Warburg and Courtauld Institutes* 3, 127–37.

Wintjes, J.
2006 'Libanius and Himerius', in Á. González Gálvez and P.-L. Malosse (eds) *Mélanges A.F. Norman* (*Topoi* Supplement 7), Lyon, 231–41.

Wirth, G.
1978 'Julians Perserkrieg. Kriterien einer Katastrophe', in R. Klein (ed.) *Julian Apostata*, Darmstadt, 455–507.

Wiseman, T. P.
1995 *Remus: A Roman myth*, Cambridge.

Witke, C.
1970 *Latin Satire: The structure of persuasion*, Leiden.

Wittkower, R.
1975 'The vicissitudes of a dynastic movement: Bernini's equestrian statue of Louis XIV', in R. Wittkower *Studies in the Italian Baroque*, Boulder, 84–102.

Womersley, D.
1994 *Edward Gibbon,* The History of the Decline and Fall of the Roman Empire, 3 vols, Harmondsworth.

Woods, D.
1995a 'Ammianus Marcellinus and the deaths of Bonosus and Maximilianus', *Hagiographica* 2, 22–55.
1995b 'Julian, Arbogastes and the signa of the Iovani and Herculani', *Journal of Roman Military Equipment Studies* 6, 61–8.
1997 'The emperor Julian and the Passion of Sergius and Bacchus', *JECS* 5, 335–67.
2000 'Julian, Gallienus, and the solar bull', *American Journal of Numismatics* 12, 157–69.

Wright, W. C.
1896 *The Emperor Julian's Relation to the New Sophistic and Neoplatonism*, London.
1913 *The Works of the Emperor Julian*, vols. 1 and 2, London.
1923 *The Works of the Emperor Julian*, vol. 3, London and New York.

Wroth, W.
1892 *A Catalogue of the Greek Coins in the British Museum*, vol. 14, *Mysia*, London.

Zanetti, A. M., Sr. and Zanetti, A. M., Jr.
1740 *Delle antiche statue greche e romane che nell'antisala della Libreria di San Marco e in altri luoghi pubblici di Venezia si trovano*, Venice.

Zanker, P.
1995 *The Mask of Socrates: The image of the intellectual in antiquity*, trans. A. Shapiro, Berkeley.

INDEX